THE **CONCISE**

McGraw- Hill
GUIDE

WRITING for COLLEGE, WRITING for LIFE

Duane   Gregory R.   Barry M.
ROEN GLAU MAID

ARIZONA STATE UNIVERSITY

Boston   Burr Ridge, IL   Dubuque, IA   New York   San Francisco   St. Louis
Bangkok   Bogotá   Caracas   Lisbon   London   Madrid
Mexico City   Milan   New Delhi   Seoul   Singapore   Sydney   Taipei   Toronto

THE CONCISE McGraw-Hill
GUIDE

WRITING for COLLEGE, WRITING for LIFE

DUANE ROEN
Arizona State University

GREGORY R. GLAU
Arizona State University

BARRY M. MAID
Arizona State University

**McGraw-Hill
Higher Education**

Boston   Burr Ridge, IL   Dubuque, IA   New York   San Francisco   St. Louis
Bangkok   Bogotá   Caracas   Kuala Lumpur   Lisbon   London   Madrid   Mexico City
Milan   Montreal   New Delhi   Santiago   Seoul   Singapore   Sydney   Taipei   Toronto

The Concise McGraw-Hill Guide: Writing for College, Writing for Life

This book is a McGraw-Hill Learning Solutions textbook and contains material from *The Concise McGraw-Hill Guide: Writing for College, Writing for Life* by Duane Roen, Gregory R. Glau, and Barry M. Maid. Copyright © 2009 by The McGraw-Hill Companies, Inc. Reprinted with permission of the publisher.

2 3 4 5 6 7 8 9 0 DOC/DOC 12 11 10

ISBN 13: 978-0-07-747312-9
ISBN 10: 0-07-747312-4

Learning Solutions Manager: Anne Kaiser
Production Editor: Patricia Koch Krieger
Printer/Binder: RR Donnelley

Brief Contents

Contents

3 Writing to Discover and to Learn   31

PART **FOUR**   Strategies for Effective Communication   389

PART SIX   Using Research for Informed Communication   499

19   Finding and Evaluating Information from Sources and the Field   501

About the Authors

Duane Roen is Professor of English at Arizona State University and Head of Humanities and Arts in the School of Applied Arts and Sciences. At ASU he served as Director of Composition for four years before directing ASU's Center for Learning and Teaching Excellence. Prior to that, he directed the Writing Program at Syracuse University, as well as the graduate program in Rhetoric, Composition, and the Teaching of English at the University of Arizona. Early in his career, he taught high school English in New Richmond, Wisconsin, before deciding to complete a doctorate at the University of Minnesota. In addition to more than 160 articles, chapters, and conference papers, Duane has published numerous books including *Composing Our Lives in Rhetoric and Composition: Stories about the Growth of a Discipline* (with Theresa Enos and Stuart Brown); *The Writer's Toolbox* (with Stuart Brown and Bob Mittan); *A Sense of Audience in Written Discourse* (with Gesa Kirsch); and *Views from the Center: The CCCC Chairs' Addresses, 1977–2005,* among others. In 2007, Duane was elected Secretary of the CCCC. Duane's interest in family history has motivated him to construct a database that lists more than 32,000 of his ancestors and to collaborate with his wife, Maureen, to write more than 14,000 pages of journal entries about their two children, Nick and Hanna.

Gregory R. Glau is Director of Writing Programs at Arizona State University, where he has taught since 1994. Greg received his MA in Rhetoric and Composition from Northern Arizona University and his PhD in Rhetoric, Composition, and the Teaching of English from the University of Arizona. Before he was appointed director in 2000, Greg directed ASU's basic writing Stretch Program. Greg is past Co-Chair of the Conference on Basic Writing (CBW) with Linda Adler-Kassner of Eastern Michigan University, and he coedited (with Linda) *BWe: Basic Writing e-Journal.* Greg is coeditor of the *Bedford Bibliography of Basic Writing,* also with Linda Adler-Kassner. Greg is also coauthor (with Craig Jacobsen) of

Scenarios for Writing. Greg has published in *WPA: Writing Program Administration*, *Rhetoric Review*, *English Journal*, *The Writing Instructor*, *IDEAS Plus*, and the *Arizona English Bulletin.* He regularly presents papers at CCCC and has also presented papers at WPA, MLA, RMMLA, the Western States Composition Conference, NCTE, and other conferences. As a teenager, Greg was an amateur magician. He maintains that interest today, and with his oldest son, Robert, he attends a convention for mentalism entertainers every year.

Barry M. Maid is Professor and Head of Multimedia Writing and Technical Communication at Arizona State University, where he led the development of a new program in Multimedia Writing and Technical Communication. He has spent most of his career in some form of writing program administration. Before coming to ASU in January 2000, he spent nineteen years at the University of Arkansas at Little Rock where, among other duties, he directed the Writing Center and the First Year Composition Program, chaired the Department of English, and helped create the Department of Rhetoric and Writing. He has written or coauthored chapters for more than a dozen books. His work has also appeared in *Kairos*, *Computers and Composition*, and the *Writing Lab Newsletter,* among other technology-oriented publications. More recently, Barry has coauthored articles on information literacy for library journals. His professional interests remain primarily with computers and writing, writing program administration, and partnerships between academia and industry. Barry enjoys long road trips. Over the past several years, he has driven along the Pacific Coast Highway from Los Angeles to Oregon, through national parks in Utah and Arizona, and through much of the Carolinas and Tennessee.

Dear Colleagues,

As longtime writing program administrators and instructors, we know that students need textbooks that address both their current and future needs. They need to see how important and valuable writing will be for them in the many diverse situations they will encounter. *The McGraw-Hill Guide* grew out of our desire to help students learn to write more effectively not only in their college courses, but also in their professional, civic, and personal lives. To do this, we designed a text that will help students to set goals for their writing, to use effective composing strategies to reach those goals, and to assess their progress toward achieving them.

In establishing goals for students, we've drawn on the learning outcomes established by the National Council of Writing Program Administrators because we know how important they have been in shaping discussions about writing curricula in the United States and other countries. These learning outcomes demonstrate the value of the full range of skills and knowledge that writers need to develop: rhetorical knowledge; critical thinking, reading, and writing; composing processes; and knowledge of conventions. *The McGraw-Hill Guide* is the first rhetoric of its kind to be developed specifically with these outcomes in mind, and the result is a text that will help students achieve these outcomes while also helping instructors teach them.

As for the future, in the twenty-first century, all writers can expect to confront increasingly varied digital contexts. Whether they need to use visual elements, implement specific design features, employ a variety of digital media, or choose an alternate genre to communicate with their readers, effective writers today have a wide range of choices to make to accomplish the goals of any particular writing task. *The McGraw-Hill Guide* helps students not only to make thoughtful choices, but also to ask thoughtful questions. We also aspire to help them find answers.

Sincerely,

Duane Roen   Gregory R. Glau   Barry M. Maid

The features of *The Concise McGraw-Hill Guide* are designed to help students answer three questions they typically ask:

- **Why** am I writing?
- **How** do I write?
- **Did** I achieve my writing goals?

Why am I writing?

Effective writers understand the situation—the purpose, context, and audience—in which they are writing. The most effective writers are strong communicators in any situation. The chapters in Parts 2 and 3 (Chapters 4–12), which present writing assignments, each focus on the purpose for which students need to write—exploring, analyzing, convincing, and so on—and provide comprehensive instruction on writing for various contexts in college and beyond.

Instructors and students have a wide variety of purposes for writing around which to organize and complete their course. Assignment chapters in Parts 2 and 3 (Chapters 4–12) focus on a wide range of writing purposes such as "Writing to Analyze," "Writing to Convince," "Writing to Explore," and "Writing to Solve Problems." This variety of writing projects maximizes the text's flexibility, both to complement instructors' unique teaching styles and to support course, department, or program goals and outcomes.

In Chapters 4–12, assignment options in the form of brief *scenarios* give students a context for writing.
A scenario gives students an audience, a purpose for writing, and a context. Each chapter in Parts 2 and 3 provides a *choice* of scenarios, so students and instructors can select from academic, professional, civic, or personal scenarios.

Writing for College

SCENARIO 1   Exploring a Major or Career

For this scenario, assume you are taking a "Career and Life Planning" class—a class devoted to helping college students decide what discipline they might like to major in. This class gives you the opportunity to explore different career paths, to learn what the educational requirements are for various majors, and to find out what job opportunities will be available in various careers and what salaries and other forms of compensation different jobs might offer.

Writing Assignment: Select one college major or career that you may be interested in pursuing and construct an exploratory paper in which you consider the various aspects of that major or career from many angles, including the preparation you would need for it and the rewards and pitfalls you might encounter if you decide to pursue it. Asking and answering questions about the major or career you are considering will form the heart of your exploratory paper.

Writing for Life

SCENARIO 2   Civic Writing: An Article about a Community Problem

As a reporter, you have been assigned to write about a community problem for your local newspaper. Select an important problem that your community is concerned about. To find a problem, read recent issues of your local paper and also speak to some residents of your community. For example, if you live in Bend, Oregon, and happen to glance through the online version of *Central Oregon Online*, you might see a list of local stories about the need to fund bridge repairs, an attempt to save horses, or problems with the water supply. All are aspects of civic life that you could write about.

The text focuses throughout on writing in all four areas of a student's life (academic, professional, civic, and personal). Although most students have an immediate need to improve their academic writing, students will see the benefits of learning to write more clearly if they examine their current literacy practices in the other areas of their lives as well.

The text emphasizes different media and genres for writing. Because many writing situations will require the use of various media and genres, in the chapters in Parts 2 and 3, many of the "Writing for Life" assignment options call for students to publish their work in a format other than a traditional, plain text, printed academic essay. In addition, Chapter 17, "Choosing a Medium, Genre, and Technology for Your Communication," gives students practical advice on, and activities for, using both basic and advanced computer tools to prepare documents for, and communicate with, different audiences in various media and genres.

WRITING ACTIVITY

Selecting a Medium

With several of your classmates, consider the following writing tasks. For each one, decide what medium might be appropriate to get your message across to the audience indicated.

- A group consisting of you and your neighbors wants to collect comments and information on a problem with an illegal dump near a school and present them to the town council.

- To increase public awareness of the different organizations on campus, your group has been asked to send information to various civic clubs such as the Rotary, Kiwanis, and Elks. With the material will be a request for donations for your school organizations.

How do I write?

Each chapter in Parts 2 and 3 illustrates the steps of the writing process with clear examples of a student writer addressing a specific writing situation. In this way, *The Concise McGraw-Hill Guide* helps students achieve their own writing goals by introducing them to the principles and guiding them through the processes of effective writing.

Options for Organization

First Inductive Approach	Second Inductive Approach	Deductive Approach
• Outline why you are making the evaluation. • Discuss/explain the criteria. • Explain how well your subject or subjects match (or fail to match) the various criteria. • Discuss which subjects are "best," according to the evaluative criteria you have established. Explain your thesis statement in your conclusion.	• Begin with a discussion of the subject or subjects that you are evaluating. • Explain its or their strengths and weaknesses. • Outline how the positive and negative points match each of your criteria. • Explain how the subject or subjects you are evaluating fulfill those criteria (this, then, is your thesis statement)	• Begin with the conclusion that you have reached about the subject or subjects (your thesis statement) • Explain why and how you reached that conclusion using a compare-and-contrast format: compare and contrast each aspect of what you are evaluating in relation to the criteria.

Guidance on the entire process of responding to an assignment is integrated into each chapter in Parts 2 and 3. The "Writing Processes" section of these chapters provides instruction at every step of the writing project, including invention, research, drafting, working with peers, revising, editing, and reflecting and self-assessing. Based on the student's purpose for writing, organizational strategies are offered in "Options for Organization" boxes which help students make sound rhetorical choices for organizing their ideas. Furthermore, because students respond best to examples of student work, a sample student paper is included in each of these chapters.

The chapters in Parts 2 and 3 include a wide variety of professional readings. Each chapter includes two professional selections by a range of authors including Maureen Dowd, Roger Ebert, Elvis Mitchell, and Tanya Barrientos. The apparatus that accompanies each reading selection encourages students to think about how the Learning Goals apply to that particular selection, as well as about ideas for their own writing.

MAUREEN DOWD

Our Own Warrior Princess

Maureen Dowd won the Pulitzer Prize for Commentary in 1999. In 1992, she received the Breakthrough Award from Women, Men and Media at Columbia University. She won the Matrix Award from New York Women in Communications in 1994. In 1996, she was named one of *Glamour*'s Women of the Year. In 1992, she was also a Pulitzer Prize finalist for national reporting.

In the following column, which first appeared in the *New York Times* on June 1, 2003, Dowd writes in a personal way about organ donation—telling the story of what her niece, Jennifer, did to help her brother, Michael. Although persuasive writing most often uses facts, statistics, and hard evidence to make its case, as you read Dowd's column consider how effective she is in using emotional appeals to persuade you.

Jennifer showed me her scar Friday. It's the most beautiful scar I've ever   1
seen. A huge stapled gash on her stomach, shaped like the Mercedes
logo. A red badge of courage. Jennifer is my niece, a 33-year-old lawyer.
On Wednesday, she had half her liver taken out at Georgetown University

Each chapter in Parts 2 and 3 emphasizes multiple forms of research. Although there are two separate chapters on research in Part 6 (Chapters 19 and 20), each chapter in Parts 2 and 3 also includes coverage of conducting research.

Each chapter in Parts 2 and 3 offers advice on using visuals. Because many writing situations today require visual as well as verbal texts, throughout the writing assignments in Parts 2 and 3, "Thinking about Visuals" sections and "Visualizing Variations" boxes encourage students to consider how they can use visuals in their writing when appropriate.

Exploring Your Ideas with Research

Research is critical to any persuasive text, for if you cannot provide evidence to support your position, you probably will not convince your reading audience.

Although you may be able to use information from your own experience as evidence, you will usually need to offer verifiable information from sources, such as facts, statistics, expert testimony, and examples.

To find evidence outside of your own experience that you need to support your claim, look for answers to the following questions:

- What facts or other verifiable information can I find that will provide solid evidence to convince my readers to agree with my position?
- What expert testimony can I provide to support my claim? What authorities on my issue might I interview?
- What statistical data support my position?
- What are other people doing in response to this issue or problem?

For help with locating sources of information, see Chapter 19; for help with documenting your sources, see Chapter 20.

The subject yo[u] help to determine scenarios above, yo[u]

- For Scenario

VISUALIZING VARIATIONS

Using Charts and Other Visuals to Support Your Claim

If you were writing in response to Scenario 1, which asks you to focus on a controversial issue, you might choose to write about global warming. Here is a dramatic image that you could use at the beginning of your paper:

A WRITER'S RESPONSIBILITIES

Establishing and Maintaining Credibility

Dealing Fairly with Opposing Views

An ethical writer must deal with opposing views fairly and honestly. If you ignore or distort opposing views, readers will think you are either ignorant, unaware, or dishonest, which will quickly weaken or destroy your ethos—your credibility.

It is perhaps only natural to tend to ignore what those who disagree with you have to say about your topic—after all, if you just ignore their views, your view will be stronger, right? However, ignoring the other side of an issue, the objections that others might have to your point of view, actually weakens your position, as your reader[s] [o]bjections and wonder why you did not deal with th[e]

And if y[ou] [y]our readers, you have an ethical obligation to note [a]nst your position. You don't necessarily have to wri[te] [I]t you may think is stronger than mine,"

(cont'd)

TechNote One way to see argumentation and persuasion in action is to look at the political discussion boards on various Web sites, blogs, and online bulletin boards. Choose a topic thread, and as you skim or read the posts, ask yourself three questions about each post you see: 1) How much credibility does the writer seem to have as a person (*ethos*)? 2) How does the writer use reason and logic to make his or her points (*logos*)? 3) What is your emotional reaction to the writer's remarks (*pathos*)? You can determine the weight a writer's comments probably carry with others by assessing your impressions of that writer's credibility, reasoning, and emotional integrity.

The text reminds students of their responsibilities as writers. Chapter 1 includes a section on writing responsibly, and the chapters in Parts 2 and 3 reinforce this important aspect of writing, with boxes that remind students that writing has consequences and that good writing is ethical writing.

TechNotes in each chapter offer hints on using technology throughout the writing process. These useful notes will help students get more from the resources that are available to them in the computer lab, in the library, and on the Web.

Did I achieve my writing goals?

The Concise McGraw-Hill Guide is designed to help students understand how others will evaluate their work and provides criteria they can use to judge their own work. Taking as their basis the Council of Writing Program Administrators *Outcomes Statement*, Chapters 4–12 integrate coverage of the four categories of learning outcomes that form the foundation of assessment practices at writing programs throughout the country: *rhetorical knowledge, critical thinking, writing processes,* and *conventions.*

Each assignment chapter is structured around the Learning Goals, so students know what the book will *do* for their writing. The Learning Goals are introduced in Chapter 1. In addition, a chart at the beginning of each chapter in Parts 2 and 3 relates the Learning Goals to the type of writing covered in that chapter, and the organization of each chapter is based on the Learning Goals, to reinforce their importance.

Each assignment chapter ends with questions for self-assessment. In the self-assessment activity, students are prompted to consider how their progress on the chapter's assignment has helped them work toward attaining the goals for the chapter, thus helping them build their knowledge of themselves as writers and thinkers.

Self-Assessment: Reflecting on Your Learning Goals

Now that you have constructed a piece of writing designed to convince your readers, go back and consider your learning goals, which you and your classmates may have considered at the beginning of this chapter (pp. 188–89). Then, reflect on all the thinking and writing that you have done in ~~the learning goals that~~ ~~g questions:~~

- *Purpose:* What have you learned about the purposes for constructing an effective persuasive text?
- *Rhetorical situation:* How did the writing context affect your persuasive text?
- *Voice and tone:* How would you describe your voice in this essay? Your tone? How do they contribute to the effectiveness of your persuasive essay? ~~ng an audience in per-~~
- *Context, medium, and genre:* How did your context determine the medium and genre you chose, and how did those decisions affect your writing?

Critical Thinking, Reading, and Writing

- *Learning/inquiry:* How did you decide what to focus on for your persuasive text? Describe the process you went through to focus on a main idea, or thesis.
- *Responsibility:* How did you fulfill your responsibilities to your readers?
- *Reading and research:* What did you learn about persuasive writing from the reading selections you read for this chapter? What research did you conduct? How sufficient was the research you did?
- As a result of writing this paper, how have you become a more critical thinker, reader, and writer? What skills do you hope to develop further?

Chapter 2 on reading helps students hone their critical reading—and thinking—skills. To help students with the second category of the Learning Goals, Chapter 2 covers the skills students need for effective college-level reading. This chapter also provides ample opportunity for students to examine and reflect on their own reading practices and habits, suggests ways to improve their reading activities, and provides journaling ideas and activities. The chapter includes a strong focus on visual literacy.

Synthesizing Information in Readings

Synthesis is more than reassembling other people's ideas and information from different sources; it calls for the thoughtful combination or integration of ideas and information with your point of view.

Synthesis can take place in all four areas of your life. For example, suppose that you would like to see a particular movie this Saturday evening. You hope to convince a group of your friends to accompany you. Because you are a movie buff, you have read several reviews of the film, you know other work by the director, and you have even read the novel on which this movie is based. In other words, you have quite a bit of information to support your case that everyone should accompany you Saturday evening to see this film. At the same time, simply sending your friends all the information you have about the film might overwhelm them. Unless you effectively structure what you have to say, one piece of information may contradict some other point that you want to make. While you want to portray what you know about the film accurately, your primary purpose is to make the case to see the film.

So how would you go about organizing your information about the film in order to convince your friends? You could focus on what you see as the most compelling reasons your friends should see the film: the novel the film is based on, along with the director of the movie. You would then provide information on the following:

- How good the novel was, with specific examples to show what you mean
- How effectively the novel has been translated to film, again, with several examples—probably quotations from reviews or other information about the film—as evidence
- Other films by the same director that you know your friends like

---

"Round-Robin" activities help students learn writing conventions. The chapters in Parts 2 and 3 each include a collaborative "Round-Robin" activity in the "Knowledge of Conventions" section that asks students to focus on a particular writing convention. These activities help students learn sentence-level conventions in the context of their own writing.

WRITER'S WORKSHOP

Round-Robin Editing with a Focus on Fragments

Because exploratory writing often includes incomplete thoughts, writers sometimes inadvertently use sentence fragments to express their thinking. A sentence fragment is missing one or more of the following elements: a subject, a verb, or a complete thought. Some fragments lack a subject, a verb, or both:

FRAGMENT   College sports are popular. *Generating lots of money for schools with successful teams.*

Other fragments have subjects and verbs, but they begin with a subordinating word like *because* or *although* and so are not complete thoughts:

FRAGMENT   *Although I have played football in high school and college.* I'm not good enough to play on a professional team.

SENTENCE   Although I have played football in high school and college, I'm not good enough to play on a professional team.

Work with two peers to look for sentence fragments. For each fragment, decide whether to connect it to a nearby sentence or to recast it into a complete sentence.

The Support Package for *The Concise McGraw-Hill Guide: Writing for College, Writing for Life*

The Concise McGraw-Hill Guide offers a rich support package for the composition classroom, with free and premium media options, a comprehensive Instructor's Resource Manual, and instructor access to *Partners in Teaching*—the McGraw-Hill faculty development Web site for composition.

Online Learning Center powered by *Catalyst 2.0* *Catalyst 2.0,* McGraw-Hill's online resource for writing, research, and editing, is available with every student and instructor copy of *The Concise McGraw-Hill Guide.*

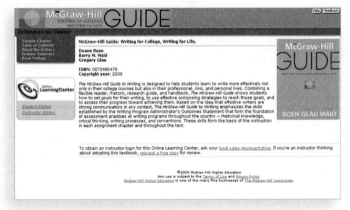

Features you'll find online include the following:

- Interactive tutorials for analyzing images and visual rhetoric
- Guides for avoiding plagiarism and evaluating sources
- Electronic writing tutors for composing informative, interpretive, and argumentative papers
- Bibliomaker software for MLA, APA, Chicago, and CSE styles of documentation
- Over 4,500 exercises with feedback in grammar, usage, and punctuation
- A state-of-the-art course management and peer review system

THE McGraw-Hill GUIDE ONLINE *The McGraw-Hill Guide Online:* This fully interactive version of the print text includes all the writing scenarios and readings from the text as well as the writing instruction and writing process coverage in a format optimized for online reading. Students can compose and submit papers in response to assigned writing scenarios, reading selections, or complete units online. In addition, they can take advantage of over two hundred "Ask the Author" video segments, all new interactive writing tutors, and a wide range of other activities and tools that facilitate writing and learning.

Partners in Teaching: **Faculty Development Web site for Composition (www.mhhe. com/englishcommunity)**   McGraw-Hill is proud to partner with many of the top names in the field to build a community of teachers helping teachers. *Partners in Teaching* features up-to-date scholarly discourse, practical teaching advice, and community support for individual instructors, graduate student programs, and professional development seminars.

The site features two main parts:

The Teaching Comp Blog and Discussion Board
This online resource is the next stage of the successful *Partners in Teaching* listserv for composition. Join in the conversation about new topics each month to discuss the latest trends, strategies, and issues in composition in our new Teaching Comp blog, moderated by Chris Anson.

Teaching Topic Modules
Created by experts, the Teaching Topics modules explore key concerns in composition today. Each module contains a wealth of information on its topic: an introductory background section, an extensive bibliography, practical teaching strategies, and helpful video mentors. In addition, instructors can download resources for teaching, including handouts, classroom PowerPoint Presentations, and Video Lecture Launchers. Combining the latest academic research with practical teaching tools, the modules provide incredible resources for new and experienced instructors.

Instructor's Resource Manual   Written by the authors of *The McGraw-Hill Guide,* this in-depth resource includes advice and chapter-by-chapter support by three of the discipline's preeminent rhetoricians. This valuable resource features suggested assignment sequences, sample syllabi, in-class activities, and discussion topics as well as classroom management techniques and advice for new instructors.

Acknowledgments

On a personal level, we'd like to thank our colleagues at Arizona State University, who've heard us talking about the project (probably more than they'd wished to!), offered constant support, and gave us good advice: Demetria Baker, O. M. "Skip" Brack, Barbara D'Angelo, Frank D'Angelo, Chitralekha Duttagupta, Ben Fasano, Janice Frangella, Maureen Goggin, Sonia Gracia-Grondin, Jeremy Helm, Glenn Irvin, Ruth Johnston, Keith Miller, Neal Lester, Silvia Llamas-Flores, Patricia Murphy, Camille Newton, Sherry Rankins Robertson, Dave Schwalm, and Linda Searcy. Duane would like especially to thank Hanna and Maureen Roen.

A number of people have made important contributions to this text and its media components. Cynthia Jeney of Missouri Western State University contributed most of the TechNotes, for which we thank her. Charlotte Smith of Adirondack Community College helped us locate reading selections, and Joanna Imm, Julie McBurney, and Judy Voss all provided editorial suggestions and guidance at various stages. Video producers Peter Berkow and Bruce Coykendahl have worked tirelessly on the videos that are part of *The McGraw-Hill Guide Online* and the Faculty Development Web site. Debora Person of the University of Wyoming provided expert commentary on the sections on library and Internet research, for which we thank her.

At McGraw-Hill, we were fortunate to have some of the best in the business helping us with this project, including Steve Debow, president of the Humanities, Social Science, and Languages group; Mike Ryan, editor in chief; Sharon Loeb, director of marketing; Allison Jones, our energetic and creative marketing manager; Ray Kelley, Paula Radosevich, Byron Hopkins, Audra Bussey, and Brian Gore, our terrific field publishers; and Jeff Brick, advertising design manager. Sherree D'Amico, our senior sales representative, and Mina Mathies, our regional manager, have both provided us with valuable advice. Betty Chen and Mia Alvar made contributions both to the text and the supplements, and Paul Banks, media development editor, has worked tirelessly on the *The McGraw-Hill Guide Online* and has provided us with useful comments on the text. Kim Menning and Jeanne Schreiber oversaw the beautiful design of the text, Janice Fehler copy edited the text, Jennifer Blankenship and Natalia Peschiera handled the photo research, and Brett Coker was responsible for seeing the text through production. We owe special thanks to Lisa Moore, now the publisher for history, arts, and the humanities, who originally helped us develop the concept and signed the project, and to Chris Bennem, senior sponsoring editor, who has guided us "editorially" in a thoughtful and kind manner. We also owe a special thanks to Carla Samodulski, senior development editor, and to Molly Meneely, who meticulously developed *The Concise McGraw-Hill Guide*. Thanks Lisa, Chris, Carla, and Molly.

The following instructors provided extremely useful advice about rhetorics at symposia sponsored by McGraw-Hill, for which we thank them:

Edith Baker, Bradley University

Charles Boyd, Genesee Community College

Amy Braziller, Red Rocks Community College-Lakewood

Jo Ann Buck, Guilford Technical Community College

Susan Callender, Sinclair Community College

Sandra Clark, Anderson University

Mary Ann Crawford, Central Michigan University

Brock Dethier, Utah State University

Anthony Edgington, University of Toledo

Steve Fox, Indiana University-Purdue University Indianapolis

Elaine Fredericksen, University of Texas-El Paso

Carolyn Handa, University of Alabama-Tuscaloosa

Christa Higgins Raney, University of North Alabama

Kim Jameson, Oklahoma City Community College

Nanette Jaynes, Wesleyan College

Peggy Jolly, University of Alabama-Birmingham

Elizabeth Kessler, University of Houston-Houston

Sandra Lakey, Pennsylvania College of Technology

Barry Mauer, University of Central Florida

John Miles, University of New Mexico-Albuquerque

Dave Reinheimer, Southeast Missouri State University

Denise Rogers, University of Louisiana-Lafayette

Mary Sauer, Indiana University-Purdue University Indianapolis

"I love the readings! They are one of the outstanding parts of the book. They are not simply didactic or chosen because they deal with politically correct topics, though they often do. They are just exceedingly well written and highly engaging pieces that both I and my students can enjoy. It's hard to choose a favorite, …"

—Geraldine Wagner, Johnson & Wales University

"Students are critical consumers today, and they want to know what they're getting for their investment in time and money. Presenting the goals and objectives up front honors their intelligence."

—Christopher Twiggs, Florida Community College

"Examples are plentiful, directions are practical, and the readings are refreshingly current. Thank goodness there are many new topics and different authors!"

—Cindy Catherwood,
Metropolitan Community
College

"This book provides a sound, student-friendly approach to writing for many purposes and in many genres, with excellent professional readings. A highlight of the text is the integration of actual student work into the writing process section of each assignment chapter."

—Steve Fox, Indiana University-
Purdue University Indianapolis

Mark Saunders, Front Range Community College, Boulder City

Kip Strasma, Illinois Central College

Gordon Thomas, University of Idaho

Donna Thomsen, Johnson & Wales University, Providence

Jeffrey Weimelt, Southeastern Louisiana University

John M. Ziebell, College of Southern Nevada

As we developed this text, we needed to test each assignment chapter in actual classrooms. We are immensely grateful to the following instructors and their students for class-testing chapters from *The McGraw-Hill Guide* and providing us with frank and valuable feedback:

Angela Adams, Loyola University-Chicago

Luisa Benton, El Centro College

Charley Boyd, Genesee Community College

Marybeth Bradley, Grand Rapids Community College

Robin Bryant, Phillips Community College
of the University of Arkansas

Laura Butler, West Texas A&M University

Regina Clemens Fox, Arizona State University

Michelle Crummey, Southwest Missouri State University

Sarah Dean, Arizona State University

James Drake, Arizona State University

Darrel Elmore, Arizona State University

Malvina Engelberg, Nova Southeastern University

Katy Grant, Arizona State University

Gwen Gray Schwartz, University of Arizona

Nanette Jaynes, Wesleyan College

Ellen Johnson, Arizona State University

Sally Lahmon, Sinclair Community College

William Lamb, Johnson County Community College

Jeanne Levy, Arizona State University

Leanne Maunu, Palomar College

Mildred Melendez, Sinclair Community College

Susan Miller, Mesa Community College

Terry Moore, Arizona State University

Karyn Reidell, Arizona State University

Jill Richards-Young, Arizona State University

Jenny Rytting, Arizona State University

Sarah Schwab, St. Louis University

Tom Skeen, Arizona State University

Carol Smith, Coastal Georgia Community College

Dana Tait, Arizona State University

Laci Talley, Baton Rouge Community College

Jillian Toomey, University of Arizona

Julie Townsend, University of North Carolina

Anna Varley, University of Arizona

Keith Yokley, Greensboro College

We are extremely grateful to all of the instructors who have provided us with their insights and suggestions as we have developed this project:

Michelle Auerbach, Front Range Community College-Boulder

Adrian Ayres Fisher, Triton College

Edith Baker, Bradley University

Larry Beason, University of South Alabama-Mobile

Luisa Benton, El Centro College

Kyle Bishop, Southern Utah University

Vicki Bott, University of Wisconsin-Milwaukee

Charley Boyd, Genesee Community College

Barbara Brown, San Jacinto College-Pasadena

Robin Bryant, Phillips Community College of the University of Arkansas

Jo Ann Buck, Guilford Technical Community College

Polly Buckingham, Eastern Washington University

> *This text comes more closely to fitting the way I teach my class in terms of building on assignments, the writing process, and the various components of the process and assignments than any other text I've used or surveyed. And as I mentioned at the beginning, I generally "force" a text to fit into my classroom; this textbook would not have to be forced to fit into my instructional goals and objectives as so many others are.*
>
> —Susie Kuilan, Northwestern State University, LA

Michael Burke, Southern Illinois University-Edwardsville

Laura Butler, West Texas A&M University

Sharon Buzzard, Quincy University

Susan Callender, Sinclair Community College

Vincent Casaregola, St. Louis University

Cindy Catherwood, Metropolitan Community College

Gary Christenson, Elgin Community College

Ann Christiansen, University of Houston-Houston

Ron Christiansen, Salt Lake Community College

Sandra Clark, Anderson University

Regina Clemens Fox, Arizona State University

Carol Conder, University of Nevada-Las Vegas

David Correll, Langston University

Mark Crane, Utah Valley State College

Mary Ann Crawford, Central Michigan University

Sarah Dean, Arizona State University

Debra Dew, University of Colorado

Anthony Edgington, University of Toledo

Jonell Farrar, San Jacinto College-Pasadena

Daniel Ferguson, Amarillo College

Steve Fox, Indiana University-Purdue University Indianapolis

Elaine Frederickson, University of Texas-El Paso

Lisa Gordon, Columbus State Community College

Jeanne Ann Graham, Ivy Tech Community College

Gordon Grant, Baylor University

Carolyn Handa, University of Alabama-Tuscaloosa

Anne Helms, Alamance Community College

Anneliese Homan, State Fair Community College

Phil Hutcheon, San Joaquin Delta Community College

Jon Inglett, Oklahoma City Community College

"The McGraw-Hill Guide: Writing for College, Writing for Life is an exceptionally thorough approach to teaching composition skills. Its focus on rhetorical techniques and critical thinking, along with its attention to writing beyond the composition classroom, make it stand apart from other composition texts. "

—Jessica Kidd, University of Alabama, Tuscaloosa

"This text approaches writing from an organic perspective—that is, the text demonstrates that good, effective writing does not come from strict adherence to genre formulas, but rather, good writing grows out of a writer's understanding of purpose, audience, and situation. "

—James Krajewski, Kansas City Kansas Community College

Peggy Jolly, University of Alabama-Birmingham

Dennis Kasum, University of South Florida

Elizabeth Kessler, University of Houston

Jessica Kidd, University of Alabama- Tuscaloosa

James Krajewski, Kansas City Kansas Community College

Julie Kratt, Cowley County Community College

Susie Kuilan, Northwestern State University

Sally Lahmon, Sinclair Community College

Sandra Lakey, Pennsylvania College of Technology

William Lamb, Johnson County Community College

Marianne Liauba, South Suburban College

Lucinda Ligget, Ivy Tech Community College

Margaret Lindgren, University of Cincinnati

Michael Mackey, Community College of Denver

Martha Marinara, University of Central Florida

Kelly Martin, Collin County Community College- Plano

Barry Mauer, University of Central Florida

Leanne Maunu, Palomar College

Mary Pat McQueeney, Johnson County Community College

Elizabeth Metzger, University of South Florida

Philip Mitchell, Dallas Baptist University

Cindy Moore, Eastern Kentucky University

Lyle Morgan, Pittsburg State University

Robin Mosher, Kansas State University

Bonnie Noonan, Xavier University of Louisiana

Michelle Pichon, Northwestern State University

Shelby Pierce, Owens Community College

Erin Pushman, Limestone College

Christa Raney, University of North Alabama

David Reinheimer, Southeast Missouri State University

"*Overall, I think this book looks really good. I'm intrigued by how much this book will change how I teach this class while really supporting the goals I already incorporate into my classroom. Excellent work!*"
—Sarah Dean,
Arizona State University

"[The McGraw-Hill Guide] ... *teaches sound rhetorical theory in an accessible and engaging manner with effective support for both students and instructors ...this text would be a useful addition to the texts that our instructors choose among.*"
—Martha Marinara,
University of Central Florida

"This is a text that addresses the many kinds of writing our students will be called upon to complete—not just in their academic lives, but in their personal and professional lives as well. This text will help faculty prepare students for the kinds of real world writing that will convince students that writing is integral to their success both in and beyond the college classroom.... We look forward to its publication."

—Donna Thomsen, Johnson & Wales University

Lois Reynolds, Pellissippi State

Paul Rodgers, Henry Ford Community College

Denise Rogers, University of Louisiana-Lafayette

Shirley Rose, Purdue University-West Lafayette

Mary Sauer, Indiana University-Purdue University Indianapolis

Mark Saunders, Front Range Community College-Boulder

Barbara Schneider, University of Toledo

William Schuh, Erie Community College

Nick Serra, Upper Iowa University

Michelle Sidler, Auburn University

Eric Stalions, Augusta State University

Ed Stieve, Nova Southeastern University

Denise Sutton, Grand Rapids Community College

David Tanner, Eastern Arizona College

Donna Thomsen, Johnson & Wales University

Christopher Twiggs, Florida Community College

Geraldine Wagner, Johnson & Wales University

Colin Wansor, Indiana University of Pennsylvania

William Waters, Northwest Missouri State University

Scott Weeden, Indiana University-Purdue University Indianapolis

Temple West, Old Dominion University

Rosemary Winslow, Catholic University of America

Lynn Woodbury, Oakton Community College

Keith Yokley, Greensboro College

Kathie Zemke, Western Illinois University

Finally, we are indebted to our reviewers who focused specifically on the manuscript of *The Concise McGraw-Hill Guide,* and we thank them for their insightful and thorough feedback that helpfully informed our work on this text.

Lori Ambacher, Gordon College

Elizabeth Baldridge, Illinois Central College

Charlotte Brammer, Samford University

Diane Canow, Johnson Community College

Billye Currie, Samford University

Terry Engebretsen, Idaho State University

Ashley Lawson, West Virginia Wesleyan College

Lynn Lewis, University of Oklahoma

Peggy Lindsey, Wright State University-Dayton

Jeanne McDonald, Waubonsee Community College

Timothy McGinn, North West Arkansas Community College

Robin Murray, Eastern Illinois University

Tony Procell, El Paso Community College-Northwest Campus

Mark Reynolds, Jefferson Davis Community College

Jessica Santini, Bismarck State College

Mary Sauer, Indiana University-Purdue University Indianapolis

Mark Saunders, Front Range Community College, Boulder County Campus

Matthew Schmeer, Johnson County Community College

Donna Strickland, University of Missouri

Debbie Williams, Abilene Christian University

Duane Roen
Gregory R. Glau
Barry M. Maid

WPA Outcomes Statement for First-Year Composition

Adopted by the Council of Writing Program Administrators (WPA), April 2000

For further information about the development of the Outcomes Statement, please see
> http://comppile.tamucc.edu/WPAoutcomes/continue.html

For further information about the Council of Writing Program Administrators, please see
> http://www.wpacouncil.org

A version of this statement was published in *WPA: Writing Program Administration* 23.1/2 (fall/winter 1999): 59-66

Introduction

This statement describes the common knowledge, skills, and attitudes sought by first-year composition programs in American postsecondary education. To some extent, we seek to regularize what can be expected to be taught in first-year composition; to this end the document is not merely a compilation or summary of what currently takes place. Rather, the following statement articulates what composition teachers nationwide have learned from practice, research, and theory. This document intentionally defines only "outcomes," or types of results, and not "standards," or precise levels of achievement. The setting of standards should be left to specific institutions or specific groups of institutions.

Learning to write is a complex process, both individual and social, that takes place over time with continued practice and informed guidance. Therefore, it is important that teachers, administrators, and a concerned public do not imagine that these outcomes can be taught in reduced or simple ways. Helping students demonstrate these outcomes requires expert understanding of how students actually learn to write. For this reason we expect the primary audience for this document to be well-prepared college writing teachers and college writing program administrators. In some places, we have chosen to write in their professional language. Among such readers, terms such as "rhetorical" and "genre" convey a rich meaning that is not easily simplified. While we have also aimed at writing a document that the general public can understand, in limited cases we have aimed first at communicating effectively with expert writing teachers and writing program administrators.

These statements describe only what we expect to find at the end of first-year composition, at most schools a required general education course or sequence of courses. As writers move beyond first-year composition, their writing abilities do not merely improve. Rather, students' abilities not only diversify along disciplinary and professional lines but also move into whole new levels where expected outcomes expand, multiply, and diverge. For this reason, each statement of outcomes for first-year composition is followed by suggestions for further work that builds on these outcomes.

RHETORICAL KNOWLEDGE

By the end of first year composition, students should

- Focus on a purpose
- Respond to the needs of different audiences
- Respond appropriately to different kinds of rhetorical situations
- Use conventions of format and structure appropriate to the rhetorical situation
- Adopt appropriate voice, tone, and level of formality
- Understand how genres shape reading and writing
- Write in several genres

Faculty in all programs and departments can build on this preparation by helping students learn

- The main features of writing in their fields
- The main uses of writing in their fields
- The expectations of readers in their fields

CRITICAL THINKING, READING, AND WRITING

By the end of first year composition, students should

- Use writing and reading for inquiry, learning, thinking, and communicating
- Understand a writing assignment as a series of tasks, including finding, evaluating, analyzing, and synthesizing appropriate primary and secondary sources
- Integrate their own ideas with those of others
- Understand the relationships among language, knowledge, and power

Faculty in all programs and departments can build on this preparation by helping students learn

- The uses of writing as a critical thinking method
- The interactions among critical thinking, critical reading, and writing
- The relationships among language, knowledge, and power in their fields

PROCESSES

By the end of first year composition, students should

- Be aware that it usually takes multiple drafts to create and complete a successful text
- Develop flexible strategies for generating, revising, editing, and proof-reading
- Understand writing as an open process that permits writers to use later invention and re-thinking to revise their work
- Understand the collaborative and social aspects of writing processes
- Learn to critique their own and others' works
- Learn to balance the advantages of relying on others with the responsibility of doing their part
- Use a variety of technologies to address a range of audiences

Faculty in all programs and departments can build on this preparation by helping students learn

- To build final results in stages
- To review work-in-progress in collaborative peer groups for purposes other than editing
- To save extensive editing for later parts of the writing process
- To apply the technologies commonly used to research and communicate within their fields

KNOWLEDGE OF CONVENTIONS

By the end of first year composition, students should

- Learn common formats for different kinds of texts
- Develop knowledge of genre conventions ranging from structure and paragraphing to tone and mechanics
- Practice appropriate means of documenting their work
- Control such surface features as syntax, grammar, punctuation, and spelling

Faculty in all programs and departments can build on this preparation by helping students learn

- The conventions of usage, specialized vocabulary, format, and documentation in their fields
- Strategies through which better control of conventions can be achieved

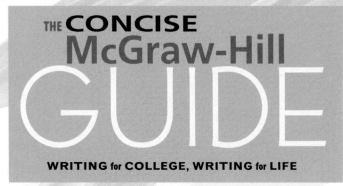

THE **CONCISE**
McGraw-Hill
GUIDE

WRITING for COLLEGE, WRITING for LIFE

1

Getting Started

Writing Goals and Objectives for College and for Life

Whenever you write in college, or for any other purpose in your life, you write to fulfill a goal. In school, you write papers and essay exam answers to demonstrate what you have learned and communicate your ideas to others. Writing is also a powerful tool for learning course material. You can use it every day to take notes during lectures and annotate assigned reading. Outside of school, you probably use—or will use—writing to perform your duties in the workplace and to make your voice heard in your community. You might also use writing to communicate with friends and family. Many of us keep in touch with our loved ones through daily e-mail exchanges or text messages.

Whether you are writing for a course or for a nonacademic reason, though, one of the most important principles of this book is that effective writers achieve their objectives with their writing. Throughout the ages, rhetoricians, scholars who study the subject of written and oral communication, have understood the importance of using language to get things done. Consider the following definitions of **rhetoric** by some well-known rhetoricians:

> Rhetoric is "the means whereby language, spoken or written, may be rendered effective."
>
> —Alexander Bain, *English Composition and Rhetoric,* 1866*

> Rhetoric is "the faculty of observing in any given case the available means of persuasion."
>
> —Aristotle, *Rhetoric*

> Rhetoric is the "symbolic means of inducing cooperation in beings that by nature respond to symbols."
>
> —Kenneth Burke, *A Rhetoric of Motives*, 1950

You have probably noticed that in each definition, the rhetorician focuses on using words—either spoken or written—to achieve some goal. Other than perhaps the yell you release when you stub your toe, most discourse, whether spoken or written, has some goal or **purpose:** to explain, to inform, to persuade, to indicate how to do something. In your college, civic, professional, and personal worlds, you use words to *do* things, to accomplish your objectives.

---

*You can find citations for all quotations in this text in the Credits section at the end of the book. For an explanation of the MLA and APA style for citing sources, which are used in many academic disciplines, see Chapter 20.

Taking our cue from the rhetoricians quoted above, we have endeavored to give each chapter in this book—especially the chapters in Parts 2 and 3, which provide writing assignments—a *rhetorical* focus. Each chapter focuses on what you as a writer want your writing to *accomplish*. The first decision any writer makes, then, is rhetorical: what would you like this writing to *do* for a particular group of readers—your **audience**—at a particular place and time? All of your subsequent writing decisions follow from your goals. Once you have determined your goals, you are prepared to decide how much and what kinds of information your audience needs to know, what kind of research you might need to conduct to collect this information, what kind of evidence will be convincing to your audience, and the best format in which to present your information.

This rhetorical approach may be different from the kind of writing you have done in the past, where you were perhaps assigned to write an essay or a research paper on a particular topic, with no notion of an audience or a purpose for that paper. But if you think about the writing that you do on your own, outside of class, you will see that you do not decide to write a letter or send an e-mail or construct a formal proposal until you figure out your purpose—what you want that letter or e-mail or proposal to do. As noted in the next section of this chapter, this rhetorical approach applies to writing that you do in various settings—not just in the classroom.

Writing in the Four Areas of Your Life

You may think that the writing skills you will learn in this course are meant to help you write successfully in your other classes as well, and of course the ability to write effective college papers is an important goal of this course and this text. Writing skills are vitally important not just in college, however, but also in the professional, civic, and personal parts of your life.

Consider how you plan to spend the twenty-four hours in each day for the next week, the next month, the next year, the next four years, the next decade, and the next six decades. If you are like most students, during the next few years you will devote much of your time to your academic studies. When you finish your academic studies, however, your time commitments will probably change. Although it is possible that you may still be a full-time student half a decade from now, it is more likely that you will devote more time to the other three parts of your life—especially to your professional life.

WRITING ACTIVITY

Balancing the Four Areas of Life

Working with two or three of your classmates, answer the following questions about the bar graph shown in Figure 1.1. Compare and discuss your responses. Your instructor may ask your small group to share its findings with the rest of the class.

- Which bar graph (1, 2, 3, or 4) comes closest to representing the current balance in your life?
- Which bar graph comes closest to representing what you consider the ideal balance for someone enrolled full-time in college? For someone enrolled part-time? For a student with family responsibilities and/or a part-time or full-time job?
- Which bar graph best represents the balance that you would like to achieve a decade from now? Two decades from now? Five decades from now?

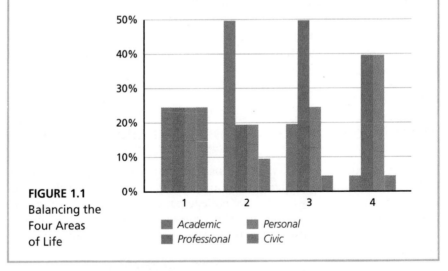

FIGURE 1.1
Balancing the
Four Areas
of Life

No matter how the four areas of your life are balanced, writing plays an important role in each of them.

Writing as a College Student

See Chapter 3 for writing-to-learn strategies.

You will be expected to do a great deal of writing in college because writing is a powerful tool both for learning and for demonstrating that learning. Students who use writing to explore course material generally learn more—and get higher grades—than students who do not. The reason for this enhanced performance is fairly simple: Writing is an effective way to become more involved with your course material.

Writing as a Professional

Almost all jobs require some writing; some require a great deal of it. Furthermore, there is a general correlation between the prestige of a job—and the level of income it generates—and the amount of writing required for that job. That is, people in important jobs that pay higher salaries tend to write more than people in lower-level jobs. The time to build essential writing skills is now while you are an undergraduate student.

Surveys of employers consistently yield results that bear out the importance of writing in the work world: employers want to hire people who can write and speak clearly and effectively, think critically, solve problems efficiently, work well in teams, and use technology thoughtfully. In other words, they prefer employees who have already developed these soft skills in college. Of course, developing these skills takes many years, so the most competitive job seekers are those who begin honing these skills as early as possible.

Writing as a Citizen

As Thomas Jefferson frequently noted, democracies—and societies in general—work best when citizens are well-educated and get involved. If you have strong feelings about certain issues and want to have a voice in how your society functions, you need to participate in your community. Of course, you can get involved by volunteering your time. But an important way to make your voice heard in a representative democracy is to write. You can write to elected officials at the local, state, and federal levels to let them know what you think about an issue and why you think the way that you do. In the civic part of your life you often will work with others—neighbors or other citizens who are involved and interested in solving problems that affect them, their neighborhood, and their community.

Writing as a Family Member or Friend

Even though writing in the academic, professional, and civic areas of life is important, the writing that you do in your personal life is probably the most important of all. We write to the people who are significant to us—whether on paper or in cyberspace—to accomplish life's daily tasks and to fulfill our needs.

Writing in the Four Areas in This Course

Because the academic, professional, civic, and personal parts of our lives are all important, this book offers numerous opportunities to write in all four areas. In each chapter in Parts 2 and 3, you have the option of writing in response to an academic or other type of situation.

Because any writing you do will have various rhetorical goals and purposes, what you will learn in this book will help you make the right kinds of writing choices whether you are writing an academic essay, working with others to construct a business proposal, writing a letter to the editor about a community problem, or writing to console an unhappy friend. In addition, the writing assignments in Parts 2 and 3 are built around **scenarios**—simulated but realistic writing situations. For each assignment, you will have a specific purpose for constructing your writing and a specific audience you are writing to.

Learning Goals in This Course

Whether you are writing for an academic, a professional, a civic, or a personal audience and purpose, you will need to draw on the same set of writing skills. Your work in this course will help you both to learn and to apply these skills to specific writing situations. To this end, throughout the text we have taken care to incorporate the learning goals developed by the Council of Writing Program Administrators (WPA), a national organization of instructors who direct composition courses. The goals are organized into four broad areas: **rhetorical knowledge; critical thinking, reading, and writing; writing processes;** and **knowledge of conventions.**

Rhetorical Knowledge

As we have noted, all writing is done for a particular purpose, in response to the needs of a specific audience. In other words, writers write in response to a **rhetorical situation.** Although each rhetorical situation is unique, there are general types of situations that require writers to use the appropriate conventions of format and structure in their writing. For example, if you are writing a lab report for a biology course, your instructor will expect you to structure your report in a certain way and use a neutral, informative tone. If you are proposing a solution to a problem in your community, your readers will expect you to describe the problem first and explain how your solution can be implemented, using a reasonable, even-handed tone and giving some attention to those who might raise objections to your proposal. The established forms of writing that are used to respond to each of these situations are known as **genres.** Genre in writing means that you follow the conventions of a kind of writing and provide, generally, what readers expect from that genre. For example, a paper for one of your college classes will generally be more formal and detailed than an e-mail you might write to your classmates, asking them to vote in an upcoming election.

From a rhetorical standpoint, you select the format to use (a letter, an e-mail, a memo, a formal report) based on what you want to accomplish. Think of format as the overall structure of the piece of writing you are constructing. For example, a letter will have a salutation, a body, and a signature. The format of that letter could vary widely—it could be organized in paragraphs or it could be given in a list. To write for others successfully, then, you need to determine how to adapt your writing to meet their expectations and needs. In other words, you need to focus on where there is a meeting of minds—yours and theirs—and where there is not. For example, if you were to write the following grocery list and take it to the store, you would probably know precisely what you had in mind. Take a moment to think about what you would bring home.

Grocery List
cereal
milk
coffee
bread
paper

If you were sick, however, and had to rely on a close family member to do your grocery shopping for you, you might have to revise the list by adding a few more details:

A Version of the Grocery List for a Family Member
Cereal
1% milk
Coffee beans
White bread
Sunday paper

If you handed the list to a neighbor, though, you would probably have to add much more specific information:

A Version of the Grocery List for a Neighbor
Grape Nuts Flakes
1% milk (half gallon)
Whole bean Starbucks Columbian coffee
Grandma Sycamore's white bread
The *New York Times*

In each case, you need to adjust your list depending on the person who will be acting on the information. When you share a great deal of lived experience with your reader, you can leave gaps in information without causing serious problems. The fewer experiences you have in common with your audience, however, the more you need to fill in those gaps while you write and revise, rather than after you have finished writing. The best way to identify those gaps is to share your writing with as many people as possible so that they can point them out.

Critical Thinking, Reading, and Writing

To get the most out of your reading, and to accomplish your goals as a writer, you need to develop and use critical thinking skills. In Chapter 2 we offer some informal reading and writing activities that promote critical thinking. While these activities will help you read more thoughtfully, many of them are also tools for generating ideas and material for the more formal writing tasks you will do in all four parts of your life.

In general, you engage in **critical thinking** when you examine an idea from many perspectives—seeing it in new ways. For example, when you write a formal argument, you will need to address others' objections to your ideas if you hope to persuade your audience to accept your point. You can also apply critical thinking to understand the relationships among language, knowledge, and power. That is, language often has a greater effect when it is used by people in positions of social, political, or economic power.

In the twenty-first century, language, when used effectively, is often far more powerful than physical weapons. Modern civilizations have written constitutions and written laws derived from those constitutions. The most politically and economically powerful people in societies tend to be those who use critical thinking and language most effectively to present their ideas.

Writing Processes

Although writing processes vary from writer to writer and from situation to situation, effective writers generally need to go through the following processes:

- Generating initial ideas
- Relating those ideas to the writing situation or assignment
- Conducting research to find support for their ideas
- Organizing ideas and support and writing an initial draft
- Revising and shaping the paper, frequently with the advice of other readers
- Editing and polishing the paper

The order of these processes can vary, and often you will need to return to a previous step. For example, while drafting you may discover that you need to find more support for one of your ideas; while revising you may find a better way to organize your ideas. In addition, effective writers develop many strategies for generating ideas, for drafting, for revising, and for editing.

When writers revise, they add or delete words, phrases, sentences, or even whole paragraphs, and they often modify their ideas. After they have revised multiple times, they then edit, attending to word choice, punctuation, grammar, usage, and spelling—the "surface features" of written texts. To have time for multiple rounds of revising and editing, of course, a writer needs to begin a writing task early. Beginning a formal paper the day before it is due rarely results in satisfactory work.

Effective writers also understand the principle that two heads are better than one. Therefore, they ask others to help them generate and refine their ideas and polish their prose. Published writers in academic, civic, and professional fields rely heavily on others as they work, often showing one another drafts of their writing before submitting a manuscript to publishers.

Because effective writers get help from others, this book provides many opportunities for your classmates—your **peers**—to help you. One key to working productively with others is to understand that they bring differing backgrounds, experiences, knowledge, and perspectives to the writing task, so it is critical to treat what others think and have to say with respect, no matter how much you agree or disagree with them.

You should also remember when working with others that the suggestions and comments they make are about your *text*, not about you. Too often writers tend to take comments and suggestions personally, as if those comments were directed at them, rather than at their text.

Knowledge of Conventions

Conventions are the table manners of writing. At times, they matter; at other times, they do not. Writing for yourself to learn course material is like eating breakfast alone at home. When you are having dinner with your employer or the president of your college, though, table manners do matter. The same principle applies when you write for readers. Effective writers know which writing conventions they should use in particular settings.

Of course, writers who are striving to make their writing more appealing to readers need to master many kinds of conventions: spelling, punctuation, sentence structure, and word choice. While some conventions are considered signs of the writer's respect for readers (correctly spelling someone's name, for instance), other conventions such as punctuation, organization, tone, the use of headers and white space, and documentation style, guide your readers to understand what you are saying.

WRITING ACTIVITY

Assessing Your Strengths and Weaknesses

In no more than two pages, assess your current strengths and weaknesses in each of the four goal areas: rhetorical knowledge; critical thinking, reading, and writing; writing processes; and knowledge of conventions. Once you have completed your assessment, share your list with two or three classmates.

Becoming a Self-Reflective Writer

By evaluating your strengths and weaknesses in each of the four learning outcomes, you have taken a step toward becoming a more reflective—and therefore a more successful—writer. Throughout this course, you will continue to build on this foundation. Toward the end of each chapter in Parts 2 and 3, you will be asked to reflect on the work you did for that chapter, so that similar writing tasks will be easier for you to complete, and so that your results will be even better in the future. When you reflect—in writing—on your own writing activities, such thinking helps you learn what worked for you (and perhaps what did not work). That kind of activity will help you the next time you face a similar writing task because reflective activity helps you to remember the best aspects of your process.

Writing in Today's World

Regardless of whether they are writing for an academic, a professional, a civic, or a personal purpose, writers today have more responsibilities than ever before because online technology makes writing available to a wide spectrum of readers. Writers who are careless in representing themselves or who use technology negligently can live to regret their lack of caution. Wise writers ask themselves the following question before publishing any of their writing electronically: What would the consequences be if this piece of writing were to appear on the front page of a local or national newspaper, a radio show, a television news program, the homepage of a Web site or a blog?

Writing Responsibly

When you write responsibly, you establish your character for your reader. The Greek philosopher and rhetorician Aristotle suggested that a writer's or speaker's *ethos*, his or her character, is one of the ways people are persuaded: readers believe you because of who you are, how you portray yourself, how you present your information, the logic you use, and the language you employ. How a writer presents himself or herself establishes that *ethos*.

Not only do writers need to present their arguments accurately and fairly, they also need to be aware of how they "sound" to their readers. You present a positive image of yourself to readers through the persona you create by the words you use. If you call opponents names and use incendiary language to describe the issue you are writing about, you will come across less convincingly than if you are logical, well-prepared, and provide solid evidence to support your case, with citations for all of your sources.

Writing Technologies

As you make decisions about writing for various audiences and purposes in the four areas of your life, you will also need to make decisions about how and when to use various kinds of technology. Recently, researchers, educators, and others have been focusing on the ways in which digital technologies are affecting—positively or negatively—how people write. Such discussions are not really that new, though. For at least several thousand years humans have understood that writing is inseparable from the technologies that make it possible. For our purposes here, **technology** is a system or practice that extends human capabilities. The system of writing that we use is actually a technology for extending human thought across time and space. Other technologies facilitate the act of writing. For example, a person can write by using an index finger to inscribe letters on sand or even soft clay tablets. With your fingernails, you can inscribe less pliable surfaces such as soft wood or a wax tablet. The point, of course, is that throughout history writers have used the best technologies available.

A generation ago it was relatively difficult to integrate words and pictures because the technology for doing so was expensive and time-consuming. However, it is now relatively easy to mix words, still pictures, video segments, audio segments, and Web links in a single digital text. These capabilities have enabled writers to become more imaginative as they compose, but these capabilities have also given writers many more choices to make as they construct texts. Throughout this text, you will be encouraged to make informed choices about the most appropriate technology to use for your audience and purpose. Chapter 17 offers additional advice on choosing a medium, genre, and technology for your written communication.

TechNote You and your friends and classmates can help each other get more out of the writing technologies that are available now or will soon become available. Don't be shy about asking friends and classmates for tips and tricks they've picked up while writing their papers with computer software. You can use your own computing knowledge as social collateral in classes where students use computers to complete assignments because some students will be more comfortable than others with the available software.

WRITING ACTIVITY

Assessing Your Uses of Technology

Think about the ways that you have used digital technologies in the past year. List a few tasks that you have done with technology in the grid below. When you have finished listing tasks, compare your list with those of several classmates.

Technological Tool	Academic Situation	Professional, Civic, or Personal Situation
E-mail		
Word-processing software		
Web browser (e.g., Mozilla Firefox, Internet Explorer)		
Web site composing tools (e.g., *Dreamweaver, Frontpage, Netscape Composer*)		
Web logs (blogs)		
Other		

Reading Critically for College and for Life

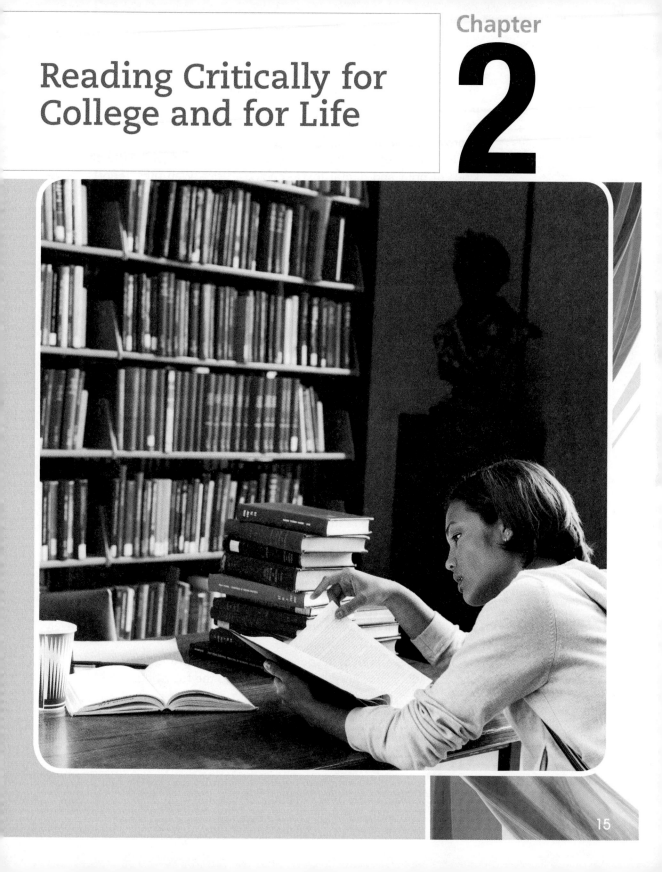

In Chapter 1, we considered how writing skills will serve you in the academic, professional, civic, and personal parts of your life—especially in your academic life. This chapter focuses on an activity that reinforces and helps you improve your writing skills: **reading.**

In your college classes, you will be asked to read (and write about) all kinds of print and digital texts—books, articles, Web sites, reports, newspaper stories, listservs, and others—for all kinds of purposes. More often than not, you will use some of what you read in the papers that you write for your college classes. The connection between what you read and how you use that material in your writing requires you to read not just casually, but *critically*.

To define the term *reading critically*, we might begin with the first word: *reading*. When we read, of course, we make meaning out of words on a page or computer screen. We can even extend our definition to include "reading" photographs, charts and graphs, Web pages, and other visual images. Actually, reading is not simply a process of figuring out, or decoding, what words mean, but rather it is the active process of constructing meaning. Just as a writer works to say something through the words and sentences of a piece of writing—to provide information, perhaps, or to make a point—a reader likewise has to work to construct the meaning of that same piece of writing.

If reading is constructing meaning, what about the second word: *critically*? When you read a text critically, you are not reading to *criticize* that text, to comment on how effective or ineffective it is, but rather to question what you read, to make connections to other articles, books, and Web pages that you have read as well as to your own experiences, and to think about how the information in the text you are reading might help you as you develop your own writing. To read critically means to read *thoughtfully*, keeping in mind what you already know. To read critically also means to read *actively*, interacting with the text as you bring your prior knowledge into play. Critical readers underline, make notes, and ask questions as they read. This chapter will give you some strategies and methods for reading actively and critically.

In college, as well as in your personal, civic, or professional life, this process of reading critically will enable you to do the following:

- **Consider an issue, a problem, or a topic in its full complexity:** Reading and thinking critically about a subject means that you examine it from many points of view.
- **Pose substantial questions that probe and test the information you are reading:** When you read actively, the questions you raise about the text will require careful analysis before you can answer them.

- **Synthesize or put together all of the information:** After reading a text critically, you should be able to gather the relevant information, data, and ideas that you have gleaned from the reading and construct a **synthesis,** an outline or summary of your perspective on the topic, based on your knowledge and your reading.

WRITING ACTIVITY

How Do You Read?

Take a few minutes to write your answers to these questions:

- What kinds of books or magazines do you like to read? Newspapers? Web sites? Blogs?
- How does the way you read a text from the World Wide Web differ from the way you read an article from a magazine or a newspaper?
- How do you read your college textbooks? How do the strategies you use to read a text for one course differ from those you use to read texts for another course?
- What strategies do you use to read long, complex nonfiction texts?
- What strategies do you use to help you understand and remember what you have read?

After you have answered the questions, share your comments with several classmates. How do your responses compare with theirs? What strategies do they use that might be helpful to you?

Using Prereading Strategies

When you write something, you usually have a purpose in mind. As we noted in Chapter 1, that reason for writing is called your **rhetorical purpose**—what you are hoping to accomplish. Likewise, before you read an article, a textbook chapter, a letter from a friend, or another piece of writing, think about your rhetorical purpose: what are you trying to accomplish by reading this text? Are you reading to be entertained, to learn new information, to understand a complex subject in more detail, or for some other reason? If you consciously think about *why* you are reading, as well as *how* you plan to read a particular text, you will have a strategy you can follow as you begin reading.

Whatever your purpose for reading, before you start to read any text, take a few minutes to preview its content and design. As you preview the text, look for the following elements:

- The title of the work, or of the particular section you are about to read
- Headings that serve as an outline of the text
- Boxes that highlight certain kinds of information
- Charts, maps, photographs, or drawings that are meant to help readers understand the information the author is providing
- Numbered or bulleted lists (such as this one) that set off certain information

Scanning these textual elements can help you get a quick sense of what you are about to read.

Think about what you bring to your reading task: In what ways does the text seem similar to or different from others of this type or on this topic that you have already read? What can you bring to the new reading that you have learned from your past experiences? If you are actively involved in the reading process and if you think of reading rhetorically—that is, if you think about what you want to get from the reading (for example, information, an explanation, directions)—then you will start with a useful map for any text you read.

After your preview, **skim** the text by reading the first and last sections or paragraphs as well as any elements that are highlighted in some way, such as boxes, section titles, headings, or terms or phrases in bold or italic type. Sometimes a box or highlighted section at the beginning of an article—often called an **abstract**—will give you a quick summary of what is ahead.

As a final step before you start to read, consider again what you are hoping to accomplish by reading this particular text. Ask yourself the following questions:

- What information—facts, statistics, graphs, data—have I noticed as I previewed the text that might help me with my writing task?
- How have I reacted so far to what I have seen in the text? Has anything startled me? Pleased me? Made me curious? Made me angry?
- What questions do I have?
- What in this text seems to relate to other texts that I have read?

Reading Actively

Now that previewing has given you a sense of what the text is about, you are ready to read actively. Here are some questions to ask yourself as you read:

- What is the writer's thesis or main point? What evidence does the writer provide to support that point? Does the writer offer statistics, facts, and expert opinion, or anecdotes (stories)?
- How reliable is the information in this text? How conscientiously does the writer indicate the sources of his or her data, facts, or examples? How reliable do these sources seem?

- What else do you know about this topic? How can you relate your previous knowledge to what this writer is saying? In what ways do you agree or disagree with the point the writer is making?

- Has the writer included examples that clarify the text? Are there photographs, drawings, or diagrams that help you understand the writer's main points? Graphs or charts that illustrate data or other statistical information? In what way(s) do the examples and visuals help you better understand the text? What information do they give you that the written text does not provide? What kinds of emotional impact do the photographs or other visual texts have?

- What information or evidence is not in this text? (Your past experience and reading will help you here.) Why do you think that the author might have left it out?

- If what you are reading is an argument, how effectively does the writer acknowledge or outline other points of view on the issue at hand?

For more on counterargument, see Chapter 14.

Annotating Effectively

When you **annotate,** you interact actively with the text as you read. To annotate a reading, make the following kinds of notes:

- Underline the main point or thesis of the reading or otherwise mark it as the key point.

- Underline key supporting points and indicate in the margins next to the corresponding paragraphs why you think each point is important.

Look for a photo of loon.

find website with loon call

16.5
x 6
99 feet

As I was paddling along the north shore one very calm October afternoon, for such days especially they settle on to the lakes, like the milkweed down, having looked in vain over the pond for a loon, suddenly one, sailing out from the shore toward the middle a few rods in front of me, set up his mild laugh and betrayed himself. I pursued with a paddle and he dived, but when he came up I was nearer than before. He dived again, but I miscalculated the direction he would take, and we were fifty rods apart when he came to the surface this time, for I had helped to widen the interval; and again he laughed long and loud, and with more reason than before. He manoeuvred so cunningly that I could not get within half a dozen rods of him. Each time, when he came to the surface, turning his head this way and that, he cooly surveyed the water and the land, and apparently chose his course so that he might come up where there was the widest expanse of water and at the greatest distance from the boat. It was surprising how quickly he made up his mind and put his resolve into execution.

What is milk weed?

rod = 16.5 feet

16.5
x50
725 feet

This reminds me of the gopher in our yard.

He attributes human qualities to the loon = anthropomorphism

FIGURE 2.1 Example of Annotations on a Page Excerpt from the chapter "Brute Neighbors" in *Walden* by Henry David Thoreau

TechNote Are you faced with one of those jargon-filled college reading assignments? When the glossary at the back of the book just isn't enough, try searching the World Wide Web for a definition. A number of good dictionaries and glossaries are available online. One trick is to use a Web search engine to find substantial definitions of complex terms. For example, if you're looking for a working definition of *existentialism*, type "define: existential" into a search engine's search screen. Often your top results will include dictionary sites, academic Web sites, and technical sites that have developed working glossaries for students, experts, and professionals.

- List any questions you have (you may find the answers as you read further).
- Respond to the text with your own remarks—especially ideas you can relate to other ideas you are familiar with.
- Jot down key terms—and their definitions—in the margins.
- Mark sections that summarize material as "summary," so you will be able to spot them more easily when you return to the text.

WRITING ACTIVITY

Annotating "A Purpose Greater Than Oneself"

"A Purpose Greater than Oneself" is an advertisement that appeared in the *New York Times* on September 23, 2001, shortly after the terrorist attack on the World Trade Center. This advertisement does not dwell on that event, however, but rather offers a statement about how the school that placed the advertisement feels and thinks about the concept of "community" and its students.

Annotate this advertisement by underlining, adding questions in the margins, and so on. As you work, keep in mind that this *is* an advertisement—yet it really does not seem to be trying to sell a product or service. To what extent do you agree? What do you think it is advertising? Why?

Share your annotations with several of your classmates, noting places where your annotations are similar as well as places where they differ.

A PURPOSE GREATER THAN ONESELF

MISS HALL'S SCHOOL

"It is in the shelter of each other that the people live." The Irish Proverb came to mind as girls and adults gathered in the school living room to hear about the wrenching terrorist attacks on this country a week and a half ago. Together, as we articulated our shock and our anger, we confirmed the power of collective spirit, determination, and resilience. Confronted with unfathomable loss, we knew that our country would prevail. In community, we performed the ancient task of teaching the next generation that hope and trust are stronger than hate.

Perhaps it took the image of America uniting after tragedy for us to understand how important it is to resist the loss of community in contemporary culture. Recent studies argue that Western societies have experienced a noticeable decrease in social capital or social connectedness over the past few decades. Suburban sprawl, busy parents, and the scatter of extended families have reduced the time we spend together and imperiled our collective strength.

And now researchers tell us that the rise in social disconnectedness parallels the rise in children's anxiety. How could it be otherwise? When our communities weaken, the individuals in them first become distrustful, then anxious. Young people need sustained, healthy interactions in order to learn how to trust themselves and others.

Adding to the rise in anxiety is girls' awareness that we expect more of them than ever before. In *The Hurried Child*, David Elkind says that today's youngsters are the "unwilling, unintended victims [of] constantly rising expectations." As a result-oriented society, we are fixated on high growth rate and strong performance as we try to compensate for the fractures in our collective life. These goals may be perfect for the GNP, but they are not sufficient for adolescents trying to become effective and balanced adults.

We are all familiar with the demands placed on young people. We expect high achievement, high test scores, admission to elite colleges, and early steps toward a brilliant career. At one time, the important challenges of school were tempered by the warmth of family and the relaxation of un-scheduled time with friends. Now, every minute not in school is scheduled. The bewildering changes in our society leave us with kids who sometimes seem to be drowning in a sea of adult requirements.

Even without the added pressure from this culture, adolescence is an uneasy time. Think of what a girl will accomplish between the ages of fourteen and eighteen. She must establish an identity, become independent from parents, learn about relationships, clarify ethical positions, grow physically, overcome awkwardness, deal with peer pressure, and maneuver through the social land mines, confronting sex, drugs, and our media-fired culture. Then, of course, she's expected to excel in Biology, Calculus, and U.S. Government and compete in team sports. Add onto that list getting into her first-choice college and keeping her room clean, and we will acknowledge that there is a lot to be uneasy about.

But a girl should not have to absorb all of the worries of the adult world just to grow up. She should not have to experience life as an unrelenting test in order to achieve. A strong community guided by wise and caring adults will empower her genius. It will let her know that she is not the only person who has ever encountered difficulty and frustration. It will connect her to others who have met serious challenges and accomplished great works. She will learn to trust the sufficiency of her person, and she will develop a purpose that is greater than herself. Instead of feeling small and anxious, she will be expansive and confident. She will relax and work from inside herself. She will do everything she needs to do and more.

Reading Visuals

While college students are most often asked to read words on paper—such as the ones you are reading now—other types of texts can be read, usually by using the same strategies you use to read sentences and paragraphs critically. However, because you see so many visual images in a typical day—on television, on billboards, in newspapers, and on the Internet—you might think that visuals are easier to read than plain old written text, but this assumption is not accurate. In fact, you often have to pay more attention to visual images, not only because they are sometimes subtler than written text, but because you are not accustomed to reading them critically.

While the process of understanding photographs, bar and line graphs, diagrams, and other visuals may seem different from that of reading and understanding textual information, you are essentially doing the same kind of work. When you read a text, you translate letters, words, and sentences into concepts and ideas; when you read a photograph or a chart (or another kind of visual image), you do the same kind of translation. Just as you read a printed text such as an article in your local newspaper for information, you also read the photographs in the newspaper or the images on your television screen to be informed.

As you read visuals, here are some questions to consider:

- What words can I use to describe the visual? That is, how can I use words to tell what the visual shows?
- If the visual is combined with written text, what does the visual add to the verbal text? What would be lost if the visual were not there? How necessary is the visual?
- Why do you think that the writer chose this particular format—photo, line drawing, chart, graph—for the visual?
- If you were choosing or designing a visual to illustrate this point, what would it look like?
- How accurately does the visual illustrate the point?
- What emotions does the visual evoke?

WRITING ACTIVITY

Reading Text and Visuals in an Advertisement

Select a full-page advertisement from a newspaper or magazine and read both the written text and the visual elements carefully, keeping in mind that nothing in an advertisement is left to chance. Each element, from the kind and size of the typeface to the colors to the illustrations or photographs, has been discussed and modified many times as the advertisement was developed and tested. On a separate piece of paper, jot down answers to the following questions:

- What is this advertiser trying to sell?
- What kinds of evidence does the advertisement use to convince you to buy the product or service?
- In what ways does the advertisement appeal to your emotions?
- What strategies does the advertiser employ to convince you of the credibility of the ad's message?

- How effective is this advertisement? Why?
- How might the various elements of the advertisement—colors, photos or other visuals, background, text—be changed to make the ad more, or less, effective?
- How much does the advertisement help potential buyers make informed decisions about this product?

If your instructor asks you to do so, share your advertisements and notes with several of your classmates. What similarities did you find in the advertisements that you selected? In what ways did the advertisements make use of visuals? What were the most effective elements of the advertisements?

Reading Web Sites

Today many of us read Web sites, which can include not only text, with type in different colors and various sizes, but also photographs or other visual elements, videos that readers can click on to view, and music. To read Web sites actively and critically, you need to examine the information on your screen just as carefully as you would a page of printed text or a visual in a magazine or newspaper, asking the questions you would ask when reading a print or visual text critically (see page 22). Because there are more aspects of the text to examine and consider, however, and also because it is often harder to establish where a text on the Web comes from, active reading becomes even more important. Consider the following additional questions when you are reading a Web page:

- The uniform resource locator (URL) of a site, its address, can give you clues about its origin and purpose. For any page you visit, consider what the URL tells you about the page, especially the last three letters—*edu* (educational), *gov* (U.S. government), *org* (nonprofit organization), or *com* (commercial). What difference does it make who sponsors the site?
- How reputable is the person or agency that is providing the information on this page? You can check the person's or agency's reputation by doing a Web search (in Google or Yahoo, for instance), using the name of the person or the agency as your keyword.
- What clues do you see as to the motives of the person or agency that is providing this information? Is there a link to an explanation of the purpose of the site? Usually such explanations are labeled something like "About [name of organization or person]."
- How current is the information on this page? Can you find a date that indicates when the page was last updated?
- If there are links on the page, how helpful is the description of each link? Are the links working, or do they lead to dead ends?

For further details about evaluating information on the Web, see Chapter 19, Finding and Evaluating Sources.

WRITING ACTIVITY

Reading Web Pages: What You Can Really See

Using the questions above, read the following Web page. Respond in writing to as many of the questions as you can. Compare your responses with those of your classmates.

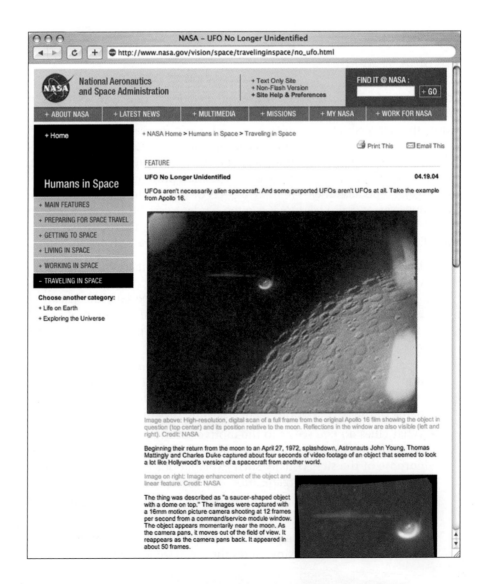

Using Postreading Strategies

After you have read an essay or other text actively and annotated it, your final step is to spend a bit of time thinking about what you have learned from it and even writing in response to it. Review your annotations and answer the following questions.

- What is the main point or idea you learned from working through this text?
- What did you learn that surprises or interests you?
- How does the information in this text agree with or contradict information on this topic you have already read or learned from your own experience?
- What questions do you still have about this text?
- Where can you find answers to those questions?
- What in this reading might be useful in your own writing?

One useful method for storing and keeping track of what you have learned from your reading is to keep a writer's journal. A journal is a handy and accessible place to write down the information and ideas you gather, as well as your reactions to and insights about the texts you read. You can use the information in your journal as a source of ideas and research for your own writing.

Starting Your Writer's/Research Journal

A writer's journal is a place where you keep track of the notes, annotations, and summaries that you make from your reading. Because any writing project longer than a page or two demands more information than you can usually store in your memory, it is vital to keep a written record of information that you discover. You can use the entries in your journal as the basis for group discussions as well as for writing tasks.

The information that you include in your journal can vary, based on the needs of the project you are working on, and the format and design will also vary to suit your purpose. In other words, your rhetorical situation will have an impact not only on the material you collect, the notes that you take, and the summaries and syntheses that you write (see pp. 28–30), but also on the physical makeup of your journal. If you are working on a project that requires a large number of illustrations, for example, you will need to include space in your journal to store them.

It is usually a good idea to keep a journal of some sort for *each* writing project you are working on, because different kinds of projects lend themselves to different kinds of journals. Consider the following questions for each journal:

- What kinds of information (data, charts, anecdotes, photos, illustrations, and so on) should you collect for this project?

- What information will help you get your message across to your intended audience?

- What information might you jot down that may lead to more complex ideas? Why would more complexity be desirable?

- What questions do you have and how might you go about finding answers to those questions?

- What kinds of illustrations might help you *show* what you mean?

As you write in your journal, you should note where ideas or quotations come from in the original texts, so that you will be able to properly cite them in your own writing. Get in the habit of noting the information you will need to cite your source, including the page number an idea or quotation comes from, and you will then have that information on hand when you write and document your papers.

For more on taking notes from and properly citing sources, see Chapter 20.

WRITING ACTIVITY

Reading a Text Critically

Assume that you have been asked to read "Choosing the Sex of Your Baby" for your Human Life Experiences class. Based on what you have learned in this chapter, consider how to read this text.

As you read the editorial, which appeared in the *New York Times* in September 2001, use the critical reading skills you have learned to do the following:

- Explain what you already knew about this topic, just from the title.

- In a brief paragraph, explain what you did before you read this text. Did you skim it?

- Annotate the first paragraph.

- Finally, jot down your answers to the following post-reading questions, providing no more than two sentences for each response.

  - What was your initial reaction and response to this text?

  - What is the main idea you learned from working through this text?

  - Did you learn anything that surprises or interests you?

  - In what ways does the information in this text reinforce or contradict other texts you have read or what you know from your own experience?

  - What questions do you still have about this text?

CHOOSING THE SEX OF YOUR BABY

THE *NEW YORK TIMES*

The public is already deeply concerned about whether the onrush of biomedical science is pushing our society into ethically troublesome areas. So it can hardly be reassured by the cavalier way in which the American Society for Reproductive Medicine has just endorsed the use of in vitro fertilization techniques to help parents determine the sex of their next child.

When last heard from on this issue, in a detailed ethics report in 1999, the society said that selecting and implanting embryos of a particular sex solely for the purpose of guaranteeing parents that their child would be a boy or a girl "should be discouraged" because of serious ethical concerns. But now, as reported by Gina Kolata in Friday's *Times*, the acting head of the society's ethics committee has ruled in a brief letter that such sex selection is permissible if parents who already have a child of one sex want to ensure that the next child is of the opposite sex.

However modest that suggestion may seem to some, it raises enormously complicated ethical issues for individuals and for the larger society. Many fertility specialists were appalled when they learned that the society had modified its position. Some cited a "slippery slope" argument, worrying that allowing parents to determine the sex of their children will inevitably lead, as science learns more and more about genetics, to designing the eye color or intelligence or other characteristics that are currently left to chance. Others worried that allowing parents to choose the sex of their children could reinforce gender discrimination in society and, if practiced widely, upset the natural balance between men and women in the population.

Such arguments must be weighed against the strong desire of some parents to have a child of a particular sex, or a mix of boys and girls, or a preferred gender order among their children. They plead that they should have maximum freedom to choose in reproductive matters that, by their lights, harm no one. The in vitro fertilization process that would be used is expensive and would thus limit the number of people who could take advantage of sex selection. The stipulation that sex selection should apply only to a second child, not to the first, eases fears of gender discrimination and the balance between men and women in the population.

Given these difficult issues, the society's latest position seems a hasty response driven by competitive pressures in the fertility industry, where some clinics see a potentially big demand for sex selection. The society, in a detailed report in May, concluded that it would be permissible to use a different method—sorting sperm to greatly increase the odds of having a child of a particular sex—for the limited purpose of achieving gender variety in a family. But extending that approach to the selection and discarding of embryos based on their sex surely deserves more consideration than a brief letter from an ethics committee chairman to the head of a fertility organization that immediately announced it would offer sex selection at its clinics in New York and Chicago. The American Society for Reproductive Medicine owes its members, and the public, a fuller examination of this issue.

Writing Effective Summaries

After they have read and annotated a text, many readers find that summarizing it also helps them to understand it better. A **summary** is a concise restatement of the most important information in a text—its main point and major supporting points.

Writing a Summary: To write an effective summary, start by listing the main points of the text, in effect outlining what you are reading. This outline forms the basis of your summary. Remember, however, that a summary is more than just a listing of the main points in an essay, book chapter, or other kind of text (the outline does that); rather, a summary provides a brief narrative structure that connects these main ideas.

STEPS FOR WRITING A SUMMARY

1. Read the text relatively quickly to get a general sense of what it is saying.
2. Read the text again, this time noting the main point of each paragraph. Mark or highlight a sentence that expresses the main point of each paragraph, and paraphrase that point—put it entirely into your own words—in the margin.
3. For a longer text, label the major sections. If the writer has provided subheadings, use them as they are or paraphrase them. If not, write subheadings.
4. After considering what you have done in the first three steps, write a statement that captures the writer's main point or thesis.
5. Working backward from Step 4, craft a paragraph—in your own words—that captures the gist of what the writer is saying.

WRITING ACTIVITY

Summarizing "A Purpose Greater Than Oneself"

In no more than one page, summarize "A Purpose Greater Than Oneself" (pp. 20–21). If your instructor asks you to, share your summary with several of your classmates.

Synthesizing Information in Readings

Synthesis is more than reassembling other people's ideas and information from different sources; it calls for the thoughtful combination or integration of ideas and information with your point of view.

Synthesis can take place in all four areas of your life. For example, suppose that you would like to see a particular movie this Saturday evening. You hope to convince a group of your friends to accompany you. Because you are a movie buff, you have read several reviews of the film, you know other work by the director, and you have even read the novel on which this movie is based. At the same time, simply sending your friends all the information you have about the film might overwhelm them. Unless you effectively structure what you have to say, one piece of information may contradict some other point that you want to make.

To organize your information, you could focus on what you see as the most compelling reasons your friends should see the film: the novel the film is based on, along with the director of the movie. You would then provide information on the following:

- How interesting the novel is, with specific examples to show what you mean
- How effectively the novel has been translated to film, using reviews or other information about the film as evidence
- Other films by the same director that you know your friends like

When you synthesize information, then, you organize the information that you have gathered to support the point that *you* want to make. When you synthesize effectively, you take the jumble of facts, data, information, and other knowledge you have on hand and put it into an understandable format that fulfills the purpose you want to accomplish. And, of course, when you cite reviewers' opinions (in the hope of convincing your friends which movie to see), you will need to indicate where the comments came from—to properly attribute what the reviewers had to say and to lend their authority to your argument. Failure to properly attribute ideas to original sources constitutes plagiarism, so you always want to indicate where your ideas and information come from.

For more on avoiding plagiarism, see Chapter 20.

As we have noted, to fully understand information and then be able to synthesize it effectively, to integrate what you read with what you already know, you must read critically, questioning, challenging, and engaging the text as you work through it. One strategy that will help you improve your critical thinking and reading is to work with others. When you work with your classmates, you learn how they read and understood a given selection. You hear their perspectives and ideas and have the opportunity to consider various points of view. Working with others also helps you learn to construct the most effective questions to ask, to help you become an active reader.

WRITING ACTIVITY

Synthesizing Information

Begin by making a list of the five features of your college or university that you like best. (If you have just begun taking classes at your school, list five features that caused you to choose this particular college or university.) After you have constructed your list, exchange it with two classmates. After the three of you have read and discussed each other's lists, combine the three lists into a single list of what the three of you agree are the top ten features of your school. List the ten items in rank order with number one as the best liked item. Your instructor may ask you to share the group's list with the whole class.

Using Your Reading in Your Writing

Information that you find in your reading can be used in many ways in your writing. If you have annotated the texts that your instructor asked you to read for a writing project in this course or another course, or the sources that you drew on for another project, you can often use those annotations in your own writing. Likewise, if you have summarized sources for a research project, you can refer to and use those summaries to spot the important points of each text you have read, and then use relevant information as evidence to support your main idea. If you have found statistical information that can be better understood in graphical form, or photographs, drawings, maps, or other illustrations, these too can become part of your text. Of course, it is always important to indicate where you found information, whose ideas you use in your text, and where statistical information came from in order to establish your credibility and avoid *plagiarizing*—representing the words or ideas of others as your own ideas or words.

In the chapters in Parts 2 and 3 of this book, you will read various kinds of selections. As you read these texts or conduct library and/or Web research to find support for your writing, you will find it helpful to use the reading strategies we have described in this chapter.

Writing to Discover and to Learn

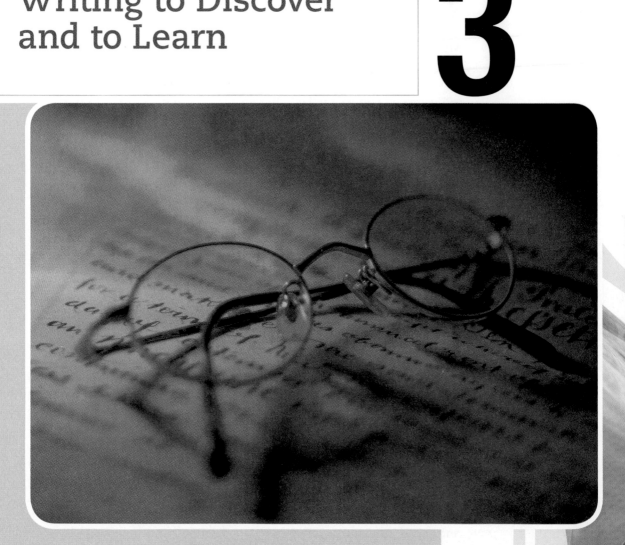

Most of the chapters in this book focus on learning to write for an audience—to accomplish a purpose involving other people. This chapter, though, provides some tried-and-true strategies for using writing to discover ideas and to learn—to accomplish a purpose for yourself. As you probably are finding out as you do more of it, writing is a way of learning, of figuring out what you know and understand about a subject and, in the process, of coming to know and understand it better. Many famous writers have commented that they cannot really know what they think about something *until* they write about it. They learn as they compose. We learn in this way, too, and we think that if you explore and experiment with some of the strategies in this chapter, writing to discover and to learn will become one of your most effective educational tools.

In addition to using strategies such as the "muddiest point" and "preconception check" to learn material from lectures, discussions, and readings in your courses, you can use some as invention strategies for formal writing assignments. Furthermore, although people typically use these tools in academic settings, they can be equally effective in professional, civic, and personal settings.

As we discussed in Chapter 2, writing about what you read for your classes can help you learn that information better, not just by rewriting to summarize your notes, but by jotting down your questions and comments, reflecting on what you have read, and noting how any new ideas and information relate to other ideas and information. In your professional life, consider how writing about what was useful in a recent business meeting, what problems came up, and what issues did not get solved might help you conduct more effective and efficient meetings in the future.

For more on critical reading strategies, see Chapter 2, pages 18–25.

In almost any situation, writing (immediately afterward) about what you *learned* from an experience will give you useful information for any similar situations you might face in the future. If you get into the habit of writing about the events, situations, and issues in your life, more often than not you will come to a more thoughtful and thorough understanding of those events and issues so that you will be able to deal with them more effectively.

The strategies that follow are tools that writers have used to figure out what they have learned and what they still need to know. Try a variety of strategies. Some may work better for you than others.

Using Invention Strategies to Discover Ideas

As you begin to explore your subject, it is a good idea to use more than one invention activity to help you generate ideas. No matter what your purpose is for writing—to share an experience, to argue a position, to propose a solution to a problem—you will need to generate information and knowledge about your topic through invention activities.

Listing

When you use listing, you jot down keywords that will remind you of ideas as you write more later. You might find it effective to establish categories within your lists to help jog your memory. If you wanted to propose a solution to a problem, you might organize keywords under "history of the problem," "how the problem affects my readers," "possible solutions," "failed solutions," and "objections to a solution."

Freewriting

When you freewrite, you simply write for a set period of time—perhaps five or ten minutes. You jot down, or type, everything that comes to mind, even if you cannot think of anything (in that case, you might write, "I can't think of anything to write," until your ideas start to flow).

Questioning

One useful way to generate information and ideas is to ask questions about your topic, audience, and purpose:

- What am I trying to accomplish in this paper?
- What do I already know about my topic?
- What might my readers already know?
- What would readers need to know to understand my point?
- What kind(s) of information (for example, graphs, tables, lists) might be useful to *show* my readers (rather than just to tell them)?
- What kinds of details and explanation can I provide?
- Where might I learn more about this subject (in the library, on the Internet, by interviewing people)?

Answering the Questions *Who? What? Where? When? Why? How?*

You can expand the questioning approach (above) by spending a few minutes jotting down answers to the reporter's questions: *who, what, where, when, why,* and *how.* You may find that your answers lead to still more questions.

- Whom does this subject affect? In what ways?
- Who is involved in making a decision about this subject?
- Who is my audience?
- What am I trying to get my audience to do?
- What can't I ask my readers to do?

- What is important here?
- What are the historical aspects of this topic?
- When might something happen to affect this situation?
- When would I like something to happen?
- Where does all of this take place?
- Why should my readers care about my paper?
- Why is this topic important?
- Why will _____ happen?
- How does the context—the "where"—affect the situation?
- How might _____ happen?
- How might _____ react to the topic I am writing about?

Brainstorming

When you brainstorm, you record on paper or on-screen the information you already know about the topic you are exploring. Once you have written down several possible topics or ideas or possible ways to focus your paper, you may have an easier time finding the one that seems most promising.

Clustering

Clustering is especially useful for figuring out possible cause-and-effect relationships. For more on clustering and an example, see page 41.

Keeping Notebooks and Journals

Writers and learners frequently maintain notebooks and journals because these forms of informal writing are useful places for recording and/or exploring ideas. Leonardo da Vinci, for example, kept notebooks for years, compiling 1,566 pages of ideas in words and images.

Double-Entry Notebook

One useful type of notebook is what composition scholar Anne Berthoff calls a **dialectical notebook** or **journal.** In a dialectical notebook, you write notes on one page and then write your questions and comments about those notes on the facing page. (Some people prefer to draw a line down the center of a page.) In effect, the two pages "speak" to each other. The **double-entry notebook,** which is a type of dialectical notebook, is one of the most commonly used writing-to-learn strategies because it can be easily adapted to so many contexts. As the name suggests, the double-entry notebook has two columns. The left column is used to present whatever kind of information is appropriate to the context. Thus, in this column, you might record lecture, lab, field, or reading notes; list the steps in a math problem; construct a timeline, or list events in chronological order. The right column is used to respond to, comment on, question, and apply the information in the left column.

For instance, Judy Bowden is enrolled in an art history course to fulfill one of the general studies requirements at her school. To understand some of the artwork that she is studying in the course, Bowden uses a variety of writing-to-learn strategies, but she frequently uses the double-entry notebook. Because her journal is electronic, she downloads public-domain artwork from the Web and pastes it into the left column of her notebook. In the right column, she writes about the work. Here is an example from Bowden's double-entry notebook.

Artwork	My Thoughts
	This is the *Black Bull* cave painting from Lascaux, France. It's amazing that this and other paintings in the cave are 10,000 to 30,000 years old. It's also amazing that 2,000 paintings and drawings in the cave have survived for so long. The details seem very sophisticated for such an old piece of art. I wonder what the four teenagers thought when they discovered the cave on September 12, 1940. If I were in an anthropology course instead of an art history course, I wonder what other things we'd learn about this painting and the others.

WRITING ACTIVITY

Your Dialectical Notebook

Select one of your college classes and go over your notes for the most recent week of classes. Construct a dialectical notebook that outlines your notes and also your reactions to, comments on, and questions about those notes.

Your instructor may want you to share your notebooks with your classmates.

Field Notebook

For more on field research, see Chapter 19, pages 525–30.

Fairly common in the sciences and social sciences, **field notebooks** are useful for students who are doing field research. A field notebook can take many forms, depending on the observations that you are making.

For instance, Lindsay Hanson is enrolled in a summer session biology course for nonmajors. One of the requirements of the course is to pick a natural habitat and observe some life-forms in that habitat. Lindsay chooses to do some bird-watching in a marsh near her campus. She decides to set up her field notebook in columns with headings, an organization that makes it easy for her to record her observations.

Date and Time	Location	Common Name	Scientific Name	Sex	Comments
6/6/07 6:20 p.m.	west shore of Widespread	red-winged blackbird	Agelaius phoeniceus	♂	The bird was sitting on the top of a weed, which was swaying in the breeze. Partly cloudy, 61°, windy
6/6/07 6:35 p.m.	south shore of Widespread	yellow-shafted flicker	Colaptes auratus	♀	The bird took off from some 8"–10" grass. Partly cloudy, 61°

WRITING ACTIVITY

Writing Your Own Field Notebook

If you have a class that requires you to do some fieldwork, construct a field notebook, including drawings or other images and your notes on your field research. If you do not have a class that requires field research, spend an hour at some place on your campus, observing and making notes on what you see in a field notebook. Use these reporter's questions to guide you:

- Who is there? What are they doing? How are they dressed? What are they carrying or working with?

- What does the place look like? Can you take photos or make drawings? What sounds and smells are in this place?

- Where is this place? How does it connect or relate to other places on campus?

- When did you visit? Why? What makes that time different from another time you might observe this place?

- Why did you select this particular spot? What other places did you consider? Why?

Rewriting Your Class Notes

Whether you use a double-entry notebook or some other method, make rewriting your class notes part of your own "homework" assignment each day. Many students who use this strategy find it helpful because, when they rewrite their class notes, they do the following:

- Put them into a more readable and organized form than the jottings they made during class.
- Think of questions about the information that had not occurred to them when they were taking the notes during class.
- Discover areas of interest that they want to find out more about.

Think of the "re" in the word *rewriting* and what it means: to resee, to reenvision, to reconsider, perhaps even to reorganize. Put another way, when you rewrite your in-class notes, use the writing as a way to help you learn, not just by transcribing your notes, but by reconsidering them and asking questions, by reseeing what you wrote (and jotting down connections you make with other ideas and texts), and by reorganizing them so they make more sense than they might have made in class. The strategies that follow can help you not just to rewrite your class notes but to comprehend and, perhaps, go beyond them.

After each of your college classes, convert your in-class notes to e-notes in a computer document. Doing so encourages you to reread your notes and put them into a more readable form. Just reading them over again helps cement the ideas into your memory—and writing them down again helps you remember them, too. Also, your notes will be easier to read when exam time comes around. Finally, your notes will be searchable, and you can copy and paste them, as needed, into your college papers.

TechNote When you take a college class, remember that your classmates can be a valuable resource. Create communication spaces on the Internet for study groups or for just yourself and one study-partner. Exchange contact information with classmates, and use it. You can exchange notes using personal blogs, e-mail, chat, instant-messaging, and other social networking/messaging sites.

Remember, though, that if you post text or images straight from sources (such as textbooks or reference works), you must cite them properly. If you want to share copyrighted work online, you must obtain permission from the source before posting someone else's intellectual property on a public site.

Minute Paper

A minute paper is a quick, useful way to reflect on a class lecture or discussion, but first we need to make a confession: this really is not a paper, but a chance just to jot down—in a minute or two—your answers to two questions:

1. What is the most important thing that I learned in class today?
2. What is the most important question that I have about today's class lecture/discussion?

For more on e-mail, instant messaging, and blogs, see Chapter 17.

For example, Conner Ames, who was enrolled in a general studies course in sociology, responded at the end of a particular class as follows:

1. Today we learned that group behavior often is different from individual behavior: people will act differently in groups than they might act alone.

This is especially true for male adolescents when a group interacts with other male adolescent groups.

2. What are more of the real-life implications of group behavior (and I also want to know more about *why* young males like me act as they do when they're in a group)?

Ames could use his question to guide further reading about group behavior. Or he could raise his question in class or on the course Web site or listserv.

Muddiest Point

As its name suggests, this strategy involves jotting down some concept or idea that is unclear or confusing and, if possible, exploring it through writing. This does not mean looking up the definition of a concept you might find confusing, but instead writing about it to clarify your thinking.

Your muddiest point may come from a paragraph in a chapter that you are reading for a course, or it may come from a class lecture or discussion. In many instances, you may be able to work through your confusion by writing. At the very least, you will crystallize the issue and provide yourself with a reminder to raise a question during the next class meeting, in an office-hour visit, in an e-mail to the professor, or on the online discussion board for the course.

Preconception Check

A *preconception* is something you think you know about a subject, before you learn more about it in class, through your reading, and from other sources of information. One strategy for overcoming preconceptions is to become aware of them, which is not always easy to do.

For instance, Tom Ambrose was enrolled in an astronomy course that fulfilled the science portion of his general studies requirements. As he read a chapter about the solar system, he encountered a subsection entitled "Why Are There Seasons on Earth?" Before he read the subsection, he realized that he had some preconceptions about why the seasons occur. He wrote the following in his learning journal for that course:

> I think that Earth has the four seasons because of the elliptical path of the planet as it orbits the Sun. When that path takes us farthest from the Sun (December–March), we have winter. When the path takes us closest to the Sun (June–August), we have summer.

This short explanation may seem trivial, but it served to make Ambrose more attuned to the explanation in his astronomy textbook. When he read that the seasons are caused by Earth's tilt on its axis, he was better prepared to process that information. He noted,

When I read the chapter, I realized the problem with my preconception. If the elliptical path of Earth's orbit were the cause of the seasons, then the whole planet would have summer in June–August. I forgot that when it's summer in the northern hemisphere it's winter in the southern hemisphere.

Paraphrasing

When you are having difficulty understanding material in a reading assignment, lecture, or class discussion, one strategy you can use to make the material more understandable is to paraphrase it—to restate it in your own words. If you have ever tried to teach something to someone, you know that the act of teaching—explaining, demonstrating, answering questions—often aids your understanding of the subject or concept. This is the rationale behind paraphrasing—by explaining something in your own words, you come to understand it better.

Jack Johnson was taking an introductory physics course for nonmajors. Early in the course, the instructor mentioned "Ockham's razor" but did not define it. Using a popular search engine to find some definitions of the term, Johnson found that it is defined as the principle of economy, or of parsimony. After reading several Web sites, Johnson felt he understood the term and wrote the following in his course journal:

> In a nutshell, Ockham's razor means this: if two theories have equal explanatory power, choose the simpler one. That is, keep it simple, Stupid—K.I.S.S. In my geology class we discussed the Grand Canyon, and I kind of now see how the simplest answer to its formation—a river and other natural weather conditions, acting over a long period of time—actually makes the most sense. If I try to get too complicated about something, I need to remember Ockham's razor: if two or more ideas seem to explain something, the simpler is probably the better answer.

For more on paraphrasing, see Chapter 20.

Organizing and Synthesizing Information

Finding and collecting information is part of learning, but effective learners need to organize and synthesize information to make it usable. As you conduct research and locate information that might be useful for your writing, do the following:

- Organize what you learn in a logical, useful manner. Often an effective way to organize your notes is to put them into a computer document; you can then use its search function to locate particular words or phrases.

- Organize your notes by putting them into a spreadsheet like Excel. If you format the spreadsheet cells to "wrap text," you create a database of notes.

For more on summary and synthesis, see pages 28–30.

- As you take notes, synthesize the information: condense it into a brief form, where the important aspects are listed, along with the reference, so you can easily locate the complete information.

Invented Interview/Unsent Letter

In an invented interview, you are the interviewer. The interviewee could be a person or a character whom you are studying or a person associated with a concept that you are studying. If you *really* could interview someone for a college class, what would you ask that person? What issues or concepts would you focus on? It is often useful to put your questions into an unsent letter format so that you have a specific audience you are writing to as you generate interview questions.

Here are some sample questions:

- In a geometry course, you might interview Pythagoras to ask him about the process that led to his development of the Pythagorean Theorem.
- In an entrepreneurship course, you might interview Bill Gates to ask him what drove him to found Microsoft.
- In an anthropology course you might interview a group of Cro-Magnons to ask about their interactions with Neanderthals.
- In a United States history course, you might ask President Harry Truman why he decided to drop atomic bombs on two Japanese cities in 1945.

Taking this concept of an invented interview further, you can conduct research to determine how your questions might have been answered if you were able to conduct such an interview.

The key to writing such interviews—and this is the case for any of the writing-to-learn strategies in this chapter—is that you need to move beyond the limits of your initial response to an event or a person, especially if your response is emotional. Use the interview as an opportunity to explore a topic from an intellectual perspective as well as an emotional perspective.

Using Charts and Visuals to Discover and to Learn

If you are like many people, you may be a visual learner: often seeing something really helps you understand it. Just as charts, graphs, tables, photographs, and other visuals help readers understand what you write about, using visuals is often a way for writers to explore ideas and really see and understand what they are writing about.

Clustering and Concept Mapping

Concept maps, or *clustering*, help us to visualize ideas that may otherwise seem abstract and also to understand relationships among ideas. For example, Figure 3.1 below shows how student writer Santi DeRosa might have developed a cluster map to help him get started with his paper about how female students help recruit male athletes for his school. According to an article in the campus newspaper, women serve as campus guides when potential athletes visit the school. When he read the article, DeRosa had concerns about the ethics of this practice, so he decided to respond by writing an essay on the issue (you can read his complete essay in Chapter 8).

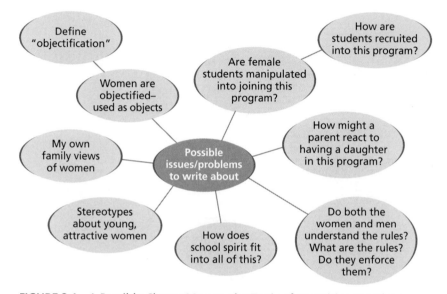

FIGURE 3.1 A Possible Cluster Map on the Topic of Recruiting Practices

Process Flowchart

A process flowchart is another visually useful tool for converting information from verbal to visual form. A flowchart allows you to translate several paragraphs of information into a clear, succinct visual that can make difficult concepts easier to understand. Rather than focusing on relationships in a system (how ideas or concepts might connect to one another), a flowchart indicates how things *move* through a system.

In his political science course, Brian Flores studied the process by which a bill moves through the U.S. House of Representatives. After reading a few pages on the process, Brian converted the material into the flowchart shown in Figure 3.2 on page 42.

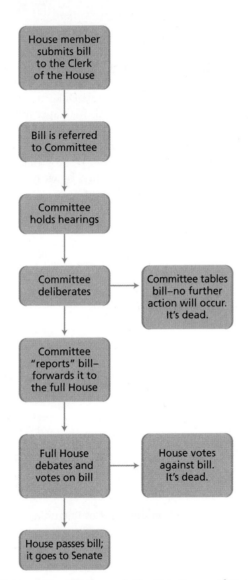

FIGURE 3.2   Following a Bill through the U.S. House of Representatives

Studying for Exams

Course grades are often based largely on tests. If you study for tests strategically, you can usually anticipate the questions that will be asked and review the course material more efficiently.

Test Questions

One way to prepare for tests is to write questions that you think your instructor may pose on them. Anticipating test questions also gives you the opportunity to anticipate your answers, thus simulating the test itself.

If you are using questions to prepare for a test, the first step is to ask the instructor about the kinds of questions that you should anticipate. Your instructor will probably indicate the formats that the questions will be in— for example, whether they will be multiple-choice, true/false, matching, short answer, and/or essay questions—and might also indicate the levels of thinking they will require: comprehension, application, analysis, synthesis, and/or evaluation.

One of the most effective strategies for writing test questions is to go through your class notes and reading notes marking sections that you think are likely to be covered on the test. Then, as soon as possible after class or after reading the textbook, write a few questions and think about the answers. If you write some questions each week, you will learn much more than if you wait until just before the test, and you will be more thorough in your coverage of the material you have studied.

Mnemonic Play

Although in many courses you will need to learn course material without having to memorize facts, there may be times when you will need to develop memory aids for some material. Here is an example that may already be familiar to you: Erin Wilson was enrolled in a general science course for nonmajors. To help her remember the order of the planets in the solar system (before Pluto's status as a planet was changed), she used the sentence: "My very educated mother just served us nine pizzas." That is, the order, beginning with the planet closest to the sun, is Mercury, Venus, Earth, Mars, Jupiter, Saturn, Uranus, Neptune, Pluto.

TechNote One way to learn material more thoroughly is to help someone else learn about it, too. Offer to help one of your former teachers from middle school or high school create a Web site about a topic you are learning more about in college. Or if you have a younger brother or sister or a child in school, offer to help his or her teacher. Use your new knowledge to create links and study notes that will help younger learners.

For advice on creating an effective Web site, see Appendix C.

For advice on taking essay examinations, see Appendix B.

PART TWO

Using What You Have Learned to Share Information

Rhetorical Knowledge

- *Audience:* Readers may or may not know you or the people you are writing about personally, but you will want to make your experience relevant to them regardless.

- *Purpose:* You may want to entertain readers and possibly to inform and/or persuade them.

- *Rhetorical situation:* Consider the constellation of factors affecting what you write—you (the writer), your readers (the audience), the topic (the experience that you're writing about), your purpose (what you wish to accomplish), and the exigency (what is compelling you to write).

- *Writer's voice and tone:* You have a *stance*—or attitude—toward the experience you are sharing and the people you are writing about. You may be amused, sarcastic, neutral, or regretful, among many possibilities.

- *Context, medium, and genre:* Your writing context, the medium you are writing in (whether print or electronic), and the genre you have chosen all affect your writing decisions.

Critical Thinking, Reading, and Writing

- *Learning/inquiry:* You need to learn the features of writing to share experiences so that you can do so effectively in any writing situation.

- *Responsibility:* You have a responsibility to represent your experiences accurately, with sensitivity to the needs of others.

- *Reading and research:* You will need to draw on your own memories, memories of relatives and friends, photographs and documents, and ideas you develop from your reading.

Writing Processes

- *Invention:* You will need to choose invention strategies that will help you recall details about your experience or experiences.

- *Organizing your ideas and details:* You will usually be organizing a series of events.

- *Revising:* You will need to read your work with a critical eye, to make certain that it fulfills the assignment and displays the qualities of this kind of writing.

- *Working with peers:* Classmates and others will offer you comments on and questions about your work.

Conventions

- *Editing:* When writers share experiences, they tend to use dialogue to report what they have said and what others have said to them. The round-robin activity in this chapter (on p. 74) addresses the conventions for punctuating dialogue.

- *Genres for sharing experiences:* Genres include personal essay, memoir, autobiography, magazine or newspaper essay, blog, letter, and accident report, as well as other possibilities.

- *Documentation:* If you have relied on sources outside of your experience, you will need to cite them using the appropriate documentation style.

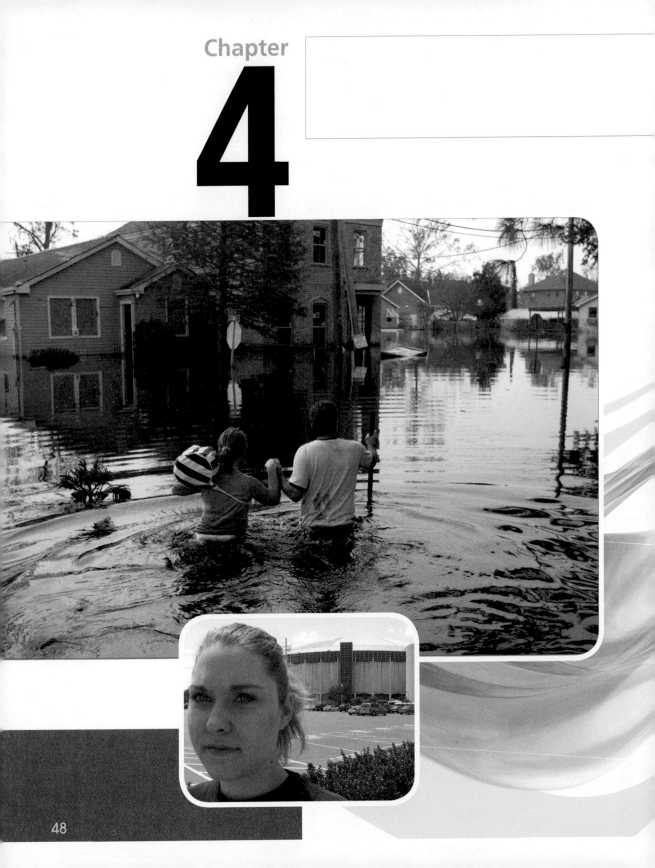

Chapter 4

Writing to Share Experiences

This excerpt from an article about the aftermath of Hurricane Katrina in September 2005, written by three reporters from the *Houston Press*, is a news item—but at the same time the writers are focusing on *stories* about real people at the Houston Astrodome, and each person, such as Nikki Ramey (shown in the smaller photograph), has an important tale to tell:

> Nikki Ramey, a 24-year-old mother, heard the media reports about refugees and volunteers who were turned away at the gate. Still, she was determined to get inside the Dome and invite a family back to her home in north Houston. So she and her friend lied to [security guard Nathan] Njakoy. They told him they were hurricane victims who had ridden one of the buses from New Orleans.
>
> The hoax worked, and Ramey could see what journalists from across the nation still could not: the Dome's ground floor, which was lined with rows of narrow cots set inches apart.
>
> Once inside, Ramey says, she approached seven families and offered to house them for free. Each family declined. Many said they wanted to stay in hopes that their own family members would eventually come to find them.

Ramey's was just one story from this monumental event. The other photograph on the facing page tells a compelling part of the story of Hurricane Katrina strictly through the image it presents.

In sharing her experience with the reporters from the *Houston Press*, Nikki Ramey was engaging in a common activity. On any given day, you share your experiences in a variety of ways. At breakfast, you might tell your roommate about the nightmare that awakened you at 3:00 in the morning, or at dinner you might tell your family about the argument that you had with your supervisor at work.

Although you may think that you share your experiences most frequently in your personal life, you have also shared your experiences in your academic life if you wrote an autobiography for your college application packet. In your professional life, you will need to narrate your experiences in résumés and letters of application, and you also will tell about your experiences in order to teach others how to do their work. In your civic life, you may decide to appear before the city council to describe how the lack of a streetlight at a busy intersection led to an automobile accident, or you may need to tell voters how your experiences make you well qualified for political office.

There are many reasons to share your experiences with other people. Writing about your experiences helps you as a writer because the act of writing requires reflection, which is a powerful tool for gaining insight into and understanding about life. Also, when you share your experiences with others, you are also offering others insight into what has worked well—and not so well—in your life. After all, for thousands of years humans have shared stories about experiences to establish and nurture social connections with one another.

Rhetorical Knowledge

When you write about your experiences in a private journal, you can write whatever and however you wish. When you write for other people, though, you need to make conscious choices about your audience; purpose; voice and tone and context, medium, and genre. You need to consider what your audience may already know about the experience that you are sharing and what your purpose is in sharing this experience with this particular audience. You also need to think about how much of your attitude toward this topic and your audience you want to reveal. Further, the effectiveness of your narrative will also be influenced by the medium and genre you choose.

Writing to Share Experiences in Your College Classes

Throughout your college career, you will often be called on to share your experiences in writing. Such writing can help you learn more effectively because it encourages you to reflect on your academic experiences. Furthermore, much academic writing takes the form of **narrative**—stories about the physical or human world. For example, one of the best-known philosophers in history, Plato, used stories as powerful teaching tools. In *The Republic*, Plato tells "The Allegory of the Cave" to illustrate what it's like to think like a philosopher.

Likewise, in your own academic life—your life in college—you may be asked to share experiences in the following ways:

- A math instructor may ask you to write about some experience in which you used a math principle or procedure to solve a problem in your everyday life.

- A music instructor may ask you to attend a concert and then write about the experience.

- An education instructor might assign you to observe a classroom and write about your observations.

Writing to Share Experiences for Life

As humans we tend to organize our lives as ongoing narratives. While your life is one long narrative, within it are thousands of shorter narratives. Those are the kinds of events you will most likely focus on when you write to record and share experiences in the professional, civic, and personal parts of your life.

Curt Schilling, one of the most successful major league baseball pitchers in recent years, partially attributes that success to his ritual of recording his experience with every batter that he faces. You can follow Curt Schilling's example by using writing to record and analyze your **professional** experiences so that you can learn from them.

To participate effectively in **civic** life, writers also frequently need to share their experiences. For democratic institutions to function effectively, citizens need to be involved with their government, especially at the local level.

In **personal** settings, you have many opportunities to record and share experiences every day. For example, at the wedding of two friends, you may be asked to tell the story of how you introduced them in high school.

Scenarios for Writing: Assignment Options

Your instructor may ask you to complete one or both of the following assignments that call for you to write about your experiences. Each assignment is in the form of a *scenario*, a brief story that provides some context for your writing. The scenario gives you a sense of who your audience is and what you need to accomplish with your writing.

Starting on page 66, you will find guidelines for completing the assignment option that you choose or that is assigned to you. Additional scenarios for college and life may be found online.

Writing for College

SCENARIO 1 Examining and Writing about a Significant and Positive Experience

This scenario asks you to examine and write about an experience in your life that you are interested in and would like to know more about—something that affected you in a positive or useful way. Such events do not always seem to be life-changing when they occur, but when we reflect back, we find that they affected us in a significant way.

Writing Assignment: Write a narrative in which you tell about an experience that affected you or someone you know in a positive way. Sometimes experiences like this are major occurrences. You might remember when a relative went off to war and how your correspondence with him or her helped you mature and grow. As an alternative, you might use a version of a tactic that disc jockeys call "brushes with greatness" or "encounters with celebrity": they ask listeners to call in and relate encounters with someone who is famous. Your narrative can be for a general academic audience, or it can be for a specific course in a discipline such as psychology or marriage and family.

Writing for Life

SCENARIO 2 Professional Writing: A Letter to a Prospective Employer

In this scenario, we ask you to focus on a recent experience that you have had as an employee or a volunteer. Consider how that experience has made you think about your future. For example, when one of the authors of this book was in college, he worked the graveyard shift (11:00 p.m. to 7:00 a.m.) in a plastics factory. As he operated the machines each night, he was reminded that he wanted a job—a career—that would allow him to work directly with people, a job that would allow him to feel the satisfaction derived from helping people achieve their goals.

Writing Assignment: Write a letter to a prospective employer narrating some experience that you have had as an employee, volunteer, or student. Indicate how that experience has prepared or inspired you for future work.

Rhetorical Considerations in Sharing Your Experiences

Audience: Who is your primary audience? Who else might be interested in this subject? Why?

Purpose: Your narrative could have several interrelated purposes. For example, if you are writing in response to Scenario 1, your narrative can serve both to entertain your audience by sharing your experience with them and to thank or honor others who contributed to your positive experience. If you are writing to a prospective employer, your purpose could be both informative and persuasive.

Voice, Tone, and Point of View: Depending on the assignment, you may or may not be a major character in your narrative. If you are relating a story in which you are a participant, you have two roles: you are its writer, and you are also a major character in it. If you are not a participant, you will need to use the third-person point of view. Your attitude toward your characters will help determine the tone of your narrative, which could be humorous, such as in "On Becoming a Writer" by Russell Baker (pp. 57–59), or more straightforward and serious.

Context, Medium, and Genre: You will always need to understand the situation that creates the occasion to write. Keeping the context of the assignment in mind, decide on a medium and a genre for your writing. How will your writing be used? If you are writing for an audience beyond the classroom, consider what will be the most effective way to present your information to this audience.

Critical Thinking, Reading, and Writing

Before you begin writing to share your own experiences, read one or more examples to get a feel for writing about experiences. You might also consider how visuals could enhance your writing, as well as the kinds of sources you might consult.

Writing about experiences has several qualities—a clear sense of purpose, a significant point, a lively narrative, and an honest representation. The writer also has a responsibility to respect the privacy of anyone who appears in a narrative. The reading selections and the visual text that appear in this section exemplify these qualities. Further, they may serve to stimulate your own inquiry and writing.

Learning the Qualities of Effective Writing about Experiences

Successful writing about experiences—often called *narrative writing*—engages your readers and keeps them interested. One of the best ways to engage readers when narrating your experiences is to incorporate real dialogue. Other strategies include providing telling details and description. The old advice to "show, don't tell" is especially important when writing about experiences.

Even when you are sharing experiences that seem self-evidently fascinating, you need to have a reason for writing about those experiences. In other words, you need to make a point.

Most readers expect the following qualities in writing that shares experience:

- **A clear sense of purpose.** When you write about your experiences, you need to provide your readers with clues that will help them understand why you are sharing this narrative. Your tone is one important clue. The amount of explanation and reflection that you include is another clue. If you are simply recording the event so that others can experience it vicariously, for example, you might include very little explanation or reflection. If, however, you want readers to learn something from your experience, or you are trying to convince them of something, you will probably use part of your paper to reflect on the significance of your experience.

- **A significant point.** Just as you need to have a clear purpose for what you are writing, you also need to use the experience you are relating to say something significant and not just ramble on aimlessly. Writers sometimes use their experiences to make a sweeping, clichéd point such as "if I knew then what I know now," which usually leads to boring, obvious writing. Points have significance for readers when they are fresh and—often—unexpected.

  One way to show significance is to explain—with examples—how the event you are telling about affected you, changed you, or improved your life. You may or may not express your point in a thesis statement, however. Many writers who share their experiences use their language, tone, and the details they choose to make their points implicitly.

- **A lively narrative.** Although your writing may include other elements, such as reflection, the foundation for writing about experience is a lively narrative. A narrative needs to answer the following questions: Who? What? Where? When? Why? and How? To answer these questions, you can use the following conventions of narrative writing:

  - *Dialogue:* Natural-sounding dialogue helps make a piece of writing immediate and lively. Dialogue—what people have to say—brings a narrative to life. Dialogue also can reveal something about the character of the people in your narrative.

  - *Vivid Description:* Detailed descriptions of the people, or *characters*, mentioned in the narrative, the place where it occurs, and the actions that take place all help involve the reader in your story. Describing people, places, actions, and objects so that your readers will recognize them and relate to them will help make your narrative memorable.

  - *Point of View:* While you will most often relate personal stories from your own point of view (first-person perspective, usually told using

For more on narration and description, see Chapter 13, pages 402–8.

the pronouns *I* and *me*), it may be more interesting or effective to tell the story from a third-person perspective—perhaps from the point of view of another participant in the event (called the "third-person limited perspective") or from the point of view of an observer who knows what each participant is doing and thinking (called the "third-person omniscient perspective").

- *A Climax or Crisis:* Effective narrative *leads* to something: a point the writer wants to make or a concept the writer wants the reader to understand. By constructing your narrative to lead readers to your main idea or point, you keep them interested, all through your narrative. Sometimes, to build suspense, your narrative can lead up to a crisis, which may or may not have already been resolved.

- **An honest representation.** As you share your experiences it's important to represent them to readers as accurately as possible. Although you can present your own perspective on any situation, it is usually important to present events without unnecessary embellishments, unless you are exaggerating for an obviously humorous purpose. Usually you are not trying to convince readers to change their ways with this kind of writing, but to honestly relate your experiences so readers can understand their significance.

Try rewriting the qualities of effective writing about experiences in a computer document, so you can keep them in mind as you write your own paper.

A WRITER'S RESPONSIBILITIES

Sharing Experiences Responsibly

When you share your experiences with other people, you need to make careful decisions about what to reveal about yourself. As you write, you will need to decide how to fulfill your responsibilities not only to your readers but also to those people who are characters in your narratives.

For instance, if you are testifying in a criminal or civil trial, you have not only an ethical but also a legal responsibility to narrate your experience as truthfully as possible. If you agree to serve as a reference for a colleague who is searching for a job, you have a responsibility to portray your experiences with that person accurately because the potential employer, as well as the employer's clients or customers, will rely on that person to perform the job well.

You also have another responsibility: if you write about criminal activity, your teacher or your classmates may feel compelled to report that activity to authorities. For certain kinds of criminal behavior—domestic violence or sexual abuse, for instance—state law may require your teacher to report the activity to the police.

Reading, Inquiry, and Research: Learning from Narratives That Share Experiences

The selections that follow are examples of writing that share experiences. As you go through each of the selections your instructor asks you to read, consider the following questions:

- How does the author make his or her experiences understandable and indicate their significance?
- What qualities of writing that share experiences does each selection exemplify?
- How can you use the techniques of sharing experiences exemplified in the selection in your own writing?

Thinking Rhetorically

Keep in mind the following questions as you read the essays that follow. Make it a practice to ask yourself these questions in all your reading—personal, academic, and professional—and you will strengthen and sharpen your abilities as a reader and as a writer.

Rhetorical Knowledge: The Writer's Situation and Rhetoric

- *Audience:* Who is the primary audience for this piece of writing? What makes you think that?
- *Purpose:* What is the author's primary purpose in writing about this experience? What other purposes might the author have?
- *Voice and Tone:* What is the author's attitude toward his or her topic? How do you know that?
- *Responsibility:* How does the author establish credibility in this piece of writing? Which specific details seem most credible?
- *Context and Format:* Though the authors' experiences are true, they relate them almost in the form of a *story*. How effective is this strategy for writing about experiences?

RUSSELL BAKER

On Becoming a Writer

Born in Virginia in 1925, Russell Baker began his professional writing career with the *Baltimore Sun* in 1947, after attending Johns Hopkins University. In 1973 he won a Pulitzer for commentary for his nationally syndicated column, "Observer," which he wrote for the *New York Times* from 1962 to 1998. Baker is the author of a Pulitzer-winning memoir *Growing Up* (1982) and *Looking Back: Heroes, Rascals, and Other Icons of the American Imagination* (2002) and has edited numerous books. Baker's writing regularly appears in the *New York Times Magazine, Sports Illustrated,* and *McCalls.* The following selection is excerpted from *Growing Up.*

The only thing that truly interested me was writing, and I knew that sixteen-year-olds did not come out of high school and become writers. I thought of writing as something to be done only by the rich. It was so obviously not real work, not a job at which you could earn a living. Still, I had begun to think of myself as a writer. It was the only thing for which I seemed to have the smallest talent, and, silly though it sounded when I told people I'd like to be a writer, it gave me a way of thinking about myself which satisfied my need to have an identity.   1

The notion of becoming a writer had flickered off and on in my head since the Belleville days, but it wasn't until my third year in high school that the possibility took hold. Until then I'd been bored by everything associated with English courses. I found English grammar dull and baffling. I hated the assignments to turn out "compositions," and went at them like heavy labor, turning out leaden, lackluster paragraphs that were agonies for teachers to read and for me to write. The classics thrust on me to read seemed as deadening as chloroform.   2

When our class was assigned to Mr. Fleagle for third-year English I anticipated another grim year in that dreariest of subjects. Mr. Fleagle was notorious among City students for dullness and inability to inspire. He was said to be stuffy, dull, and hopelessly out of date. To me he looked to be sixty or seventy and prim to a fault. He wore primly severe eyeglasses, his wavy hair was primly cut and primly combed. He wore prim vested suits with neckties blocked primly against the collar buttons of his primly starched white shirts. He had a primly pointed jaw, a primly straight nose, and a prim manner of speaking that was so correct, so gentlemanly, that he seemed a comic antique.   3

I anticipated a listless, unfruitful year with Mr. Fleagle and for a long time was not disappointed. We read *Macbeth.* Mr. Fleagle loved *Macbeth* and wanted us to love it too, but he lacked the gift of infecting others   4 with his own passion. He tried to convey the murderous ferocity of Lady Macbeth one day by reading aloud the passage that concludes.

> . . . I have given suck, and know
> How tender 'tis to love the babe that milks me.
> I would, while it was smiling in my face,
> Have plucked my nipple from his boneless gums. . . .

The idea of prim Mr. Fleagle plucking his nipple from boneless gums was too much for the class. We burst into gasps of irrepressible snickering. Mr. Fleagle stopped.

"There is nothing funny, boys, about giving suck to a babe. It is the— the very essence of motherhood, don't you see."   5

He constantly sprinkled his sentences with "don't you see." It wasn't   6
a question but an exclamation of mild surprise at our ignorance. "Your pronoun needs an antecedent, don't you see," he would say, very primly. "The purpose of the Porter's scene, boys, is to provide comic relief from the horror, don't you see."

Late in the year we tackled the informal essay. "The essay, don't you   7
see, is the . . ." My mind went numb. Of all forms of writing, none seemed so boring as the essay. Naturally we would have to write informal essays. Mr. Fleagle distributed a homework sheet offering us a choice of topics. None was quite so simple-minded as "What I Did on My Summer Vacation," but most seemed to be almost as dull. I took the list home and dawdled until the night before the essay was due. Sprawled on the sofa, I finally faced up to the grim task, took the list out of my notebook, and scanned it. The topic on which my eye stopped was "The Art of Eating Spaghetti."

This title produced an extraordinary sequence of mental images.   8
Surging up out of the depths of memory came a vivid recollection of a night in Belleville when all of us were seated around the supper table—Uncle Allen, my mother, Uncle Charlie, Doris, Uncle Hal—and Aunt Pat served spaghetti for supper. Spaghetti was an exotic treat in those days. Neither Doris nor I had ever eaten spaghetti, and none of the adults had enough experience to be good at it. All the good humor of Uncle Allen's house reawoke in my mind as I recalled the laughing arguments we had that night about the socially respectable method for moving spaghetti from plate to mouth.

Suddenly I wanted to write about that, about the warmth and good   9
feeling of it, but I wanted to put it down simply for my own joy, not for Mr. Fleagle. It was a moment I wanted to recapture and hold for myself. I wanted to relive the pleasure of an evening at New Street. To write it as I wanted, however, would violate all the rules of formal composition I'd

learned in school, and Mr. Fleagle would surely give it a failing grade. Never mind. I would write something else for Mr. Fleagle after I had written this thing for myself.

When I finished it the night was half gone and there was no time 10 left to compose a proper, respectable essay for Mr. Fleagle. There was no choice next morning but to turn in my private reminiscence of Belleville. Two days passed before Mr. Fleagle returned the graded papers, and he returned everyone's but mine. I was bracing myself for a command to report to Mr. Fleagle immediately after school for discipline when I saw him lift my paper from his desk and rap for the class's attention.

"Now, boys," he said, "I want to read you an essay. This is titled 'The 11 Art of Eating Spaghetti.'"

And he started to read. My words! He was reading *my words* out loud 12 to the entire class. What's more, the entire class was listening. Listening attentively. Then somebody laughed, then the entire class was laughing, and not in contempt and ridicule, but with openhearted enjoyment. Even Mr. Fleagle stopped two or three times to repress a small prim smile.

I did my best to avoid showing pleasure, but what I was feeling was 13 pure ecstasy at this startling demonstration that my words had the power to make people laugh. In the eleventh grade, at the eleventh hour as it were, I had discovered a calling. It was the happiest moment of my entire school career. When Mr. Fleagle finished he put the final seal on my happiness by saying, "Now that, boys, is an essay, don't you see. It's—don't you see—it's of the very essence of the essay, don't you see. Congratulations, Mr. Baker."

For the first time, light shone on a possibility. It wasn't a very hearten- 14 ing possibility, to be sure. Writing couldn't lead to a job after high school, and it was hardly honest work, but Mr. Fleagle had opened a door for me. After that I ranked Mr. Fleagle among the finest teachers in the school.

QUESTIONS FOR WRITING AND DISCUSSION: LEARNING OUTCOMES

Critical Thinking: Responding to the Writer's Ideas

1. How do Baker's experiences in high school English compare with your experiences?

2. How does Baker help readers understand what it means to become a writer?

Composing Processes and Knowledge of Conventions: The Writer's Strategies

1. Why do you think Baker uses dialogue in describing Mr. Fleagle's class rather than simply summarizing or paraphrasing what Fleagle said?

2. Baker is well known for his use of precise language, carefully selecting just the right word to express what he means. Where is that care most evident in this essay?

Inquiry and Research: Ideas for Further Exploration

1. In *Growing Up*, Baker narrates many other stories from his life. In your school library, or online, read more stories about Baker's life. Find one that you consider to be especially compelling. What are the qualities or features of that story that you can use in your writing?

TANYA BARRIENTOS

Se Habla Español

Tanya Maria Barrientos has written for the *Philadelphia Inquirer* for more than twenty years. Barrientos was born in Guatemala and raised in El Paso, Texas. Her first novel, *Frontera Street*, was published in 2002, and her second, *Family Resemblance*, was published in 2003. Her column "Unconventional Wisdom" runs every week in the *Inquirer*. This essay originally appeared in the collection *Border-Line Personalities: A New Generation of Latinas Dish on Sex, Sass & Cultural Shifting*.

The man on the other end of the phone line is telling me the classes I've called about are first-rate: native speakers in charge, no more than six students per group. 1

"Conbersaychunal," he says, allowing the fat vowels of his accented English to collide with the sawed-off consonants. 2

I tell him that will be fine, that I'm familiar with the conversational setup, and yes, I've studied a bit of Spanish in the past. He asks for my name and I supply it, rolling the double *r* in Barrientos like a pro. That's when I hear the silent snag, the momentary hesitation I've come to expect at this part of the exchange. Should I go into it again? Should I explain, the way I have to half a dozen others, that I am Guatemalan by 3 birth but pura gringa by circumstance? Do I add the humble little laugh I usually attach to the end of my sentence to let him know that of course I see the irony in the situation?

4 This will be the sixth time I've signed up to learn the language my parents speak to each other. It will be the sixth time I've bought workbooks and notebooks and textbooks listing 501 conjugated verbs in alphabetical order, with the hope that the subjunctive tense will finally take root in my mind.

5 In class, I will sit across a table from the "native speaker," who won't question why the Irish-American lawyer, or the ad executive of Polish descent, has enrolled but, with a telling glance, will wonder what to make of me.

6 Look, I'll want to say (but never do). Forget the dark skin. Ignore the obsidian eyes. Pretend I'm a pink-cheeked, blue-eyed blonde whose name tag says Shannon. Because that is what a person who doesn't innately know the difference between corre, corra, and corrí is supposed to look like, isn't it? She certainly isn't supposed to be earth-toned or be from my kind of background. If she happens to be named García or López, it's probably through marriage, or because an ancestor at the very root of her family trekked across the American line three or four generations ago.

7 I, on the other hand, came to the United States at age three, in 1963, with my family and stopped speaking Spanish immediately.

8 College-educated and seamlessly bilingual when they settled in West Texas, my parents (a psychology professor and an artist) embraced the notion of the American melting pot wholeheartedly. They declared that their two children would speak nothing but inglés. They'd read in English, write in English, and fit into Anglo society beautifully. If they could speak the red, white, and blue without a hint of an accent, my mother and father believed, people would be forced to look beyond the obvious and see the all-American kids hidden inside the ethnic wrapping.

9 It sounds politically incorrect now. But America was not a hyphenated nation back then. People who called themselves Mexican-Americans or Afro-Americans were considered dangerous radicals, while law-abiding citizens were expected to drop their cultural baggage at the border and erase any lingering ethnic traits. Role models like Vikki Carr, Linda Ronstadt, and Raquel Welch[1] had done it and become stars. So why shouldn't we?

10 To be honest, for most of my childhood I liked being the brown girl who defied expectations. When I was seven, my mother returned my older brother and me to elementary school one week after the school year had already begun. We'd been on vacation in Washington, D.C., visiting the Smithsonian, the Capitol, and the home of Edgar Allan Poe. In the

---

[1] Three popular entertainers of Hispanic orgin.

Volkswagen, on the way home, I'd memorized "The Raven," and I'd recite it with melodramatic flair to any poor soul duped into sitting through my performance. At the school's office, the registrar frowned when we arrived.

"You people. Your children are always behind, and you have the nerve to bring them in late?" 11

"My children," my mother answered in a clear, curt tone, "will be at the top of their classes in two weeks." 12

The registrar filed our cards, shaking her head. 13

I did not live in a neighborhood with other Latinos, and the public school I attended attracted very few. I saw the world through the clear, cruel vision of a child. To me, speaking Spanish translated into being poor. It meant waiting tables and cleaning hotel rooms. It meant being left off the cheerleading squad and receiving a condescending smile from the guidance counselor when you said you planned on becoming a lawyer or a doctor. My best friends' names were Heidi and Leslie and Kim. They told me I didn't seem "Mexican" to them, and I took it as a compliment. I enjoyed looking into the faces of Latino store clerks and waitresses and, yes, even our maid, and saying "yo no hablo español." It made me feel superior. It made me feel American. It made me feel white. 14

It didn't matter that my parents spoke Spanish and were successful. They came from a different country, where everyone looked alike. In America, fitting in with the gringos was key. I didn't want to be a Latina anything. I thought that if I stayed away from Spanish, the label would stay away from me. 15

When I was sixteen, I told my father how much I hated being called Mexican—not only because I wasn't, but also because the word was hurled as an insult. He cringed and then he made a radical plan. That summer, instead of sending me to the dance camp in Aspen that I wanted to attend, he pointed me toward Mexico City and the Ballet Nacional. 16

"I want you to see how beautiful Mexico is," he said. "That way when anybody calls you Mexican, you will hold your head up." 17

I went, reluctantly, and found out he was right. I loved the music, the art, the architecture. He'd planted the seed of pride, but it would take years for me to figure out how to nurture it. 18

Back at home, my parents continued to speak only English to their kids while speaking Spanish to each other. 19

My father enjoyed listening to the nightly Mexican newscast on television, so I came to understand lots of the Spanish I heard. Not by design, but by osmosis. So, by the time I graduated from college, I'd become an odd Hispanic hybrid—an English-only Latina who could comprehend Spanish spoken at any speed but was reluctant to utter a word of it. Then came the backlash. In the two decades I'd worked hard to isolate myself from the stereotype I'd constructed in my own head, society shifted. The nation had changed its views on ethnic identity. 20

College professors had started teaching history through African-American and Native American eyes. Children were being told to forget about the melting pot and picture America as a multicolored quilt instead.

Hyphens suddenly had muscle, and I was left wondering where I fit in. The Spanish language was supposedly the glue that held the new Latino-American community together. But in my case it was what kept me apart. I felt awkward among groups whose conversations flowed in and out of Spanish. I'd be asked a question in Spanish and I'd have to answer in English, knowing that raised a mountain of questions. I wanted to call myself Latina, to finally take pride, but it felt like a lie. So I set out to learn the language that people assumed I already knew.

After my first set of lessons, which I took in a class provided by the newspaper where I worked in Dallas, I could function in the present tense. "Hola Paco, ¿qué tal? ¿Qué color es tu cuaderno? El mío es azul."[2] My vocabulary built quickly, but when I spoke my tongue felt thick inside my mouth, and if I needed to deal with anything in the future or the past I was sunk. I suggested to my parents that when I telephoned we should converse only in Spanish, so I could practice. But that only lasted a few short weeks. Our relationship was built in English and the essence of it got lost in the translation.

By my mid-twenties I had finally come around to understanding that being a proud Latina meant showing the world how diverse the culture can be. As a newspaper reporter, I met Cubans and Puerto Ricans and brown-skinned New Mexicans who could trace their families all the way back to the conquistadores. I interviewed writers and teachers and migrant workers, and I convinced editors to put their stories into print. Not just for the readers' sake, but for my own. I wanted to know what other Latinos had to say about their assimilation into American culture, and whether speaking Spanish somehow defined them. What I learned was that they considered Spanish their common denominator, linking them to one another as well as to their pasts. With that in mind, I traveled to Guatemala to see the place where I was born, and basked in the comfort of recognizing my own features in the faces of strangers. I felt connected, but I still wondered if without flawless Spanish I could ever fill the Latino bill.

I enrolled in a three-month submersion program in Mexico and emerged able to speak like a sixth-grader with a solid C average. I could read Gabriel García Márquez with a Spanish-English dictionary at my elbow, and I could follow ninety percent of the melodrama on any given telenovela.

21

22

23

24

25

---

[2] Hello Paco. What's happening? What color is your notebook? Mine is blue.

But I still didn't feel genuine. My childhood experiences were different from most of the Latinos I met. I had no quinceañera, no abuelita teaching me to cook tamales, no radio in the house playing rancheras. I had ballet lessons, a high school trip to Europe, and a tight circle of Jewish friends. I'd never met another Latina like me, and I began to doubt that they existed.   26

Since then, I've hired tutors and bought tapes to improve my Spanish. Now I can recite Lorca. I can handle the past as well as the future tenses. But the irregular verbs and the subjunctive tense continue to elude me.   27

My Anglo friends call me bilingual because I can help them make hotel reservations over the telephone or pose a simple question to the women taking care of their children. But true speakers discover my limitations the moment I stumble over a difficult construction, and that is when I get the look. The one that raises the wall between us. The one that makes me think I'll never really belong. Spanish has become a pedigree, a litmus test showing how far from your roots you've strayed. Of course, the same people who would hold my bad Spanish grammar against me wouldn't blink at an Anglo tripping over a Spanish phrase. In fact, they'd probably be flattered that the white man or woman was giving their language a shot. They'd embrace the effort. But when I fumble, I immediately lose the privilege of calling myself a full-fledged Latina. Broken Spanish doesn't count, except to set me apart from "authentic" Latinas forever.

My bilingual friends say I make too much of it. They tell me that my Guatemalan heritage and unmistakable Mayan features are enough to legitimize my membership in the Latino-American club. After all, not all Poles speak Polish. Not all Italians speak Italian. And as this nation grows more and more Hispanic, not all Latinos will share one language. But I don't believe them. I think they say those things to spare my feelings.   28

There must be other Latinas like me. But I haven't met any. Or, I should say, I haven't met any who have fessed up. Maybe they are secretly struggling to fit in, the same way I am. Maybe they are hiring tutors and listening to tapes behind the locked doors of their living rooms, just like me. I wish we all had the courage to come out of our hiding places and claim our rightful spot in the broad Latino spectrum. Without being called hopeless gringas. Without having to offer apologies or show remorse.   30

If it will help, I will go first.   31

Aquí estoy.[3]   32

Spanish-challenged and pura Latina.   33

---

[3] I am here.

QUESTIONS FOR DISCUSSION AND WRITING: LEARNING OUTCOMES

Critical Thinking: Responding to the Writer's Ideas

1. In many ways, this essay is about how Barrientos is trying to fit in to American culture and society. Where have you tried to fit in, and what have your struggles been?

2. What are the potential advantages of being multilingual?

Composing Processes and Knowledge of Conventions: The Writer's Strategies

1. Barrientos tells of her experiences in the first person. How would it alter the effectiveness and interest of this essay if it had been written in the third person? Why?

2. Barrientos now and then writes in Spanish. How do the Spanish sentences affect her essay?

Inquiry and Research: Ideas for Further Exploration

1. Interview several family members about their language background and experiences. In a brief paper, explain how their experiences compare to those related by Barrientos.

 ## Thinking about Visuals That Share Experiences

Photographs can also serve to share experiences, sometimes more effectively than written text. On any given day, we are surrounded by images that tell stories—some mundane, some tragic, some comic, and so on.

The photograph in Figure 4.1 on page 66 shares an experience with which most people are familiar. As you look at this photograph, consider these questions about the effective use of photographs to share experiences:

- What kind of story does this photograph tell?

- What details in the picture speak to you?

- What might this grandmother have to say if she were to write about this experience?

- Does this photograph speak to a larger theme about how fragile people are when they are young? About the relationship between young and old? Is a photograph more, or less, effective at making a point or expressing a theme than a written narrative about this relationship would be?

FIGURE 4.1
A Grandmother
and Her Grandson

Writing Processes

As you work on the assignment scenario that you have chosen, keep in mind the qualities of effective writing about experiences (see pp. 53–55).

Technote

Are your files stored in folders (directories) on your computer? If so, have you established a system of organization for them? Have you ever lost track of where you have stored a song, video, project, or paper on your computer? Before it happens again, take some time to organize your folders and files.

- Start by looking at the names of all of the folders you've already created. Did you use some principle for naming and organizing them? That is, are they alphabetized? Named according to project or media type (such as music, video, and so on)?

Or are the names more or less random?

- See if you can find relationships among the names of your folders, and look for ways to group folders and files and store them together in one folder.

- Establish a separate folder for each course you are taking.

Taking a little time to organize your files and folders today can save you time and prevent confusion when you need to retrieve files you are working on and quickly locate documents you must print and hand in.

In the pages that follow, you will engage in various writing processes to help you generate ideas and draft, revise, and edit your writing. These processes are *recursive*, which means that you will probably revisit each stage numerous times as you work.

If you are considering several possible topics, put your notes into a separate computer document for each one. Once you determine which topic you will write about, it will be easy to access and use those notes. As you work on your project, make certain that you save your computer files frequently. Also, savvy writers back up their computer files in two or more places—on an internal or external hard drive of the computer, on a USB flash drive, and/or on a rewritable CD or DVD.

Invention: Getting Started

As you begin to explore your subject, it is a good idea to use more than one invention activity to help you come up with ideas. Especially when you are writing to share experiences, the more detail that you generate about the experience through invention, the better you will be able to convey the experience and its meaning to your readers. As you begin the process, consider the following questions:

- What do I already know about the experience that I am writing about?
- What feelings, attitudes, or notions do I already have about this experience?
- What questions can I ask about the experience? That is, what gaps do I have in my memory of it or knowledge about it that might help me understand what information a reader might need?
- Who would know about my experience (a relative or friend)? What questions might I ask that person in an interview?
- What do I know about my audience? What don't I know that I should know? Why might they be interested in reading my text?
- What might my audience already know about my subject? Why might they care about it?
- To what extent will sensory details—color, shape, smell, taste—help my reader understand my topic? Why?
- What visuals might I use to help my readers understand my experience?

Completing invention activities such as the ones suggested in the first writing activity should yield a wealth of information that you can draw on for your first draft. (Doing your invention work in electronic form, rather than on paper, lets you easily use the writing you generate in your paper at the drafting stage.) As with any kind of writing, invention activities improve with peer feedback and suggestions. Consider sharing the invention work you have done so far with several classmates or friends in order to understand your rhetorical situation more clearly and to generate more useful information.

Finally, if you already keep a journal, you might skim through it to find ideas for your writing. If you don't already keep a journal, you might do so while you are getting started on this writing project. Who knows—you might even start a lifelong habit of writing in a daily journal.

TechNote Use technology to help you "unjam" that writer's block! Some writers find it hard to get started when they are asked to share personal experiences in class, either because they are overcome by shyness or overwhelmed by the number and variety of experiences and interests they are excited to write about. If writer's block sets in, one way to get your ideas and memories flowing is to use your personal network and communication skills to tap a vital resource: the people who know you well. Send a couple of e-mails, a text message, an instant message, or even an I-Voice message to family members or close friends. Ask them to reminisce briefly about events, occurrences, or activities you've shared. You might be pleasantly surprised at the memories and ideas they share that will inspire you.

For more on descriptive writing, see Chapter 13.

For help with strategies for discovery and learning, see Chapter 3.

Exploring Your Ideas with Research

While a paper in which you share experiences may not seem to require research, even "mining" your own memory—and looking through childhood memorabilia—is a form of research. You may find it useful to go back through old family files, letters, documents, and photo albums—all wonderful sources of information. See the box below for more on generating ideas from photographs and documents.

Depending on the scenario you are responding to, you may also need to interview family members or friends about the experiences you are exploring. Be sure to record their stories carefully; their recollections will enliven your own text. Always try to ask them for remembered dialogue—what people said—as those remembered sentences will help you show (rather than just tell) about the experience you are writing about.

For more on conducting interviews, see Chapter 19, pages 527–29.

Use an electronic journal to record images, URLs, and other electronic pieces of information that you find as you are conducting your research. Such an e-journal makes it easy for you to add those e-documents once you start drafting your paper.

VISUALIZING VARIATIONS

Using Photos and Documents as Sources

If you are writing in response to Scenarios 1 or 2 (p. 52), you may be able to use photographs and documents to help you generate ideas and recall or reconstruct events. The photograph above is of the great-great-grandparents of the wife of one of the authors of this book. Look at photographs of the experience you are writing about in your past and speculate about the person or people, using the following questions:

1. What do the clothes the people in the photograph are wearing tell you about them?
2. What do their expressions reveal—or fail to reveal—about them?

3. Are you looking at old photographs similar to this one? If so, compare the facial expressions in your photos to the one above. Does everyone in your old photographs always look glum (ours do!)?

The photograph below, taken in Wisconsin circa 1955, includes one of the authors of this book and his siblings. Use the following questions to speculate about this photograph or a similar one from your past.

1. On what day of the week do you think the photograph was taken? What evidence supports that assumption?
2. During what time of year was the photograph taken? Why do you think that?
3. What do the expressions on the people's faces tell you about the situation?

In addition to photographs, you might have a letter, diary, or other document that you or your relatives or ancestors wrote that can give you insight into your experience or their experiences. Use the following questions to generate more ideas about this assignment:

1. When and where was the document written? What was the writer's purpose in writing it? How can you tell?
2. What does the document reveal about the writer's experiences or about your experiences at the time?
3. How significant does the experience seem? In what ways did the experience in the document change the writer's, or your, life?

If you participated in the experience shown in the photograph or described in the document, use the following questions to generate ideas about it:

1. How is your memory of the experience the same as, or different from, the experience as it is depicted in the photograph(s) or document?
2. If you wanted to write a brief story about the people in one of the photographs above, or in one of your photographs, what would you say?

(cont'd)

(continued)

3. What experiences have you had in taking photographs? What stories do you try to tell when taking photographs or videos? How do you try to do so?

Consider including a copy of the photograph or a selection of photographs and quoting from the document in your final paper.

Organizing Your Ideas and Details

Once you have generated ideas and details about your subject using invention activities and, if necessary, research, consider how you might organize this material. The questions that you need to ask yourself when deciding on your organization are all rhetorical:

- Who is your audience?
- Why might they be interested in your narrative—and how can you make them interested?
- What is your purpose for writing—that is, what do you want your readers to understand about you or the event you are narrating?

The answers to these questions can help you decide what you need to emphasize, which in turn will help you choose an organization.

It is usually helpful to try *several* organizational strategies in early drafts because seeing your words on paper—in various ways—will help you decide what strategy will work best for you. Most often, writing about experiences is sequential: the writer starts at some specific point in the past and then moves to a later time or to the present.

An alternative would be to use the narrative technique known as **flashback.** In a flashback, commonly used in film, something that happened in the past is shown "just the way it happened" and then the narrator returns to the present to reflect on the event's significance.

Here are three possible organizational structures that you might use for a piece of writing that shares experiences:

Options for Organization

Chronological Approach	Flashback Approach	Crisis Approach
• Straightforward chronology—narrate the experience from beginning to end. • Relate key details surrounding the event or experience.	• Begin in the present. • Flash back to the events and experiences you want to share and relate them in sequence. • Relate key details surrounding the events.	• Begin with the crisis point in the event or experience. • Go back to the beginning and tell the story to the end. • Relate key details surrounding the event or experience.

- Note the impact of the experience on your life or the lives of others who were part of the experience.
- Reflect on the significance of the experience. (optional)

- Look back on those events and experiences in terms of the impact they had on your life, or the lives of others.
- Reflect on the significance of the experiences. (optional)

- Reflect on the significance of the event and experience. (optional)

Constructing a Complete Draft

Once you have chosen the organizational approach that works best for your audience and purpose, you are ready to construct the rest of your draft. Before you begin your draft, review all your invention material to see what needs to be included and what might be left out. To make these decisions, consider your purpose for sharing this experience with others: What is the significance of the experience? How can you help readers see the significance?

You will also want to discover the method of writing a first draft that works best for you. Some writers prefer drafting large chunks at once. Others prefer drafting small pieces over time. Remember that you do not have to compose your essay in a linear way—from beginning to end. You might find it easiest to jump in somewhere in the middle.

Introduction: One of the qualities of a successful narrative is that it grabs and holds readers' attention. A number of strategies for beginning your narrative can help get your readers interested, including the following:

- *Start your narrative with a surprising event or piece of dialogue.* Tanya Barrientos (her essay appears on pp. 60–64) starts her essay by telling of a phone conversation and then adds a word readers may not know or expect: "*Conbersaychunal.*"

- *Start with interesting details*, to draw the reader in through sensual, descriptive words and phrases.

- *Start with a comment that might startle your readers.*

For more on introductions, see Chapter 13.

Body: The main part, or body, of your narrative is the place to tell your story. Use dialogue and telling details to develop the story and reveal the character of the people in your narrative. To hold your readers' interest, you should usually build your narrative to a crisis or climax, unless you are writing for an informative purpose and are required to maintain a neutral tone (or unless you are beginning with the crisis point of the narrative—see p. 70). Choose the verb tense that will best serve the purpose of your narrative. If you use past-tense verbs to narrate the experience, you remind readers that it happened in the past and that you have had time to reflect on it. If you use present-tense verbs, you make the event seem as if it is happening now, and you will seem to reveal its significance to yourself and to your readers at the same time. Also, you might consider using photographs to complement the words you are using to tell the story.

Conclusion: Your conclusion should tie things together for your readers by explaining or suggesting the significance of the experience or experiences you have shared. Here are some strategies for concluding a paper in which you have shared experiences:

- Review the subject's most important aspects.
- Explain the subject's significance.
- Suggest avenues for a reader's further inquiry.
- Refer back to the introduction of your narrative.

For more on conclusion, see Chapter 13

Title: You might think that you need to come up with a title before you start writing, but often it is more useful to get a first draft down on paper or into a computer file and then consider possible titles. As with the introduction, an effective title for a narrative intrigues readers and makes them want to read the text.

Revising

Just finishing a complete draft may give you a justified sense of accomplishment. However, you are only part of the way to a successful piece of writing; you still need to revise and then edit the draft. It is a good idea to let your draft sit for a while after you have finished it. When you return to it, you are much more likely to find sections that need to be revised: places where details need to be added, other places where details may need to be removed, still others where some of your words or sentences need to be shifted from one place to another.

Technology can help you revise and edit your writing more easily. Use your word processor's track-changes tool to try out changes. After you have had time to think about the possible changes, you can "accept" or "reject" them. If your classmates are offering feedback on your draft, they can also use track changes, the comment tool, or the peer-commenting feature of the software. Friends or family members may also be willing to read your draft and offer useful suggestions.

WRITER'S WORKSHOP

Responding to Full Drafts

Working with one or two classmates, read each paper and offer comments and questions that will help each of you see your papers' strengths and weaknesses. Consider the following guidelines and questions as you do:

- Write a brief narrative comment that outlines your first impression of this draft. How effectively does the title draw you into the narrative? Indicate what you like about the draft—that is, provide positive and encouraging feedback to the writer.

- Comment specifically on the introduction: What is effective about it? What suggestions can you make on how to improve the introduction?

- What significant point is the writer making about the experience he or she is relating? How might the writer be able to make that point more clearly?

- Why is the writer relating this experience or these experiences? What in this piece of writing helps you see why the experience or experiences were important to the writer?

- How lively is the narrative? Where has the writer gone beyond simply telling readers about the experience or experiences to showing it or them? How might the writer use more dialogue?

- How has the writer used description to make people, places, and scenes vivid for readers? Where is more description needed?

- How effectively does the story build in terms of reaching a climax, holding the readers' attention throughout, and making logical sense in how one action follows another?

- How honestly has the writer explained the experience? If not, why do you question it?

- Reread the conclusion. What could be added or changed to make it more effective? How well does it bring the narrative to a satisfying conclusion?

Responding to Readers' Comments

Once they have received feedback from peers, teachers, writing tutors, and others, all writers have to determine what to do with that feedback.

Pay close attention to what your readers tell you. As with any group of readers, some of your peer reviewers might not understand your point, or they may misunderstand something you wrote. It is up to you either to accept or to ignore their comments and suggestions. Other comments, though, deserve your attention because they are the words of interested, caring readers speaking to you about how to improve your text. They offer perspectives that you may not have. You may find that comments from more than one reader contradict each other. In that case, use your own judgment to decide which reader's comments are on the right track.

Knowledge of Conventions

When effective writers edit their work, they attend to the conventions that will help readers understand their ideas. These include genre conventions, documentation, format, usage, grammar, punctuation, and mechanics. By attending to these conventions in your writing, you make reading a more pleasant experience for readers.

Editing

After you revise, you need to go through one more important step: editing and polishing. When you edit and polish your writing, you make changes to your sentence structure and word choice to improve your style and to make your writing clearer and more concise. You also check your work to make sure it adheres to conventions of grammar, usage, punctuation, mechanics, and spelling.

Because it is sometimes difficult to identify small problems in a piece of writing you have been mulling over for some time, it often helps to distance yourself from the text before your last read so you can approach the draft with fresh eyes. Some people like to put the text aside for a day or so; others try reading aloud; and some even read from the last sentence to the first so that the content, and their familiarity with it, does not cause them to overlook an error. Because checking conventions is easier said than done, though, we strongly recommend that you ask classmates, friends, and tutors to read your work to find sentence problems that you do not see.

To assist you with editing, we offer here a round-robin editing activity focused on punctuating dialogue, which is a common concern in writing to share experiences.

WRITER'S WORKSHOP

Round-Robin Editing with a Focus on Punctuating Dialogue

When writers share their experiences, they often use dialogue to make the scenes and events vivid for readers, but writers who use dialogue need to be aware of the conventions for punctuating it.

All dialogue needs to be enclosed in quotation marks to set it off from the rest of the text. If the dialogue is presented within the context of a sentence, the phrase that introduces the dialogue ends with a comma and then the dialogue begins with a quotation mark:

Embarrassed that she caught me sleeping, I said quickly, "No, Ms. Cain. I'm fine."

Note that if the dialogue is not introduced within a sentence, it usually starts a new paragraph that begins with a quotation mark.

Periods and commas go inside the quotation marks, but question marks and exclamation points go either inside or outside of the quotation marks, depending on whether they are part of the quotation itself.

"Jessica, are you awake yet?" my father asks.

"It was terrible! Coach was in such a bad mood!"

Work with two peers to edit one another's papers for problems in punctuating dialogue. Compare notes to see if you have any questions about the conventions for punctuating dialogue. If you are uncertain about a rule, consult reading selections in this book with punctuated dialogue, such as "On Becoming a Writer" (pp. 57–59) or "Se Habla Español" (pp. 60–64); check the rules in a grammar handbook; or ask your instructor for assistance.

Genres, Documentation, and Format

If you are writing an academic paper, follow the conventions for the discipline in which you are writing and the requirements of your instructor. If you have chosen to write a letter to a prospective employer, you should also follow the conventions of a business letter.

Student Jessica Hemauer Shares Her Experiences

Jessica Hemauer, a student in a first-year composition course, wrote an essay called "Farm Girl" about her experience of growing upon a farm. As you read Hemauer's essay, think about what makes it an effective example of writing about experiences.

JESSICA HEMAUER

Farm Girl

BEEP! BEEP! BEEP! It's 5:00 a.m. My eyes are heavy with sleep and struggle to open. I think to myself, "A typical ten-year-old child does not have to wake up at five in the morning to do chores!"

I hit the snooze button, hoping desperately that the cows will, for once, feed and milk themselves. Seconds away from falling back into a deep sleep, I hear my father's heavy footsteps outside my bedroom door. They stop and my door opens with a creak. "Jessica, are you awake yet?" my father asks. Without a word, knowing from past experience that an argument won't get me anywhere, I stagger out of my warm twin bed, trudging dejectedly past the figure at the narrow doorway. I continue down the hall toward the small bathroom to find my sisters, Angie and Melissa, and my brother, Nick, already awake.

We all proceed with our usual morning routine, which consists of washing our faces, brushing our teeth, and taking turns on the white porcelain throne. In the lower level of the old farmhouse, our outside clothes await. My mother makes it a rule to keep them there so that they won't stink up the rest of the house. As soon as we open the door to the basement, we can smell the putrid aroma of cows that has seeped from our clothing into the damp cool air. We take our turns going down the steep, narrow steps, using the walls on either side for extra guidance. As we dress, not a single word is spoken because we all feel the same way, "I hate this!" However, most of the time our choice of vocabulary is much more creative.

Nick opens the basement door leading outside to the barn. There is a brisk and bitter wind accompanied by icy snowflakes that feel like needles digging into our faces. We don't turn back. We desperately want to, but we know my father is patiently waiting for us to help him milk and feed the cows before school starts at 8:30 a.m. We lift our scarves and pull down our hats so only our squinted eyes show. We lower our bodies to dodge the fierce winds and trudge a half mile to the red barn, which is somehow standing sturdily in the dreadful blizzard.

When we finally reach the barn, Nick, leading the pack, grabs the handle of the heavy wood door and props it open for my sisters and me to pass through. Nick goes immediately to help my father herd the cows and get them into their proper stalls to be milked. Meanwhile, my sisters and I go to the milk house to sanitize the milking machines, prepare all the milking equipment, and set up a station with towels and charts of the cows that are being medicated.

While Melissa and my father milk the one hundred cows, Nick and Angie feed them, and I feed the newborn calves. Because I am the youngest

One of Hemauer's peer readers wrote the following comment:

I like how the real details (like all of the smells) help me "be there" with you.

Notice the sensory details in this paragraph.

in the family, this is my favorite chore because I rarely have the chance to look after someone or feel like I am taking care of him or her. I have always had older siblings who look after me, watching every step I take, making sure that I don't get into trouble. We all work together — that's critical. When I feed the calves, I am finally the one in charge. It is a nice feeling, being on the opposite end of the spectrum. They are my responsibility. Little do I realize it, but this is the beginning of a lifetime of responsibilities.

After the calves are fed, other chores have to be done. Cleaning out various huts and pens and laying down fresh straw are a part of our daily duties. This is the worst of the jobs I have to do. It is so dusty that I can hardly breathe at times, but we all know it has to be done so there is no sense complaining. My brother, sisters, and I work together to get the chores done as quickly as possible. Typically, we finish with the chores and return to the house around 7:30 in the morning.

7

We make our way back to the farmhouse, drape our clothes on a fold-ing chair next to the washing machine in the basement, and crawl up the stairs. The delicious smell of smoked bacon and cheese omelets grows more intense with each step. Our stomachs aching with hunger, we take turns in the shower, cleaning ourselves as fast as possible in order to get to the breakfast table. My father eats quickly and is back outside on the farm by the time my sisters or I run by the kitchen, grabbing a glass of fresh squeezed orange juice and a piece of toast as we yell frantically at the bus, "Wait!" It seems our daily lives operate in shifts, not like a real family.

8

Again, note the sensory details in Hemauer's paper: the smells, being hungry, fresh OJ, etc.

When I finally arrive at school, I have already been up for four hours doing chores on the farm in the bitter cold. The other kids in my private grade school have just rolled out of their beds inside their subdivision homes an hour before the bell rang. The school day always goes by fast. While my other classmates are thinking about what television show they are going to watch after school, I am thinking about the chores that await me once I get off the yellow school bus.

9

One peer reader had the following comment:

I don't see why the information about your parents is important—can you clarify or explain?

School has always been my social life. I want to join teams or differ-ent clubs, but I always have to consider how my chores on the farm will get done, which makes it difficult for me to get involved. If I join a team that practices after school, I can't participate. If I join a club that meets before school, I can't attend the meetings. Being a farm girl means that I can't be like the other kids in my class. Not being able to participate in school activities like my friends makes me feel left out and depressed. The topic of conversation at the lunch table never involves me.

10

Hemauer deleted two paragraphs from her first draft about her parents that took the essay off track.

"Hey, Carrie, how was basketball practice last night?" Susan asks as she pulls out a chair from the lunch table and sets her plastic tray down next to the tall, broad, blond-haired girl.

"It was terrible! Coach was in such a bad mood!" Carrie shoves a hand-ful of French fries into her mouth, spilling catsup down the front of her

11

One peer reviewer made this suggestion:

I'd like to hear more about school and the people there.

Note the details and specific examples that Hemauer provides to really show what she means (rather than just telling).

white tee shirt without noticing. "He made us run sprints for every shot we missed. And Kelly was missing all her shots last night. I'm so sore today."

Carrie starts rubbing her legs when she notices the streak of catsup on her shirt. She begins to wipe it off with one of her napkins, with little success. **12**

"Hey, Carrie, how was the student council meeting this morning? Did you decide if we're going to have a formal dance this winter?" **13**

"Yeah, we're having it on the Saturday before Christmas. Are you going to come?" **14**

I sit listening in silence. The twenty-minute lunch period always feels like eternity. While everyone around me continues talking and laughing, I sit there next to them silently eating my French fries, listening carefully, trying to laugh at the right times. **15**

In eighth grade I really want to play basketball, and after begging and pleading with my parents, they finally say I can join the team as long as I continue to help with chores in the morning before school and after practice. I quickly agree. I become the basketball team's starting point guard. I am thrilled to be on a team, and I finally feel like I am starting to have a life like the other kids. Now I am included in the conversations at lunch, and I feel like a part of the group. I never tell anyone that I have to go home after practice and work on the farm, or that I wake up every morning at five to help with chores. None of my friends, teachers, or coaches know. I don't think they would care and I don't want them to know that I am different. **16**

In high school I become more involved with the school. Coincidently, my father's farm continues to grow. We are now up to two hundred cows, and my dad still wants to expand the farm. During my freshman year I continue to work on the farm before and after school, making sure that I can still play on the basketball team. A few times a teacher catches me with my eyes closed during class. One time my teacher, Ms. Cain, comes over to my wooden desk, where my head is resting on top of a math textbook. She taps her knuckles on the hollow wood and says, "Jessica, are you okay? Do you need to go to the health room?" Raising my head, embarrassed that she caught me sleeping, I say quickly, "No, Ms. Cain, I'm fine. I'm sorry for being rude and causing a disruption. I promise to be more attentive." **17**

Shortly after freshman year, my father arranges a meeting with my entire family. He explains that he wants our farm to continue to grow, and this means that he needs more help on the farm than his children can provide. In fact, he says that he would rather not have us work on the farm anymore, unless we want to. He would rather have us be more involved in school and go on to college. After this meeting, I feel happy and relieved, and I can tell my father is relieved too. He knows that my siblings and I have sacrificed our school activities and social lives to help with the family business, and I know that this is his way of saying thank you. **18**

From this moment on, I become more involved with my school. I join 19
the homecoming club, audition for musicals and plays, serve as the
president of the student council as well as president of my class. I also
became more social with my friends. I even take on a waitressing job at
a resort in a neighboring town. During all these activities, I always notice
that I stick out from the group. In school people come up to me and ask
how I manage my time so well, without getting stressed out. When I'm
with a group of my friends, I always seem to be more mature than they
are, leading the group while others try to follow in my footsteps. When it
comes to my job, I am always on time, never calling in sick and never
complaining about a task I have been asked to do.

One night after work, I sit down in front of the full-length mirror in 20
my bedroom and start thinking about the past years. I had believed that
joining various clubs and social activities would make me fit in with my
peers. But in fact, it has not. I still stick out. And the more I think about
it, the more I realize why. My life growing up has been much different
from the lives of my peers. From an early age, I had to learn how to manage my time so that I could do my chores and attend school. When I
started to play basketball, I had to manage my time even more carefully.
I have always had a challenging amount of responsibility, and I have
learned to complete tasks in a timely fashion. The work that I had to do
on the farm was far from glamorous. I have done some of the worst jobs
conceivable, so I have a higher tolerance for work than most people.
Though I hated it growing up, working on the farm has taught me many
lessons about life, and it has shaped me into the individual I am today.

Each day of my life there are times when I reflect back to working on 21
the farm. And every day people notice that I am different from the rest of
my peers. At school, teachers and organization leaders are impressed by
my time management skills and the amount of responsibility I take on.
At work, my boss continues to ask me where he can find some more hard
working people. I simply tell him, "Try hiring some farm girls. I hear they
turn out pretty good."

QUESTIONS FOR WRITING AND DISCUSSION: LEARNING OUTCOMES

Rhetorical Knowledge: The Writer's Situation and Rhetoric

1. **Purpose:** Why did Hemauer write this essay? How might different audiences see different purposes?

2. **Audience:** Who do you see as Hemauer's audience? What can you point
   to in the text that supports your claim?

3. **Voice and Tone:** How does Hemauer establish her *ethos*—her credibility—in this essay?

4. **Responsibility:** What is Hemauer's responsibility to her readers? To the members of her family? How does she fulfill those responsibilities?

5. **Context and Format:** Hemauer is writing an essay for readers who are probably not familiar with life on a farm. How does this context affect her essay?

Critical Thinking: Responding to the Writer's Ideas

1. Even though you may have had a much different childhood from Hemauer's, can you relate to some of her experiences? What does she do to develop interest in the subject of her essay?

2. What do you see as the significance of Hemauer's story?

Composing Processes and Knowledge of Conventions: The Writer's Strategies

1. How do descriptive and narrative details function in the essay? Point to several places where Hemauer "shows" instead of "tells."

2. What is the main point of Hemauer's essay? How do the details in the essay support that point?

Inquiry and Research: Ideas for Further Exploration

1. Search the Web to find other narratives—especially blog entries—in which college students reflect on their life and work experiences. How do they compare to Hemauer's narrative about her farm-life experience?

Self-Assessment: Reflecting on Your Learning Goals

Now that you have constructed a piece of writing to share experiences, revisit your learning goals, which you and your classmates may have considered at the beginning of this chapter (see pp. 46–47). Here are some questions to help you focus on what you have learned from this assignment. Respond to the questions in writing and discuss your responses with classmates. If you are constructing a course portfolio, your responses to these questions can also serve as invention work for the portfolio.

Rhetorical Knowledge

- *Audience:* What did you learn about your audience as you wrote about your experience or experiences?

- *Purpose:* How successfully do you feel you fulfilled your purpose?

- *Rhetorical Situation:* What was your rhetorical situation? How have you responded to the rhetorical situation?
- *Voice and Tone:* How did you reveal your personality? What tone did you use?
- *Context, Medium, and Genre:* What context were you writing in? What medium and genre did you choose, and how did those decisions affect your writing?

Critical Thinking, Reading, and Writing

- *Learning/Inquiry:* What did you discover about writing about experiences while you were working on this assignment? What did you discover about yourself? About your experiences?
- *Responsibility:* How did you fulfill your responsibility to your readers? To the people you wrote about?
- *Reading and Research:* Did you rely on your memories, or did you conduct additional research for this assignment? If so, what sources did you consult? How did you use them?

Writing Processes

- *Invention:* What invention strategies were most useful to you?
- *Organizing Your Ideas and Details:* What organization did you use? How successful was it?
- *Revising:* What one revision did you make that you are most satisfied with? What are the strongest and the weakest parts of the paper you wrote for this chapter? Why?
- *Working with Peers:* How did your instructor or peer readers help you by making comments and suggestions about your writing? List some examples of useful comments that you received. How could you have made better use of the comments and suggestions you received?
- Did you use photographs or other visuals to help you describe your experience or experiences? If so, what did you learn about incorporating these elements?
- What "writerly habits" have you developed, modified, or improved on as you constructed the writing assignment for this chapter?

Knowledge of Conventions

- *Editing:* What sentence problem did you find most frequently in your writing? How will you avoid that problem in future assignments?
- *Genre:* What conventions of the genre you were using, if any, gave you problems?
- *Documentation:* Did you use sources for your paper? If so, what documentation style did you use? What problems, if any, did you have with it?

Rhetorical Knowledge

- *Audience:* Because you are learning as you write, you will often be the main audience. Who else can you visualize reading your work? What will that person or those people expect to find in it? How can you appeal to those readers as well?

- *Purpose:* Your purpose might be simply to learn more about the topic, but often exploratory writing leads to the unexpected and unfamiliar, so you need to be prepared to be surprised.

- *Rhetorical situation:* Consider the myriad of factors that affect what you write—you (the writer), your readers (the audience), the topic (the subject you are exploring), your purpose (what you wish to accomplish), and the exigency (what is compelling you to write). In an exploratory essay, you are writing to raise questions and to let them guide your inquiry; your readers are reading your text so that they can grapple with those same questions.

- *Writer's voice and tone:* Generally, exploratory writing has an inquisitive tone. Of course, sometimes an exploratory essay can have a humorous tone.

- *Context, medium, and genre:* The genre you use to present your thinking is determined by your purpose: to explore. You will need to decide on the best medium and genre to use to present your exploration to the audience you want to reach.

Critical Thinking, Reading, and Writing

- *Learning/inquiry:* By reading and writing as an explorer, you gain a deeper understanding of diverse and complex perspectives.

- *Responsibility:* You have a responsibility to represent diverse perspectives honestly and accurately.

- *Reading and research:* Your research must be accurate and as complete as possible, to allow you to consider the widest possible array of perspectives.

Writing Processes

- *Invention:* You will need to choose invention strategies that will help you thoughtfully contemplate diverse perspectives.

- *Organizing your ideas and details:* You will need to find the most effective way to present perspectives to your readers, so they can easily understand them.

- *Revising:* You will need to read your work with a critical eye, to make certain that it fulfills the assignment and displays the qualities of effective exploratory writing.

- *Working with peers:* Your classmates will make suggestions that indicate parts of your text they find difficult to understand so you can work to clarify.

Conventions

- *Editing:* When you explore, you might tend to leave your thoughts—and sentences—incomplete. To help you avoid this pitfall, the round-robin activity in this chapter (on p. 112) deals with sentence fragments.

- *Genres for exploratory writing:* Possible genres include exploratory essays, profiles, and more informal types of exploratory writing such as blogs, journals, and diaries.

- *Documentation:* If you have relied on sources outside of your own experience, you will need to cite them using the appropriate documentation style.

Chapter 5

A.

B.

C.

A. Photo taken on July 20, 1969, by Neil A. Armstrong of Edwin E. "Buzz" Aldrin during the Apollo 11 mission to the moon.

B. The Mars Rover, one of two "robot geologists" that landed on the surface of Mars in January 2004.

C. A view of the star cluster NGC 346 in the Small Magellanic Cloud, a satellite galaxy of the Milky Way, taken by the Hubble Space Telescope.

Writing to Explore

When you hear the word *exploration*, you may envision astronauts or explorers of earlier centuries, people who physically ventured to previously uncharted territory. When astronauts Neil Armstrong and Edwin E. "Buzz" Aldrin went to the moon in 1969, they were looking for answers to questions that humans have asked for thousands of years: What is the moon like? What is it composed of? What does Earth look like from the moon? More recently, the Hubble Space Telescope has enabled explorers to view remote parts of the universe such as the brilliant star cluster NGC 346. And today's space explorers are often not astronauts but robots—like the Mars Rover, also shown here.

Although we commonly associate exploration with physical travel, there are many other kinds of explorations. Indeed, some of the most valuable explorations are those that take place in your own mind. Often, through the act of writing, you can discover new ideas or new perspectives.

Playwright Edward Albee once noted, "I write to find out what I'm talking about." In addition to exploring what you already know, exploratory writing gives you the chance to ask questions and to consider what else you would like to find out.

Exploring various perspectives on issues, concepts, places, or people will help you to work your way through ideas and problems in college and in the professional, civic, and personal areas of your life. You may already have used exploratory thinking and writing in deciding where to go to college. In your professional life, you might be asked to research possible locations for a new branch office of your company, exploring the advantages and disadvantages of each. Or, at some point in your personal life, you may need to decide whether to stay home with a young child or find an appropriate daycare facility so that you can work outside the home or attend school. In your civic life, you may research a charity to which you are thinking of donating to make sure it is what it claims to be.

In each of these explorations, you investigate a particular subject closely. You will often need to explore an idea or a concept—or a decision you need to make—in detail, from various perspectives, before you can really see and understand the overall situation, gain some insight, or make a difficult decision.

Rhetorical Knowledge

When you write to explore, consider how your exploration will help you gain some greater understanding and how you can help your readers understand your topic in a new way and why you want them to gain this understanding. You will also need to decide what medium and genre will help you communicate your exploration most effectively to your audience.

Writing to Explore in Your College Classes

Your college classes, which are generally designed to fulfill requirements for a specific major and college degree, give you wonderful opportunities to explore your current interests and discover new ones. Taking a college class in almost any field allows you to begin exploring that field, reading its literature and listening to and interacting with people who are experts in the field. Each class you take also gives you the chance to explore the subject area in writing. During your college career, you may write the following kinds of papers:

- In a history class, your instructor may encourage you to explore several perspectives on the Cuban Missile Crisis in 1962. Such an exploration might then lead to a writing project in which you argue that certain events and factors were the actual causes of this crisis.

- In a nutrition class, your instructor asks you to explore several perspectives on vegetarian diets. Here, too, your exploration could lead to a paper in which you demonstrate specific effects of vegetarianism or in which you argue for or against such a diet.

- For a communication course, your instructor may ask you to explore whether there is evidence that men and women have different communication styles.

For information on writing a cause-and-effect analysis, see Chapter 10. For information on writing to convince, see Chapter 8.

Writing to Explore for Life

Just as you will undoubtedly write to explore in your academic life, you are likely to use different kinds of exploratory writing in other areas of your life. You may enjoy keeping a journal of your personal life. In your professional life, creating scenarios may help you explore options and make difficult decisions. In your civic life, you may also have opportunities to use exploratory writing.

In much of the exploratory writing you will do in your **professional** life, you will find yourself exploring various options. To what extent will hiring Ms. X instead of Mr. Y make a difference to the business? A teacher might ask what effect one lesson plan would have on a group of students compared to a different lesson plan? Parents might explore the possibilities of different schools for their children or different neighborhoods to live in. While it is impossible to predict the future, by engaging in exploratory writing we can often better understand the consequences of taking a particular action.

People working for the good of a community often deal with *best options*—solutions to problems for which there may not be a single perfect result but rather many possible outcomes. Therefore, those involved in **civic** life can find exploratory writing especially useful.

Your **personal** life offers many opportunities for exploratory writing. You may respond regularly to e-mails or notes from friends, family members, and classmates in which you explore the possibilities for a group gift for someone important to all of you, propose convenient times for getting together, or consider a new wireless carrier. You may keep a journal or diary, where you can explore your thoughts, ideas, responses, and feelings in a private conversation with yourself.

TechNote The ultimate form of writing to explore might be a personal or professional online journal, or *blog*. A blog can be a fun place to explore issues and events of the day while developing your voice, style, and expressive self. If your teacher recommends blogging, a good place to get started with ideas for a blog might be Maggie Mason's book *No One Cares What You Had for Lunch: 100 Ideas for Your Blog* (Peachpit Press; August 11, 2006).

For more on blogs, see Chapter 17.

Scenarios for Writing: Assignment Options

Your instructor may ask you to complete one or both of the following assignments that call for exploratory writing. Each assignment is in the form of a *scenario*, a brief story that provides some context for writing. The scenario gives you a sense of who your audience is and what you need to accomplish with your writing.

Starting on page 104, you will find guidelines for completing whatever assignment option you choose. Additional scenarios for college and life may be found online.

Writing for College

SCENARIO 1 Exploring a Major or Career

For this scenario, assume you are taking a "Career and Life Planning" class—a class devoted to helping college students decide what discipline they might like to major in. This class gives you the opportunity to explore different career paths, to learn what the educational requirements are for various majors, and to find out what job opportunities will be available and what salaries and other forms of compensation different jobs might offer.

Writing Assignment: Select one college major or career that you may be interested in pursuing and construct an exploratory paper in which you consider the various aspects of that major or career from many angles, including the preparation you would need for it and the rewards and pitfalls you might encounter if you decide to pursue it. Asking and answering questions about the major or career you are considering will form the heart of your exploratory paper.

Writing for Life

SCENARIO 2   Constructing a Personal Exploration in a Letter to a Friend

For this exploratory writing assignment, think of something you really believe in. You might want to discuss your views on raising children, supporting aging parents, choosing a simpler lifestyle, discovering some important truth about yourself, or some other quality or belief that makes you who you are. (Because religious beliefs are so personal, you may want to select a strongly held opinion that does not involve your religion.)

Writing Assignment: Write down in a sentence or two something you believe in strongly. Now explore the basis for your belief. Consider what in your background, education, history, family, friendships, upbringing, and work experiences has helped you come to the conclusions you have reached about the topic. Why do you believe what you do? Put your text into the form of a letter to a good friend.

Rhetorical Considerations for Exploratory Writing

Audience: Although your instructor in your college class is your main audience for this paper, you are also part of your audience—this assignment is designed to help you think through some possible educational and career choices, or to explore some of your personal beliefs. Your classmates are also your audience, as some of them may also be considering these issues and ideas, and they will learn from your research and perhaps ask questions and think of ideas they had not yet considered.

Purpose: Your purpose is to explore the various aspects of your topic in enough detail and depth to lead you to a greater understanding of it and what you believe about it.

Voice, Tone, and Point of View: As a student, you already have your own ideas, knowledge, background, and experiences. As you explore your topic, you will step back to consider whether your preconceptions about it are accurate. Your stance should be objective, and you should be open to the different possibilities you will discover. The point of view you take should be one of *questioning*—what can you learn by exploring your topic?—but the tone you use can range from humorous to serious.

Context, Medium, and Genre: Because you will be exploring an area you are already interested in, you will have the incentive to learn more as you research and write. The knowledge you gain may benefit you later. For example, you may be able to use the information you have acquired from this assignment to write a causal analysis or a proposal paper. If you are writing for an audience beyond the classroom, consider what will be the most effective way to present your information to this audience. You might write a letter to a friend, prepare a formal report for colleagues at work, or construct a Web site.

For more on choosing a medium and genre, see Chapter 17 and Appendix C. For more on writing a causal analysis, see Chapter 10. For more on writing a proposal paper, see Chapter 11.

Critical Thinking, Reading, and Writing

Before you begin to write your exploratory paper, consider the qualities of successful exploratory writing. It also helps to read one or more examples of this type of writing. Finally, you might consider how visuals could enhance your exploratory writing, as well as the kinds of sources you will need to consult.

Unlike many other kinds of writing, where writers have a good idea of their intent, exploratory writing frees writers to take intellectual chances and to see where different, and sometimes unusual, possibilities may lead. Although effective exploratory writing involves taking intellectual chances and finding alternatives that you may not have thought of before, your writing will not be successful if you simply write anything you please. Effective exploratory writing is based on reasonable options and uses information culled from solid research.

Learning the Qualities of Effective Exploratory Writing

As you think about how you might construct an exploratory paper, consider that readers probably expect the unexpected from this kind of text. Effective exploratory writing will include the following qualities:

- **A focus on a concept or question.** Rather than focusing on a specific, narrowly provable thesis, exploratory writing is more open-ended. Writers are more than likely trying to answer a question, to lay the groundwork for a solution to a problem, or to redefine a concept. For instance, a writer might pose a question such as this one: "We had a large number of traffic fatalities in my city last year. What possible solutions might I explore?"

- **An inquisitive spirit.** Any explorer begins with an interest in finding out more about the subject. Ask questions that you really want to answer, and let the answers lead you to further questions. While you want to make sure your queries are grounded in reality, you should not feel constrained by conventional thinking. For instance, Albert Einstein used "thought experiments" to explore time and space in ways conventional experiments could not. As a result, he developed his revolutionary theory of relativity.

- **A consideration of the range of perspectives in a subject.** As you explore your subject, you need to be willing to see it from different vantage points and to consider its positive and negative aspects. Effective exploratory writing looks at a topic from as many angles as possible. This can be difficult to do sometimes, as we often get locked in to our own way of thinking. In exploratory writing, however, it is vital to look at alternative views and to understand that others may have a different perspective than yours.

- **Expansive coverage of a subject.** Effective exploratory writing does not try to make a case or attempt to persuade you as writer or your reader of something, but rather examines all aspects of the topic, often developing a **profile** of its subject. You need to look at as much information about your subject as possible, while realizing that not all information is good or relevant. You will use your critical reading and thinking skills to help determine the reliability and relevance of the information you have gathered. Because exploratory writing is often inductive in nature, you might find it useful to organize your details in categories, using a cluster chart or listing.

For more on inductive thinking, see Chapter 14. For more on cluster charts and listing as strategies, see Chapter 3.

In a computer document, you might find it helpful to put the above qualities of effective exploratory writing into your own words, and then refer to those notes as you conduct research and write your paper.

A WRITER'S RESPONSIBILITIES

Exploring Ideas

Writers who are considering and examining multiple viewpoints have a responsibility to their readers to present those viewpoints as accurately as possible. In exploratory writing, you can express your opinions, responses, and reflections, but you must be careful not to misrepresent the viewpoints of others. Because you may not feel comfortable, at least initially, with all the points of view you will be exploring, you need to make sure you are using reliable information that readers can verify themselves. You do not have to accept all of the perspectives you examine, but you do have an ethical responsibility to treat them all honestly and with respect.

Your purpose is to open yourself and your readers to different possibilities. If you find yourself limiting the perspectives you explore because you feel uncomfortable with some of them, you are limiting your and your readers' options.

Reading, Inquiry, and Research: Learning from Texts That Explore

The readings that follow are examples of exploratory writing. Each offers perspectives on a subject. As you read each one, consider the following questions:

- What makes this reading an interesting and useful exploration?
- After reading the selection what else do you want to learn about the subject? Why?
- How can you use the techniques of exploratory writing in your own writing?

Thinking Rhetorically

Keep in mind the following questions as you read the essays that follow. Make it a practice to ask yourself these questions in all your reading—personal, academic, and professional—and you will strengthen and sharpen your abilities as a reader and as a writer.

Rhetorical Knowledge: The Writer's Situation and Rhetoric

- *Audience:* Who is the primary audience for this piece of writing? What makes you think that?
- *Purpose:* What is the author's primary purpose in this exploration? How do you know? What other purposes might the author have in exploring this topic?
- *Voice and Tone:* What is the author's attitude toward his or her topic? How do you know that?
- *Responsibility:* How does the author establish credibility in this piece of writing? How does the author handle his or her preconceptions or biases about the subject matter?
- *Context and Format:* Locate the time and place where the reading was originally published. Consider how the initial context affects the author's writing and your reading of the essay.

KENNETH CHANG

Scientist at Work—Terence Tao: Journeys to the Distant Fields of Prime

After working on his Ph.D. in physics at the University of Illinois for seven years, Kenneth Chang transferred to the University of California, Santa Cruz to study science writing. He has written for numerous outlets, including the *Los Angeles Times*, the *Greenwich Times*, the *Newark Star-Ledger*, and ABCNews.com. Since 2000, Kenneth Chang has regularly written science articles for the *New York Times*. A good example of a profile exploring the world of a mathematician, the following article was first published in the *New York Times* in March 2007.

Four hundred people packed into an auditorium at U.C.L.A. in January to listen to a public lecture on prime numbers, one of the rare occasions that the topic has drawn a standing-room-only audience.   1

Another 35 people watched on a video screen in a classroom next door. Eighty people were turned away.   2

The speaker, Terence Tao, a professor of mathematics at the university, promised "a whirlwind tour, the equivalent to going through Paris and just seeing the Eiffel Tower and the Arc de Triomphe."   3

His words were polite, unassuming and tinged with the accent of Australia, his homeland. Even though prime numbers have been studied for 2,000 years, "There's still a lot that needs to be done," Dr. Tao said. "And it's still a very exciting field."   4

After Dr. Tao finished his one-hour talk, which was broadcast live on the Internet, several students came down to the front and asked for autographs.   5

Dr. Tao has drawn attention and curiosity throughout his life for his prodigious abilities. By age 2, he had learned to read. At 9, he attended college math classes. At 20, he finished his Ph.D.   6

Now 31, he has grown from prodigy to one of the world's top mathematicians, tackling an unusually broad range of problems, including ones involving prime numbers and the compression of images. Last summer, he won a Fields Medal, often considered the Nobel Prize of mathematics, and a MacArthur Fellowship, the "genius" award that comes with a half-million dollars and no strings.   7

"He's wonderful," said Charles Fefferman of Princeton University, himself a former child prodigy and a Fields Medalist. "He's as good as they come. There are a few in a generation, and he's one of the few."   8

Colleagues have teasingly called Dr. Tao a rock star and the Mozart of Math. Two museums in Australia have requested his photograph for   9 their permanent exhibits. And he was a finalist for the 2007 Australian of the Year award.

"You start getting famous for being famous." Dr. Tao said. "The Paris Hilton effect." 10

Not that any of that has noticeably affected him. His campus office is adorned with a poster of "Ranma 1/2," a Japanese comic book. As he walks the halls of the math building, he might be wearing an Adidas sweatshirt, blue jeans and scruffy sneakers, looking much like one of his graduate students. He said he did not know how he would spend the MacArthur money, though he mentioned the mortgage on the house that he and his wife, Laura, an engineer at the NASA Jet Propulsion Laboratory, bought last year. 11

After a childhood in Adelaide, Australia, and graduate school at Princeton, Dr. Tao has settled into sunny Southern California. 12

"I love it a lot," he said. But not necessarily for what the area offers. 13

"It's sort of the absence of things I like," he said. No snow to shovel, for instance. 14

A deluge of media attention following his Fields Medal last summer has slowed to a trickle, and Dr. Tao said he was happy that his fame might be fleeting so that he could again concentrate on math. 15

One area of his research—compressed sensing—could have real-world use. Digital cameras use millions of sensors to record an image, and then a computer chip in the camera compresses the data. 16

"Compressed sensing is a different strategy," Dr. Tao said. "You also compress the data, but you try to do it in a very dumb way, one that doesn't require much computer power at the sensor end." 17

With Emmanuel Candès, a professor of applied and computational mathematics at the California Institute of Technology, Dr. Tao showed that even if most of the information were immediately discarded, the use of powerful algorithms could still reconstruct the original image. 18

By useful coincidence, Dr. Tao's son, William, and Dr. Candès's son attended the same preschool, so dropping off their children turned into useful work time. 19

"We'd meet each other every morning at preschool," Dr. Tao said, "and we'd catch up on what we had done." 20

The military is interested in using the work for reconnaissance: blanket a battlefield with simple, cheap cameras that might each record a single pixel of data. Each camera would transmit the data to a central computer that, using the mathematical technique developed by Dr. Tao and Dr. Candès, would construct a comprehensive view. Engineers at Rice University have made a prototype of just such a camera. 21

Dr. Tao's best-known mathematical work involves prime numbers— 22
positive whole numbers that can be divided evenly only by themselves
and 1. The first few prime numbers are 2, 3, 5, 7, 11 and 13 (1 is excluded).

As numbers get larger, prime numbers become sparser, but the 23
Greek mathematician Euclid proved sometime around 300 B.C. that there
is nonetheless an infinite number of primes.

Many questions about prime numbers continue to elude answers. Euclid 24
also believed that there was an infinite number of "twin primes"— pairs of
prime numbers separated by 2, like 3 and 5 or 11 and 13—but he was unable
to prove his conjecture. Nor has anyone else in the succeeding 2,300 years.

A larger unknown question is whether hidden patterns exist in the 25
sequence of prime numbers or whether they appear randomly.

In 2004, Dr. Tao, along with Ben Green, a mathematician now at the 26
University of Cambridge in England, solved a problem related to the Twin
Prime Conjecture by looking at prime number progressions—series of
numbers equally spaced. (For example, 3, 7 and 11 constitute a progression of prime numbers with a spacing of 4; the next number in the
sequence, 15, is not prime.) Dr. Tao and Dr. Green proved that it is always
possible to find, somewhere in the infinity of integers, a progression of
any length of equally spaced prime numbers.

"Terry has a style that very few have," Dr. Fefferman said. "When he 27
solves the problem, you think to yourself, 'This is so obvious and why
didn't I see it? Why didn't the 100 distinguished people who thought
about this before not think of it?'"

Dr. Tao's proficiency with numbers appeared at a very young age. "I 28
always liked numbers," he said.

A 2-year-old Terry Tao used toy blocks to show older children how to 29
count. He was quick with language and used the blocks to spell words
like "dog" and "cat."

"He probably was quietly learning these things from watching 30
'Sesame Street,'" said his father, Dr. Billy Tao, a pediatrician who immi-
grated to Australia from Hong Kong in 1972. "We basically used 'Sesame
Street' as a babysitter."

The blocks had been bought as toys, not learning tools. "You expect 31
them to throw them around," said the elder Dr. Tao, whose accent swings
between Australian and Chinese.

Terry's parents placed him in a private school when he was 3½. They 32
pulled him out six weeks later because he was not ready to spend that
much time in a classroom, and the teacher was not ready to teach someone like him.

At age 5, he was enrolled in a public school, and his parents, admin- 33
istrators and teachers set up an individualized program for him. He

proceeded through each subject at his own pace, quickly accelerating through several grades in math and science while remaining closer to his age group in other subjects. In English classes, for instance, he became flustered when he had to write essays.

"I never really got the hang of that," he said. "These very vague, undefined questions. I always liked situations where there were very clear rules of what to do." 34

Assigned to write a story about what was going on at home, Terry went from room to room and made detailed lists of the contents. 35

When he was 7½, he began attending math classes at the local high school. 36

Billy Tao knew the trajectories of child prodigies like Jay Luo, who graduated with a mathematics degree from Boise State University in 1982 at the age of 12, but who has since vanished from the world of mathematics. 37

"I initially thought Terry would be just like one of them, to graduate as early as possible," he said. But after talking to experts on education for gifted children, he changed his mind. 38

"To get a degree at a young age, to be a record-breaker, means nothing," he said. "I had a pyramid model of knowledge, that is, a very broad base and then the pyramid can go higher. If you just very quickly move up like a column, then you're more likely to wobble at the top and then collapse." 39

Billy Tao also arranged for math professors to mentor Terry. 40

A couple of years later, Terry was taking university-level math and physics classes. He excelled in international math competitions. His parents decided not to push him into college full-time, so he split his time between high school and Flinders University, the local university in Adelaide. He finally enrolled as a full-time college student at Flinders when he was 14, two years after he would have graduated had his parents pushed him only according to his academic abilities. 41

The Taos had different challenges in raising their other two sons, although all three excelled in math. Trevor, two years younger than Terry, is autistic with top-level chess skills and the musical savant gift to play back on the piano a musical piece—even one played by an entire orchestra— after hearing it just once. He completed a Ph.D. in mathematics and now works for the Defense Science and Technology Organization in Australia. 42

The youngest, Nigel, told his father that he was "not another Terry," and his parents let him learn at a less accelerated pace. Nigel, with degrees in economics, math and computer science, now works as a computer engineer for Google Australia. 43

"All along, we tend to emphasize the joy of learning," Billy Tao said.   44
"The fun is doing something, not winning something."

Terry completed his undergraduate degree in two years, earned a   45
master's degree a year after that, then moved to Princeton for his doctoral studies. While he said he never felt out of place in a class of much
older students, Princeton was where he finally felt he fit among a group
of peers. He was still younger, but was not necessarily the brightest student all the time.

His attitude toward math also matured. Until then, math had been   46
competitions, problem sets, exams. "That's more like a sprint," he said.

Dr. Tao recalled that as a child, "I remember having this vague idea   47
that what mathematicians did was that, some authority, someone gave
them problems to solve and they just sort of solved them."

In the real academic world, "Math research is more like a marathon,"   48
he said.

As a parent and a professor, Dr. Tao now has to think about how to   49
teach math in addition to learning it.

An evening snack provided him an opportunity to question his son,   50
who is 4. If there are 10 cookies, how many does each of the five people
in the living room get?

William asked his father to tell him. "I don't know how many,"   51
Dr. Tao replied. "You tell me."

With a little more prodding, William divided the cookies into five   52
stacks of two each.

Dr. Tao said a future project would be to try to teach more non-   53
mathematicians how to think mathematically—a skill that would be
useful in everyday tasks like comparing mortgages.

"I believe you can teach this to almost anybody," he said.   54

But for now, his research is where his focus is.   55

"In many ways, my work is my hobby," he said. "I always wanted to   56
learn another language, but that's not going to happen for a while. Those
things can wait."

QUESTIONS FOR WRITING AND DISCUSSION

Critical Thinking: Responding to the Writer's Ideas

1. What do you find most interesting in Chang's essay about Terence
   Tao? Why do you find this aspect of the essay interesting?

2. Why do you think Chang includes information about three areas of Tao's
   life—the academic, the personal, and the professional?

Composing Processes and Knowledge of Conventions: The Writer's Strategies

1. Why does Chang use so many quotations in the profile? Why do you think he uses quotations instead of paraphrases in particular places?
2. Because he writing for a newspaper, Chang cites his sources within the body of his article rather than using a formal system of documentation. How do his sources lend credibility to his writing? What other sources of information might he have cited?

Inquiry and Research: Ideas for Further Exploration

1. Conduct research on some person whom you find interesting. Write a profile of that person.

MICHAEL WOLFF

Bipolar Iraq

Michael Wolff, who grew up in New Jersey, has written widely about the Internet since 1991. Among his most popular books are *Net Guide*, a manual for using the Internet, and *Burn Rate*, a exposé on the early days of the Internet business boom. A regular columnist for *Industry Standard* and for *New York Magazine*, Wolff frequently tackles controversial and complex topics. The essay the follows was first published in *New York Magazine* in November 2003.

Here are the two opposite story lines: 1
(1) It's working.   2
(2) It's a quagmire.   3
Let's fill them out a little more: 4
(1) Iraqis are back in the markets and on the street; schools are   5
opening, businesses getting going again, institutions returning to life. By virtually every happiness-quotient measure, the state of being among the vast majority of Iraqis is more positive now than it was during the reign of Saddam Hussein—and it will be even more positive in the near future. As social experiments go—revivifying a materially and psychologically broken nation—there is every reason to be optimistic (and even proud) about this one.

(2) We've gotten ourselves into an ever-expanding war with a fanati- 6
cal and well-armed resistance. What's more, growing numbers of ideological defenders are traveling to this battlefield, which threatens to turn
Iraq, along with Israel and the Palestinian territories, into a permanent
Muslim versus non-Muslim front and international tripwire. We're stuck
in a situation with consequences and financial burdens that we cannot
estimate. This is the definition of quagmire. And by the logic of quagmire,
the situation only ever becomes more intractable and the consequences
more fearful and destabilizing.

As you read those quick précis, your inclination is, invariably, to pick 7
one. They can't, after all, really exist together. Or, if perchance they do
exist together now, one will inevitably come to overshadow the other.
Obviously, if you're a Bush person, you choose the former, and if you're
an anti-Bush person, you choose the latter. In some sense, in fact, these
are not even alternative views of the reality in Iraq as much as opposite
worldviews applicable to almost any situation.

(1) There is, quite simply, the patent superiority of the American way. 8
When people are exposed to it, it spreads like a virus. We have not only
righteousness on our side but modernity and economic reality. Eighty-
seven billion dollars changes any equation. Everything seems messy,
inchoate, ugly, fraught, without organization; but at some point in the
organizational process, rationality and benefit will begin to become clear.
Upside will outweigh downside. Ambivalence and self-doubt are the real
killers here. Long-term investment and staying the course are the solutions and the way to get a big return.

(2) An incredible arrogance chronically pervades the American 9
mind-set. Our lack of self-doubt makes us stupid. We're blinded to the
intractable problems set against us: not just to a deep cultural antipathy
but to a million details on the ground that the guys at the Pentagon or at
Centcom HQ in Florida don't have the patience or the language skills or
the in-country intelligence to think through. What's more, because we
pride ourselves on "can-do" and turn up our noses at intellectual and
abstract analysis, we never really or accurately appreciate cause and
effect. We're always the victims of the law of unintended consequences.
Because we're too big and too quick, we necessarily upset the ecology in
ways that will certainly come back to haunt and terrorize us.

(1) Essentially good news.   10

(2) Inevitably bad news.   11

Which brings us to the Chinook helicopter—and before that the 12
attack on the Al Rashid Hotel, and before that the U.N. attack.

The fervent bad-news-ites seem to believe that the Bushies under- 13
stand the kind of mess they're (we're) in and are doing everything they
can to disguise (spin) it and to blame someone else for it. But the more

interesting and complex and difficult possibility is that they don't see it as a mess at all.

For them, these bad-news incidents represent an illusion created by the small resistance, the leftover Baathists. These thugs and irregulars. What we have here are isolated acts meant to sow widespread fear—it's just, well, terrorism. The odd thing, of course, is that such terrorism is exactly why we went to war—so it's rather disorienting to have it dismissed now as somehow inconsequential in relation to the bigger picture. 14

It's not bad news, the Bushies seem to be saying, as much as bad PR—or the other side's good PR. The bad guys have effectively influenced the media coverage without, the Bushies seem genuinely convinced, affecting the reality. Life in Iraq gets better and better—except for the fact that these scumballs know how to generate bad press for the Americans who are making life in Iraq better and better. 15

Hence the Bushies have countered with a campaign to generate good news. There is even the sense—again, a reality inversion—that the best way to deal with terrorism is in the court of public opinion rather than on the battlefield. 16

So the good-news offensive. The mainstream media—because it is overly liberal and crassly superficial—is emphasizing the (minimal) bloodshed and ignoring the story of a liberated nation. And there has been the careful parsing of the story: carving the Sunni triangle from the rest of a (largely) pacified country; rushing in American pollsters (and then parsing those results); separating good imams from bad imams. 17

And, indeed, there has been a sudden rush of not unconvincing good-news accounts. Life was terrible. Life is better. Nothing worked. Now many things are working. Average Iraqis may not be embracing the American occupation, but they are sure grateful not to have Saddam around (cue the torture tapes that the Pentagon released to Fox News). Life, as seen by in-country reporters, is returning to normal. 18

But there are the bodies. 19

The Bush people, as they argue their story line, have to distract people's attention from the dead. The president doesn't mention the bodies; doesn't attend funerals. Body-bag shots are on the media proscribed list. You can sense their frustration in this regard—that the bodies are always, annoyingly, the story. This is partly a military-civilian disconnect. Our job, you can hear Rumsfeld saying, is to minimize casualties, not to eliminate them. In sheer military terms—troops deployed versus casualties sustained—it's not even that bad. Arguably (although it's an argument you lose by making it), the kill ratio indicates a big success. I mean, you can't really fight a war if everybody is precious—if nobody is expendable. 20

And yet, the great nonmilitary sensibility of the country, and of the media, sees each body as a story, and multiple bodies as a bigger story, and the aggregate of bodies as a really damning piece of evidence.   21

There is a socio-military calculation on the part of reporters and politicians (both Democrats and Republicans) and, one would assume, military people as well, as to how much is too much. What's sustainable and what's a big problem?   22

When the number of soldiers killed in the aftermath exceeded the number of people killed in the actual war, that was seen as a problematic milestone.   23

When the total number of people killed in Iraq II surpassed the total number killed in Iraq I, that got serious.   24

Oh yes, and significant multi-casualty incidents are major bad news. Mogadishu levels would be very dicey. Beirut levels in the Reagan era might well put the whole proposition over the top.   25

Now, what the Bush administration is arguing is, in effect, that our enemies know these numbers. That they cannot damage us enough to truly harm us or even to actually hamper our mission, but they can inflict enough damage to frighten us (or frighten you—or frighten the media)—precisely because our tolerance for damage has been set artificially low.   26

Not least of all by Democrats and by the biased media!   27

And so we move from a military war to a political one.   28

This is the exact opposite of the wars of the last generation—of the Clinton approach or even of the first Bush administration—that constant and obsessive cost-reward analysis.   29

Of not being caught out there without a way back. Retreating from Mogadishu. Not following Saddam into Baghdad. Of always making the calculation about when the consensus might divide. Of not making people choose sides. Of not letting there be two stories told at once.   30

The Bush people don't believe there are two sides. Not two right sides, anyway. This mission is sacrosanct. The WMD canard and the sexing of intelligence reports happened, not least of all, to protect the mission. Nobody is going to go for broke in an elective war—it had to be a necessary war.   31

There's no debate. There's polling (of course) but no interest in consensus. Stubbornness (Rumsfeldness) is both virtue and strategy. If you refuse to engage in any back-and-forth but just say what you believe relentlessly, repetition eventually changes perceptions.   32

Righteousness went out of favor in the post–Cold War world (incrementalism, globalism, complex systems analysis came in). But   33 righteousness is surely back. The righteous don't compromise, don't negotiate, don't wimp out. The righteous (even if they had planned not to have to) take casualties (unlike that thoroughly nonrighteous Clinton, who hated to take casualties).

There's no longer even a pretense that this is about conventional 34 success measures (indeed, failure suddenly seems part—even a necessary part—of the great ultimate success). The *we're-not-quitters* stance of the Bushies (and that the Democrats are, ipso facto, quitters) is explicitly disconnected from any talk about how we're actually going to win.

The arguable merit of the Bush position—life is certainly better in 35 Iraq—is subsumed by its larger, relentless, messianic, and fatalistic ambitions.

We're at the bear-any-burden stage. That is, in most political terms, 36 a wildly unpopular place to be. We are, after all, selfish, self-obsessed Americans.

So the only way they're going to sell this is to turn it from a problem- 37 solving issue into an ideological one. "We are fighting that enemy in Iraq, in Afghanistan today so that we do not meet him again on our own streets, in our own cities," said the president.

It's a setup. We're going to have to choose position (1) or position (2). 38

The Democrats and Howard Dean play into that hand (Bush-bashing 39 is probably good for the Bushies).

It's them or us. 40

Winners or losers. 41

Lefties or real Americans. 42

We've been here before, and we know how badly it turns out. 43

QUESTIONS FOR WRITING AND DISCUSSION

Critical Thinking: Responding to the Writer's Ideas

1. What is your immediate response to Wolff's exploration of the United States's activities in Iraq?

2. Why does Wolff offer so many dichotomies in his essay? How would Wolff's essay be different if he had used continua rather that dichotomies? That is, what if he had tried to figure out how the situation might lie somewhere on the following continuum:

|--------------------------------------|

It's good.   It's bad.

Composing Processes and Knowledge of Conventions: The Writer's Strategies

1. How effectively does Wolff present the alternative perspectives in this piece? How might he improve his presentation?
2. What exactly is Wolff exploring?

Inquiry and Research: Ideas for Further Exploration

1. Given what has happened in Iraq since Wolff's essay was published on November 17, 2003, how might Wolff revise the essay to reflect the current situation in Iraq?

Thinking about Visuals That Explore

Visuals are helpful tools for exploring because they often compress a great deal of verbal and numerical information into a single element. Here, for example, is a bar graph from the United States Bureau of Labor Statistics showing projected job growth in service-providing industries over a decade. Notice the relationship between the information presented in the bar graph and the verbal information that accompanies it.

Excerpted from "Tomorrow's Jobs"

U.S. Bureau of Labor Statistics
(http://www.bls.gov/oco/oco2003.htm)

Service-providing industries

The long-term shift from goods-producing to service-providing employment is expected to continue. Service-providing industries are expected to account for approximately 18.7 million of the 18.9 million new wage and salary jobs generated over the 2004–14 period (*see the chart on the next page*).

Education and health services

This industry supersector is projected to grow faster, 30.6 percent, and add more jobs than any other industry supersector. About 3 out of every 10 new jobs created in the U.S. economy will be in either the healthcare and social assistance or private educational services sectors.

. . .

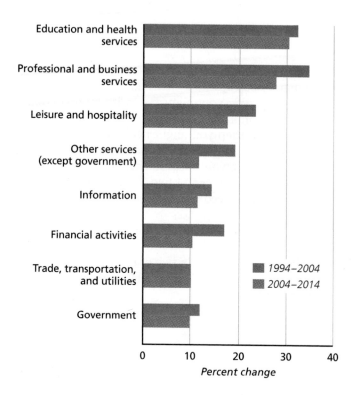

Professional and business services

This industry supersector, which includes some of the fastest growing industries in the U.S. economy, will grow by 27.8 percent and add more than 4.5 million new jobs.

. . .

Information

Employment in the information supersector is expected to increase by 11.6 percent, adding 364,000 jobs by 2014. Information contains some of the fast-growing computer-related industries such as software publishers; Internet publishing and broadcasting; and Internet service providers, Web search portals, and data processing services.

If you were using the graph above and the accompanying text to explore potential college majors (Scenario 1), you might consider the following kinds of questions:

1. How does the bar graph help you to see future trends in service-industry job categories?
2. How do these trends influence your thinking about potential careers?
3. How do the bar graph and the text complement each other?

Writing Processes

As you work on the assignment you have chosen, remember the qualities of an effective exploratory paper, which are listed on pages 89–90. Also remember that writing is recursive—you might start with an invention activity or two and then conduct some research, which leads to more invention work and then a first draft; but then you might need to do more invention work to help flesh out your draft and conduct more research to answer questions that come up as you explore your ideas further, and then you'll revise your draft and possibly find another gap or two. . . . So while the activities listed below imply that writers proceed step-by-step, the actual process of writing is usually messier.

For a tip on organizing your computer files, see page 66.

As you work on your project, make sure that you save your computer files frequently because any work that you don't save could be lost. Savvy writers back up their computer files in two or more places—on an internal or external hard drive of the computer, on a USB flash drive, and on a rewritable CD or DVD, for example.

Invention: Getting Started

The invention activities below are strategies that you can use to help you get some sense of what you already know about a subject. Whatever invention method(s) you use (or that your instructor asks you to employ), try to answer questions such as these:

- What do I already know about my subject?
- What preconceptions—positive, negative, neutral—do I have?
- Why am I interested in exploring this subject?
- What questions about the subject would I most like answers to? Who might I be able to talk to about this subject?
- What do I know about my audience? What can I say to interest them in my subject?
- What might my audience already know about my subject? What questions might they have?
- What is my purpose in exploring this subject? What would I like the end result of my research and writing to be? More knowledge? Information that I might use to pursue some goal?

Doing your invention work in electronic form, rather than on paper, lets you easily use this early writing as you construct a draft.

As with any kind of writing, invention activities improve with peer feedback and suggestions. Consider sharing the invention work you have done so far with several classmates or friends in order to understand your rhetorical situation more clearly and to generate more useful information.

Exploring Your Ideas with Research

While your opinions and ideas—and especially your questions—are central to any exploratory writing that you do, as you explore your subject, you need to answer the questions you raise. Getting those answers usually requires *research*, which can include reading books and periodical articles at the library, reading articles in your local newspaper, interviewing people who know more than you do about your subject, conducting searches online, and using other means of gathering information. The information that you discover through your research, such as data, statistics, examples, descriptions,

---

Technote

Writing to explore is not about getting and giving information or simple answers. Exploration involves the very hard work of experiencing and understanding *different perspectives*. A good way to learn about different or unusual perspectives is to read news reports from around the world—not just those published by American news services such as the Associated Press and Knight-Ridder, but news reports published in foreign newspapers and news magazines. Most of the major publications (and plenty of smaller ones) are now available in English translation.

The following are some examples of Web sites maintained by foreign news organizations:

Pravda (Russian)
http://english.pravda.ru/

London Times
http://www.timesonline.co.uk/tol/global/

Japan Times
http://www.japantimes.co.jp

Agence France-Presse
http://www.afp.com/english/home/

---

images, and expert testimony, can help you respond to the questions that prompted your exploration.

Before you start your research, review your invention work to remind yourself of all that you know about your subject and the questions you have about it. Use the reporter's questions of *who, what, where, when, why,* and *how* to get started. After you have decided what information you need, determine what kind of research you need to conduct to gather that information, and conduct research in the library and on the Internet.

You could conduct several kinds of research in response to the scenarios on pages 87–88. For Scenario 1, for example, in which you explore potential majors, you might visit the Web sites of various departments to gather information about degree programs, courses offered, and careers of alumni. You might also visit the Web sites of companies that hire graduates in the fields that you are exploring. You could even search newspapers and the Internet to find job advertisements in those fields. You might interview graduating seniors to ask them about their experiences in the majors that you are

For help with locating sources of information, see Chapter 19; for help with taking notes and documenting your sources, see Chapter 20.

exploring or people who hold the kinds of jobs that require those majors. Finally, you could search for and read blogs maintained by people who write about their professional fields and careers.

Reviewing Your Invention and Research

After you have conducted your research, you need to review your invention work and notes. You may be tempted to decide on a thesis statement—a statement that summarizes the main point of your exploration—at this point. Even though you might already have a general idea of the conclusion your research is leading you to, it is often hard to know for certain what your thesis will be. Your thesis should come *from* your exploration. It is best to decide on your thesis after you have done a lot of invention work (listing, brainstorming, clustering, and so on) and research, or even after you construct your first draft.

For more on developing a thesis, see Chapter 13.

Organizing Your Ideas and Details

Because the purpose of writing an exploratory text is to examine an idea or concept from various perspectives, you will need to organize your thoughts in a useful manner. The questions that you need to ask yourself when deciding on your organization are all rhetorical.

- Who is your audience?
- Why might they be interested in your exploratory writing, or how can you make them interested in it? One way to emphasize the importance of your exploration to your audience is to show them why your subject is interesting to you.
- What is your purpose for writing—that is, why do your readers need to explore this topic with you?

Here is a brief outline of three possible organizational approaches to writing an exploratory paper:

Options for Organization

Classifying Ideas	Comparing and Contrasting Ideas	Relating Causes and Effects
• Begin with your questions, perhaps from the least to the most important. • Explain each question in detail—and then provide possible answers.	• Note how many possible perspectives there may be on your subject and how they relate to one another. • Explore each perspective in detail	• Start from what happens first and move to later events. • Explore and explain the various possible causes or effects.

- By looking at each question in detail, you may find that classifying both questions and answers is a useful method of organization.
- Offer follow-up questions that may lead to further exploration.
- You may conclude by suggesting that your exploration does not answer all the questions and that other, specified, questions now need to be asked.

- Because you began by noting multiple perspectives, comparison and contrast might be a useful method of organization.
- By exploring your topic through various lenses, you come to a better understanding of your subject and are able to explain it for your readers, especially in relation to the different points of view on it.
- Having presented multiple perspectives on your topic, indicate which conclusion your exploration has led you to.

- Use specific examples to show how one cause or effect logically leads to the next. This is a variation on a cause-and-effect paper. In an exploratory paper you *consider* possible causes and effects; in a cause-and-effect paper, you *argue* that specific phenomena are causes or effects.
- You may choose to end your paper with what seems like the final effect—keeping the entire paper chronological.

Constructing a Complete Draft

Once you know your subject, have your ideas down on paper or stored in a computer file, and have conducted research, you are ready to construct your initial draft. It is possible that you will find a suitable organizational approach before you begin drafting, but you may also find it—or decide to change it—as you are drafting or even after you have constructed a draft. Also, as you write the first version of your exploratory paper, do not worry about editing your work.

Introduction: One of the qualities of a successful piece of exploratory writing is that it grabs and holds readers' attention. There are a number of strategies for beginning your paper that will help you hook your readers.

- *Take your readers on the journey.* Let your readers know from the beginning that this is an exploration. Let them be your travel companions. In "Scientist at Work—Terence Tao: Journeys to the Distant Fields of Prime," Kenneth Chang (p. 92), indicates that his essay will be a journey through his title and his opening anecdote, in which Tao promises an audience at a lecture "a whirlwind tour."

- *Ask one or more questions.* By asking a question or questions, you present options and directions. Your exploratory writing will help you and your reader find solutions.

- *Establish multiple perspectives.* Let your readers know from the very beginning that they will look at an issue from different points of view.

In the opening to "Bipolar Iraq" (p.97), Michael Wolff offers two conflicting story lines for the U.S. military involvement in Iraq.

Body: The body of your paper will lead you and your readers through your exploration process. You may choose one or several different kinds of organization. You might try classification, for example, where by grouping ideas in like categories, you discover similarities. However, comparison and contrast, where you discover both similarities and differences, might be more helpful. Or you might discover that cause and effect is the most powerful kind of organization for your paper.

Conclusion: Following your exploration, your conclusion should leave your readers feeling satisfied.

- If in your exploration you discover that there will be consequences if certain events occur, you may choose to present these final consequences.
- If you discover that your exploration has only led to even more questions, you may simply state the new questions that need to be researched.
- Finally, if your exploration does lead you to a reasonable conclusion, state that conclusion, explaining to readers how you reached it.

Title: You might think that you need to come up with a title before you start writing, but often it is more useful to get a first draft down on paper or into a computer file and then consider possible titles. For an exploratory paper, your title should indicate your subject and give your reader a reason to want to explore it with you. The titles "Bipolar Iraq" and "Journeys to the Distant Fields of Prime," for example, indicate that their authors have a unique approach to their subjects.

VISUALIZING VARIATIONS

Using Visuals to Make Your Exploration Clear

An appropriate image can add visual appeal to any exploratory writing. If you are exploring some personal interest, consider using a visual or visuals to show why you find your topic appealing. Suppose you collect state quarters, and, as your collection has grown, you have become more interested in the images on the backs of the quarters, the stories behind them, and the artists who designed them.

As you think about presenting your profile of quarter collecting to your readers, you decide which of the quarters' images will be most intriguing to them and which will best demonstrate your exploration. You might choose the Nevada quarter, for instance, released in 2006.

The image on the Nevada quarter tells a story about the state, but you need to do some exploration to discover what that story is. Your exploration might lead you to the Web site for the United States Mint (http://www.usmint.gov), where you find the story behind the "design of three galloping wild horses, sagebrush, the sun rising behind snow-capped mountains and the State's nickname, 'The Silver State,' inside a banner" and how it was chosen from five candidates.

Although you could certainly use words, the photo of the image will help readers see it more clearly. Using this image as an example, consider the best way to use an image or images to enhance your exploratory writing for your readers. Use the following questions to guide you:

- What can an image or images add that the words alone cannot show?

- How can I use the image to surprise readers—to offer them something unexpected?

- Should the image(s) I use be in color or black-and-white? What would be most effective?

- What kinds of images would draw readers into my text, make them want to read and learn more?

- How can the image(s) I select help show my exploration?

Revising

Revising means re-seeing and re-thinking your exploratory text. The most effective way to revise your work is to read it as if you are reading it for the first time. Reading your work in this way is difficult to do, of course—which is why writers often put their work aside for a period of time. The more you can see your writing as if for the first time, the more you will respond to it as your real readers might, questioning and exploring it. As you reread the first draft of your exploratory writing, here are some questions to ask yourself:

- What are the most important questions, the ones I would really like to have answered? How well have I answered them?
- How well have I answered the questions that will help me understand every facet of my subject?
- How well do I understand the draft? What parts are confusing or need more information? What research might I need to conduct to further clarify my ideas?
- What information, if any, might I provide as a visual?

Technology can help you revise and, later, edit your writing more easily. Use your word processor's track-changes tool to try out revisions and editing changes. After you've had time to think about the possible changes, you can "accept" or "reject" them. Also, you can use your word processor's comment tool to write reminders to yourself when you get stuck with a revision or some editing task.

Because it is so difficult even for experienced writers to see their emerging writing with a fresh eye, it is almost always useful to ask classmates, friends, or family members to read and comment on drafts.

WRITER'S WORKSHOP

Responding to Full Drafts

As you read and respond to your classmates' papers (and as they comment on yours), focus on the exploratory nature of this assignment, but from a reader's perspective. Be sure to ask questions of their writing and respond to their ideas by exploring your reactions and responses to their thoughts.

Working in pairs or groups of three, read each others' papers, and then offer your classmates comments that will help them see their papers' strengths as well as places where they need to develop their ideas further. Use the following questions to guide your responses to the writer's draft:

- Write a brief comment that gives your first impression. How interested are you in reading beyond the first paragraph? Why? Do you have any suggestions for improving the title?
- In a paragraph, indicate what you like about the draft—that is, provide positive and encouraging feedback to the writer. How interesting, educational, or useful did you find this exploration? Why?
- What is the focus of the paper? How does the focus emerge as you read? How well do you understand how the writer comes to her conclusion?
- How easily can you follow the writer's thought process? Comment on how the writer's exploratory writing helps you better understand the questions or problems posed in the introduction.
- How thoroughly does the writer explore the subject? How might the writer explore it more fully? If there are places in which the writer is simply restating information that is already known and obvious, how might those parts be changed?

(cont'd)

(continued)

- How viable are the differing perspectives? How appropriate are the writer's sources?
- Reread the conclusion. How logically does it follow from the rest of the paper? Were you surprised by the conclusion? What are other possible conclusions based on the information the writer has presented?
- In another paragraph, outline what you see as the main weaknesses of this paper—and suggest how the writer might improve the text.

Responding to Readers' Comments

Once they have received feedback on their writing from peers, teachers, friends, and others, all writers have to figure out what to do with that feedback. Since your text is *your* responsibility, you must determine how to deal with reader responses to your work. You may decide to reject some comments, of course; other comments, though, deserve your attention, as they are the words of real readers speaking to you about how to improve your text. You may find that comments from more than one reader contradict each other. In that case, you need to use your own judgment to decide which reader's comments are on the right track.

Knowledge of Conventions

When effective writers edit their work, they attend to the conventions that will help readers move through their writing effortlessly. These include genre conventions, documentation, format, usage, grammar, and mechanics. By paying attention to these conventions in your writing, you make reading a more pleasant experience for readers.

Editing

The last task in any writing project is editing—the final polishing of your document. When you edit and polish your writing, you make changes to your sentence structure and word choice to improve your style and to make your writing clearer and more concise. You also check your work to make sure it adheres to conventions of grammar, usage, punctuation, mechanics, and spelling. Use the spell-check function of your word-processing program, but be sure to double-check your spelling personally. If you have used sources in your paper, make sure you are following the documentation style your instructor requires.

See Chapter 20 for more on documenting sources using MLA or APA style.

As with overall revision of your work, this final editing and polishing is most effective if you can put your text aside for a few days and come back to it with fresh eyes. Because checking conventions is easier said than done, though, we strongly recommend that you ask classmates, friends, and tutors to read your work to find sentence problems that you do not see.

To assist you with editing, we offer here a round-robin editing activity focused on sentence fragments, a common concern in all writing.

WRITER'S WORKSHOP

Round-Robin Editing with a Focus on Fragments

Because exploratory writing often includes incomplete thoughts, writers sometimes inadvertently use sentence fragments to express their thinking. A sentence fragment is missing one or more of the following elements: a subject, a verb, or a complete thought. Some fragments lack a subject, a verb, or both:

FRAGMENT   College sports are popular. *Generating lots of money for schools with successful teams.*

Other fragments have subjects and verbs, but they begin with a subordinating word like *because* or *although* and so are not complete thoughts:

FRAGMENT   *Although I have played football in high school and college.* I'm not good enough to play on a professional team.

SENTENCE   Although I have played football in high school and college, I'm not good enough to play on a professional team.

Work with two peers to look for sentence fragments. For each fragment, decide whether to connect it to a nearby sentence or to recast it into a complete sentence.

Genres, Documentation, and Format

If you are writing an academic paper, follow the conventions for the discipline in which you are writing and the requirements of your instructor. However, if you are exploring potential majors (Scenario 1), you might choose to write a letter or an e-mail message to family members, especially if any of them are providing financial support for your education. If you are doing a personal exploration (Scenario 2), you might want to write a journal entry—one that does not have a wide public readership. If you have chosen to do a personal exploration, you might avoid writing a blog entry, because blogs can have thousands of readers—including potential employers.

For advice on writing in different genres, see Appendix C. For guidelines for formatting and documenting papers in MLA or APA style, see Chapter 20.

If you have used material from outside sources, including visuals, give credit to those sources, using the documentation style required by the discipline you are working in and by your instructor.

Student Rick Mohler Shares His Exploration

Rick Mohler was taking a "Career and Life Planning" class at his local community college and was a assigned to respond to Scenario 1 on page 87. Rick was interested in a lot of areas—especially sports—but he was not quite sure what he might want to pursue as a career.

As you read the final version of Rick Mohler's exploratory paper, consider what makes it effective. Following the reading you will find some questions to help you conduct your own exploration of this paper.

RICK MOHLER

A Sporting Career?

If you ask most people to name a career in sports, they'll usually say, "professional athlete," because that is the most visible (and well-paid) career option. But what about those of us who have the desire, but not the size, speed, or talent? Are there other career options available to us, and if so, what are they?

I'm one of those people. I doubt that I have the size or speed to make the pros, but I want a career in sports, as do many others. Perhaps my "wonderings" here can help others as they try to decide what career path they may want to follow.

My favorite sport is football—and it's also America's choice. While the players have the faces and names that fans recognize, they are only one part of the big picture that is NFL football. Many other people make the games happen, keep the players in good condition, and tell the rest of America all about the sport. Coaches, weight trainers and conditioning coaches, publicists, writers, and photographers all have a part to play in the game of football.

The career path that excites me most is being a sportswriter. The job has an artistic element that appeals to me. As a sportswriter, I wouldn't just describe what took place at a game or event—I would really try to paint a picture. Maybe someday I'll even be able to write something as famous as Grantland Rice's description of the Notre Dame football team:

> Outlined against a blue-gray October sky, the Four Horsemen rode again. In dramatic lore they are known as Famine, Pestilence, Destruction and Death. These are only aliases. Their real names are Stuhldreher, Miller, Crowley and Layden. They formed the crest of

One of Mohler's classmates made this comment on his paper:

Another question I thought of is about how many possible careers in sports are there?

Notice how he provides information to answer this peer-review question.

One of Mohler's classmates wrote this comment on an early draft:

Why are you interested in these two careers? What about them attracts you? I really do not know what a person in either position does all day long. Maybe to focus the paper a little more, you ought to focus on just one career.

Notice how Mohler does just what his classmate suggested, focusing on one specific career path.

the South Bend cyclone before which another fighting Army football team was swept over the precipice at the Polo Grounds yesterday afternoon as 55,000 spectators peered down on the bewildering panorama spread on the green plain below.

Though not all sportswriters become as famous as Rice, they are everywhere. Local newspapers as well as national television networks need them, so there are plenty of employment opportunities. Just as most sports have both amateur and professional athletes, a sportswriter can start as an amateur and advance to the pros. It seems to make sense to begin working for a student newspaper, especially since I've always been a fairly good writer.   6

Last week's College Press, for example, included seven sports-related articles, all written by student writers. Two touched on football, and perhaps the most interesting article was about spring workouts for our football players.   7

John Wilson, the spring workouts College Press writer, was kind enough to give me an interview. I asked him what kind of background an aspiring sports-writer needs. "It's not as easy as it sounds," Wilson told me. "I'm an English major, which really helps, and while that combined with my interest in and knowledge of sports is good, what's hard for me is the process of writing."   8

I asked Wilson what he meant about writing and effort, and he gave me a description of how he typically covers a game: 9

It's just a lot of work. You have to go to the game and take notes. Then you interview some of the people involved—the coaches, the players, etc. Then you figure out some angle or slant that you want to focus on—one big play, or how a coach made a great call, or whatever. Then, finally, you have to write it all into a coherent form.   10

I told Wilson that the process he described was just what I was learning in my college writing class. "You have to write fast as well as accurately," Wilson said. He also told me that he likes the challenge. I can see that appealing to my competitive nature.   11

Because I wanted to find out what a professional sportswriter might do, Wilson also suggested I contact Brad Taylor, the high school sports editor of a large newspaper in my hometown.   12

My communications with Brad Taylor proved even more interesting. Taylor explained the path he took to become a sportswriter. Like me, he had played football in high school but wasn't good enough to play in college. He was a history major in college but also wrote for the College Press, becoming sports editor his senior year. As much as he enjoyed sports-writing, he didn't think it was a real career. He expected to go   13 either to law school or graduate school in history and become a history professor.

Despite being accepted by some really good law schools and gradu-   14
ate schools, he chose to start work on a masters degree at a local college. For a number of reasons, school wasn't as exciting as he thought
it would be. On a whim, he went to the sports department of the large
local paper. They asked if he had clippings, and he brought some of his
college articles. They offered him a job as a stringer covering high
school football.

Taylor told me that something clicked when he started covering   15
high schools. He got a real thrill talking to the coaches and the players.

Eventually, he dropped out of graduate school when offered a full-   16
time reporting job. Over time he became editor for all of high school
sports. I could hear the excitement in his voice. It reminded me of
the times in my old high school locker room—the joy after winning and
the disappointment after losing, the camaraderie among teammates, the
team meetings to discuss strategy. I wouldn't mind reliving that again—
even if it's a vicarious experience.

Works Cited

Rice, Grantland. "The Four Horsemen." University of Notre Dame Archives.
    5 May 2003. <http://lamb.archives.nd.edu/rockne/rice.html>.
Taylor, Brad. Personal E-mail. 7 May 2003.
———. Personal Interview. 9 May 2003.
Wilson, John. Personal Interview. 30 Apr. 2003.

Mohler ended his first version with the words "locker room," and a peer reviewer asked about his ending:

This is a good story, but I'd like to see more in your conclusion. What's so good about your old locker room?

Notice how Mohler has now added some information to answer his classmate's question.

QUESTIONS FOR WRITING AND DISCUSSION

Rhetorical Knowledge: The Writer's Situation and Rhetoric

1. **Audience:** Who is the intended audience for Mohler's essay? What in the essay makes you think so?
2. **Purpose:** What does Mohler hope will happen when people read his essay?
3. **Voice and Tone:** How would you describe Mohler's tone in his essay?
4. **Responsibility:** How responsibly has Mohler reported information about being a sportswriter to you? To himself? Why do you think so?
5. **Context and Format:** Mohler wrote this paper for a college course. If you were an editor for your local newspaper, would you consider hiring Mohler as a sportswriter? Why or why not? What qualities in his exploratory essay would help you make this decision?

Critical Thinking: Responding to the Writer's Ideas

1. What is your first reaction to Rick Mohler's exploratory paper?

2. What is the main point of Mohler's essay? How well does he focus the essay? How does he support his main idea? What questions do you still have about his subject?

Composing Processes and Knowledge of Conventions: The Writer's Strategies

1. In what ways does Mohler establish his *ethos*, or his credibility, in this exploratory essay?

2. How effective is Mohler's conclusion? Why?

Inquiry and Research: Ideas for Further Exploration

1. In what other ways might Mohler have researched his choice? What sources might he have investigated?

Self-Assessment: Reflecting on Your Learning Goals

Now that you have constructed a piece of exploratory writing, go back and consider your learning goals, which you and your classmates may have considered at the beginning of this chapter (see pp. 82–83). Reflecting on your writing process and the exploratory text you have constructed—and putting such reflections down *in writing*—is another kind of exploration: you are exploring, thinking about, and commenting on your own work as a writer. Here are some questions to answer that focus on what you have learned from this assignment:

Rhetorical Knowledge

- *Audience:* What have you learned about addressing an audience in exploratory writing?
- *Purpose:* What have you learned about the purposes of exploratory writing?
- *Rhetorical Situation:* How did the writing context affect your exploratory text?
- *Voice and Tone:* How would you describe your voice in this project? Your tone? How do they contribute to the effectiveness of your exploratory essay?

- *Context, Medium, and Genre:* How did your context determine the medium and genre you chose, and how did those decisions affect your writing?

Critical Thinking, Reading, and Writing

- *Learning/Inquiry:* How did you decide what to focus on in your exploratory writing? How did you judge what was most and least important in your exploratory writing?
- *Responsibility:* How did you fulfill your responsibility to your readers?
- *Reading and Research:* What did you learn about exploratory writing from the reading selections you read for this chapter? What research did you conduct? How sufficient was the research you did?
- As a result of writing this exploration, how have you become a more critical thinker, reader, and writer? What critical thinking, reading, and writing skills do you hope to develop further in your next writing project? How will you work on them?

Writing Processes

- *Invention:* What invention strategies were most useful to you? Why?
- *Organizing Your Ideas and Details:* What organization did you use? How successful was it?
- *Revising:* What one revision did you make that you are most satisfied with? What are the strongest and the weakest parts of the paper or other piece of writing you wrote for this chapter? Why?
- *Working with Peers:* How did your instructor or peer readers help you by making comments and suggestions about your writing? How could you have made better use of the comments and suggestions you received? How could your peer readers help you more on your next assignment? How might you help them more, in the future, with the comments and suggestions you make on their texts?
- If you used photographs or other visuals to help present your exploration to readers, what did you learn about incorporating these elements?
- What "writerly habits" have you developed, modified, or improved on as you constructed the writing assignment for this chapter?

Conventions

- *Editing:* What sentence problem did you find most frequently in your writing? How will you avoid that problem in future assignments?
- *Genre:* What conventions of the genre, if any, gave you problems?
- *Documentation:* If you used sources for your paper, what documentation style did you use? What problems, if any, did you have with it?

Rhetorical Knowledge

- *Audience:* Consider what your readers need to know—and how you can interest them in that information. What about your subject might your audience be *most* interested in? What information might readers consider unusual?

- *Purpose:* You want readers to understand the information you are sharing, so your writing must be clear. Considering what your audience might *do* with the information you provide will help you decide how best to provide the information to your readers.

- *Rhetorical situation:* In an informational essay, you are writing to share information; your readers are reading your text to learn about (and—you hope—to understand) that information.

- *Writer's voice and tone:* Generally, informational writing has a neutral tone because you as the writer are trying, not to convince or explore, but rather to inform your readers. Of course, sometimes an informational essay can have a humorous tone.

- *Context, medium, and genre:* The genre you use to present your information is determined by your purpose: to inform. Decide on the best medium and genre to use to present your information to the audience you want to reach.

Critical Thinking, Reading, and Writing

- *Learning/inquiry:* Because you are helping your readers learn about the subject of your text, decide on the most important aspects of your topic and explain them in a clear, focused way.

- *Responsibility:* You have a responsibility to represent your information honestly and accurately.

- *Reading and research:* Your research must be accurate and as complete as possible, to allow you to present thoughtful, reliable information about your subject.

Chapter 6

Writing Processes

- *Invention:* You will need to choose invention strategies that will help you generate and locate information about your topic.

- *Organizing your ideas and details:* You will need to find the most effective way to present your information to your readers so they can easily understand it.

- *Revising:* You will need to read your work with a critical eye, to make certain that it fulfills the assignment and displays the qualities of good informative writing.

- *Working with peers:* Your classmates will make suggestions that indicate the parts of your text they found difficult to understand so you can work to clarify.

Conventions

- *Editing:* Informative writing benefits from the correct use of modifiers, so the round-robin activity on page 146 focuses on avoiding misplaced or dangling modifiers.

- *Genres for informative writing:* Possible genres include newspaper or magazine articles, informative letters, informative essays, and Web documents.

- *Documentation:* If you have relied on sources outside of your experience, cite them using the appropriate documentation style.

Chapter

6

The *New York Times* Online (February 23, 2007)

Writing to Inform

We all deal with *information* every day of our lives. We learn about facts, ideas, and ways of doing things and then communicate such information to others through spoken or written words and, at times, graphic or other visual means.

Many newspaper articles are examples of informative writing. The headlines from the *New York Times Online* do not seem to contain elements of persuasion, argumentation, or evaluation—the primary goal of headline writers is simply to provide information. We could argue, of course, that any type of writing has elements of persuasion, and by selecting certain words and emphasizing particular facts, a writer will influence a reader's response. However, the goal of most informative writing, especially the informative writing you will do in college, *is* to be as neutral as possible, so it is the writer's responsibility to present information impartially.

Not all newspapers or magazines make a similar effort to present information in an unbiased way, of course. A tabloid like the *National Enquirer* does not even attempt to appear neutral. Even in less flamboyant settings, however, informative writing does not need to be dull.

As a college student, you read informative writing in your textbooks and other assigned reading and are expected to write informative responses on tests and provide information in the papers your teachers assign. While you may think that you encounter informative writing only in your textbooks and in newspapers or magazines, you can easily find examples of such reading and writing in each area of your life. In your professional life, for example, you may need to read (or construct) a training manual, while in your civic life, you may be called on to write a voter guide about two candidates, presenting their positions without revealing your personal views.

Rhetorical Knowledge

When you provide information to readers, you need to consider what your readers might already know about your topic as well as what other information you have learned about through your research that would be useful to them. You will also need to decide what medium and genre will help you get that information across to your audience most effectively.

Writing to Inform in Your College Classes

Much of the writing you will do for your college classes will be informative. The purpose of most of the reading you will do in college is to learn new information—and many writing assignments will require you to relate new facts and concepts to other facts and concepts you have already read and learned about, as in the following examples:

- Your psychology instructor may ask you to read several essays or books about recovered memory and to *synthesize* the information they contain—to explain to a reader the most important points made in each text and how the information in one text agrees or disagrees with the information in the others.
- Your art instructor may ask that you trace the development of a specific approach to art, providing examples and details that show its evolution over time.
- Your political science instructor may ask you to examine "presidential bloopers," where presidential candidates did or said something awkward—and explain in writing how those instances affected the next election.

Writing to Inform for Life

In addition to your academic work, you will also construct informative texts for the other areas of your life, including your professional career, your civic life, and your personal life.

Much of the writing done in **professional settings** is designed to inform and often to teach. If you have or have had a job, for example, consider what you know about this job, including everyday activities and interactions, the tools or equipment you use or used, and so on. Now consider how you would explain the details of your job to someone who is going to take it over: What information would that person need to know to do your job effectively? How can you best relay that information to your replacement? What you have just considered are the details that make up a training manual, a type of informative writing that most businesses have in one form or another.

Likewise, much **civic writing** is designed to provide information to residents, voters, neighbors, and other citizens to help them decide issues or take advantage of community resources and programs. Perhaps citizens are being encouraged to participate in a community program such as a citizen's watch campaign, a civic event that would almost certainly require informative writing.

You will also do a great deal of informative writing in your **personal life,** ranging from notes to family members to e-mail conversations with relatives and friends. While you no doubt feel more comfortable jotting down information for your friends and family than you do for other audiences, you probably feel especially obligated to provide accurate and useful information because you care about your personal relationships.

Scenarios for Writing: Assignment Options

The following writing assignments call for you to construct informative texts. Each is in the form of a *scenario*, a brief story that provides some context for your writing. The scenario gives you a sense of who your audience is and what you need to accomplish. Starting on page 136, you will find guidelines for completing whatever assignment option you choose or that is assigned to you. Additional scenarios for college and life may be found online.

Writing for College

SCENARIO 1   Are Students Really Slobs?

Does your room—whether on campus or in a private home—look like the student's dorm room shown in Figure 6.1 on page 124?

Your sociology class has been focusing on student behavior. Just last week a classmate mentioned the problem of trash on campus: "Our campus is a big mess because students just don't care," she said. "They ignore the trash cans and recycling boxes and just toss their garbage everywhere!"

Although the following scenario focuses on littering, if you prefer you may write about some other issue on your campus. Your task is not to propose a solution for the issue; rather, your task is to inform other members of the campus community that a problem exists.

Writing Assignment: Construct an informative paper, based on two sets of information: (1) your observations of the problem on campus, and (2) interviews you conduct with at least two of your classmates, asking them what

TechNote A digital camera is an ideal tool for any assignment that asks you to make observations. Once you have transferred the photographs of your subject to your computer, it is easy to add them to your text. Be sure, though, to get written permission from any people you photograph before using photographs of them in your work.

FIGURE 6.1
A Student's Dormitory
Room

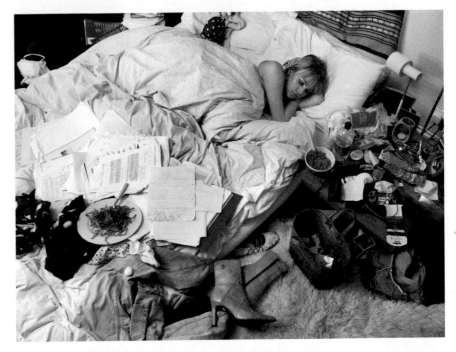

their thoughts are on why some students don't use trash cans as they should, or on the alternate problem you have chosen to write about.

Writing for Life

SCENARIO 2   Civic Writing: An Article about a Community Problem

As a reporter, you have been assigned to write about a community problem for your local newspaper. Select an important problem that your community is concerned about. To find a problem, read recent issues of your local paper and also speak to some residents of your community. For example, if you live in Bend, Oregon, and happen to glance through the online version of *Central Oregon Online*, you might see a list of local stories about the need to fund bridge repairs, an attempt to save horses, or problems with the water supply. All are aspects of civic life that you could write about.

Writing Assignment: Write an article for your local newspaper in which you explain the local problem or issue that interests you in detail so your readers will understand all aspects of and perspectives on it. Keep in mind that your article will be published on the front page of the newspaper, not in the editorial section, so your text must be as neutral as possible. (As an alternative, you can create a Web site, poster, or brochure about the problem—see the Visualizing Variations box on pp. 142–43.)

Rhetorical Considerations in Informative Writing

Audience: Who is your primary audience? Who else might be interested in your subject? Why?

Purpose: As noted in Chapter 3, writing can be a powerful tool for learning, so use the information you collect and write about as a way to increase your knowledge of your subject, as well as the knowledge of your readers. Bear in mind as you write that your purpose is not to convince readers to agree with an opinion you hold about your subject, but rather to inform them about it in neutral terms.

Voice, Tone, and Point of View: If you have a limited knowledge of your topic, your stance, or attitude, will be that of an interested investigator and your tone will usually be neutral. If you are writing about a topic that you know well, take care to keep any biases out of your writing. If you are writing about a problem, you should present all opinions about the problem, including those you disagree with, fairly. Your point of view will usually be third person.

Context, Medium, and Genre: Keeping the context of the assignment in mind, decide on a medium and a genre for your writing. How will your writing be used? If you are writing for an audience beyond the classroom, consider what will be the most effective way to present your information to this audience.

For more on choosing a medium and genre, see Chapter 17 and Appendix C.

Critical Thinking, Reading, and Writing

Before you begin to write your informative paper, read examples of informative writing. You might also consider how visuals can inform readers, as well as the kinds of sources you will need to consult.

Writing to provide information has several qualities—a strong focus, relevant, useful information that is provided in an efficient manner, and clear, accurate explanations that enable readers to understand the information easily. The reading selections and the visual text that appear in the next sections can serve to stimulate your inquiry and writing. Finally, informative writing almost always requires that you go beyond your current knowledge of a topic and conduct careful research.

Learning the Qualities of Effective Informative Writing

As you think about how you might compose an informative paper, consider what readers expect and need from an informative text. As a reader, you probably look for the following qualities in informative writing:

- **A focused subject.** In *The Elements of Style*, his classic book of advice to writers, author and humorist E. B. White suggests, "When you say something, make sure you have said it. The chances of your having said it are only fair." White's comment is especially applicable to informative writing. The best way to "make sure you have said" what you want to say is to have a clear focus. What information about your subject is the most important? If you could boil down your information into one sentence, what would it be? Condensing the important aspects of your information into a single sentence forces you to craft a thesis statement, which in turn helps you connect all your details and examples back to that main point.

For more on thesis statements, see Chapter 13.

- **Useful and relevant information.** People often read to gain information: they want to learn how their favorite sports team is doing, to find the best way to travel from one place to another, to learn why high blood pressure is a health concern. So how can you present your information so that readers understand what they might *do* with it, and how it relates to their lives? Perhaps there is an unusual or a humorous angle on your subject that you can write about. And if you *synthesize* the information you have—explain the most important points made in each source you have consulted and how the information in one source agrees or disagrees with that in the other sources you have read—you will provide readers with a more thorough understanding of your subject.

- **Clear explanations and accurate information.** Information needs to be presented clearly and accurately so it is understandable to readers who do not have background knowledge about your subject. Consider your information as if you knew nothing about the subject. Examples are almost always a useful way to help explain ideas and define terms. *Comparison and contrast* can be useful when you need to explain an unfamiliar subject—tell the reader what a subject is like and what it is not like. One strategy that will help you write clear, accurate papers is to take careful notes when you conduct research.

For more on using examples and comparison and contrast, see Chapter 13. For more on conducting research and taking notes, see Chapters 19 and 20.

- **Efficiency.** Information should usually be presented concisely. To help readers grasp the information, you might want to provide them with a road map, an outline of what you have in mind, at the beginning of the paper so they will know what to expect. Another way to present data efficiently is to "chunk" your writing—put it into sections, each dealing with a different aspect of the subject, making it easier for readers to understand. As you plan your paper, you should also consider whether it would be helpful to present your information in a table, graph, chart, or map. Consider how the title of your informative text not only will help your reader understand your focus, but also will help to draw readers in, motivating them to read your paper.

For more on the use of visuals to enhance your explanations, see Chapter 18.

In an electronic form that you can copy and paste, you might jot down the main ideas from the qualities of effective informative writing above. Later, you can paste them into your working draft to remind you of the qualities that make an effective informative text.

A WRITER'S RESPONSIBILITIES

Presenting Informative Writing Conscientiously

People often use information from their reading to help them make a decision, to support an idea in their writing, or to teach someone else. It is important, therefore, that you present accurate information and that you are aware of any biases, or pre-conceived ideas, you may bring to your writing about a topic—biases that might cause you to present that information in a way that is other than neutral. Ethical writers also take care to present reliable data. For example, you cannot say, "the majority of students who attend this college think that the school does a good job of recycling on campus," unless you have asked a sufficiently large and representative group of your classmates and are reasonably certain that you are presenting a true majority opinion.

Reading, Inquiry, and Research: Learning from Texts That Inform

The following reading selections are examples of informative writing. As you read, consider the following questions:

- What makes this reading selection useful and interesting? What strategies does its author use to make the information understandable for readers?
- What parts of the reading could be improved by the use of charts, photographs, or tables? Why? How?
- How can you use the techniques of informative writing exemplified here in your writing?

Thinking Rhetorically

Keep in mind the following questions as you read the essays that follow. Make it a practice to ask yourself these questions in all your reading—personal, academic, and professional—and you will strengthen and sharpen your abilities as a reader and as a writer.

Rhetorical Knowledge: The Writer's Situation and Rhetoric

- *Audience:* Who is the primary audience for this piece of writing? How effective is the author at addressing this audience? What can you point to in the article or essay to support your position?
- *Purpose:* What is the author's primary purpose in informing her audience? What realm (personal, professional, civic, or academic) does the article or essay fit into? Why?
- *Voice and Tone:* What is the author's attitude towards his or her topic? How do you know that?

- *Responsibility:* How does the author address different perspectives on her subject? Has the author also met her obligation to write with clarity?
- *Context and Format:* Given the topics of the reading selection, how effectively has the author organized her writing? How might the inclusion of visuals, such as tables, charts, photos, and graphs, have helped the author to inform her readers?

CAROL EZZELL

Clocking Cultures

Carol Ezzell has been a science writer since the early 1990s and currently works as a writer and an editor at *Scientific American,* specializing in biology and biomedicine. She has also worked for *Nature, Science News, Bio/World* and the *Journal of NIH Research.* An award-winning writer, Ezzell has been recognized for her science journalism by the National Association of Science Writers and the Pan American Health Organization. In 2000, she won a Science in Society Journalism award for her article "Care for a Dying Continent," about how AIDS has affected women and girls in Zimbabwe. This article was originally published in the September 2002 issue of *Scientific American.*

Show up an hour late in Brazil, and no one bats an eyelash. But keep someone in New York City waiting for five or 10 minutes, and you have some explaining to do. Time is elastic in many cultures but snaps taut in others. Indeed, the way members of a culture perceive and use time reflects their society's priorities and even their own worldview.   1

Social scientists have recorded wide differences in the pace of life in various countries and in how societies view time—whether as an arrow piercing the future or as a revolving wheel in which past, present and future cycle endlessly. Some cultures conflate time and space: the Australian Aborigines' concept of the "Dreamtime" encompasses not only a creation myth but a method of finding their way around the countryside. Interestingly, however, some views of time—such as the idea that it is acceptable for a more powerful person to keep someone of lower status waiting—cut across cultural differences and seem to be found universally.   2

The study of time and society can be divided into the pragmatic and the cosmological. On the practical side, in the 1950s anthropologist Edward T. Hall, Jr., wrote that the rules of social time constitute a "silent language" for a given culture. The rules might not always be made explicit, he stated, but they "exist in the air. . . . They are either familiar and comfortable or unfamiliar and wrong."   3

In 1955 he described in *Scientific American* how differing perceptions of time can lead to misunderstandings between people from separate cultures. "An ambassador who has been kept waiting for more than half an hour by a foreign visitor needs to understand that if his visitor 'just mutters an apology' this is not necessarily an insult," Hall wrote. The time system in the foreign country may be composed of different basic units, so that the visitor is not as late as he may appear to us. You must know the time system of the country to know at what point apologies are really due. . . . Different cultures simply place different values on the time units.

Most cultures around the world now have watches and calendars, uniting the majority of the globe in the same general rhythm of time. But that doesn't mean we all march to the same beat. "One of the beauties of studying time is that it's a wonderful window on culture," says Robert V. Levine, a social psychologist at California State University at Fresno. "You get answers on what cultures value and believe in. You get a really good idea of what's important to people." Levine and his colleagues have conducted so-called pace-of-life studies in 31 countries. In *A Geography of Time*, published in 1997, Levine describes how he ranked the countries by using three measures: walking speed on urban sidewalks, how quickly postal clerks could fulfill a request for a common stamp, and the accuracy of public clocks. Based on these variables, he concluded that the five fastest-paced countries are Switzerland, Ireland, Germany, Japan and Italy; the five slowest are Syria, El Salvador, Brazil, Indonesia and Mexico. The U.S., at 16th, ranks near the middle. Kevin K. Birth, an anthropologist at Queens College, has examined time perceptions in Trinidad. Birth's 1999 book, *Any Time Is Trinidad Time: Social Meanings and Temporal Consciousness*, refers to a commonly used phrase to excuse lateness. In that country, Birth observes, "if you have a meeting at 6:00 at night, people show up at 6:45 or 7:00 and say, 'Any time is Trinidad time.'" When it comes to business, however, that loose approach to timeliness works only for the people with power. A boss can show up late and toss off "any time is Trinidad time," but underlings are expected to be more punctual. For them, the saying goes, "time is time." Birth adds that the tie between power and waiting time is true for many other cultures as well.

The nebulous nature of time makes it hard for anthropologists and social psychologists to study. "You can't simply go into a society, walk up to some poor soul and say, 'Tell me about your notions of time,'" Birth says. "People don't really have an answer to that. You have to come up with other ways to find out."

Birth attempted to get at how Trinidadians value time by exploring how closely their society links time and money. He surveyed rural residents and found that farmers—whose days are dictated by natural events, such as sunrise—did not recognize the phrases "time is money," "budget your time" or "time management," even though they had satellite TV and were familiar with Western popular culture. But tailors in the same areas were aware of such notions. Birth concluded that wage work altered the tailors' views of time. "The ideas of associating time with money are not found globally," he says, "but are attached to your job and the people you work with."

How people deal with time on a day-to-day basis often has nothing   8
to do with how they conceive of time as an abstract entity. "There's often a disjunction between how a culture views the mythology of time and how they think about time in their daily lives," Birth asserts. "We don't think of Stephen Hawking's theories as we go about our daily lives."

Some cultures do not draw neat distinctions between the past, pres-   9
ent and future. Australian Aborigines, for instance, believe that their ancestors crawled out of the earth during the Dreamtime. The ancestors "sang" the world into existence as they moved about naming each feature and living thing, which brought them into being. Even today, an entity does not exist unless an Aborigine "sings" it.

Ziauddin Sardar, a British Muslim author and critic, has written   10
about time and Islamic cultures, particularly the fundamentalist sect Wahhabism. Muslims "always carry the past with them," claims Sardar, who is editor of the journal *Futures* and visiting professor of postcolonial studies at City University, London. "In Islam, time is a tapestry incorporating the past, present and future. The past is ever present." The followers of Wahhabism, which is practiced in Saudi Arabia and by Osama bin Laden, seek to re-create the idyllic days of the prophet Muhammad's life. "The worldly future dimension has been suppressed" by them, Sardar says. "They have romanticized a particular vision of the past. All they are doing is trying to replicate that past."

Sardar asserts that the West has "colonized" time by spreading the   11
expectation that life should become better as time passes: "If you colonize time, you also colonize the future. If you think of time as an arrow, of course you think of the future as progress, going in one direction. But different people may desire different futures."

QUESTIONS FOR WRITING AND DISCUSSION: LEARNING OUTCOMES

Critical Thinking: Responding to the Writer's Ideas

1. What is the most interesting piece of information in Ezzell's article? Why? The least interesting? Why?

2. What is the main idea—or thesis—in Ezzell's essay? How well does Ezzell provide support for this idea? Why do you think that?

Composing Processes and Knowledge of Conventions: The Writer's Strategies

1. Ezzell uses information and quotations from experts throughout her essay. How does she present this information? What does the presence of these experts add to the essay?

2. Prepare a quick outline of this essay. What does this outline reveal about the way Ezzell has organized her information for readers?

Inquiry and Research: Ideas for Further Exploration

1. Prepare a list of questions that you still have about time and cultures. Interview several of your friends, asking them the questions that you have listed, and then explain, in no more than two pages, their answers to your questions.

KATIE HAFNER

Growing *Wikipedia* Revises Its "Anyone Can Edit" Policy

Katie Hafner has written widely about technology. Her books include *Cyberpunk: Outlaws and Hackers on the Computer Frontier* (with John Markoff, 1991), *The House at the Bridge: A Story of Modern Germany* (1995), *Where Wizards Stay Up Late: The Origins of the Internet* (with Matthew Lyon, 1996), and *The Well: A Story of Love, Death and Real Life in the Seminal Online Community* (2001). She writes regularly for the *New York Times* and *Newsweek*. She also has written articles for *Wired,* the *New Republic,* and *Esquire.* As a student, she studied German literature and culture. This article, published in the *New York Times* in 2006, concerns *Wikipedia,* the well-known online encyclopedia. As you read Hafner's article, think about your experience with conducting research—and how you decide what is correct and accurate information and what is not.

Wikipedia is the online encyclopedia that "anyone can edit." Unless   1
you want to edit the entries on Albert Einstein, human rights in China or Christina Aguilera.

Wikipedia's come-one, come-all invitation to write and edit articles, 2
and the surprisingly successful results, have captured the public imagination. But it is not the experiment in freewheeling collective creativity
it might seem to be, because maintaining so much openness inevitably
involves some tradeoffs.

At its core, *Wikipedia* is not just a reference work but also an online 3
community that has built itself a bureaucracy of sorts—one that, in
response to well-publicized problems with some entries, has recently
grown more elaborate. It has a clear power structure that gives volunteer
administrators the authority to exercise editorial control, delete unsuit-
able articles and protect those that are vulnerable to vandalism.

Those measures can put some entries outside of the "anyone can 4
edit" realm. The list changes rapidly, but as of yesterday, the entries for
Einstein and Ms. Aguilera were among 82 that administrators had "protected" from all editing, mostly because of repeated vandalism or disputes over what should be said. Another 179 entries—including those for
George W. Bush, Islam and Adolf Hitler—were "semi-protected," open to
editing only by people who had been registered at the site for at least
four days. . . .

While these measures may appear to undermine the site's demo- 5
cratic principles, Jimmy Wales, *Wikipedia*'s founder, notes that protection
is usually temporary and affects a tiny fraction of the 1.2 million entries
on the English-language site.

"Protection is a tool for quality control, but it hardly defines *Wikipedia*," 6
Mr. Wales said. "What does define *Wikipedia* is the volunteer community
and the open participation."

From the start, Mr. Wales gave the site a clear mission: to offer free 7
knowledge to everybody on the planet. At the same time, he put in place
a set of rules and policies that he continues to promote, like the need to
present information with a neutral point of view.

The system seems to be working. *Wikipedia* is now the Web's third- 8
most-popular news and information source, beating the sites of CNN
and Yahoo News, according to Nielsen *NetRatings*.

The bulk of the writing and editing on *Wikipedia* is done by a geo- 9
graphically diffuse group of 1,000 or so regulars, many of whom are
administrators on the site.

"A lot of people think of *Wikipedia* as being 10 million people, each 10
adding one sentence," Mr. Wales said. "But really the vast majority of
work is done by this small core community."

The administrators are all volunteers, most of them in their 20's. 11
They are in constant communication—in real-time online chats, on "talk"
pages connected to each entry and via Internet mailing lists. The

volunteers share the job of watching for vandalism, or what Mr. Wales called "drive-by nonsense." Customized software—written by volunteers—also monitors changes to articles.

Mr. Wales calls vandalism to the encyclopedia "a minimal problem, a dull roar in the background." Yet early this year, amid heightened publicity about false information on the site, the community decided to introduce semi-protection of some articles. The four-day waiting period is meant to function something like the one imposed on gun buyers. 12

Once the assaults have died down, the semi-protected page is often reset to "anyone can edit" mode. An entry on Bill Gates was semi-protected for just a few days in January, but some entries, like the article on President Bush, stay that way indefinitely. Other semi-protected subjects as of yesterday were Opus Dei, Tony Blair and sex. 13

To some critics, protection policies make a mockery of the "anyone can edit" notion. 14

"As *Wikipedia* has tried to improve its quality, it's beginning to look more and more like an editorial structure," said Nicholas Carr, a technology writer who recently criticized *Wikipedia* on his blog. "To say that great work can be created by an army of amateurs with very little control is a distortion of what *Wikipedia* really is." 15

But Mr. Wales dismissed such criticism, saying there had always been protections and filters on the site. 16

Wikipedia's defenders say it usually takes just a few days for all but the most determined vandals to retreat. 17

"A cooling-off period is a wonderful mediative technique," said Ross Mayfield, chief executive of a company called Socialtext that is based on the same editing technology that *Wikipedia* uses. 18

Full protection often results from a "revert war," in which users madly change the wording back and forth. In such cases, an administrator usually steps in and freezes the page until the warring parties can settle their differences in another venue, usually the talk page for the entry. The Christina Aguilera entry was frozen this week after fans of the singer fought back against one user's efforts to streamline it. 19

Much discussion of *Wikipedia* has focused on its accuracy. Last year, an article in the journal *Nature* concluded that the incidence of errors in *Wikipedia* was only slightly higher than in *Encyclopaedia Britannica*. Officials at *Britannica* angrily disputed the findings. 20

"To be able to do an encyclopedia without having the ability to differentiate between experts and the general public is very, very difficult," said Jorge Cauz, the president of *Britannica*, whose subscription-based online version receives a small fraction of the traffic that *Wikipedia* gets. 21

Intentional mischief can go undetected for long periods. In the article   22
about John Seigenthaler Sr., who served in the Kennedy administration, a
suggestion that he was involved in the assassinations of both John F. and
Robert Kennedy was on the site for more than four months before Mr.
Seigenthaler discovered it. He wrote an op-ed article in *USA Today* about the
incident, calling *Wikipedia* "a flawed and irresponsible research tool."

Yet Wikipedians say that in general the accuracy of an article grows   23
organically. At first, said Wayne Saewyc, a *Wikipedia* volunteer in Vancouver,
British Columbia, "everything is edited mercilessly by idiots who do stupid
and weird things to it." But as the article grows, and citations slowly
accumulate, Mr. Saewyc said, the article becomes increasingly accurate.

Wikipedians often speak of how powerfully liberating their first contri-   24
bution felt. Kathleen Walsh, 23, a recent college graduate who majored in
music, recalled the first time she added to an article on the contrabassoon.

"I wrote a paragraph of text and there it was," recalled Ms. Walsh.   25
"You write all these pages for college and no one ever sees it, and you
write for *Wikipedia* and the whole world sees it, instantly."

Ms. Walsh is an administrator, a post that others nominated her for   26
in recognition of her contributions to the site. She monitors a list of
newly created pages, half of which, she said, end up being good candidates for deletion. Many are "nonsense pages created by kids, like 'Michael
is a big dork,'" she said.

Ms. Walsh also serves on the 14-member arbitration committee,   27
which she describes as "the last resort" for disputes on *Wikipedia*.

Like so many Web-based successes, *Wikipedia* started more or less by   28
accident.

Six years ago, Mr. Wales, who built up a comfortable nest egg in a brief   29
career as an options trader, started an online encyclopedia called Nupedia.
com, with content to be written by experts. But after attracting only a few
dozen articles, Mr. Wales started *Wikipedia* on the side. It grew exponentially.

For the first year or so, Mr. Wales paid the expenses out of his own   30
pocket. Now the Wikimedia Foundation, the nonprofit organization that
supports *Wikipedia*, is financed primarily through donations, most in the
$50 to $100 range.

As the donations have risen, so have the costs. The foundation's   31
annual budget doubled in the last year, to $1.5 million, and traffic has
grown sharply. Search engines like Google, which often turn up *Wikipedia*
entries at the top of their results, are a big contributor to the site's traffic,
but it is increasingly a first stop for knowledge seekers.

Mr. Wales shares the work of running *Wikipedia* with the administra-   32
tors and four paid employees of the foundation. Although many decisions
are made by consensus within the community, Mr. Wales steps in when

an issue is especially contentious. "It's not always obvious when something becomes policy," he said. "One way is when I say it is."

Mr. Wales is a true believer in the power of wiki page-editing technology, which predates *Wikipedia*. In late 2004, Mr. Wales started Wikia, a commercial start-up financed by venture capital that lets people build Web sites based around a community of interest. Wiki 24, for instance, is an unofficial encyclopedia for the television show "24." Unlike *Wikipedia*, the site carries advertising. 33

Mr. Wales, 39, lives with his wife and daughter in St. Petersburg, Fla., where the foundation is based. But Mr. Wales's main habitat these days, he said, is the inside of airplanes. He travels constantly, giving speeches to reverential audiences and visiting Wikipedians around the world. 34

Wikipedia has inspired its share of imitators. A group of scientists has started the peer-reviewed *Encyclopedia of Earth*, and *Congresspedia* is a new encyclopedia with an article about each member of Congress. 35

But beyond the world of reference works, *Wikipedia* has become a symbol of the potential of the Web. 36

"It can tell us a lot about the future of knowledge creation, which will depend much less on individual heroism and more on collaboration," said Mitchell Kapor, a computer industry pioneer who is president of the Open Source Applications Foundation. 37

Zephyr Teachout, a lawyer in Burlington, Vt., who is involved with *Congresspedia*, said *Wikipedia* was reminiscent of old-fashioned civic groups like the Grange, whose members took individual responsibility for the organization's livelihood. 38

"It blows open what's possible," said Ms. Teachout. "What I hope is that these kinds of things lead to thousands of other experiments like this encyclopedia, which we never imagined could be produced in this way." 39

QUESTIONS FOR WRITING AND DISCUSSION: LEARNING OUTCOMES

Critical Thinking: Responding to the Writer's Ideas

1. What in Hafner's text do you want to learn more about? What questions do you still have?

2. Hafner addresses the delicate balance between the importance of accuracy and the advantages of openness—that anyone can contribute to *Wikipedia*. If you were an editor of *Wikipedia*, how would you maintain that balance?

Composing Processes and Knowledge of Conventions: The Writer's Strategies

1. Hafner covers a good deal of ground in this reading selection, yet she has a central idea. What is her central idea, or focus? How does she maintain it?

2. Because she is a journalist writing for a newspaper, Hafner cites her sources within the body of her article rather than using a formal system of documentation. How do her sources lend credibility to her writing? What other sources of information might she have cited?

Inquiry and Research: Ideas for Further Exploration

1. Research a concept or issue on the Web. Make a list of the information you collect that seems contradictory. How might you reconcile those inconsistencies, to figure out what *is* accurate?

Thinking about Visuals That Inform

For more on using visuals in your own writing, see Chapter 18.

Tables, graphs, and charts are all excellent ways to inform readers about statistical data. Figure 6.2 on page 137 is a bar graph showing the national debt of the United States. As you look at this bar graph, consider these questions about the effective use of bar graphs and other visuals to inform readers:

- How do you react to this graph?
- What does this information mean to you, personally? How might a table or another type of chart be used to convey this information?
- How do you think our (rapidly) growing national debt might affect you and your family in the future?
- Is this visual neutral, or does it have a point of view? Look for other visuals that describe the national debt, either in a print publication or on the Web. How are those visuals used?

Writing Processes

As you work on the assignment scenario you have chosen, keep in mind the qualities of an effective informative paper (see pp. 125–26). Also remember that writing is more a circular than a linear process. So while the activities listed below imply that writers go through them step-by-step, the actual

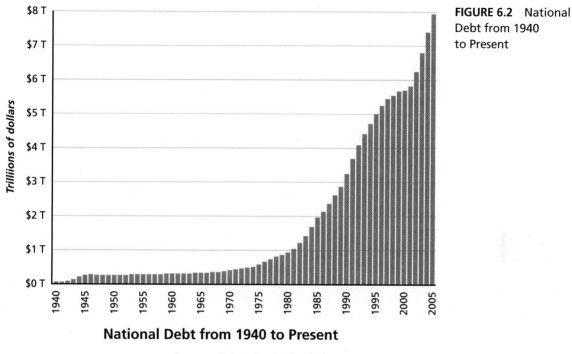

National Debt from 1940 to Present

FIGURE 6.2 National Debt from 1940 to Present

Source: U.S. National Debt Clock
http://www.brillig.com/debt_clock/

process of writing is usually messier. You will keep coming back to your earlier work, adding to it and modifying the information to be more accurate as you conduct more research and become more familiar with your topic.

As you work on your project, make certain that you save your computer files frequently because any work that you do not save could be lost. Also, savvy writers back up their computer files in two or more places—on the hard drive of the computer, on a USB flash drive, and/or on a rewritable CD or DVD.

Invention: Getting Started

Use invention activities to explore, on paper or on your computer screen, the information that you want to include in your first draft. It is also useful to keep a journal as you work on any writing project, for your journal is a place where you can record not just what you learn but also the questions that arise during your writing and research activities.

For more on using journals, see Chapters 2 and 3.

Try to answer these questions while you do your invention work:

- What do I already know about the topic that I am writing about?
- What feelings or attitudes do I have about this topic? How can I keep them out of my text so that my writing is as free of bias as possible?

- What questions can I ask about the topic?
- Where might I learn more about this subject (in the library, on the Web)? What verifiable information on my topic is available?
- Who would know about my topic? What questions might I ask that person in an interview?
- What do I know about my audience? What don't I know that I should know? Why might they be interested in reading my text?
- What might my audience already know about my subject? Why might they care about it?
- To what extent will sensory details—color, shape, smell, taste, and so on—help my reader understand my topic? Why?
- What visual aids might I use to better inform my readers?

For more on descriptive writing, see Chapter 13.

Doing your invention work in electronic form, rather than on paper, lets you easily use this early writing as you construct a draft.

As with any kind of writing, invention activities improve with peer feedback and suggestions. Consider sharing the invention work you have done so far with several classmates or friends in order to understand your rhetorical situation more clearly and to generate more useful information.

Exploring Your Ideas with Research

While you can sometimes draw exclusively on your experience in a piece of informative writing, especially in personal writing contexts, in academic, professional, and civic writing situations you will usually need to include information gained from outside research.

Assume, for example, that you would like to inform a group of your friends about a local homeless shelter. You would probably want to list the services the shelter provides, indicate the various ways people can become involved with the shelter, and cite financial data on what percentage of each cash donation goes to support the shelter's clients. To provide this information to your readers, you would need to conduct some form of research.

Research provides you with the statistical data, examples, and expert testimony that will enable you to give your audience enough information, and the right kind of information, on your topic. As with any other aspect of your writing, the kind and amount of research you will need to do will depend on your rhetorical situation: who your audience is and what you are trying to accomplish. If you are writing a paper for a sociology course on aspects of male group behavior, you would need to locate articles in scholarly journals, as well as statistical data, which you could present in a chart. If you are writing about a problem in your community, you would need to read articles and government documents, and you might also interview government officials.

As you work on the scenario you have chosen (see pp. 123–24), you could conduct several kinds of research. Where you are researching a problem on campus or in your community, you will need to conduct interviews with students or with people affected by the problem. As an alternative, you might consider conducting a survey of a representative sample of students or people within the community. You will also need to observe the problem.

Gather, read, and take notes on your topic from outside sources. You might use an electronic journal to record images, URLs, and other electronic pieces of information that you find as you research. Such an e-journal makes it easy for you to add those e-documents once you start drafting your paper.

For help with locating sources of information, see Chapter 19; for help with documenting your sources, see Chapter 20.

TechNote

The results of a search for sources on your topic can let you know if your informative topic is unwieldy. If you find that a search brings up thousands of Web sites with information about your topic, it is probably too broad to be manageable. For example, when a search engine such as Google returns more than 1 million links for the topic "West Nile Virus," you'll need to use strategies that will narrow the topic so that your ideas and your research will be more focused. Adding search terms based on your specific interests and concerns can help.

Adding search terms narrows your exploratory Web search to an aspect of the West Nile Virus. (Tip: Separate your terms or phrases in the search window with quotation marks.) The terms "West Nile Virus" + "horse vaccine" narrows the results to 1,150 sites that are likely to give information about equine vaccination against West Nile virus—a more focused topic, but still fairly broad. Adding a third term—"Missouri"—narrows the topic further, resulting in 108 sites and getting you closer to a topic of immediate interest. Adding yet a fourth term—"Kansas City"—yields only 5 sites, possibly indicating a topic of interest to others, yet limited enough to provide the focus needed for an essay.

For an essay-length informative piece, then, think about focusing on a local—or even a personal—aspect of a larger issue. "West Nile Virus: Is Kansas City Doing Its Part?" is a working topic that may glean information that is fresh, new, and useful.

For more on using search engines, see Chapter 19.

Reviewing Your Invention and Research

After you have conducted your research, review your invention work and notes and think about the information you have collected from outside sources. You may be tempted to decide on a thesis statement—a statement that summarizes your main point—at this time. Even though you might already have a general idea of what you want your informative paper to focus on, until you get some of your ideas and research on paper, it is often hard to know what your thesis will be. Your thesis should come *from* the writing you do about your topic. Once you have done a lot of invention work (listing, brainstorming, clustering, and so on) and research, you may be ready to decide on your working thesis. Or you can wait until after you construct your first draft.

For more on deciding on a thesis, see Chapter 13.

Organizing Your Information and Research

Once you have some sense of what you would like your informative paper to include, you need to consider how you might organize this material. The questions you need to ask yourself when deciding on your organization are all rhetorical:

- Who is your audience?
- Why might they be interested in your subject, or how can you make them interested in it? (One way to indicate why your subject is important to your audience is to explain how your audience will be affected by it.)
- What is your purpose for writing—that is, what do you want to *inform* your readers about?
- What are the most important ideas, concepts, or statistics that you want your readers to learn about from your text?

The answers to these questions can help you decide what you need to emphasize, which in turn will help you choose an organization.

Here are three possible organizational approaches for writing an informative paper:

Options for Organization

First Approach	Second Approach	Third Approach
• Start with an unusual or surprising piece of information about your subject. • Present the information, starting from the least unusual or surprising idea and moving to the most. • Use specific examples, quotations, statistics, and so on to illustrate your topic. • End your paper by restating a unique or surprising aspect of your topic.	• Begin with a question to help readers see why they might want to read about your topic. • Outline the information, starting with the least significant piece of information and working toward the most important. • Use specific examples, quotations, statistics, and so on to illustrate your topic. • Your conclusion might answer the question that you started with.	• Set the stage—what is the situation that your readers may be interested in? • Broaden your initial explanation with specific details, quotations, and examples so your reader can "see" what you are writing about. • Compare and contrast your subject with another one, to help readers understand the information. • Conclude your paper by reinforcing your reader's connection to your topic.

Constructing a Complete Draft

Once you have chosen the organizational approach that works best given your audience and purpose, you are ready to finish constructing your draft. Look back over the information you have generated through your invention activities and collected through your research, as well as any comments made by your classmates. You should also re-examine your focus or your thesis (if you have one) and decide if you need to modify it.

Remember that you will learn more about your subject as you write, and your ideas will probably change as you compose the first draft of your informative essay. Consider, too, what visual aids your readers might find useful.

Introduction: A successful piece of informative writing grabs and holds readers' attention. The following strategies can help you hook your readers:

- *Define any important terms that the reader might not know.* Defining terms does not mean listing their dictionary definitions, but rather explaining those terms in the context of your explanation of your subject. For an especially effective opening, you might get readers' attention by defining a familiar term in an unexpected way.
- *Start your text with unusual or surprising information.*
- *Get down to business by bluntly stating your thesis.* A straightforward statement like "Denver's new sign code is causing businesses to lose money" often gets readers' attention. Journalists, who are trained to put the most important information up front, often use this approach.
- *Start with a provocative example or two.*

Body: Think of the body of your informative text as the place to provide all of the information that you want your readers to know and to understand. This is the section where you will present your data: quotations, graphs, tables, charts. The body of your paper is always the longest part, and, while you are not trying to prove anything in an informative essay, you are providing information to your readers, and most of it will appear in this section.

Conclusion: Your conclusion should tie your paper together for your readers by explaining or suggesting the significance of the information you have given them: why it is useful or interesting to them. Here are some strategies for concluding an informative paper:

- *Summarize your main points.*
- *Explain the subject's most critical part.* Carol Ezzell uses a quotation from an expert to indicate what is most significant about her topic: "If you colonize time, you also colonize the future" (p. 128).
- *Outline again the subject's most important aspects.*

Title: You might think that you need to come up with a title before you start writing, but often it is more useful to get a first draft on paper or into a computer file and then consider possible titles. Your paper's title should indicate what your paper is about, but it should also capture your readers' interest and invite them to read your paper.

- *Use a title that readers will wonder about.* For example, "Clocking Cultures" makes readers wonder what this essay could be about.
- *Start with something current.* Katie Hafner titles her article, "Growing *Wikipedia* Revises Its 'Anyone Can Edit' Policy." Anyone familiar with *Wikipedia* will want to read more.

VISUALIZING VARIATIONS

Using a Web Site, Poster, or Brochure to Inform Your Readers

If you are working with Scenario 2 (p. 124), which calls for civic writing, one way to present your information to your readers would be to construct a Web site, poster, or brochure instead of a newspaper article.

The following Web site from EasyVoter.org is designed to provide information on issues that are important to California voters, as well as information on how to vote.

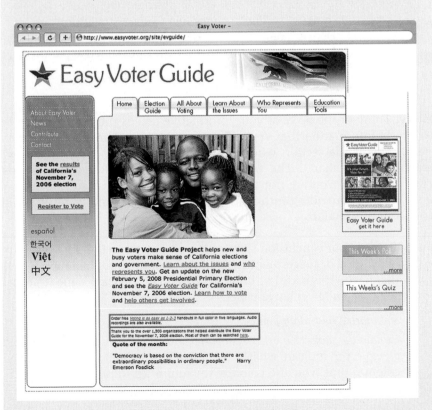

Using this Web site as an example, consider the best way to present the information you have researched to the voters in your area. Use the following questions to guide you:

1. Who do you see as your audience for your document? What information do you already know about them?
2. What is the best format in which to put your information? Which format—a Web site, poster, or brochure—would be easiest for your audience to gain access to?
3. Should you illustrate your Web site, poster, or brochure with tables or photos? Why?
4. What kind(s) of charts would be effective? Ineffective? How might you test a chart to see if it would be useful to include in your document?
5. If you create a Web document, what hyperlinks would you want to include? How effective are the hyperlinks in the document on page 142, and what makes them that way?

Revising

Revising means re-seeing and re-thinking your informative text. The most effective way to revise your work is to read it as if you are reading it for the first time. Reading your own work in this way is difficult to do, of course—which is why writers often put their work aside for a period of time. The more you can see your writing as if for the first time, the more you will respond to it as your real readers might, questioning and probing and exploring it. As you reread the first draft of your informative writing, here are some questions to ask yourself:

1. What else might my audience want or need to know about my subject?

2. How else might I encourage my audience to learn more about my subject?

3. What information did I find that I did not include in my paper? (Effective research always results in more information than you can include, so consider what you left out that you might include in your next draft.)

4. Have I clearly explained any terms my readers might not know?

5. Could some of my information be better presented as a graph or chart or in a photograph?

Technology can help you revise and edit your writing more easily. Use your word processor's track-changes tool to try out revisions and editing changes. After you've had time to think about the possible changes, you can "accept" or "reject" them. Also, you can use your word processor's comment tool to write reminders to yourself when you get stuck with a revision or some editing task.

Because it is so difficult to see our own emerging writing with a fresh eye (even for experienced writers), it is almost always useful to ask classmates, friends, or family members to read and comment on drafts of your papers.

WRITER'S WORKSHOP

Responding to Full Drafts

As you read and respond to your classmates' papers (and as they comment on yours), focus on the informative nature of this assignment, but from a reader's perspective. Be sure to ask questions of their writing and respond to their ideas by exploring your reactions and responses to their thoughts.

Working in pairs or groups of three, read each others' drafts, and then offer your classmates comments that will help them see their papers' strengths as well as places where they need to develop their ideas further. Use the following questions to guide your responses to the writer's draft:

- Write a brief narrative comment that outlines your first impression of this draft. How effectively does the title draw you into the paper? Why?

- Indicate what you like about the draft—that is, provide positive and encouraging feedback to the writer.

- Comment on the writer's focus. If the paper loses focus, indicate where.

- What part(s) of the text are especially informative? What information was interesting and/or new to you?

- Comment specifically on the introduction: What is effective about it? What suggestions can you make on how to improve the introduction?

- What do you think is the author's thesis or main point? How could it be expressed or supported more effectively?

- In the main part of the paper, are there parts that are confusing? Where would you like more details or examples to help you see what the author means? What parts could use more explanation or definitions?

- How clear is the author's informative writing? If there are places that seem wordy or unclear, how might the author revise to address those problems?

- How accurate does the information seem? How does the author indicate the sources of statistics and other information that are not common knowledge?

- Reread the conclusion. How well does it tie everything together? To what extent does it make you want to learn more about this topic?

- In another paragraph, outline what you see as the main weaknesses of this paper—and suggest how the writer might improve the text.

- If you are working with what might be called a non-traditional text (a Web page, for example, or a brochure), comment on the special attributes of that kind of text and how effectively the piece functions.

- If there are visual aspects of the document, comment on how effectively they illustrate the point being made. How much do the visuals add to a reader's overall understanding of the information?

Responding to Readers' Comments

Once they have received feedback from peers, teachers, and others, all writers have to decide what to do with that feedback. Because the text is *your* paper, you as the writer are responsible for dealing with reader responses to your work. You may decide to reject some comments, of course, and that decision is yours. As with any reader, some of your peer reviewers might not understand your main point, or they may misunderstand something you wrote—so it is up to you either to accept or to ignore their comments and suggestions. Other comments, though, deserve your attention, as they are the words of real readers speaking to you about how to improve your text. You may find that comments from more than one reader contradict each other. In that case, you need to use your own judgment to decide which reader's comments are on the right track.

Knowledge of Conventions

When effective writers edit their work, they attend to the conventions that will help readers—the table manners of writing. These include genre conventions, documentation, format, usage, grammar, punctuation, and mechanics. By attending to these conventions in your writing, you make reading a more pleasant experience for readers.

Editing

The last task in any writing project is editing. When you edit and polish your writing, you make changes to your sentence structure and word choice to improve your style and to make your writing clearer and more concise. You also check your work to make sure it adheres to conventions of grammar,

See Chapter 20 for more on documenting sources.

usage, punctuation, mechanics, and spelling. Use the spell-check function of your word-processing program, but be sure to double-check your spelling personally. If you have used sources in your paper, make sure you are following the documentation style your instructor requires.

As with overall revision of your work, this final editing and polishing is most effective if you can put your text aside for a few days and come back to it with fresh eyes. We strongly recommend that you ask classmates, friends, and tutors to read your work as well.

To assist you with editing, we offer here a round-robin editing activity focused on finding and correcting problems with modifiers.

WRITER'S WORKSHOP

Round-Robin Editing with a Focus on Modifiers

Informative writing benefits from the careful use of **modifiers**—words or groups of words that describe or limit other words—such as adjectives, adverbs, infinitives, participles, prepositional phrases, and relative clauses. Working in small groups, read one another's papers, looking for two common problems: misplaced and dangling modifiers

When a modifier is misplaced, it is too far away from the word or phrase it is modifying, so that it appears to be modifying something else. To correct the problem, the modifier needs to be moved.

MISPLACED   Student Jim Roberts told me ~~at orientation or anywhere else~~ no one had
                                                                at orientation or anywhere else
             mentioned the school's recycling program to him ∧.

A modifier is dangling when the word or phrase it modifies does not appear in the sentence to all. You can correct the problem by adding the word or phrase.

                                                            students need to be provided with
DANGLING   In order to know about the recyling program, ~~Meyers suggests that~~
                                                        ∧   *according to Meyers*
            information ~~be provided~~ at all orientation meetings ∧.

Compare notes to see if you have questions about modifiers, and consult a grammar handbook or ask your instructor for assistance.

Genres, Documentation, and Format

If you are writing an academic paper, follow the conventions for the discipline in which you are writing and the requirements of your instructor. If you are constructing an article for your local newspaper (Scenario 2), check the newspaper's editorial page or its Web site to see what the requirements are for length and format. If you have used material from outside sources, including visuals, give credit to those sources, using the documentation style required by the discipline you are working in and by your instructor.

For advice on writing in different genres, see Appendix C. For guidelines for formatting and documenting papers in MLA or APA style, see Chapter 20.

Student Craig Broadbent Informs His Readers

Craig Broadbent, a first-year student, chose to write in response to Scenario 1. Based on his observations around campus, Craig chose to write about litter in his essay titled "Watch for the Blue Barrels" which follows. As you read Broadbent's essay, think about what makes it effective.

CRAIG BROADBENT

Watch for the Blue Barrels

Have you ever wondered what all of those blue barrels that are scattered around campus are for . . . and if you know what they're for, do you wonder why students don't seem to use them? Those blue barrels are the heart of our campus-wide recycling program, and it is critical not only that students know what they are, but also that they *use* the barrels.   1

Joan Meyers, who coordinates our campus recycling program, says that it has been in place for more than ten years now, but receives little publicity. My purpose here is to outline what we're doing about recycling on campus, to show what the costs and income are from the program, and finally, based on several interviews, to suggest the reasons that students don't use the blue barrels.   2

What is recycling and why should we care about it? Recycling is the reuse of some product. We all know that reusing plastic, aluminum cans, newspaper, glass, and other items by recycling them saves energy (and thus helps our air pollution problem) and can also save money. Recycling is environmentally sound—the more paper, plastic, and metal products that we can reuse, the less we have to make. That's the case even though things are usually not recycled into what they were to start with. That is, aluminum cans, Meyers told me, rarely are recycled to make more aluminum cans. But they are recycled and made into   3

One peer suggestion Broadbent received was the following:

I'd like more tables and charts, if you have them—they help me see what you mean.

To address this reader's concern, Broadbent added this paragraph and also Table 1.

other products (frying pans, for instance). Therefore, recycling saves trees and other natural resources.

Not only that, but if certain items are <u>not</u> recycled, they can be around forever. That is, if we don't recycle some household items, they never seem to "waste away." For example, the University of British Columbia reports that some items can last huge amounts of time: glass bottles last a million years and plastic bottles <u>never</u> go away, as shown in Table 1.   4

Even seemingly minor items like cigarette butts can last as long as twelve years, and empty soda cans—unless they are recycled—can last   5

Table 1
Rates of Disintegration of Common Waste Products

Product	Time it takes
Cotton Rags	1–5 months
Paper	2–5 months
Rope	3–14 months
Orange Peels	6 months
Wool Socks	1–5 years
Cigarette butts	1–12 years
Plastic coated paper cartons	5 years
Plastic bags	10–20 years
Leather shoes	25–40 years
Nylon fabric	30–40 years
Tin cans	50–100 years
Aluminum cans	80–100 years
Plastic 6-pack holder rings	450 years
Glass bottles	1 million years
Plastic bottles	Never

Source: "Facts about Litter." <u>UBC Waste Management Litter Reduction Program</u>. University of British Columbia. 23 June 2003 <http://www.recycle.ubc.ca/litter.html>.

for up to one hundred years. They can also cost the college a great deal of money to clean up. Fig. 1 shows some cost information from the University of Nebraska at Lincoln, a school comparable to our own.

?

Did you know...

✓ UNL spends in excess of $180,000 per year just "picking-up" litter?

✓ An average of 10,700 labor hours were spent last year to pick-up campus litter?

✓ Cigarette butts are the #1 litter problem

Help us keep Campus clean.

Don't Litter.

Fig. 1 Costs of cleaning up litter at the University of Nebraska—Lincoln Botanical Garden and Arboretum. "Did You Know?" The Garden. 6 Sept. 2002. University of Nebraska—Lincoln. 3 June 2003. <http://busfin.unl.edu/LS/litter/litter.html>.

Joan Meyers notes that our recycling program not only keeps the campus cleaner, since items are collected in the blue barrels instead of perhaps being thrown on the ground, but it also generates some $5,000 a year in revenue for the school. Ms. Meyers also told me that our college could make as much as $30,000 a year from recycling if we all recycled all the newspapers, cans, and other waste that we now throw away.

Another comment Broadbent received from his peer review session pointed out a problem:

The weakest part is the interview information, which made me want to read more of what other people had to say.

Note how he has now included a good deal of information from the students he interviewed:

Broadbent's peer made this comment on his earlier draft:

Your conclusion was weak—maybe you could add what students ought to be doing now? Put another way, what do you want your readers to do with this (interesting) information?

Note how he now addresses what students can do to become more involved with their campus recycling program.

Students, though, don't use the program, sometimes because they're not aware of it. Student Jim Roberts told me that no one had mentioned the school's recycling program to him, at orientation or anywhere else. Another student, Tracy Worsam, even asked about the program at her orientation, but no one there seemed to know much about it, other than to say "we have some blue barrels around campus." Finally, I interviewed several students who live in that old house on the edge of campus. It's not really a fraternity but more of a boarding house. They all told me that *they* never littered, even though their yard was a mess (Wilson, Marble, and Addams). Maybe my interview with them—and the information I gave them about the blue barrel program—will help. Maybe if they understood recycling and had blue barrels in a convenient location, they would recycle their plastic, paper, and glass items.

7

A search through several back issues of the Campus Reporter may explain why not many students are really aware of the blue barrel program. During the last few months, only one small advertisement about the campus recycling program has appeared in the Reporter, and no articles about the program were published.

8

In order to know about and understand the recycling program, students need to be provided with information at all orientation meetings, and weekly advertisements need to be run in the Campus Reporter, according to Joan Meyers. In the meantime, students who would like to learn more about the recycling program on campus, and how they can help, can contact Meyers at JoanMeyers@Ourcollege.edu.

9

Works Cited

"Did You know?" The Garden. 6 Sept. 2002. University of Nebraska—Lincoln Botanical Garden and Arboretum. 27 June 2003 <http://busfin.unl.edu/LS/litter/litter.html>.

"Facts about Litter." UBC Waste Management Litter Reduction Program. University of British Columbia. 23 June 2003 <http://www.recycle.ubc.ca/litter.html>.

Meyers, Joan. Personal interview. 17 Mar. 2004.

Roberts, Jim. Personal interview. 15 Mar. 2004.

Wilson, James, Stacy Marble, and Sam Addams. Personal interview. 17 Mar. 2004.

Worsam, Tracy. Personal interview. 15 Mar. 2004.

QUESTIONS FOR WRITING AND DISCUSSION: LEARNING OUTCOMES

Rhetorical Knowledge: The Writer's Situation and Rhetoric

1. **Audience:** How effective is Broadbent at appealing to the audience that this information is intended for—students at a college or university? What can you point to in the article to demonstrate what you mean?

2. **Purpose:** In addition to its informative purpose, what other purposes does this paper have?

3. **Voice and Tone:** What is Broadbent's attitude toward his subject? How does he indicate this attitude in his tone?

4. **Responsibility:** What can you point to in Broadbent's informational essay that gives the text its *ethos*? To what extent do you believe the information that Broadbent presents here? Why?

5. **Context and Format:** How has Broadbent's context—his college campus— affected his paper? How might he have written about the same subject differently in another context?

Critical Thinking: Responding to the Writer's Ideas

1. What ideas in Broadbent's essay seem the most important to you? Why?

2. How effectively does Broadbent inform the reader? What examples can you point to in the text that provide useful information?

Composing Processes and Knowledge of Conventions: The Writer's Strategies

1. How effective are the visuals that Broadbent includes? What is your opinion of the sources he uses? What other sources might he have consulted?

2. What is your opinion of Broadbent's conclusion?

Inquiry and Research: Ideas for Further Exploration

1. Go to your college's main Web page and search for "recycling." In no more than one page, outline what you learn.

Self-Assessment: Reflecting on Your Learning Goals

Now that you have constructed a piece of informative writing, go back and consider your learning goals, which you and your classmates may have considered at the beginning of this chapter (see pp. 118–19). Write notes on what you have learned from this assignment.

Rhetorical Knowledge

- *Audience:* What did you learn about your audience as you wrote your informative paper?

- *Purpose:* How successfully do you feel you fulfilled your informative purpose?

- *Rhetorical situation:* How did the writing context affect your informational text? How did your choice of topic affect the research you conducted and how you presented your information to your readers? What do you see as the strongest part of your paper? Why? The weakest? Why?

- *Voice and tone:* How would you describe your voice in this essay? Your tone? How do they contribute to the effectiveness of your informational essay?

Critical Thinking, Reading, and Writing

- *Learning/inquiry:* How did you decide what to focus on in your informative paper? Describe the process you went through to focus on a main idea, or thesis.

- *Responsibility:* How did you fulfill your responsibility to your readers?

- *Reading and research:* What did you learn about informative writing from the reading selections you read for this chapter? What research did you conduct? Why? What additional research might you have done?

Writing Processes

- *Invention:* What invention strategies were most useful to you?

- *Organizing your ideas and details:* What organization did you use? How successful was it? Why?

- *Revising:* What one revision did you make that you are most satisfied with? Why? If you could make an additional revision, what would it be?

- *Working with peers:* How did your instructor or peer readers help you by making comments and suggestions about your writing? How could you have made better use of the comments and suggestions you received?

- Did you use photographs or other visuals to help you inform your readers? If so, what did you learn about incorporating these elements?
- What "writerly habits" have you developed, modified, or improved on as you constructed the writing assignment for this chapter?

Knowledge of Conventions

- *Editing:* What sentence problem did you find most frequently in your writing? How will you avoid that problem in future assignments?
- *Genre:* What conventions of the genre you were using, if any, gave you problems?
- *Documentation:* Did you use sources for your paper? If so, what documentation style did you use? What problems, if any, did you have with it?

Rhetorical Knowledge

- *Audience:* You should determine who will benefit from your analysis. What do the audience members probably already know? What will you need to tell them?

- *Purpose:* When you analyze a complex situation, process, or relationship, you can help others understand the subject more thoroughly. Your purpose is usually informative, although you also in a sense intend to persuade the reader that your analysis is insightful.

- *Rhetorical situation:* In an analysis, you break down your subject into parts or categories to help your reader understand it more clearly.

- *Writer's voice and tone:* When you write an analysis, you are trying to give readers a better understanding of something. You need to be detailed and thorough, but you should avoid an all-knowing attitude that might be interpreted as arrogant.

- *Context, medium, and genre:* You will need to decide on the best medium and genre to use to present your analysis to the audience you want to reach. Often, you can use tables, charts, and graphs as well as words to depict an analysis.

Critical Thinking, Reading, and Writing

- *Learning/inquiry:* By reading and writing analytically, you gain a deeper understanding of issues and the ability to make more informed decisions. This kind of thinking will help you avoid easy answers to complex issues.

- *Responsibility:* Effective analysis leads naturally to critical thinking. When you engage in analysis, you see the nuances of all the potential relationships involved in your subject.

- *Reading and research:* Analysis can involve close observation as well as interviews and online and library research.

Chapter 7

Writing Processes

- *Invention:* Various invention activities—brainstorming, listing, clustering—can help you consider the parts of your subject and how they relate to one another. The writing-to-learn strategies from Chapter 3 can also help you explore your subject.

- *Organizing your ideas and details:* If your subject is large, you might break it down into more understandable parts, or you might begin with individual parts and examine each one in detail. You will need to make sure that the individual pieces of information you are analyzing are presented clearly and logically.

- *Revising:* You will need to read your work with a critical eye, to make certain that it fulfills the assignment and displays the qualities of good analytical writing.

- *Working with peers:* Listen to your classmates to make sure that they understand your analysis. What do they say about how well your details justify your conclusion?

Conventions

- *Editing:* Wordiness can be a problem in any kind of writing. The round-robin activity on page 180 will help you check your analysis for wordy sentences.

- *Genres for analytical writing:* Usually analyses are written as formal documents (as opposed to, say, a letter that might be intended to inform a reader), so most times your analysis will be a formal report or an academic essay.

- *Documentation:* If you have relied on sources outside of your own experience, you will need to cite them using the appropriate documentation style.

What are you afraid of?

Writing to Analyze

To get a clearer understanding of a subject such as the irrational fear of spiders or snakes that many people suffer from, scientists need to analyze it, to break it down. An **analysis** examines an issue or topic by identifying the parts that make up the whole. You can gain a much clearer understanding of your subject when you look closely at the individual pieces that constitute the whole. Perhaps you have read an analysis of a current news story in a magazine such as *Time* or *US News and World Report.* Maybe you've heard a film critic analyzing the trends in summer movies, or read an analysis of a provocative new advertising campaign that started with a controversial ad first run during the Super Bowl. An analysis of a *phobia,* defined as an uncontrollable (and sometimes irrational) fear of some situation, object, or activity, would require you to examine the various aspects of that phobia.

While psychologists analyze subjects such as phobias to understand mental processes better and, perhaps, bring unwanted anxieties under control, analysis can also be a helpful tool in your everyday life. You have probably analyzed the college you are currently attending: examining its catalog to consider the variety of courses offered, perhaps reading through faculty lists to consider who you might be able to study with, and considering other factors. Likewise, using analysis in your writing can help you come to a deeper understanding of your subjects and share that understanding with your readers.

Rhetorical Knowledge

When you write an analysis, you need to consider how it will help your readers understand your topic in a new way and why you want them to gain this understanding. You will also need to decide what medium and genre will help you get your analysis across to your audience most effectively.

Writing to Analyze in Your College Classes

Much of the writing and thinking you will be asked to do in college will be analytical. Although academic disciplines vary widely, all of them use the process of analysis because when you analyze something, you almost always come to a more complete understanding of that idea or item.

In your college career, you may be asked to construct written analyses in many of your classes:

- In a chemistry class, you might be asked to break down an unknown compound to find what elements are present and write a lab report on your findings.
- In a business class, you might analyze whether a certain corporation's stock is a safe investment by investigating such factors as its market share, earnings statements, track record in the field, and potential for growth.
- In a literature class, you might be asked to analyze how an author develops the hero of a novel to be a sympathetic character.
- In an American history class, you may analyze what political circumstances led to the ratification of an amendment to the U.S. Constitution.

The work needed to perform an analysis usually requires you to make close observations or conduct research so you will have a command of your subject. Writing an analysis also forces you to put your understanding of that subject into your own words. Whenever you express something in your own way, you automatically learn more effectively.

Writing to Analyze for Life

In the professional, civic, and personal areas of your life, you also will construct analyses of various ideas, products, and situations.

The kind of analytical writing you do in your **professional life** will depend on your career, yet the odds are that at some point you will be asked to do an analysis and write a report on your findings. For example, an attorney analyzes legal rulings, the strengths and weaknesses of a client's case, and the arguments presented in court. A physician analyzes her patient's symptoms as she attempts to diagnose the illness and prescribe a cure. The list of possibilities is endless, but it's clear the quality of your analytical thinking and writing will influence your ultimate success.

All too often our first impulse in our **civic life** is emotional. You may get angry when the city council decides to demolish an old building, or you might enthusiastically support a local developer's plan to buy unused farmland. Despite your personal feelings on the issues, your voice will be taken much more seriously if you engage in a balanced, in-depth analysis.

Interestingly, in our **personal lives,** we often tend to analyze events or conversations after they have happened, determining what was useful, what was a problem, and what we might do the next time. You may have had a conversation with a close friend that left both of you feeling unhappy. After the encounter, you replay the conversation in your mind, trying to take apart what was said by whom and figure out what went wrong. You may then write a note to the other person, explaining your analysis of the situation and what you propose to do to make amends.

Scenarios for Writing: Assignment Options

Your instructor may ask you to complete one or both of the following analytical writing assignments. Each assignment is in the form of a *scenario*, a situation that provides some context for the analysis you will construct. The scenarios are designed to provide a sense of who your audience is and what you want to accomplish with your analytical writing, including your purpose; voice, tone, and point of view; context; and genre.

Starting on page 172, you will find guidelines for completing the assignment option that you choose or that is assigned to you. Additional scenarios for college and life may be found online.

Writing for College

SCENARIO 1   Analyzing a Subject That Matters to You

This scenario asks you to construct an analysis of a subject from any area of your academic life. Choose a complex subject that you would like to look at in depth and about which you think you have insights to offer.

Writing Assignment: Think of something that functions effectively. Possibilities include a championship sports team, a successful business, an effective charitable organization, or a popular TV show. Analyze the topic you selected by breaking down its components, describing and explaining what they are and how they function, outlining how each piece works in conjunction with the others, and offering insights into the subject. Your analysis should be for a course in the subject area to which the topic belongs; for example, you would analyze a championship sports team for a physical education course or a successful business for a business administration course.

Writing for Life

SCENARIO 2   Professional Writing: A Business Report
Analyzing Part of Your Future Career

Think forward to the day when you are ready to apply for jobs in your chosen field. Select an image or advertisement related to your future career—the position you plan to seek after you graduate from college. You might select the following, for example:

- A movie advertisement, if you are planning to work as an actor, director, screenwriter, or another role in the film industry
- An advertisement for a product produced by or a service provided by the company you hope to work for
- An image from a company's annual report
- A company's logo
- A Web page from a nonprofit or government agency for which you hope to work

Writing Assignment: For this writing project, analyze the image or advertisement that you selected. Your task is not to evaluate the image or advertisement, but rather to analyze its various aspects (color, point of view, text, size, shading) to understand how the image or advertisement works.

Rhetorical Considerations in Analytical Writing

Audience: Although your teacher and classmates are your initial audience for your analysis, also consider a wider audience. What kinds of analysis will be most interesting to this group of readers?

Purpose: By researching and analyzing the problem, issue, concept, options, or object, you will be providing your readers with an analysis that will allow them to make more informed decisions.

Voice, Tone, and Point of View: You have probably chosen your topic because you have a personal interest in the subject. What preconceptions do you have? How can you avoid letting them oversimplify your analysis? How can you use voice and tone to establish credibility, so your readers believe your analysis?

Context, Medium, and Genre: Keeping the context of the assignment in mind, decide on a medium and a genre for your writing. How will your analysis be used? Who might be interested in reading your analysis? If you are writing for an audience beyond the classroom, consider what will be the most effective way to present your analysis to this audience.

For more on choosing a medium and genre, see Chapter 15 and Appendix C.

Critical Thinking, Reading, and Writing

Before you begin to write your analysis, consider the qualities of successful analytic writing. It also helps to read one or more examples of analysis to see these qualities in action. Finally, you might consider how visuals can add to an analysis, as well as the kinds of sources you will need to consult.

As we have seen, effective analytical writing focuses on a complex subject, thoroughly explains the parts of that subject and their relationship to one another, and is almost always based on research rather than on personal experience. An analysis is usually focused and straightforward, with insights and a conclusion that ties the aspects of your subject together for readers.

Learning the Qualities of Effective Analytical Writing

An effective analysis will help you and your readers better understand your subject. To accomplish this, you need to make sure your analysis includes the following qualities:

- **A focus on a complex subject.** Any subject worth analyzing—a political position, a book, a war strategy—will be complex (if it were not complex, you would not need to analyze it). It will consist of many parts or features, and these parts will interact with one another in complicated ways.

- **A thorough explanation of the parts and how they relate to one another.** An effective analysis identifies and explains the parts of a subject in sufficient detail and builds the foundation for your analysis. Your first step will be to identify the component parts or aspects of your subject and then consider how those component parts function separately and together. For a subject such as a new school tax bond, you might consider aspects like the following:
  - Benefits
    - to the students
    - to the local tax base
    - to the teachers, administration, and support staff

- Problems and costs
  - costs in the form of debt that will need to be paid off
  - interest charges
- What happens if the community does not fund the schools in this way?
  - Will school taxes need to be raised?
  - Will the quality of the school suffer?

After you have identified the parts or aspects of your subject, you need to gain a thorough understanding of each one so that you can explain it to your readers.

- **Research-based rather than personal-based writing.** With the exception of an informal analysis of a subject you know well, such as an analysis of a film or restaurant for a friend or family member, a formal analysis usually requires research. Your understanding of the subject is seldom enough to inform a thorough analysis. If you were analyzing the bond proposal, for example, you would need to read the entire proposal, interview the officials or citizen groups behind it, and examine recent school budgets.

For more on conducting research, see Chapters 19 and 20.

- **A focused, straightforward presentation.** An effective analysis focuses on the subject's component parts, always working to show how they combine to make up the whole subject. All aspects of your text must focus on some central theme or idea that connects all parts or aspects of the analysis together.

  Like an informative text, an analysis is usually neutral in tone—the writer's primary purpose is not to persuade, but rather to explain how the writer's subject functions.

- **Insights.** The purpose of analysis is to provide more meaningful insights into a topic or an issue. Taking something apart (even metaphorically) to analyze it provides insights into how each part functions, how each aspect relates to every other aspect and to the whole.

- **A conclusion that ties parts together.** Any writing project needs to reach a conclusion, but for an analysis a thoughtful conclusion is critical. In an analysis your conclusion does much more than just state your major claim (as a *thesis statement* usually does). While your paper serves to explain each aspect of the subject you are analyzing, in your conclusion you have the opportunity to outline how those parts function together and also to explain whether you believe that those parts function together effectively or not.

For more on thesis statements, see Chapter 13.

In a computer file, you might summarize each quality of an effective analysis in your own words, and then refer to that summary as you conduct research and write your paper.

A WRITER'S RESPONSIBILITIES

Constructing Analytical Writing in the Sciences

Effective analytical writing is thorough, examining and explaining as many details as possible. If you are working in a field that has particular procedures in place, you have an obligation to follow the accepted procedures faithfully. Scientists must follow specific procedures and policies in order for their experiments to be considered valid, for example. If you are working in a scientific field, you will need to document everything you do—from taking notes on your process, to constructing drawings that illustrate the process, to verifying measurements with specific instruments. You also must clearly and accurately present any statistical data, with all supporting evidence and detail, and you must explain relationships between variables in your experiment.

To construct an effective scientific analysis, you may be expected to follow the four-step *scientific method*:

1. You observe and describe a phenomenon or group of phenomena.
2. You formulate a hypothesis to explain the phenomena. In physics, for example, the hypothesis often proposes a cause for the phenomenon.
3. You then use your hypothesis to predict the existence of other phenomena or to predict quantitatively the results of new observations.
4. You and other independent researchers test your predictions by conducting experiments.

Source: The four steps are adapted from Frank Wolfs. "Appendix E: Introduction to the Scientific Method." http://teacher.nsrl.rochester.edu/phy_labs/AppendixE/AppendixE.html. Downloaded 12/13/03.

Reading, Inquiry, and Research: Learning from Texts That Analyze

The reading selections that follow are examples of analytical writing. As you read the texts, ask yourself the following questions:

- What makes this analysis effective? What might I point to in the reading selection that helps me understand the analysis?

- What qualities of an effective analysis (see pp. 161–62) does the reading selection exhibit?

- What parts of the analysis still leave me with questions?

- How can I use these analytical techniques in my writing?

Thinking Rhetorically

Keep in mind the following questions as you read the essays that follow. Make it a practice to ask yourself these questions in all your reading—personal, academic, and professional—and you will strengthen and sharpen your abilities as a reader and as a writer.

Rhetorical Knowledge: The Writer's Situation and Rhetoric

- *Audience:* Who is the primary audience for this piece of writing? How effectively does the author understand and reach his or her audience? What can you point to in the essay that supports your claim? Who else might be interested in reading this analysis?
- *Purpose:* What is the author's primary purpose in writing this analysis?
- *Voice and tone:* What is the author's tone in his or her analysis? What does it contribute to the author's credibility?
- *Responsibility:* What can you cite from the essay to show how the author fulfills his or her responsibility to accurately present the subject?
- *Context and format:* How effectively has the author organized his or her analysis? How might the inclusion of visuals, such as tables, charts, photos, and graphs, have made the analysis more clear?

JAMES M. LANG

Putting In the Hours

James M. Lang is a public speaker, workshop leader, and assistant professor of English at Assumption College. Essays from his regular column for the *Chronicle of Higher Education* about life on the tenure track were compiled into the book *Life on the Tenure Track: Lessons from the First Year* (2005). Lang is also the author of *Learning Sickness: A Year with Crohn's Disease* (2004). This essay was originally published on May 16, 2003, as part of Lang's column in the *Chronicle*.

Most casual observers of the North American professor assume his   1
natural habitat to be the classroom, where he engages in those behaviors commonly associated with his species: speaking to audiences of young people in a loud voice, marking with writing utensils on green or white boards, receiving and distributing pieces of paper.

But the casual observer may overlook that this species usually   2
spends an equal, if not greater, part of his week in his den, holding what

his institution terms "office hours." At small, liberal-arts colleges in New England, like the one where our observations have been centered, he and his colleagues are, in fact, required to hold 10 office hours each week—time set aside for advisees and students who want to consult with the professor outside of the normal classroom hours.

Working our way up and down the halls of one faculty office building, checking out the office-hour schedules posted below the nameplates, and observing the work and leisure habits of these specimens through their half-opened doors, we have been able to classify, according to their office-hour behavior, some subspecies of the North American professor. 3

The Early Bird: Whether he actually likes mornings or not, the Early Bird schedules all of his office hours before 10 a.m.—in other words, before most of his students have rolled out of bed. The Early Bird can be assured that he will have fewer office visits than his next-door neighbor, who has scheduled all of her hours after noon. 4

The Early Bird has done nothing technically wrong, of course; he probably keeps his office hours more regularly than most faculty members. But the Early Bird also knows exactly what he is doing. He doesn't particularly want students visiting during office hours, and he has found the best legal means of ensuring that they don't. 5

The Door Closer: The Door Closer knows that students are far more likely to knock on an open door than a closed one, so he wards off all but the most desperate and devoted of his students by keeping his door completely shut during office hours. For extra effect, he will lock it, forcing students to realize that they are interrupting him by compelling him to walk to the door and open it. 6

We have actually observed students walk up to a professor's office, see the door closed, and walk away dispirited—only to watch the office's occupant emerge moments later, heading to the departmental office for a coffee refill. Like the Early Bird, the Door Closer has not violated the letter of his contract; he relies instead upon simple and subtle discouragement. 7

The Counselor: The Door Closer's antithesis, the Counselor props his door open as wide as it will allow, faces his desk towards the doorway, and peeks out expectantly at every passing footfall. The Counselor wants students to visit him in his office. The Counselor wants to know how they're doing. The students actually divulge this information to the Counselor: They tell him about their roommates, and their relationships, and their home lives. The Counselor loves it. 8

Other faculty members are baffled by the Counselor, and slightly suspicious of him. They suspect—and they are probably right—that their own names come up occasionally in the Counselor's office, and that the Counselor listens to student complaints about them with a sympathetic ear. 9

The Chatterer: Chatterers, whether they want students in their office   10
or not, like to spend their office hours socializing. They stop in to visit
other colleagues who are having office hours, they linger in the departmental office to check their mail or fill their coffee mug, and they welcome long lines at the copy machine. As a rule, nonchattering faculty
members tend to appreciate Chatterers most at paper-grading time,
when frequent interruptions to their work are happily tolerated. When
they are trying to prepare for a class they have to teach in 30 minutes,
the average faculty member sees his Chattering neighbor as a nuisance.

Most Chatterers are people who simply like to talk, and practice   11
their chatting habits in other realms of their lives as incessantly as they
do at the office.

We have noticed a subspecies of Chatterers, though: people who   12
live by themselves, especially those newly arrived at the college, without much of a social network outside the campus. For this species, the
time they spend in the office provides them with their primary socializing opportunity. Back in their apartments, it's a book or the television.
During office hours they get to communicate with other members of
their species.

The Fugitive: The counterpart to the lonely Chatterer, the Fugitive   13
has a houseful of living creatures—spouses, children, dogs, cats, her-
mit crabs—and sees the office as his refuge from the chaos that constantly threatens to overwhelm his home life. Fugitives can best be
recognized by their relaxed attitude during office hours. However much
work they have to do at the office, it can't be any more stressful than
what they have to deal with at home. Fugitives usually have at least
one extremely comfortable chair in their office, and can occasionally
be spotted sitting in that chair and staring off into space, just enjoying
the peace and quiet.

In the interests of scientific objectivity, we should disclose that the   14
author of this paper is a Fugitive.

He has a recliner purchased from the Salvation Army, and the most   15
relaxing part of his day are those moments when he can balance a cup
of tea on the armrest, kick off his shoes, and read the material he has
assigned for class. He has a little refrigerator in his office, and he has
expressed his desire to install a television/VCR as well.

"If you ever kick me out," he has been known to remark to his wife,   16
with just a hint of hopefulness, when he has all three kids in the tub and
the phone and the doorbell are ringing and the cats are scratching at the
door, "I'll be able to move right into my office."

"Don't get your hopes up," she has been known to respond.   17

But the truth of the matter is, he is not always or exclusively a Fugitive. Sometimes he engages in behaviors associated with the Chatterer, and the Door Closer, and sometimes the Early Bird too (he draws the line at the Counselor—much as he loves his students, he does not want to hear about their latest relationship problems). 18

He holds one office hour on Friday morning from 8:30 to 9:30 a.m., before his first class. In an entire semester, he has had one visitor during that office hour, and she came under extreme duress, when all other options were exhausted. He counts three Chatterers in his department among his closest friends, so he often welcomes the opportunity to talk with them, even occasionally instigating such conversations. And he will close his door when he is having one of those weeks when the paper stack never seems to diminish, no matter how many he grades. So we have begun to suspect that these observations are perhaps more appropriately classified as behaviors rather than subspecies types. 19

Most North American professors do have a dominant behavior that characterizes their office-hour activity, but most also engage in multiple behaviors in the course of a single week. 20

Given the early and exploratory nature of these observations, we would welcome notes from fellow field researchers who have studied the office-hour habits of the North American professor, and have observed other forms of both common and unusual behaviors. 21

QUESTIONS FOR WRITING AND DISCUSSION: LEARNING OUTCOMES

Critical Thinking: Responding to the Writer's Ideas

1. What is your initial reaction to Lang's analysis? Do you find it humorous? Why?

2. How accurate are Lang's categories and sub-categories? Why? How much do you agree with his analysis? Why?

Composing Processes and Knowledge of Conventions: The Writer's Strategies

1. Consider Lang's overall organization by making a sentence or scratch outline of it (outline the text by writing, in one sentence, what each

paragraph has to say). How effective is his organization? Why? In what other way(s) might this essay be organized?

2. Lang starts his essay with this line: "Most casual observers of the North American professor assume his natural habitat to be the classroom . . ." (paragraph 1). What effect does Lang have by making his essay sound like an animal observation?

Inquiry and Research: Ideas for Further Exploration

1. Visit two of your professors in their offices. How do they compare to Lang's professors? Be specific in your description.

TAMARA DRAUT

All Work and No Play

Tamara Draut is the director of the Economic Opportunity Program at Demos, a public policy center. She has written widely on economic security, and her op-ed pieces frequently appear in major newspapers. She is also a frequent guest commentator on television and radio talk shows. The following selection is an excerpt from her book *Strapped: Why America's 20- and 30-Somethings Can't Get Ahead* (2006).

In the fall of 1997, Shaney, who is now 27, enrolled in the University of Arkansas. She chose the state college because it was close to home and the nearby private colleges were financially out of the question. Shaney's excellent grades in school scored her a $10,000 scholarship to help cover the cost of tuition for four years. The scholarship was an enormous relief for Shaney and her family. Neither of her parents had gone to college and they couldn't offer any financial support for her studies. With tuition covered by the scholarship, Shaney was confident she could earn enough for room and board through part-time jobs. She opted out of living in the dorms, choosing instead to get an apartment with a friend from high school.

Shaney worked a lot of hours during school, holding down two or three jobs at all times. During summers, Shaney was unable to capitalize on internship opportunities that would have helped her gain better work experience because the pay was too low and she had to continue to earn.

She waited tables instead, trying to save as much money as she could before school started again in the fall. She regrets not being able to accept an internship that would have helped her build more impressive and relevant experience for her résumé.

Shaney's college days were a far cry from the keg parties and dorm room shenanigans that dominate our popular conception of college. Tuition increases made her scholarship money run out sooner than expected. Because Shaney was a French major, she opted to study abroad in France for a year, which she paid for with student loans. She also took out loans to deal with tuition increases. All told, Shaney left school with $25,000 in student loans. After working two or three jobs for the last four years, Shaney was looking forward to being done with school and having a regular nine-to-five job and her nights once again free.

For all of Shaney's hard work, she graduated into one of the worst job markets in recent history and has yet to find a job. Staring down the barrel of $25,000 in loans, Shaney is understandably worried about her financial future. She's begun to question the value of going to college and finds herself wondering whether it wasn't all a waste of time.

Stress-filled college days like Shaney's are much more common than they were twenty or thirty years ago. Full-time on-campus students work more hours at paying jobs while in college than did students in the 1970s or 1980s. According to an analysis of U.S. Department of Education survey data, today three quarters of full-time college students are holding down jobs. Like Shaney, nearly half of them work twenty-five hours or more a week. Working while going to school isn't inherently a bad thing—in fact, some studies show that working on-campus for fifteen hours or less per week can help foster better academic performance. On-campus jobs, which are often work-study slots, provide a chance for students to deepen their connections to the campus through contact with other students, faculty, and staff. The problem is that more and more students are working off-campus at multiple jobs and for longer hours. Students who work twenty-five hours or more a week are much more likely to report that work affected their grades and interfered with their class schedule. Grades suffer as studying time declines and so does the free time to participate in academic clubs and social activities.

Not everyone can handle the added stress of long work hours on top of college. Too often students give up under the pressure. As anyone who has made it past their first two years of college can attest, the second half is when college becomes really interesting; it's the whole four-year package that provides the analytical, problem-solving, and writing skills that distinguish a bachelor's degree from an associate's degree. But when an 18-year-old is borrowing $8,000 or more a year and working twenty-five hours a week to pay for college, it changes the equation. Under these conditions, a boring class is no longer just a snooze fest—it's an extremely *expensive* snooze fest. It's not surprising that under a debt-for-diploma and work till you drop environment, one third of students drop out after their first year of college. And first-generation college students are almost twice as likely as students with college-educated parents to drop out before their second year.

This is why the percentage of students who actually earn their bachelor's degree hasn't risen nearly as fast as enrollments would suggest. Just over half (53 percent) of all students who enroll in four-year colleges end up getting their bachelor's degrees within five years. Not surprisingly, there are wide disparities by class and race in who completes college. Within five years of entering college, 40 percent of students from the top socioeconomic quartile (25 percent) will earn a four-year degree as compared to only 6 percent of students in the lowest quartile. Over a quarter of white students who enter college will earn a bachelor's degree, whereas only about 15 percent of black and Hispanic college students will complete their degrees.

7

QUESTIONS FOR WRITING AND DISCUSSION: LEARNING OUTCOMES

Critical Thinking: Responding to the Writer's Ideas

1. As a college student, what is your initial reaction to Draut's analysis?
2. What point do you think Draut is trying to make here? What conclusions is Draut drawing from her analysis of the information she is presenting?

Composing Processes and Knowledge of Conventions: The Writer's Strategies

1. Draut begins this piece with an example of one student in financial straits because of student loans. She then generalizes to other groups and shows how financial problems can lead to dropping out. How effective do you find this method—starting with an example of a real person?
2. Draut uses many statistics, which she works into her text. How effective is this strategy?

Inquiry and Research: Ideas for Further Exploration

1. Find out the graduation rate for your college or university. Is your school doing anything to improve it? If so, what? If the problem is primarily financial, what, if anything, can an institution of higher education do to address it?

Thinking about Visuals That Analyze

Often businesses use flowcharts to visually describe how something happens within their company. Such a visual aid not only provides a description of how items, products, ideas, or people move through their business, but also serves as a visual analysis of how things work.

Figure 7.1 is an example of a flowchart showing which aspects of a transaction are "costs" to a particular business and which aspects are "value added."

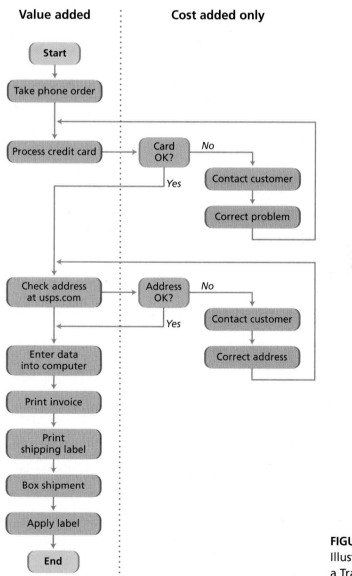

FIGURE 7.1 A Flowchart Illustrating Aspects of a Transaction

As you look at the flowchart, consider these questions about the effective use of flowcharts in analyses:

- How does the flowchart provide information on how things fit together?
- How does it show how the parts of the whole work in an ideal setting? In real settings?
- What does the chart show that would be hard to show with text alone?

Writing Processes

As you work on the assignment you have chosen, remember the qualities of an effective analytical paper, which are listed on pages 161–62. Also remember that writing is recursive—you might start with an invention activity or two and then conduct some research, which leads to more invention work and then a first draft; but then you might need to do more invention work to help flesh out your draft and conduct more research to fill in any gaps in information you spot; and then you will revise your draft and possibly find another gap or two. . . . So while the activities listed below imply that writers go through them step-by-step, the actual process of writing is usually messier.

As you work on your project, make certain that you save your computer files frequently because any work that you don't save could be lost. Also, savvy writers back up their computer files in two or more places—on an internal or external hard drive of the computer, on a USB flash drive, and/or on a rewritable CD or DVD, for example.

For a tip on organizing your computer files, see page 66.

Invention: Getting Started

As with your other writing assignments, the more invention activities you can draw on, the more information you will have available. Try to answer these questions while you do your invention work:

- What do I already know about the subject that I am considering for my analysis?
- What insights do I already have to offer?
- Where might I learn more about the topic I am considering? Should I go to the library, use the Web, interview people, and/or make observations? What verifiable information am I likely to find?
- What do I know about my audience?
- What might my audience already know about my possible topic? How can I make my insights convincing for them?

- What questions do I need to answer before I can begin (and complete) my analysis?

Doing your invention work in electronic form rather than on paper lets you easily use your invention work as you construct a draft.

As with any kind of writing, invention activities improve with peer feedback and suggestions. Consider sharing the invention work you have done so far with several classmates or friends in order to understand your rhetorical situation more clearly and to generate more useful information.

Exploring Your Ideas with Research

Research is critical to any analysis. If you do not examine and consider each aspect of your subject in depth, how can you analyze it? Researching a subject for analysis can include reading books and articles, interviewing those who may know more about subject than you do, conducting searches online, and other means of gathering information. Research materials such as data, figures, statistics, examples, descriptions, images, and testimony can help you explain the different parts or aspects of your subject.

Before you begin your research, consider what your focal point should be. For example, you may want to research how electronic telecommunications such as cell phones and the Internet are helping families to keep in touch more often and to share more information. You may choose to focus on how college students who live away from home are keeping in touch with their parents. Look over your invention work to remind yourself of all that you know about your subject, and the questions you came up with about it. Use the reporter's questions of *who*, *what*, *where*, *when*, *why*, and *how* to get started on your research. After you have decided what information you need, determine what kind of research you need to conduct in order to gather that information, and conduct research in the library and on the Web.

You almost always will get the most useful information for an analysis if you conduct what is called *primary research:* you examine the subject and collect the data yourself. Primary research can include interviewing, field research where you take notes or measurements, making your own direct observations, and surveys.

Use an electronic journal to record images, URLs, interview notes, and other electronic pieces of information that you find as you are conducting your research. Such an e-journal makes it easy for you to add those e-documents once you start drafting your paper.

Reviewing Your Invention and Research

After you have conducted your research, you need to review your invention work and notes and think about the information you have collected from

For more on developing a thesis, See Chapter 13.

outside sources. You may be ready to decide on a working thesis statement—a statement that summarizes the main point of your analysis—at this point. Even though you might already have a general idea of the conclusion your analysis is leading you to, until you get some of your ideas and research on paper, it is often hard to know for certain what your thesis will be. Your thesis should come *from* your analysis. It is helpful to decide on your thesis when you have done a lot of invention work (listing, brainstorming, clustering, for example) and research. You might even wait until after you construct your first draft.

Organizing Your Information

Once you have some sense of what your analysis will include, you need to consider how you might organize this material. The questions that you need to ask yourself when deciding on your organization are all rhetorical:

- Who is your audience?
- Why might they be interested in your analysis, or how you can make them interested in it? (One way to emphasize the importance of your analysis to your audience is to show them why they need to understand your subject.)
- What is your purpose for writing—that is, why do your readers need this analysis?
- What is the most important aspect of your subject?

For more on classification and cause-and-effect, see Chapter 13.

The answers to these questions can help you decide on what you need to emphasize, which in turn will help you choose an organization.

Here are three organizational structures that you might consider for your analytical paper.

Options for Organization

Defining Parts	Classification	Relating Causes and Effects
• Explain why the subject you are analyzing is important to your readers. • Provide examples of how readers might be affected by the subject. • Provide background information, so readers can see the whole subject of your analysis.	• Start with a question about your subject that readers probably do not know the answer to. • Explain why knowing the answer to this question will benefit your readers. • Using the writing strategy of *classification* to explain your subject, label and explain each aspect or part.	• Begin with information about your subject that may surprise your readers. • Explain how an analysis of your subject will lead to more surprises and better understanding. • Use the writing strategy of *cause-and-effect* to show how each aspect or part of your subject causes or is affected by the other aspects or parts.

- Use a strategy of description to explain each aspect or part of your subject.

- Provide examples to show what you mean.

- Conclude by showing how each aspect or part works together.

- Provide specific examples to illustrate each category.

- Conclude by showing how the aspects or parts function together to make up the whole of your subject.

- Provide specific examples to show what you mean.

- Conclude by outlining how parts of your subject function together.

Constructing a Complete Draft

Once you have chosen the most effective organizational approach, you are ready to construct the rest of your draft. Consider how you might use the invention materials you have generated and how you might integrate the research information you have gathered.

As you write your first draft, remember the main point that you are trying to make (if you have decided on one). In an analysis, you will want to make sure that your discussion of the parts or aspects of your subject helps to support what it is that you are trying to say about the whole.

There are many ways to write a first draft. It may seem to make the most sense to you to start at the first sentence and then move to the end; however, many writers, once they are comfortable with their organization, write individual pieces of their draft and then put them all together.

Introduction: Regardless of the organizational approach that you have chosen, you need to begin with a strong introduction that captures your readers' attention and introduces the subject you are analyzing. To accomplish these two goals in an introduction, you might use one of the following strategies:

- *Explain (briefly) why an analysis of your subject might be of interest.* In "Putting In the Hours" (p. 164), James Lang suggests that it might be interesting to consider the behavior of his subject, the North American college professor.

- *Provide a brief outline of what most people know about your subject.*

- *Explain (briefly) why your analysis is important.* Just as Tamara Draut does in "All Work and No Play" (p. 168), you may want to look at how the problem affects one person and then generalize to show how it affects many people.

- *Provide a fact about the subject you are analyzing that will surprise or concern your readers.*

Body: You can use various writing strategies to effectively analyze your subject:

- *Classify and label each aspect of your subject.* In "Putting In the Hours" (p. 164), James Lang organizes his descriptions of professors and their offices by labeling them: the "Early Bird," the "Door Closer," the "Chatterer," and so on. He then describes each type.

- *Define the various parts of your subject—explaining what each is and how it relates to the other parts.* If you were to analyze a PDA (personal digital assistant, sometimes called a "Smartphone"), for example, you would probably focus on its features: operating system, software, phone, memory, processor speed.
- *Compare and contrast each aspect of your subject, so readers can see the differences and similarities.* For instance, you might compare the functional features of two PDAs.
- *Focus on the cause-and-effect relationship of each aspect of your subject,* to show how one aspect causes, or is caused by, one or more other aspects. This approach would work well if you were analyzing a complex machine such as a car or an airplane.

For more on classification, definition, comparison and contrast, and causal analysis, see Chapter 13.

Conclusion: In your conclusion, review the major parts or aspects of your subject, explaining the following:

- How they relate to one another
- How they function together
- How all of the aspects of your subject lead to the conclusion you have reached

Title: As you compose your analysis, a title may emerge, but often it will not occur to you until late in the process. Because an analysis is by definition complex, you are probably not going to be able to summarize your main ideas in your title, but it should be something that catches your readers' attention and makes them want to read your essay.

VISUALIZING VARIATIONS

Using Charts and Graphs to Make Your Analysis Clear

You might discover that an effective way to show your analysis is by the means of a chart or graph such as a flowchart (see p. 171), a pie chart, a bar graph, or a line graph. For example, the data below focus on the changes in tuition costs at a fictional college, in percentages, between 2004 and 2008:

Changes in Tuition, 2004–2008

	Our college	Other colleges
2004	4.00%	5.60%
2005	6.50%	7.70%
2006	4.70%	5.00%
2007	3.70%	6.10%
2008	5.20%	7.10%

If you wanted to show these data in a graph, you could present it in several ways. A line graph would look like this:

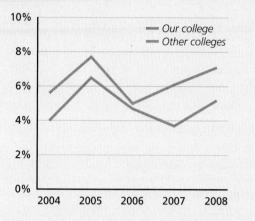

If you displayed the same data in a bar graph, it would look like this:

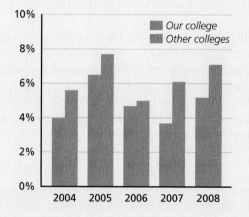

- What type of chart or graph best shows and explains how your college's tuition has changed in relation to other colleges' tuition? Why?

- How would it affect your audience's understanding if you used more than one kind of chart or graph in your analysis?

TechNote If you are working with numbers and statistical information for your analysis, consider putting them into an Excel document. The Excel program can automatically convert your data into a table or graph.

Revising

Many writers find that it is useful to let their work "sit" for a period of time—to put it aside for a day or two and then revise it. Taking a break lets them come back to their paper as if they are seeing it for the first time. When you approach your work this way, you will find it easier to notice parts that are not explained in enough detail, or examples that are confusing, or places where an illustration or graph might show what you mean more clearly than the text does.

As you revise your early drafts, hold off on doing a lot of heavy editing. When you revise you will probably change the content and structure of your paper, so time spent working to fix problems with sentence style or grammar, punctuation, or mechanics at this stage is often wasted.

When you reread the first draft of your analysis, here are some questions to ask yourself:

- What else might my audience want or need to know about my subject?
- How else might I interest my audience in my analysis of this subject?
- What did I find out about my subject that I did not include in my paper? (Effective research always results in more information than you can include, so consider what you left out that you might include in your next draft.)
- Have I clearly explained any terms my readers might not know?
- Could some aspects of my analysis be better presented as a graph or chart?

Technology can help you revise and edit your writing more easily. Use your word processor's track-changes tool to try out revisions and editing changes. After you have had time to think about the possible changes, you can "accept" or "reject" them. Also, you can use your word processor's comment tool to write reminders to yourself when you get stuck with a revision or some editing task.

Because it is so difficult to see emerging writing with a fresh eye (even for experienced writers), it is almost always useful to ask classmates, friends, or family members to read drafts of your papers and comment on them.

WRITER'S WORKSHOP

Responding to Full Drafts

As you read and respond to your classmates' papers (and as they comment on yours), focus on the analytical nature of this assignment, but from a reader's perspective. Be sure to ask questions of their writing and respond to their ideas by exploring your reactions and responses to their thoughts.

Working in pairs or groups of three, read one another's papers, and then offer your classmates comments that will help them see their papers' strengths as well as places where they need to develop their ideas further. Use the following guidelines and questions to guide your responses to the writer's draft:

- In a paragraph, comment on your first impression of this draft. How effectively does the title draw you into the paper? Why?

- Indicate what you like about the draft—that is, provide positive and encouraging feedback to the writer.

- Comment specifically on the introduction: What is effective about it? What suggestions can you make on how to improve the introduction?

- How well do you understand what the author is trying to do in this paper? How well does the writer stay on track? Does the paper wander a bit? Where? What questions are left unanswered?

- How has the writer demonstrated an awareness of readers' knowledge, needs, and/or expectations for the analysis?

- Comment on how effective you found this paper to be as an analysis. How has the writer covered—or failed to cover—all of the parts or aspects of the subject adequately? What *other* aspects of the subject should be included? That is, what did the author miss in this analysis that would help you better understand the subject?

- What is your opinion of the author's insight into the subject? How meaningful is it? Does it pass the "so what?" test?

- What do you think is the author's thesis or main claim for the analysis? How could it be expressed or supported more effectively?

- In the main part of the paper, are there parts that are confusing or concepts that are unclear? Where would you like more details or examples to help you see what the author means?

- Comment on the writer's tone. Is it straightforward and neutral?

- How accurate and appropriate is the supporting evidence? Point out any questionable statistics, inaccurate facts, or questionable authorities. How clearly does the author indicate the sources for statistics and other supporting information?

- Reread the conclusion. How well does it tie everything together?

- If there are visual aspects of the document, comment on how effectively they illustrate the point being made.

- In another paragraph, outline what you see as the main weaknesses of this paper—and suggest how the writer might improve the text.

Responding to Readers' Comments

Once they have received feedback from peers, teachers, and others, writers have to decide how to deal with those comments and suggestions. It is important to consider carefully what your readers are saying to you. You may decide to reject some comments, of course, because they are not consistent with your goals for your paper. For example, some readers may disagree with your point of view or conclusion. You may find that comments from more than one reader contradict each other. In that case, you need to use your own judgment to decide which reader's comments are on the right track.

Knowledge of Conventions

When effective writers edit their work, they attend to the conventions that will help readers—the table manners of writing. These include genre conventions, documentation, format, usage, grammar, punctuation, and mechanics. By attending to these conventions in your writing, you make reading a more pleasant experience for readers.

Editing

The last task in any writing project is editing—the final polishing of your document. When you edit and polish your writing, you make changes to your sentence structure and word choice to improve your style and to make your writing clearer and more concise. You also check your work to make sure it adheres to conventions of grammar, usage, punctuation, mechanics, and spelling. Use the spell-check function of your word-processing program, but be sure to double-check your spelling personally. If you have used sources in your paper, you should make sure you are following the documentation style your instructor requires.

See Chapter 20 for more on documenting sources.

As with overall revision of your work, this final editing and polishing is most effective if you can put your text aside for a period of time and come back to it with fresh eyes. Because checking conventions is easier said than done, though, we strongly recommend that you ask classmates, friends, and tutors to read your work to find editing problems that you may not see.

To assist you with editing, we offer here a round-robin editing activity focused on finding and correcting problems with wordy sentences, a constant challenge for many writers.

WRITER'S WORKSHOP

Round-Robin Editing with a Focus on Wordiness

Wordiness—using more words than necessary—is a common concern for writers and their readers. Wordy sentences take longer to read, and having a large number of them in your paper will increase your reader's workload and decrease your paper's effectiveness.

Work with two peers to edit one another's papers for wordiness. Ask yourself questions like, "Is the writer repeating herself?" "Has he included phrases that don't add meaning to the sentence?" Circle sentences that can be made more concise and make suggestions on how to tighten them. Compare notes to see if you have any questions about wordiness, and ask your instructor for assistance.

Genres, Documentation, and Format

If you are writing an academic paper, you will need to follow the conventions for the discipline in which you are writing and the requirements of your instructor. On the other hand, if you are constructing a formal business report for Scenario 2, you will need to follow the model for a business analysis report.

If you have used material from outside sources, including visuals, credit those sources, using the documentation style required by the discipline you are working in and by your instructor.

For advice on writing in different genres, see Appendix C. For guidelines for formatting and documenting papers in MLA or APA style, see Chapter 20.

Student Sarah Washington Shares Her Analysis

Student writer Sarah Washington decided to analyze a campus issue. When her instructor mentioned the issue of campus parking, Sarah knew she had found her subject. As you read her essay, "Campus Parking: Love it or Leave It," think about what makes it effective.

SARAH WASHINGTON

Campus Parking: Love It or Leave It

Like many others, I've been frustrated by the parking situation   1
since I first started school here. While talking to other students, I've discovered that we're all not very happy about the parking. It's too expensive, and there are never enough spots. Juniors and Seniors, it's

been this way since they came here. Every year it seems as though the parking fees go up, and every year it seems as though it's harder to find a good parking spot. An analysis of the parking situation on campus will help anyone concerned with parking (and that includes most students) understand how parking "works" at our college. I am focusing my analysis on two aspects of campus parking: the number of spaces, including how many spaces are actually needed, and also the costs for parking on campus, especially compared to what other colleges charge.

Campus Data

When I interviewed Mr. Michael Nguyen, head of Parking and Transit, he gave me the following background information:

> A total of 13,485 students are registered this semester.
> Of those, 4,735 live on campus.
> A total of 2,700 resident students (that is, students who live on campus) have cars.
> There are 512 full-time faculty members; 193 part-time faculty.
> There are 398 staff employees.

Analysis

Looking at the numbers Mr. Nguyen provided, I was able to make the following quick determinations. If everyone drove to campus and needed to be there at the same time, the campus would need 12,913 parking spots (the total of all the faculty, staff, and students who are either non-residential or have cars). That means the university would have to provide close to 13,000 parking spots, or around 5,500 additional spots. This is especially important because, according to Nguyen, the campus presently has 6,100 parking spots.

However, even at 9:00 am on Monday not every one of those 13,000 people will be on campus, and not everyone who is on campus drives. I have friends who live in apartments close enough to campus to allow them to walk to class. And, after talking to Nguyen, I realized that not only are all students not on campus at the same time, but all faculty aren't necessarily on campus at the same time either. In addition, some students, and to a lesser degree, faculty and staff, carpool. All of these variables act to reduce the number of parking spaces really needed on campus. Clearly the severity of the parking problem requires further analysis.

One classmate wrote this comment on Washington's paper:

Interesting introduction, but I'm not sure what the purpose of your paper is. Are you going to try to inform readers of parking problems or persuade us to do something?

Now, Washington clearly indicates what she is trying to accomplish: to analyze the parking situation.

In her earlier draft, Washington got this comment from one of her peer reviewers to this sentence from her first draft: "My initial response was no wonder I always felt I could never find a parking spot."

Also interesting but you have a lot of your personal feelings in your paper. If I understood your paper's purpose I'd know better whether it's appropriate for them to be in it.

In her final version, she has removed her personal comment as she continues to outline the details of her analysis.

Staff surveys done by the Parking Office indicate that 15% of the staff either carpool or use some other means of transportation. Therefore, around 340 spots are necessary to support employees, not counting the faculty. Assuming that, at the busiest time of day, 60% of the full-time faculty and 50% of the part-time faculty need to be on campus, and they all drive their own vehicles and don't carpool, then the campus will need around 410 additional spots.   5

It may be more difficult to determine the real number of spots that students need. However, assuming that at the busiest time of the day 70% of the nonresident students are present on campus, since many students live close enough to walk and are more likely to carpool, 70% of those students will probably need parking. At these times, then, the campus will need approximately 4,500 student spaces—not counting the necessary 2,700 spaces by the resident halls.   6

Therefore, when all of these numbers are added together, it seems that the campus may need in the neighborhood of 7,950 parking spots, or a little more than 61%, of the initial estimate of more than 13,000 spots. The campus really can use some more parking at peak periods, but only around 500 spots—not my initial estimate of 5,500 spots.   7

Parking Costs

This analysis reveals that the college is close to the number of parking spots it needs, but cost is another part of the whole campus parking picture. The cost of parking on our campus—which for students is $200 per semester—does not seem out of line with what other universities cost, except for Iowa State University, which charges students only $45 per year to park ("ISU Proposes Parking Enhancement, Fee Increase").   8

Other schools charge varying amounts:

The University of Georgia: "prime parking" is $360 a year (Stroer).
The University of Texas at Austin: students can park in surface
    lots for $89 a year, but if they live off-campus and want garage
    parking, it runs from $240 to $336 per year ("Spring 2004 Garage
    Student Permit Availability").

Parking costs at our school, it appears, are not out of line with other colleges.   9

Determining how many parking spots are needed on a campus is not an exact science. There are many variables involved and those variables may change from semester to semester. In addition to the raw   10

A classmate asked this question and made this comment on Washington's draft:

Who is "we" here? I'm not sure why you're using "we" so much—sounds strange.

She revised her draft to remove the word *we*, which also helped to make her sentences more concise.

In her first draft, Washington received this comment from a classmate:

Now you're ending, and you're back to the number of parking spaces, without ever explaining what all that information about parking has to do with anything.

Note how she now offers a more effective conclusion to her text.

numbers, I discovered that part of the problem with parking is a result of the desirability of the lots. Everyone wants to be close to where they're going, but that "where" keeps changing. During the morning, students all seem to want to park in the lots closer to the academic buildings where their classes are being held. Later in the day, more vehicles can be found in the lot that serves the student union and the library. Students can help the situation by simply planning their days on campus a little better. For example, if they have classes in the morning and plan on staying on campus for most of the day, they might have a much easier time finding a parking spot over by the library rather than in crowded lots near the classroom buildings. Where parking is concerned, a little strategy can go a long way.

Works Cited

"ISU Proposes Parking Enhancement, Fee Increase." 3 Feb. 2004. <http://www.iastate.edu/~nscentral/releases/2002/jan/parking.shtml>.

Nguyen, Michael. Personal interview. 2 Feb. 2004.

"Spring 2004 Garage Student Permit Availability." 4 Feb. 2004. <http://www.utexas.edu/parking/parking/springStudentPermit.htm>.

Stroer, Joan. "Proposed parking plan drives costs up dramatically." 4 Feb. 2004. <http://www.onlineathens.com/stories/021902/uga_0219020032.shtml>.

QUESTIONS FOR WRITING AND DISCUSSION: LEARNING OUTCOMES

Rhetorical Knowledge: The Writer's Situation and Rhetoric

1. **Audience:** What audience does Washington have in mind for this essay? How can you tell?

2. **Purpose:** An analysis should help readers understand a subject. What can you point to in Washington's paper that indicates her purpose?

3. **Voice and tone:** How would you describe the tone Washington uses in her paper? Would a different tone (more strident, perhaps, or more subdued) have made her analysis more, or less, effective? Why?

4. **Responsibility:** How accurately does Washington represent statistical information? How can you tell? How credible is Washington's analysis? Why?

5. **Context and format:** Washington is writing as a college student concerned about parking on her campus. How does this context affect her use of language, appeals, and evidence in her analysis?

Critical Thinking: Responding to the Writer's Ideas

1. What is your initial response to Washington's analysis? What in her text causes your response?

2. To what extent does Washington's report give you insight into how parking might work at other public places serving large groups of drivers?

Composing Processes and Knowledge of Conventions: The Writer's Strategies

1. Construct a scratch or sentence outline of Washington's analysis (jot down, next to each paragraph, no more than a one-sentence description of what that paragraph contains. You will end up with a brief outline). How effective is her organization? Why?

2. How effectively does Washington use statistics or data to support her claims? What can you cite from her essay to demonstrate your conclusion?

Inquiry and Research: Ideas for Further Exploration

1. At your library find a journal or magazine that covers the area you think you want to major in, and locate an example of an analysis. In no more than two pages, explain why that text is or is not an effective analysis.

Self-Assessment: Reflecting on Your Learning Goals

Now that you have constructed a piece of analytical writing, go back and consider your learning goals, which you and your classmates may have considered at the beginning of this chapter (see pp. 154–55). Write notes on what you have learned from this assignment.

Rhetorical Knowledge

- *Audience:* What have you learned about addressing an audience in analytical writing?

- *Purpose:* What have you learned about the purposes for constructing an analysis?

- *Rhetorical situation:* How did the writing context affect your analytical text? How did your choice of topic affect the research you conducted and how you presented your analysis to your readers? What do you see as the strongest part of your analysis? Why? The weakest? Why?

- *Voice and tone:* How would you describe your voice in this essay? Your tone? How do they contribute to the effectiveness of your analytical essay?

Critical Thinking, Reading, and Writing

- *Learning/inquiry:* Describe the process you went through to focus on a main idea, or thesis. How did you judge what was most and least important in your analysis?
- *Responsibility:* How did you fulfill your responsibility to your readers?
- *Reading and research:* What did you learn about analytical writing from the reading selections you read for this chapter? What research did you conduct? How sufficient was the research you did?
- As a result of writing this analysis, how have you become a more critical thinker, reader, and writer? What skills do you hope to develop further?

Writing Processes

- *Invention:* What invention strategies were most useful to you?
- *Organizing your ideas and details:* What organization did you use? How successful was it?
- *Revising:* What one revision did you make that you are most satisfied with? If you could make an additional revision, what would it be?
- *Working with peers:* How did your instructor or peer readers help you by making comments and suggestions about your writing? How could you have made better use of the comments and suggestions you received?
- Did you use photographs or other visuals to help you explain your analysis to readers? If so, what did you learn about incorporating these elements?
- What "writerly habits" have you developed, modified, or improved on as you constructed the writing assignment for this chapter?

Conventions

- *Editing:* What sentence problem did you find most frequently in your writing? How will you avoid that problem in future assignments?
- *Genre:* What conventions of the genre you were using, if any, gave you problems?
- *Documentation:* Did you use sources for your paper? If so, what documentation style did you use? What problems, if any, did you have with it?

If you are constructing a course portfolio, file your written reflections so that you can return to them when you next work on your portfolio.

3

Using What You Have Learned to Write Arguments

LEARNING GOALS FOR PERSUASIVE WRITING

Rhetorical Knowledge

- *Audience:* When you are writing to convince your readers, your success will depend on how accurately you have analyzed your audience: their knowledge and attitudes toward your topic.

- *Purpose:* A convincing text is meant to persuade readers to accept your point of view, but it can also include an element of action—what you want readers to do once you've convinced them.

- *Rhetorical situation:* Think about all of the factors that affect where you stand in relation to your subject—you (the writer), your readers (the audience), the topic (the issue you are writing about), your purpose (what you wish to accomplish), and the exigency (what is compelling you to write your persuasive essay).

- *Writer's voice and tone:* When you write to persuade, you are trying to convince readers to think or act in a certain way. The tone you use will of course influence how they react to your writing: consider how you want to sound to your readers. If your tone is subdued and natural, will that convince your readers? If you come across as shrill and shouting, will that convince your readers?

- *Context, medium, and genre:* You will need to decide on the best medium and genre to use to present your persuasive essay to the audience you want to reach. Often, you can use photographs, tables, charts, and graphs as well as words to provide evidence that supports your position.

Critical Thinking, Reading, and Writing

- *Learning/inquiry:* Writing to persuade helps you learn the important arguments on all sides of an issue, so such writing deepens your own understanding.

- *Responsibility:* As you prepare to write persuasively, you will naturally begin to think critically about your position on the subject you are writing about, forcing you to examine your initial ideas, based on what you learn through your research. Persuasive writing, then, is a way of learning and growing, not just of presenting information.

- *Reading and research:* You will usually need to conduct interviews and online and library research in order to gather evidence to support the claims you are making in your persuasive writing.

188

Chapter 8

Writing Processes

- *Invention:* Various invention activities such as brainstorming, listing, and clustering can help you consider the arguments that you might use to support your persuasive essay, or the opposing arguments you need to accommodate or refute.

- *Organizing your ideas and details:* Most often, you will state the main point—your thesis—clearly right at the start of your persuasive essay and then present the evidence supporting that point. Other methods of organization are useful, however, depending on your audience and context.

- *Revising:* You will need to read your work with a critical eye, to make certain that it fulfills the assignment and displays the qualities of effective persuasive writing.

- *Working with peers:* Listen to your classmates as they tell you whether or not you have persuaded them, and why. They will give you useful advice on how to make your essay more persuasive and, therefore, more effective.

Conventions

- *Editing:* Citing sources correctly adds authority to your persuasive writing. The round-robin activity on page 216 will help you edit your work to correct problems with your in-text citations and your works-cited or references list.

- *Genres for persuasive writing:* Possible genres include academic essays, editorials, position papers, letters to the editor, newspaper and magazine essays—even e-mails or letters you might send to friends or family members to persuade them about a problem or issue.

- *Documentation:* You will probably need to rely on sources outside of your experience, and, if you are writing an academic essay, you will be required to cite them using the appropriate documentation style.

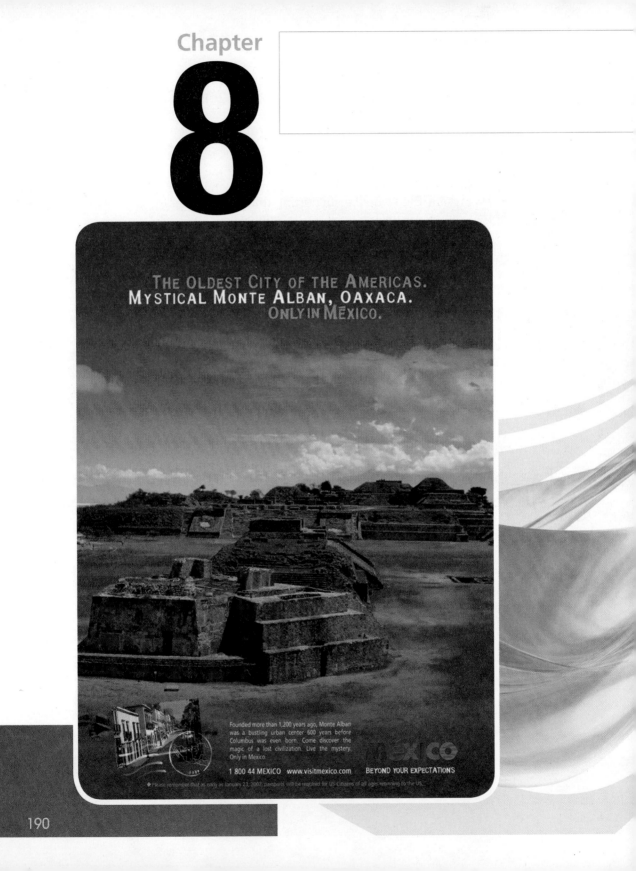

THE OLDEST CITY OF THE AMERICAS.
MYSTICAL MONTE ALBAN, OAXACA.
ONLY IN MEXICO.

Founded more than 1,200 years ago, Monte Alban
was a bustling urban center 600 years before
Columbus was even born. Come discover the
magic of a lost civilization. Live the mystery.
Only in Mexico

1 800 44 MEXICO   www.visitmexico.com   BEYOND YOUR EXPECTATIONS

mexico

◆ Please remember that as early as January 23, 2007, passports will be required for US Citizens of all ages returning to the US.

Writing to Convince

Think of the last time you wrote something. Whether it was a formal academic paper, a letter, or an informal note such as a text message to a friend, your writing was most likely designed to convince someone about something—to persuade your reader that he or she should accept your particular point of view. In fact, most purposes for writing—to inform, to explain, to analyze—to some degree almost always involve persuasion.

You encounter **persuasive writing**—writing designed to convince readers to agree with the writer's position—many times a day. Notice, for example, the persuasive appeals in the advertisement here. The top line noting that Monte Alban is "The oldest city of the Americas" is an ethical appeal because it shows that the ad writers are knowledgeable about the area's history. The same holds true for the details that appear below the photograph. At the same time, these historical details can be considered logical appeals because they are pieces of information. "Live the mystery" is, of course, an emotional appeal, as is the color photograph that showcases the breathtaking beauty of Monte Alban. How effectively does this advertisement convince you to visit this place?

Advertisements, of course, are clearly intended to convince the reader to buy something—a product or service or trip to Mexico. For most of the persuasive writing you will do, you will have a more limited audience than the audience for an advertisement or a newspaper editorial, but the strategies that you will use to assert your point of view and persuade readers are the same.

Rhetorical Knowledge

When you write to persuade, you need to have a specific purpose in mind, a good sense of your audience, and an idea of what might be an effective way to persuade that audience. You need to make a point and provide evidence to support that point, with the goal of persuading your readers to agree with your position.

Writing to Convince in Your College Classes

Many—if not most—of the papers you will be asked to write for your college classes will be persuasive. While your college assignments will often specifically require that you inform or analyze, they will frequently include an element of persuasion. Here are some examples:

- In a literature course, your instructor asks you to write a persuasive essay in which you argue that the concept of the Oedipal complex is appropriate for analyzing Hamlet's behavior.
- Your sociology professor asks you to develop and support a thesis about deviant behavior in prisons.
- Your mechanical engineering professor asks you to argue for or against using a particular material in a specific situation.

Writing to Convince for Life

Although persuasive writing is common in college and university courses, it plays an even larger role in professional, civic, and personal settings. Consider these examples of **professional writing**:

- A product-development team writes a memo to company executives to convince them to manufacture a product it has designed and tested.
- An attorney writes a memo to fellow members of the local bar association, asking them to work *pro bono* (for free) for a specific group.
- A division manager writes an e-mail to convince the human resources manager to hire a particular applicant.

Persuasive writing is also present in **civic settings**. Civic leaders and other participants in the political process—mayors, city council members, school board members, town supervisors, volunteers, and ordinary citizens—are all involved in persuasion. In fact, it is difficult to imagine a political process without persuasion as its major component. For instance, concerned citizens might write to their city council to argue that a streetlight needs to be installed at an intersection where many accidents have occurred.

In **personal settings**, you constantly negotiate with those around you as you make life decisions, often working to convince others that your views and ideas are best.

- You might write to persuade a family member to send you money for tuition.
- You might write to a friend or family member to encourage him or her to have a medical test if that person is having trouble making a decision.

 ## Scenarios for Writing: Assignment Options

Your instructor may ask you to complete one or both of the following assignments that call for persuasive writing. Each of these assignments is in the form of a *scenario*, which gives you a sense of who your audience is and what you need to accomplish with your persuasive writing.

Starting on page 205, you will find guidelines for completing whatever scenario you decide—or are asked to—complete. Additional scenarios for college and life may be found online.

Writing for College

SCENARIO 1 An Academic Argument about a Controversial Issue

What controversial issues have you learned about in other college classes? Here are some possibilities:

- **Political science:** In what ways did the ethical issues some senators and members of the House of Representatives faced immediately before the 2006 election affect the results of that election?
- **Business ethics:** How effective is the threat of criminal punishment in preventing insider trading of stocks?
- **Psychology:** How should the courts use the concept of insanity to determine culpability in criminal cases?

Writing Assignment: Select a controversial issue or problem from one of your classes and compose a paper convincing readers in that class that your position on the issue is valid.

Writing for Life

SCENARIO 2   Civic Writing: An Editorial about a Campus–Community Problem

Every college campus has problems, ranging from scarce parking to overcrowded computer labs to too much vehicle traffic to too little community involvement. Many of these problems, such as too much traffic, extend into the neighborhoods near the campus.

Writing Assignment: Write an editorial for your campus newspaper in which you identify a campus problem that also affects the surrounding community and then persuade your readers that the problem exists and that it needs to be taken seriously. Although you need to do more than simply provide information about the problem (that is an informative paper, covered in Chapter 6), you do not need to suggest detailed solutions to the problem (that is a proposal, covered in Chapter 11). Your goal is to convince your readers that your campus has a serious problem and that this problem has a negative impact on the surrounding neighborhoods.

Rhetorical Considerations for Persuasive Writing

Audience: While your instructor and classmates are your initial audience for this assignment, you should also consider other audiences for your persuasive writing. What would you like them to believe or do? How might they respond to your argument? How might you best convince them?

Purpose: Your main purpose is to make your audience aware of the issue and convince them it is significant and that your position is the most reasonable one. You might also want to convince them to *do something* about it.

Voice, Tone, and Point of View: Why are you interested in the issue? What are your attitudes toward the issue and the audience? How will you convey those attitudes to your audience?

Context, Medium, and Genre: Although you are writing this persuasive paper to fulfill a college assignment, most issues worth writing about are important beyond the classroom. How might your views make a difference to your community? Keeping the context of the assignment in mind, decide on the most appropriate medium and genre for your writing. If you are writing for an audience beyond the classroom, consider what will be the most effective way to present your argument to this audience. You might write an e-mail message to a friend, prepare a memo for colleagues at work, or write a brochure or op-ed article for members of your community.

For more on choosing a medium and genre, see Chapter 17 and Appendix C.

Critical Thinking, Reading, and Writing

As we have seen, effective persuasive writing focuses on an issue and provides sufficient and compelling evidence to convince readers that the writer's position on that issue is correct, or at least worthy of respect. Before you begin to write your own persuasive paper, read one or more persuasive essays to get a feel for this kind of writing. Finally, you might consider how visuals could make your writing more convincing, as well as the kinds of sources you will need to consult.

When you write to convince, you will often need to draw on material from other sources by conducting research. To research effectively, you must read the material critically and evaluate it carefully, to make certain that the evidence you are offering as proof really does support your claims. Of course, thinking critically also means that you need to consider other points of view about your issue and decide whether those views are compatible or in conflict with your view.

For more on gathering and evaluating information from sources, see Chapter 19.

Learning the Qualities of Effective Persuasive Writing

Much of the writing that you do is intended to convince someone to agree with you about something, typically about an issue. An **issue** is a subject or problem area that people care about and about which they hold differing views. Issues of current concern in the United States include tax cuts, campaign finance reform, and school vouchers. Subjects about which people tend to agree—for example, the importance of education in general—are not usually worth writing arguments about.

Persuasive writing that achieves the goal of convincing readers has the following qualities:

- **Presentation of the issue.** You need to present your issue in a way that will grab your readers' attention and help them understand that an issue exists and that they should be concerned about it. For example, if you are attempting to convince buyers to purchase cellular phones with antivirus protection, you first need to demonstrate the existence and danger of viruses. Another way to present an issue is to share an anecdote about it, or you might also offer some statistics that clearly demonstrate the prevalence of cell phone viruses.

- **A clearly stated, arguable claim.** A **claim** is the assertion that you are making about the issue. Your claim should be clear, of course; a confusing claim will not convince readers. Any claim worth writing about also needs to be arguable: a statement about which reasonable people may disagree. For example, "All cell phone us-

TechNote One way to see argumentation and persuasion in action is to look at the political discussion boards on various Web sites, blogs, and online bulletin boards. Choose a topic thread, and as you skim or read the posts, ask yourself three questions about each post you see: 1) How much credibility does the writer seem to have as a person (*ethos*)? 2) How does the writer use reason and logic to make his or her points (*logos*)? 3) What is your emotional reaction to the writer's remarks (*pathos*)? You can determine the weight a writer's comments probably carry with others by assessing your impressions of that writer's credibility, reasoning, and emotional integrity.

ers should purchase anti-virus software" is an arguable claim; a reader could disagree by saying, "Cell phone viruses are not a major threat." However, no one would disagree with the statement "Computer viruses can be annoying and disruptive." Therefore, it is not arguable and not an effective claim for a piece of persuasive writing.

- **An awareness of audience.** Because your task as a writer is to convince other people, it is crucial to be aware of the needs, situations, and perspectives of your audience. In any audience, you can expect some members to be more open to your claim than others:
  - If someone already agrees with you, persuasion is unnecessary.
  - If someone mildly disagrees with you or is undecided, persuasion has a good chance of working.
  - If someone strongly disagrees with you, there is little chance that persuasion will work.

- **Convincing reasons.** Writers of convincing arguments offer support for what they are asking their reader to believe or to do. Think of the reasons you use to support your point as the other part of a *because* statement, with the claim being the first part. ("Animal fur should not be used in clothing *because* synthetic fur is available and looks like real fur.")

- **Sufficient evidence for each reason.** After considering the degree to which the audience agrees or disagrees with your claim, you need to provide enough evidence, and the kind(s) of evidence, that will convince your readers and, if applicable, persuade them to act accordingly. Evidence includes statistics, expert opinion, examples, and anecdotes (stories).

- **Appeals based on logic, emotion, and the writer's character.** Effective persuasive writers carefully decide when to use three kinds of appeals—*logos* (appeals based on logic), *pathos* (appeals to the audience's emotions), and *ethos* (appeals based on the writer's character or credibility). Appeals based on logic are generally the most effective. Emotional appeals can be effective with audience members who are predisposed to accept your claims. Appealing to an audience's emotions is risky, however, because critical thinkers will reject this type of appeal unless it is accompanied by logical and ethical appeals. Appeals based on the writer's authority and credibility—ethical appeals—can be powerful, especially when coupled with logical appeals.

For more on strategies for argument, including dealing with opposing views, see Chapter 14.

- **An honest discussion of other views.** For any arguable claim or thesis, there will be at least one other point of view besides yours. To be effective, the writer of a persuasive text needs to acknowledge and deal with possible objections from the other side. You already make this kind of **counterargument** naturally. For example, when you are told that you "cannot register for this course because you have not completed the prerequisite," you probably already have an answer to that objection such as, "You're right, but I received approval from the dean because of my prior professional experience."

If you think that another perspective has merit, you should certainly **acknowledge** it and even **concede** that it is valid. Another possibility is a Rogerian approach (see Chapter 14), in which both sides negotiate a compromise position. Perhaps you can offer a compromise by incorporating aspects of the other perspective into your thesis. Of course, if other perspectives on your issue are without merit, you will need to **refute** them by indicating how they are inappropriate, inadequate, or ineffective.

- **A desired result.** The goal of persuasive writing is convincing readers to change their minds about an issue or at least to give your view serious consideration. Often the goal is to get your reader to act in some way—vote for a candidate, write a letter to the school board, or buy some product.

In a computer file, put the above qualities of effective persuasive writing into your own words, and then refer to those notes as you conduct research and write your paper.

A WRITER'S RESPONSIBILITIES

Establishing and Maintaining Credibility

Dealing Fairly with Opposing Views

An ethical writer must deal with opposing views fairly and honestly. If you ignore or distort opposing views, readers will think you are either ignorant, unaware, or dishonest, which will quickly weaken or destroy your ethos—your credibility.

It is perhaps only natural to tend to ignore what those who disagree with you have to say about your topic—after all, if you just ignore their views, your view will be stronger, right? However, ignoring the other side of an issue, the objections that others might have to your point of view, actually weakens your position, as your readers will most likely know of the objections and wonder why you did not deal with these other perspectives.

And if you are going to be honest with your readers, you have an ethical obligation to note that there are arguments against your position. You don't necessarily have to write, "Here is another position that you may think is stronger than mine,"

(cont'd)

(continued)

but you do need to acknowledge that "other sides to this issue include XXX," and then explain why your position is still the stronger one.

Avoiding Logical Fallacies

Using faulty logic intentionally will weaken your credibility and annoy your audience. Using faulty logic unintentionally will indicate that you are not a critical thinker. If you include logical fallacies such as *stacking the deck*, in which you provide only one point of view, or use *red herrings*, in which you use misleading evidence that serves only to distract your readers, you are not presenting an ethical text. That is, instead of writing to persuade you are writing to mislead. See Chapter 14, pages 436–39 for more on avoiding logical fallacies.

Reading, Inquiry, and Research: Learning from Texts That Persuade

The readings that follow are examples of persuasive writing. As you read the persuasive selections your instructor assigns, consider the following questions:

- What makes this selection convincing?
- To what extent am I convinced by the writer's reasons and evidence? Why?
- What parts of the selection could be improved? In what ways?
- How can I use the techniques of persuasive writing exemplified here in my own writing?

Thinking Rhetorically

Keep in mind the following questions as you read the essays that follow. Make it a practice to ask yourself these questions in all your reading—personal, academic, and professional—and you will strengthen and sharpen your abilities as a reader and as a writer.

Rhetorical Knowledge: The Writer's Situation and Rhetoric

- **Audience:** What audience does this reading selection aim to convince? How effectively does the author address this audience? What can you point to in the article to support your position?
- **Purpose:** What is the author's primary purpose in writing about this topic? What other purposes might the author have?

- **Voice and Tone:** What can you point to in this piece of writing that gives the author his or her *ethos* in writing about this subject? How does the tone contribute to—or detract from—the author's credibility?
- **Responsibility:** What has the author done to write responsibly in his or her writing to convince?
- **Context and Format:** Locate the time and place where the reading was originally published. Consider how the initial context affects the author's writing and your reading of the essay.

ANNE APPLEBAUM

When Women Go to War

Anne Applebaum, a member of the *Washington Post* editorial board, writes a column that usually appears each Wednesday. Applebaum was born in Washington, D.C. She has a degree from Yale University and was a Marshall Scholar at the London School of Economics and St. Antony's College, Oxford. She was awarded the Charles Douglas-Home Memorial Trust award for journalism in the ex-Soviet Union in 1992. In 1996, her book *Between East and West* was given an Adolph Bentinck prize for European nonfiction. This essay first appeared as a column in the *Post* in 2003.

The argument about women in combat is over. In fact, it was over three years ago, when two female sailors were among the victims of the bombing of the USS Cole. Women had been serving aboard U.S. combat ships only since 1994, yet these deaths—the first time any female sailor had been killed in hostile action onboard—did not lead to a reversal of policy. No special outrage accompanied the sight of "women in body bags" being brought home for burial, as many had predicted, either then or during the 1991 Persian Gulf War. Now, as we fight a new Gulf war, women constitute nearly a sixth of the armed forces. More than 90 percent of service positions, including most combat positions, are open to women. Although these facts have been noted once or twice in recent days, they have provoked no special angst. Right now, women are flying helicopters, launching missiles and dropping bombs on Iraqi cities, and American civilization has not collapsed as a result.

But if the argument about women in combat is over, the conversa- 2
tion about women in the military should not be—just as the conversation about women in the law, or in business, or in factories did not
end when more women took those jobs. To see why, look no further
than this week's front pages, some of which feature the face of Army
Spec. Shoshana Johnson, a POW in Iraq and the single mother of a 2-
year-old. Johnson's fate is heartbreaking, but it is not entirely unique.
Johnson's child is one of tens of thousands who have been left behind while their mothers—or their mothers *and* their fathers—go off
to war.

Is there anything wrong with that? That is, is there anything 3
wrong with the fact that Johnson was where she was when she was,
"in harm's way," as the Army puts it? Some think not. Carolyn Becraft,
assistant secretary of the Navy in the Clinton administration, puts
the case like this: "This is a volunteer military. Everyone who stays
is there of their own free will. This is their job. These are the conditions of their employment. If they have children, they still have to be
available for worldwide deployment." Official policy is no different,
and no wonder. After the long struggle for acceptance, higher-ranking
women in particular loathe the idea of treating mothers and fathers
differently.

Dig a little deeper, though, and the angst is palpable. Very far 4
off the record, one high-ranking Pentagon official admits to being
deeply disturbed by photographs of women hugging their babies before leaving for war. "We're the United States of America. How can
we ask a young woman to leave her infant?" A military women's
Web site burns with acrimony. "My husband is on a ship already and
we are overseas. I have no one to care for my child if we are both
underway," writes one. Another has no sympathy: "As a childless
single woman working hard to cover up the slack that foolish preg-
nant women like you give the military, I and others have every right
to be mad." The awareness of a stereotype—that women get preg-
nant on ships in order to be sent home—leads another to describe
the "shame" she felt after a planned pregnancy led to her discharge
from the Navy and to write of how she longs, once again, "to serve
my country with pride."

Should she be able to? In civilian life, it would be easy. Where- 5
as many among the first generation of female lawyers, like the first
generation of female fighter pilots, took two-week maternity leaves or
refused to have children at all, those in the second generation—my
generation—happily take off a year, or five years, or work three days
a week indefinitely. This isn't because younger women have sold out,

but because they, and the working world, have made a series of imperfect compromises. Women give up some seniority, and sometimes some money. In exchange, they get some time. Many, if not all, find this a fair compromise.

It is in this sense that the military now needs to catch up to the civilian world, to make that same generational shift. The American military offers its enlisted men and women enormous choices of training and education. Why shouldn't they also be offered the chance to take a few years off, and then to reenlist, with no stigma attached? The military takes dozens of factors into consideration when it deploys people. Why shouldn't single mothers be deliberately kept out of harm's way? Military traditions make some of these questions starker and harder than they would be in civilian life, but it doesn't make them illegitimate. In fact, it is only when the armed forces are comfortable enough with women to treat them differently, and only when military mothers are comfortable enough to be treated differently, that we will know they have truly arrived. 6

QUESTIONS FOR WRITING AND DISCUSSION

Critical Thinking: Responding to the Writer's Ideas

1. What is Applebaum's claim?
2. To what extent do you agree with Applebaum—that is, how much has she convinced you? Why?

Composing Processes and Knowledge of Conventions: The Writer's Strategies

1. How successfully has Applebaum used *logos*, *pathos*, and *ethos*? How might she have used any of these three appeals more convincingly?
2. Where does Applebaum address counterarguments, and how does she do so? How effective is she in doing this?

Inquiry and Research: Ideas for Further Exploration

1. Search for "women in war" at your college library or by using an Internet search engine. In no more than two pages, outline the most persuasive arguments you found both in favor of and against women going to war.

MAUREEN DOWD

Our Own Warrior Princess

Maureen Dowd won the Pulitzer Prize for Commentary in 1999. In 1992, she received the Breakthrough Award from Women, Men and Media at Columbia University. She won the Matrix Award from New York Women in Communications in 1994. In 1996, she was named one of *Glamour*'s Women of the Year. In 1992, she was also a Pulitzer Prize finalist for national reporting.

In the following column, which first appeared in the *New York Times* on June 1, 2003, Dowd writes in a personal way about organ donation—telling the story of what her niece, Jennifer, did to help her brother, Michael. Although persuasive writing most often uses facts, statistics, and hard evidence to make its case, as you read Dowd's column consider how effective she is in using emotional appeals to persuade you.

1 Jennifer showed me her scar Friday. It's the most beautiful scar I've ever seen. A huge stapled gash on her stomach, shaped like the Mercedes logo. A red badge of courage. Jennifer is my niece, a 33-year-old lawyer. On Wednesday, she had half her liver taken out at Georgetown University Hospital to save the life of her uncle (my brother Michael), who had gotten hepatitis years ago from a tainted blood transfusion.

2 The complicated and risky operation for the two, side by side, went from 7:30 am. until after 10 pm. Then, when a Medivac helicopter arrived with a matching liver for another patient, the same team of doctors had to start on another emergency six-hour liver transplant.

3 The night nurse told Jennifer she was an oddity. "We don't see many live donors," she said. "Not many people are that generous."

4 Or brave. Jennifer's morphine drip wasn't attached properly the first night after the operation, and no one knew it. She felt pain, but didn't want to be a wimp by complaining too loudly. Instead, she was Reaganesque, cracking jokes and wondering where the cute doctors were.

5 She survived the first night after this excruciating operation au naturel, like Xena the Warrior Princess. If all goes well, her liver will grow whole again in several weeks, as will Michael's half.

6 Unlike her father, who charged people a nickel to see his appendix scar when he was 10, she let me look for free. As we sat in her room, watching Mariah Carey singing with a bare midriff on the "Today" show, I worried a little how she would take the disfigurement.

7 She's a fitness fanatic, who works as a personal trainer in her spare time. She's single, out in the cruel dating world. And we live in an airbrush

culture, where women erase lines with Botox, wrinkles with lasers, and fat with liposuction. I told Jen scars are sexy; consider that great love scene in "Lethal Weapon 3" when Mel Gibson and Rene Russo, as police officers, compare scars.

Jennifer has every quality of heart, spirit, mind and body a woman   8 could want. She's smart, funny, generous, loyal, principled, great looking and, obviously, adventurous.

"Write a column about me," she smiled, tubes coming out of every   9 part of her body, as I left her room.

I knew what she meant. She didn't want me to write about her   10 guts, but to encourage others to have the guts to donate organs. When she came to, she asked for the green ribbon pin that encourages organ donation. Her exquisite doll-like transplant surgeon, Dr. Amy Lu, in white coat and black high-heeled mules, still on the job after 21 hours in the operating room, removed her pin and gave it to Jennifer.

As Neal Conan said on NPR Thursday: "More than 80,000 Ameri-   11 cans are on waiting lists for organ donations, and most will never get them. Thousands on those lists die every year. One big reason for the shortage is that families are reluctant to give up their relatives' organs. Even when people filled out a donor card or checked the organ donor box on their driver's license, family members often refuse. The need is so acute and so frustrating that more and more doctors are wondering whether financial incentives might persuade some families to change their minds and save lives." (Iran has wiped out its kidney transplant wait by offering rewards.)

As the New York Organ Donor Network Web site notes: "One donor   12 can save up to eight lives through organ donation and improve dozens of lives through corneal, bone, skin and other tissue transplants. Across the U.S., 17 men, women and children of all races and ethnic backgrounds die every day for lack of a donated organ."

I'm one of the scaredy-cats who never checked the organ donation   13 box or filled out the organ and tissue donor card.

Some people don't do it because they have irrational fears that doc-   14 tors will be so eager to harvest their organs, they'll receive subpar care after an accident.

I had nutty fears, too, straight out of a Robin Cook medical thriller,   15 that they might come and pluck out my eyes or grab my kidney before I was through with them.

On Friday, Michael's birthday, I got the card online, filled it out and   16 stuck it in my wallet. If Jennifer is brave enough to do it alive, how can I be scared of doing it dead?

BRIAN J. G. PEREIRA, M.D.

Letter Responding to Dowd

Brian Pereira is a Professor of Medicine at the Tufts University School of Medicine. Dr. Pereira is a nationally recognized expert on kidney disease and nephrology. He is the President of the National Kidney Foundation, Chairman of the International Nephrology Network, and has served on the editorial board of many scientific journals. Dr. Pereira also serves as a director of Kidney Care Partners, Wellbound Inc., and Satellite Health Care Inc.

This letter, in response to Dowd's essay, appeared in the *New York Times* a few days after Dowd's column was published.

To the Editor:
Re "Our Own Warrior Princess" (column, June 1):

Maureen Dowd's inspiring story of her niece's live liver donation points to an emerging trend in transplantation. 1

The year 2001 was the first in which there were more living donors than nonliving donors in the United States. Because of new techniques for kidney removal and the medical success of live liver transplantation, more people are considering saving lives through organ donation while they are alive. 2

A recent survey by the National Kidney Foundation found that one in four Americans would consider donating a kidney or a piece of their liver or lung to a complete stranger. 3

This is not just talk. The real numbers are encouraging. In 2002, 353 people became living liver donors, and 6,234 were live kidney donors. 4

While the need for organ donors continues to grow, people like Ms. Dowd's niece represent hope for a future when the transplant waiting list will cease to exist. 5

BRIAN J. G. PEREIRA, M.D.
Pres., National Kidney Foundation
Boston, June 2, 2003
New York Times

QUESTIONS FOR WRITING AND DISCUSSION

Critical Thinking: Responding to the Writer's Ideas

1. Has Dowd's column affected your views about becoming an organ donor? If so, how?

2. Dowd's column includes an implicit definition of bravery. What is this definition? How does Dowd use it to convince her readers?

Composing Processes and Knowledge of Conventions: The Writer's Strategies

1. Dowd uses a personal story to make her point. How effective is this writing strategy? Why?

2. How does Dowd establish her *ethos* in this article? How does Pereira establish his *ethos* in his letter?

Inquiry and Research: Ideas for Further Exploration

1. What questions do you still have about organ donation? Where can you go to get answers to those questions?

Thinking about Visuals That Persuade

Photographs can be extremely persuasive; their appeal to a viewer's emotions is immediate. Suppose you are reading a paper whose author is trying to persuade you that there have been problems at a particular intersection, with drivers continually running red lights and causing accidents. Would the photograph shown in Figure 8.1 on page 206 get your attention?

Consider, for example, how you could use a photograph such as this one—depicting a recent accident on the road that leads into your campus from a nearby neighborhood—to illustrate the editorial written in response to Scenario 2 on page 194 (a campus–community problem).

As you think about the use of photographs as part of arguments to persuade, consider the following questions:

- How does the photograph connect to the main point the writer is trying to make?
- In what way(s) does the picture help convince the reader?
- The photograph obviously makes an appeal to a viewer's emotions. Is the appeal fair in each case? Why or why not?
- What other type of visual might you use for each of these arguments?

Writing Processes

As you work on the assignment that you have chosen, remember the qualities of an effective and convincing persuasive paper, listed on pages 195–97.

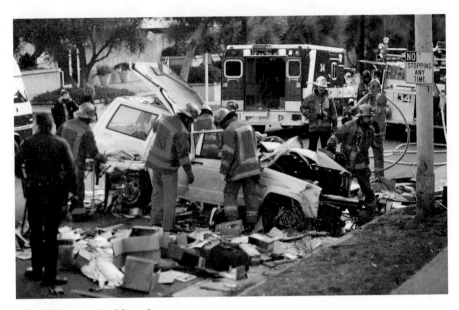

FIGURE 8.1 An Accident Scene

Also remember that writing is recursive—you might start with an invention activity or two and then conduct some research, which leads to more invention work and then a first draft; but then you might need to do more invention work to come up with additional reasons and conduct more research to add more support or refute an opposing argument; and then you will revise your draft and possibly find another gap or two. . . . So while the activities listed below imply that writers proceed step-by-step, the actual process of writing is usually messier: you will keep coming back to your earlier work, adding to it, modifying the information to be more accurate as you conduct additional research and become more familiar with your issue.

If you are considering several issues for your persuasive text, put your notes into a separate computer document for each one. Once you determine the focus of your paper, it will be easy to access and use the notes on that issue. As you work on your project, make sure that you save your computer files frequently because any work that you do not save could be lost. Also, savvy writers back up their computer files in two or more places—on an internal or external hard drive of the computer, on a USB flash drive, and/or on a rewritable CD or DVD.

For a tip on organizing your computer files, see page 66.

Invention: Getting Started

The invention activities below are strategies that you can use to help you get some sense of what you already know about the issue you have chosen. Whatever invention method(s) you use (or that your teacher asks you to use), try to answer questions such as these:

- What do I already know about this issue?
- What is my point of view on this issue?
- Where might I learn more about this issue? What verifiable information is available?
- What might my audience already know? What might their point of view be?
- What do I know about my audience? What don't I know that I should know?
- What questions do I have about the issue?
- What are some other views on this issue?

Doing your invention work in electronic form, rather than on paper, lets you easily use your invention work as you construct a draft.

As with any kind of writing, invention activities improve with peer feedback and suggestions. Consider sharing the invention work you have done so far with several classmates or friends in order to understand your rhetorical situation more clearly and to generate more useful information.

For more on listing, questioning, freewriting, and other strategies for discovery and learning, see Chapter 3.

Exploring Your Ideas with Research

Research is critical to any persuasive text, for if you cannot provide evidence to support your position, you probably will not convince your reading audience.

Although you may be able to use information from your own experience as evidence, you will usually need to offer verifiable information from sources, such as facts, statistics, expert testimony, and examples.

To find evidence outside of your own experience that you need to support your claim, look for answers to the following questions:

For help with locating sources of information, see Chapter 19; for help with documenting your sources, see Chapter 20.

- What facts or other verifiable information can I find that will provide solid evidence to convince my readers to agree with my position?
- What expert testimony can I provide to support my claim? What authorities on my issue might I interview?
- What statistical data support my position?
- What are other people doing in response to this issue or problem?

The subject you focus on and the kind of essay you are constructing help to determine the kind of research you conduct. For example, for the scenarios above, you could conduct several kinds of research:

- For Scenario 1 (p. 193), which asks you to focus on a controversial issue, assume that you have decided to write about whether the threat of criminal punishment helps to prevent the insider trading to stocks. What kinds of research might you conduct? At your library, a search of business publications such as the *Wall Street Journal, Business Week,* and *Forbes* would be a good place to start. But in addition, you could also interview some local business executives so you could get their perspectives for your paper. You could interview local law enforcement officials and attorneys to get their take on whether the threat of punishment helps stop insider trading.

- For Scenario 2 (p. 194), where you focus on a problem in your campus community, that same kind of "local" research—interviewing your classmates, for example—will provide useful information for your paper. Consider all of the comments you could get, for instance, if you were writing about an issue involving your classrooms, such as the condition of the building or the time the classes are scheduled, or a campus issue, such as campus safety, student fees, or athletics. Speaking with campus officials and administrators will also give you useful information for your paper. In addition, a search of the campus newspaper archives in your college's library may provide good background information on the issue you are writing about.

- One way to learn about other perspectives on your subject is to read online blogs or join Listservs that focus on the topic of your essay. These ongoing electronic conversations often can provide multiple perspectives and ideas on the issue you are writing about—which then can help you with your own thinking and research.

Reviewing Your Invention and Research

After you have conducted your research, you need to review your invention work and notes and the information you have collected from outside sources. Once you have a general idea of the conclusion your research is leading you to, you can develop a "working" thesis statement: if you had to make a point now, based on what you have learned, what would it be? It is called a working thesis because your main point or thesis will inevitably change as you continue to conduct research and learn more. And, as you know, through the process of writing itself, you will *For more on deciding on a thesis, see Chapter 13.* learn about your topic, so give yourself permission to modify and develop this initial thesis statement as you draft and revise your text. Once you have written several drafts, have received feedback on them, and have revised them, you will be better able to determine what your final thesis statement should be.

Organizing Your Information

Because the purpose of writing a persuasive text is to convince your readers to accept your point of view, you will need to organize your reasons and evidence strategically. The questions that you need to ask yourself when deciding on your organization are all rhetorical:

- Who is your audience? What is your readers' position on your issue likely to be? If they are undecided, you might try a classical or an inductive approach, both of which are discussed below. If they are likely to hold an opposing view, then a refutation approach, also discussed below, may be the better choice.
- Why might they be interested in your persuasive writing, or how can you make them interested in it?
- What is your purpose for writing—that is, why do you need to convince readers of this position?

When you construct a persuasive paper, you have to determine the most effective organizational approach for your purpose and audience. One method of organizing an argument, called the *classical scheme*, was first outlined by Aristotle nearly 2,400 years ago. If you are using the classical scheme, this is the sequence you will follow:

introduction → main claim → evidence supporting claim → discussion of other perspectives (acknowledging, conceding, and/or refuting them) → conclusion.

Aristotle's approach is also called the **deductive method** because you state your claim and then help the reader understand, or deduce, how the evidence supports your claim. The advantage of this method is that you state your position and make your case early, before your reader starts thinking about other perspectives.

Another organizational approach is commonly known as the **inductive method.** When using this approach, you first present and explain all of your reasons and evidence, then draw your conclusion—your main claim. The advantage is that your reader may come to the same conclusion before you explicitly state your position and will therefore be more inclined to agree with your point of view.

Because persuasive writing must usually acknowledge and incorporate or refute opposing viewpoints, a third organizational method starts by presenting the views of the other side. In this method, you first deal with objections to your claim and then state your position and provide reasons and evidence to support it. This is an especially effective strategy if the opposing view or views are widely held.

Here are three organizational structures that you might consider for your persuasive paper.

Options for Organization

The Classical (Deductive) Approach	The Inductive Approach	Refutation Approach
• Introduce the issue and state your thesis. • Explain the importance of the issue. • Present your reasons and evidence—why readers should agree with you. • Answer objections—either incorporate or refute other points of view. • Conclude—often with a call to action.	• Introduce the issue. • Offer reasons and evidence for your claim. • Draw your conclusion—your main claim. • Deal with other viewpoints either before or after presenting your claim. • Conclude—often with a call to action.	• Introduce the issue. • List opposing views. • Deal with each objection in turn. • Introduce your position and explain why it makes sense, offering reasons and evidence. • Conclude—often with a call to action.

Constructing a Complete Draft

Once you have chosen the best organizational approach for your audience and purpose, you are ready to construct your draft. After you have reviewed your invention writing and research notes, developed a working thesis, and carefully considered all of the reasons and evidence you have generated, construct a complete first draft.

As you work, keep the following in mind:

- You may discover you need to do more invention work and/or more research as you write.

- As you try out tentative claims and reasons, ask your classmates and other readers about the kinds of supporting evidence they consider convincing.

For more on choosing visuals, see Chapter 18.

- Consider whether photographs or other visuals might help support your thesis.

- If you become tired and the quality of your thinking or your productivity is affected, take a break.

Introduction: Regardless of your organizational approach, you need to have a strong **introduction** to capture your readers' attention and introduce the issue. To accomplish these two goals in an introduction, you might do one or more of the following:

- *Share an anecdote that clearly exemplifies the issue.* Maureen Dowd begins her column on organ donation (p. 202) with the story of her niece's bravery in choosing to donate part of her liver to her uncle.

- *Provide a brief history of the issue.*

- *Provide a fact or statistic about the issue that will surprise—and possibly concern—readers.* In her article about women in combat (p. 199), Anne Applebaum begins by informing readers of something they may not realize:

  > The argument about women in combat is over. In fact, it was over three years ago, when two female sailors were among the victims of the bombing of the USS Cole.

- *Explain (briefly) why your persuasive text is important.*

- *Ask an intriguing question about your subject.* Student writer Santi DeRosa opens his paper (p. 217) by asking a key question:

  > Are women at Arizona State University being treated as objects by the very university that has a responsibility to treat them with equality and dignity and not as second-class citizens?

Body: You can use various writing strategies, including defining all terms your reader might not understand within the body of your text to effectively persuade your reader. This is the area of your paper where you will provide supporting examples or evidence for each reason you offer, use visual aids (photographs, charts, tables) to support your position, and use rhetorical appeals—*ethos, logos, pathos* (p. 196)—to help convince your readers.

For more on rhetorical appeals and argument strategies, see Chapter 14.

Conclusion: In your conclusion you need to restate or allude to your thesis and let your readers know what you would like them to do with the information they learned from your essay. Conclusions in persuasive writing often do the following:

- *Explain your main thesis or point—what you want to persuade your reader about.*

- *Summarize how each supporting point adds evidence to support your main point.* In a long, involved argument, a summary can help readers recall the main points that you are making.

- *Reach out to the audience.*

- *Include a "call to action."* Maureen Dowd ends "Our Own Warrior Princess" with a description of herself filling out an organ donor card and the strong implication that readers should do so as well.

Title: As you compose your persuasive writing, a title should emerge at some point—perhaps late in the process. The title should reflect the point you are trying to make, and it should catch your readers' attention and make them want to read your essay. However, it may be risky to state your major claim in the title. If you state a controversial claim in your title, you take the chance that some readers will choose not to read your argument. On the other hand, there are times when stating a bold claim in the title is appropriate—especially if readers may not even have considered the topic.

VISUALIZING VARIATIONS

Using Charts and Other Visuals to Support Your Claim

If you were writing in response to Scenario 1, which asks you to focus on a controversial issue, you might choose to write about global warming. Here is a dramatic image that you could use at the beginning of your paper:

But while you could focus on an image like this one as a way to help make your points, you could also use charts and graphs to convince your reader, as they can provide useful information. This chart shows the global variation in temperatures from 1860 to 2000:

If you were to combine this chart with the following information from the same source, you would be providing your reader with a useful chart along with some specific data to explain it.

(cont'd)

(continued)

The temperature values in the data set are provided as **differences** from a mean of 15 degrees C. These data have been analyzed by scientists to show a 0.5 degrees C increase in global temperatures. However, this finding is under dispute because some claim that the amount of error in the data is too large to justify the conclusion. This data set has been created using the follwing steps:

- Data was collected from land based stations, from ocean buoys, and from ships.

- For each year data has been averaged to come up with a yearly average.

- Data is smoothed to accommodate historical changes that skew the data (e.g., weather stations near cities record artificially high temperatures because [cities] create what is called an "urban heat island effect").

If it were appropriate to put a political spin into your essay, you could use a cartoon like this one to make your point.

Copyright ©2005 Brian Narelle. Reprinted by permission of Brian Narelle, www.narellecreative.com

The President's indifference to global warming was starting to show.

Remember that the whole idea of using charts, photographs, or even cartoons in your essays is to help support the point you are trying to make in your text in a way that will help readers not only understand but also be convinced by your argument.

- Which visual is the best example of an emotional appeal? Of a logical appeal? Are any of these visuals examples of an ethical appeal? Why or why not?

- How might someone opposed to the claim that global warming is a current danger argue against the appeals presented by these three visuals?

Revising

Once you have a full draft of your persuasive text, you still have much to do. First, however, you should set the draft aside so that you can gain some critical distance. You should then read it with fresh eyes. When you approach your work this way, you will find it easier to notice reasons that are irrelevant, evidence that is not fully developed, or places where a compelling photograph might add to the impact of your argument.

As you work to revise your early drafts, do not be concerned about doing a great deal of heavy editing. When you revise you will probably change the content and structure of your paper, so time spent fixing problems with sentence style or grammar, punctuation, or mechanics at this stage is often wasted.

When you reread the first draft of your persuasive writing, here are some questions to ask yourself:

- How clearly and persuasively am I making my point? Am I sure my readers can understand it? How easily will they be able to restate the thesis?
- How effectively does all of my evidence support that main point? (Sometimes it is easy to include evidence that seems persuasive but that does not support the point you are arguing for.)
- Are there other photographs, charts, or graphs that might help make my point?
- Are there parts of my paper that might confuse a reader? If so, how might I clarify them?
- Do I restate or allude to my main point at the end of my paper and also explain to the reader what I would like him or her to do (to vote, to write a letter to the editor, to *do* what I have been arguing for)?

Technology can help you revise and edit your writing more easily. Use your word processor's track-changes tool to try out revisions and editing changes. After you have had time to think about the possible changes, you can "accept" or "reject" them. Also, you can use your word processor's comment tool to write reminders to yourself when you get stuck with a revision or some editing task.

Because it is so difficult even for experienced writers to see their emerging writing with a fresh eye, it is almost always useful to ask classmates, friends, or family members to read and comment on drafts of your persuasive writing.

WRITER'S WORKSHOP

Responding to Full Drafts

Working with one or two classmates, read each paper and offer comments and questions that will help each of you see your papers' strengths and weaknesses. Consider the following guidelines and questions as you do:

(cont'd)

(continued)

- Write a brief narrative comment outlining your first impression of this draft. How effective is the title at drawing you in? Why? What are your overall suggestions for improvement? What part(s) of the text are especially persuasive? What reasons could use more support? Indicate what you like about the draft, and provide positive and encouraging feedback to the writer.

- Comment on the writer's focus. Does the paper wander a bit? If so, indicate where.

- Comment on how convincing you found the paper. Explain, in a brief paragraph, how much you were persuaded by the paper.

- Comment on the effectiveness of the introduction. What suggestions can you make to improve it?

- What is the author's thesis or main claim? Could it be expressed or supported more effectively? If so, how?

- Are there parts that are confusing? Where would you like more details or examples to help clarify the writer's meaning?

- How accurate and appropriate is the supporting evidence? Has the writer included questionable statistics or concepts? How clearly does the author indicate the sources of statistics and other supporting evidence that may not be common knowledge?

- Might visuals such as charts, tables, photographs, or cartoons strengthen the writer's case and make the text more convincing?

- How clearly and effectively does the writer present any opposing points of view? How might this presentation be improved? How effectively does the writer answer opposing viewpoints? How might the writer acknowledge, concede, and/or refute them more effectively?

- How well has the writer demonstrated an awareness of readers' knowledge, needs, and/or expectations? How might the writer demonstrate greater awareness?

- How carefully has the writer avoided logical fallacies?

- Reread the conclusion. What could be added or changed to make it more effective? How well does it tie everything together? If action is called for, to what extent does it make you want to take action?

Responding to Readers' Comments

Once they have received feedback on their writing from peers, instructors, friends, and others, all writers have to figure out what to do with that feedback.

As with all feedback, it is important to really listen to it and consider what your reader has to say. Then it is up to you, as the author, to decide how to come to terms with these suggestions. You may decide to reject some comments, of course; other comments, though, deserve your attention, as they are the words of real readers speaking to you about how to improve your text. It is especially important to deal with comments from readers that indicate that they are unconvinced by your argument. You sometimes may find that comments from more than one reader contradict each other. In that case, you need to use your own judgment to decide which reader's comments are on the right track.

Knowledge of Conventions

When effective writers edit their work, they attend to the conventions that will help readers process their work. These include genre conventions, documentation, format, usage, grammar, and mechanics. By attending to these conventions in your writing, you make reading a more pleasant experience for readers.

Editing

See Chapter 20 for more on documenting sources using MLA or APA style.

The last task in any writing project is editing—the final polishing of your document. When you edit and polish your writing, you make changes to your sentence structure and word choice to improve your style and to make your writing clearer and more concise. You also check your work to make sure it adheres to conventions of grammar, usage, punctuation, mechanics, and spelling. Use the spell-check function of your word-processing program, but be sure to double-check your spelling personally. If you have used sources in your paper, make sure you are following the documentation style your instructor requires.

As with overall revision of your work, this final editing and polishing is most effective if you can put your text aside for a few days and come back to it with fresh eyes. Because checking conventions is easier said than done, though, we strongly recommend that you ask classmates, friends, and tutors to read your work to find editing problems that you cannot see.

To assist you with editing, we offer here a round-robin editing activity focused on citing sources correctly.

WRITER'S WORKSHOP

Round-Robin Editing with a Focus on Citing Sources

Working in small groups, look over both the in-text citations and the works-cited or references lists in your papers. For example, you might notice a problem with an in-text citation that is supposed to be in MLA style, such as this one:

> In the last line of the story, however, Rudebeck quotes Zach Krula, a freshman offensive lineman. Zach says, "We've got a lot of hot girls, we might as well utilize them" (Rudebeck 1).

(cont'd)

(continued)
In MLA style, it is not necessary to include the source's name in parentheses if the name has been given within the text.

As you work with your peers, consult Chapter 20 of this text, which provides guidelines for using MLA or APA style when citing sources.

Genres, Documentation, and Format

If you are writing an academic paper in response to Scenario 1, you will need to follow the conventions for the discipline in which you are writing and the requirements of your instructor. If you are writing an editorial for your college newspaper (Scenario 2), you should check the newspaper's editorial page or its Web site to see what the requirements are for length and format and what information you need to include when you submit the editorial.

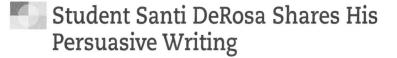

Student Santi DeRosa Shares His Persuasive Writing

Student writer Santi DeRosa read an article in his college paper about how female students help to recruit male athletes for his school. According to the article, women serve as campus guides when potential athletes visit the school, a widespread practice. DeRosa had concerns about the ethics of this practice, so he decided to respond by writing an essay on the issue for his writing class.

SANTI DEROSA

The Objectification of Women: Whose Fault Is It?

Are women at Arizona State University being treated as objects   1
by the very university that has a responsibility to treat them with equality and dignity and not as second-class citizens? All anyone needs to do is look at the athletics department to see the way women are treated here at ASU. What I don't understand is why in the year 2003 women are still allowing themselves to be used in such a way.

In the past week I have read two news articles in the State Press 2 about recruiting practices at ASU that made me a little perplexed. Maybe it's because I have a son the age of the female students in the articles, or maybe it's because I have a wife, a sister, a mother, and nieces whom I respect as people and as women, but these articles upset my sense of right and wrong. Objectification of women, sexual or otherwise, should never be allowed or condoned.

In the first article I read, "Risky Behavior Not Policed in ASU 3 Recruiting," reporter Joe Watson explains how high school football players who visit ASU for the purpose of being recruited are met by coeds from the "ASU Sun Devil Recruiters." Thirty-five of thirty-seven student recruiters are females. Is this just a coincidence? I don't think so. Schools from all over the country use the same practices to recruit high school players. Watson conducted an informal survey of 117 Division 1-A football programs nationwide and found many with similar proportions of female to male recruiters. Louisiana State has 55 females; Alabama leads the way with 100 females (1).

As Watson reports, ASU advertises every spring for new recruiters. 4 Most come from sororities. The football coaches say they prefer using women because that's the way the other schools do it. They maintain that the players coming to ASU to be recruited would be uncomfortable if they were greeted by men because they are used to female recruiters.

This justification is just an excuse to ignore a potential problem. 5 Most of the players who come to ASU to be recruited are 17 and 18 years old. There have been many reports of under-age drinking at local clubs and parties and sometimes sex, according to some senior recruiters. The people interviewed for the article who support the "hostess" program defend it by saying that "the recruiters perform respectable duties during high school recruits' campus visits" (Watson 2). Does the responsibility of "performing respectable duties" end when they leave the campus for a party? I believe that Becky Stoltz, a fourth-year recruiter at ASU who was interviewed for the article said it best: "It's a disaster waiting to happen." Big problems have in fact already happened at the University of Colorado, where a recruiting aide was indicted for improper conduct after a three-month grand-jury investigation of illegal recruiting practices, including allegations of sexual assault (Lambert).

Over the last hundred years, women have traveled a rocky road 6 to greater equality. At the turn of the twentieth century women didn't have many of the rights we take for granted today, such as the right to

Santi DeRosa and his instructor brainstormed a number of objections to the recruiting practices for him to develop in his revised draft, including this one:

I need to develop the idea that these practices use women for their bodies.

Note how DeRosa develops this objection.

DeRosa and his instructor also came up with the following objection for him to develop:

The program reinforces age-old notions of prostitution.

Note how he adds details and specific examples to support this part of his persuasive text.

own property and the right to vote. By staying strong, working together, and maintaining their dignity, women eventually gained these rights for themselves and their daughters and granddaughters.

In my own family, my grandmother and great-grandmother took care of their family in Italy while my grandfather came to America to set up a decent life for them. My grandmother held things together for six years until her husband was able to go back and get her. Although she did not have the same rights as a man of that time, she never gave up hope and never lost her pride. In this country she worked as a seamstress, as so many Italian women did, in order to help the family make it through bad times and to provide a better life for her children. My mother also worked a full-time job as a seamstress in a factory while taking care of her home and family, as women did in the 1950s and 1960s. However, women of that time were being taken for granted, and their roles had to change. Women wanted more, and through their strength of conviction, they got it—more equitable pay for their work. However, over the last forty years, the great strides women have made have been somewhat squandered. Women have made impressive gains in their professional lives, but they have also come to be seen, more and more, as objects.

The objectification of women in popular culture and sports is not new. During the 1950s and 1960s, the advertising industry started to portray women in roles outside the kitchen, but it also created a perspective on women that objectified them. To consider women in terms of the way they look is objectification. Examples of this are common: (1) Female newscasters chosen for their appearance, (2) the Dallas Cowboy cheerleaders—and cheerleading squads for other teams, and (3) beautiful women appearing in advertisements for beer and automobiles.

Amanda Bonzo, in an opinion piece in the online journal The Digital Collegian, writes the following about this process of objectification:

> In our society, a woman's body is objectified daily on television, music videos, advertisements. What do we do with objects? We buy, sell, trade them. . . . We tame them through rape and domestic abuse. Finally, we destroy them.

And Casey Jacketta, writing for the University of New Mexico's Daily Lobo, notes the following:

> I was pleased that my favorite show, "Law and Order," was on. Then, as I kept watching, I realized that the assistant district attorney, played by Angie Harmon — a woman — didn't say a word in court.

This troubled me, so I changed the channel to MTV. This upset me even more! All I saw was a bunch of barely clothed women shaking their bodies for the male singer's pleasure. (1)

We see what these writers are talking about daily in advertising [11] and in other media such as television, movies, and music. It is unfortunate that the sexual objectification of women sells products, and unless women understand that advertisers, filmmakers, college athletic departments, and others are taking advantage of them, this exploitation will never change. Barbara Fredrickson and her colleagues explain that this process causes women to start to view themselves the way others view them; as a consequence, "[a] woman views her own body as an object (or each piece as a separate object)" (274).

Objectification is often disguised as free speech and free expression, [12] which are both noble principles, although they are often misused. What I don't understand is how any woman would allow herself to be used in this way. In the case of ASU recruiters, objectification is disguised as school spirit.

In the second news article I read, "'Hot' Recruiters Draw Prospects," [13] Megan Rudebeck seems to be defending the program. Ms. Rudebeck not only talked to the coaches that run the program; she spoke with recruiters and players as well. She almost had me convinced that I might be overreacting. After all, here is a woman who is defending the way the recruiting program works. In the last line of the story, however, Rudebeck quotes Zach Krula, a freshman offensive lineman. Zach says, "We've got a lot of hot girls, we might as well utilize them" (1). That quotation made me wonder why Ms. Rudebeck wasn't insulted by that comment. Is she, as well as the women who are part of the program, so brainwashed by the need to get quality players onto the football team that they are willing to overlook the fact that they are being "utilize[d]"?

The use of women as sexual objects in mass media advertising, tele- [14] vision, and music has made the practice so commonplace that we fail to see that it degrades our society. It amazes me that the women of the ASU recruiting staff have not made the connection. It amazes me that Ms. Rudebeck and the ASU coaching staff say they don't see what's going on, and that students, faculty, the alumni, and the administration buy into this degrading and potentially dangerous practice. I hope that a copy of Joe Watson's article makes it into the hands of each of the recruiter's parents and the Board of Regents. This practice is an insult to the women of ASU, as well as to every woman in the last century who has sacrificed in order to achieve social equality.

DeRosa also needed to develop this objection to the recruiting program:

It operates under the guise of school spirit.

He added information from another article (by Megan Rudebeck) that puts a positive spin on the practice DeRosa is criticizing and provides a defense of the program; he then refutes Rudebeck's argument.

Works Cited   14

Bonzo, Amanda. Letter. The Digital Collegian. 20 Nov. 2000. 4 Feb. 2003 <http://www.collegian.psu.edu/archive/2000/11/11-20-00tdc/11-20-00dops-letter-1.asp>.

Fredrickson, Barbara L., Tomi-Ann Roberts, Stephanie M. Noll, Diane M. Quinn, and Jean M. Twenge. "That Swimsuit Becomes You: Sex Differences in Self-Objectification, Restrained Eating, and Math Performance." Journal of Personality and Social Psychology, 75 (1998): 269–84.

Jacketta, Casey. "Women's Lib Has Not Ended Objectification." Daily Lobo. 25 Nov. 2002. 3 Feb. 2003 <http://www.dailylobo.com/news/2002/11/25/Opinion/Column. Womens.Lib.Has.Not.Ended.Objectification-332561.shtml>.

Lambert, Liz. "Maxcey Indicted in CU Grand Jury Probe." 6 Sept. 2004. <http://9news.com/cu/>.

Rudebeck, Megan. "'Hot' Recruiters Draw Prospects." The State Press 18 Oct. 2002: 1–2. 3 Feb 2003 <http://www.asuwebdevil.com/main.cfm?include=detail&storyid= 300645>

Watson, Joe. "Risky Behavior Not Policed in ASU Football Recruiting." The State Press. 9 Dec. 2002: 1–2. 3 Feb. 2003 <http://www.asuwebdevil.com/main.cfm?include=detail&storyid= 339775>.

QUESTIONS FOR WRITING AND DISCUSSION

Rhetorical Knowledge: The Writer's Situation and Rhetoric

1. **Audience:** What audience does DeRosa have in mind for this essay? How can you tell?

2. **Purpose:** What purpose(s) does DeRosa have for writing this essay? How well does he achieve his purpose(s)?

3. **Voice and tone:** How does DeRosa's voice and tone help to establish his ethos? Is his tone appropriate? Why or why not?

4. **Responsibility:** How effectively does DeRosa represent opposing views on the issue of using female students as recruiters? In what ways, if any, could he represent their views more fairly?

5. **Context and format:** DeRosa is writing as an ASU student but also as a husband and father. How does this context affect his use of language, appeals, and evidence?

Critical Thinking: Responding to the Writer's Ideas

1. What is your initial response to DeRosa's essay? What can you point to in the text that causes you to respond in this way?

2. What is DeRosa's main point, or claim? To what extent do you agree with it? Why?

Composing Processes and Knowledge of Conventions: The Writer's Strategies

1. How convincing is the evidence DeRosa supplies? What other evidence might he have used?

2. What organizational method does DeRosa use? How effective is it? What other method(s) might he have used?

Inquiry and Research: Ideas for Further Exploration

1. Conduct a search (at your school library or on the Web), focusing on the events that DeRosa describes in his family history (paragraph 7). What similarities can you find to the family story that DeRosa relates in his text?

Self-Assessment: Reflecting on Your Learning Goals

Now that you have constructed a piece of writing designed to convince your readers, go back and consider your learning goals, which you and your classmates may have considered at the beginning of this chapter (pp. 188–89). Then, reflect on all the thinking and writing that you have done in constructing your persuasive paper. To help reflect on the learning goals that you have achieved, respond in writing to the following questions:

Rhetorical Knowledge

- *Audience:* What have you learned about addressing an audience in persuasive writing?

- *Purpose:* What have you learned about the purposes for constructing an effective persuasive text?
- *Rhetorical situation:* How did the writing context affect your persuasive text?
- *Voice and tone:* How would you describe your voice in this essay? Your tone? How do they contribute to the effectiveness of your persuasive essay?
- *Context, medium, and genre:* How did your context determine the medium and genre you chose, and how did those decisions affect your writing?

Critical Thinking, Reading, and Writing

- *Learning/inquiry:* How did you decide what to focus on for your persuasive text? Describe the process you went through to focus on a main idea, or thesis.
- *Responsibility:* How did you fulfill your responsibilities to your readers?
- *Reading and research:* What did you learn about persuasive writing from the reading selections you read for this chapter? What research did you conduct? How sufficient was the research you did?
- As a result of writing this paper, how have you become a more critical thinker, reader, and writer? What skills do you hope to develop further?

Writing Processes

- *Invention:* What invention strategies were most useful to you?
- *Organizing your ideas and details:* What organizational approach did you use? How successful was it?
- *Revising:* What one revision did you make that you are most satisfied with? If you could go back and make an additional revision, what would it be?
- *Working with peers:* How did your instructor and peer readers help you by making comments and suggestions about your writing? List some examples of how you revised your persuasive text based on comments from your instructor and your peer readers. How could you have made better use of the comments and suggestions you received? How could your peer readers help you more on your next assignment? How might you help them more, in the future, with the comments and suggestions you make on their texts?
- Did you use photographs, charts, graphs, or other visuals to help you convince your readers? If so, what did you learn about incorporating these elements?

- What "writerly habits" have you developed, modified, or improved on as you constructed the writing assignment for this chapter? How will you change your future writing activities based on what you have learned about yourself?

Conventions

- *Editing:* What sentence problem did you find most frequently in your writing? How will you avoid that problem in future assignments?
- *Genre:* What conventions of the genre you were using, if any, gave you problems?
- *Documentation:* Did you use sources for your paper? If so, what documentation style did you use? What problems, if any, did you have with it?

If you are constructing a course portfolio, file your written reflections so that you can return to them when you next work on your portfolio.

Rhetorical Knowledge

- *Audience:* When you are writing an evaluation, determine who will benefit from your evaluation. Who needs to make decisions about the subject of your evaluation? What do the audience members probably already know about your subject? What will you need to tell them? How can you best explain the criteria on which you will base your evaluation?

- *Purpose:* When you evaluate, you make a judgment based on specific criteria. Your purpose is not to say just "I think the Toyota truck is better than the Chevy," but to convince your reader to agree with your judgment.

- *Rhetorical situation:* Consider the many factors that affect where you stand in relation to your subject. If you have some personal interest in your evaluation (you love Ford automobiles, for example) you will have a different stance about evaluating the new Mustang than a more neutral party might.

- *Writer's voice and tone:* When you construct an evaluation, you are trying to explain your reasoned judgment. If you come across as a know-it-all, rather than as someone trying to explain how you came to your evaluative judgment, your readers may lose interest or suspect your judgment.

- *Context, medium, and genre:* You will need to decide on the best medium and genre to use to present your evaluation to the audience you want to reach. Often, you can use tables, charts, and graphs as well as words to help show how the subject you are evaluating compares to other similar items.

Critical Thinking, Reading, and Writing

- *Learning/inquiry:* By observing, listening to, and/or reading about the subject of your evaluation, and then by writing about it, you gain a deeper understanding of its qualities and the ability to make more informed judgments about it. This kind of thinking will help you make more informed decisions throughout your college and professional careers.

- *Responsibility:* Effective evaluative writing leads naturally to critical thinking. When you engage in evaluating something, you have to consider all aspects of that item, not only to determine the criteria on which you will base your evaluation, but also to construct a reasoned argument for your evaluation.

- *Reading and research:* To evaluate a subject, you not only need to examine it in detail (which means you need to conduct research), but you also need to examine similar items (which means you need to research them, too).

Writing Processes

- *Invention:* Various invention activities—brainstorming, listing, clustering—can help you consider all aspects of the subject you are evaluating.

- *Organizing your ideas and details:* The act of evaluating necessarily means that you think about the various aspects of your subject. That process can help you organize your thinking, and later your writing, into categories, based on your criteria.

- *Revising:* You will need to read your work with a critical eye, to make certain that it fulfills the assignment and displays the qualities of effective evaluative writing.

- *Working with peers:* Listen to your classmates to make sure that they understand your evaluation. What do they say about how well your details justify your conclusion?

Conventions

- *Editing:* Effective evaluations usually require careful word choice. The round-robin activity on page 258 will help you improve your word choice.

- *Genres for evaluative writing:* In many situations your evaluation will be a formal report or an academic paper. Evaluations written about movies, restaurants, or other products or services are not quite as formal as college assignments, however. Evaluations, especially of fellow employees, are also a common type of writing for employees in many businesses.

- *Documentation:* If you have relied on sources outside of your experience, you will need to cite them using the appropriate documentation style.

Writing to Evaluate

In 1997, the American Film Institute (AFI) announced a list of 100 greatest American films. The list was chosen by a panel of "leaders from across the film community." In 2007, the AFI updated this list, which now includes one film released since 2000: *Lord of the Rings: The Fellowship of the Ring*. *Citizen Kane*, however, retained its spot at the top of list.

American Film Institute's Greatest Movies, 1–25

1. *Citizen Kane* (1941)
2. *The Godfather* (1972)
3. *Casablanca* (1942)
4. *Raging Bull* (1980)
5. *Singin' in the Rain* (1952)
6. *Gone With the Wind* (1939)
7. *Lawrence of Arabia* (1962)
8. *Schindler's List* (1993)
9. *Vertigo* (1958)
10. *The Wizard of Oz* (1939)
11. *City Lights* (1931)
12. *The Searchers* (1956)
13. *Star Wars* (1977)
14. *Psycho* (1960)
15. *2001: A Space Odyssey* (1968)
16. *Sunset Boulevard* (1950)
17. *The Graduate* (1967)
18. *The General* (1927)
19. *On the Waterfront* (1954)
20. *It's a Wonderful Life* (1946)
21. *Chinatown* (1974)
22. *Some Like It Hot* (1959)
23. *The Grapes of Wrath* (1940)
24. *E.T. – The Extra-Terrestrial* (1982)
25. *To Kill a Mockingbird* (1962)

Evaluations are part of everyday life. When you decide which classes to take, what to eat for breakfast, or which candidate to support, you decide which choice is best for you and act accordingly. As you think about all the choices you confront in your life, consider why you make the ones that you do.

You make such decisions by evaluating your available choices based on certain **criteria,** or standards. For example, if you are evaluating a product, you may consider factors such as price, brand name, location, and size. Usually, you will base your evaluation on a combination of criteria—and you will inevitably weigh some criteria more heavily than others. The price of a new washing machine may matter more to one person while the brand may be more important to another.

Whether you realize it or not, you have years of practice in judging the trustworthiness of others' evaluations and the relevance of the criteria they use. When a newspaper endorses a political candidate, your familiarity with the newspaper and its editorial policy influences your view of that endorsement. If you are a movie fan, you have probably already come to some conclusions about the excerpt from the American Film Institute's evaluation of the "Greatest Movies" (shown on the opening pages of this chapter) based on your agreement or disagreement with its list of films. Your experience with everyday evaluations will help you determine the criteria for the evaluations you write in the different situations you will encounter in your life.

Rhetorical Knowledge

When you write an evaluation, you need to consider the criteria on which you will base your evaluation as well as how you will come up with that criteria. What aspects of the work, product, service, or idea should you examine for your evaluation? How can you best make an evaluative judgment about it? You will also need to decide what medium and genre will help you get your evaluation across to your audience most effectively.

Writing to Evaluate in Your College Classes

As a college student, you will be expected to read evaluations in most of your classes. While you may think most academic writing consists of logical arguments or the presentation of information or new theories or perspectives, you will also be asked to write evaluations in many of your college courses:

- Your psychology instructor may ask you to read brief summaries of experiments and evaluate how well the experiment's design served to answer the research question.
- Your political science instructor might ask you to rate the effectiveness of a political campaign.
- Your business and marketing instructor might ask you to evaluate several potential store locations.

Finally, in much of your academic writing, you will have to evaluate the sources and evidence you select to support your thesis statements.

Writing to Evaluate for Life

In addition to the evaluations you will consider and write while in college, you no doubt make evaluations every day in the professional, civic, and personal areas of your life.

In your **professional life,** your writing may often have an evaluative purpose. For example, if you have employees reporting to you, you will probably be asked to evaluate their job performances. You may consider criteria that include both verifiable information (does your employee arrive at work on time?) and opinions (is he or she an effective leader?). You will need to provide facts to support your judgments while sufficiently explaining your opinions.

In your **civic life,** you will often evaluate people and proposals and then make decisions or recommendations. Suppose that a local power company is planning to expand a power plant in your neighborhood, and you are a member of a committee that is evaluating the impact of the expansion. Before drafting its report, your committee will need to establish appropriate criteria for evaluating the plant, including the impact that the plant will have on property values and rents and the change it will cause in the local landscape. To provide a responsible, credible perspective, your committee will need to make your criteria explicit.

Without even realizing it, we often make evaluations when writing in our **personal life.** An e-mail to a relative may include comments about favorite restaurants, teachers, or newfound friends. On the one hand, we might feel more comfortable making evaluations for our friends and family. On the other, we may feel especially obligated to provide a useful evaluation because we care about the relationship.

Scenarios for Writing: Assignment Options

Your instructor may ask you to complete one or both of the following writing assignments that call for evaluation. Each of these assignments is in the form of a scenario, which gives you a sense of who your audience is and what you need to accomplish with your evaluative writing.

Starting on page 247, you will find guidelines for completing whatever assignment option you decide—or are asked—to complete. Additional scenarios for college and life may be found online.

Writing for College

SCENARIO 1   What Are the Rules? An Academic Evaluation

You may currently live (or may previously have lived) in a communal setting such as a dormitory, a military barracks, a summer camp, or a house or apartment with roommates. In that setting you are probably aware of rules and regulations (if you were in the military, you were definitely aware of them), yet you may not have thought about whether they are fair or not, or even if there are punishments for not obeying the rules. Or you may be living with one or both of your parents, who probably insist on certain rules (for example, rules about guests, cleanliness, a curfew, music level, what you can hang on the walls). Your audience will be your instructor and your classmates.

Consider questions such as these:

- Who controls what happens in the living quarters?
- What are the rules for living in the particular setting (communal or parental)? Are they fair and reasonable?
- Who is paying for the living quarters? Do they (should they) have total control of what happens in them? What, if any, restrictions are there?
- Should parents be allowed to place restrictions on college-age students who live at home? What rules would be reasonable?
- If an organization such as a college or the government controls the living quarters, can they monitor e-mail? Internet access?

Writing Assignment: Write an evaluation of the rules of the communal setting in which you currently live or once lived (for example, a dorm room such as that shown in Figure 9.1 or an apartment with others), or of your parent's or parents' rules. You will need to do some research on what the rules are and consider what you might use as criteria for evaluating them.

FIGURE 9.1
A College
Dormitory Room

Writing for Life

SCENARIO 2   Personal Writing: An Opinion Essay
Evaluating a Cultural Subject

Is there a cultural event taking place on your campus or in your community that you have a personal connection to and would like to evaluate? Or is there a place, such as a museum (Figure 9.2) or theater, where you would like to spend some time in a cultural pursuit: listening to music, watching a film, examining works of art? This assignment gives you an opportunity to evaluate a subject that matters to you personally.

Writing Assignment: Construct an evaluation of a cultural artifact, event, or place, explaining in detail the criteria on which you base your evaluation as well as how the cultural event or place fits your criteria. For this assignment—which asks for a personal evaluation—focus on a subject that matters to you, and then develop criteria based on your personal ideas. That is, decide how your subject—the book, play, building, work of art, or other cultural artifact, event, or place—makes you feel, what it brings to your mind, how it inspires a reaction within you.

FIGURE 9.2   How might you evaluate New York's Guggenheim Museum?

Rhetorical Considerations in Evaluative Writing

Audience: While your instructor and classmates are your initial audience for this assignment, you should also consider other audiences for your evaluative writing, depending on the scenario you have chosen. You need to consider whether the members of your audience will agree with you about the criteria for evaluating your subject, or whether you will need to convince them to accept your criteria.

Purpose: Your purpose is to evaluate your subject in terms of the criteria you decide on and persuade your audience to accept your judgment of it.

Voice, Tone, and Point of View: You have probably chosen your subject because you have a personal interest in it. What preconceptions about it do you have? How can you avoid letting them color your evaluation, perhaps leading you to a simplistic judgment? How can you use voice and tone to establish credibility, so your readers believe your evaluation and judgment?

For more on choosing a medium and genre, see Chapter 17 and Appendix C.

Context, Medium, and Genre: Keeping the context of the assignment in mind, decide on a medium and genre for your evaluation. How will your evaluation be used? If you are writing for an audience beyond the classroom, consider what will be the most effective way to present your evaluation to this audience. You might write an e-mail message to a friend, prepare a report for colleagues at work, or construct a Web site for members of your community.

◗ Critical Thinking, Reading, and Writing

Before you begin to write your own evaluation, read one or more evaluations to get a feel for this kind of writing. You might also consider how visuals could enhance your evaluative writing, as well as the kinds of sources you may need to consult.

To write an effective, responsible evaluation, you need to understand your subject and the reasons for your evaluation of it. You will need to choose valid criteria, organize your writing logically, and present your evaluation in a way that fulfills your responsibility to your readers. To do this, you need to think critically about your own views as well as those of any outside sources. Thinking critically does not necessarily mean that you will criticize, but rather that you will carefully consider which criteria are most and least important and how different aspects of your subject relate to each other.

Learning the Qualities of Effective Evaluative Writing

As we have seen, most writing is purposeful—you want to accomplish something. Focusing on the outcome should be the starting point for everything you write, and for an evaluation you want to make a reasoned, thoughtful, and justifiable judgment. You need to outline the criteria on which you will base your evaluation and then explain, in terms your readers can understand, how the subject of your evaluation fits the criteria.

Evaluative writing that achieves its goal has the following qualities:

- Clearly defined and explained criteria. Readers expect an evaluation to be based on specific criteria that are germane to the item being evaluated. You would evaluate an array of backpacks in a sporting-goods store using different criteria from what you would use to evaluate, say, a television news program. Readers deserve to have the criteria on which you are basing your evaluation defined, in detail, so they can understand your reasoning.

    If you are evaluating a work of art, you would use—and explain—criteria appropriate for evaluating art: for example, aesthetic appeal, the impact the work has on the viewer, and how well it represents a specific genre.

- Comparisons based on the criteria. Especially when you are evaluating products or services, you will need to show how your subject can be measured against other, similar, subjects and then explain this basis of comparison. You will compare like with like, showing how each aspect of the item you are evaluating rates in comparison with the same (or a similar) aspect of a similar item.

    You can make comparisons based on numerical information ("Tire brand C has a 50 percent longer tread life rating than Brand B, and twice as long as Brand A"). A table can help your readers see the basis of your claim.

Tire Brand	Tread Life Rating
Brand A	30,000 miles
Brand B	40,000 miles
Brand C	60,000 miles

Because this numerical information is verifiable and is not a matter of opinion, it can be persuasive evidence for your overall evaluation.

Finally, you can make comparisons based on more subjective crite-ria, such as your definition of "quality": You might note that a back-pack "should have this kind of fabric, this type of zipper, a lifetime warranty, and straps made out of this material." Then you would go on to outline how each backpack matches (or perhaps does not match) each of your criteria.

When you compare, it is important not to slant your evaluation by leaving out negative information or highlighting only those details that make the product, service, or work you favor seem to be the best. Instead, explain and compare honestly so your readers can reach their own conclusions about the effectiveness of your evaluation. You may find that the item you judge to be best is weak when measured on the basis of one or more of your criteria. It is vital to your overall credibil-ity to account for such shortcomings. Just because something is com-paratively weak in one or more areas does not mean that it can't still come out on top in your evaluation.

- **Evidence that supports your claims.** To accept your evaluation, your reader needs to understand that you are not just making assertions about your subject, but that you actually have evidence to support your claims. Evidence can include the following:

  - Testimony: "I've owned Ford automobiles for twenty years, and they've never let me down."

  - Statistical information: "A recent study by the National Highway Traffic Safety Administration found that nearly 50 percent of the 11,500 cars, pickup trucks, vans, and sport-utility vehicles the agen-cy checked had at least one tire with half-worn tread. Another 10 percent had at least one bald tire." (*Consumer Reports*)

  - Detailed description: the more details you can provide, the easier it will be for a reader to understand what you mean.

- **An analysis and explanation of how any visual elements affect your evaluation.** When they evaluate textbooks, teachers often consider how the visual elements in the books might help students learn more effectively. If you were a science teacher, for example, you might focus on the photographs or drawings in the various books under consideration and cite examples from the texts in your evaluative comments.

- **A clearly-stated judgment.** Readers can either agree or disagree with your conclusions, but if you have written a successful evaluation, they will understand how you arrived at your judgment.

In a computer document, put the above qualities of effective writing into your own words, and then refer to those notes as you conduct research and write your paper.

A WRITER'S RESPONSIBILITIES

Constructing Ethical Evaluations

As humans, we all make judgments, yet we rarely analyze the process that we use to make those judgments. However, whenever you make an evaluation, your judgments will have an impact, and because of that impact, you have certain responsibilities. When you make an evaluation in a civic writing situation, you have a responsibility to all who will be affected by the decision that will eventually be made. Remember, too, that the audience for a civic evaluation will include some who will disagree, and that potential for disagreement makes your honesty and sense of responsibility even more important. If you misrepresent some aspect of your evaluation, someone can use that distortion to discredit your entire evaluation. Writing an ethical evaluation means you must present statistics and other data accurately, without skewing them in your favor. If you have asked only a few of your classmates about the effectiveness of your campus recycling program, for example, you cannot say, "The majority of students who attend my college think that campus recycling is effective."

Reading, Inquiry, and Research: Learning from Texts That Evaluate

The reading selections that follow are examples of evaluative writing. As you read through the selections that your instructor assigns, consider the following questions:

- How clearly are the evaluative criteria explained?

- To what extent do I agree with the evaluation? Why?

- How well do I understand why the writer evaluated this subject as he did? That is, how clearly has the writer explained his judgment?

- How familiar am I with the subject that is being evaluated? What does my knowledge add to my reading of this text?

- What else would I like to know about the subject being evaluated? How can I learn more about it?

- How can I use the techniques of evaluative writing, as demonstrated here, in my own writing?

As you read an essay, take notes, jot down questions, and make observations about the essay, preferably in a computer file. If you want to use the information in your own writing, you will already have the main points in a digital format.

Thinking Rhetorically

Keep in mind the following questions as you read the two reviews of *Harry Potter and the Sorcerer's Stone* that follow. Make it a practice to ask yourself these questions in all your readings—personal, academic, and professional—and you will strengthen and sharpen your abilities as a reader and as a writer.

Rhetorical Knowledge: The Writer's Situation and Rhetoric

- *Audience:* Before the film was released, many people had read *Harry Potter and the Sorcerer's Stone*. As a result, critics Mitchell and Ebert are aware that many readers will know what will happen in the movie while others will not want to have the plot "spoiled" for them. How adequately do these reviewers present information for both audiences?

- *Purpose:* Film reviewers have one main task: to explain what they see as the strengths and weaknesses of the film being reviewed. How well do these two reviewers fulfill that task here? What can you point to in their reviews to illustrate your comments?

- *Voice and Tone:* Ebert seems to take a kinder, gentler stance toward the film than does Mitchell. What can you quote from the text to show this contrast?

- *Responsibility:* As critics for major American newspapers—the *Chicago Sun-Times* (Ebert) and the *New York Times* (Mitchell)—both reviewers have responsibilities to their readers. If you were such a critic, what might you see as your responsibilities to your readers?

- *Context and Format:* Consider the way this film had been highly anticipated by a huge audience. How does that seem to affect both reviews, do you think?

ROGER EBERT

Harry Potter and the Sorcerer's Stone

Roger Ebert has been the film critic for the *Chicago Sun-Times* since 1967. He is probably best known for his partnership with the late Gene Siskel in the television show "Siskel and Ebert at the Movies," which popularized the simple thumbs-up, thumbs-down critique of films. Today, Ebert's show with co-host Richard Roeper is seen in over 200 television markets across the country. Ebert was born in Urbana, Illinois, in 1942, and every year the city hosts the Roger Ebert Overlooked Film Festival, which Ebert founded in 1999. He is also the author of fifteen books including *The Great Movies; I Hated, Hated, HATED This Movie*; and *Roger Ebert's Book of Film*. You can read Ebert's weekly film reviews at rogerebert.suntimes.com. Ebert's review of *Harry Potter and the Sorcerer's Stone* originally appeared in the *Chicago Sun-Times* on November 16, 2001.

Ebert likes *Harry Potter and the Sorcerer's Stone* much more than does fellow reviewer Elvis Mitchell, whose review appears on pages 241–45. If you have seen this film, whom do you agree with?

Harry Potter and the Sorcerer's Stone is a red-blooded adventure movie, dripping with atmosphere, filled with the gruesome and the sublime, and surprisingly faithful to the novel. A lot of things could have gone wrong, and none of them have: Chris Columbus' movie is an enchanting classic that does full justice to a story that was a daunting challenge. The novel by J. K. Rowling was muscular and vivid, and the danger was that the movie would make things too cute and cuddly. It doesn't. Like an Indiana Jones for younger viewers, it tells a rip-roaring tale of supernatural adventure, where colorful and eccentric characters alternate with scary stuff like a three-headed dog, a pit of tendrils known as the Devil's Snare and a two-faced immortal who drinks unicorn blood. Scary, yes, but not too scary—just scary enough. 1

Three high-spirited, clear-eyed kids populate the center of the movie. Daniel Radcliffe plays Harry Potter, he with the round glasses, and like all of the young characters he looks much as I imagined him, but a little older. He once played David Copperfield on the BBC, and whether Harry will be the hero of his own life in this story is much in doubt at the beginning. 2

Deposited as a foundling on a suburban doorstep, Harry is raised by his aunt and uncle as a poor relation, then summoned by a blizzard of letters to become a student at Hogwarts School, an Oxbridge[1] for 3

---

[1] an academic program run jointly by Oxford and Cambridge universities

magicians. Our first glimpse of Hogwarts sets the tone for the movie's special effects. Although computers can make anything look realistic, too much realism would be the wrong choice for Harry Potter, which is a story in which everything, including the sets and locations, should look a little made up. The school, rising on ominous Gothic battlements from a moonlit lake, looks about as real as Xanadu[2] in *Citizen Kane,* and its corridors, cellars and great hall, although in some cases making use of real buildings, continue the feeling of an atmospheric book illustration.

At Hogwarts, Harry makes two friends and an enemy. The friends   4
are Hermione Granger (Emma Watson), whose merry face and tangled curls give Harry nudges in the direction of lightening up a little, and Ron Weasley (Rupert Grint), all pluck, luck and untamed talents. The enemy is Draco Malfoy (Tom Felton), who will do anything, and plenty besides, to be sure his house places first at the end of the year.

The story you either already know, or do not want to know. What is   5
good to know is that the adult cast, a who's who of British actors, play their roles more or less as if they believed them. There is a broad style of British acting, developed in Christmas pantomimes, which would have been fatal to this material; these actors know that, and dial down to just this side of too much. Watch Alan Rickman drawing out his words until they seem ready to snap, yet somehow staying in character. Maggie Smith, still in the prime of Miss Jean Brodie[3] is Prof. Minerva McGonagall, who assigns newcomers like Harry to one of the school's four houses. Richard Harris is headmaster Dumbledore, his beard so long that in an Edward Lear[4] poem, birds would nest in it. Robbie Coltrane is the gamekeeper, Hagrid, who has a record of misbehavior and a way of saying very important things and then not believing that he said them.

Computers are used, exuberantly, to create a plausible look in the   6
gravity-defying action scenes. Readers of the book will wonder how the movie visualizes the crucial game of Quidditch. The game, like so much else in the movie, is more or less as I visualized it, and I was reminded of Stephen King's theory that writers practice a form of telepathy, placing ideas and images in the heads of their readers. (The reason some movies don't look like their books may be that some producers don't read them.)

---

[2] newspaper magnate Charles Foster Kane's "castle" in the film *Citizen Kane*
[3] an unorthodox teacher, played by Maggie Smith, who had an unusual—and risky—relationship with some of her students
[4] writer of "nonsense" poetry

If Quidditch is a virtuoso sequence, there are other set pieces of almost equal wizardry. A chess game with life-size, deadly pieces. A room filled with flying keys. The pit of tendrils, already mentioned, and a dark forest where a loathsome creature threatens Harry but is scared away by a centaur. And the dark shadows of Hogwarts library, cellars, hidden passages and dungeons, where an invisibility cloak can keep you out of sight but not out of trouble. 7

During *Harry Potter and the Sorcerer's Stone*, I was pretty sure I was watching a classic, one that will be around for a long time, and make many generations of fans. It takes the time to be good. It doesn't hammer the audience with easy thrills, but cares to tell a story, and to create its characters carefully. Like *The Wizard of Oz, Willy Wonka and the Chocolate Factory, Star Wars* and *E.T.*, it isn't just a movie but a world with its own magical rules. And some excellent Quidditch players. 8

ELVIS MITCHELL

The Sorcerer's Apprentice

Elvis Mitchell began doing film reviews on public radio as an undergraduate at Wayne State University in Detroit. He has worked as a film critic for National Public Radio "Weekend Edition," the *Detroit Free Press*, the *Village Voice*, the *Fort Worth Star-Telegram, Spin* magazine, and the Independent Film Channel. From 1999 until 2004 Mitchell was a film critic for the *New York Times*. More recently he has been a visiting professor at Harvard, teaching film criticism and African-American film, and became a production consultant for Columbia Pictures. His review originally appeared in the *New York Times* on November 16, 2001.

Mitchell does not seem to like *Harry Potter and the Sorcerer's Stone*. If you have seen the film, do you agree with his comments?

The world may not be ready yet for the film equivalent of books on tape, but this peculiar phenomenon has arrived in the form of the film adaptation of J. K. Rowling's *Harry Potter and the Sorcerer's Stone*. The most highly awaited movie of the year has a dreary, literal-minded competence, following the letter of the law as laid down by the author. But it's all muted flourish, with momentary pleasures, like Gringott's, the bank staffed by trolls that looks like a Gaudí[1] throwaway. The picture is so 1

---
[1] Antoni Gaudí is a Spanish architect, famous for his unusual designs.

careful that even the tape wrapped around the bridge of Harry's glasses seems to have come out of the set design. (It never occurred to anyone to show him taping the frame together.)

The movie comes across as a covers act by an extremely competent tribute band—not the real thing but an incredible simulation—and there's an audience for this sort of thing. But watching *Harry Potter* is like seeing *Beatlemania* staged in the Hollywood Bowl, where the cheers and screams will drown out whatever's unfolding onstage.   2

To call this movie shameless is beside the point. It would probably be just as misguided to complain about the film's unoriginality because (a) it has assumed that the target audience doesn't want anything new and (b) Ms. Rowling's books cannibalize and synthesize pop culture mythology, proof of the nothing-will-ever-go-away ethic. She has come up with something like *Star Wars* for a generation that never had a chance to thrill to its grandeur, but this is *Young Sherlock Holmes* as written by C. S. Lewis from a story by Roald Dahl.   3

The director, Chris Columbus, is as adept as Ms. Rowling at cobbling free-floating cultural myths into a wobbly whole. The first film from a Columbus script, *Gremlins*, had the cheeky cheesiness of an urban legend written for Marvel Comics. Mr. Columbus probably felt like the right choice for *Harry Potter* because he has often used the same circuit boards as Ms. Rowling to design his fables. His *Home Alone* movies, *Mrs. Doubtfire* and *Stepmom* employ the theme of abandonment by parents as if it were a brand name. And like Mr. Columbus's films, Ms. Rowling's novels pull together archetypes that others have long exploited. This movie begins with a shot of a street sign that will cause happy young audiences to erupt in recognition, as the dry-witted giant Hagrid (Robbie Coltrane) and Professor McGonagall (Maggie Smith) drop a baby at the Doorstep of Destiny.   4

Years later Harry (Daniel Radcliffe), sporting the jagged thunderbolt scar across his forehead, is living there with his terrors of an aunt (Fiona Shaw) and uncle (Richard Griffiths).   5

Harry is the kid all kids dream they are. His special abilities are recognized by people other than the ones who have raised him. Hagrid returns to rescue him from his tiny room under the stairs and clues Harry in about the boy's inner force, which is why he doesn't fit into the world of Muggles, the nonmagical and nonbelievers.   6

Harry is shown the way to Hogwarts, an English boarding school for wizards run by Professor Dumbledore (Richard Harris), where Harry pals up with the gawky but decent Ron (Rupert Grint) and the bossy, precocious Hermione (Emma Watson). The instructors, who rule the classrooms   7 with varying degrees of imperiousness, include the acid Snape (Alan Rickman) and the mousy stutterer Quirrell (Ian Hart).

The casting is the standout, from the smaller roles up; it seems 8 that every working British actor of the last 20 years makes an appearance. John Hurt blows through as an overly intense dealer in magic equipment, schooling Harry on selecting his tools. While shopping for his magic equipment, Harry comes across the Sorcerer's Stone, a bedeviled jewel whose power affects his first year at the enchanted school.

Mr. Radcliffe has an unthinkably difficult role for a child actor; all 9 he gets to do is look sheepish when everyone turns to him and intones that he may be the greatest wizard ever. He could have been hobbled by being cast because he resembles the Harry of the book cover illustrations. It's a horrible burden to place on a kid, but it helps that Mr. Radcliffe does have the long-faced mournfulness of a 60's pop star. He also possesses a watchful gravity and, shockingly, the large, authoritative hands of a real wizard.

The other child actors shine, too. Ms. Watson has the sass and smarts 10 to suggest she might cast a spell of her own on Harry in the coming years and, one supposes, sequels. Mr. Grint has a surprising everyman quality, but the showstopper is Tom Felton as Draco Malfoy. This drolly menacing blond with a widow's peak is Harry's plotting foe, and he has the rotted self-confidence of one of the upperclassmen from Lindsay Anderson's "If." There has never been a kid who got so much joy from speaking his oddball name.

Ms. Shaw and Mr. Griffiths are enjoyably swinish, the most resolute 11 of Muggles. Mr. Rickman, whose licorice-black pageboy has the bounce of a coiffure from a hair products ad, is a threatening schoolroom don who delivers his monologues with a hint of mint; his nostrils flare so athletically that he seems to be doing tantric yoga with his sinuses. The mountainously lovable Mr. Coltrane really is a fairy-tale figure that kids dream about.

The movie's most consistently entertaining scene features a talking 12 hat, and that's not meant as an insult. The Sorting Hat, which has more personality than anything else in the movie, assigns the students to the various dormitories; it puts Harry, Ron and Hermione together.

But the other big set pieces are a letdown. The Quidditch match—the 13 school sport that's part polo, part cricket and part Rollerball, played on flying brooms—has all the second-rate sloppiness of the race in *Stars Wars—Episode 1: The Phantom Menace*. It's a blur of mortifyingly ordinary computer-generated effects.

Given that movies can now show us everything, the manifestations   14
that Ms. Rowling described could be less magical only if they were delivered
at a news conference. And the entrance that may be as eagerly awaited
as Harry's appearance—the arrival of Voldemort (Richard Bremmer),
the archvillain—is a disappointment, a special effect that serves as a
reminder of how much he stands in Darth Vader's shadow.

This overly familiar movie is like a theme park that's a few years   15
past its prime; the rides clatter and groan with metal fatigue every time
they take a curve. The picture's very raggedness makes it spooky, which
is not the same thing as saying the movie is intentionally unsettling.

No one has given Harry a pair of Hogwarts-edition Nikes, nor do he,   16
Hermione and Ron stop off to super-size it at the campus McDonald's:
exclusions that seem like integrity these days. (There's no need for product placement. The Internet is likely to have a systems crash from all the
kids going online to order maroon-and-gold scarves, which Harry and his
dorm mates wear.)

Another kind of exclusion seems bothersome, though. At a time   17
when London is filled with faces of color, the fleeting appearances by
minority kids is scarier than Voldemort. (Harry's gorgeous owl, snow
white with sunken dark eyes and feather tails dappled with black, gets
more screen time than they do.)

Mr. Columbus does go out of his way to give a couple of lines to a   18
little boy with a well-groomed head of dreadlocks. This movie may not be
whiter than most, but the peering-from-the-sidelines status accorded to
minorities seems particularly offensive in a picture aimed at kids. It's no
different in the books, really, but young imaginations automatically correct for this paucity.

A lack of imagination pervades the movie because it so slavishly fol-   19
lows the book. The filmmakers, the producers and the studio seem pan-
icked by anything that might feel like a departure from the book—which
already feels film-ready—so *Harry Potter and the Sorcerer's Stone* never takes
on a life of its own.

Someone has cast a sleepwalker's spell over the proceedings, and at   20
nearly two and a half hours you may go under, too. Its literal-mindedness
makes the film seem cowed by the chilling omnipresence of its own
Voldemort, Ms. Rowling, who hovered around the production.

The movie is so timid it's like someone who flinches when you   21
extend a hand to shake. This film is capable of a certain brand of magic:
it may turn the faithful into Muggles.

Harry Potter and the Sorcerer's Stone is rated PG (Parental Guidance 22 suggested), probably so that kids older than 12 won't think it's baby stuff. It includes scenes of magic someone must have found intense and threatening and a soupçon of strong language.

QUESTIONS FOR WRITING AND DISCUSSION

Critical Thinking: Responding to the Writer's Ideas

1. What is your initial reaction to Ebert's review? To Mitchell's review?

2. If you have seen this film and subsequent Harry Potter films, how do the films compare?

3. Make a list of the evaluative criteria that Ebert uses to judge this film. How fair is the evaluation that he makes? Why?

4. Do the same with Mitchell's review: list his evaluative criteria. How fair is Mitchell's evaluation? Why?

5. Of the two reviewers, which one do you see as being fairer in his review? Why?

Composing Processes and Knowledge of Conventions: The Writer's Strategies

1. What is the strongest part of Ebert's review? Why? Of Mitchell's review? Why? What do you consider to be the least effective part of each review? Why?

2. One criterion for an effective evaluation is that the writer explains the criteria on which he or she bases the evaluation. In what ways does Ebert do this? In what ways does Mitchell?

3. Ebert uses many examples from Rowling's novel in his own text. How helpful are they for purposes of constructing a film review? Why?

Inquiry and Research: Ideas for Further Exploration

1. In your library or on the Internet, find reviews of some of the other films that Ebert mentions—the *Indiana Jones* movies, *Citizen Kane, Star Wars*—and compare those reviews to Ebert's review of the Harry Potter movie. How effective are they as evaluations, compared to Ebert's comments?

Thinking about Visuals That Evaluate

We have already seen how a simple list of great films can help explain an evaluation in the American Film Institute's list at the beginning of this chapter (p. 229), and we have also seen how a simple table can help a writer make evaluative comparisons clear for readers, as in tire tread rating on page 235. How else might you as a writer use a visual aid to help explain your evaluation?

Figure 9.3 is an evaluation checklist of criteria from the federal government's Small Business Administration used to evaluate how well a business does its job. While the checklist is simple and brief, it could serve at least as a starting point for developing specific criteria for each item in more detail. What evidence would you look for in a company's past history to demonstrate how effectively it met that criteria?

Notice how the photographs of the tires in Figure 9.4 add to this excerpt from *Consumer Reports* on how to evaluate tire conditions:

> Worn tires—especially bald ones—can be deadly on wet roads, where the grooves aren't deep enough to channel water out from beneath the tread. The result is hydroplaning, where the tread skims the water's surface and the vehicle no longer responds to the steering wheel. Wet-weather braking and snow traction also decrease as tires wear.
>
> Tires are considered bald when one or more of their grooves reaches 2/32 of an inch deep, compared with about 10/32 of an inch for new tires (tread wear is usually measured in 1/32-inch increments). Manufacturers have made bald tires easier to spot by placing a series of molded horizontal bars at the base of the grooves. The bars become flush with surrounding tread when wear reduces a groove's depth to 2/32 of an

Evaluation criteria checklist

- Product/service delivered on time and within budget

- Experienced project management staff

- Excellent customer services

- Product met or exceeded needs

- Would recommend to others

FIGURE 9.3
A Checklist of Criteria for Evaluating Small Businesses

FIGURE 9.4
Examining Tire Treads

PINCHING PENNIES
Grooves reveal more of Lincoln's head as tires wear; wet-weather grip declines long before the top is visible.

GAUGING WEAR A tread-depth gauge shows wear more precisely. Wear bars approach the tread surface as grooves get shallow.

inch. That's also the point where tires will flunk a state safety inspection—and where tread must be worn for you to collect on a tire's tread-wear warranty.

Unfortunately, 2/32 of an inch may be too late if you drive in rain or snow. Based on our tests of new and half-tread-depth tires, you may want to consider replacing the ones on your car or truck closer to the 5/32-inch groove depth that marks the half-tread point on many tires.

Consider how each of these visual aids makes an evaluation more effective as well as more interesting to a reader.

- How does each visual serve the writer's evaluative purpose?
- How effectively does the visual help the reader understand the point of the evaluation?
- What other type of visual might be used in each situation?
- Besides lists of criteria and photographs, what other visuals can help writers explain an evaluation to readers?
- What other types of visual aids might help the reader better understand and agree with the evaluation?

Writing Processes

As you work on the assignment that you have chosen, remember the qualities of an effective and convincing evaluative paper, which are listed on pages 235–36. Also remember that writing is recursive—you might start with an invention activity or two and then conduct some research, which leads to more invention work and then a first draft; but then you might need to do more invention work to help flesh out your evaluation and conduct more research to add more criteria or more support; and then you'll revise your draft and possibly find another gap or two. So while the activities listed below imply that writers proceed step-by-step, as you actually write, you will keep coming back to your earlier work, modifying the criteria and strengthening the support for your claim.

As you work on your project, make certain that you save your computer files frequently because any work that you do not save could be lost. Also, savvy writers back up their computer files in two or more places—on an internal or external hard drive of the computer, on a USB flash drive, and/or on a rewritable CD or DVD, for example.

Invention: Getting Started

Invention activities can help you decide what you might want to evaluate before you make your evaluation. Writers often find it useful to work through several invention activities for any particular writing task. Regardless of the invention activities you do, try to answer these questions while you work:

- What do I already know about the subject (film, TV program, performance, place, product, service, or other subject) that I am thinking about evaluating?
- What makes each potential subject suitable for evaluation?
- What criteria can I establish for my evaluation? On what basis should I make my judgment? How can I compare it with other, similar, items?
- What kinds of explanation can I provide about each of my criteria?
- Where might I learn more about the subject (in the library, on the Web, by interviewing people)?
- What verifiable information about my subject is available (price, size, production information, historical information)?
- Are any of my criteria potentially just a matter of opinion and, if so, how might I explain them? How can I define criteria such as "quality" or "comfort" or "more reasonable" or "fairness"?
- What might my audience already know about my subject? What do I know about my audience? What don't I know that I should know?

Doing your invention work in electronic form, rather than on paper, lets you easily use your invention work as you construct a draft.

As with any kind of writing, invention activities improve with peer feedback and suggestions. Consider sharing the invention work you have done so far with several classmates or friends in order to understand your rhetorical situation more clearly and to generate more useful information.

Constructing and Supporting Evaluative Criteria

To evaluate any subject, you need to begin by considering the basis on which you will make your evaluation, as well as how you might support your criteria.

You evaluate a consumer product like a backpack differently than you evaluate a potential job, a work of art, a film, a CD, a computer game, or an evening news broadcast, so consider the various aspects of the subject on which you might base your evaluation. Here are just a few possibilities:

- Physical aspects such as size, weight, shape, taste, smell, and sound

- Quality, including warranty period, type of warranty offered, component quality (steel vs. plastic, for example), and power aspects (size of amplifier)

- Aesthetic aspects, meaning how the item feels to use (drive, listen to, sit in, wear), color, and proportion

- Entertainment-value aspects (what will you use this product for?)

- Comparative aspects, such as the following:
  - Why might this stock be a good investment?
  - Which career would give me the greatest satisfaction? Why?
  - Which airline is the safest?
  - What is the best place to study? Why?
  - Which employee should I promote to manager?
  - Which political candidate should get my vote?

In most evaluations, you will need to show how your subject can be measured against other, similar, subjects and explain the basis of your comparison. If you are comparing two automobiles, for example, you would probably compare both cars in terms of price, gas mileage, and maintenance, among other criteria.

For more on making comparisons, see Chapter 13.

Once you have a basis for comparison, the first step in deciding the criteria for your evaluation is to look over your invention work and consider what you have learned so far about your subject. Try to answer these questions:

- What do you consider the most important aspect of your subject? Would most people agree that this aspect is most important?

- What other qualities, either positive or negative, does this subject have? Which are more important to you, and which are less important?

- If you are evaluating a subject for its usefulness, what must it do? How can you determine that your subject will do what you want or need it to?

- If you are evaluating a product or service, think about what you will use it for. If you are evaluating a child's car seat, for example, the most important criterion will probably be safety. What do you mean by the term *safe*, and how can you tell if a particular car seat is safe?

- If a product or service needs to be reliable, what do you mean by that term, and how can you determine reliability?

- What criteria are absolutely necessary for the subject to possess? What must it have? What criteria are important, but perhaps not as necessary? How can you assign a value or weight to each criterion?

- What research might help you to make your evaluation? What can you learn at the library? Will a search of the World Wide Web help? What would you gain from talking with others or conducting a survey?

Exploring Your Ideas with Research

While personal opinions are sometimes sufficient evidence for an evaluation, in more formal settings you will need to support your claims with outside research. One advantage of conducting research is that the information you find will help you form your judgment about your subject. Its is important not to make that judgment too soon—often you won't know what you really think until you have done a lot of invention work, conducted much of your research, and have even written a draft or two.

For help with locating sources of information and with field research, see Chapter 19; for help with taking notes and documenting your sources, see Chapter 20.

Research, of course, can give you solid evidence—verifiable information, such as figures, statistics, data, or expert testimony—to help support your final evaluation. The kind and amount of research you will need to do will vary according to the rhetorical situation: who your audience is and what you are trying to accomplish. Use the reporter's questions of *who, what, when, where, why,* and *how* to get started on your research. After you have determined the information you need, decide what kind of research you need to conduct in order to gather that information, and conduct research in the library and on the Internet. You may also find it necessary to do field research.

As you review your notes, look for information that will help you show how your subject does, or does not, meet a given criterion. Look as well for any conclusions that others have drawn about the subject of your evaluation—and consider if and how your own evaluation differs from theirs. While you can use others' opinions in support of your own conclusion, hearing and reading what others have said will often provide new ideas and suggest additional avenues for research.

As you conduct your research, you may find that other writers have reached judgments that differ from yours. You will want to address—and counter—their opinions in your own comments, since doing so will strengthen your evaluation.

Reviewing Your Invention and Research

After you have conducted your research, you need to review your invention work and notes and think about the information you have collected from outside sources and how that information matches the criteria you have for your evaluation. You may be ready to decide on a working thesis statement— a statement that summarizes the main point of your evaluation—at this point. Even though you might already have a general idea of the conclusion your evaluation is leading you to, your thesis should come *from* your complete evaluation. It is best to decide on your thesis when you have done a lot of invention work (listing, brainstorming, clustering, and other strategies) and research. You might even wait until after you construct your first draft.

Organizing Your Evaluation

Once you have some sense of the criteria you will use and how your subject matches those criteria, you need to consider how you might organize your evaluation. The questions that you need to ask yourself when deciding on your organization are all rhetorical:

- Who is the audience for your evaluation?
- Why might they be interested in your evaluation, or how you can make them interested in it?

TechNote

If there's one thing computers are good at, it's establishing hierarchies (systems of ranking, prioritizing, and organizing things). When you're writing an essay that evaluates something, the computer screen can serve as a kind of workshop space, where you can move around ideas, concepts, criteria, issues, and controversies.

You can use different programs— and sometimes different windows within the same software application— to design charts, outlines, tables, Venn diagrams, timelines, and other visual space-holders for your information. Use color, line, shape, and space to move information around on the plane of the computer screen, looking for categories and interesting interrelations among your ideas and segments of information.

For more on design and visuals, including examples of different kinds of graphics, see Chapter 18.

- What is your purpose for writing—that is, what will your readers learn about your subject by reading your evaluation? How will that knowledge help them with their evaluation?

For more on the inductive and deductive methods, see Chapter 8, pages 209–10.

The answers to these questions can help you decide what you need to emphasize, which in turn will help you choose an organizational approach.

Here is a brief outline of three possible organizational approaches for writing an evaluation.

Options for Organization

First Inductive Approach	Second Inductive Approach	Deductive Approach
• Outline why you are making the evaluation. • Discuss/explain the criteria. • Explain how well your subject or subjects match (or fail to match) the various criteria. • Discuss which subjects are "best," according to the evaluative criteria you have established. Explain your thesis statement in your conclusion.	• Begin with a discussion of the subject or subjects that you are evaluating. • Explain its or their strengths and weaknesses. • Outline how the positive and negative points match each of your criteria. • Explain how the subject or subjects you are evaluating fulfill those criteria (this, then, is your thesis statement)	• Begin with the conclusion that you have reached about the subject or subjects (your thesis statement) • Explain why and how you reached that conclusion using a compare-and-contrast format: compare and contrast each aspect of what you are evaluating in relation to the criteria.

Constructing a Complete Draft

Once you have generated some initial thoughts and ideas, selected the criteria for judging your subject, and reviewed your notes from the reading and research you have done, your next step is to write a first draft, which is often called a working draft. Your first draft is your opportunity to expand, explain, and develop your ideas.

Before beginning your draft, review the writing you have done so far. What are the relative advantages of evaluating several items or of concentrating on just one? Why? Review the criteria that you have developed and decide which you want to emphasize. If your instructor and/or peers have given you suggestions, consider how you will incorporate their advice into your evaluation. As you prepare to write, ask yourself the following questions:

- What is the most effective way to explain my criteria?
- In what ways does the subject of my evaluation match up with (or fail to match up with) the criteria I have selected?
- What is my final evaluation?
- How can I express my main point effectively as a thesis statement?

As you draft your evaluation, stop occasionally to read your work, imagining that you are reading it for the first time. Because your draft is an exploratory text, ask yourself the following questions:

For more on comparison, definition, and description, see Chapter 13.

- How have I compared my subject with other, similar items?
- How effectively have I added details demonstrating how well the subject matches my criteria?
- What visual information might I use to explain my evaluation?
- How clear is my final judgment?

Introduction: One of the qualities of a successful evaluation is that it grabs and holds readers' attention. Some strategies that will help you hook your readers include the following:

- *Begin by explaining why you are making the evaluation—your rhetorical purpose—followed by a discussion of your criteria.* It is also often helpful to include an explanation of why you selected these criteria. This is usually the approach taken by articles in consumer magazines such as *Consumer Reports*.
- *Indicate your conclusion at the beginning.* You will then explain in the body of your text why and how you reached that conclusion. Both of the reviews of *Harry Potter and the Sorcerer's Stone* reprinted in this chapter begin with the critic's judgment.
- *Set the scene for your evaluation.* Depending on your topic, you might open your evaluation with a description of your subject.

Body: If you are using an inductive method, you indicate what you want to evaluate and on what basis at the beginning, and as you work through the process (and through the body of your evaluation), you answer as you go. If you are using the deductive method, you begin by stating your judgment, and then use the body of your paper to support it, often by comparing and contrasting your subject with other subjects of the same type.

Conclusion: Regardless of the organizational method you decide to employ, you need to make sure that your judgment of your subject—your evaluation—is clearly stated. Remember that in an evaluation, your ultimate conclusion is usually your thesis statement, or main point, but your conclusion also can serve other purposes. A conclusion in evaluative writing often does the following:

- *Summarizes how each supporting piece of evidence helps support your main point.* In a lengthy, detailed evaluation, a summary of your findings can help readers recall the main points that you are making.
- *Reaches out to your audience.* An appeal to the audience is an especially effective way to end an evaluation, as often you want them to not only agree with your evaluation but also to do something with what they have learned.

Title: As you compose your evaluative writing, a title should emerge at some point—perhaps late in the process. The title should reflect your judgment of your subject, and it should catch your readers' attention and make them want to read your essay.

VISUALIZING VARIATIONS

Using Visuals to Support Your Evaluation

If you decided to respond to Scenario 2 (p. 233), which asks that you evaluate a cultural subject, you might include photographs to illustrate what you are evaluating.

For instance, the three authors of this text live in Arizona—part of what is called the Old West. We still have cowboys and cowgirls, and rodeos and parades are part of our tradition. If we were evaluating the local rodeo or a Fourth of July parade, we could find any number of photographs that would illustrate the event. What if our criteria for evaluating this cultural event included *plenty of activities, tradition,* and *audience involvement?*

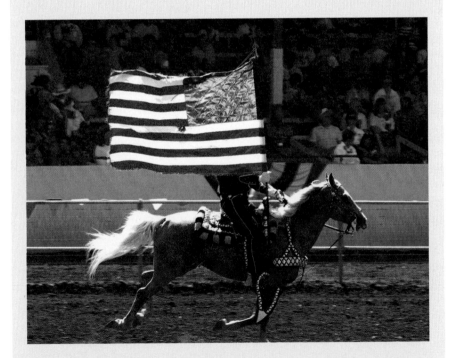

Think about what this photograph shows and what it might suggest to a reader:

- Part of American history; part of a long-standing tradition

- Movement; action

- The involvement of animals; this horse is decorated with fancy hardware

- Lots of people watching in the audience

What do you think this picture would add to our evaluation of a local rodeo?

For any photograph you are considering, then, ask yourself the following questions:

- What might this photograph show about my subject?

- How can I select a photograph that will support a point I want to make and help me justify my overall judgment about my subject?

TechNotes It is always a good idea to store the photographs you find in your research in a separate computer file, so you will have easy access to them when you start constructing your evaluation. Charts and graphs are also useful visuals for evaluations. If you find that you need to include numbers and statistical information in your evaluation, consider putting them into an Excel document. The Excel program has a function that allows you to easily convert your numerical data into a table or graph.

For more on using visuals, see Chapter 18.

Revising

Once you have a full draft of your evaluation, you still have much to do. First, however, you should set the draft aside so that you can gain some critical distance. You should then read it with fresh eyes. When you approach your work this way, you will find it easier to notice criteria that are irrelevant, support that is not fully developed, or places where a compelling photograph or other visual might add to the impact of your argument.

As you work to revise your early drafts, hold off on doing a great deal of heavy editing. When you revise you will probably change the content and structure of your paper, so time spent working to fix problems with sentence style or grammar, punctuation, or mechanics at this stage is often wasted.

When you reread the first draft of your evaluation, here are some questions to ask yourself:

- Have I effectively explained or indicated my criteria, so the reader knows on what basis I am making my evaluation?

- What else might my audience want or need to know about my subject?

- How else might I interest my audience in my evaluation of this subject?

- What did I find out about my subject that I did not include in my evaluation? (Effective research always results in more information than you can include, so consider what you left out that you might include in your next draft.)

- How clearly have I defined any terms my readers might not know?

- Could some aspects of my evaluation be better presented as a graph or chart?

Technology can help you revise and edit your writing more easily. Use your word processor's track-changes tool to try out revisions and editing changes. After you have had time to think about the possible changes, you can "accept" or "reject" them. Also, you can use your word processor's comment tool to write reminders to yourself when you get stuck with a revision or some editing task.

Because it is so difficult even for experienced writers to see their emerging writing with a fresh eye, it is almost always useful to ask classmates, friends, or family members to read drafts of your persuasive writing.

WRITER'S WORKSHOP

Responding to Full Drafts

Working with one or two other classmates, read each evaluation and offer comments and questions that will help each of you see your papers' strengths and weaknesses. Consider the following questions as you do:

- Write a brief narrative comment outlining your first impression of this draft. How effective is the title at drawing you in? Why? What are your overall suggestions for improvement? What part(s) of the text are especially strong?

- How clear and understandable is the point of the evaluation?

- How has the writer explained the subject of the evaluation? How might the writer develop the explanation further to make it more effective?

- How clearly and thoroughly has the writer explained and justified the criteria? What details need to be added or clarified?

- How effectively has the writer applied his or her criteria?

- How adequately are all assertions supported with evidence?

- If the writer makes comparisons, how clear are they? Where might additional comparisons be called for?

- How could the writer more clearly match the criteria to the subject? Are there any criteria that the writer discusses but never applies to the subject?

- What terms need to be defined?

- How effective is the organization of this evaluation? How logically are the points connected to the writer's thesis? Point out any gaps that you notice. What evidence is provided in support of each contention?

- How might visuals such as charts, tables, graphs, or photographs help the writer explain or support his or her criteria more effectively?

- How clearly does the writer present any opposing points of view on this subject? How effectively does the writer answer opposing viewpoints? How might the writer acknowledge and/or refute them more effectively?

- How adequately is the writer's overall evaluation supported by the evidence he or she has presented? Would you, the reader, reach the same conclusion? Why or why not?

Responding to Readers' Comments

Once they have received feedback on their writing from peers, instructors, and others, all writers have to figure out what to do with that feedback. As with all feedback, it is important to listen carefully to it and consider what your reader has to say. Then it is up to you, as the author, to decide *how* to come to terms with these suggestions.

Knowledge of Conventions

When effective writers edit their work, they attend to the conventions that will help readers understand their writing. These include genre conventions, documentation, format, usage, grammar, and mechanics. By attending to these conventions in your writing, you make reading a more pleasant experience for readers.

Editing

After you revise, you have one more important step—editing and polishing. When you edit and polish, you make changes to your sentence structure and word choice to improve your style and to make your writing clearer and more concise. You also check your work to make sure it adheres to conventions of grammar, usage, punctuation, mechanics, and spelling. If you have used sources in your paper, you should make sure you are following the documentation style your instructor requires.

Because it is sometimes difficult to identify small problems in a familiar text, it often helps to distance yourself so that you can approach your draft with fresh eyes. Some people read from the last sentence to the first so that the content, and their familiarity with it, doesn't cause them to overlook an

See Chapter 20 for more on documenting sources using MLA or APA style.

error. We strongly recommend that you ask classmates, friends, and tutors to read your work to help you find editing problems that you may not see.

To assist you with editing, we offer here a round-robin editing activity focused on careful word choice, which is a common concern in writing to evaluate.

WRITER'S WORKSHOP

Round-Robin Editing with a Focus on Careful Word Choice

Evaluative writing often requires careful word choice (diction). It is critical to select words that clearly represent what you intend to say. For example, notice how the revision to this word choice problem improves the clarity of this sentence:

rely on

We don't have time to prepare a full-blown meal, so we ˄ ~~have created~~ fast food to fit with our fast-paced lives.

People in general have not "created" fast food, but they have come to rely on the convenience that it provides.

Working with several peers, consult a good college dictionary and the portion of a handbook that covers word choice. If you are uncertain about a specific word choice, ask your instructor for help.

Genres, Documentation, and Format

For advice on writing in different genres, see Appendix C. For guidelines for formatting and documenting papers in MLA or APA style, see Chapter 20.

If you are writing an academic paper in response to Scenario 1, you will need to follow the conventions for the discipline in which you are writing and the requirements of your instructor. If you are working on Scenario 2, an opinion essay, you can be somewhat more informal than you would be for an academic paper.

If you have used material from outside sources, including visuals, you will need to give credit to those sources, using the documentation style required by the discipline you are working in and by your instructor.

Student Annlee Lawrence Shares Her Evaluation

Student writer Annlee Lawrence decided to write an evaluation of the meals available at some local fast-food restaurants. Here is her final draft.

ANNLEE LAWRENCE

Who Has the Healthiest Burger?

Did you know that McDonald's Corporation operates more than thirty thousand restaurants in more than one hundred countries on six continents? In the United States, McDonald's represents 43% of the total fast-food market (Super-Size Me). Restaurants that are part of the McDonald's organization feed more than forty-six million people a day— more than the entire population of Spain. While the global reach of McDonald's and other fast-food chains is impressive, it is also dangerous. As Surgeon General David Satcher comments, "Fast food is a major contributor to the obesity epidemic" (Super-Size Me).

It's no wonder that 60% of Americans are overweight or obese. Obesity, if left unchecked, will soon surpass smoking as the leading cause of preventable death in America. So why can't we seem to stay away from our beloved Big Macs or Whoppers? Probably because our lives demand it at times. Busy Americans often don't have time to prepare a home-cooked meal, so they rely on fast food to fit in with their fast-paced lives. Unfortunately, then, fast food is a part of today's society, but obesity can be avoided through moderation of consumption. According to guidelines published by the Office of the Surgeon General, most fast food contains high—and therefore unhealthy—levels of calories, fat, and cholesterol, three dangerous aspects of an unhealthy lifestyle. But some fast-food meals are not as bad for you as others. For this evaluation, I chose three popular meals: the Whopper Combo from Burger King, Wendy's Classic Single Combo, and McDonald's Quarter Pounder Combo.

When I researched the nutritional content of these three meals, I found that all three have high calorie content (see Fig. 1). The Whopper Combo from Burger King has been a favorite of Americans for generations. But is it as good for your body as it is to your taste buds? When I researched the nutritional information, I discovered that this meal has a grand total of 1260 calories. By contrast, Wendy's Classic Single Combo has 990 calories, and McDonald's Quarter Pounder Combo has 980.

The Burger King Whopper meal not only has the highest calorie count, it also has the highest fat content at 58 grams of total fat (see Fig. 2). The next lowest is Wendy's Combo meal at 41 grams of total fat. The lowest of the three is McDonald's Quarter Pounder Combo at 34 grams of fat.

Last but not least is the cholesterol content (see Fig. 3). A high level of cholesterol in the blood can increase the risk of heart disease. Once again, the Burger King Whopper meal has the highest level at 85 milligrams. McDonald's Quarter Pounder Combo has the next highest

1

2

3

4

5

One of Lawrence's classmates commented on her criteria:

These seem like good criteria, but why did you choose them? Do you need a stronger reason for your criteria here?

Notice how Lawrence offers support for her criteria: information from the Surgeon General's guidelines.

One peer reviewer had this comment:

This is a lot of statistics . . . Can you may be give all this in a table or chart?

Note how Lawrence put that data into three charts.

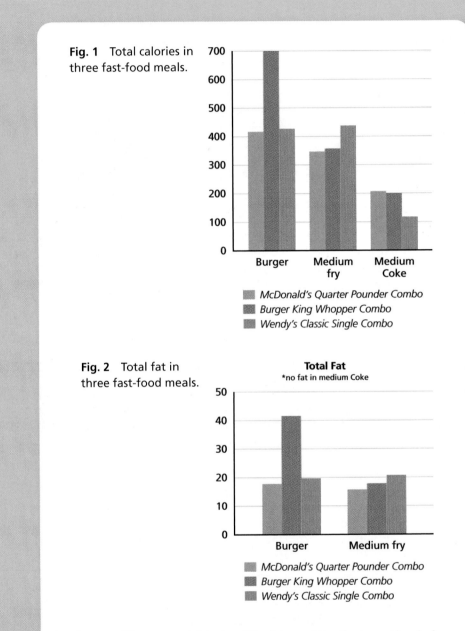

Fig. 1 Total calories in three fast-food meals.

Legend:
- McDonald's Quarter Pounder Combo
- Burger King Whopper Combo
- Wendy's Classic Single Combo

Fig. 2 Total fat in three fast-food meals.

Total Fat
*no fat in medium Coke

Legend:
- McDonald's Quarter Pounder Combo
- Burger King Whopper Combo
- Wendy's Classic Single Combo

level at 70 milligrams, and this time Wendy's meal has the lowest level of cholesterol at 65 milligrams.

So if you are in a hurry and feel like grabbing a burger, you are probably better off getting the McDonald's Quarter Pounder meal, which has fewer calories and lower fat content than the other two meals. This

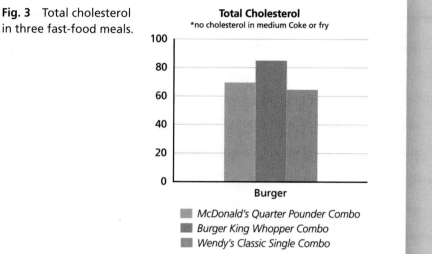

Fig. 3   Total cholesterol in three fast-food meals.

doesn't mean, however, that you should make a habit of eating at McDonald's or any other fast-food restaurant chain, especially if you have a genetic predisposition to high cholesterol levels. Obviously, as the movie Super-Size Me proved, even the "healthy" fast food isn't good for you when consumed on a regular basis. But if eaten in moderation, fast food is one of the best things to happen to busy Americans.

Works Cited

AOA Fact Sheets. American Obesity Association. 2 May 2005. 14 Oct. 2005.
    <http://www.obesity.org/subs/fastfacts/obesity_US.shtml>.
Burger King Nutritional Information. 18 Aug. 2004. <http://www.bk.com/
    Nutrition/PDFs/brochure.pdf>.
McDonald's USA Nutrition Facts for Popular Menu Items. 3 Apr. 2005.
    <http://www.mcdonalds.com/app_controller.nutrition.index1
    .html>.
McDonald's Investor Fact Sheet 2006. 14 Oct. 2005. <http://mcd.mobular
    .net/mcd/90/8/26/>.
Super-Size Me. Dir. Morgan Spurlock. Hart Sharp Video. 2004.
United States. Office of the Surgeon General. Dietary Guidelines for Ameri-
    cans 2005. 12 Jan. 2005. 10 Apr. 2005. <http://www.healthierus.gov/
    dietaryguidelines/index.html>.
Wendy's U.S. Nutrition Information. 3 Apr. 2005. <http://www.wendys
    .com/food/US_Nutrition_2003.pdf>.

One of Lawrence's classmates pointed out in her first draft that she had problems with her documentation:

Don't you have a quote in the first paragraph from the Surgeon General? There's no citation for it here.

Lawrence added a citation for the Surgeon General's *Dietary Guidelines*.

QUESTIONS FOR WRITING AND DISCUSSION

Rhetorical Knowledge: The Writer's Situation and Rhetoric

1. **Audience:** Who do you see as Lawrence's audience? What can you point to in the text that supports your claim?

2. **Purpose:** Lawrence seems to have another purpose for her evaluation, in addition to writing this paper for a class assignment: to help her classmates. How well does she fulfill that larger purpose?

3. **Voice and tone:** What voice/tone strategies does Lawrence use to establish her *ethos*? What passages can you point to in the text that help demonstrate her credibility on this issue?

4. **Responsibility:** How effectively does Lawrence represent the facts about calories and other nutritional data in her evaluation?

5. **Context and format:** Lawrence is writing as a college student who eats fast food. How does that affect her credibility in this evaluation?

Critical Thinking: Responding to the Writer's Ideas

1. What is your initial response to Lawrence's essay? How much do you agree with her evaluation? Why?

2. Lawrence focuses on only three criteria for her evaluation. How sufficient is that, do you think, for her to construct an effective evaluation? Why?

Composing Processes and Knowledge of Conventions: The Writer's Strategies

1. How effective is the evidence that Lawrence provides? What other evidence might she have used?

2. How effectively does Lawrence use the quotation and information from the Surgeon General?

Inquiry and Research: Ideas for Further Exploration

1. Interview several of your classmates, explaining Lawrence's conclusions. What is their reaction to her evaluation? Might it influence their dining decisions in the future?

Self-Assessment: Reflecting on Your Learning Goals

Now that you have constructed a piece of evaluative writing, go back and reconsider your learning goals, which you and your classmates considered at the beginning of this chapter (pp. 226–27). To help reflect on the learning goals that you have achieved, respond in writing to the following questions:

Rhetorical Knowledge

- *Audience:* What have you learned about addressing an audience in evaluative writing?

- *Purpose:* What have you learned about the purposes for constructing an evaluation?

- *Rhetorical situation:* How did the writing context affect your evaluative text? How did your choice of subject affect the research you conducted and how you presented your evaluation?

- *Voice and tone:* How would you describe your voice in this essay? Your tone? How do they contribute to the effectiveness of your evaluation?

- *Context, medium, and genre:* How did your context determine the medium and genre you chose, and how did those decisions affect your writing?

Critical Thinking, Reading, and Writing

- *Learning/inquiry:* Describe the process you went through to focus on a main idea, or thesis. How did you judge what was most and least important in your evaluation?

- *Responsibility:* How did you fulfill your responsibility to your readers?

- *Reading and research:* What did you learn about evaluative writing from the reading selections in this chapter? What research did you conduct? How sufficient was the research you did?

- As a result of writing this evaluation, how have you become a more critical thinker, reader, and writer? What skills do you hope to develop further in your next writing project?

Writing Processes

- *Invention:* What invention strategies were most useful to you?

- *Organizing your ideas and details:* What organization did you use? How successful was it?

- *Revising:* What are the strongest and the weakest parts of the paper you wrote for this chapter? Why? If you could go back and make an additional revision, what would it be?

- *Working with peers:* How did your instructor or peer readers help you by making comments and suggestions about your writing? List some examples of useful comments that you received. How could you have made better use of the comments and suggestions you received?

- Did you use photographs or other visuals to help explain your evaluation to readers? If so, what did you learn about incorporating these elements?

- What "writerly habits" have you developed, modified, or improved on as you constructed the writing assignment for this chapter? How will you change your future writing activities, based on what you have learned about yourself?

Conventions

- *Editing:* What sentence problem did you find most frequently in your writing? How will you avoid that problem in future assignments?

- *Genre:* What conventions of the genre you were using, if any, gave you problems?

- *Documentation:* Did you use sources for your paper? If so, what documentation style did you use? What problems, if any, did you have with it?

If you are preparing a course portfolio, file your written reflections so that you can return to them when you next work on your portfolio.

Rhetorical Knowledge

- *Audience:* Your success will partially depend on how well you have analyzed your audience. How can you make your audience interested in this cause-and-effect relationship? What might this audience already know or believe about this relationship? How will your audience benefit from what you have to say? What evidence will convince this audience that this relationship exists?

- *Purpose:* Your main purpose is argumentative: to convince readers that a cause-and-effect relationship exists. Your purpose may be first to identify a cause and then determine its effect(s). Or your purpose may be to determine a series of causes and effects—often called a *causal chain*—where one cause leads to an effect, which then causes a second effect, and so on.

- *Rhetorical situation:* Think about all of the factors that affect where you stand in relation to your subject—what is compelling you to write your causal analysis essay?

- *Writer's voice and tone:* You will need to present yourself as a logical writer who provides reliable information. If readers perceive you as uninformed, illogical, or inflexible, you will lose credibility.

- *Context, medium, and genre:* You will need to decide on the best medium and genre to use to present your causal analysis to the audience you want to reach. Visuals such as flowcharts are often an effective way of helping audiences understand causal relationships.

Critical Thinking, Reading, and Writing

- *Learning/inquiry:* When you write about causes and effects, you must think critically about whether an actual cause-and-effect relationship exists. It may be coincidental that one event happens right after another or that two phenomena often occur together; the events or phenomena may not have a causal relationship.

- *Responsibility:* You have a responsibility to recognize that causes and effects may be more complex than you first realize. Any given phenomenon or event is likely to have many causes and to produce many effects. Determining what is and is not a cause (or an effect), or determining which of several causes (or effects) is most important, may require considerable time and thought.

- *Reading and research:* As you conduct research about a causal relationship, make sure you understand the nature of the relationship well enough to be able to document the causality. Also, as you conduct research, always ask, "How could X cause Y, specifically?"

Writing Processes

- *Invention:* Begin by recording possible answers to the question you are considering (for example, why do gasoline prices fluctuate?), using an invention strategy such as brainstorming or listing. As you write, you will undoubtedly come up with more questions about a possible cause-and-effect relationship.

- *Organizing your ideas and details:* Once you have recorded some ideas, you can think about how to organize your main points and what supporting evidence you need to provide.

- *Revising:* You will need to read your work with a critical eye, to make certain that it fulfills the assignment and displays the qualities of a good causal analysis.

- *Working with peers:* Peer review is a crucial part of the process of writing a causal analysis because it enables you to get a sense of how an audience will respond to your claim that a cause-and-effect relationship exists. Peers can be especially useful in helping you think critically about possible causes for an effect or possible effects of a cause.

Conventions

- *Editing:* When you edit a causal analysis—or anything that you write—make sure that the subordinate clauses in your paper are attached to independent clauses and are therefore part of complete sentences. The round-robin activity in this chapter will help you look for and correct this type of sentence fragment (p. 295).

- *Genres for cause-and-effect writing:* In your college classes, writing about cause-and-effect relationships is usually academic writing, so you will be required to follow the conventions for an academic essay. Other, nonacademic, writing situations may call for a variety of genres, including memos, essays, Web log (blog) postings, letters to the editor, and even formal position papers.

- *Documentation:* You will probably need to rely on sources outside of your experience, and if you are writing an academic essay, you will be required to cite them using the appropriate documentation style.

Chapter 10

Writing to Explain Causes and Effects

Here is the space weather report from NASA for one day in October 2003:

> Giant sunspots 484 and 486 remain visible on the sun, posing a continued threat for X-class solar explosions. Indeed, on Sunday, Oct. 26, 2003, there were two such blasts—one from each sunspot. The explosions hurled coronal mass ejections (CMEs) into space and somewhat toward Earth.
>
> Because of these events, sky watchers should be alert for auroras during the nights ahead. . . . Forecasters estimate a 25 percent chance of severe geomagnetic storming when the incoming CMEs sweep past Earth and deliver (probably glancing) blows to our planet's magnetic field.

Things happen, and we are often curious about how and why. We wonder what causes natural phenomena such as the northern lights (aurora borealis), we want to know what caused the extinction of certain species, and we have a vested interest in knowing the causes of diseases such as cancer, Alzheimer's, or schizophrenia.

Consider the events that take place in your life: You are always surrounded by *changes* that occur, *trends* you can observe (and wonder why they happen), *behavior* that is unusual or surprising. All have *causes*, reasons why they happened. In fact "why?" is probably the best question you can ask as you explore any cause-and-effect relationship.

In some cases, discovering the cause is an end in itself. For instance, we may one day know precisely why the dinosaurs became extinct about sixty million years ago, but we may not be able to use that information to change life as it is currently lived on Earth. In other cases, though, we can use information gained from causal analysis to eliminate or avoid the causes of certain effects. For instance, in recent years scientists have come to understand—and share with the public—the strong cause-and-effect relationship between tobacco use and certain kinds of cancer.

Rhetorical Knowledge

When you write about causes and effects, you need to have a specific purpose in mind, some sense of your audience, and an idea of an effective way to substantiate the cause-and-effect relationships you are considering. How can you prove your claim that a cause-and-effect relationship exists?

Writing about Causes and Effects in Your College Classes

Many of the assignments for your college classes will ask you to determine the causes of an event, a trend, or a phenomenon. Here are some examples:

- Your dance instructor may ask you to explain why and how dance steps and movement have evolved over time.
- Your biology instructor may ask you to explain what causes leaves to turn color and drop from trees in certain parts of the world in the fall.
- In a sociology course, you might investigate the possible effects of anti-poverty programs on the crime rate in low-income neighborhoods.

Writing about Causes and Effects for Life

Much of the writing constructed in **professional settings** is designed to solve problems. The first step in solving any problem is determining why the problem exists:

- *Why* is quality control so much better at one plant than it is at the others?
- *Why* can't we increase sales to the level we need to become profitable?

Many professionals in the work world spend a good deal of their time determining causes and effects:

- A team of medical researchers writes a paper reporting on a study that reveals a cause-and-effect relationship between Vitamin C deficiency and osteoporosis.
- A teacher wonders why some students have difficulty reading and studies them to find out the causes of their problems.

When writers focus on **community issues,** they often need to find and explain answers to *why* questions:

- A citizens' group submits a written report to the county health board arguing that more restaurant inspections lead to fewer incidences of *E. coli* food poisoning.

- A homeowner writes a letter to the editor of a county newspaper arguing that a nearby golf course is the source of the chemical residue recently discovered in local well water.

You will also encounter many occasions for thinking and writing about causes and effects in **personal settings.** It is critical to understand why things happen, and journals are an excellent place to explore such cause-and-effect relationships. For example, a young couple might keep a daily journal on the activities of their infant daughter. After a few weeks, when they reread their entries, they might notice a pattern suggesting that when they feed their daughter one kind of formula, she sleeps fewer hours at night.

Scenarios for Writing: Assignment Options

Your instructor may ask you to complete one or both of the following assignments that call for writing about causes or effects. Each of these assignments is in the form of a scenario, which gives you a sense of who your audience is and what you need to accomplish with your causal analysis.

Starting on page 287, you will find guidelines for completing whatever assignment option you decide—or are asked to—complete. Additional scenarios for college and life may be found online.

Writing for College

SCENARIO 1   An Academic Paper on Causes and Effects in One of Your Other College Courses

Consider the topics that you are studying in your courses this semester that involve causes and effects. To complete this assignment, you must first decide which of those topics interests you and then come up with a question about that topic that will lead you to investigate causes and/or effects. Here are some possibilities:

- **Geology:** What causes an earthquake? What are the effects of continental drift?

- **Music:** How did hip-hop change popular music? What led to the development of jazz?

- **Art:** How did the invention of the camera affect the kinds of painting that artists did in the nineteenth century?

- **Physics:** What causes the lift that makes it possible for airplanes to fly?

Alternatively, you might consider some general cause-and-effect relationships that you have noticed in your college community, in a class, in a department, or on campus. For example,

- **College:** Why does the cost of attending college always seem to increase?
- **Community:** Why do some neighbors around the college resent having students rent homes nearby?
- **Classroom:** Why do some students take so long to finish college?

Writing Assignment: For this assignment, you can choose among several options. One possibility is to select an effect and then write about its causes. Another possibility is to select a cause and then write about its effects. Your goal is to convince an audience of instructors and students in the discipline that your causal analysis is credible.

Writing for Life

SCENARIO 2   Professional Writing: A Report on Causes and/or Effects That Affect Your Employer

Think about the kinds of causes and effects that you encounter on your current job or that you expect to encounter in your future profession. Here are some possibilities to get you thinking:

- What causes a business to succeed or to fail?
- What causes customers to choose one product over similar products that competitors offer?
- What causes employees to remain loyal to an organization?
- What causes a company or an organization to treat its workers well or poorly? What are the effects of the way a manager treats employees?
- What causes employees to leave a company or other type of organization voluntarily? What are the effects of employees leaving an organization?
- What are the effects of rudeness at work?
- What causes high or low morale in the workplace? What are the effects of high or low morale?

Writing Assignment: Write a report for your supervisor—along with a cover memo—in which you identify a cause-and-effect question important to your organization and write a causal analysis in response to that question. If you are writing about a problem, you need to do more than simply provide information about it (that is an informative paper, covered in Chapter 6), but you do not need to suggest detailed solutions to the problem (that is a proposal, covered in Chapter 11). Your goal is to convince your readers that the causes or effects that you are proposing are plausible.

Rhetorical Considerations in Cause-and-Effect Writing

Audience: While your instructor and classmates are your initial audience, you should also consider other audiences for your causal analysis. What evidence will convince your readers that you are making a valid claim about a cause-and-effect relationship?

Purpose: Your general purpose is to convince readers that a cause-and-effect relationship exists. Beyond that, your purpose is either to establish the causes of something (an effect), to establish the effects of something (a cause), or to show how a series of causes and effects are related. It is critical to provide sufficient evidence to show that a cause-and-effect relationship actually exists.

Voice, Tone, and Point of View: Why are you interested in the cause-and-effect relationship that you have chosen to write about? What preconceptions about it do you have? What are your attitudes toward the topic and the audience? How will you convey those attitudes?

Context, Medium, and Genre: Keeping the context of the assignment in mind, decide on a medium and a genre for your writing. How will your writing be used? If you are writing for an audience beyond the classroom, consider what will be the most effective way to present your information to this audience. You might write an e-mail message to a friend, prepare a report for colleagues at work, or construct a Web site for members of your community.

For more on choosing a medium and genre, see Chapter 17 and Appendix C.

■ Critical Thinking, Reading, and Writing

Before you begin to write your causal analysis, read examples of writing about causes and effects to get a feel for this kind of writing. You might consider how visuals could enhance your causal analysis, as well as the kinds of sources you will need to consult.

The qualities of writing about causes and/or effects include a focused presentation of the effect(s) or cause(s), a clearly stated claim that a cause-and-effect relationship exists, and sufficient evidence to support the claim. The writer also has the responsibility to research carefully, to avoid logical fallacies, and to consider other points of view. These qualities and responsibilities are discussed in the section that follows.

Learning the Qualities of Effective Writing about Causes and Effects

When you consider what causes what, or what the effects of something are, you need to convince others that the relationship you see in fact exists. Here are the qualities of writing that analyzes causes and/or effects successfully:

- **Presentation of focused cause(s) or effect(s).** At the beginning of your essay, you need to introduce the event, activity, or phenomenon for which you wish to establish cause(s), or effect(s), or both. To focus the causes or effects, you should limit the time period that you are considering. This does not mean you cannot write about long periods of time (for a geology paper, you almost have to do so), but rather that you always keep the time period in mind as you determine exactly what to focus on so you can reasonably cover your topic given the limits of your assignment.

- **A clearly stated claim that a cause-and-effect relationship exists.** After you have done enough research to be certain that a cause-and-effect relationship exists, you will be prepared to state the nature of that relationship. State the claim so that readers understand it, especially since they may know little or nothing about your topic.

- **Sufficient evidence to support your claim.** To support your claim, present evidence that readers will consider persuasive. Such evidence may consist of the following:

  - The results of empirical studies or historical research found in scholarly and popular books, in journals, and on Web sites.

  - Your own observations, experience, or reading.

  - Testimony from interested or affected parties ("Interviews with other students indicate that . . .") or experts ("Professor X, a noted authority, asserts that . . .").

  - The use of examples that demonstrate that your suggested cause or causes actually do cause the effect.

- **Clear, logical thinking.** People often jump to conclusions when they see two events happening at the same time and assume there is a cause-and-effect relationship (see the discussion of *post hoc, ergo propter hoc* in the box on pp. 275–76). So consider these issues as you search for cause-and-effect relationships:

  - **Does the effect have a single cause, or multiple causes?** Things are rarely as simple as they first appear to be. More often than not, an effect will have multiple causes. Carefully analyze and research all the causes that may contribute to a particular effect.

  - **What are the contributing causes, and do they lead to a precipitating cause?** Often, a number of causes together contribute to what might be called a *precipitating* cause, the final cause that sets the effect in motion. Several contributing causes might set up a single precipitating cause. For example, while the football fan might blame the kicker who missed a last-second field goal for the team's loss of the important game, there surely were many other reasons that contributed to the loss (dropped passes, poor execution of running plays, and other missed opportunities).

- **Is a particular cause remote or immediate?** It is sometimes useful to examine a chain of causes so that you understand what came first, what happened next, and so on. Writing down the sequence of causes and effects will help you see the events in the **causal chain** as they happened over time.

- **Is a particular cause necessary or sufficient?** A **necessary cause** is one that must be present for the effect to occur. A **sufficient cause** is one that, if present, always triggers a particular effect. For example, for a teenager to be able to borrow the family car, his or her family must have a car—that cause is *necessary* to the effect of the teenager being able to borrow it. The teenager's forgetting to put gas into the family car before bringing it back, however, is a *sufficient* cause for the parents to refuse to lend it again; other causes would be sufficient as well (bringing the car home dirty or after running into a utility pole and denting the fender are also possible causes for the parents' decision), so forgetfulness is not a necessary cause.

- **Anticipation of possible objections or alternative explanations.** While your causal analysis may be highly plausible, there are almost always other possible causes for the same effect or other possible effects of the cause that you are considering. Be prepared to acknowledge those other potential causes or effects and to show why your causes or effects are more likely.

For more on writing effective arguments, including claims, evidence, types of appeals, and counterarguments, see Chapter 14.

In a computer file, put the above qualities of effective writing into your own words, and then refer to those notes as you conduct research and write your paper.

A WRITER'S RESPONSIBILITIES

Determining True Causes and Effects

Events that happen at the same time may or may not be related causally—you need to take care to be sure you are not asserting a relationship that does not in fact exist, or mistaking a cause for an effect, or vice versa. An ethical writer works diligently to avoid the logical fallacy of *post hoc, ergo propter hoc,* a Latin phrase meaning "after this, therefore because of this." If you argue that X caused Y simply because X preceded Y, you are guilty of this logical fallacy.

(cont'd)

(continued)

What are some examples of *post hoc, ergo propter hoc* thinking that you have recently witnessed?

Often in cases where two events happen at the same time and are probably causally related, it still may not be obvious which is the cause and which is the effect. For instance, educational experts have observed that students with low self-esteem often underperform in school. But do people who have low self-esteem perform poorly in school because they have low self-esteem, as has been assumed in the past? Or do they have low self-esteem because they perform poorly in school, as some psychologists now believe? A responsible writer needs to consider both of these possibilities.

Reading, Inquiry, and Research: Learning from Texts That Explain Cause-and-Effect Relationships

The readings that follow are examples of writing about causes and effects. As you read them, consider the following questions.

- To what extent is the writer focused on causes, on effects, or on both causes and effects? What specific elements of the selection support your judgment?

- What parts of the selection seem the strongest? Why do you think so?

- How can you use the techniques of cause-and-effect writing exemplified here in your writing?

As you read an essay, jot down questions and make observations about the essay, preferably in a computer file. Then, if you want to use the information in your writing, you will already have the main points in a digital format.

Thinking Rhetorically

Keep in mind the following questions as you read the essays that follow. Make it a practice to ask yourself these questions in all your reading—personal, academic, civic, and professional—and you will strengthen and sharpen your abilities as a reader and as a writer.

Rhetorical Knowledge: The Writer's Situation and Rhetoric

1. **Audience:** Who is the primary audience for this piece of writing? How effectively does the author understand and reach this audience?

2. **Purpose:** What is the author's primary purpose in writing this causal analysis? How successfully does he fulfill his purpose?

3. **Voice and Tone:** What is the author's tone in his or her causal analysis? What does it contribute to the author's credibility?

4. **Responsibility:** What can you cite from the essay to show how the author fulfills his or her responsibility to demonstrate clear, meaningful connections between cause(s) and effect(s)?

5. **Context and Format:** Locate the time and place where the reading was originally published. Consider how the initial context affects the author's writing and your reading of the essay.

JUAN WILLIAMS

The Ruling That Changed America

Juan Williams is the author of *Thurgood Marshall: American Revolutionary*, the non-fiction bestseller *Eyes on the Prize: America's Civil Rights Years, 1954–1965*, and *This Far by Faith: Stories from the African American Religious Experience*. He was born in Colon, Panama, but moved to Brooklyn, New York, in 1958. In an interview for the Web site *Tolerance.org*, Williams said, "Since I was born in 1954 my whole education is tied to the Brown case. I attended public schools in Brooklyn, New York, during the 1960s [and] those schools were very integrated. . . . I went to schools with Jewish children, Irish children, Italian children, and a stunning range of immigrant children from around the world."

Williams attended Haverford College and graduated with a degree in philosophy in 1976. For more than 20 years, Williams was an editorial writer, op-ed contributor, and White House reporter for the *Washington Post*. His work has appeared in *Newsweek, Fortune, Atlantic Monthly, Ebony, Gentlemen's Quarterly*, and the *New Republic*. Williams is currently a senior correspondent for National Public Radio.

This essay originally appeared in the April 2004 issue of the *American School Board Journal*.

F ifty years later, the *Brown* decision looks different. At a distance from   1
the volcanic heat of May 17, 1954, the real impact of the legal, political, and cultural eruption that changed America is not exactly what it first appeared to be.

On that Monday in May, the high court's ruling outlawing school   2
segregation in the United States generated urgent news flashes on the radio and frenzied black headlines in special editions of afternoon newspapers. One swift and unanimous decision by the top judges in the land was going to end segregation in public schools. Southern politicians reacted with such fury and fear that they immediately called the day "Black Monday."

South Carolina Gov. James Byrnes, who rose to political power with   3
passionate advocacy of segregation, said the decision was "the end of
civilization in the South as we have known it." Georgia Gov. Herman
Talmadge struck an angry tone. He said Georgia had no intention of
allowing "mixed race" schools as long as he was governor. And he touched
on Confederate pride from the days when the South went to war with the
federal government over slavery by telling supporters that the Supreme
Court's ruling was not law in his state; he said it was "the first step toward
national suicide." The Brown decision should be regarded, he said, as
nothing but a "mere scrap of paper."

Meanwhile, newspapers for black readers reacted with exultation.   4
"The Supreme Court decision is the greatest victory for the Negro people
since the Emancipation Proclamation," said Harlem's *Amsterdam News*. A
writer in the *Chicago Defender* explained, "neither the atomic bomb nor
the hydrogen bomb will ever be as meaningful to our democracy." And
Thurgood Marshall, the NAACP lawyer who directed the legal fight that
led to *Brown*, predicted the end of segregation in all American public
schools by the fall of 1955.

Slow Progress, Backward Steps

Ten years later, however, very little school integration had taken place.   5
True to the defiant words of segregationist governors, the Southern states
had hunkered down in a massive resistance campaign against school
integration. Some Southern counties closed their schools instead of
allowing blacks and whites into the same classrooms. In other towns,
segregationist academies opened, and most if not all of the white children left the public schools for the racially exclusive alternatives. And in
most places, the governors, mayors, and school boards found it easy
enough to just ask for more time before integrating schools.

That slow-as-molasses approach worked. In 1957, President Eisen-   6
hower had to send troops from the 101st Airborne into Little Rock just to
get nine black children safely into Central High School. Only in the late
'60s, under the threat of losing federal funding, did large-scale school
integration begin in Southern public schools. And in many places, in both
the North and the South, black and white students did not go to school
together until a federal court ordered schoolchildren to ride buses
across town to bring the races together.

Today, 50 years later, a study by the Civil Rights Project at Harvard   7
University finds that the percentage of white students attending public
schools with Hispanic or black students has steadily declined since 1988.
In fact, the report concludes that school integration in the United States

is "lower in 2000 than in 1970, before busing for racial balance began." In the South, home to the majority of America's black population, there is now less school integration than there was in 1970. The Harvard report concluded, "At the beginning of the 21st century, American schools are now 12 years into the process of continuous resegregation."

Today, America's schools are so heavily segregated that more than two-thirds of black and Hispanic students are in schools where a majority of the students are not white. And today, most of the nation's white children attend a school that is almost 80 percent white. Hispanics are now the most segregated group of students in the nation because they live in highly concentrated clusters. 8

At the start of the new century, 50 years after Brown shook the nation, segregated housing patterns and an increase in the number of black and brown immigrants have concentrated minorities in impoverished big cities and created a new reality of public schools segregated by race and class. 9

The Real Impact of *Brown*

So, if *Brown* didn't break apart school segregation, was it really the earthquake that it first appeared to be? 10

Yes. Today, it is hard to even remember America before *Brown* because the ruling completely changed the nation. It still stands as the laser beam that first signaled that the federal government no longer gave its support to racial segregation among Americans. 11

Before Brown, the federal government lent its power to enforcing the laws of segregation under an 1896 Supreme Court ruling that permitted "separate but equal" treatment of blacks and whites. Blacks and whites who tried to integrate factories, unions, public buses and trains, parks, the military, restaurants, department stores, and more found that the power of the federal government was with the segregationists. 12

Before Brown, the federal government had struggled even to pass a law banning lynching. 13

But after the Supreme Court ruled that segregation in public schools was a violation of the Constitution, the federal attitude toward enforcing second-class citizenship for blacks shifted on the scale of a change in the ocean's tide or a movement in the plates of the continents. Once the highest court in the land said equal treatment for all did not allow for segregation, then the lower courts, the Justice Department, and federal prosecutors, as well as the FBI, all switched sides. They didn't always act to promote integration, but they no longer used their power to stop it. 14

An irreversible shift had begun, and it was the direct result of the   15
Brown decision.

The change in the attitude of federal officials created a wave of   16
anticipation among black people, who became alert to the possibility of
achieving the long-desired goal of racial equality. There is no way to offer
a hard measure of a change in attitude. But the year after *Brown*, Rosa
Parks refused to give up her seat to a white man on a racially segregated
bus in Montgomery, Ala. That led to a yearlong bus boycott and the emer-
gence of massive, nonviolent protests for equal rights. That same year,
Martin Luther King Jr. emerged as the nation's prophet of civil rights for
all Americans.

Even when a black 14-year-old, Emmit Till, was killed in Mississippi   17
for supposedly whistling at a white woman, there was a new reaction to
old racial brutality. One of Till's elderly relatives broke with small-town
Southern tradition and dared to take the witness stand and testify against
the white men he saw abduct the boy. Until Brown, the simple act of a
black man standing up to speak against a white man in Mississippi was
viewed as futile and likely to result in more white-on-black violence.

The sense among black people—and many whites as well—that a   18
new era had opened created a new boldness. Most black parents in Little
Rock did not want to risk harm to their children by allowing them to join
in efforts to integrate Central High. But working with local NAACP officials, the parents of nine children decided it was a new day and time to
make history. That same spirit of new horizons was at work in 1962 when
James Meredith became the first black student to enroll at the University
of Mississippi. And in another lurch away from the traditional support of
segregation, the federal government sent troops as well as Justice Department officials to the university to protect Meredith's rights.

The next year, when Alabama Gov. George Wallace felt the political   19
necessity of making a public stand against integration at the University
of Alabama, he stood only briefly in the door to block black students and
then stepped aside in the face of federal authority. That was another
shift toward a world of high hopes for racial equality; again, from the
perspective of the 21st century, it looks like another aftershock of the
Brown decision.

The same psychology of hope infected young people, black and   20
white, nationwide in the early '60s. The Freedom Rides, lunch-counter
sit-ins, and protest marches for voting rights all find their roots in Brown.
So, too, did the racially integrated 1963 March on Washington at which
Martin Luther King Jr. famously said he had a vision of a promised land
where the sons of slaves and the sons of slave owners could finally join
together in peace. The desire for change became a demand for change in

the impatient voice of Malcolm X, the militant Black Muslim who called for immediate change by violent means if necessary.

In 1964, a decade after *Brown*, the Civil Rights Act was passed by a Congress beginning to respond to the changing politics brought about by the landmark decision. The next year, 1965, the wave of change had swelled to the point that Congress passed the Voting Rights Act.   21

Closer to the Mountaintop

This sea change in black and white attitudes toward race also had an impact on culture. Churches began to grapple with the Christian and Jewish principles of loving thy neighbor, even if thy neighbor had a different color skin. Major league baseball teams no longer feared a fan revolt if they allowed more than one black player on a team. Black writers, actors, athletes, and musicians—ranging from James Baldwin to the Supremes and Muhammad Ali—began to cross over into the mainstream of American culture.   22

The other side of the change in racial attitudes was white support for equal rights. College-educated young white people in the '60s often defined themselves by their willingness to embrace racial equality. Bob Dylan sang about the changing times as answers "blowing in the wind." Movies like "Guess Who's Coming to Dinner" found major audiences among all races. And previously all-white private colleges and universities began opening their doors to black students. The resulting arguments over affirmative action in college admissions led to the Supreme Court's 1978 decision in the *Bakke* case, which outlawed the use of quotas, and its recent ruling that the University of Michigan can take race into account as one factor in admitting students to its law school. The court has also had to deal with affirmative action in the business world, in both hiring and contracts—again as a result of questions of equality under the Constitution raised by *Brown*.   23

But the most important legacy of the *Brown* decision, by far, is the growth of an educated black middle class. The number of black people graduating from high school and college has soared since *Brown*, and the incomes of blacks have climbed steadily as a result. Home ownership and investment in the stock market among black Americans have rocketed since the 1980s. The political and economic clout of that black middle class continues to bring America closer to the mountaintop vision of racial equality that Dr. King might have dreamed of 50 years ago.   24

The Supreme Court's May 17, 1954, ruling in *Brown* remains a landmark legal decision. But it is much more than that. It is the "Big Bang" of all American history in the 20th century.   25

QUESTIONS FOR WRITING AND DISCUSSION

Critical Thinking: Responding to the Writer's Ideas

1. Before reading Williams's article, how aware were you of the wide impact of *Brown vs. Board of Education*? Can you think of another Supreme Court ruling that has had as significant an impact? What was the impact?

2. Williams tries to show that the impact of *Brown vs. Board of Education* went beyond education. To what extent was the decision a sign of the times—an effect? To what extent was the Supreme Court caught up in the mood of the country? To what extent did the decision itself cause other effects?

Composing Processes and Knowledge of Conventions: The Writer's Strategies

1. Because for many people, fifty years after the fact, *Brown vs. Board of Education* is simply an entry in history books, how does Williams make the decision real for his current readers?

2. Williams structures his argument to show that *Brown vs. Board of Education* did not accomplish what it intended, but that it eventually did more. How effective is his argument? Why?

Inquiry and Research: Ideas for Further Exploration

1. Investigate other Supreme Court decisions. Which seem to have had greater impact than expected at the time they were made? What was the impact?

BRUCE NUSSBAUM

Where Are the Jobs?

Bruce Nussbaum is the editorial page editor at *BusinessWeek*, and author of the book *Good Intentions: How Big Business and the Medical Establishment Are Corrupting the Fight against AIDS*. In 2005, Nussbaum was honored with a place on the "I.D. Forty," which is the *International Design* magazine's list of the forty most influential people in the world of design. This essay originally appeared in *BusinessWeek* in 2004.

Americans live in a faith-based economy. We believe deeply in education, innovation, risk-taking, and plain hard work as the way to a better life. But that faith is being eroded. The link between strong growth and job creation appears to be broken, and we don't know what's wrong with it. Profits are soaring, yet no one is hiring. Angry voices are blaming Benedict Arnold CEOs who send jobs to India and China. If highly educated "knowledge" workers in Silicon Valley are losing their jobs, who is really safe?

The truth is that we are living through a moment of maximum uncertainty. The economy is at an inflection point as new forces act upon it. Yet the shape and impact of these forces remains unknown. Outsourcing looms large as a potential threat because no one knows how many jobs and which industries are vulnerable. And productivity seems problematic because it's hard to see where the rewards for all the cost-cutting and hard work are going. Meanwhile, the Next Big Thing that is supposed to propel the economy and job growth forward after the Internet boom isn't obvious. As a result, CEOs are reluctant to place big bets on the future. Workers hunker down. And those laid off are at a loss trying to retrain. How can they, when they don't know where the new jobs will be and who will be hiring? It's not even clear what college students should major in anymore. No wonder this feels like a new age of uncertainty.

The Real Culprit

Yet there are things we do know. The real culprit in this jobless recovery is productivity, not offshoring. Unlike most previous business cycles, productivity has continued to grow at a fast pace right through the downturn and into recovery. One percentage point of productivity growth can eliminate up to 1.3 million jobs a year. With productivity growing at an annual rate of 3 percent to 3.5 percent rather than the expected 2 percent to 2.5 percent, the reason for the jobs shortfall becomes clear: Companies are using information technology to cut costs—and that means less labor is needed. Of the 2.7 million jobs lost over the past three years, only 300,000 have been from outsourcing, according to Forrester Research Inc. People rightly fear that jobs in high tech and services will disappear just as manufacturing jobs did. Perhaps so. But odds are it will be productivity rather than outsourcing that does them in.

We know also where the benefits of rising productivity are going: higher profits, lower inflation, rising stocks, and, ultimately, loftier prices for houses. In short, productivity is generating wealth, not employment. Corporate profits as a share of national income are at an all-time high. So is net worth for many individuals. Consumer net worth hit a new peak, at $45 trillion—up 75 percent since 1995—and consumers have more than recouped their losses from the bust.

We know, too, that outsourcing isn't altogether a bad thing. In the '90s, high-tech companies farmed out the manufacture of memory chips, computers, and telecom equipment to Asia. This lowered the cost of tech gear, raising demand and spreading the IT revolution. The same will probably happen with software. Outsourcing will cut prices and make the next generation of IT cheaper and more available. This will generate greater productivity and growth. In fact, as venture capitalists increasingly insist that all IT startups have an offshore component, the cost of innovation should fall sharply, perhaps by half.

We know something about the kinds of jobs that could migrate to Asia and those that will stay home. In the '90s, the making of customized chips and gear that required close contact with clients remained in the U.S., while production of commodity products was outsourced. Today, the Internet and cheaper telecom permit routine service work to be done in Bangalore. But specialized jobs that require close contact with clients, plus an understanding of U.S. culture, will likely remain.

America has been at economic inflection points many times in the past. These periods of high job anxiety were eventually followed by years of surging job creation. The faith Americans have in innovation, risk-taking, education, and hard work has been sustained again and again by strong economic performance.

There's no question that today's jobless recovery is causing many people real pain. The number of discouraged workers leaving the workforce is unprecedented. Labor-force participation is down among precisely the most vulnerable parts of the workforce—younger and nonwhite workers. Some are going back to school, but many are simply giving up after fruitless searches for decent jobs. If the participation rate were at its March 2001 level, there would be 2.7 million more workers in the labor force looking for jobs. This would push the unemployment rate up to 7.4 percent, not the current 5.6 percent.

History has shown time and again that jobs follow growth, but not necessarily in a simple, linear fashion. America has a dynamic, fast-changing economy that embodies Joseph A. Schumpeter's ideal of creative destruction. We are now experiencing the maximum pain from the wreckage of outmoded jobs while still awaiting the innovations that will generate the work of the future. While America's faith in its innovation economy has often been tested, it has never been betrayed. Given the chance, the economy will deliver the jobs and prosperity that it has in the past.

QUESTIONS FOR WRITING AND DISCUSSION

Critical Thinking: Responding to the Writer's Ideas

1. As college students, you will be entering the job market in the next several years. What does Nussbaum say either to encourage or discourage you about your prospects?

2. Nussbaum's central idea is that increased worker productivity in the United States, not outsourcing, is the primary cause for the reduction in job growth. How believable is he? Why?

Composing Processes and Knowledge of Conventions: The Writer's Strategies

1. Nussbaum's first sentence uses the phrase "faith-based economy." His closing paragraph returns to the notion that we need to have faith that our economy will rebound—even if it takes some time. How effective do you find the strategy of ending an essay with an echo of where it began? Why?

2. The title of this article is "Where Are the Jobs?" How directly does the article address that question? What evidence can you offer to support your judgment?

Inquiry and Research: Ideas for Further Exploration

1. What factors besides productivity and outsourcing might have an impact on job creation?

TechNote

Graphics, and even video, can help you explain complex cause-and-effect relationships. If your instructor allows, see if you can find a short video clip (one to three minutes long) that shows the causal relationship you are explaining. Many Web search engines include video searches. Or you might explore a large video site such as YouTube (http://youtube.com). If you have access to a digital video camera, or if you own a video-capable cell phone or smart phone, you can create a short video clip yourself. For example, if you are writing about the effects of proper stance and follow-through on curveball execution in baseball, you could ask a campus baseball player to demonstrate while you record video of various techniques. Consider recording a voice-over that explains the movements involved.

Thinking about Visuals That Indicate Cause-and-Effect Relationships

Visuals can often explain the effect of an event better than words can. The map in Figure 10.1 shows that some aftershocks of an 1895 earthquake that was centered in southeastern Missouri were felt as far away as the Atlantic seaboard, the Gulf Coast, and even north of Green Bay, Wisconsin.

If you were writing a paper about earthquakes, how would a map help illustrate a cause-and-effect relationship? Might a photo illustrate the damages caused by an earthquake?

As you think about these visual aids, consider these questions about the effective use of visuals in showing a cause-and-effect relationship:

- How does the map provide information about the cause-and-effect relationship?
- What does the map illustrate for a reader that it would be hard to show with text alone?
- What other types of visuals might be useful in illustrating cause-and-effect relationships?
- How might visuals mislead readers about cause-and-effect relationships?

FIGURE 10.1 Map Showing the Intensity of the 1895 Earthquake

The 1895 M6.0 Charleston, MO earthquake affected an area 20X greater than an equivalent magnitude quake in California

◗ Writing Processes

As you work on your assignment, remember the qualities of an effective cause-and-effect paper (see pp. 274–75) and remember that the writing process is recursive—that is, writers move back and forth among all of the activities. After you engage in invention strategies and conduct some research, you may start writing, or you may decide to do some more research.

If you are considering several topics for your causal analysis, put your notes into a separate computer document for each subject. Once you determine the focus of your analysis, it will be easy to access and use those notes. Also, as you work on your project, make sure that you save your computer files frequently. Savvy writers back up their computer files in two or more places—on an internal or external hard drive of the computer, on a USB flash drive, and/or on a rewritable CD or DVD, for example.

For a tip on organizing your computer files, see page 66.

Invention: Getting Started

The more invention activities that you use, the more effective your causal analysis will be. As you work, try to answer these questions:

- What do I already know about this event, phenomenon, or trend?
- What do I know about its cause(s) or effect(s)?

- Where can I learn more about the causal relationships involved? What relevant personal experiences or observations can I contribute?
- What might my audience already know about the cause-and-effect relationship I am exploring?
- What might my audience's point of view be?
- What questions do I have? What do I want and need to find out?

As with any kind of writing, invention activities improve with peer feedback and suggestions. Consider sharing the invention work you have done so far with several classmates or friends in order to understand your rhetorical situation more clearly and to generate more useful information.

Exploring Your Ideas with Research

Usually when you are writing about cause-and-effect relationships, you will need to provide evidence to support your claims. Although you may be able to draw on your own experience to provide evidence, you will also need to offer verifiable information such as facts, statistics, expert testimony, experimental results, and examples. For instance, if you were writing about cause-and-effect relationships in the areas of health or safety, two good sources of information are the Centers for Disease Control or the U.S. Department of Transportation, both of which have Web sites filled with reliable information.

To find evidence from outside of your own experience, you will need to do research to answer questions such as the following:

- What facts or other verifiable information will provide solid evidence that a cause-and-effect relationship actually exists? Where can I find this information? What sources will be most reliable?
- What expert testimony can I provide to support my thesis about causes or effects or both? What authorities might I interview?
- What statistical data support my contention that a cause-and-effect relationship exists?
- How can I best explain the data to my readers so that (1) they can easily understand them and (2) the evidence I provide supports my conclusions?

The subject you focus on, and the kind of essay you are constructing, helps to determine the kind of research you conduct. For example, you could conduct several kinds of research:

- For Scenario 1, in which you focus on a topic in one of your courses, interviewing classmates, professors, and/or administrators is a useful way to learn about different perspectives.

- For Scenario 2, regarding an issue in the company you work for, a search through past memos and other records often will provide information that might help you see cause-and-effect relationships.

Reviewing Your Invention and Research

After you have conducted your research, review your invention work and the information you have collected from outside sources. Once you have a general idea of the cause(s) and/or effect(s) your research is leading you to, try to develop what is called a *working thesis statement:* If you had to explain the cause-and-effect relationship now, based on what you have learned, what would it be? Through the process of writing itself, you will learn more about your topic and possible cause-and-effect relationships, so you will modify and develop the working thesis statement as you draft and revise your text.

Organizing Your Cause-and-Effect Paper

Once you have a working thesis and supporting evidence for your cause-and-effect paper, you need to consider how you might organize your text. The questions to ask yourself are all rhetorical:

- Who is the audience for your paper?
- Why might they be interested in your reasoning about causes and/or effects, or how can you make them interested in it?
- What is your purpose for writing—that is, why do your readers need to understand this cause-and-effect relationship? What will your readers learn about your subject by reading your paper?

Once you have determined your purpose, you can choose the organizational approach that is best suited to it. Here are three possible organizational approaches that you might choose for your paper.

Options for Organization

Identify an Effect and Then Determine Its Cause(s)	Identify a Cause and Then Determine Its Effect(s)	Determine a Series of Causes and Effects
• Introduce the effect.	• Introduce the cause.	• Introduce one of the causes or one of the effects.
• Explain the importance of the effect.	• Explain the importance of the cause.	• Explain the importance of the cause or the effect that you have identified.
• List possible causes.	• List possible effects.	
• Assert probable cause-and-effect relationship(s).	• Assert probable cause-and-effect relationship(s).	• List possible causes and effects.

(cont'd)

(continued)

Identify an Effect and Then Determine Its Cause(s)	Identify a Cause and Then Determine Its Effect(s)	Determine a Series of Causes and Effects
• There may be several causes. • Provide evidence to support your claim about cause-and-effect relationship(s). • Address skeptics' doubts—others say these causes do not cause the effect, so address those objections. • Conclusion.	• There may be several effects. • Provide evidence to support your claim about cause-and-effect relationship(s). • If others might see different effects from your cause, address their objections. • Conclusion.	• Assert probable chain of causes and effects. • Provide evidence to support your claim about series of causes and effects. • Address skeptics' doubts. • Conclusion.

Constructing a Complete Draft

Once you have chosen the organizational approach that works best given your audience and purpose, you are ready to construct the rest of your draft. As you work, keep the following in mind:

- Draw on your invention work and your research. If necessary, do more invention work and/or more research.

For more on constructing visuals, see Chapter 18.

- As you try out tentative ideas about possible causes and/or possible effects, ask peers about what they consider necessary to support your ideas.

- Ask yourself and peers whether visuals might help make your case.

Introduction: In order to write an introduction that captures readers' attention, you might want to try one of the following strategies:

- *Give your audience a reason for being interested by vividly portraying how this topic makes a difference in their lives.*

- *Make a statement that suggests the unexpected.* Juan Williams uses this strategy in "The Ruling That Changed America" (p. 277):

  > Fifty years later, the *Brown* decision looks different. At a distance from the volcanic heat of May 17, 1954, the real impact of the legal, political, and cultural eruption that changed America is not exactly what it first appeared to be.

- *Examine a surprising causal relationship (that you can substantiate) to hold an audience's interest.*

Body: There are many strategies you can use to show cause and effect. In the body of your causal analysis you may list and discuss possible causes and effects. You will likely also refute skeptics' claims. For example, in a causal analysis on the dangers of smoking, you might note that while many smokers may feel their habit endangers only themselves, research data indicates the harmful effects of second-hand smoke. You could then present the data as evidence.

Conclusion: In your conclusion you need to reinforce the connections between the causes and effects that you have established. Do not assume your reader will make the same connections you have. Ask yourself the following questions:

- How effectively have you shown that the effect was a result of the cause?
- How well have you tied together all of the different ideas you have been working with?
- How clearly have you articulated your perspective so your audience has no doubt about what you have been trying to prove?
- Have you given your reader a sense of closure?

Title: As you construct your cause-and-effect paper, a title should emerge at some point—often late in the process. The title should reflect the cause-and-effect claim that you are considering.

VISUALIZING VARIATIONS

Choosing Visuals That Illustrate Cause-and-Effect Relationships

If you have prepared a causal analysis for a civic or professional writing situation, you will often need to present the results of your analysis to a group. If you were to prepare an oral presentation using either *PowerPoint* slides or transparencies and an overhead projector, what content would you need to include on your slides or transparencies, and how would you format them? Here are some aspects of PowerPoint slides or transparencies that you would need to keep in mind:

For more on oral presentations, including the use of PowerPoint, see Chapter 16.

- Slides allow you to "show" as well as "tell." What information will you "show" and what will you "tell"?
- How can you use graphics (charts, graphs, photographs) most effectively as part of your presentation?
- When you prepare presentation slides, your writing becomes very visible. Make sure to edit your slides carefully.
- Programs for creating presentation slides often provide options for background templates. How can you pick a background that will complement your slides?

For example, for a presentation to a civic association, consider how to format an overhead transparency showing an increase in the number of bicycle/pedestrian accidents during the past year. You might start with plain black type.

(cont'd)

(continued)

In the past year, bicycle/pedestrian accidents have increased 70%

You also could add some shading to highlight the most important part of the sentence:

In the last year, bicycle/pedestrian accidents have increased 70%

You could include a slide with a bar graph to illustrate the problem:

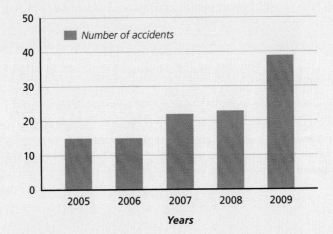

For any visual that you are considering, ask yourself the following questions:

- What might this photograph show about the cause-and-effect relationship I am arguing for?

- How do I select a chart or graph that will support a point I want to make and help me justify my overall judgment?

- What other kind of illustration (drawing, table) might help show that a cause-and-effect relationship exists?

Revising

Once you have a draft, put it aside for a day or so. This break will give you the chance to come back to your text as a new reader might. Read through and revise your work, looking especially for ideas that are not explained completely, terms that are not defined, and other problem areas. As you revise your early drafts, hold off on doing a great deal of heavy editing. When you revise you will probably change the content and structure of your paper, so time spent working to fix problems with sentence style or grammar, usage, punctuation, or mechanics at this stage is often wasted.

When you reread the first draft of your paper, here are some questions to ask yourself:

- How effectively have I explained or indicated my thesis so the reader knows my view of the cause-and-effect relationship and what I intend to prove?

- What else might my audience want or need to know about my subject?

- How else might I interest my audience in my causal analysis?

- What did I find out about my subject that I did not include in my causal analysis? (Effective research always results in more information than you can include, so consider what you left out that you might include in your next draft.)

- Have I clearly explained and defined any terms my readers might not know?

- Could some aspects of my causal analysis be better presented visually?

Technology can help you revise and edit your writing more easily. Use your word processor's track-changes tool to try out revisions and editing changes. After you've had time to think about the possible changes, you can "accept" or "reject" them. Also, you can use your word processor's comment tool to write reminders to yourself when you get stuck with a revision or some editing task.

Your instructor may also ask you to share your work with your classmates and ask them for suggestions and ideas. Friends or family members may also be willing to read your draft and offer useful suggestions.

WRITER'S WORKSHOP

Responding to Full Drafts

Working with one or two classmates, read each paper and offer comments and questions that will help each of you see your paper's strengths and weaknesses. Consider the following guidelines and questions as you do:

- Write a brief narrative comment that outlines your first impression of this draft. How effectively does the title draw you into the paper? Why? What part(s) of the text are especially effective for showing a cause-and-effect relationship? Provide positive and encouraging feedback to the writer.

- How well does the writer stay on track? If he or she loses focus, indicate where.

- How logical is the paper? Explain, in a brief paragraph, the strengths and weaknesses you see in the writer's logic.

- How effective is the introduction? What suggestions can you make to improve the introduction?

- What do you think is the author's thesis or main point? How could it be expressed or supported more effectively?

(cont'd)

(continued)

- In the main part of the paper, are there parts that need more explanation? Where would you like more details or examples?

- How credible is the writer's case that a relationship exists? How credible are the writer's sources?

- Might visuals such as charts, tables, graphs, or photographs help the writer to explain or support his or her claims about causes and/or effects more simply and clearly?

- How clearly and effectively does the writer present any opposing points of view on this subject? How effectively does the writer answer opposing viewpoints?

- What could be added or changed to make the conclusion more effective? To what extent does it make you want to learn more about this topic?

- In a brief paragraph, outline what you see as the main weaknesses of this paper—and suggest how the writer might improve the text.

Responding to Readers' Comments

Once they have received feedback on their writing from peers, teachers, friends, and others, writers have to figure out what to do with that feedback. As with any feedback, it is important to listen to it carefully and consider what your reader has to say. Then it is up to you, as the author, to decide *how* to come to terms with these suggestions. You may find that comments from more than one reader contradict each other. In that case, use your own judgment to decide which reader's comments are on the right track.

Knowledge of Conventions

In your college classes, writing about a cause-and-effect relationship is usually academic writing, so you will be required to follow the conventions for an academic essay. Other situations may call for a variety of genres, including memos, essays, blog postings, letters to the editor, and even formal position papers. Such documents often include tables, charts, graphs, or photos. Be aware of the conventions for any genre you use.

Editing

After you revise, you have one more important step—editing and polishing. At the editing stage, make changes to your sentence structure and word choice to improve your style and to make your writing clearer and more concise. Also check your work to make sure it adheres to conventions of grammar, usage, punctuation, mechanics, and spelling. Use the spell-check function of your word-processing program, but be sure to double-check your spelling personally (your computer cannot tell the difference between *compliment* and *complement*). If you have used sources in your paper, make sure you are following the documentation style your instructor requires.

See Chapter 20 for more on documenting sources using MLA or APA style.

As with overall revision of your work, this final editing and polishing is most effective if you can put your text aside for a few days and come back to it with fresh eyes. We strongly recommend that you ask classmates, friends, and tutors to read your work to find editing problems that you may not see. To assist you with editing, we offer here a round-robin editing activity focused on making sure that subordinate clauses are attached to independent clauses.

WRITER'S WORKSHOP

Round-Robin Editing with a Focus on Subordinate Clauses

Writing about causes and effects benefits from the careful use of **subordinate clauses**. A subordinate clause has a subject and a verb, but it cannot stand on its own because it begins with a subordinating conjunction (such as *although*, *because*, *while*, *if*, or *since*) and is a sentence fragment:

FRAGMENT   *Because my car did not start this morning.*

Because subordinate clauses cannot stand on their own, they need to be attached to an independent clause:

SENTENCE   *Because my car did not start this morning,* I was late for class.

or

SENTENCE   I was late for class *because my car did not start this morning.*

Working with several classmates, look for the subordinate clauses in your papers, and make sure they are attached to independent clauses. If you are uncertain about a specific convention for using subordinate clauses, consult a handbook or ask your instructor.

Genres, Documentation, and Format

If you are writing an academic paper in response to Scenario 1, follow the conventions appropriate for the discipline in which you are writing and the requirements of your instructor. However, if you are responding to Scenario 2, you may decide to write a report with a cover memo. In that case, follow the acceptable format for memos and you will also need to format your report so that it meets the needs and requirements of your intended audience.

For advice on writing in different genres, see Appendix C. For guidelines for formatting and documenting papers in MLA or APA style, see Chapter 20.

If you have used material from outside sources, including visuals, give credit to those sources, using the documentation style required by the discipline you are working in and by your instructor.

Student Deborah Schlegel Shares Her Causal Analysis

Deborah Schlegel became interested in the topic of global warming in her environmental studies class. She decided to write a cause-and-effect essay about global warming in response to the first scenario (see p. 271). Below is her finished cause-and-effect paper.

DEBORAH SCHLEGEL

Weather Forecast: Bikinis or Parkas?

Climate researchers have recently come up with good and bad news   1
about the global warming crisis. The good news first—maybe it wasn't such a bad idea to move to hot Phoenix after all, and we may not have to worry about global warming. The bad news? Teenagers may have spent too much money on summer clothes. A growing number of scientists are warning that global warming may cause really big-time global cooling—an ice age.

To understand how this seeming contradiction could happen, we'll   2
follow a path that leads from the Arctic ice cap to the Atlantic Ocean and around the world on the same ocean current the turtles rode in <u>Finding Nemo</u>. But first we start with the current crisis, global warming. I also want to note that while some politicians do <u>not</u> believe that global warming is a real and serious problem, the majority of scientists—the great majority—are positive that the earth is warming up, and that humans are a primary cause of global warming.

One classmate wrote to Schlegel the following comment:

I suggest that you provide more information after your first paragraph, to give us more background on how the climate works and how do we know that?

In her final draft, Schlegel provides significant background.

The arguments are endless over what is causing our global temperatures to rise. Is it the higher amounts of greenhouse gases such as CO_2 and aerosols in the atmosphere caused by humans? Is it the higher amounts of greenhouse gases like methane being pumped into the atmosphere by the large numbers of cows living on this planet? Or is it something totally unavoidable, such as where we are in the sunspot cycle or the increased solar output of our sun? Whatever the causes are, temperatures are rising, and it is this increase that is the beginning of the story.

When temperatures heat up, increased amounts of fresh water enter the northern Atlantic Ocean. This effect happens for two reasons. First, the warmer temperatures cause the Arctic ice cap and the sea ice that surrounds it to melt. Second, runoff into the ocean increases, caused by increased rain and snow in the northern latitudes of North America. NASA's Earth Observing System (EOS) science report ("The Earth Observing System Science Plan") points to the models on global climate change, all showing that these are the two ways global warming will cause the amount of fresh water entering the Atlantic Ocean to increase. Clearly, increased global temperatures cause an increase in fresh water entering the Atlantic Ocean.

Earth's oceans are ringed by several ocean currents linked together, forming what is called the Global Ocean Conveyor. Like a conveyor belt, these currents move water around the globe, cooling the atmosphere above them when they're carrying cold water on the surface and warming the atmosphere when they carry warm surface water. This giant conveyor belt is driven by very cold, very salty water that sinks to the bottom of the ocean and creeps along slowly—also moving the water above it. The turtles in the film Finding Nemo rode a portion of the Global Ocean Conveyor that slides around Australia and down its east coast (not as quickly as shown in the movie, but then, that was fiction). The portion of this conveyor in the Atlantic, the Gulf Stream, is an important force in driving the whole system.

How fast the Gulf Stream moves is determined by thermohaline circulation—what the temperature of the water is (thermo-) and how salty it is (-haline). Ideally, the Gulf Stream brings warm, salty water from the equatorial and Caribbean regions up to the North Atlantic. There the winds of the jet stream, moving from west to east, take out a fair amount of the heat and move it to the North Atlantic regions and Europe. The journal Natural Science likens the amount of heat sent on via the jet stream ". . . to the total energy output of a million nuclear power plants" ("A New European Ice Age?"). That's why Europe has such balmy temperatures for its latitude. London is as far north as Moscow, the Aleutian Islands and Edmonton, Canada. Rome shares its latitude, but not its

3

4

5

6

One of Schlegel's peers wondered about using other strategies besides the word "we."

This is pretty informal, especially the use of 'we.' I realize that you're trying to draw your readers in to make them interested in your paper—how else might you do so?

While Schegel still sometimes uses the word we, she also engages her readers by asking questions.

Mediterranean weather, with Upper Mongolia and northern Montana. The East Coast of the United States also benefits from warmer temperatures through this heat transfer.

As the surface water of the Gulf Stream cools, it becomes denser, 7 sinks to a depth of about two kilometers, and begins its slow progress around the world. As the dense water leaves an area, it pulls in new water from the equatorial and Caribbean regions, and the cycle continues. That is, the cycle continues as long as the water traveling north becomes denser and sinks. However, an increase in cold, fresh water entering the North Atlantic cools the surface temperatures and, because it's fresh water, makes the ocean currents less salty. Cooler surface temperatures and less salty currents, in turn, cause a slowdown in the Gulf Stream. If there is a lot of cold, fresh water, the surface temperatures no longer have enough heat to transfer to the jet stream as it passes over, nor are the waters salty enough to sink and continue driving the Global Ocean Conveyer. The Global Ocean Conveyer could stop. No more nice winters for London, Rome, and the rest of Europe. But that's not all.

The end of the Global Ocean Conveyer would mean an end to warm 8 surface water arriving from the equatorial regions and the Caribbean. The jet stream would no longer be able to pick up warm air to distribute over Europe, causing that area to become colder. The jet stream would be delivering colder air to each point east of Europe—Northern Asia and the Northern Pacific. Onshore winds would no longer be warming the East Coast of North America—that area would become colder. Because the jet stream would be passing over colder water and colder landmasses, the weather everywhere would be affected. Any place that currently depends on warming from ocean currents, directly or indirectly, would become colder.

The results of these colder temperatures when winter comes would 9 be devastating. The North Atlantic regions, the British Isles, Europe, Japan, and the Pacific Northwest normally receive heavy rains in the winter. If their winter temperatures were colder, this precipitation would fall instead as snow. Snow would fall in many places that had never or rarely seen it previously. Snow stays on the ground during the entire winter in the northern latitudes, waiting for the warm winds of spring (called chinooks in the northern United States and Canada) to melt it. But without a Global Ocean Conveyor, the system that transfers warm temperatures from the tropics to the northern climates via the ocean currents would no longer exist. So this snow would stay on the ground.

Those who've lived in northern climates, where it snows all winter, 10 know that once it snows, the temperatures go down further and stay down. With no warm winds coming, the same effect would happen in the scenario just described. To make matters worse, the snow on the ground would reflect sunlight back up, making the temperatures even colder. This surface reflection of incoming solar radiation is called <u>albedo</u>. NASA's Earth Observing System satellites have measured the albedo value of non-melting snow-covered surfaces at 80% to 90% ("The Earth Observing System Science Plan"). This means that 80% to 90% of the sunlight falling on these snow-covered areas will reflect back into space, leaving only 10% to 20% of the heat. With many more regions of the Earth covered with snow, the reflection of sunlight would cause temperatures to fall even further in a vicious cycle. Snow and ice would also act as an insulating blanket to keep ground temperatures cold. It takes a large amount of energy to warm up this insulated blanket, but that energy would no longer be available.

When snow keeps falling, it packs down, becoming ice. The more 11 snow, the thicker the ice. As the ice thickens, more stress is put on the deep ice. When enough stress is placed on it, the ice begins to move or flow—it advances. In fact, this is the definition of a glacier—an ice sheet that advances. An ice age occurs when widespread glaciers advance. In our scenario, we would now be in an ice age.

You shouldn't sell off your tank tops and shorts yet, though. Not 12 everyone in the scientific community agrees with this scenario. In fact, scientists have never agreed on a cause for the ice ages that have occurred in the past. Because no one was recording and preserving data then, we have no record of the events leading up to the ice ages or the events that caused them to end. What scientists do have is physical evidence—clues they can put together and run through computer models to see how they relate to what's happening in our climate today.

One group of disbelievers argues that this new theory isn't what 13 we've traditionally thought causes ice ages, so it can't be trusted. Every new theory in science since Copernicus announced that the sun doesn't travel around the Earth has confronted similar resistence. Past theories of the causes of ice ages include the occurrence of massive volcanic eruptions or increased amounts of space dust from meteors or comets, events that put large amounts of dust and particles into the atmosphere and block out the sun; decreases in the amount of the sun's energy reaching the earth caused by variations in Earth's orbit, lessened solar output, or changes in the Earth's tilt; or events that block ocean and air currents such as the shifting of the continental plates or the lifting up of massive mountain ranges like the Himalayas. These theories all have problems. An ice age has not followed every time one of these events has occurred, and some ice ages have occurred without any of these events happening first. If any of these theories are valid, they must be only a part of the picture, not the main contributing factor.

A student reader caught an error of fact:

It was Copernicus, not Galileo, who first suggested the earth moves around the sun. Make sure your facts are right!

Like any good researcher, Schlegel makes sure all her facts are correct in her final draft.

Another group of critics questions whether the specific models used   14
to predict the events in our scenario indicate that our current situation
will in fact lead to an ice age. These critics question whether any model
could predict such a complex future event. Computer models are only as
good as the data being used in them, so before accepting the results of
these models we must consider the validity of the research. Was it done
by a scientifically reputable institution? Was it published in a reputable,
peer-reviewed journal? Were the results of the model replicated by other
reputable institutions?

In considering possible causes of ice ages, we have good sources of   15
computer modeling. Several studies looking at the effects of global
warming have come up with models that support a global cooling.
The government-funded Geophysical Fluid Dynamics Lab working with
Princeton University has used a computer model to look at the effects on
our climate of CO_2 increases. The global warming that resulted led to a
shutdown of the Global Ocean Conveyor. The model indicated that this
shutdown would occur within a decade and that the conveyor would
take several centuries to recover (Raphael). Scientists at the Physics Institute of the University of Bern in Switzerland duplicated these results
using a different model (Stocker and Schmitter).

Researchers at Woods Hole Oceanographic Institute on Cape Cod   16
looked at evidence gathered over the past ten or fifteen years and concluded that we may be heading for the colder climate predicated by
our scenario. As the President and Director of the Institute, Dr. Robert
B. Gagosian, puts it, "... we've seen ominous signs that we may be headed
toward a potentially dangerous threshold. If we cross it, Earth's climate
could switch gears and jump very rapidly—not gradually—into a completely different mode of operation."

Scientists at the Woods Hole Oceanographic Institute found that in   17
the past decade, the North Atlantic waters have become dramatically
fresher—they are losing their saltiness (Gagosian). If this trend continues, we may get to see firsthand whether or not the predictions of these
models are accurate.

While computer climate models have not existed long enough for us   18
to see if their long-term predictions will hold, we can look at evidence we
have from past eras and see what happened before previous ice ages
occurred. While studying fossilized remains of plankton algae drilled
from the bottom of the mid-Atlantic, Scott Lehman and Julian Sachs,
former University of Colorado–Boulder researchers now at Columbia
University's Barnard College, found that the temperature of the Atlantic
dropped prior to the beginning of ice ages and rose prior to their ending.
These temperature changes were abrupt and "seem to be almost entirely

One classmate had this
comment:

I'd like to read even
more on the human
causes of global
warming and climate
change. Are there any
illustrations that you
found in your research
that might help
readers *see* what you
mean?

One of the ways that
Schlegel responded was
to include the illustration
on the following page.

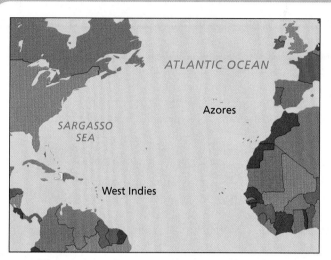

Fig. 1   Temperatures in the Sargasso Sea during the Last Ice Age. "Study Hints at Extreme Climate Change." CNN. 28 Oct. 1999. 1 Nov. 2003. <http://www.cnn.com/NATURE/9910/28/climate.change.enn/>.

ocean driven" (qtd. in "Study Hints at Extreme Climate Change"). These temperature changes seem to indicate changes in how the Gulf Stream was distributing warmer water. Lehman and Sachs also note that the "temperatures in the Sargasso Sea during the last ice age fluctuated up to 9 degrees Fahrenheit" (Fig. 1).

Dr. Richard Alley, a professor of geosciences at Pennsylvania State University, says that Global Ocean Conveyer disruptions and sudden climate changes are "nothing new—only the realization that they have occurred [is]" (qtd. in Wood). He states that while we used to think climate changes, like aging, happened gradually, recent studies of ice cores dating back 100,000 years show sudden shifts. Alley notes that "Large, abrupt and widespread climate changes occurred repeatedly in the past across most of the Earth, and followed closely after freshening of the North Atlantic" (qtd. in Wood).   19

While we can't predict the future with absolute certainty, we can look at past trends and see where we might be going. Where are we now? The Gulf Stream and Global Ocean Conveyor are still running, although one climate scientist, Dr. Andrew Weaver at the University of Victoria in British Columbia, suspects they might be slowing down. His work shows that the Scandinavian Glacier is growing and suggests this may be the result of less warm air reaching that far corner of the North Atlantic (Wood). Records of past climates suggest that when the Gulf Stream   20 stops, it does so within a few decades of the first sign that it is slowing down (Raphael).

And we continue to see increases in those factors that may cause the currents to stop. The Geophysical Fluid Dynamics Lab found CO_2 levels are continuing to rise 0.4% per year and have risen 28% since preindustrial times, indicating continued global warming. A Danish study from the University of Bremen found a decrease in the amount of Arctic sea ice each year since 1978, with 2002 seeing the smallest amount of ice observed for at least 100 years (Kaleschke). The melting of this sea ice is a continuing source of fresh water for the North Atlantic.   21

So what is happening now? Water temperatures off Atlantic City, New Jersey, were colder in 2003 than in any other year since 1911, when record keeping began ("Atlantic Surf" B10). These colder water temperatures were seen as far south as Florida. In fact, the water temperatures along the East Coast were almost three degrees Fahrenheit below normal. Next time you see a sale on parkas, take another look. And you might want to start selling those tank tops and shorts after all!   22

Works Cited

"A New European Ice Age?" Natural Science. 1 Nov. 1997. 24 Oct. 2003 <http://naturalscience.com/us/cover/ cover5.html>.

"Atlantic Surf Seekers Get Big Chill." Arizona Republic. 4 Nov. 2003. B10.

Gagosian, Robert B. "Triggering Abrupt Climate Change." Argentinean Foundation for a Scientific Ecology Web site. 24 Oct. 2003 <http://mitosyfraudes.8k.com/Calen/ TriggerIceAge.html>.

Kaleschke, Lars. "New Trend of Arctic Sea Ice Decrease?" Sept. 2002. University of Bremen, Denmark. 1 Nov. 2003 <http://iup.physik.uni-bremen.de:8084/decade.html>.

Raphael, Catherine. "Climate Impact of Quadrupling Atmospheric CO_2— An Overview of GFDL Climate Model Results." Geophysical Fluid Dynamics Lab. 24 Oct. 2003 <http://www.gfdl.gov/~tk/climate_dynamics/index.html>.

Stocker, T. F., and A. Schmittner. "Influence of CO_2 Emission Rates on the Stability of the Thermohaline Circulation." 1997 University of Bern, Switzerland. 24 Oct. 2003 <http://www.climate.unibe.ch/~stocker/abstracts/stocker97nat.html>.

"Study Hints at Extreme Climate Change." CNN. 28 Oct. 1999. 1 Nov. 2003 <http://www.cnn.com/NATURE/9910/28/climate.change.enn/>.

"The Earth Observing System Science Plan." Goddard Space Flight Center. 1999. 1 Nov. 2003 <http://eospso.gsfc.nasa.gov/science_plan/>.

"The Great Ice Age." US Department of the Interior/US Geological Survey. 1 Nov. 2003 <http://pubs.usgs.gov/gip/ice_age/ice_age.pdf>.

Weart, Spencer. "Past Cycles: Ice Age Speculations." The Discovery of Global Warming. 2003. American Institute of Physics. 24 Oct. 2003 <www.aip.org/history/climate/cycles.htm>.

Wood, Anthony R. "After Mild Winters, a Possible Sea Change." Philadelphia Inquirer. 8 Dec. 2002. 1 Nov. 2003 <http://www.philly.com/mld/inquirer/4689103.hrm?template+contentMdules/printstory.jsp>.

QUESTIONS FOR WRITING AND DISCUSSION

Rhetorical Knowledge: The Writer's Situation and Rhetoric

1. **Audience:** Who is the intended audience for this essay? What in the essay makes you think so?
2. **Purpose:** What is Schlegel's purpose in writing this essay? What does she want her readers to understand?
3. **Voice and tone:** What tone does Schlegel take in this essay? How does this tone affect her credibility?
4. **Responsibility:** How responsibly has Schlegel written? How effectively does she present and counter opposing viewpoints?
5. **Context and format:** Schlegel is writing as a student in a first-year writing course. How does this context affect her writing? If Schlegel were writing in a different context, how might her essay change?

Critical Thinking: Responding to the Writer's Ideas

1. What is your initial response to Schlegel's essay?
2. Does Schlegel focus mainly on causes? Effects? A series of causes and effects?

Composing Processes and Knowledge of Conventions: The Writer's Strategies

1. How well do you think Schlegel has researched her topic? How can you tell? What additional research might she have done?
2. What part(s) of Schlegel's essay are the most convincing? Why? The least convincing? Why?

Inquiry and Research: Ideas for Further Exploration

1. Interview several friends about the causes and/or effects of global warming, and record their comments. Write about the similarities and differences that you discover in the comments you have received.

Self-Assessment: Reflecting on Your Learning Goals

Now that you have constructed a piece of writing that explains causes and effects, review your learning goals, which you and your classmates may have considered at the beginning of this chapter (see pp. 266–67). To help reflect on the learning goals that you have achieved, respond in writing to the following questions:

Rhetorical Knowledge

- *Audience:* What have you learned about addressing an audience in this kind of writing?

- *Purpose:* What have you learned about the purposes for writing about causes and effects?

- *Rhetorical situation:* How did the writing context affect your writing about cause(s) and/or effect(s)? How did your choice of subject affect the research you conducted?

- *Voice and tone:* How would you describe your voice in this essay? Your tone? How do they contribute to the effectiveness of your writing about cause(s) and/or effect(s)?

- *Context, medium, and genre:* How did your context determine the medium and genre you chose, and how did those decisions affect your writing?

Critical Thinking, Reading, and Writing

- *Learning/inquiry:* While working on your paper, did you learn anything you might be able to generalize about in the causal relationship you focused on? If so, what might that be?

- *Responsibility:* How did you show that the effect or effects you wrote about were really the result of the cause or causes you identified?

- *Reading and research:* What did you learn from the reading selections you read for this chapter? What research did you conduct? What additional research might you have done?

- What skills have you learned while being engaged in this project? How do you hope to develop them further in your next writing project?

Writing Processes

- *Invention:* What invention skills have you learned in writing about causes and effects? Which skills were most useful to you?

- *Organizing your ideas and details:* Describe the process you used to identify the causes and then the effects you wrote about. How did you decide to organize your paper, and how successful was your organization?

- *Revising:* What one revision did you make that you are most satisfied with? If you could go back and make an additional revision, what would it be?

- *Working with peers:* How have you developed your skills in working with peers? How did you make use of feedback you received from both your instructor and your peers? How could your peer readers help you more with your next assignment? How might you help them more, in the future, with the comments and suggestions you make on their texts?

- Did you use visuals to explain your cause(s) or effect(s) to readers? If so, what did you learn about incorporating these elements?

- What "writerly habits" have you developed, modified, or improved on as you constructed the writing assignment for this chapter? How will you change your future writing activities, based on what you have learned about yourself?

Conventions

- *Editing:* What sentence problem did you find most frequently in your writing? How will you avoid that problem in future assignments?

- *Genre:* What conventions of the genre you were using, if any, gave you problems?

- *Documentation:* Did you use sources for your paper? If so, what documentation style did you use? What problems, if any, did you have with it?

If you are constructing a course portfolio, file your written reflections so that you can return to them when you next work on your portfolio.

Rhetorical Knowledge

- *Audience:* To convince your audience to accept your solution, you need to pay careful attention to your readers' views on and attitudes toward the problem. Who will be interested in your solution? What are their needs, their values, their resources? What arguments are most likely to convince this audience?

- *Purpose:* One purpose of any proposal is to convince readers of the existence of a problem and the need for a solution. Another purpose is to convince readers that the solution(s) you propose is (are) the best one(s) possible. If your solution involves money, you will also have to convince your readers that implementing your solution is cost-effective.

- *Rhetorical situation:* Think about all of the factors that affect where you stand in relation to your subject. What is compelling you to write your proposal essay?

- *Writer's voice and tone:* When you write to solve problems, you will need to be persuasive. As a result, you will need to make sure your tone engages your readers and does not in any way threaten or offend them.

- *Context, medium, and genre:* You will need to decide on the best medium and genre to use to present your proposal to the audience you want to reach. Visuals such as charts, graphs, or photographs may help you make your case.

Critical Thinking, Reading, and Writing

- *Learning/inquiry:* When you propose a solution, you first need to think critically to determine whether the problem exists and needs to be solved and whether your proposed solution is viable. You will also need to think critically about the kind of evidence that will convince your readers. Further, you will need to evaluate a range of possible solutions to find one or more that are not only viable but also effective.

- *Responsibility:* As you read solutions proposed by others, you have the responsibility to consider their solutions fairly as well as critically. You cannot simply ignore other good ideas simply because you do not agree with them.

- *Reading and research:* Readers will find your solution more acceptable if you have carefully and critically examined the problem and the issues surrounding your solution, supporting it with strong evidence, not unproven assumptions and assertions.

Writing Processes

- *Invention:* As with other kinds of writing, you should start by recording on paper or computer disk the ideas that you have about your problem, using an invention strategy such as brainstorming or listing. After recording your own initial ideas and findings, you will also need to conduct research to find information that will support your proposed solution.

- *Organizing your ideas and details:* Once you have some ideas down, you can then think of how you might want to organize your main points, what evidence you might need to provide to support those points, and how you might deal with competing solutions to the problem.

- *Revising:* As you write, you will undoubtedly learn what you think about your problem and solution, and you may even qualify or change your opinion about it. Once you have a draft, you will need to read your work with a critical eye to make certain that it fulfills the assignment and displays the qualities of an effective proposal.

- *Working with peers:* Make sure you "test" your solution on your classmates. If they have trouble accepting your idea, your readers will likely have the same problem.

Conventions

- *Editing:* One of the hallmarks of effective proposals to solve problems is the use of inclusive language—language that makes diverse readers feel like part of the team that is solving the problem. The round-robin activity in this chapter (pp. 333–34) addresses the issue of inclusive language.

- *Genres for writing to solve problems:* In your college classes, proposing a solution usually involves academic writing, so you will probably be required to follow the conventions for an academic essay. Other, nonacademic writing situations may call for a variety of genres, including reports, Web sites, editorials, brochures, letters to the editor, newspaper columns, blog entries, and formal proposals.

- *Documentation:* When writing to solve problems, you will probably need to rely on sources outside of your own experience. Make sure you document them using the appropriate style.

Chapter 11

Writing to Solve Problems

You see, hear, and read about problems and possible solutions to those problems all the time. In developing countries, governments and nongovernmental organizations struggle with problems such as poverty or disease. Closer to home, your community might experience a high dropout rate in your local school system or a shortage of affordable housing. When you write to **propose solutions,** you first identify an existing problem and then suggest one or more possible ways to solve it. For example, the Web site on the opposite page, ACCION International has identified world poverty as a problem and has proposed a possible solution. For example, ACCION started its lending program more than forty years ago, providing loans to what it calls "Microentrepreneurs," so those business owners can grow their own small companies. In turn, the interest they pay provides funding for even more small business loans.

When you are faced with a smaller-scale problem than world poverty, perhaps one in your own life or your friends' lives, you will often propose your own solution to it. When you suggest counseling to an unhappy friend, you are proposing a solution—a known treatment—to an emotional problem: depression. When you recommend a heating and air conditioning repair company to a friend with a broken furnace, you are proposing a solution—the repair company—to a more practical problem: the faulty furnace.

When you propose any solution, however, others may already have suggested different solutions to the same problem. Therefore, you must support your own proposal with convincing evidence—not just opinions—and demonstrate that the proposal has a reasonable chance of success.

Rhetorical Knowledge

If you want to propose a solution that your audience will take seriously, you will need to pay careful attention to rhetorical issues. Readers of any proposal will ask themselves, "Why should I believe *you*?" Therefore, all successful proposals have one important aspect in common: the establishment of a credible *ethos*. The nature of your subject and your audience will help determine the balance between logical arguments and emotional appeals that you will need to maintain.

Writing to Solve Problems in Your College Classes

In many of your classes, your instructor may present you with a problem and ask you to propose a solution. Here are some examples:

- In a political science class, you might be asked to propose a solution for the problems that surround the role of the Electoral College in presidential elections.
- In a course in environmental studies, you might be asked to propose ways to reduce U.S. dependence on fossil fuels.
- In a geology course, you might be asked to write a research proposal for the problem of erosion in a nearby gully or canyon.

Writing to Solve Problems for Life

As common as it is to propose solutions in academic settings, this kind of thinking and writing is even more prevalent in the other areas of your life. Many people feel that all they ever do in their **professional lives** is propose solutions to problems. For instance, the following examples all call for proposals:

- An employee writes to her company's personnel director to propose a solution to the high turnover rate in her division.
- A new member of a company's product-development division writes to her supervisor to suggest ways to reduce the time and costs required to develop and test new products.

People who are active in their communities often find themselves proposing solutions as part of their **civic life.** Because problems continually emerge—and old problems often reemerge—every community constantly needs ideas to help solve its problems. You might, for example, write a letter to a local newspaper in which you propose a plan for raising funds for a non-profit organization, a food bank, or a homeless shelter.

In your **personal life,** you will also encounter problems that need to be solved. Many of them will be small, but some will no doubt be large and potentially life altering. Suppose your mother, who lives alone, is suffering from a worsening case of Alzheimer's disease. You might send an e-mail to your siblings, proposing several possible solutions that you will then discuss by phone in a conference call. Or suppose your child is having a problem at school. You might send a letter to your child's teacher, suggesting a possible solution.

Scenarios for Writing: Assignment Options

Your instructor may ask you to complete one or both of the following assignments that call for a solution to a problem. Each of these assignments is in the form of a *scenario,* which gives you a sense of who your audience is and what you need to accomplish with your proposal. The list of rhetorical considerations on pages 312–13 encourages you to think about your audience; purpose; voice, tone, and point of view; and context, medium, and genre for the scenario you have chosen.

Starting on page 325, you will find guidelines for completing whatever assignment option you decide—or are asked—to complete. Additional scenarios for college and life may be found online.

Writing for College

SCENARIO 1   Solving a Social Problem from One of Your Courses

Think about a problem—local, national, or global—that you have learned about in another class you are taking this term. To complete this assignment, assume that the instructor for this class has asked you to choose a problem and propose a solution for it, which you will present to your classmates. You must first decide which problem you wish to address and then look at various options available for solving the problem. Here are some possible social problems to consider:

- **Education:** In some states, the high school dropout rate is relatively high compared to rates in other states.
- **Criminal Justice:** In some cities, motorists run red lights more frequently than they do in other communities.
- **Business Administration:** In many sectors of the U.S. economy, relatively few women have high-level management positions.
- **Health:** The incidence of diabetes is relatively high among some segments of the population in the United States.

Writing Assignment: Propose a solution to the problem that you have selected. Be sure to focus on solving one aspect of the problem, thus narrowing it down to a manageable size for a three- to five-page paper.

Writing for Life

SCENARIO 2   Civic Writing: A Letter to an Official Proposing a Solution to a Community Problem

Think about some problem in your community that has affected you, your family, or someone close to you. Perhaps you have been affected by a situation like one of these:

- Some in the community are convinced that a local factory, power plant, or other facility might be an attractive target for terrorists.
- The community's only grocery store, laundromat, or hardware store is about to close.
- A new family in your neighborhood has decided to paint its house an ugly color, or decorate the front lawn with pink flamingos, or its members play loud music late at night.
- A major chain of big-box superstores wants to build an enormous new store on the outskirts of your town, threatening the livelihood of local merchants.

As you consider possible topics, you will need first to figure out what the problem is so that you can define it—and prove its existence—to others.

Writing Assignment: Construct a letter to a local official outlining and explaining the problem in your community and then identifying and proposing a workable solution to that problem.

Rhetorical Considerations

Audience: While your instructor and classmates will be the primary audience, you should also consider other audiences for your proposal, depending on the scenario you have chosen. What will your audience know about this problem? Why should they be concerned about it? How can you make your solution(s) seem reasonable to them? What kinds of responses would you expect them to have to your proposal?

Purpose: Your purpose is to identify a particular problem, convince readers that it needs attention, and propose a viable solution.

Voice, Tone, and Point of View: You may choose to write about a problem that you have strong feelings about. How much has your view of the problem—or even your view that it *is* a problem—been determined by your own value system? How will you deal with your preconceptions about the problem, and how might these preconceptions affect your tone? What attitudes, if any, do you hold toward members of your audience, and how might that affect how you present your information?

Context, Medium, and Genre: Keeping the context of the assignment in mind, decide on a medium and a genre for your writing. How will your writing be used? If you are writing for an audience beyond the classroom, consider what will be the most effective way to present your proposal to this audience.

For more on choosing a medium and genre, see Chapter 17 and Appendix C.

Critical Thinking, Reading, and Writing

Before you begin to write your own proposal, you need to consider the qualities of a successful proposal. It also helps to read one or more proposals to get a feel for this kind of writing. Finally, you might consider how visuals could enhance your proposal, as well as the kinds of sources you will need to consult.

Effective writing that solves problems contains a clearly defined problem and a well-articulated solution that is targeted for a specific audience. In addition, this kind of writing will include convincing evidence for the proposed solution's effectiveness as well as a well-documented review of alternative solutions. Finally, an effective proposal will include a call to action.

Learning the Qualities of Effective Proposals

A piece of writing that proposes a solution to a problem should include the following qualities:

- **A clearly defined problem.** An effective proposal first establishes the existence of a problem that is both understandable and manageable within the scope of the assignment.

For more information on cause and effect, see Chapter 10.

- **An awareness of the audience.** Your readers need to believe that the problem you are writing about actually exists and that your proposed solution will work. Therefore, you should use what your audience already knows and believes to shape your proposal. For instance, if your audience readily accepts that there is a problem, you need not spend time and effort on establishing that; you can focus almost exclusively on the proposed solution. If, however, your readers may be unaware of the problem, or may not believe it *is* a problem, you will need to spend time making them aware of it and convincing them to be concerned about it.

- **A well-explained solution.** Your readers need both to understand your solution and to find it reasonable. One way to help any audience understand your proposal is to use language that the audience understands, and to provide definitions of unfamiliar terms.

- **Convincing evidence for the effectiveness of the solution.** You will need to prove that your solution is viable and the best answer to the problem by supporting your assertions with evidence such as expert testimony, case studies, experimental studies, and examples of similar solutions to similar problems. A solution needs to be feasible, affordable, and effective.

  You will also need to anticipate readers' objections to your proposed solutions so that you can address them. The cost of any solution almost always comes up as an objection, so you need to be prepared to deal with that objection ("While this solution is expensive in the near future, I will demonstrate how the costs will actually save us money in the long run.").

- **A well-documented review of alternative solutions.** While your proposed solution should be able to stand on its own merits, for your proposal to convince the most skeptical readers, you must also acknowledge alternative ways to solve the problem and then carefully show why the alternatives will not work, or work as well, thus demonstrating that your solution is the best option.

- **A call to action.** There is little point to proposing a solution to a problem unless someone actually implements that solution. At the end of your proposal, you should urge those who can take action to solve the problem to do so.

Rewrite the qualities of an effective proposal in your own words to help you better remember and understand them as you research your solution and develop your proposal.

A WRITER'S RESPONSIBILITIES

Constructing Writing to Solve Problems

When you propose a solution to a problem, you have multiple responsibilities. You have a responsibility to be honest about the scope and magnitude of the problem: Who is affected and how much are they affected? In addition, if there are costs associated with your proposal, it is your responsibility to provide an accurate estimate of those costs.

You also have a responsibility to consider a range of viable solutions and to evaluate carefully the effectiveness, affordability, and limitations of each. By doing so, you establish your credibility with your readers by demonstrating that you have looked at a number of solutions, that you have thoroughly investigated each one, and that you have made a carefully considered recommendation. By presenting each option fairly and by showing how *your* solution is the best, you also make your own position more credible and believable.

Reading, Inquiry, and Research: Learning from Texts That Propose Solutions

The following selections all propose solutions. As you read the selections your instructor assigns, consider the following questions:

- How effective is the writer at convincing you that there is a problem that needs to be addressed?

- To what extent has the writer offered a workable solution?

- How convincing is the evidence? Why? What other information would it take to convince you?

- How effectively does the writer anticipate opposing views, look at alternative solutions, and otherwise show that he or she has considered the problem in depth?

- How can you use the techniques of proposal writing exemplified here in your own writing?

As you read an essay, take notes, jot down questions, and make observations about the essay in a computer file. If you want to use the information in your own writing, you will already have the main points in a digital format.

Thinking Rhetorically

Keep in mind the following questions as you read the essays that follow. Make it a practice to ask yourself these questions in all your reading—personal, academic, and professional—and you will strengthen and sharpen your abilities as a reader and as a writer.

Rhetorical Knowledge: The Writer's Situation and Rhetoric

1. **Audience:** Who is the primary audience for this piece of writing? How effectively has the author addressed that audience? To what other audience(s) might this proposal be made?

2. **Purpose:** What is the author's primary purpose? What other purposes might the author have?

3. **Voice and Tone:** What is the author's attitude toward his or her topic? What can you point to in the essay that gives its author *ethos*?

4. **Responsibility:** What can you point to in the essay to show how the author is accurately using statistical information?

5. **Context and Format:** How effective is the format of the essay? Why?

MICHELLE MISE POLLARD

The Nursing Crisis: The Solution Lies Within

As a nursing student at the University of North Carolina, Charlotte, Michelle Pollard wrote this paper for the *Journal of Undergraduate Nursing Scholarship*. In it, she vividly describes the nursing shortage in the United States, as well as some ways to solve the shortage.

Abstract

The nursing crisis, in our country, has reached such epidemic proportions   1
that congressional testimony indicates a need for immediate action.
Exploring the causes, finding clues to the attrition, and understanding the
implications of this worsening shortage can help us to search for solutions.
This paper attempts to express how solutions may lie within the nursing
profession itself to stop the outflow of nurses from the profession and to
increase the inflow of new individuals to the profession.

Introduction

On September 25th 2001, a congressional hearing took place to address the   2
problem of the current nursing shortage, which has reached critical proportions. Members of the House of Representatives met and heard nurses tell
stories of poor working conditions that include inadequate staffing, heavy
workloads, use of mandatory overtime, lack of sufficient support staff, and
inadequate wages. One such nurse from a Washington area hospital said
eliminating mandatory overtime, setting better nurse to patient ratios and
giving staff nurses a voice in hospital policy were more important than
higher pay. "Until you fix the working environment, the salary issue is kind
of moot" (Romig, 2001, p. 733). The current nursing shortage, unlike those of
the past, appears to be headed toward a path of rapid decline.

This unstable environment in the healthcare setting has been blamed   3
on many issues that stem from changes in healthcare to societal attitudes
about the nursing profession. Steps can be taken and words spoken that
can lessen the declivity[1] of nursing professionals. This has become an

---

[1] declining number

issue that affects all Americans and immediate steps need to be taken to stop the worsening progression of this threat to healthcare as we know it.

Exploring the Causes

An aging population of patients that are often in need of more intense and specialized care from qualified medical professionals, of which nurses comprise the largest percentage, is adding fuel to the fire of this worsening crisis (Heinrich, 2001). The increase in the number of higher acuity patients with the added burden of a shrinking nursing population results in a bleak picture for the future of the profession.

According to congressional testimony by the House Education and Workforce Committee, the nursing workforce is aging and there are not enough new nurses entering the profession to replace those retiring or leaving (Heinrich, 2001). According to Senator Jim Jeffords (2001), I-Vt, the average age of a nurse is presently between 42–45 and by 2010 nearly 40% of the nursing workforce will be over the age of 50 and nearing retirement. "Our nation has suffered from nursing shortages in the past. However, this shortage is particularly severe because we are losing nurses from both ends of the pipeline," Jeffords said.

Clues to Attrition

Not only are the majority of nursing professionals aging, but many young people are choosing other careers. A recent study reported that women graduating from high school in the 1990s are 35% less likely to become nurses than women who graduated in the 1970s (Heinrich, 2001). Women today have more job options, many of which offer better pay, more job satisfaction, and perceived better working conditions ("Nursing Shortage," 2001).

Experienced nurses are opting out of nursing after many years, as well, looking for less stressful and more lucrative careers. A survey done by the Federation of Nurses and Health Professionals found that half of the currently employed RNs had considered leaving the patient care field for reasons other than retirement over the past two years (Heinrich, 2001).

Understanding the Implications

The shortage of qualified nursing personnel is an issue that affects anyone who is a provider or consumer of healthcare in this country. Consumers are affected directly by quality of care from nurses who feel they are overworked and overstressed due to the increasing demands on their time. Physicians are affected, as well, in their everyday practice and dealings with nurses and patients. According to one physician, "we are increasingly feeling the strain of a hospital nursing staff who are stretched too thin" (Stapleton, 2001, p. 30). The situation inevitably leads to a question of quality of care in settings such as hospitals.

As employers of the largest segment of healthcare professionals, administrators of hospitals and other facilities are also directly affected by the nursing shortage. A poll by the American Hospital Association (AHA) reports from a survey of 700 hospitals that there are approximately 126,000 nationwide RN positions currently vacant ("Publication," 2001). Maryland, for example, reported a statewide vacancy rate for hospitals of 14.7%, up from 3.3% in 1997. California reported a vacancy rate of 20% among its hospitals (Heinrich, 2001).   9

Proposing Solutions

There is no tried and true solution to a problem that has been seen before by this profession, but how do we stop the downward spiral as we lose current and future nurses to other, more attractive career choices? Efforts made to improve the workplace environment may both reduce the likelihood of nurses leaving the field and encourage more young people to enter the nursing profession. Governmental agencies can help bring new nurses into the profession by offering money for tuition assistance as well as all related expenses. Hospitals and other healthcare agencies can offer more attractive employment packages and listen first-hand to the issues surrounding the dissatisfaction of their nursing staff. Nurse managers that work closely with top administrators and have voices that leaders listen to can take a stand for nursing as a whole. The reports show that nurses would have increased job satisfaction if they had better working relationships with supervisors who have real power and autonomy (Welch, 2001, p. 24). But the majority of the burden for improving the job satisfaction lies within each of us as nurses.   10

Improving the workplace environment has to start from within the profession itself. As Mueller (2001) notes in an article in *Creative Nursing*, "we know we are proceeding into a serious global nursing shortage. . . . And we are discovering that some of the solutions lie within each one of us" (p. 3). As nurses we have voices that can be heard through all the administrative and governmental offices, but we must find ways to speak collectively and constructively. Oftentimes nurses are not assertive in telling the story of what it is that causes them to be dissatisfied, and many degrade the profession by complaining and not acting to improve it. Do we not hurt ourselves as well as the profession by discouraging qualified individuals from choosing nursing as a career? To express   11 ourselves completely and honestly, we must first look to develop personally and professionally. We, as nurses, need to implement a plan of action to further enhance our professionalism and solicit new members. My suggestions for such a plan include:

- First, "Do no harm"; do not degrade the profession by words, actions, or deeds.
- Become a teacher, mentor, role model to young professionals.
- Develop a strategy for community awareness and respect for the profession.
- Strive to continue to elevate our own personal standards and the standards of our profession (i.e., educational requirements should be MSN[2] for managers and teachers).
- Find ways to enhance the collective voice of nursing in your workplace, state, country.
- Finally, have pride and enjoy the wonderful and rewarding career that you have chosen.

These ideas can help our profession gain a sense of why it is we are   12
important to society and why we are irreplaceable to the healthcare system. By continuing to discuss only the negative nursing experiences, we discourage many prospective nurses from entering the profession altogether. Nurses need to share stories of how wonderful and rewarding a career in nursing can be. "I have never been bored or disinterested in nursing because I've been able to have so many roles in many settings . . . nursing is intellectually stimulating as I read articles in nursing, attend conferences and meetings and use that knowledge in my practice . . . I could share that I have had the pleasure of participating in the professional growth and development and that almost everyday new opportunities present themselves to me because I am a nurse . . . and that I haven't regretted a day or a moment for having chosen nursing as a career" states Christine Mueller, RN, PhD (2001, p. 5).

It is stories like these that will bring those future nurses into a career   13
that can be more rewarding than most. How many other careers allow you to be a part of the milestones of life like birth and death, recovery from illness and trauma, and make a difference in the lives of those who cross your path? Nurses are the backbone of the patient care setting, offering holistic care unlike any offered by other members of the healthcare team. And as nurses we have an obligation to save our profession from further deterioration and overall worsening of the nursing shortage.

---

[2] Master of Science in Nursing degree

Whether you are a bedside nurse or a top nursing executive, it is the   14
responsibility of us all to make our voices heard throughout the halls of
our hospitals, state legislatures, and this country. We must show why it
is important to improve conditions and what a wonderful and rewarding
career nursing is and can be to many individuals who have much to offer
this outstanding and admirable profession. If we, ourselves, have
immense pride and respect for what it is we do, we have to influence others to share this frame of mind in order to make a difference in the
careers we have chosen. Be proud and speak loudly, letting everyone
know what a noble and caring profession it is that we share.

References

Workforce: The people part of getting ready [Electronic Version]. (2001, October). *AHA News, 37* (40), 6.

Boehner, J. (2001, September 25). *Nursing shortage.* FDCH Congressional testimony.

Bozell, J., Holcomb, S., & Kornman, C. (2002). Cut to the chase [Electronic version]. *Nursing Management, 33*(1), 39–40.

Heinrich, J. (2001, July 10). *Emerging nurse shortages due to multiple factors.* FDCH government account reports. Retrieved from http://ehost-vgw20.epnet.com

Jeffords, J. (2001, November 1). *Jeffords' legislation to strengthen nursing profession passes health committee.* FDCH press releases. Retrieved from http://ehostvgw20.epnet.com

Mueller, C. (2001). The breadth and depth of nursing. [Electronic version]. *Creative nursing, 7*(4), 3–5.

Nursing shortage: It's likely to get worse before it gets better [Electronic version]. (2001, August). *Occupational Health Management, 11*(8), 85.

Parker, C. (2001). Nursing shortage, working conditions intertwined at congressional hearing [Electronic version]. *AHA News, 37*(39), 1.

Publication paints a bleak picture [Electronic version]. (2001, August). *Occupational Health Management, 11*(8), 89.

Romig, C. (2001). The nursing shortage demands action now—state and federal legislation passed [Electronic version]. *AORN Journal, 74*(5), 733.

Stapleton, S. (2001). Where's the nurse? [Electronic version]. *American Medical News, 44*(23), 30.

Thompson, T. (2001, September 28). Tommy Thompson holds news conference on the nursing shortage. *FDCH Political Transcripts.* Retrieved from http://ehostvgw20.epnet.com.

Welch, M. (2001–2002). The nursing shortage may be permanent [Electronic version]. *Connecticut Nursing News, 74*(4), 24.

QUESTIONS FOR WRITING AND DISCUSSION: LEARNING OUTCOMES

Critical Thinking: Responding to the Writer's Ideas

1. How aware were you of the impending crisis in nursing in the United States? How might this problem affect you or your family members?

2. What is Pollard's solution? How concrete is it?

Composing Processes and Knowledge of Conventions: The Writer's Strategies

1. Pollard lists ways the nursing profession can help itself in six bullet points. All of these steps seem easy to do from the outside. To what extent will these solutions have an impact on the problem?

2. What in the essay do you disagree with? That is, what aspects of Pollard's proposed solution do you think are unworkable?

Inquiry and Research: Ideas for Further Exploration

1. Interview a nurse about his or her career. In no more than two pages, explain his or her "take" on a nursing career.

MICHAEL BÉRUBÉ

How to End Grade Inflation

Michael Bérubé teaches literature and cultural studies at Penn State University. Professor Bérubé is the author of *Public Access: Literary Theory and American Cultural Politics* (1994) and has co-edited *Higher Education Under Fire: Politics, Economics, and the Crisis of the Humanities* (1994), and *Bad Subjects: Political Education for Everyday Life* (1998). He has also published in the *New York Times, the Boston Globe, the Village Voice,* and numerous academic journals. This article originally appeared in the *New York Times* on May 4, 2004.

Last month, Princeton University announced it would combat grade inflation by proposing that A-minuses, A's and A-pluses be awarded to no more than the top 35 percent of students in any course. For those of us in higher education, the news has come as a shock, almost as if   1

Princeton had declared that spring in central New Jersey would begin promptly on March 21, with pleasant temperatures in the 60's and 70's through the end of the semester. For until now, grade inflation was like the weather: it got worse every year, or at least everyone said so, and yet hardly anybody did anything about it.

There is nothing inherently wrong with grade inflation. Imagine a   2
system of scoring on a scale from 1 to 6 in which everyone gets a 5 and above, or a scale of 1 to 10 in which the lowest posted score is around 8.5. Such are the worlds of figure skating and gymnastics. If colleges employed similar scoring systems, the class valedictorian would come in with a 4.0, followed closely by hundreds of students above 3.95, trailed by the class clown at 3.4.

Critics would argue that we must be perilously close to such a sys-   3
tem right now. Several years ago, Harvard awarded "honors" to 90 percent of its graduates. For its part, Princeton has disclosed that A's have been given 47 percent of the time in recent years, up from 31 percent in the mid-1970's. Perhaps grade inflation is most severe at the most elite colleges, where everyone is so far above average that the rules of the Caucus Race in "Alice in Wonderland" apply: everybody has won, and all must have prizes. At the school where I teach, Penn State, grade inflation over the same period has not been nearly so drastic. In the spring semester of 1975, the average G.P.A. was 2.86; in 2001 it had risen to only 3.02.

Still, we don't grade all that toughly. English departments have basi-   4
cally worked on the A/B binary system for some time: A's and A-minuses for the best students, B's for everyone else and C's, D's and F's for students who miss half the classes or threaten their teachers with bodily harm. At Penn State, A's accounted for 47 percent of the grades in English in 2002. The numbers are similar for sociology, comparative literature and psychology—and indeed for the College of Liberal Arts as a whole. The sciences and engineering, notoriously, are stingier.

What to do? If we so desired, we could recalibrate grades at Penn   5
State, at Princeton or at any college in the country. The principle is simple enough, and it's crucial to every diving competition: we would merely need to account for each course's degree of difficulty.

Every professor, and every department, produces an average grade—an   6
average for the professor over her career and an average for the discipline over the decades. And if colleges really wanted to clamp down on grade inflation, they could whisk it away statistically, simply by factoring those averages into each student's G.P.A. Imagine that G.P.A.'s were calculated on a scale of 10 with the average grade, be it a B-minus or an A-minus, counted as a 5. The B-plus in chemical engineering, where the

average grade is, say, C-plus, would be rewarded accordingly and assigned a value of 8; the B-plus in psychology, where the average grade might be just over B-plus, would be graded like an easy dive, adequately executed, and given a 4.7.

After all, colleges keep all the necessary statistics—by year, by course and by department. We know perfectly well which courses require a forward somersault with two and a half twists from the pike position for an A, and which courses will give B's for cannonballs. We could even encourage professors and entire departments to increase their prestige by lowering their average grade and thereby increasing their "degree of difficulty." Students who earn A's in difficult courses would benefit—as would students who earn B's. 7

Incorporating "degree of difficulty" into students' G.P.A.'s would turn campuses upside down; it would eliminate faculty capriciousness precisely by factoring it in; and it would involve nothing more than using the numbers we already have at our disposal. It would be confusing as hell. But it would yield a world in which the average grade was never anything more or less than the middle of the scale. 8

QUESTIONS FOR WRITING AND DISCUSSION

Critical Thinking: Responding to the Writer's Ideas

1. What is your response to Bérubé's essay?

2. Bérubé seems to be implying that any letter grading is inherently subjective and masks a real, objective numerical grade. Do you agree with this assumption? Why or why not?

Composing Processes and Knowledge of Conventions: The Writer's Strategies

1. How seriously do you think Bérubé intends readers to take his ideas? What can you point to in the essay to support your answer?

2. Is Bérubé's use of statistics appropriate within the essay he has constructed?

Inquiry and Research: Ideas for Further Exploration

1. Interview several of your classmates about their views on grade inflation. Then interview several of your instructors about the same topic. In no more than two pages, write about the similarities and differences you found.

Thinking about Visuals That Present a Problem and Give a Solution

Sometimes the most effective way of presenting your case is to show your audience the problem and the solution. You can illustrate problems and solutions in a number of ways.

Consider the case of the old Los Arcos Mall, in Scottsdale, Arizona. The mall was closed, the site abandoned, and the location subsequently became a problem for the community. Arizona State University presented a solution to the Los Arcos problem. The university proposed to enter into a partnership with the city of Scottsdale to build a mixed-use complex that would include technology research, commercial space, a hotel-conference center, and multifamily residential units.

As part of the proposal for the site, the partners provided the architect's rendering of the project, called SkySong, which appears in Figure 11.1.

As you look at this visual aid, consider these questions about the effective use of visuals in illustrating a proposal:

- How does the visual provide information about the proposal?
- What does the visual illustrate for a reader that would be hard to show with text alone?

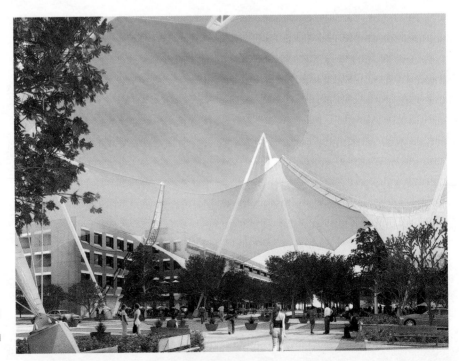

FIGURE 11.1
An Architect's
Rendering of SkySong
Source: Courtesy SkySong,
rendering by Pei Cobb Freed
& Partners

- What other types of visuals might be useful in a proposal? How might they convince an audience to accept the writer's solution?
- How might a visual such as the architect's rendering shown here be used to mislead readers about the feasibility of a proposed solution?

Writing Processes

As you work on your assignment, remember the qualities of an effective paper that proposes a solution to a problem (see pp. 313–14), and recall the recursive nature of the writing process—that is, after you engage in invention and conduct some research, you may start writing, or you may decide to do some more research. In fact, the more writing experience you get, the more you will realize that no piece of writing is ever finished until your final draft.

For a tip on organizing your computer files, see page 66.

Be sure to save your work frequently and back it up in two or more places—on an internal or external hard drive, on a USB flash drive, and on a rewritable CD or DVD.

Invention: Getting Started

As with any writing that you do, the more invention activities that you can draw on, the more effective your paper will be. Try to answer these questions while you do your invention work:

- What do I already know about the problem?
- What possible solutions do I already have in mind to propose?
- Where might I learn more about this problem (in the library, on the Internet, by interviewing people, by conducting a survey)? What personal experience might I have that is relevant?
- What might my audience already know about this problem?
- What might their point of view be?
- What questions do I have about the problem or about possible solutions?

Remember, invention activities improve with peer feedback and suggestions. Consider sharing the invention work you have done so far with several classmates or friends in order to understand your rhetorical situation more clearly and to generate more useful information.

Exploring Your Ideas with Research

Once you have used invention techniques to decide on a problem and explore what you know about it, you need to conduct research to explore the problem further as well as possible solutions to it.

Although your own experience may provide some evidence for the effectiveness of your proposed solution, personal experience usually needs to be supplemented by other forms of evidence: quotations from experts, examples, statistics, and estimates of time and financial resources drawn from reliable sources. One way to organize your research is to use the qualities of effective proposals to guide your research activities. Here are some possibilities:

- **A clearly defined problem:** As you do research on your problem, look at how others have defined it and narrowed it to make it more manageable.

- **An awareness of your audience:** Your research should give you a sense of how other writers have defined and addressed their audiences. Also, you should note how other writers have treated people's perceptions of the problem that you are trying to solve. What do they assume that people know about the problem? What do they assume that people do not know about the problem? How much do they assume that people care about the problem?

- **A well-articulated solution:** For most kinds of problems in the world, you will not be the first person to propose solutions. Look at how other writers have articulated their solutions.

- **Convincing evidence for the solution's effectiveness:** You will need to find evidence that your proposed solution is viable. Look for expert testimony, the results of experimental research, and case studies.

- **A well-documented review of alternative solutions:** You cannot be certain that your proposed solution is the most effective one unless you have carefully reviewed a range of possible solutions. As you consider them, keep an open mind—you might find a solution that is more effective than the one that you first offered.

- **A call to action:** As you do your research, look at the language that other writers have used to inspire their readers to action.

TechNote Your writing about problems and solutions can be improved if you investigate the kinds of solutions that would satisfy the larger community. To do so, you can use online resources to conduct primary research. To collect data or feedback from members of the community that will be affected by your solution, you can create a survey to collect their opinions, observations, and ideas, either developing a simple email distribution list and sending a small number of good questions to targeted respondents or taking advantage of free spaces for collecting peoples' opinions and reactions on popular sites such as Facebook, MySpace, and SurveyMonkey.

For advice on conducting primary research, see Chapter 19.

Reviewing Your Invention and Research

After finding sources and reading them critically, you should begin thinking about a tentative thesis—your statement of your proposed solution. Keep an open mind, though. As you draft and revise your proposal, you may continue to refine your thesis. People who develop the best solutions usually leave open the possibility that a better solution could occur to them at any time.

Organizing Your Information

Once you know the problem you will be writing about and the solution you will be proposing, you need to consider how you might organize this material. The questions that you need to ask yourself are all rhetorical:

- Who is your audience?
- Why might they be concerned about the problem you are discussing, and why might they be willing to accept your solution? Is it in your audience's best interest to find a solution for your problem?
- What is your purpose for writing—that is, why do your readers need this solution?
- What is the most important aspect of the problem you are proposing to solve?

One method for organizing a solution to a problem is the **whole-problem pattern.** If you are following this pattern, you first grab the readers' attention and introduce the problem and then use the paragraphs that follow to explain and illustrate it. If you think that readers are already familiar with the problem, this part of the paper could be fairly short, consisting of only a paragraph or two. If you think that readers are not familiar with the problem, however, then you might need to devote several pages to explaining and illustrating it. Then, offer your proposed solution or set of solutions, respond to objections that you think readers might have, and conclude with a call to action, encouraging your readers to do what you are proposing.

A second organizational approach is to **segment the problem.** This approach is useful if the problem is relatively complex and has several components. First, you explain and illustrate the problem, but in a general way. Next, you focus on each part of the problem that needs special attention, offering a solution and responding to objections that you anticipate specific to each part. Finally, you offer suggestions for implementation and conclude with a call to action.

A third organizational approach, which involves a **sequence of steps,** is appropriate if the solution has multiple steps. After introducing the problem, you offer an overview of a series of steps that will solve the problem. You then explain each step in detail, provide evidence that it will work, and address any objections to it.

Here is a summary of these three organizational structures:

Options for Organization

Whole-Problem Pattern	Segmenting the Problem	Sequence of Steps
• Introduce the problem and its background.	• Introduce the problem and its background.	• Introduce the problem and its background.
• Explain the problem.	• Explain the problem.	• Explain the problem.
• Offer a solution or set of solutions.	• Explain one part of the problem, offer a solution, respond to objections.	• Offer a multi-step solution with an overview of the steps.
• Respond to anticipated objections to the solution.		• Offer a detailed explanation of the first step.

(cont'd)

(continued)

Whole-Problem Pattern	Segmenting the Problem	Sequence of Steps
• Offer suggestions for implementing the solution. • Conclude with a call to action.	• Explain another part, offer a solution, respond to objections. • Deal similarly with remaining parts. • Offer suggestions for implementing the solution. • Conclude with a call to action.	• Offer a detailed explanation of the second step. • Deal with any additional steps that might be necessary. • Conclude with a call to action.

Constructing a Complete Draft

Once you have chosen the organizational approach that works best given your audience and purpose, you are ready to construct the rest of your draft. Remember that your thinking about the problem and its solution(s) will evolve as you write, so as you work on the draft, keep the following in mind:

- Draw on your invention work and your research. As you draft, you may discover that you need to do more invention work and/or more research.
- As you try out tentative solutions to the problem, ask peers about the kinds of evidence you need to demonstrate that the solution is viable.

For more on constructing
visuals, see Chapter 18.

- Ask yourself and peers whether visuals might help make your case.

Introduction: Regardless of your organizational approach, you need to begin with a strong **introduction** to capture your readers' attention and introduce the problem that you are proposing to solve. To accomplish these two goals, you might do one or more of the following:

- *Provide a brief history of the problem.*
- *Quote an authority who knows the problem well.* In "The Nursing Crisis," Michelle Mise Pollard begins her report with an account of a nurse's testimony to Congress.
- *Cite salient statistics that demonstrate the nature of the problem.*

- *Provide information about the problem that will surprise—and possibly concern—readers.* In his second paragraph, Michael Bérubé makes the startling assertion that "there is nothing wrong with grade inflation."

Body: When you propose a solution to a problem, you should determine the most effective organizational approach for the purpose you are trying to achieve and the audience that you are addressing. The reading selections in this chapter, for example, use the organizational approaches outlined on pages 327–28 to good effect. Whether you present a whole problem, segment the problem, or give a step-by-step solution, be sure to show why other solutions will not work or have already failed. Sometimes a problem has not been solved because previous solutions have only addressed its symptoms, not its root cause. If this is the case, you need to show that your solution will take care of the root problem.

- *Present a whole problem and then give solutions.* Although she has no one solution to the whole problem of the nursing shortage, Pollard does propose that any real solution will succeed only if all of the people who have a stake in solving this problem work together to find a solution and not just try to fix small pieces of it.
- *Give a step-by-step solution to the problem.* Though satirical in nature, Michael Bérubé's "How to End Grade Inflation" does present his readers with a step-by-step process for addressing grade inflation.

Conclusion: In your conclusion you need to review your proposed solution, reach out to your audience, and, usually, call for readers to take action to implement the proposal. Your conclusion could include the following:

- An outline of the problem you are working to solve.
- A summary of your main points, with an explanation of why your solution would work.
- A call to action—what you would like your reader to *do* now that he or she knows about the problem and your suggested solution.

Title: As you work on the process of composing your proposal, a title should emerge at some point—often very late in the process. The title should, of course, reflect the problem that you are addressing and might or might not hint at the solution. If you hint at a controversial solution in the title, however, you risk alienating readers whom you might otherwise win over with the strength of your argument.

VISUALIZING VARIATIONS

Alternative Forms for Solving Problems

Assume that rather than writing about a problem area such as the one that existed at the former site of Arizona's Los Arcos Mall (pp. 324–25) and design a brochure that includes visuals to show what could replace the eyesore.

What pictures or drawings might be useful to a potential customer, keeping in mind that the project is reaching out not only to businesses but also to people who might want to live in SkySong?

For the residential part of the project, this visual and exerpt from the descriptive text that accompanies it is designed to catch a potential renter's eye:

Source: Courtesy SkySong, rendering by Pei Cobb Freed & Partners

- 325 one-, two-, and three-bedroom floor plans ranging in size from ±551 to ±1,583 SF
- 1,000 space parking garage for residents and tenants
- Private balconies
- In-unit washers and dryers
- Community pool, spa, and exercise facility
- State-of-the-art high-speed Internet and communications facilities
- Connectivity with office-research facilities at SkySong

The following visual and details are directed at possible business clients:

- Two 4-story buildings, each approximately 150,000 square feet, frame the Eastern half of the east-west boulevard intersecting the center. Built with flexibility in mind, the buildings are designed to accommodate any tenant's space needs whether small start-up companies, expanding businesses, or regional operations.

Consider these questions:

- Although these are all drawings, and not photographs, each one has the look and feel of a photograph. Why might the people who rendered these drawings want them to *seem real*, as if the buildings and people, really exist?

- What do these drawings contribute to the proposal for SkySong? What could similar drawings contribute to a proposal in the form of a brochure?

Revising

Once you have a draft, put it aside for a day or so. This break will give you the chance to come back to your text as a new reader might. Read through and revise your work, looking especially for ideas that are not explained completely, terms that are not defined, and other problem areas. As you work to revise your early drafts, hold off on doing a great deal of heavy editing. When you revise you will probably change the content and structure of your paper, so time spent working to fix problems with sentence style or grammar, punctuation, or mechanics at this stage is often wasted.

As you revise, here are some questions to ask yourself:

- How effectively have I explained and outlined the problem(s), so my readers can understand those issues?

- What *else* might my audience want or need to know about my subject?

- How might I explain my solution(s) in sufficient detail and with enough examples so my readers can see how my ideas are logical solutions to the problem?

- How clearly have I explained and defined any terms my readers might not know?

- What other visual aids might help explain the problem and/or my solution?

Technology can help you revise and edit your writing more easily. Use your word processor's track-changes tool to try out revisions and editing changes. After you've had time to think about the possible changes, you can "accept" or "reject" them. Also, you can use your word processor's comment tool to write reminders to yourself when you get stuck with a revision or some editing task.

Many writers improve their ability to reconsider their own writing by having others respond to their text, which enables them to see how a real audience *reads* their proposal.

WRITER'S WORKSHOP

Responding to Full Drafts

Working with one or two other classmates, read each paper and offer comments and questions that will help each of you see your papers' strengths and weaknesses. Consider the following guidelines and questions as you do:

- Write a brief narrative comment that outlines your first impression of this draft. How effectively does the title draw you into the paper? What part(s) of the text are especially effective at explaining the problem or the writer's proposed solution?

- How successfully do the title and the introduction grab readers' attention? What other attention grabbers might the writer try?

- How well has the writer explained the problem to someone who is unfamiliar with it? How might the writer explain it more effectively?

- How effective is the organizational approach?

- How carefully did the writer document sources in this draft? What does he or she need to do with sources in the next version of the proposal?

- How well has the writer explained the proposed solution?

- How well has the writer addressed objections that skeptics might raise?

- How has the writer suggested ways to implement the proposed solution?

- Might visuals such as charts, tables, graphs, or photographs help the writer to present the problem or its solution more effectively?

- How effectively does the conclusion call people to action? What else might the writer do?

- In a brief paragraph, outline what you see as the main weaknesses of this paper—and suggest how the writer might improve the text.

Responding to Readers' Comments

Once you have received feedback from your classmates, your instructor, and others about how to improve your text, you have to determine what to *do* with their suggestions and ideas. The first thing to do with any feedback is to really listen to it and consider carefully what your readers have to say. You may decide to reject some comments, of course; other comments, though, deserve your attention. You may find that comments from more than one reader contradict each other. In that case, you need to use your own judgment to decide which readers' comments are on the right track.

Knowledge of Conventions

By paying attention to conventions when they edit their work, effective writers help to meet their readers' expectations. Experienced readers expect proposals to follow accepted conventions, especially if they are written for the business world. These include genre conventions, documentation, format, usage, grammar, and mechanics. Following these conventions allows your readers to concentrate on the content of what you are writing.

Editing

After you revise, you need to go through one more important step: editing and polishing. When you edit and polish your writing, you make changes to improve your style and to make your writing clearer and more concise. You also check your work to make sure it adheres to conventions of grammar, usage, punctuation, mechanics, and spelling. If you have used sources in your paper, you should make sure you are following the documentation style your instructor requires.

See Chapter 20 for more on documenting sources using MLA or APA style.

Because it is sometimes difficult to identify small problems in a familiar text, it often helps to distance yourself from it so that you can approach the draft with fresh eyes. Some people like to put the text aside for a day or so; others try reading aloud, some even read from the last sentence to the first so that the content, and their familiarity with it, doesn't cause them to overlook an error. We strongly recommend that you ask classmates, friends, and tutors to read your work to help find editing problems.

To assist you with editing, we offer here a round-robin editing activity on inclusive language, an important concern when writing proposals.

WRITER'S WORKSHOP

Round-Robin Editing with a Focus on Inclusive Language

When you propose solutions to problems, you need to be especially careful to use inclusive language—language that does not exclude people based on gender, ethnicity, marital status, or disability. Using inclusive language makes readers feel that they are included in the group that is solving the problem.

(cont'd)

(continued)

Look for instances in your work where the writer may have inadvertently used language that excludes a group based on gender, ethnicity, marital status, or disability. If you are uncertain about whether a particular word or phrase is a problem, consult a grammar handbook or ask your instructor.

Genres, Documentation, and Format

For advice on writing in different genres, see Appendix C. For guidelines for formatting and documenting papers in MLA or APA style, see Chapter 20.

If you are writing an academic paper in response to Scenario 1, you will need to follow the conventions appropriate for the discipline in which you are writing. For Scenario 2, you may need to follow the conventions of a business letter.

Student Esther Ellsworth Proposes a Solution

Student writer Esther Ellsworth, who is planning to major in biology, decided to look at the problems of current land-use policy in Arizona—as well as solutions to these problems. Here is her final draft.

One of Ellsworth's classmates made the following comment on her initial draft:

You probably need to do more of an introduction that grabs our attention more than this does.

Ellsworth responded with a new opening paragraph that attempts to catch the reader's attention by alluding to various American myths.

ESTHER ELLSWORTH

Comprehensive Land Use Planning in Arizona

The *American West*. What visions of grandeur that phrase brings to mind! Repeating it aloud, I think of tumultuous rivers, steep mountains, deep canyons, wide expanses of desert, large stands of trees. I think of pioneers migrating to this area, of people coming in search of something more than they ever had before—money, adventure, freedom from religious persecution, rebirth—something to be found in the wide open spaces of the land. I think of the native peoples who have inhabited this territory for centuries, not claiming ownership but instead simply living on the land for generations. I think of this place that I and so many others have called home.   1

Land—open land—is central to the identity of a western state. It is the very fact that our cities are two or three hours apart, that we have open areas without any significant development, that gives the West its   2 character. Yet, more and more, we are losing this characteristic. Developers keep speculating, turning once-rural areas into huge planned communities. Cities keep sprouting up and spreading out, encroaching on the wilderness around them. And people keep moving to Arizona, attracted by the state's open land and renowned natural beauty, by the good weather and good recreation.

This population growth, and the urban expansion that accompanies it, is beginning to destroy Arizona's outdoor flavor. Because we have no statewide plan for land use, development goes unchecked and undirected; cities sprawl, and growth also hits both rural communities and historically unsettled areas. As people watch, the open land for which Arizona is famous begins to disappear; office buildings, housing developments, and utility plants swallow it up. Residents see this occurring, and they become worried about state land preservation and planning. People recognize that Arizona's lack of conservation measures is a problem, but they do not know what to do about it. They do not understand that a series of legislative actions can create the plan for comprehensive land use that Arizona needs.

Land conservation is necessary for several reasons. First of all, open spaces can be used by virtually every member of the public, allowing all people to enjoy the outdoors. Guarding environments from exploitation by developers and businesses keeps public land available for all citizens' benefit. Protected environments provide space for everyone, space where people can go hiking or camping, where they can go boating or bird watching, where they can hunt or fish. With protected environments, people are free to enjoy the land in its most natural, undisturbed state.

Open space is also important ecologically. By preserving the native species and genetic variation of an area, open space preserves biodiversity. Animals and plants thrive in unrestricted territories, because the land gives them access to migratory routes, new habitats, and new mating populations (Nabhan 37–39). Thus, land conservation allows Arizona's unique creatures and ecosystems to prosper: Our state is home to many protected species, and it is the site of several reintroduction efforts for California condor and Mexican wolf populations, both of which are endangered. Arizona is also one of the only places in the world to have Sonoran Desert flora and fauna, and regions like southern Arizona's "sky island" mountain ranges (the Tucson Mountains, Santa Ritas, and Catalinas) or northern Arizona's Colorado Plateau provide research opportunities for numerous scientists ("Colorado" 1; Ellsworth). The importance of preserving this state's biodiversity, for both species protection and academic study, is clear.

Some people claim that preservation of biodiversity should not receive as much attention as it does, that it stands in the way of states' economic health. Today, however, the opposite of that statement is true: Preserving

3

4

5

6

Ellsworth received this comment from a classmate:

Here you might do something to build a link between these paragraphs—perhaps some language about the proposal.

Her response was to add language that helps to serve as a bridge between the two paragraphs.

biodiversity in Arizona is financially important and beneficial for everyone involved. Ecotourism, or "visitation to natural areas that involves no consumptive use of those areas," is an extremely profitable and reliable economic foundation for many communities (Leones 56). Ecotourism also happens to be one of Arizona's primary methods of attracting visitors to the state; each year, about five million people come to see the Grand Canyon alone, and the money they spend supports local economies ("Grand" 1). If the Canyon were only a hole in the ground without an incredibly diverse ecosystem, if it did not host an amazing variety of animals and plants, people would not be nearly so anxious to see it. But the canyon is <u>not</u> just a "hole in the ground," and like many areas in our state, its unadulterated natural beauty makes it attractive to visitors. This sort of beauty—found also in places like the Chiricauha Mountains and the West Fork of Oak Creek—brings visitors, and ultimately better financial health, to the state.

For all of these reasons, open space is worthy of conservation. We realize, as Arizona citizens, that land use and planning are issues we need to address; they affect so many aspects of our lives that we cannot ignore them any longer. In Arizona, there is a growing need to develop a statewide vision for land appropriations, and the public has to decide how to set aside land for conservation.

7

In order to have viable land use programs, we must have projects that are supported by all members of the community. The Sierra Club might advocate one approach while the governor's office and utility companies prefer another, and if no one is willing to construct a third, compromise plan, conservation efforts will fail. Many people want to approach land use planning as a problem to be solved quickly, as something they can look at once and then leave behind (Martori), but such thinking is also sure to fail. Because Arizona's land use patterns and needs will always change, it is impossible to establish policy that will not require periodic review. To be successful in conservation efforts, Arizona leaders and citizens must consider land use to be an ongoing concern, something that will be part of every future campaign and administration. "Governing growth will always require a perspective and process capable of balancing strong and independent values," ASU Public Affairs Professor John Stuart Hall says, and he is certainly correct (14). Just like education, immigration, and criminal justice concerns, land use will have to become part of Arizona's core political dialogue.

8

As we discuss land protection and development, we must also be careful not to turn our conversations into tense political debates. This inclination toward divisiveness inhibits the communication and consensus that are necessary for the successful establishment of a statewide land use plan. If people argue continuously, they have difficulty understanding one another's worries, and they do not work well together. Until Arizona's citizens decide

9

In response to a very short paragraph that briefly alluded to community involvement and political dialogue, one student made the following comment:

Can you add something here about how to conduct these dialogues in ways that will help to solve the problem rather than make it worse?

Ellsworth's response was to expand paragraph 8 in order to "show" community involvement and political dialogue rather than merely "tell" about it.

to establish common ground in conservation discussions, until they recognize a shared desire to take care of the state's land, they will not make much progress with planning. "We must struggle together," Phoenix writer Larry Landry states in one opinion piece, "to replace animosity with civility in our dialogue on the future of our community, to recognize the need to bring balance into the growth versus no-growth debate . . ." (80). Until this happens, conservation efforts will have little success.

Advocates of land preservation in Arizona must consider the state's present territory divisions and usage plans. Right now, about 80% of the state is undeveloped. Most of these areas are managed by American Indian tribes, local and state governments, the Bureau of Land Management, and the U.S. Forest Service ("Overview" 29). A person could rightly ask, then, why more preservation efforts are necessary if so much land is already held in the public's interest. The most direct response to this query, the reason we need further conservation measures, is that many people have tried to develop commercial and residential sites in these so-far-undisturbed areas—areas meant for the general public's use—and under present laws, such action is permissible. Under Arizona law, individuals and companies are allowed to purchase territory from the State Land Department, even though the areas are designated State Trust Lands (properties to be leased or sold only for the benefit of education and criminal justice programs). Because of the present structure, the Land Department manages to sell areas without much oversight from courts or the public. Citizens therefore have no way to preserve State Trust Lands for conservation, and they lose much of "the open landscape [that is] so vital to [Arizona's] functioning ecosystem" (Walsh 143). If, as some argue, we do not need to reconsider State Trust Land rules, how, then, can we ever hope to preserve our open areas from development? If, on the other hand, we reserve the right to decide the future of the Trust Lands, we can create conservation codes for the state, designating certain areas for preservation and leaving others open to the possibility of development. By taking this step, we can decide to save many of Arizona's wild areas from urbanization, and we can officially pledge to protect our environment's biodiversity.

People have tried to solve Arizona's land conservation dilemma several times in the past, but they have not developed an all-encompassing preservation program. As recently as three weeks ago, when Arizona voters passed Proposition 303 (the Preserve Arizona Initiative), they did not effect the kind of change that can really save the state's open lands from development. Under Preserve Arizona, $20 million of state funding will be available every year to help local governments purchase land for conservation. But with this measure, citizens still have little assurance that

10

11

Here, one of Ellsworth's classmates asks for some historical perspective:

What have people tried to do in the past? What will be the benefits of your proposed solution?

Her response is to describe some past Arizona efforts at land management.

Arizona's significant tracts of open space will be protected. The Preserve Arizona plan will help to guard small parcels from development by setting aside land in projects like the Scottsdale McDowell Mountain Preserve, but in the end, it will only create a fragmented string of conservation parks.

The passage of Preserve Arizona also presents the challenge of linking small conservation areas to one another. If animals and plants living in Preserve Arizona territories are to thrive, each of the small protected parcels must be connected to other wild spaces. According to some people, such a requirement makes it necessary for cities to implement "greenbelt" or growth boundary policies. (A greenbelt is a permanent conservation area around a city; a growth boundary is a temporary development limit that is adjusted every few years.) But while these actions are helpful biologically, allowing animals to migrate, they are unlikely to solve the problem of open space preservation. Growth boundaries are simply too unpopular among politicians and developers to be viable conservation methods. Many officials maintain that boundaries make housing costs skyrocket, and politicians therefore hate the idea of implementing boundaries here in Arizona (DeGrove 88). It is wise to be skeptical of complaints against boundaries, however. In Portland, Oregon, which has had a growth boundary since 1973, residents have not noted significant cost-of-living increases (DeGrove 88), and Arizona cities could choose to adopt some version of the urban boundary idea, making it work in conjunction with Preserve Arizona. But neither boundary-specification nor Preserve Arizona is comprehensive enough to protect this state's land resources.

In addition to Preserve Arizona and urban boundary plans, the state needs to develop two major policies: It must adjust State Trust Land rulings to designate some of these territories as permanent conservation spaces, and it must give individuals a way to designate their own properties as conservation lands.

Arizona lawmakers need to work with national officials to adjust the federal regulations that make it impossible to designate State Trust Lands as permanent preservation zones. The easiest way to do this would be to create, with the federal government's approval, a "Conservation Area" classification within the State Land Department. The new designation would give an undeveloped area permanent status as a non-development zone; its land would remain free of structures, and only the state government, with public approval, could build roads or utilities on it. The property could still generate revenue for the state by being leased to ranchers and farmers ("Overview" 29), but cities would never be allowed to encroach on the territory, companies would never be allowed

One classmate wants to know if there are other options:

Is there anything else that needs to be done to solve the problem?

Ellsworth responds by mentioning alternative options.

12

13

14

to mine the land, and power plants would never pollute the area's air. The space would be free of concrete and steel; it would be open to animals, plants, and people.

Some Arizona residents would definitely object to setting aside these 15 lands as Conservation Areas; the idea of non-development zoning is anathema for them because it seems like a restriction of freedom. But land conservation actually <u>guarantees</u> citizens' freedoms. It may prohibit certain individuals from disturbing the land, but it allows all citizens the freedom to use the area, and it is thus the most fair use for all involved. Through leasing to ranchers and farmers, Conservation Areas provide money for state education and criminal justice programs, and they ensure the preservation of places that are important and beneficial to all of Arizona. Also, not all State Trust Lands would become Conservation Areas; about 10 percent would still remain available for the Land Department to sell, lease, or preserve as it deems appropriate.

Once the Conservation Area system is in place, private individuals 16 would have a means of designating their own properties for preservation. Currently, tax systems make it very difficult for large landowners to keep their areas free of development. If individuals who own large pieces of land do not use the territory for commercial purposes, like farming or ranching, they pay exorbitant property taxes. Upon reaching retirement age, many of these people find that they cannot afford to keep their land because the taxes are simply too high. Individuals who want to preserve their family's heritage and land have no way to do so, and consequently much of Arizona's agricultural and ranching lands have been sold to developers in the past few decades. If we were to allow landowners to make their properties Conservation Areas, however, and give them a tax break for doing so, we would make possible another way to preserve open spaces. It is true that each of the territory additions would be rather small (Arizona's remaining tracts of private land are not very extensive), but nonetheless, they would increase the amount of preserved open space in Arizona.

In almost any discussion of land use, developers and environmen- 17 talists put themselves at odds, polarizing the conversation and refusing any compromise. Therefore, if they are ever to recognize their roles as stewards of the land, both groups will have to take a step back from the argument. They must leave behind their extreme beliefs—advocating either no growth planning or total growth restriction—because both of these approaches are harmful to the state. If Arizona's open space is exploited, it will not be able to yield profit *for* <u>anyone</u> in the future, and if all development is stopped, we will endanger our present economic health. The best approach to the question of land use, instead, is compromise. Our cities will continue to grow, but we can slow their rapid

One of Ellsworth's classmates asked,

What about people who think that your proposal will restrict freedom and harm commerce?

She responds by trying to anticipate the position of potential critics and give arguments to show that her proposal will not restrict freedom.

expansion by preserving areas in and around them. We can also preserve large tracts of land in the state's rural regions, thereby preventing the urbanization of these areas.

One classmate pointed out that Ellsworth didn't really have a conclusion in her initial draft.

She responded with a concluding paragraph.

Restricting growth and planning for conservation does not limit   18
individual freedom; instead, these actions free us all from future problems with land use. They free us to enjoy the open spaces of Arizona. They free us to use the land for recreation and sustainable commerce (ranching and agriculture). By controlling cities' growth and general land use, we ensure every individual's ability to enjoy state lands in the years to come. We ensure the survival of our unique environment, and we ensure the beauty of this territory. Developing a comprehensive land use plan for Arizona will not be easy, but the legislation is possible, and developing it is a challenge we ought to accept.

Works Cited

"Colorado Plateau Information Network." 22 Nov. 1998 <http://ecosys. usgs.nau.edu/>.

DeGrove, John M. "State Responses to Urban Growth: Lessons for Arizona." Growth in Arizona: The Machine in the Garden. Tempe: Morrison Institute for Public Policy/ASU, 1998.

Ellsworth, Clare. Personal interview. 25 Oct. 1998.

"Grand Canyon National Park." 22 Nov. 1998 <http://www.nps.gov/grca/>.

Hall, John Stuart. "Arizona's Growth Continuum and Policy Choices." Growth in Arizona: The Machine in the Garden. Tempe: Morrison Institute for Public Policy/ASU, 1998.

Landry, Larry. "Restore the Focus on Planning." Growth in Arizona: The Machine in the Garden. Tempe: Morrison Institute for Public Policy/ ASU, 1998.

Leones, Julie, and Bonnie Colby. "Tracking Expenditures of the Elusive Nature Tourists of Southeastern Arizona." Journal of Travel Research 36.3 (1998): 56.

Martori, Peter. "Land Use and Urban Growth in Arizona." Flinn Foundation Public Policy Seminar Series, Session 1.17, Oct. 1998.

"Overview of Growth in Arizona: Critical Statistics." Growth in Arizona The Machine in the Garden. Tempe: Morrison Institute for Public Policy/ASU, 1998.

Nabhan, Gary Paul, and Andrew R. Holdsworth. "State of the Desert Biome." Growth in Arizona: The Machine in the Garden. Tempe: Morrison Institute for Public Policy/ASU, 1998.

Walsh, James P. "Losing Ground: Land Fragmentation in Rural Arizona." Growth in Arizona: The Machine in the Garden. Tempe: Morrison Institute for Public Policy/ASU, 1998.

Since the draft originally submitted to classmates didn't contain any formal documentation, one classmate reminded Ellsworth to add it:

Of course, in your revised version, you'll need to include all of your citations.

Ellsworth included a formal list of works cited in her final draft.

QUESTIONS FOR WRITING AND DISCUSSION: LEARNING OUTCOMES

Rhetorical Knowledge: The Writer's Situation and Rhetoric

1. **Audience:** Who is the intended audience for Ellsworth's proposal? What makes you think that?

2. **Purpose:** What does Ellsworth hope will happen when people read her proposal?

3. **Voice and tone:** How has Ellsworth used language to help establish her *ethos* as someone who is knowledgeable about the problem of land use?

4. **Responsibility:** Comment on Ellsworth's use of sources to support her proposal. How responsibly has she used her sources? Why?

5. **Context and format:** Ellsworth wrote this paper for a first-year writing course. How is that context evident in the paper? If she were to change this piece of writing to an editorial for her local newspaper, what revisions would she need to make? If she were to make a poster representing the land-use problem and her solution, what would be on the poster?

Critical Thinking: Responding to the Writer's Ideas

1. What is your initial response to Ellsworth's paper?

2. How is Ellsworth's paper similar to other proposed solutions that you have read?

Composing Processes and Knowledge of Conventions: The Writer's Strategies

1. How effectively does Ellsworth organize her proposal? What other organization would have worked?

2. How does Ellsworth provide evidence that her solution is viable? What other evidence might she have provided?

Inquiry and Research: Ideas for Further Exploration

1. Interview family members and neighbors about their own feelings on what is happening to your own community and the surrounding areas.

Self-Assessment: Reflecting on Your Learning Goals

Having finished your proposal assignment, take some time now to reflect on the thinking and writing you have done. It is often useful to go back and reconsider your learning goals, which you and your classmates may have considered at the beginning of this chapter (see pp. 306–7). In order to better reflect on these learning goals, respond in writing to the following questions:

Rhetorical Knowledge

- *Purpose:* What have you learned about the purposes for writing a proposal?
- *Audience:* What have you learned about addressing an audience for a proposal?
- *Rhetorical situation:* How did the writing context affect your writing about the problem you chose and the solution you proposed? How did your choice of problem and solution affect the research you conducted and how you made your case to your readers?
- *Voice and tone:* What have you learned about the writer's voice in writing a proposal? How did your voice and tone contribute to the effectiveness of your proposal?

Critical Thinking, Reading, and Writing

- *Learning/inquiry:* As a result of writing a proposal, how have you become a more critical thinker, reader, and writer?
- *Responsibility:* What have you learned about a writer's responsibility to propose a good and workable solution?
- *Reading and research:* What research did you conduct for your proposal? Why? What additional research might you have done?
- What critical thinking, reading, and writing skills do you hope to develop further in your next writing project? How will you work on them?

Writing Processes

- *Invention:* What invention skills have you learned in writing your proposal? Describe the process you went through to identify the problem and the solution you wrote about. How helpful was this process? What research skills have you developed while writing your proposal?
- *Organizing your ideas and details:* How did you decide to organize your paper, and how successful was your organization? What drafting skills have you improved? How will you continue to improve them?

- *Revising:* What revising skills have you improved? What one revision did you make that you are most satisfied with? If you could go back and make an additional revision, what would it be?
- *Working with peers:* How did you make use of the feedback you received from both your instructor and your peers?
- How have you developed your skills in working with peers? How could your peer readers help you more on your next assignment? How might you help *them* more?
- Did you use visuals to help you explain your problem and solution? If so, what did you learn about incorporating these elements?
- What "writerly habits" have you developed, modified, or improved upon as you constructed the writing assignment for this chapter? How will you change your future writing activities, based on what you have learned about yourself?

Conventions

- *Editing:* What sentence problem did you find most frequently in your writing? How will you avoid that problem in future assignments?
- *Genre:* What conventions of the genre you were using, if any, gave you problems?
- *Documentation:* Did you use sources for your paper? If so, what documentation style did you use? What problems, if any, did you have with it?

If you are constructing a course portfolio, file your written reflections so that you can return to them when you next work on your portfolio.

Rhetorical Knowledge

- *Audience:* When you write about a creative work, you have to assess your audience's knowledge, interests, and biases carefully. For example, if you are writing about a story that you think few of your readers will be familiar with, then you may need to describe characters or narrative details. If you are writing about an obscure painting, you may need to describe details about the work more fully than you otherwise would. On the other hand, if you think that your audience is familiar with your subject, you can refer more casually to plot points or characters or aspects of the painting. You also need to consider whether your readers will have a negative or positive view of the work.

- *Purpose:* At the most basic level your ultimate purpose for writing about a creative work is to convince your readers that your perspective on that work is valid. Beyond that, you will usually have a secondary purpose, such as entertaining or informing your readers.

- *Rhetorical situation:* Consider the many factors that affect where you stand in relation to your subject. As you write about any work of art, it is crucial to clarify your stance for your readers.

- *Writer's voice and tone:* When you write about a creative work, you are trying to give readers a better understanding of the work. You need to be detailed and thorough, but you should avoid an "all knowing" or inflexible attitude that can be interpreted as arrogant. Instead, you should appear open to other interpretations.

- *Context, medium, and genre:* You will need to decide on the best medium and genre to use to write about the work at hand. For some works, such as plays or films, and especially for art, a visual may help you present your analysis.

Critical Thinking, Reading, and Writing

- *Learning/inquiry:* Reading a creative work critically means going beyond simple comprehension. Works of literature have layers of meaning, so it is important to read them carefully, thoughtfully, and more than once. Works of visual art almost always present a myriad of possible interpretations as well. As you read, you need to analyze the work and synthesize and evaluate your ideas.

- *Responsibility:* Effective writing about any creative work often leads to critical thinking. When you write about literature, you see the nuances in the work, and it is vital to present those aspects in a responsible and accurate manner.

- *Reading and research:* Writing about a creative work can involve close reading as well as online and library research to discover what others have written about the work.

Writing Processes

- *Invention:* Various invention activities—brainstorming, listing, clustering— can help you consider the parts of your subject and how they relate to one another. If you are reading a literary work, you may also find it helpful to annotate the work.

- *Organizing your ideas and details:* If your subject is large (for example, a novel or film, or several paintings, or a body of short stories), you might break it down into smaller parts, or you might begin with individual parts and examine each one in detail. You will need to make sure that each part of your analysis is presented clearly and logically.

- *Revising:* As you write, you will undoubtedly learn what you think about the work you are analyzing, and you may even qualify or change your ideas about it. You will need to read your paper with a critical eye, to make certain that it fulfills the assignment and displays the qualities of writing effectively about a creative work.

- *Working with peers:* Listen to your classmates to make certain that they understand what you are saying about the work. What do they say about how well your details justify your assertions?

Conventions

- *Editing:* One of the conventions of an effective analysis of any creative work is the use and proper documentation of quotations. The round-robin activity in this chapter (p. 381) addresses the issue of using and documenting quotations correctly as well as using the appropriate tense to write about events in a literary work.

- *Genres for writing about literature:* Usually a text about a creative work is written as a formal essay.

- *Documentation:* If you have relied on sources outside of your own experience, you will need to cite them using the appropriate documentation style, which would usually be the MLA style.

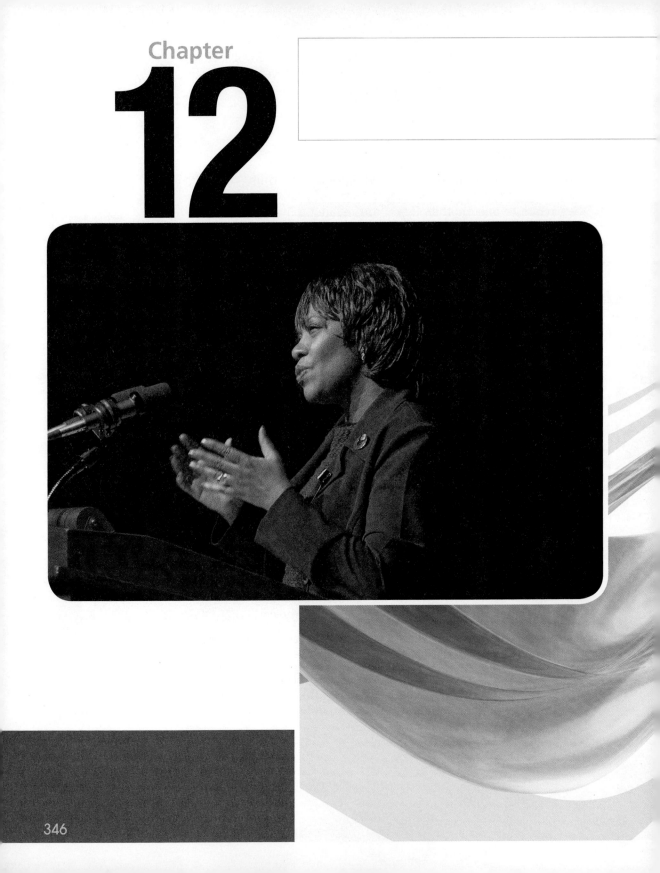

Writing about a Creative Work

Geometry

I prove a theorem and the house expands:
the windows jerk free to hover near the ceiling,
the ceiling floats away with a sigh.

As the walls clear themselves of everything
but transparency, the scent of carnations   5
leaves with them. I am out in the open

and above the windows have hinged into butterflies,
sunlight glinting where they've intersected.
They are going to some point true and unproven.

—Rita Dove

Is poetry what *you* think of when you think of "literature" or "creative work"? When you think of "literature," do you think of a poem like "Geometry" by poet Rita Dove? Or do you associate the word "literature" with some other literary genre? You may associate writing about literature exclusively with academic courses, and certainly writing about literature is a common assignment in many high school and college English classes.

However, people think and write about literature and other creative works in many places outside of the classroom. In presentations in civic and professional situations, speakers often allude to a scene or a character from a well-known novel, play, television series, or film to make a point. In your personal life, you may have already joined the legions of people who post brief reviews of books on the Web sites of book vendors such as Amazon.com. And "literature" isn't necessarily restricted to books, short stories, plays, and poetry—it can be defined more broadly to include film and television shows, graphic novels, hypertext, song lyrics—basically, any story told in any kind of medium. Throughout your life, as you engage in countless spoken and written conversations about a novel you have read, a film you have seen, or the lyrics of your favorite song, you'll be continuing to think, talk, and write about literature. Literature is about life—lived and imagined—so you will have many opportunities to connect it to all four areas of your life.

Rhetorical Knowledge

You will usually write about creative works to help your readers understand that work in a new way. You need to think about why you want them to gain this understanding. You also need to decide what medium and genre will help you communicate with your audience most effectively.

Writing about a Creative Work in Your College Classes

This chapter will offer you strategies for writing about creative works. Here are some academic situations that might call for this kind of writing:

- In a women's studies course, your professor asks you to provide a feminist perspective on the main character in a novel by Virginia Woolf.
- In a history course, your professor instructs you to analyze how well a film portraying a real event, such as *Titanic* or *Pearl Harbor*, matches historical records of the event.
- In your political science course, you are asked to analyze the impact of a work of fiction on public events, such as the impact of the novel *Uncle Tom's Cabin* on the debate about slavery in the nineteenth century.

Writing about a Creative Work for Life

If you are writing about a creative work in a professional, civic, or personal situation, you will consider literary texts or works of art in any number of ways, including explaining or evaluating ideas and concepts in the work(s) you read, comparing and contrasting ideas from them, and extracting information from them and relating it to your own situation.

Savvy **professionals** know that to make a complex idea understandable or to demonstrate that they share common ground with an audience, literary techniques and allusions to well-known fictional characters are often useful. An executive encouraging his employees to donate to charities during the holiday season might contrast their generosity to Charles Dickens's famous literary cheapskate, Ebenezer Scrooge, for example.

Many people also use literature to help them make points in their **civic lives.** Allusions to literature, films, or television shows can be powerful tools for helping audiences see the common ground that you share. The film *Mr. Smith Goes to Washington,* in which the main character filibusters the U.S. Senate, is often used to make the point that the country always needs strong, intelligent, and honest representatives in government. In the **personal area of life,** even people who do not think they are interested in literature often talk and write about the stories they see, read, and hear. When you see a film that your friends or family have also seen, you probably discuss it with them over dinner or in an email exchange. You might also write about movies or books or music or art at blog sites devoted to these topics, or you may contribute book or film reviews or lists of recommendations to online databases or sites such as Amazon.com, which allows readers to post comments and reviews.

Scenarios for Writing: Assignment Options

Your instructor may ask you to complete one or both of the following assignments that call for writing about a creative work. Each of these assignments is in the form of a *scenario*, which gives you a sense of who your audience is and what you need to accomplish with your writing. The list of rhetorical considerations on pages 350–51 encourages you to think about your audience; purpose; voice, tone, and point of view; and context, medium, and genre for the scenario you have chosen.

Starting on page 370, you will find guidelines for responding to whatever assignment option you decide—or are asked—to complete. Additional scenarios for college life may be found online.

Writing for College

SCENARIO 1 Writing a Literary Analysis for This Course

No matter what major you choose, especially in the humanities and social sciences, instructors in your college classes will probably require you to write about literature or other kinds of "stories," whether they are fiction or nonfiction, verbal or visual, and these stories will be open to numerous interpretations. This assignment will help you develop the skills to write about a wide range of literary works in a variety of fields such as history, economics, art, anthropology, education, business, and biology, among other disciplines.

Writing Assignment: Write an essay in which you analyze some feature (character, setting, point of view, plot, theme, style) in the work of literature chosen either by you or by your instructor.

Writing for Life

SCENARIO 2   Personal Writing: A Recommendation to a Friend or Family Member

When you read a wonderful book, see a movie that thrills you, or view an art collection that moves you, you probably want friends and family to share your enjoyment. Conversely, you do not want anyone you care about to waste their time reading a book or seeing a film that you consider pointless, dull, or even offensive. This scenario gives you the chance to influence the reading or viewing habits of people close to you.

Writing Assignment: Choose a novel, play, short story, poem, or film that you especially like. In a letter to a friend or family member, recommend that he or she read or see the work. Describe and show how the author has developed or used any of the following elements effectively: a character, the setting, the point of view, a provocative theme, a distinctive style. You can also write about how the work affects you. Be sure to point to specific evidence from the work to support your assertions.

Rhetorical Considerations

Audience: In addition to your instructor and classmates, your audience might also include a wide range of readers—perhaps family, friends, or subscribers to a listserv that focuses on a particular author, director, or genre of literature, film, or some other medium.

Purpose: Your purpose for writing this analysis is to convince readers that your analysis of the creative work is valid and to add to readers' understanding of the work. You might want to analyze a character, explain your view of the symbolism, or persuade your readers that they ought to view or read the work. This assignment allows you to explore a work that interests you in depth, and then to explain to your readers the *why* behind that interest—what in the story, film, novel, or play is valuable to you, and why.

Voice, Tone, and Point of View: Choose a writer's role that fits your purpose: What are you trying to accomplish? What preconceptions or biases do you bring to your writing? Letting your reader know your biases and preconceptions will add to your credibility. If you are writing in response to Scenario 2, for example, consider your relationship with the friend or family member to whom you are writing the recommendation. How might your recommendation affect that relationship?

Context, Medium, and Genre: Define a context that relates to your purpose for writing. Who might be interested in what you have to say about this work? Where and how can you reach that audience? Depending on the assignment—and in consultation with your instructor—you could use any number of genres. Possibilities include a standard academic essay, a letter to the author or your friend or family member, a Web posting, a dialogue with the author or a character, or an annotated timeline.

Critical Thinking, Reading, and Writing

Before you begin to write, you need to consider the qualities of this type of writing. It also helps to read a sample analysis of a creative work. Finally, you might consider how visuals could enhance your consideration of a cinematic work, as well as the kinds of sources you might consult to inform your own perspective on a work.

Learning the Qualities of Effective Writing about a Creative Work

Although in some instances you may be asked simply to explore a work of literature or art or music, in most cases you will be expected to make a point about the work you are writing about and provide evidence to support that point. As with most academic writing, you do not necessarily have to convince your readers to accept your point of view, but you do want readers to understand and appreciate your perspective. You may be asked to do the following:

For more on writing an evaluation, see Chapter 9.

- Evaluate the work.
- Analyze the entire work or some aspect of it (character, plot, theme, setting, sounds, colors, symbolism, imagery, or another element).
- Compare a character or characters to characters in other works.
- Explain the historical significance of the work.
- Explain how the work causes a reaction in the reader/viewer and explore why that reaction occurs.

Effective writing about creative works includes these elements:

- A clear thesis about the work. Your main point or thesis statement should clearly state your main idea about the work in a single sentence or two. In the rest of your essay, you should support, explain, and expand on this main point.

*For more information
about supporting
assertions, see
pages 195–96.*

- **Textual support for your assertions.** When writers make claims about a work, they need to point to specific evidence in the work that provides support for their claims. Using evidence from a short story or other literary work usually involves paraphrasing or directly quoting phrases, clauses, or sentences from the text or lines or stanzas from a poem. To provide evidence from a film, you would need to describe specific scenes.

- **Attention to the elements of the work.** If you are reading a work of literature, for example, you need to read it more closely than you would read other kinds of texts, such as a newspaper or even a college textbook.

    When you read a literary work such as a short story, which we will focus on in this chapter, you are reading not just for information—what happens in the story—but also for character development, theme, figurative language, and other elements that are commonly found in literary works. In other words, you are reading for the **literary qualities** of the text:

    - **Character.** Who is the story about? Who does what? How? Why?

    - **Setting.** The time and location of the story.

    - **Point of view.** The perspective of the narrator—the person telling the story. The narrator may or may not be a character in the story. The story may be told from a first-person (*I*) perspective, or from a third-person (*he, she, they*) perspective, and the narrator may or may not know what other characters are thinking.

    - **Plot.** The sequence of events in a story—what happens. In a work of fiction such as a short story or film, the plot usually reaches a crisis point or climax and then a resolution.

    - **Theme.** A theme is what the story means, the general statement that the story makes about life. It is analogous to the thesis of an essay. Some common themes in fiction deal with life's big questions, such as why seemingly good people suffer or what "love" is.

    - **Style.** Ernest Hemingway once said that the hard part of writing is "getting the words right." We see that famous quotation as a comment about writing style, which involves sentence structure and variation, word choices, the use of irony, and overall tone. In fact, writing style is one way literary authors define themselves and their texts. Here is an example of Hemingway's style from the opening of his short book *The Old Man and the Sea*. How would you describe his style?

        He was an old man who fished alone in a skiff in the Gulf Stream and he had gone eighty-four days now without taking a fish. In the first forty days a boy had been with him. But after forty days without

fish the boy's parents had told him the old man was now definitely and
finally *salao*, which is the worst form of unlucky, and the boy had gone
at their orders in another boat which caught three good fish the first
week. It made the boy sad to see the old man come in each day with
his skiff empty and he always went down to help him carry either the
coiled lines or the gaff and harpoon and the sail that was furled around
the mast. The sail was patched with flour sacks and, furled, it looked
like the flag of permanent defeat.

- **Figures of speech/imagery.** Literary works often contain **figurative
  language,** which evokes images in the reader's mind, and symbols.
  Writers use **symbols** within a work to represent or indicate other
  things. Writers also use **metaphors** to represent one thing as if it were
  another ("her hair is velvet"), **similes** to say that one thing is similar
  to another using the word *like* ("her smile is like the sun"), and **imagery** to generate a group of closely related details that, taken together,
  evoke an idea.

  *For more on the elements
  of creative works, see pages
  373–74.*

- **Sufficient context.** The amount of evidence and the kinds of evidence
  you provide your audience depends on who you see as that audience and
  what they need to know about the work if they are to accept your claim.
  Your audience's existing familiarity with the work helps you determine
  how much you will need to summarize or how much detail to include,
  what characters you will need to describe, and what else from the story
  you need to explain so that readers will understand your point.

  One effective strategy for approaching this assignment is to read
  or view the creative work you're interested in several times. The first
  time, you might simply read or view the work to comprehend or
  understand it. The second time, you might read or view the work with
  an eye for kinds of literary features described in the list above. During
  this second reading, make notes in the margins or in a journal. After
  that second reading, review your marginal comments to see what in
  the work seems to have grabbed your attention the most. For instance,
  your comments may focus on characterization more than anything
  else. If so, consider that focus to be a cue to pay extra attention to
  characterization as you read or view the work a third time.

  *For more on reading
  critically and writing
  to learn, see Chapters 2
  and 3.*

A WRITER'S RESPONSIBILITIES

Writing about a Creative Work

When you write about creative works, you need to balance several kinds of responsibilities. First, you have a responsibility to present your own thinking about the
work you are writing about instead of simply repeating the thoughts of others.
Second, you have a responsibility to support your assertions about the work that
you are analyzing. The best way to support your ideas is to excerpt or paraphrase

(cont'd)

(continued)

relevant passages from the text carefully, making sure to present them accurately, document them correctly, and avoid claiming others' ideas or words as your own. You are also obligated to consider those passages that could be used to refute your assertions. Third, you have a responsibility to use excerpts from the work fairly, in context. Using an excerpt out of context is a distortion, and readers who are familiar with the work will quickly recognize your dishonesty.

For more on documenting sources properly, see Chapter 20.

Reading, Inquiry, and Research: Learning from Literary Works

Literature can take you places you may never get to, show you lives very different from—or similar to—your own, and help you understand your own life, feelings, and relationships. And when you *write* about literature, you open up a new world of learning. Putting your thoughts into some order and onto paper, you can learn more about what you think and believe about ideas implicit in the story, novel, poem, or play you are considering.

DON DELILLO
Videotape

Born to Italian immigrant parents in New York City in 1936, Don DeLillo earned his bachelor's degree from Fordham University in 1958. He is well known for his fifteen novels, including *White Noise* (1985), which won the National Book Award. He has also written plays, as well as the screenplay for the 2005 film *Game 6*, which tells the story of a playwright obsessed with the 1986 World Series between the Boston Red Sox and the New York Mets. This story first appeared in *Antaeus* in 1994 and was later included in his novel *Underworld* (1997).

It shows a man driving a car. It is the simplest sort of family video. You   1
see a man at the wheel of a medium Dodge.

It is just a kid aiming her camera through the rear window of the   2
family car at the windshield of the car behind her.

You know about families and their video cameras. You know how   3
kids get involved, how the camera shows them that every subject is

potentially charged, a million things they never see with the unaided eye. They investigate the meaning of inert objects and dumb pets and they poke at family privacy. They learn to see things twice.

It is the kid's own privacy that is being protected here. She is twelve years old and her name is being withheld even though she is neither the victim nor the perpetrator of the crime but only the means of recording it.   4

It shows a man in a sport shirt at the wheel of his car. There is nothing else to see. The car approaches briefly, then falls back.   5

You know how children with cameras learn to work the exposed moments that define the family cluster. They break every trust, spy out the undefended space, catching Mom coming out of the bathroom in her cumbrous robe and turbaned towel, looking bloodless and plucked. It is not a joke. They will shoot you sitting on the pot if they can manage a suitable vantage.   6

The tape has the jostled sort of noneventness that marks the family product. Of course the man in this case is not a member of the family but a stranger in a car, a random figure, someone who has happened along in the slow lane.   7

It shows a man in his forties wearing a pale shirt open at the throat, the image washed by reflections and sunglint, with many jostled moments.   8

It is not just another video homicide. It is a homicide recorded by a child who thought she was doing something simple and maybe halfway clever, shooting some tape of a man in a car.   9

He sees the girl and waves briefly, wagging a hand without taking it off the wheel—an underplayed reaction that makes you like him.   10

It is unrelenting footage that rolls on and on. It has an aimless determination, a persistence that lives outside the subject matter. You are looking into the mind of home video. It is innocent, it is aimless, it is determined, it is real.   11

He is bald up the middle of his head, a nice guy in his forties whose whole life seems open to the hand-held camera.   12

But there is also an element of suspense. You keep on looking not because you know something is going to happen—of course you do know something is going to happen and you do look for that reason but you might also keep on looking if you came across this footage for the first time without knowing the outcome. There is a crude power operating here. You keep on looking because things combine to hold you fast—a sense of the random, the amateurish, the accidental, the impending. You don't think of the tape as boring or interesting. It is crude, it is blunt, it is relentless. It is the jostled part of your mind, the film that runs through your hotel brain under all the thoughts you know you're thinking.   13

The world is lurking in the camera, already framed, waiting for the boy or girl who will come along and take up the device, learn the instrument, shooting old Granddad at breakfast, all stroked out so his nostrils gape, the cereal spoon baby-gripped in his pale fist. 14

It shows a man alone in a medium Dodge. It seems to go on forever. 15

There's something about the nature of the tape, the grain of the image, the sputtering black-and-white tones, the starkness—you think this is more real, truer-to-life, than anything around you. The things around you have a rehearsed and layered and cosmetic look. The tape is superreal, or maybe underreal is the way you want to put it. It is what lies at the scraped bottom of all the layers you have added. And this is another reason why you keep on looking. The tape has a searing realness. 16

It shows him giving an abbreviated wave, stiff-palmed, like a signal flag at a siding. 17

You know how families make up games. This is just another game in which the child invents the rules as she goes along. She likes the idea of videotaping a man in his car. She has probably never done it before and she sees no reason to vary the format or terminate early or pan to another car. This is her game and she is learning it and playing it at the same time. She feels halfway clever and inventive and maybe slightly intrusive as well, a little bit of brazenness that spices any game. 18

And you keep on looking. You look because this is the nature of the footage, to make a channeled path through time, to give things a shape and a destiny. 19

Of course if she had panned to another car, the right car at the precise time, she would have caught the gunman as he fired. 20

The chance quality of the encounter. The victim, the killer, and the child with a camera. Random energies that approach a common point. There's something here that speaks to you directly, saying terrible things about forces beyond your control, lines of intersection that cut through history and logic and every reasonable layer of human expectation. 21

She wandered into it. The girl got lost and wandered clear-eyed into horror. This is a children's story about straying too far from home. But it isn't the family car that serves as the instrument of the child's curiosity, her inclination to explore. It is the camera that puts her in the tale. 22

You know about holidays and family celebrations and how somebody shows up with a camcorder and the relatives stand around and barely react because they're numbingly accustomed to the process of being taped and decked and shown on the VCR with the coffee and cake. 23

He is hit soon after. If you've seen the tape many times you know from the handwave exactly when he will be hit. It is something, naturally, that you wait for. You say to your wife, if you're at home and she is 24 there, Now here is where he gets it. You say, Janet, hurry up, this is where it happens.

Now here is where he gets it. You see him jolted, sort of wire-shocked—then he seizes up and falls toward the door or maybe leans or slides into the door is the proper way to put it. It is awful and unremarkable at the same time. The car stays in the slow lane. It approaches briefly, then falls back.

You don't usually call your wife over to the TV set. She has her programs, you have yours. But there's a certain urgency here. You want her to see how it looks. The tape has been running forever and now the thing is finally going to happen and you want her to be here when he's shot.

Here it comes, all right. He is shot, head-shot, and the camera reacts, the child reacts—there is a jolting movement but she keeps on taping, there is a sympathetic response, a nerve response, her heart is beating faster but she keeps the camera trained on the subject as he slides into the door and even as you see him die you're thinking of the girl. At some level the girl has to be present here, watching what you're watching, unprepared—the girl is seeing this cold and you have to marvel at the fact that she keeps the tape rolling.

It shows something awful and unaccompanied. You want your wife to see it because it is real this time, not fancy movie violence—the realness beneath the layers of cosmetic perception. Hurry up, Janet, here it comes. He dies so fast. There is no accompaniment of any kind. It is very stripped. You want to tell her it is realer than real but then she will ask what that means.

The way the camera reacts to the gunshot—a startled reaction that brings pity and terror into the frame, the girl's own shock, the girl's identification with the victim.

You don't see the blood, which is probably trickling behind his ear and down the back of his neck. The way his head is twisted away from the door, the twist of the head gives you only a partial profile and it's the wrong side, it's not the side where he was hit.

And maybe you're being a little aggressive here, practically forcing your wife to watch. Why? What are you telling her? Are you making a little statement? Like I'm going to ruin your day out of ordinary spite. Or a big statement? Like this is the risk of existing. Either way you're rubbing her face in this tape and you don't know why.

It shows the car drifting toward the guardrail and then there's a jostling sense of two other lanes and part of another car, a split-second blur, and the tape ends here, either because the girl stopped shooting or because some central authority, the police or the district attorney or the TV station, decided there was nothing else you had to see.

This is either the tenth or eleventh homicide committed by the Texas   33
Highway Killer. The number is uncertain because the police believe that
one of the shootings may have been a copycat crime.

And there is something about videotape, isn't there, and this par-   34
ticular kind of serial crime? This is a crime designed for random taping
and immediate playing. You sit there and wonder if this kind of crime
became more possible when the means of taping and playing an event—
playing it immediately after the taping—became part of the culture. The
principal doesn't necessarily commit the sequence of crimes in order to
see them taped and played. He commits the crimes as if they were a
form of taped-and-played event. The crimes are inseparable from the
idea of taping and playing. You sit there thinking that this is a crime that
has found its medium, or vice versa—cheap mass production, the
sequence of repeated images and victims, stark and glary and more or
less unremarkable.

It shows very little in the end. It is a famous murder because it is on   35
tape and because the murderer has done it many times and because the
crime was recorded by a child. So the child is involved, the Video Kid as
she is sometimes called because they have to call her something. The
tape is famous and so is she. She is famous in the modern manner of
people whose names are strategically withheld. They are famous without names or faces, spirits living apart from their bodies, the victims and
witnesses, the underage criminals, out there somewhere at the edges of
perception.

Seeing someone at the moment he dies, dying unexpectedly. This is   36
reason alone to stay fixed to the screen. It is instructional, watching a
man shot dead as he drives along on a sunny day. It demonstrates an
elemental truth, that every breath you take has two possible endings.
And that's another thing. There's a joke locked away here, a note of cruel
slapstick that you are completely willing to appreciate. Maybe the victim's a chump, a dope, classically unlucky. He had it coming, in a way, like
an innocent fool in a silent movie.

You don't want Janet to give you any crap about it's on all the time,   37
they show it a thousand times a day. They show it because it exists, because
they have to show it, because this is why they're out there. The horror
freezes your soul but this doesn't mean that you want them to stop.

QUESTIONS FOR WRITING AND DISCUSSION

1. **Your Personal Response:** What is your initial emotional reaction to this
   story? Why do you think you feel this way?

2. **Character:** What is the effect of having a twelve-year-old girl videotape the murder of the man driving the car?

3. **Setting:** The story has two settings—the setting for the events in the videotape and the setting for the viewing of the tape in the story. How do you as a reader mentally process these two settings simultaneously?

4. **Point of view:** What is the point of view of the story's narrator? Why do you think that DeLillo chose to use this point of view?

5. **Plot:** What is the structure of the story's plot?

6. **Theme:** What is DeLillo saying about violence and death?

7. **Style:** Find examples of figurative language in the story.

8. **For Further Exploration:** Many people have written about DeLillo's story. Search the Web to find some of those responses. How do they compare with your reactions to the story?

AMY TAN

Alien Relative

Author Amy Tan was born in Oakland, California, in 1952 to Chinese immigrant parents. Tan went to high school in Switzerland and attended many colleges before graduating from San Jose State University. The publication of *The Joy Luck Club* (1989), about the relationships between Chinese women and their Chinese-American daughters, launched her writing career and eventually led to a film version of the novel. Tan is also the author of *The Kitchen God's Wife* (1991), *The Hundred Secret Senses* (1995), and two children's books. Her most recent works include *The Bonesetter's Daughter* (2001), *The Opposite of Fate*, a book of nonfiction, and *Saving Fish from Drowning* (2005). This story was originally published in the anthology *Charlie Chan Is Dead: An Anthology of Contemporary Asian American Fiction* (1993).

I was there at San Francisco Airport when Helen arrived in this country   1
from Formosa. That was in 1956, maybe sooner than that. In any case, back then she was called Hulan, "Lake Mist." She said her mother named her that because she came into this world like the Queen of Clouds rising from the water at dawn. But I think Helen just made that up. I think probably her mother called her that because she was born already crying a lake of tears.

As I was saying, I was there at the airport with my husband and children, waiting for Hulan to come, this woman I call sister, although she is no such thing. I just said that for the Immigration officials, so I could sponsor her—also because I owed Hulan a debt I had to repay. She helped me leave my first marriage, that time I was married to a bad man. Actually, she did not really help, only promised not to interfere. In China, that was almost like helping. As for myself, I really did help Hulan. I helped her come to this country. In America, that meant I had to interfere. 2

"Hey!" I called when I saw Hulan come out of the Customs swinging door, her face bouncing up and down in the crowd. And just like her name, she had mist in her eyes, crying so hard she couldn't see us. It was seven years since the last time I saw her, but she looked as if it had been twice as long, she was so old. Her hair was unstylish, same as always, only now it was hanging down just like a washerwoman's, no curly parts to frame her round face. And she wore an ugly fur coat, the skins bent all stiff to pieces, like an old dead dog dried out on the road. So of course I didn't recognize it, my mink coat, I mean, the same one I loaned her in Shanghai last time I saw her, when I was still dreaming I could buy ten just like it in my rich new American home. Oh, I was mad when I found out later that her ruined coat was mine! 3

But, as I was saying, that day at the airport, at the Customs door, our whole family was happy to welcome her—her husband and her children, too. I was standing on my tiptoes, holding my young daughter's hand. Actually, I squeezed Pearl's hand too hard. I didn't mean to, of course, but then, with so much waiting and excitement, and then to finally see Hulan, my old friend who knew all the troubles of my life—well, how did I know what I had done until Pearl screamed, "Let me go, Mommy, let me go!" In front of all those people, she said that. All my life, it seems, Pearl's been saying the same thing. Let me go. 4

Anyway, we were there, only a few faces away, and still Hulan couldn't see us. Of course she couldn't—she didn't have her glasses on. So my husband, Johnny, lifted our four-year-old son high in the air to call Hulan's attention our way. And little Samuel shouted, "Whoa, horsey! Whoa!" and waved three cowboy hats, two white, one black, two for boys, one for girl, because that's how many children Hulan had. Finally Hulan saw us, and cried back, "Brother! Sister!" I think she called us that just in case the Immigration officials were watching. 5

She pushed her way through the crowd. Her husband, Henry, came next, just like a person still dream-walking, not believing he was really here. He was holding the baby, Bao-bao Roger. Then came Ming-fei Mary, so small for eight years old . . . then two suitcases . . . one box . . . no more. 6

Right away I noticed: Only two children, why not three? Where was 7
their middle child, the son who was six years old?

"Feng-yi Frank, where is he?" I asked, still looking. 8

"Oh, he is coming," Hulan answered slowly, "only later." 9

Johnny and I looked behind her, thinking she meant one minute 10
later. Then one minute later, when we were still waiting and looking,
Henry finally explained it this way: "The money you sent for five tickets,
later it was enough for only four."

And still we didn't understand, until Hulan began to cry in a scared 11
way. "You already did so much. How could we ask for more?" Then Henry
sat down on a suitcase and covered his face. And Ming-fei Mary started
wailing. And little Bao-bao saw all this, turned his mouth down, and cried
loud, too.

So that's how we found out: They left Feng-yi behind. Too polite to 12
ask for more money! Too polite to let their middle son come to America!
Oh, isn't that the Chinese way—to make all that pain seem like just a
small inconvenience?

That day at the airport I can never forget. We were all standing 13
together at last, so many happy people rushing by us. My heart hurt,
filled with Hulan's troubles, my stomach ached, mixed with my own
anger. I wanted to shout at Hulan, "So stupid! So stupid!" Because I was
remembering how much we too had suffered. How Johnny worked
overtime, one-dollar-eighty-five for an hour, stacking boxes weekends
and nights. How I always bought the fatty pork, twenty cents' saving
here and there. How I scolded Pearl so hard for one sock missing, until
she shouted, "Leave me alone," and I left her with a big slap mark on
her face instead. All those sacrifices to bring so much unhappiness to
America!

Of course, we tried to send for Feng-yi right away, as soon as we had 14
more money. But then we found out: no applications for nephews, ten-
years waiting list for sons, but first you must be a citizen, no breaking the
rules. So, it was seven years more before Hulan and Henry received their
citizenship papers, four years more before they were brave enough to tell
the authorities, "We have another son." Eleven years altogether before
they finally got Feng-yi Frank back. And telling it this way, I make it sound
simple.

Anyway, that was long time ago, more than twenty years gone by, all 15
those troubles now forgotten. Today Hulan's an American. Now days she
calls herself Helen. Now she thinks life is so easy, doing everything the
American way. Like what she said yesterday. I was complaining about my
daughter, Pearl, how she never comes to visit, how she never tells me
anything over the phone, just, "Oh, Mom, we're fine, don't worry."

And Helen said, "You want her to visit you more often, it's easy. You invite her to your house. That's the American way. These days, kids don't drop in, drop out. You have to ask. Come on this date, such-and-such a time. Like an appointment, see, easy to make." 16

And I wanted to tell Helen: Easy? You don't remember? It's not so easy to claim back your child. 17

I was with her, standing in long lines at the Department of Justice. You think Hulan could speak up for herself, a mother who left her son behind? So I came along to use the American rules to push us through first one line then another, one place to get forms, one place to ask questions. 18

Finally we found the right line, but the woman authority acted like she was too busy stamping official documents—toong! toong!—oh yes, what she was doing was more important than us. Helen pushed forward the application, the one that said, "Petition for Alien Relative." I whispered to Helen from behind, "Talk, talk, tell her your situation." 19

"I came to this country," Helen began, "but forgot my son." 20

"Forgot?" the woman said, still stamping, not even looking up. "How can you forget a son?" 21

"No, no! I can never forget my son," Hulan said, leaning back, scared. "This is not what I meant." The woman authority now looked at Hulan. Hulan looked at me. And I knew what she wanted to say, all those things she told me at her kitchen table these past eleven years. So I stepped to the counter and I told the Immigration authority how this could happen, how you can lose a child, and really, this was nobody's fault. 22

They were sitting in a courtyard in Formosa, Henry and Hulan, when our telegram came. They took it inside their room, so the neighbors could not see, these strangers who envied you if you had even one grain of rice more. But already, people were whispering, "Overseas! They got a telegram from overseas!" 23

Hulan dried their hands, it was so steamy hot that day. Then carefully, so carefully, she used a small knife to cut open the envelope and read our one-page message, the words we tried to say clearly, so there would be no delay: "The Red Cross, the church sponsor, all of us are saying to come now, come through. There is an opening. The money is being wired to you." 24

They walked out of their room, into the courtyard. They looked at their neighbors, who were by their doors watching. Hulan had waited for the day she could do this. "Soon this room will be available," she announced, just like a victor. "We are moving to America!" 25

Then came the first problem. Their daughter had a TB test, and it said maybe the TB was active, maybe not. In any case, Ming-fei Mary 26 couldn't leave. So they gave an official some of their plane ticket money to say it was not, and later it really turned out it was not. "But in those days," Helen argued with me later, "who knew which way things would go for you without paying a price?"

Now they had only enough money to buy four plane tickets. They didn't think ahead that this would happen, that's how it is when you are scared. So Henry said, "We should write to Winnie and Johnny, ask them for more money." 27

But Hulan said, "They will think we were careless! Besides, too much time will be wasted before they can answer us yes or no." Because they both knew: In Formosa, wait too long and you can lose your chance forever. Just that day, they had heard it on the radio: at a black-market booth, hundreds of people had pushed and shoved, shouted and fought— then fourteen people were hurt, two people crushed—over one special visa to America, which turned out to be illegal. 28

For two days and two nights, they argued and cried, deciding what to do. Hulan even tried to sell the mink coat, the same one I gave her before I left China. But then the pawnshop man told Hulan the coat was dirty, trying to bargain her down. So Hulan washed that mink coat with soap and water, washed it until there was nothing left to sell. After that, Henry decided what to do. 29

"I will stay," he said. "You and the children, you go first." He was once a military official. He knew how to be brave like that, ordering his family to a second-place victory. 30

But Hulan scolded him bitterly, "What good is a family in America with no father to feed them? I will stay." 31

Then Henry shouted, "Crazy woman! No mother to guide her children to the right opportunities? You want them to become wild Americans? We are all staying then." 32

That evening they felt too sick to eat. They lay wide awake on their bed, grieving silently over the opportunity they could no longer use. Then they looked at their three sleeping children, crowded on another bed in the same room, two boys, one girl, growing bigger every day. I have done the same with my own children, so I know. And seeing this, all their anger turned to grief. Because at that moment, as with every moment, neighbors were arguing: "That's my pot! Who said you can use it to cook your smelly food!" Then more people were shouting, "Your food stinks worse!" Every day they heard this, the cursing and shouting, accusing and pleading. They were listening to all this hopelessness coming from rooms filled with people who had once been so rich and powerful in different parts of China, and were now the same kind of poor in one courtyard in Formosa. 33

In the middle of the night, when the courtyard was finally quiet, Hulan and Henry rose from the bed and went outside. They sat on the ground, looked at the sky, but not at each other. 34

Hulan spoke first: "Ming-fei's health, it's always been poor." 35

Then Henry said, "And little Bao-bao—so helpless! Only one year old." 36

After that they were silent for a long time. The night was black, no stars, no moon. They heard no crickets, felt no cooling wind. Finally Hulan spoke in a trembly voice. 37

"Yesterday afternoon I saw Feng-yi holding a cocoon in his hand. Just like this, so softly. He was blowing his breath on it, thinking this would make the butterfly pop out and play." 38

"Six years old, and already so clever," said Henry. 39

"So patient, so playful," Hulan said, now starting to cry. 40

"Strong," said Henry, then more loudly, "and obedient, too." 41

"Our favorite," Hulan whispered in a hoarse voice, "and he knows this, too. Old enough to never forget us." 42

That morning, Hulan grasped her middle child to her heart and promised him, "I will never forget you, never lose you." And Feng-yi smiled, not knowing what she meant. 43

In the evening, they took Feng-yi to visit his grandmother. Actually, she was not the real grandmother but a bondservant who married Henry's father after the real grandmother died. In any case, the old lady was glad to take in the little boy. Although, after she put the boy to bed, she scolded Hulan and Henry: "Leaving China was bad enough. Now you're going to America, where it is even worse. What will become of us Chinese people?" They went to the airport that night, when Feng-yi was already dreaming. 44

On the airplane, they practiced everything about the new country in their minds. They imagined a large Immigration official greeting them with pale eyes and a sly mouth, smiling and encouraging them, "Say anything. In our country, you are free to say anything. Do you love our government?" 45

"Yes," they practiced saying in English. "We love America, very, very much, more than China, more than Formosa." 46

And then they imagined this pale-eyed man asking them more questions, trickier ones: "Then where is your other son, the one on this document? Why did you leave him behind? Is he a Communist spy?" 47

"Oh no, not a spy, just a little boy. He loves America, too." 48

"Then why didn't you bring him?" 49

"He was sick, too sick to come." 50

"I see, and the rest of you, did you bring this same sickness here?" 51

"Actually he is not sick, nobody is. It's just that we didn't have the money to bring him. This is the truth, only that reason, no money." 52

"What! You came to our country with not enough money? You came here to beg? Police! Police!" 53

Before they landed, the visa papers with their names had one name crossed out. I always thought that was a bad-luck thing to do, crossing Feng-yi's name out, like wishing he would be banished from the world—which, of course, is what happened four months later. 54

I read the letter in Hulan's kitchen. That grandmother, who was not even the real grandmother, wrote to say she was returning to China. "Fukkien food is bad for the stomach," she wrote. "I would rather die in Shanghai than live in Formosa. No more running away. We are going home, Feng-yi and I." 55

"Henry did this!" cried Hulan. "I insisted I should be the one to stay, Feng-yi should go. Now look what's happened!" 56

"I said we all should stay," Henry shouted back. "But you! You were dreaming of American cars, a car we could drive back to Formosa to fetch Feng-yi back!" 57

Day after day, year after year, we heard them arguing like that. I used to sit in Hulan's kitchen. So many times I had to watch the steam rise from her cook pot, the mist clouding her eyes, while she whispered to me—every birthday, every festival day, every time I brought my same-age daughter to her house—how she would never forget him. 58

Let me tell you, that little boy, Feng-yi, none of us could forget him. For so many years we could not see him. We could not hear him. We could not write to him. He was just a little boy, living in Red China, cut off from the world. But I remember, it was just like he was living in Hulan's kitchen all those years, shouting back, as powerful as any angry ghost. 59

"My sister, she only forgot to claim her son on the paper," I explained to the Immigration authority. "Now do you understand?" 60

The authority was not smiling. She said, "Then here's what you should do." 61

For her forgetfulness, Hulan and Henry had to hire an expensive immigration lawyer. The lawyer they found in the Yellow Pages was Chinese but born in this country. Hulan didn't listen when I told her, "A Chinese name doesn't mean Chinese thinking." 62

Sure enough, this lawyer said—in English—that we needed proof, "a birth certificate," to show this Alien Relative on the application paper had a true relationship with his mother. 63

"In China," I told the lawyer carefully, "you don't need a certificate to be born. See, when a baby is born, if he is crying, this is proof he is born live. If a woman sacrifices her own breast to feed him, this is proof she is his mother. Okay?" 64

"What you need," the lawyer said to Hulan, "is an affidavit witnessed   65
by a notary public, signed by witnesses who knew you in China when
your son was born."

Hulan shook her head quickly and said, "All those people are dead."   66
But what she really meant was, "All those people are scared to death."
Who would be willing to sign an official document when they had their
own problems to hide? Maybe they were renting a room for two, when
they really had eight or ten people living inside. Maybe they told the officials they were working one job, nine-to-five, but it was really three
jobs—graveyard, overtime, weekends—and who knew if all that extra
work was illegal to do. In any case, why should anyone lift a hand to help
only to have it chopped off?

"Chinese people always help each other out," said the lawyer.   67

Lucky for Hulan, I remembered Old Auntie Du, her aunt married to   68
her father's brother from long time ago. And this old aunt, over seventy
years old, knew she would die soon anyway.

"They can kick me out of this country, okay!" laughed Auntie Du.   69
"Send me back to China, doesn't matter. Anyway, I want to be buried
there."

Old Auntie Du signed the affidavit, and she told the notary public   70
several times, "I was right there. These two eyes, these two hands—right
there inspecting the cord that tied mother to son, son to mother. Write
that down."

Six months later, Feng-yi Frank, the Alien Relative on the petition,   71
arrived at the airport. We were there, at the Customs swinging door, same
as in 1956, only now it was 1967. Henry brought his never-forgotten son
a cowboy hat. Samuel and Pearl brought their new cousin Silly Putty and
a water pistol. And Hulan, I remember, she brought her dreams. Her face
had two dark spots under her eyes, two hungry hollows in her cheeks. So
many nights of dreaming awake!

I saw how her eyes grew big with hope, staring at each little boy who   72
walked through the Customs door. Her feet were ready to run toward this
one—then that one—here, no, over there!

I was the first to know it was Feng-yi Frank standing in front of us.   73
And Hulan was right, when she left her son, he was old enough never to
forget. He stared right at his mother, nobody else. That's when Helen's
eyes looked up, turned scared, searching for her memory.

His smooth, plump chin, the one she used to lift to her face to kiss,   74
now it pointed down at her, rough and bony hard. His soft little hands,
the ones that reached up to her, demanding to be held, now they held
tight onto two boxes tied with string, and he didn't even put them down
when Hulan hugged him American-style.

But his eyes—they had changed the most, she whispered to me later. Not curious, not eager, never looking back or farther ahead. He seemed to see only what was in front of him, and he showed no opinion in his eyes about any of it. That son, already seventeen years old when he arrived, never let his mother forget what she had done. 75

Maybe I should have felt more sorry for Hulan. But then I thought, She never told Feng-yi she was sorry. I heard what she said: how Formosa, then America, then China were the reasons for the long delay. "How could I fight three countries?" she told him at the beginning. Later, she bragged about all her hardships to bring him over: "Lawyers, money, affidavit—more complicated than you think!" 76

Now Feng-yi is an American, life is so easy. He tells everyone to call him Frank. He is almost forty, same as my daughter, Pearl. He lives with his mother and father. Lucky he still has a living father, not like my children. Every evening he has dinner at home, so polite, saying thank you, no thanks when his mother says, "Eat more, eat more!" At night he goes to his job as a security guard, signing people in, signing people out. And when he gets up late in the afternoon, he smokes too many cigarettes, or plays video games on his TV set, or lies underneath an old greasy car and sings to its stomach, "How much is that doggie in the window, the one with the waggle-ly tail." 77

An American lady from our church once asked Frank, "What was it like living in China, aren't you so glad to be here?" And Frank said, "China wasn't too bad, just boring, same old clothes, nothing to do. Oh, and they didn't let you have pets." 78

Helen then told that church lady how much Frank always wanted a dog. And that's what he got, a fancy poodle dog, for his twenty-fifth birthday. Puffy head, puffy tail. I tell you this, though, that dog, all those years, lived outside on a cold little porch, because Helen didn't want it to messy up her house. And I saw that dog every time I went to visit—I saw it through the sliding glass door. It was matted and dirty, so skinny, shaking and dancing in a circle every time he saw Frank come home. But Frank didn't even look at that doggie in the window. Although sometimes he still sang that same song, the one with the waggle-ly tail. 79

I heard Helen complain only one time, about her son, I mean. We were watching Frank, and Frank was watching cars race round and round on the TV set. He sat up, he sat back, he shook his fist and shouted, "Go, you sonabitch, go!" That's when Helen whispered to me, "Look what the Communists did to my son." 80

I still see Helen almost every day. But she doesn't tell me her troubles. She doesn't cry in her kitchen. She doesn't take my advice anymore. Now she thinks she's giving me advice, helping me. Like the other day. We were sitting in her kitchen, near the sliding glass door. I was watching her dog lying outside, so sad. She was telling me how I should call Pearl. 81

"Make her some Chinese dumplings," Helen said. "Invite her to come eat. She eats your food, she's just like your little girl again, thanking her mommy." 82

I pretended not to listen. What does she know? Why should I let her interfere? So instead I told her, "That poodle dog looks sick, real bad." 83

And she said, "Oh, that dog's okay. It's just old." 84

The next day that dog died. I was in Helen's kitchen a few days after it happened. I didn't say anything about the dog that was no longer there. I didn't tell Helen how I made the dumplings, how Pearl didn't come. We were just sitting and drinking tea, same as always. Then Helen started to scratch her ankles, then her legs, until she cried out, "Why are those fleas still pinching me? That dog's already dead!" 85

And I didn't explain to her, because I know how Helen has become. She doesn't understand, not anymore, how something can still hurt you after it's gone. 86

QUESTIONS FOR WRITING AND DISCUSSION

1. **Your Personal Response:** What is your overall emotional reaction to this story?

2. **Character:** How would you describe the relationship between the narrator and Hulan?

3. **Setting:** Various events in the story take place in China, Formosa (Taiwan), and the United States. How do these multiple settings affect the story?

4. **Point of View:** Why do you think Tan uses a first-person narrator for this story? How would the story be different if Helen, or Feng-yi, were the narrator?

5. **Plot:** Which events seem to be caused by or result from others?

6. **Theme:** What is Tan saying about the choices people make in life?

7. **Style:** What aspects of Tan's style—her sentence structure, word choice, and tone—seem particularly striking to you?

8. **For Further Exploration:** Interview the oldest relative you can locate, asking about his or her early life experiences, especially if this person immigrated to the United States. In no more than two pages, indicate what new information you learned about your family from this interview.

Thinking about Visuals When Writing about Creative Works

If you are writing about a visual medium such as film, you might find it useful to include visuals as part of your discussion. For instance, artists construct *storyboards* and other drawings to illustrate what a movie will look like, what the characters in the film will wear, how specific scenes will appear for publicity purposes, and for other reasons. Figures 12.1 and 12.2 are illustrations from the film *Harry Potter and the Sorcerer's Stone*.

Other visuals that might be available for writing about films include publicity stills and frame enlargements. (If you post your writing on the Web, however, you will probably need permission to include these images.) As you look at these visuals, consider these questions about the effective use of visuals in writing about a creative work:

- In what ways does each illustration illuminate the film?
- What does the illustration show a reader that it would be hard to show with text alone?
- What other types of visuals might be useful in writing about the film?

FIGURE 12.1
Harry Potter in a Classroom at Hogwarts School

FIGURE 12.2 Students
Approach Hogwarts
School in Boats

Writing Processes

As you read, view, or listen to the creative work you are writing about, you might find it fruitful to use some of the reading strategies presented in Chapter 2 and the strategies for discovery and learning presented in Chapter 3 to help you to engage more fully and more critically in the work. As you read, view, or listen to the work, you should look for the literary qualities discussed on page 352 and remember the qualities of an effective paper about a creative work (see pp. 351–54).

As we have noted throughout this book, the writing process is recursive—you will often need to return to earlier writing activities as you work on your assignment, and you will always need to return to the work you are writing about for fresh evidence, for more inspiration, and (possibly) for a new perspective.

If you are considering several works for your analysis, put your notes into a separate computer document for each work. Once you determine the focus of your analysis, it will be easy to access and use those notes. Also, make certain that you save your computer files frequently. Savvy writers back up their computer files in two or more places—on an internal or external hard-drive of the computer, on a USB flash drive, and on a rewritable CD or DVD, for example.

For a tip on organizing your computer files, see page 66.

Invention: Getting Started

You should use a variety of invention activities to select and then explore your creative work. Keep in mind that doing your invention work in electronic form, rather than on paper, makes it easy to use that work later as you construct a draft.

Selecting a Creative Work to Write About

If your instructor has not assigned a particular creative work, spend some time exploring short stories or other works. Try to answer these questions while you do your invention work:

- Which works have you recently read or seen that interest you the most? Why?
- Which works have evoked the strongest emotional responses in you? What are those emotions?
- Which works have made you think the most?

VISUALIZING VARIATIONS

Using Visuals to Illustrate an Analysis of a Creative Work

Suppose you are writing about a film based on a graphic novel, which is a cross between a novel and a comic book, with the illustrations telling most of the story. As you consider possible subjects for your analysis, you might find a photo like this one from the *X-Men* films, a series you enjoyed immensely:

Browsing on the Internet, you might also find images such as these, from the graphic novels the *X-Men* films were based on:

(cont'd)

(continued)

What other kinds of illustrations might help you to analyze an aspect of the film and/or novels for your readers?

As you think about using a visual in your writing about a creative work, consider the following:

- What visual information would you include as part of your analysis?

- What textual information would you include as part of your analysis to explain the images?

- On what basis would you select one image instead of another?

Recording Your Initial Responses

Once you select the creative work, begin recording your emotional and intellectual responses to it. If you do not do this important step, you may be tempted to adopt someone else's views in place of your own. Record your responses by writing answers to the following questions:

- What kinds of emotions does this work evoke in you?
- How does this work make you think about life?
- In one sentence, what is the theme of this work?
- What language in the work do you find most interesting or effective?

Finding a Feature to Analyze

The following questions will help you think analytically about the various features of a story, whether you are writing about a short story, a novel, a film, or a narrative in some other genre or medium. Keep in mind that to consider each aspect of a creative work thoroughly, you will need to read it and take notes carefully and thoughtfully—never just skim. Your notes will help you learn what you think about the story, decide what you will finally focus on, and gather evidence from the text itself to support the claim you will make in your essay.

Character: There are many ways to analyze characters. To find an approach that works and that interests you, consider using a concept that you have learned in another course. Here are some possibilities:

- In a psychology course, you may have learned about psychological concepts you can apply to a character—for instance, the six stages people go through when accepting death or the Oedipus complex.

- In a sociology course, you may have learned about social stratification or other concepts that you can use to interpret the motivations of a character or group.

You can also analyze characters by thinking about them in the same way you think about people in general. You might ask the following questions:

- What motivates the actions of this character?

- What do you admire or dislike about this character? Why?

- How effectively does this character communicate with other characters? What factors seem to influence those interactions the most?

- What role does this character play in the story?

- Why do other characters treat this character as they do?

Setting: The physical setting is where a story takes place.

As you read or view the creative work to analyze the setting, consider the following kinds of questions:

- What information can you glean from the details provided about the setting?

- How does the setting affect the atmosphere in which the story occurs? How does the setting affect the events that take place in the story?

- If the story is set in some specific time in history, how historically accurate are the details? What is the effect on readers of aspects of the setting such as language used by the characters, technology, dress, food—qualities that change over time?

Point of view: *Point of view* is a term describing what the narrator knows (and does not know). In some stories the narrator is *omniscient;* he or she knows what all of the characters are thinking. In other stories, the narrator's knowledge is limited to what one character is thinking. If the narrator is a character in the story, his or her knowledge will be limited to what he or she sees, hears, or thinks.

As you contemplate point of view, consider the following questions:

- Is the narrator a character (first-person narration)? Is the narrator someone outside the story (third-person narration)? If the narration is third-person, is the narrator omniscient? Or is the narrator limited to describing what characters do and say rather than what they think?
- Why do you think that the author used this particular point of view to tell the story?
- How would the story be different if the author had used another point of view?

Plot: A *plot* is what happens in the story—the events that take place during its course. Most plots involve a *conflict*, either between characters, within a character, or between a character and nature or circumstance. In many stories, the conflict leads to a problem or crisis, which is then resolved.

To write about the plot of a particular story, consider the following kinds of questions:

- How are the events in the story related to one another?
- When do events begin and end?
- How do specific events in the story affect individual characters?
- How is the crisis resolved?

Theme: Most creative works have a message or an idea—a point the author is trying to get across to readers. To explore the theme of a work, you might consider the following questions:

- How does the story make you think about life or people?
- What, if anything, is the moral of this story?

Style: Although many stylistic devices are used in literature and film, you are probably familiar with some of the more common ones.

- A *simile* is an indirect comparison that includes the word *like* or *as.* (*His coat was like a faded carpet.*)
- A *metaphor* is a direct comparison in which one thing is described as something else. (*The hummingbird was a tiny blue helicopter.*)
- *Personification* involves attributing human qualities to animals, objects, or even ideas. (*Sensing my frustration, the computer screen promptly went blank.*)

- *Hyperbole* is exaggeration so extreme that it is clearly not meant to be taken literally (*His car was the size of a canal barge*), while *understatement* is a statement surprising in its lack of force (*"We're experiencing some difficulties," the pilot said as we noticed the distinct smell of smoke*).

- *Irony* is a tone in which the writer's meaning contrasts sharply with what is stated. (*"Oh I'm thrilled to be here," she said from her hospital bed.*)

Consider the following questions about style:

- What uses of language are especially interesting? Why?

- Can you find examples of simile, metaphor, personification, hyperbole, and understatement in the work? Identify any that you notice.

- Does the writer use irony in any way? How is it used, and why?

TechNote

You can find many classic works of literature online in powerful literature archives. Usually these are editions and translations that are in the public domain. You can download these works from a reputable Web site such as Project Gutenberg (http://www.gutenberg.org/catalog/), then copy and paste them into a word processor. If a work is stored on your computer, you can then perform simple yet interesting types of *quantitative analysis*, which is useful for investigating and writing about the way the author uses words and phrases to develop themes and stylistic patterns in the work. For example, you can use your word processor's "Find" feature to do the following:

- Count the number of times the author uses a certain word or words, which can support the argument that the repetition of a word or idea creates a "cumulative" effect on readers

- Focus on the consistency with which the author uses the word or words and what that might mean

- Argue that the word is used primarily by a specific character or group of characters

- Examine the actual grammar and syntax of passages in which the word appears, to show how the author explores its implications

Using technology to search for words and phrases can also turn up surprising results. Sometimes words and phrases we would expect to find are not present in the work. (Tip: Sometimes words are present in different forms. If you are looking for the word *noting*, for example, make sure you search for *note* and *notice* as well.)

As with any kind of writing, invention activities improve with peer feedback and suggestions. Consider sharing the invention work you have done so far with several classmates or friends in order to understand the creative work more clearly and to generate more useful information.

Exploring Your Ideas with Research

From your brainstorming and other invention work, select one possible focus for your analysis of the work—plot, character, narrative development, point of view, theme, or style. If you had to phrase your main idea in one sentence, what would it be? Write the sentence on the top of a sheet of paper.

Reread or view again the work, looking for evidence that might support your claim, and write down each quotation or example that you find.

For some writing situations or assignments, you may want or need to read what others have written about the work you are studying. If you are consulting outside sources, remember to record your own responses to the work before you read what others think about it, so you are in a position to consider others' views more critically.

Your instructor may ask you to share your research notes with several of your classmates, not only so that you can see what subjects they are working on, but also so you can help one another determine if you have sufficient evidence to support the claim you intend to make.

Organizing Your Ideas and Details

Once you know the aspect of the work you will focus on and have a tentative or working thesis as well as evidence from the work, you need to consider how you might organize this material. The questions that you need to ask yourself when deciding on your organization are all rhetorical:

- Who is your audience? Will they be familiar with the work you are writing about? If they are not familiar with it, how much will you need to tell them about it?

- What is your purpose for writing—that is, why will your readers be interested in your analysis of this work?

Once you have determined your audience and purpose, here are three possible organizational approaches that you might choose for your paper.

Options for Organization

A Deductive Approach	An Inductive Approach	A Narrative Approach
• State, right at the beginning, the conclusion (thesis statement) that you have reached about the subject or subjects of your analysis.	• Explain, with examples, each piece of textual evidence that supports your thesis statement or claim, but without expressly stating that claim.	• Lead the reader through the story, event by event. Start by stating your thesis or claim.

- Explain why and how you reached that conclusion by providing textual evidence—quotations, examples—that support your claim.

- Conclude by briefly explaining all of the connections to your point—how they support your main claim.

- Each piece of evidence leads your reader to the conclusion that you are trying to assert.

- At the end state your claim, to which your readers have been led by the evidence you have provided.

- Each discussion of an event or each citation of dialogue from the story is evidence for your claim—that is, each supports the assertion you are making about the story.

- When you reach the end of the story, you will have presented all of your textual evidence.

Constructing a Full Draft

Once you have chosen the organizational approach that works best given your audience and purpose, you are ready to construct the rest of your draft. As you work on your draft, keep returning to the major claim that you are making. Use evidence from the work itself to support your assertions.

Remember that you will learn more about your topic as you write about it. As you draft your paper, you might even discover a more interesting claim or a claim for which you have more support, so keep an open mind.

Introduction: Because in writing about a creative work you are making a point about some aspect of that work—its theme, symbolism, or use of metaphor, for example—it is often effective to start your analysis by stating your own point or thesis, especially if your readers are familiar with the work and if your thesis is bold or provocative. You might also want to try one of the following strategies:

- Start with a compelling quotation or incident from the work, such as Kurtz's famous last exclamation from Joseph Conrad's novel *The Heart of Darkness:* "The Horror! The Horror!"
- Start with an incisive observation from a well-known critic.
- Start with a question that helps the reader become involved with your essay.
- Provide an eye-catching visual and comment to interest your reader.
- Express a surprising opinion about the work, one that goes "against the grain" of typical opinion.

Body: There are many ways to organize a paper about a creative work. In almost every case, you will state your claim, an assertion about the work, and then support that claim with evidence from the text. Usually, you will want to state your claim early in your essay, and then use the rest of your essay to provide supporting evidence for it. An alternative is the *inductive* approach, in which you present your evidence first, showing how it leads to your conclusion, which you state at the end of your analysis.

Conclusion: In the conclusion, you tie your essay together. Here are some possible ways to conclude your analysis:

- Refer back to the quotation or incident with which you began the essay.
- End with a compelling observation about a character or other element of the story.
- Restate all of the main ideas of your essay, noting how they connect to and support your thesis.

Title: The title for your analysis of a creative work should give your reader some sense of your main idea or thesis, a hint about what your essay tries to show.

Revising

Once you have a draft, put it aside for a day or so. This break will give you the opportunity to come back to your text as a new reader might. Read through and revise your work, looking especially for ideas that are not explained completely, places where you need more evidence from the work, and other problem areas. As you work to revise your early drafts, hold off on doing a great deal of heavy editing. When you revise you will probably change the content and structure of your paper, so time spent working to fix problems with grammar, punctuation, or mechanics at this stage is often wasted.

As you revise, here are some questions to ask yourself:

- How clearly have I presented my claim about the work?
- How well have I provided sufficient evidence from the work to support my claim?
- What visual could I include that would help me make my point about the work?
- How well do I connect every piece of evidence (quotations from experts, examples from the work itself) to my main claim?

Technology can help you revise and edit your writing more easily. Use your word processor's track-changes tool to try out revisions and editing changes. After you have had time to think about the possible changes, you can "accept" or "reject" them. Also, you can use your word processor's comment tool to write reminders to yourself when you get stuck with a revision or some editing task.

WRITER'S WORKSHOP

Responding to Full Drafts

Working with one or two other classmates, read each others' papers, and then offer your classmates comments that will help them see their papers' strengths as well as places where they need to develop their ideas further. Consider the following guidelines and questions as you do:

- Read for a first impression of the text. Then, in a brief paragraph, outline your initial response.

- Write a one-sentence summary of the author's main point or thesis. If your summary does *not* match what the author thinks is the main point, that discrepancy will help the writer see what needs to be revised.

- Write a brief paragraph outlining what you liked about the essay. What part(s) of the text are especially effective?

- In another paragraph, indicate what you found problematic about the essay—what you needed more information about, what questions the essay did not answer, what areas of confusion exist in the text.

- How effective is the introduction at leading a reader into the text?

- How well do you understand the point the author is making about the creative work? What could the author do to further clarify the main point? How convinced are you that the author's thesis is sound? Why?

- Where does the text need more examples or details to show rather then tell? What claims are well-supported? Which need more evidence?

- How much background information about the work does the author provide? Is this context sufficient? Why or why not?

- Has the writer documented all quotations from the work correctly? If the writer used outside sources, has he or she correctly documented information and quotations taken from them?

- How logical is the organization?

- Might a visual such as a photograph help the author to make his or her point about the work more vividly?

- How effective is the conclusion at connecting the writer's ideas and reinforcing the main point of the essay?

Responding to Readers' Comments

After receiving feedback from classmates, teachers, and others, you have to decide how to deal with their comments and suggestions. The first thing to do with any feedback is to listen to it and consider carefully what your readers have to say.

You may decide to reject some comments, of course, because they are not consistent with your goals for your paper. Other comments, though, deserve your attention. You may find that comments from several readers contradict each other. In that case, you need to use your own judgment to decide which readers' comments will best help you achieve your goals.

Knowledge of Conventions

When effective writers edit their work, they attend to the conventions of proper documentation, usage, grammar, punctuation, and mechanics. By following these conventions in your writing, you make reading a more pleasant experience for readers because then they don't have to work hard to understand what your main point is and how you support that point.

See Chapter 20 for more on documenting sources.

In any essay that you write about literature, you will probably need to include quotations from the work you are writing about, and you may need to quote from the work of others who have written about that work of literature. Therefore, you will need to pay close attention to the conventions of quoting and documenting primary and secondary sources. When you write about literature you will also be expected to discuss events and actions in the story in the present tense, as if they were happening now. The round-robin activity on page 381 will help you to check your essay for your adherence to these two conventions.

Editing

After you revise, you need to go through one more important activity: editing and polishing. When you edit and polish your writing, you make changes to improve your style and to make your writing clearer and more concise. You also check your work to make sure it adheres to conventions of grammar, usage, punctuation, mechanics, and spelling. Use the spell-check function of your word processing program, but be sure to double-check your spelling personally (your computer cannot tell the difference between *their, they're,* and *there,* but you can).

Because it is sometimes difficult to identify small problems in a familiar text, it often helps to distance yourself from it so that you can approach the draft with fresh eyes. Some people like to put the text aside for a day or so;

others try reading aloud, some even read from the last sentence to the first so that the content, and their familiarity with it, doesn't cause them to overlook an error. We strongly recommend that you ask classmates, friends, and tutors to read your work to help find sentence-level problems.

WRITER'S WORKSHOP

Round-Robin Editing with a Focus on Writing about Literary Texts

For this activity, work with two of your classmates. Make sure you each have copies of the work that you are quoting from. First, concentrate on the quotations that each of you has used to support your claims about the literary text. In particular, pay attention to the following:

- The accuracy of the quotations. Check each quoted excerpt to make certain that it matches the original source exactly.

- MLA conventions for introducing quotations and citing the sources of the quoted excerpts, both in the text and on the works-cited page. (See pages 538–65 in Chapter 20.)

Now look for places within your text where you talk about events within the work. Check to make sure that you are using the present tense, not the past tense, when describing those events.

There seems to be some conflict or tension in their marriage that ~~was~~ *is*

somehow amplified by the main character's viewing of this tape.

Genres, Documentation, and Format

If you are writing an academic paper in response to Scenario 1, you will need to follow the conventions appropriate for the discipline in which you are writing and the requirements of your instructor. However, if you are responding to Scenario 2, you may decide to write a posting for a Web site, start your own blog, write a letter, or use some other format.

If you have used material from outside sources, including visuals, you will need to give credit to those sources, using the documentation style required by the discipline you are working in and by your instructor.

For advice on writing in different genres, see Appendix C. For guidelines for formatting and documenting papers in MLA style, see Chapter 20.

Student Hanna Earley Shares Her Writing about a Creative Work

Student writer Hanna Earley had a strong emotional response to "Videotape" by Don DeLillo (pp. 354–58), so she decided to analyze the story and write about it for Scenario 1.

HANNA EARLEY

That Doesn't Mean We Want Him to Stop: Suspense in Don DeLillo's "Videotape"

One reader wrote to Earley that her first title, "Suspense," was

functional but didn't really motivate people to read your essay.

Earley changed the title to make it more compelling.

We've heard the phrases—page-turner, nail-biter, cliff-hanger—but they all communicate one idea: suspense. It doesn't matter how we experience it, hairs rising on our necks, sweaty palms, or slinking down in the movie seat, but it's that distinctive mix of excitement and fear, hope and dread, that pushes us to find the answer to the primary question: What happened? So in a short story such as Don DeLillo's "Videotape," in which the answer to "What happened?" is revealed almost from the outset, how does he keep us reading, transfixed to the page as his characters are to the videotape and the event it reveals?

The premise is simple, a man's murder caught on tape by a child. DeLillo delivers the news at the beginning of the ninth in a series of brief, expository paragraphs delivered in the same sparse prose as the rest: "It is not just another video homicide. It is a homicide recorded by a child who thought she was doing something simple . . . " (1064). Despite what we might expect, however—that all excitement and suspense would be lost once the main event is revealed—DeLillo still manages to create suspense, keeping our anxiety and interest until, and perhaps beyond, the end of the story: "The horror freezes your soul but this doesn't mean that you want them to stop" (1067).

One reader thought the first draft of Earley's introduction fell a little flat:

Maybe add some details to help the reader get into the paper?

Earley added details about how people experience suspense to the opening paragraph.

DeLillo achieves this effect, of perpetuating suspense through the story despite a revealed outcome, by keeping his reader literally on edge. The first way that DeLillo keeps us on the edge is his use of second-person narration, constantly beckoning the reader into the story with "you." "You see a man at the wheel of a medium Dodge," we learn in the first paragraph, and so we as readers feel situated inside the story itself, almost as if participating. The tone is conversational, as if to establish common ground or ordinariness here. But in fact, this situation is anything but ordinary. As soon as the reader is drawn into the story with the "you" sentence structures, DeLillo starts to show that "you" is a specific

1

2

3

character, perhaps similar to the reader but completely outside the reader. For example, "you" have a wife and "[y]ou don't usually call your wife over to the TV set . . . now the thing is finally going to happen and you want her to be here when he's shot" (1065). Clearly there is a whole set of circumstances here in which the reader is not involved. So when we are both drawn into and rejected from the story, we are somehow both participant and observer, but also neither, therefore unsettling our own points of view. We are left somewhere in-between, on the edge of the story itself. DeLillo's pulling of the reader into the story, but use of "you" as a particular man with a particular point of view and circumstance, triggers the ambivalence and doubt we associate with suspense. "And you keep on looking," we read, and we do.

Building upon the disconcerting and suspense-building use of second-person voice, DeLillo also generates uncertainty and anxiety by placing the central story—the murder caught on film—within the frame of a larger story, that of a man watching the videotape in his living room and thinking about his wife and the argument they'd be having about the videotape if she were there. As the moment of the murder approaches, we learn, "Now here is where he gets it. You say, Janet, hurry up, this is where it happens" (1065). Clearly, there is something about the videotape and the nature of the murder that the main character wants to express to his wife. In fact, the underlying tension in the marriage seems almost intensified by the main character's viewing of the videotape: "You want to tell her it is realer than real, but then she will ask you what that means" (1065). At this moment, he seems more connected to the video-tape than to his partner in life. So as we proceed through the story, two storylines develop, and as a result, we have two reasons to read, two vehicles for suspense. Not only do we want to learn how the tape ends—what becomes of the child? The shooter?—but we want to know what is happening in this relationship and why this narrator keeps talking about his wife as he watches. Therefore, DeLillo once again puts us on edge; we hover between the two "stories," one foot in each, waiting for the resolution of both, which heightens our feelings of suspense. As the video-tape rolls forward, the anxiety of the main character likewise escalates; he is unsure what he is even trying to communicate by encouraging her to watch, when he admits, "What are you telling her? Are you making a little statement? Like I'm going to ruin your day out of ordinary spite. Or a big statement? Like this is the risk of existing?" (1066). In the end, both stories are left somewhat open-ended. As for the tape, ". . . [it] ends here, either because the girl stopped shooting or because some central author-ity . . . decided there was nothing else you had to see" (1066), and as for the relationship, we can only anticipate more conflict, as we learn "[y]ou

4

don't want Janet to give you any crap about it's on all the time, they show it a thousand times a day" (1067). Arguably, the readers' sensations of suspense, unease, and uncertainty extend beyond the end of the text, as do the uncertainties surrounding the murder and this man's relationship.

In addition to his narrative strategies of second-person voice and a   5 frame story surrounding the main event, DeLillo also achieves suspense through his use of detail. Occasionally, the story is very detailed; for example, "[Children] break every trust, spy out the undefended space, catching Mom coming out of the bathroom in her cumbrous robe and turbaned towel, looking bloodless and plucked" (1063) or "[The girl filming the videotape] feels halfway clever and inventive and maybe slightly intrusive as well" (1064). But these details are speculation, not truth, since they come from the main character's imagination. The key events of the story, however, get very little detail, such as "It shows a man driving a car" (1063) or "[h]e is bald up the middle of his head, a nice guy in his forties whose whole life seems open to the hand-held camera" (1064). Most noticeably, the death of the driver is clean and almost graceful: "[y]ou don't see the blood, which is probably trickling behind his ear and down the back of his neck. . . . [T]he twist of the head gives you only a partial profile. . . . " (1066). All the details of the actual event are full of uncertainty ("seems open," "probably," "partial"), so we readers are hindered from painting a clear picture in our minds—our images of the story are as grainy as the tape itself and our uncertainty adds to our feeling of suspense.

After all, "It shows very little in the end" (1066); like the victim's car,   6 the narrator seems to approach the details, but falls back, drifting away before we can really understand what's before us. When we read, "If you've seen the tape many times you know from the handwave exactly when he will be hit. It is something, naturally, that you wait for" (1065), it seems the anticipation of the gunshot is more important than any detail about the murder itself. Likewise, DeLillo downplays the details in order to heighten the anticipation. We read in suspense, looking to see and understand the events, but we can never quite obtain the full picture.

In "Videotape," the reader is constantly on edge: on the edge   7 between participant and observer by way of the second-person voice, on the edge between two storylines by way of the framing device, and on the edge between knowledge and ignorance as details are uncertain or withheld. It is no wonder, then, that even though we know the central event of the story, we are plagued by uncertainty, doubt, anxiety, and the urge to find out more, all of which are manifested in the concept we call suspense. DeLillo, when speaking about the video-tape, practically tells us outright his strategy for suspense: "You keep on looking not because you know something is going to happen—of course you do know something is going to happen and you look for that reason but you . . . keep on looking because things combine to hold you fast—a sense of the random, the amateurish, the accidental, the impending" (1064). So even though we know all along that the driver on the videotape will be shot, he will die, and his car will drift back out of the camera frame as a child watches and a murderer escapes, DeLillo compels us to read to the end. We're looking for more than an answer to "What happened?" It is something else, more elu-sive or accidental, something in our relationships and ourselves, something to do with that child's "clear-eyed" wander into horror, something "realer than real" (1065).

Work Cited

DeLillo, Don. "Videotape." Responding to Literature: Stories, Poems, Plays, and Essays. 5th ed. Ed. Judith A. Stanford. New York: McGraw, 2006. 1063–67.

QUESTIONS FOR WRITING AND DISCUSSION: LEARNING OUTCOMES

Rhetorical Knowledge: The Writer's Situation and Rhetoric

1. **Audience:** What audience does Earley have in mind for this essay? How can you tell?

2. **Purpose:** What purpose(s) does Earley have for writing this essay? How well does she achieve this (these) purpose(s)? How easily can you tell what her main point is?

3. **Voice and tone:** How would you describe the tone Earley uses in this essay?

4. **Responsibility:** How accurately does Earley portray what happens in the story? How responsibly does she use quotations?

5. **Context and format:** Earley is writing for her composition class. How might her essay differ if she were writing about this story for a psychology or a sociology class?

Critical Thinking: Responding to the Writer's Ideas

1. What is your initial response to Earley's essay?

2. How effectively does Earley support her claims? Why do you think so?

Composing Processes and Knowledge of Conventions: The Writer's Strategies

1. What are the major strengths of Earley's analysis? Why do you perceive them to be strengths?

2. What outside sources might she have consulted to support her points more effectively? What other quotations might she have used to further support her points?

Inquiry and Research: Ideas for Further Exploration

1. In your library or on the Internet, look up "reader response criticism" and in an essay of no more than three pages, explain how someone using the "reader response" approach would examine "Videotape."

Self-Assessment: Reflecting on Your Learning Goals

When you have finished with this assignment, reflect on all the thinking and writing that you have done while writing about a creative work. It is often useful to go back and consider your learning goals, which you and your classmates may have considered at the beginning of this chapter (see pp. 344–45). To help reflect on the learning goals that you have achieved, respond in writing to the following questions:

Rhetorical Knowledge

- *Purpose:* How successfully do you feel you fulfilled your purpose in writing about a creative work?

- *Audience:* What did you learn about your audience as you wrote about the work you chose?

- *Rhetorical situation:* How did the writing context affect how you wrote about the work? How did your choice of topic affect the research you conducted and how you presented your argument to your readers?

- *Voice and tone:* How would you describe your voice in this essay? Your own tone? How do they contribute to the effectiveness of your writing?

Critical Thinking, Reading, and Writing

- *Learning/inquiry:* How did you decide what to focus on in your writing about the work you chose? Describe the process you went through to focus on a main idea (or thesis). How did you judge what was most and least important in your evidence from the work?

- *Responsibility:* How did you fulfill your responsibility to your readers?

- *Reading and research:* What did you learn about writing about creative works from the reading selections you read for this chapter? What research did you conduct? Why? What additional research might you have done?

- What critical thinking, reading, and writing skills do you hope to develop further in your next writing project? How will you work on them?

Writing Processes

- *Invention:* What invention strategies were most useful to you?

- *Organizing your ideas and details:* What organization did you use? How successful was it?

- *Revising:* What one revision did you make that you are most satisfied with? If you could go back and make an additional revision, what would it be?

- *Working with peers:* How did your instructor or peer readers help you by making comments and suggestions about your writing? How could you have made better use of the comments and suggestions you received?

- Did you use photographs or other visuals as part of your analysis? If so, what did you learn about incorporating these elements?

- What "writerly habits" have you developed or improved upon as you constructed the writing assignment for this chapter? How will you change your future writing activities, based on what you have learned?

Knowledge of Conventions

- *Editing:* What sentence problem did you find most frequently in your writing? How will you avoid that problem in future assignments?

- *Genre:* What conventions of the genre you were using, if any, gave you problems?
- *Documentation:* Did you use sources for your paper? If so, what documentation style did you use? What problems, if any, did you have with it?

If you are constructing a course portfolio, file your written reflections so that you can return to them when you next work on your portfolio.

PART FOUR

Strategies for Effective Communication

Using Strategies That Guide Readers

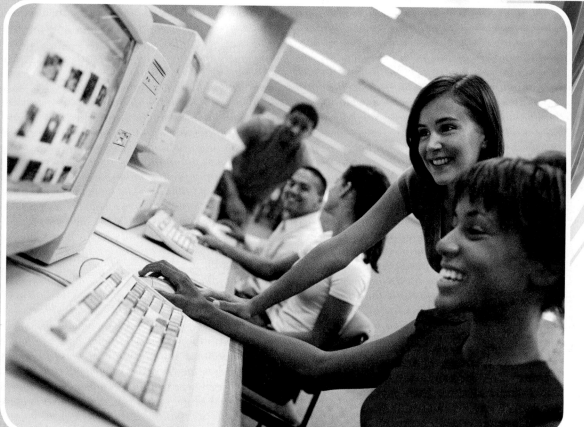

The chapters in Parts 2 and 3 of this book provide guidelines for writing that have various purposes. Whatever your purpose, you can use a range of **rhetorical strategies** to help readers to understand your writing.

Because sentences and paragraphs are the basic building blocks of any piece of writing, you will need strategies for writing them effectively. This is especially true for developing your thesis statement, because if readers do not understand your main point, they will not understand your text. At the level of the individual sentence, the individual paragraph, and the full piece of writing, you will need strategies to help readers make connections. Frequently, you will want to describe, define, classify, narrate, or compare and contrast events, objects, or concepts and will need strategies to organize your paragraphs accordingly. In most pieces of writing, you will use some combination of these organizing and connecting strategies. This chapter looks in turn at each type of rhetorical strategy—writing strong thesis statements, writing paragraphs, establishing connections within and across paragraphs, and organizing ideas.

Announcing a Thesis or Controlling Idea

A **thesis** announces the main point, major claim, or controlling idea in an essay. A clear thesis helps readers because it prepares them for what they will be reading.

Although a thesis statement can focus your attention as you write, it is usually a good idea to write your thesis statement after you have done invention work and research. Invention activities can help you clarify your thinking about a topic. Research can help you learn more about it. Once you have done invention and research, a thesis statement can help you construct a well-focused draft. Of course, the exact wording of your thesis statement might continue to change as you draft your paper—and even as you revise and edit it for readers.

The strongest and most helpful thesis statements do more than simply state facts, provide personal feelings, or offer vague generalities. If your thesis statement merely states a fact, it just informs the reader about that fact; it is not arguable. If you offer a personal feeling as a thesis ("I don't like coffee"), people could certainly argue with it, but your evidence would be purely subjective ("I don't care for the flavor") and therefore not persuasive. If your thesis statement is general and vague ("Movies are more expensive now than they were at this time last year"), there might not be much to write in support of your thesis. Providing two figures—the average price of movies last year and the average price this year—proves your assertion. Or it may be hard to get a grip on how to support your thesis. It would be difficult to decide what evidence to use to support a generalization like "Animals have a hard time living in zoos," for example. The best thesis statements are limited and focused and offer some sense of the support that is forthcoming.

WEAK	I can't stand war movies.
REVISED	*Letters from Iwo Jima* is an effective war movie because it forces Americans to view, and even sympathize with, combatants traditionally seen as enemies.
REASON	There is no way to support your personal feeling—that you do not like war movies—with evidence. But you could provide evidence for the ways *Letters from Iwo Jima* helps viewers see enemy combatants in a new light.
WEAK	The National Hockey League is in trouble.
REVISED	The National Hockey League has lost fan support because of the 2004–2005 lockout.
REASON	The weaker version is too general and vague. The revised version gives a specific reason for the trouble.

It also is important to *qualify* your thesis statement by using terms like *probably* or *likely* to make it more acceptable to an audience.

WRITING ACTIVITY

Looking for Weak Thesis Statements

Examine a copy of your campus or local newspaper, looking at the various articles for examples of weak thesis statements. Bring some examples to share with your classmates, and be prepared to indicate how you would improve the weak statements you located.

Writing Paragraphs

A **paragraph** is a collection of connected sentences that focus on a single idea. To guide readers through a piece of writing, arrange paragraphs in a logical order and make the connections among them clear. They also need to support your purpose, which is often to assert a main point, or thesis. But first of all, of course, you need to structure each paragraph effectively. Consider the following simple example, which could appear in a paper about Abraham Lincoln's career.

> During his years as president, 1861–1865, Abraham Lincoln experienced great stress from a combination of causes. **First,** the Civil War, which broke out weeks after his March 1861 inauguration, wore on him daily until its end in April 1865. **Second,** typhoid took the life of Willie, his beloved eleven-year-old son, in February 1862. **Third,** his wife, Mary

Todd Lincoln, suffered from depression and other forms of mental illness, problems that became more acute during the years in the White House.

While the specifics may vary, effective paragraphs generally have the following features:

- **A Focus on a Single Main Idea.** Readers expect that a paragraph will contain a single main idea related to the topic of the piece of writing. The more tightly you focus a paragraph on a main idea, the more you will help readers navigate through the paragraph. Note that in the example paragraph about President Lincoln every sentence is focused on the causes of Lincoln's stress. If you want to alert your readers about other specific information that will come later in your paper, use a *forecasting sentence* (the sentence in the paragraph about Lincoln that mentions Mary Lincoln's depression could forecast that the paper will have more to say about that topic).

- **A Topic Sentence.** A topic sentence guides readers because it expresses a paragraph's main idea, the idea that the other sentences in the paragraph support or develop. In the example about Lincoln, the first sentence, which is underlined, serves as the topic sentence. The topic sentence often comes first because this placement helps readers see at the outset how the sentences in the paragraph fit together.

- **Different Levels of Specificity.** All paragraphs have at least two levels of specificity. In the paragraph about Lincoln, the topic sentence clearly introduces the idea of stress and its various causes, and the second, third, and fourth sentences are more specific, each discussing a particular cause.

- **Use of Connective Words and Phrases.** Used within a paragraph, connective words and phrases, discussed in more detail on pages 398–99, can show precisely how the sentences in the paragraph support the topic sentence and relate to one another. In the example paragraph, the words *First, Second*, and *Third* (in bold type) tell readers that each of the sentences they begin offers a separate cause of Lincoln's stress.

- **A Logical Connection to the Next Paragraph.** When readers finish a paragraph, they expect that the next paragraph will be connected to it in some readily apparent way. After reading the paragraph that focuses on the sources of stress that Lincoln experienced, readers expect that the next paragraph will also be related to Lincoln's stress. The final task of an effective paragraph, then, is to relate to the paragraph that follows it.

Placement of Topic Sentences

In the paragraph about Lincoln, the topic sentence is the first sentence, a placement that lets readers know right away what the paragraph will be about. Sometimes, however, you will want to place a topic sentence at the end of a paragraph in order to develop suspense or to summarize information. Placing a topic sentence at the end of a paragraph can be an especially effective strategy in persuasive writing because it allows the writer to present evidence before making an assertion. Here is such an example from Joseph Pace's essay "Let's Go Veggie!":

> Less than a quarter of our agricultural land is used to feed people directly. The rest is devoted to grazing and growing food for animals. Ecosystems of forest, wetland and grassland have been decimated to fuel the demand for land. Using so much land heightens topsoil loss, the use of harsh fertilizers and pesticides, and the need for irrigation water from dammed rivers. <u>If people can shift away from meat, much of this land could be converted back to wilderness.</u>

> Joseph Pace, "Let's Go Veggie!"

Sometimes a paragraph has no topic sentence. Instead, the topic sentence is implied. In cases where the point is fairly clear to readers, a writer may decide to leave it unstated.

Moving to a New Paragraph

Paragraph breaks signal that a writer is moving from one idea to another—even if the shift is a small one. Consider the example paragraph on Lincoln in which every sentence is related to causes of stress. We could develop that paragraph further by adding sentences that maintain that focus. Look at what happens, though, when we add a sentence that does not fit the focus on causes of stress:

> . . . Third, his wife, Mary Todd Lincoln, suffered from depression and other forms of mental illness, problems that became more acute during the years in the White House. <u>To alleviate the stress, Lincoln often read the plays of Shakespeare.</u>

The last sentence in this paragraph does fit the general topic of Lincoln's experience with stress, but it does not fit the tight focus on causes in this paragraph, a focus established by the topic sentence. Instead, it introduces a related but new idea. The solution is to make the last sentence the topic sentence of the next paragraph:

> . . . Third, his wife, Mary Todd Lincoln, suffered from depression and other forms of mental illness, problems that became more acute during the years in the White House.
>
>   <u>To alleviate the stress, Lincoln often read the plays of Shakespeare.</u> Among those that he read most frequently were *King Lear*, *Richard III*, *Henry VIII*, *Hamlet*, and *Macbeth*. About his favorite play, *Macbeth*, he

wrote the following in a letter to the actor James H. Hackett on August 17, 1863: "I think nothing equals *Macbeth*. It is wonderful."

Notice that this new paragraph provides details about Lincoln and stress that are even more specific than the ones in the preceding paragraph.

Opening Paragraphs

The opening paragraphs of an essay announce the topic and the writer's approach to that topic. Because writers often develop a fuller understanding of their topic as they write, many choose to draft an opening paragraph *after* they have drafted and revised the rest of an essay. In an opening paragraph the writer needs to establish a relationship with readers and help them connect the topic to what they already know and care about. Some common strategies for opening paragraphs include the following:

- Tell an interesting anecdote.
- Raise a thought-provoking question.
- Provide salient background information.
- Offer a view that the writer and readers hold in common.
- Forecast the rest of the essay.

WRITING ACTIVITY

Introductions

For each of the following excerpts from opening paragraphs, describe the strategy that the writer is using.

> The official poverty rate in 2003 was 12.5 percent, up from 12.1 percent in 2002. In 2003, 35.9 million people were in poverty, up 1.3 million from 2002. For children under 18 years old, both the poverty rate and the number in poverty rose between 2002 and 2003, from 16.7 percent to 17.6 percent, and from 12.1 million to 12.9 million, respectively.
>
> U.S. Census Bureau, "Poverty: 2003 Highlights"

> The most vulnerable victims of poverty are the world's children. Over 27,000 children die *every day*—more than 10 million per year—most from preventable diseases and malnutrition. Yet, the handful of preventable diseases that kill the majority of these children can be treated and prevented at very little cost. Measles can be prevented with a vaccine costing just 65 cents. Diarrheal disease, which results

from poor sanitation and unsafe drinking water, can be treated with pennies' worth of oral rehydration salts. Malaria kills nearly one million children each year, despite the fact that treatment for acute malaria costs less than one dollar.

"Child Survival," Results (results.org)

Tina Taylor was a model of what welfare reform was supposed to do. Taylor, 44, a single mother, had spent six years on public assistance. After 1996, when changes were made in welfare law to push people into work, she got a job that paid $400 a week and allowed her family to live independently. For the first time in a long time, she could afford to clothe and feed her two children, and even rent a duplex on the beach in Norfolk.

Griff Witte, "Poverty Up as Welfare Enrollment Declines; Nation's Social Safety Net in Tatters as More People Lose Their Jobs"

Concluding Paragraphs

Readers remember best what they read last. Although you should not simply restate what your essay is about in your conclusion, you can use it to do the following:

- Restate your main point (your thesis) and remind readers of your key points.
- Emphasize the significance of your perspective on your topic.
- Bring your writing to closure.

WRITING ACTIVITY

Conclusions

For each of the following concluding paragraphs, explain what the writer has done and decide how effective you think each conclusion is.

Each day of my life there are times when I reflect back to working on the farm. And every day people notice that I am different from the rest of my peers. At school, teachers and organization leaders are impressed by my time management skills and the amount of responsibility I take on. At work, my boss continues to ask me where he can find some more hard working people. I simply tell him, "Try hiring some farm girls. I hear they turn out pretty good."

Jessica Hemauer, "Farm Girl" (Chapter 4)

> The Supreme Court's May 17, 1954, ruling in *Brown* remains a landmark legal decision. But it is much more than that. It is the "Big Bang" of all American history in the 20th century.
>
> Juan Williams, "The Ruling That Changed America" (Chapter 10)

Using Cohesive Devices

Within paragraphs, effective writers use a variety of cohesive devices to show readers how sentences are connected to one another. The major devices include connective words and phrases, word repetition, and pronoun reference. To help readers understand how paragraphs are related to one another, writers use transitional sentences as well as headings.

Using Connective Words and Phrases

You can guide readers with logically connected sentences and paragraphs, making these connections explicit through use of **connective words and phrases.** These connections fall into three main categories: temporal, spatial, and logical. Some of the more common words and phrases expressing these connections are as follows:

TEMPORAL CONNECTIONS

Time: now, then, during, meanwhile, at this moment

> I worked all weekend. *Meanwhile,* my colleagues watched football all day Saturday and Sunday.

Frequency: often, occasionally, frequently, sometimes

> Sally likes unplanned trips. *Sometimes,* she'll even show up at the airport and then decide where to fly for the weekend.

Temporal order: first, second . . . ; next; before (that); after (that); last; finally

> Let's eat dinner. *After that,* let's see a movie.

SPATIAL CONNECTIONS

Location: nearby, outside, inside

> I stood by the window. *Outside,* a moose ran down the street.

Spatial Order: first, second, . . . ; last, next

> Jane sat in the corner. *Next to her* sat Jill.

LOGICAL CONNECTIONS

Addition: further, furthermore, moreover, additionally, in addition, and, also

> Martha Flynn is a powerful council member in our city. *Further,* she may be headed for other powerful positions in the future.

Opposition/Contrast: on the other hand, however, in contrast, on the contrary, but, conversely, nevertheless, yet, instead, rather

> I don't eat meat for ethical reasons. *On the other hand,* I do wear leather shoes.

Comparison: likewise, similarly, analogously

> George H. W. Bush led the United States to war in the 1990s. *Likewise,* George W. Bush led the United States to war in 2001.

Causation: because, as a result, as a consequence, therefore, thus, accordingly, consequently, so, then, on account of

> He didn't pay his phone bill. *As a result,* the phone company discontinued his service.

Clarification: in other words, that is, that is to say

> He rarely does his homework. *In other words,* he's not a very good student.

Qualification: under the [these] circumstances, under other circumstances, under these conditions, in this context

> John McCain spent years as a prisoner of war in North Vietnam. *Under these circumstances,* it's remarkable that he is so well adjusted.

Conclusion: finally, in summary, to sum up, in conclusion

> The new Toyota Camry has been rated one of the safest cars on the road. *Therefore,* we should consider buying one.

Illustration: for example, for instance, in particular, specifically

> Luz wears colorful clothes. *For example,* yesterday she wore a bright red sweater to her math class.

Using Word Repetition

Repeating a word or phrase—either the exact word or phrase or a form of it—from one sentence to the next helps readers make a connection between those two sentences:

> In a new study on the occurrence of dating **violence** among teenagers, University of Arkansas researchers found that 50 percent of high schoolers have experienced some form of physically **violent** behavior in their relationships. More surprising, the research revealed that male and female students perpetrate **violence** at an equal rate and that, of the two, females may be inflicting more serious forms of abuse on their partners.
>
> Megan Mooney and Patricia Petretic-Jackson, "Half of High School Students Experience Dating Violence, UA Study Shows"

Using Pronoun Reference

Pronouns substitute for nouns. When writers use pronouns to replace nouns, those pronouns point backward or forward to the nouns that they replace:

> During **his** years as president, 1861–1865, Abraham Lincoln experienced great stress from a combination of causes. First, the Civil War, which broke out weeks after **his** March 1861 inauguration, wore on **him** daily until its end in April 1865. Second, typhoid took the life of Willie, **his** beloved eleven-year-old son, in February 1862. Third, **his** wife, Mary Todd Lincoln, suffered from depression and other forms of mental illness, problems that became more acute during the years in the White House.

WRITING ACTIVITY

Focusing on Cohesive Words

Working alone or with one or two classmates, identify the cohesive devices (and lack of cohesive devices) in the following paragraph. Also, improve the paragraph by adding any cohesive devices that you think might strengthen connections between sentences.

The want to consume is nothing new. It is has been around for millennia. People need to consume resources to survive. However, consumption has evolved as people have ingeniously found ways to help make their lives simpler and/or to use their resources more efficiently. Of course, with this has come the want to control such means. Hence, the consumption patterns have evolved over time based on the influence of those who can control it. As a result, there is tremendous waste within this system, to maintain such control and such disparities.

Anup Shaw, "Creating the Consumer"

Using Transitional Sentences and Paragraphs

Writers use transitional sentences and paragraphs to help readers move from one section of an essay to another. These sentences or paragraphs often summarize what has come before and forecast what will come next. Here are some examples:

- Those are the advantages of an interest-only home loan. Now let me explain their major disadvantages.

- Although after that presentation I admired her intellect even more, her next decision caused me seriously to question her judgment.

Using Headings

In short pieces of writing, you probably will not need to use headings. Headings are also rarely used in certain types of writing—for instance, in writing to share experiences and in letters. For longer pieces of writing and in certain genres, though, headings and even subheadings can help readers more quickly understand the focus of the paragraphs that come after them. They give readers information about the paragraphs they precede both that they are a related group and that they are all on the same topic, specified in the heading.

To guide readers effectively with headings, keep the following guidelines in mind when you write them:

- Generally, only one level of heading is necessary for a five-page paper.

- All content under a heading should relate to that heading.

- Make your headings and subheadings specific.

  | VAGUE | Properties of Glass |
  | SPECIFIC | Chemical Properties of Glass |

- At each level, make headings and subheadings parallel in grammatical structure, font type, and level of specificity.

  | NOT PARALLEL | The Chemistry of Glass, Physical Properties |
  | PARALLEL | Chemical Properties, Physical Properties |

- Design headings so that they stand out from the text.

  | DOESN'T STAND OUT | Common Uses of Glass |
  | DOES STAND OUT | **Common Uses of Glass** |

For more on headings in MLA and APA style, see Chapter 20.

If you are writing an academic paper, you should follow the requirements of the documentation style you are using for the style of your headings.

WRITING ACTIVITY

Focusing on Headings and Subheadings

Working on your own or with several classmates, consider the headings in "The Nursing Crisis: The Solution Lies Within" (pp. 316–20 in Chapter 11). How do the headings help guide readers?

Using Organizing Strategies

In much of the writing that you do in this course, in other courses, and in other areas of life, you will use organizing strategies to guide your readers. Among the most useful strategies are narrating, describing, defining, classifying, and comparing and contrasting.

Writing Narratives

Both in everyday speech and in many kinds of writing, **narration** is a common strategy. When you narrate, you relate an event or a series of events or, in the case of a process, you give a series of steps. Most narratives are organized by time, or **chronologically,** from the beginning to the end of an event, a series of events, or a process. Obviously, narration is relevant to much of our discourse in all areas of our lives because our lives are filled with events and processes:

- At dinner, you tell your family or friends about an event at school or work that day.
- In a science course, you record what happened when you conducted a laboratory experiment.
- As a witness to a traffic accident, you tell the investigating police officers what happened.

In this section we will consider two kinds of narratives: narratives that relate an event or a series of events and narratives that relate a process.

NARRATING SINGLE EVENTS OR A SERIES OF EVENTS

Often in everyday conversation, you narrate single events and narrating a single event is also a common way of organizing part or all of a piece of writing. You might write an essay about an event that affected your life, an article on the opening of a store in your neighborhood, or a research report on the Montgomery bus boycott in 1955, a major event in the struggle for civil rights. You can also narrate a series of events in a piece of writing. You might write an account of your life, of the growth of the McDonald's restaurant chain, or of the American civil rights movement in the 1950s and 1960s.

Whether you are narrating one event or a series of events, you need to give your readers a clear picture of what happened by providing sufficient detail. When you narrate an event or a series of events, you will most often order your details chronologically—what happened first, what happened next, and so on. As an alternative, however, you might discuss the importance of the event or events first, and then proceed to the details so that your readers will understand why they, too, ought to be interested in what happened.

For more on narrating an event or a series of events, see Chapter 4.

CHRONOLOGICAL STRUCTURE

Because life's events occur chronologically, it is usually easiest to narrate them that way. It is also usually easier for readers to process narratives that unfold chronologically. Even a short narrative paragraph such as the following one can suggest a chronological ordering of events:

> Once my aunt found a freckle on her chin, at a spot that the almanac said predestined her for unhappiness. She dug it out with a hot needle and washed the wound with peroxide.
>
> Maxine Hong Kingston, "No Name Woman"

POINT OF VIEW

The narrator of a story can have several points of view, so when you construct a narrative, you will need to select a point of view to write from.

In the *first-person* point of view, the narrator tells the story from the perspective of a participant or character in the story:

> When I went to kindergarten and had to speak English for the first time, I became silent.
>
> Maxine Hong Kingston, "Tongue Tied"

In a narrative told from a *third-person* point of view, the narrator is not a participant or character in the story. The narrator consistently uses third-person pronouns or proper nouns to talk about the actions of characters:

> On December 1, 1963, shortly after President Kennedy's assassination, Malcolm X addressed a public rally in New York City. He was speaking as a replacement for Elijah Muhammad as he had done many times before. After the speech, during a question and answer period, Malcolm X made the remark that led to his suspension as a Muslim minister. In answer to a question, "What do you think about President Kennedy's assassination?" Malcolm X answered that he saw the case as "The chickens coming home

to roost." Soon after the remark, Malcolm X was suspended by Elijah Muhammad and directed to stop speaking for ninety days.

John Henrik Clarke, from the Introduction to *Malcolm X: The Man and His Times*

DEVELOPING TENSION

Narratives with tension are more interesting to readers. To establish tension in narratives, writers can show conflicts between characters who hold differing values or perspectives. For example, the following sentences develop tension:

- My mother's parents didn't want her to marry my father, so the young couple eloped on a blustery day in November.
- Tom and I were best friends, but then one day I saw him stuff a DVD into his shirt in a department store.

RESOLVING THE TENSION OR CONFLICT

Just as readers are intrigued by narrative tension, they are interested in seeing how tensions are resolved or not resolved by the end of the story. Most readers look forward to a sense of closure by the end of the story.

INCORPORATING VISUALS IN NARRATIVES

When you narrate a series of events, you obviously have the opportunity to cover a significant period of time, as well as the complications involved in a more extended narration. If the chronology becomes complex, you might find it useful to guide readers with a summarizing visual such as a timeline. Figure 13.1, for instance, is a brief timeline for the flu epidemic of 1918.

NARRATING PROCESSES

When you narrate a process, you tell how something is done (informative/ explanatory process narrative), or you tell others how to do something (instructional/directive process narrative).

Informative/Explanatory Process Narratives: Informative or explanatory process narratives tell readers how something is done so that they can understand a process, not so that they can replicate the process. For example, you might write an informative process analysis about the following:

- How a legislative bill becomes a law
- How a seed germinates
- How a company's supply chain works

Instructional/Directive Process Narratives: While the purpose of informative or explanatory process narratives is to enhance the reader's understanding of a process, the purpose of an **instructional** or a **directive process**

FIGURE 13.1 Timeline for the 1918 Flu Epidemic

narrative is to help readers learn how to do something. For instance, you might explain the following processes so that readers can replicate them:

- How to make a great pizza at home
- How to use the online library catalogue at your school
- How to fill out a ballot petition

Writing Descriptions

When you describe, you sketch people, places, and things verbally, rather than visually. Usually, you will aim to establish some dominant impression—an overall feeling about what you are describing, such as the feeling evoked in the following passage:

> A dark mist lay over the Black Hills, and the land was like iron. At the top of the ridge I caught sight of Devil's Tower upthrust against the gray sky as if in the birth time the core of the earth had broken through its crust and the motion of the world was begun. There are many things in nature that engender an awful quiet in the heart of man; Devil's Tower is one of them.
>
> N. Scott Momaday, "The Way to Rainy Mountain"

TechNote To construct a timeline like this one, you can use the timeline template available in *Microsoft Word*. It works best to construct the timeline in a separate *Word* document. Once you have prepared your timeline, you can insert the timeline file into the *Word* document that comprises your whole project. Alternatively, you can cut and paste the timeline into a *PowerPoint* slide and then insert the slide into your document file. As a *PowerPoint* slide, it's more easily moved within your document file.

Because it is so common, **description** will be part of many of your writing projects in all four areas of life. However, the approach you take to description will depend on what you are describing. Here we focus on three approaches that can be especially effective—naming, sensory, and spatial.

Naming in Description

When you describe someone or something, you need to name that person or thing, as well as its features. For example, if you were to describe the room where you sleep, you might name objects such as the bed, artwork, walls, ceiling, and floor. Here is an excerpt from Robert Sullivan's book *Rats: Observations on the History and Habitat of the City's Most Unwanted Inhabitants*:

> A rat is a rodent, the most common mammal in the world. *Rattus norvegicus* is one of the approximately four hundred different kinds of rodents, and it is known by many names, each of which describes a trait or a perceived trait or sometimes a habitat: the earth rat, the roving rat, the barn rat, the field rat, the migratory rat, the house rat, the sewer rat, the water rat, the wharf rat, the alley rat, the gray rat, the brown rat, and the common rat. The average brown rat is large and stocky; it grows to be approximately sixteen inches long from its nose to its tail—the size of a large adult human male's foot—and weighs about a pound, though brown rats have been measured by scientists and exterminators at twenty inches and up to two pounds. The brown rat is sometimes confused with the black rat, or *Rattus rattus*, which is smaller and once inhabited New York City and all of the cities of America but, since *Rattus norvegicus* pushed it out, is now relegated to a minor role.

A Sensory Approach to Description

A thorough sensory description includes details from all five senses—sight, sound, taste, smell, and touch. In a vivid sensory description, the reader experiences vicariously what the writer has described. To generate such a description, you might use the questions in the following table. With minor modifications, you can use these questions to develop descriptions of a wide range of items, from roasted marshmallows to a favorite place from your childhood.

Sensory Details of _____

Sense:	Questions to Consider:	Responses:
Sight	What does it look like?	
	What do I see when I look at it?	
Hearing	What sounds does it make?	
	What sounds are associated with it?	

Taste	How does it taste?
	What tastes are similar to it?
	What tastes are associated with it?
Smell	What does it smell like?
	What smells are similar to it?
	What smells are associated with it?
Touch	What does it feel like to the touch?
	What tactile associations do I have with it?

Of course, for some subjects you will rely on details from only one or two senses and may not use others at all. The sense you will use most commonly and extensively when writing description is sight. It is important to remember that other senses can also have an impact on readers, however. The sense of smell, for example, tends to evoke memory in humans more powerfully than any other sense.

In the following description of "good bread," notice how the writer appeals to several of the senses:

> Good bread. Its pleasure is deeply soul satisfying. It's not a superficial pleasure. It's down deeper than that. It may come from a perfect crust, with texture, definition, a caramelized crusty crunch with just the right give and not too thick. And it may come from a light, airy crumb, and you know it's been crafted by gentle, knowing hands that have shaped thousands of loaves just like this. And it may come from that lingering, wheaty fullness that makes you think of a soft sun-tinted breeze flowing its tide through a field of just-ripe, golden, amber-at-sunset wheat, ready for harvest.
>
> Ken's Artisan Bakery and Café (Portland, Oregon),
> "What Is Good Bread?"

A Spatial Approach to Description

When you describe something *spatially*, you describe it in terms of both its own physical dimensions and its relationship to the objects around it. An approach that is primarily spatial can include sensory details as well, and spatial description often includes a visual, which may even be the predominant part of the description. For example, Figure 13.2 is an x-ray of a child's hand. The paragraph below is a brief spatial description of the x-ray.

> The hand is composed of many small *bones* called carpals, metacarpals and phalanges. The two bones of the lower arm—the radius and the ulna—meet at the hand to form the wrist.

FIGURE 13.2 An X-ray of a Child's Hand

The *carpal bones* are a set of eight short bones forming the wrist; they are disposed on two rows of four bones each. These bones, the size of a marble, provide the wrist's litheness and mobility.

The palm of the hand is composed of five *metacarpal bones* laid out from the wrist, as a fan. The articulation of the first metacarpal bone with the carpal bones, permits the movement of touching, with the thumb, the tips of all fingers.

It is from this movement that the human hand can acquire the efficiency necessary to grab and manipulate objects.

Every hand is composed of 14 long bones named the *phalanges*. These bones compose the fingers and the thumb. Each finger has three phalanges and the thumb only two.

McGill University, School of Architecture

WRITING ACTIVITY

Writing an Effective Description

Working on your own or with several classmates, choose a topic to describe. First, generate a list of questions that an interested reader might have about the topic you have chosen. Second, answer each of the questions to generate descriptive details. Third, use those details to write a short descriptive paragraph, using the approaches described above.

Your instructor may ask you to share your description with the rest of the class.

For more on two types of writing that use description extensively, see Chapter 4, Writing to Share Experiences, and Chapter 7, Writing to Analyze.

Writing Definitions

Definitions help you to make certain that your readers understand the terms that you are using. Clear definitions are especially important if you are writing about a topic that you know more about than your readers do, about an issue over which there are differences of opinion—including over the meanings of terms—or about a topic for which precision is crucial. You will find occasions to use definitions in all four areas of life:

- In a letter to one of your U.S. senators, you define "the working poor" as you make an argument for legislation that will assist low-income families.

- When you take a friend to a baseball game, you define "earned run average" when "ERA" appears after a pitcher's name on the big screen in left field.

- In an economics course, you define "gross domestic product" in a paper about economic growth in India and China.

Kinds of Definitions

You can use any of several kinds of definitions depending on how much information your readers need. Sometimes you can define a term by simply giving your readers a **synonym,** a more familiar word or phrase that could be used in place of the term you are defining. However, defining a word with a synonym has limitations. Consider some synonyms for the word *war: warfare, combat, conflict, fighting, confrontation, hostilities,* and *battle.* Each has differences in meaning, and, depending on the context, these words cannot necessarily be used interchangeably.

More useful than a synonym in many cases is an essential definition. **Essential definitions** are sentence definitions that include three parts: (1) the name of what is being defined, (2) the general category for the item being defined, and (3) the form or function that distinguishes the item being defined from other similar items in the same general category. Here is an example:

Name	Category	Form or Function
A toaster	is a small kitchen appliance	that browns bread.
A mixer	is a small kitchen appliance	that combines ingredients.

If a synonym or an essential definition is not enough, you can incorporate it in an extended definition. An **extended definition,** which can take up one or more paragraphs in a piece of writing, may include both of these briefer types of definition, as well as additional information and examples. It is especially helpful when you need to define a concept that is abstract or complex. For instance, here is an extended definition of a *mugwump:*

> This archetypal American word derives from the Algonquian dialect of a group of Native Americans in Massachusetts. In their language, it meant "war leader." The Puritan missionary John Eliot used it in his translation of the Bible into their language in 1661–63 to convey the English words "*officer*" and "*captain*."
>
> *Mugwump* was brought into English in the early nineteenth century as a humorous term for a boss, bigwig, grand panjandrum, or other person in authority, often one of a minor and inconsequential sort. This example comes from a story in an 1867 issue of *Atlantic Monthly:* "I've got one of your gang in irons—the Great Mugwump himself, I reckon—strongly guarded by men armed to the teeth; so you just ride up here and surrender."
>
> It hit the big time in 1884, during the presidential election that set Grover Cleveland against the Republican James G. Blaine. Some Republicans refused to support Blaine, changed sides, and the *New York Sun* labelled them *little mugwumps*. Almost overnight, the sense of the word changed to *turncoat*. Later, it came to mean a politician who either could not or would not make up his mind on some important issue, or who refused to take a stand when expected to do so. Hence the old joke that a mugwump is a person sitting on the fence, with his mug on one side and his wump on the other.
>
> Michael Quinion, *World Wide Words*

Notice that the definition indicates what a mugwump is, explains the origin of the word and its history, and provides a concrete example.

WRITING ACTIVITY

Identifying Features of a Definition

Consider the following definition of a Luddite:

> A Luddite is a person who fears or loathes technology, especially new forms of technology that threaten existing jobs. During the Industrial Revolution, textile workers in England who claimed to be following the example of a man named Ned Ludd destroyed factory equipment to protest changes in the workplace brought

For more on a type of writing that uses definitions extensively, see Chapter 8, Writing to Convince.

about by labor-saving technology. The term Luddite is derived from Ludd's surname. Today, the term Luddite is reserved for a person who regards technology as causing more harm than good in society, and who behaves accordingly.

Tech Target Network

1. What are the features of this definition?
2. How might you clarify the definition to make it easier for readers to visualize a Luddite?

Writing Classifications

When you classify, you group—or divide—items into categories based on a principle of classification. There are three principles of division: completeness, exclusiveness, and consistency.

- **Completeness** means that all items need to be included in a classification. If you were classifying automobiles, you would need to make certain that SUVs were included in your scheme.

- **Exclusiveness** means that none of your categories should overlap with any other category. For example, the categories *movies about monsters* and *scary movies* don't work because some movies about monsters are scary (*The Thing*) and would fit in both categories.

- **Consistency** means that the same criteria need to be used to determine the contents of each category. If you are classifying animals and two of your categories are *mammals* and *birds*, your third category should not be *extinct animals* because that introduces different criteria into your system.

Many topics can be classified, which means that you will find classification a useful organizing strategy for many kinds of writing:

- Before purchasing a laptop computer for business travel, you might classify some possible laptops you are considering by weight—ultra-light (under three pounds), light (three to five pounds), moderate (six to eight pounds), heavy (more than eight pounds).

- In deciding which candidates to support in an election, you classify them according to their stated positions on those issues that are important to you.

- As you write a menu for your next week's meals, you use the categories in the food pyramid (see p. 412).

For more on a type of writing that uses classification extensively, see Chapter 7, Writing to Analyze.

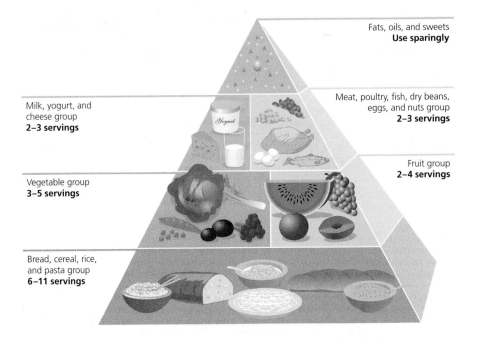

Fats, oils, and sweets
Use sparingly

Milk, yogurt, and
cheese group
2–3 servings

Meat, poultry, fish, dry beans,
eggs, and nuts group
2–3 servings

Fruit group
2–4 servings

Vegetable group
3–5 servings

Bread, cereal, rice,
and pasta group
6–11 servings

FIGURE 13.3
The Food Pyramid

Writing about Comparisons and Contrasts

The related strategies of **comparison**—looking at how subjects are similar—and **contrast**—looking at how they are different—are common not just in writing but in thinking. People find that they are crucial tools in thinking about and differentiating many aspects of the world around them.

In all areas of life, you will use comparison and contrast:

- In an art history class, you might compare and contrast the features of two schools of art such as impressionism and surrealism.
- In an e-mail to a friend, you might compare and contrast two romantic comedies that you recently saw at movie theaters.
- You might compare and contrast the features of two network servers that your company is considering for purchase.

Approaches to Comparison and Contrast

The two major approaches to comparing and contrasting two items are point-by-point and block. In the **point-by-point approach,** you discuss the two items together for each point of comparison/contrast. In the **block approach,** you discuss all of your points of comparison/contrast about one item first and then all points about the other item second. Here are two abbreviated outlines for a paper comparing the sports of baseball and fast-pitch softball, each using one of the two organizational approaches.

Point-by-Point Approach

I. Pitching
  A. Method
    1. Overhand or sidearm in baseball
    2. Underhand in fast-pitch softball
  B. Speed
    1. Up to 100 miles per hour in baseball
    2. Up to 70 miles per hour in fast-pitch softball
II. Field dimensions
  A. Mound
    1. Elevated to about 12 inches in baseball
    2. Level with the field in fast-pitch softball
  B. Infield
    1. Ninety feet between bases in baseball
    2. Sixty feet between bases in fast-pitch softball
  C. Outfield
    1. Over 400 feet to the centerfield fence in baseball
    2. Usually no more than 300 feet to the centerfield fence in fast-pitch softball
III. Equipment
  A. Balls
    1. A baseball is approximately 2.75 inches in diameter
    2. A fast-pitch softball is approximately 3.5 inches in diameter
  B. Bats
    1. Baseball bats are usually over 2.5 inches in diameter
    2. Fast-pitch softball bats are usually under 2.3 inches in diameter

Block Approach

I. Baseball
  A. Pitching
    1. Overhand or sidearm
    2. Up to approximately 100 miles per hour
  B. Field Dimensions
    1. Pitcher's mound approximately twelve inches high
    2. Ninety feet between bases
    3. Over 400 feet to centerfield fence

    C. Equipment
       1. Baseball approximately 2.75 inches in diameter
       2. Bats usually over 2.5 inches in diameter
II. Fast-Pitch Softball
    A. Pitching
       1. Underhand
       2. Up to 70 miles per hour
    B. Field Dimensions
       1. Pitcher's circle level with the field
       2. Sixty feet between bases
       3. Usually no more than 300 feet to centerfield fence
    C. Equipment
       1. Softball approximately 3.5 inches in diameter
       2. Bats usually under 2.3 inches in diameter

If you are comparing two items with many features, you should usually use the point-by-point approach so that readers don't get lost. Regardless of the approach that you use, however, you can help guide your readers by doing the following:

- Focusing on the major similarities and differences.
- Including the same points of comparison/contrast for both items.
- Covering the points in the same order for both subjects.
- Using transition words to move from point to point.

WRITING ACTIVITY

Comparing/Contrasting

Read "Bipolar Iraq" on pages 97–101 in Chapter 5, "Writing to Explore." Construct an outline of the major points of comparison/contrast between the two positions about the Iraq War that Wolff describes. Does the writer use a point-by-point approach or a block approach?

Using Outlines and Maps to Organize Your Writing

Regardless of the organizing strategies that you use, outlines and visual maps can be helpful tools for getting and staying organized as you write. Use the kind of outline or map that fits best with your own situation and writing process.

SCRATCH OUTLINES

Scratch outlines work well early in the process of composing. As rough sketches of your thoughts, they can help you get ideas on paper without much concern for the final organization of the project. A scratch outline might be little more than a list of ideas in the order in which they might appear in the final project.

FORMAL OUTLINES

Formal outlines can be useful once you have done some invention work and research and have a clearer sense of what you want to include in your draft and how you want to arrange the material. In a formal outline, you arrange your ideas in a series of levels. The first level is marked with roman numerals (I, II, III), the second level with capital letters (A, B, C), the third level with numbers (1, 2, 3), and the fourth level with lowercase letters (a, b, c). Each level must have at least two entries. The entries in a formal outline can be in sentences (a sentence outline) or in words or phrases (a topic outline) as in the following example:

Solving the Problem of Childhood Obesity

I. Opening story about obesity
II. Background/history of obesity
III. Description and explanation of the problem
    A. Statistical overview of the problem
    B. Causes of the problem
        1. Poor nutrition (food pyramid)
        2. Large serving sizes
        3. Lack of exercise
    C. Consequences of problem
        1. Diabetes
        2. Cardiovascular problems in adulthood
IV. Possible solutions
    A. Instruction for parents on how to read nutritional labels
    B. Education for children and parents about serving sizes
    C. Recommendation that schools require physical education, and that parents engage their children in more exercise
V. Conclusion

If you wanted a more detailed plan, with sentences that you could actually use in your paper, you could prepare a sentence outline like the following:

Solving the Problem of Childhood Obesity

I. Many children, such as Heather H., begin the cycle of dieting and gaining weight as early as age 10.

II. Obesity has been increasing in the United States, especially among children and adolescents.

III. Here are some recent, and quite startling, statistics about childhood obesity.

IV. There are several reasons for this problem, including poor nutrition, ever-increasing portion sizes, and children's reluctance to exercise.

    A. The first reason is that today's children, who live in one of the wealthiest countries in the world, suffer from poor nutrition.

    B. Another reason is that we all seem to expect large serving sizes in every restaurant these days.

    C. Finally, many children don't exercise, preferring to stay indoors for video games and online chats with their friends.

V. The consequences of childhood obesity can be dire.

    A. Diabetes can be one major and severe consequence.

    B. Childhood obesity also leads to cardiovascular problems when children grow up.

VI. Fortunately, some doctors and other experts are turning their time and attention to this problem, and have come up with some unique ideas.

    A. Parents need to learn how to read food labels, so here are some instructions for doing so.

    B. Both children and parents need to understand what a reasonable "serving size" looks like.

    C. Several exercise programs are available that schools can provide to young students—exercise that will be fun and helpful to them.

VII. Childhood is too important a time to spend obsessing about weight, but children should be encouraged to eat a healthful diet and exercise regularly to avoid the dieting treadmill that Heather H. and others like her are on.

TREE DIAGRAMS

Like outlines, tree diagrams such as Figure 13.4 show hierarchical relationships among ideas.

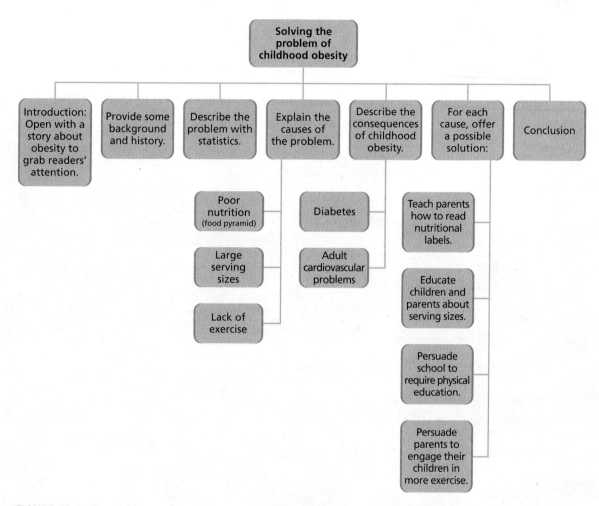

FIGURE 13.4   Tree Diagram for a Paper on Childhood Obesity

Often in our culture, the word **argument** has a negative connotation, as if to *argue* really means to *fight* about something, as children sometimes do on a playground, or as angry athletes sometimes do. Or, the word *argument* conjures up images of a loud and raucous debate, where the debaters do anything and everything to "win." But the term *argument* in many academic, professional, and civic settings and in most writing situations means to debate with someone about an issue or to attempt to convince someone to accept your point of view. That does not mean your debating partners, listeners, or readers will end up agreeing with you (or you with them), but rather that, at the end of your argument, your audience will say, "I understand what you mean and can appreciate your position. I don't necessarily agree with everything you've said, but I can see where you're coming from." This kind of *argument* must have as its thesis an assertion that is debatable, not a certainty, and must generate responses somewhere on the following continuum:

Strongly Disagree <---> **Strongly Agree**

Assertions that are capable of evoking such responses are appropriate **thesis statements** or **claims** for arguments.

The fundamental aim of an argument is to move the audience along this continuum of responses toward agreement or strong agreement if possible, but in any case farther away from strong disagreement.

Effective arguers get to know their audiences well enough to understand where on this continuum their responses to a thesis are likely to lie, and they choose argument strategies based on that knowledge of their audience. Of course, effective arguers realize that some members of the audience will be willing to move farther along the continuum than others.

If "winning" an argument means that the other side sees, understands, and appreciates your position, then your goal is to present your thesis and supporting evidence in a logical manner, so that your reader can at least understand—and perhaps agree with—your position.

WRITING ACTIVITY

Considering Your Audience

Construct two brief letters, no longer than a page. For each letter, assume that you want twenty-four-hour, seven-day-a-week access to your college's library.

- For your first letter, your audience is your classmates. How would you argue for your position in a letter to them? What "shared needs" would you list, to show what needs you have in common?

- For your second letter, your audience is the president of your college or university. How would you argue for your position to him or her?

With several classmates, discuss the differences between your letters.

Argument and Persuasion

When you present an argument, you want readers at a minimum to under-stand what you mean and to see your perspective. The concept of *argument*, then, is somewhat different from and broader than that of **persuasion.** When you have persuaded someone, you have convinced that person to believe something (this legislative bill is better than that one) or to do some-thing (provide the funding needed for longer library hours).

In a sense, an argument is the means of persuasion: You cannot persuade someone about anything without an effective argument. So, while you cer-tainly hope that you will be able to persuade the president of your school to increase library hours, your overall goal is to construct and present a sound, effective argument. Put another way, after members of your audience read your argument they may or may not agree with you in part or in full, but if your argument is effective, they will at least think, "I understand this writer's position, and he or she has made a strong case."

Each of the chapters in Part 3 of this book asks you to construct a certain kind of argument, with the goal of attempting to persuade your readers in a variety of ways. For example, Chapter 8 ("Writing to Convince") asks you to argue for a position on a controversial issue, while Chapter 9 ("Writing to Evaluate") asks for your judgment on the quality of a product, event, place, or other subject. In both cases, you may not necessarily cause your readers to change their minds—by switching sides on the issue or rushing out to see the film you recommended—but rather, they will understand your position and the reasons and evidence that support that position. Likewise, for Chapter 10 ("Writing to Explain Causes and Effects"), Chapter 11 ("Writing to Solve Problems"), and Chapter 12 ("Writing about a Creative Work"), you are asked to argue a debatable claim, whether it be a cause-and-effect relationship, a solution to a problem, or an interpretation of a short story or other work of art. Readers may not completely agree with your claim, but if it is soundly argued, they should at least be willing to consider it.

Rhetorical Appeals

The philosopher Aristotle was one of the first to notice that effective speakers use three kinds of appeals to help make their arguments convincing. An

appeal in this sense is a means of convincing your audience to agree with your argument, and perhaps of convincing them to do something. You already use these various appeals in your daily conversations when you want to convince your friends to do something with you, for example, or to talk your parents, or children, into going somewhere.

Logical Appeals

Logical appeals (or, using the Greek word, *logos*) are appeals made through your use of solid reasoning and appropriate evidence, including statistical and other types of data, expert testimony, and illustrative examples.

Always consider what kind(s) of evidence will best convince your audience:

No matter what kind of evidence you use to support your argument, that evidence must come from reliable sources. For more information on evaluating sources, see Chapter 19.

- For example, if you are writing to evaluate something (perhaps a film, a restaurant, or an art museum), quoting known and accepted authorities on the subject is often persuasive.

- If you are writing to solve a problem, historical information also is often useful, showing, for instance, how other communities have dealt with similar issues or problems.

Ethical Appeals

Ethical appeals (or appeals to *ethos*) focus on your character. When you establish your *ethos*, you communicate to readers that you are credible, intelligent, knowledgeable, fair, and perhaps even altruistic, concerned about the welfare of others. You can establish your ethos by doing the following:

- Presenting yourself as knowledgeable about your subject matter.

- Acknowledging points of view that differ from your own position, and dealing fairly with them. Sometimes dealing with an alternative position can be as simple as writing, "Other people might say that _____ is less costly than what I'm proposing, and they would be right—my plan does cost more. But the benefits far outweigh the cost, and here is why —"

- Providing appropriate information, including facts and statistics, for the audience you are addressing. Some audiences will be receptive to statistical information; others will be more receptive to quotations from experts in the field. Other audiences might look for both types of evidence.

If you present yourself in these ways, readers are more likely to be receptive to your argument.

Emotional Appeals

Appeals to readers' emotions (or *pathos*) can help readers connect with and accept your argument. However, effective arguers use emotional appeals judiciously, avoiding appeals that astute readers might consider exploitive.

There are many ways to appeal to readers' emotions. Here are some possibilities:

- Identify who is or will be affected positively or negatively by a situation or course of action that you are arguing for and ask the audience to identify with them.
- Show how the situation or course of action has emotionally affected people elsewhere.
- Arouse indignation over a current situation by showing how it is inconsistent with a community's value or concerns.

You use all three appeals frequently in everyday life. To convince a reluctant friend to go to see a particular film with you, for example, you might mention that the film, while new and relatively unknown, received an award from the Sundance Film Festival, an ethical appeal in which you draw on the *ethos* of the famous film festival; you might point out that the early showings cost only half as much as the nighttime shows (a logical appeal); or you might plead that you have no one else to go with and hate going to movies alone, clearly an emotional appeal.

The Rhetorical Triangle: Considering the Appeals Together

Most effective arguments combine rhetorical appeals because audiences respond to a variety of appeals. The three kinds of appeals complement one another, as is suggested by the rhetorical triangle shown in Figure 14.1. Each aspect of an act of communication—the writer, the reader, the message—is connected to the other two aspects.

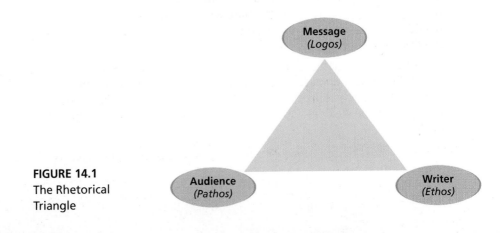

FIGURE 14.1
The Rhetorical Triangle

WRITING ACTIVITY

With two of your classmates, write a brief note to the chair of the College of Business, suggesting several possible internship projects that would count as course credit at community-service agencies. Use each of the rhetorical appeals to make your case. Possible agencies include the following:

- United Way

- Literacy Volunteers

- Kiwanis Club

- A local food pantry or homeless shelter

- The local Chamber of Commerce

Three Approaches to Argument

To aid you in responding to the assignments that call for argument in Part 3 of this text, in this chapter we cover three approaches to argument—classical, Toulmin, and Rogerian. All three approaches are widely used in effective arguments, so understanding how they function will help you not only to understand the arguments you read or hear, but also to construct your own written arguments.

Classical Strategies for Arguing

About 2400 years ago, the Greek philosopher Aristotle formalized what we now call the **classical scheme** of argument by listening to effective public speakers and then figuring out what made their arguments effective. Amazingly, Aristotle's ideas remain relevant today: You already use this approach in argument all the time. If you are using the classical scheme, this is the sequence you follow:

Aristotle

- Introduction
- Main claim
- Evidence supporting claim
- Discussion of other perspectives (acknowledging, conceding, and/or refuting them)
- Conclusion

This approach is called the **deductive** way to reason because you state your claim and then help the reader understand (or deduce) how the evidence supports your claim. Here is a simplified example of how the deductive approach might work in asking for a raise:

• Introduction and main claim	I'd like to talk with you about getting a raise. I've been with the company for two years now, and for several reasons I feel that I deserve a raise at this point in my career here.
• Evidence supporting claim	First, I am very effective now at doing work in the office as well as working with customers outside the office.
	Second, I've taken classes to learn several new software programs, and I'm now fully proficient at using them.
	Third, I've shown that I can take on lots of responsibility because I've handled several important projects in the past two years.
	Fourth, my end-of-year rankings have consistently improved.
• Discussion of other perspectives (acknowledging, conceding, and/or refuting them)	Now, I know there was that one dissatisfied customer, but if you'll recall, I managed to satisfy her (at last!) by providing extra service.
• Conclusion	Therefore, I deserve a raise.

The advantage of the deductive method is that you state your position and make your case before your reader starts thinking about other perspectives. Because readers understand what your point is *early* in your text, they find it easier to follow your argument.

If you are using another method, commonly known as the **inductive** approach, you first present and explain all of your reasons and evidence, then draw your conclusion—your main claim. In other words, you provide the evidence first and then the conclusion at the end. The advantage is that your reader may come to the same conclusion before you explicitly state your position and will therefore be more inclined to agree with your view.

For more on deductive and inductive reasoning, see Chapter 8.

Parts of a Classical Argument

Thinking about the parts or components of an argument makes the task of arguing more manageable. When you put the parts together, the results can lead to an effective whole.

The classical argument as presented here has five parts occurring in a certain order. However, as you write your own arguments, you may find that not every part is essential in every case and you may also find it useful to rearrange or combine the parts. The five parts are as follows:

1. **Introduction** (*exordium*): In the introduction you gain the attention of the audience and begin to establish your credibility. To accomplish this, you need to have analyzed your audience so that you understand what might get their attention and what you might do to establish yourself as a credible authority on the topic. Your overall goal in the introduction is to prepare your audience to be receptive to your case.

TechNote

If you have ever listened closely to the words of popular songs, whether they are examples of rock, blues, jazz, musical theater, hip-hop, or rhythm and blues, you've probably noticed that many song lyrics follow the patterns of argument.

If you are asked to write an essay that persuades, consider searching your music collection for interesting and powerful metaphors, statements, and stories you can use as quotations. Whether you collect CDs, download tunes from the Web, listen to podcasts, or even write and produce your own music, it is possible to consider your own collection of music as a collection of **arguments**. Be careful, though, to provide context and reasons for choosing the particular quotations that seem to support your view.

Often, you can insert a sound file into a *PowerPoint* presentation, which can add an interesting dimension to an in-class persuasive oral presentation. Be cautious about posting any music online, however. All music—no matter how brief the excerpt—is protected by copyright and is not considered fair use unless it is in the public domain.

---

2. **Narration** (*narratio*): Here you briefly explain the issue and provide some background or context for the argument you will make, as well as explain why it is important. If your readers understand why the issue is important to *them*, they are more likely to be interested and involved in your argument.

3. **Confirmation** (*confirmatio*): This is the main body of your argument. Here you offer evidence to support your thesis or claim. Evidence can consist of facts, statistics, expert opinion, and other information that supports your claim.

4. **Refutation** (*refutatio*): If you can argue about a statement, that means ideas or values are in dispute—that is, an issue is undecided and there is another side, or point of view, to your argument. Dealing with that objection, or **counterargument,** is a crucial step: If you fail to deal with the opposition's counterarguments, your readers may think that you are unaware of them and consider you ignorant, or they may think that you are trying to conceal their existence and suspect that you are dishonest.

   To refute counterarguments, you first need to discover what they are through research or audience analysis. For example, as you share ideas and drafts with your classmates, ask them what arguments "the other side" might make to address this issue or problem.

   As you consider opposing viewpoints, you need to decide how to handle them. Refutation is only one of several options. Some counterarguments may not be significant enough to merit further consideration; it may be enough simply to acknowledge them. If you were trying to convince students to vote in a campus election, you might simply acknowledge the objection that one vote does not make a difference: "I understand what you mean, because I used to think that way. And it's true that one vote rarely makes 'the difference' in any election." Or you might decide to refute the objection, noting that "what one person can do is to talk to other people, and convince them that they need to vote, and talk to them about the issues, and then all of a sudden that one person has gotten a lot of other people involved."

   Other ways to deal with objections to your argument include the following:

   • Agreeing that *part* of the opposing view is valid, and then demonstrating how the rest of the argument is unsound.

   • Discrediting any authorities they cite in their favor ("Since Jones wrote that, three studies have been published showing that his conclusions were incorrect . . .").

5. **Conclusion:** (*peroration*): Here you conclude your argument and, possibly, call for action. In the conclusion, you can do one or more of the following:

   • Summarize your case.

   • Stir readers' emotions.

   • Suggest an action or actions that the audience might take.

   • Refer back to the start of your essay, tying everything together.

   • List (briefly) your main points, touching on your evidence for each—basically listing why your argument makes sense.

Example: the Classical Scheme in Action

JARON LANIER

Beware the Online Collective

A pioneer in virtual reality research, Jaron Lanier invented the term *virtual reality*. In the early 1980s, he started VPL, which was the first company to offer virtual reality software. Along with his work in computer science, he is also a composer and an author. He received CMU's Watson Award in 2001 and was a finalist for the first Edge of Computation Award in 2005. In 2006, the New Jersey Institute of Technology awarded him an honorary doctorate. Among his many other awards is the first Virtual Reality Industry Award for Applications, which he shared with VPL client Matsushita in 1992. The following opinion piece first appeared in *Time* magazine in 2006.

It's funny being an "old timer" in the world of the Internet. About six years ago, when I was 40 years old, a Stanford freshman said to me, "Wow Jaron Lanier—you're still ALIVE?" If there's any use to sticking around for the long haul—as computers get so much more powerful that every couple of years our assumptions about what they can do have to be replaced—it might be in noticing patterns or principles that may not be so apparent to the latest hundred million kids who have just arrived online.

There's one observation of mine, about a potential danger, that has caused quite a ruckus in the last half-year. I wrote about it initially in an essay called "Digital Maoism."

Here's the idea in a nutshell: Let's start with an observation about the whole of human history, predating computers. People have often been willing to give up personal identity and join into a collective.

Historically, that propensity has usually been very bad news. Collectives tend to be mean, to designate official enemies, to be violent, and to discourage creative, rigorous thought. Fascists, communists, religious cults, criminal "families"—there has been no end to the varieties of human collectives, but it seems to me that these examples have quite a lot in common. I wonder if some aspect of human nature evolved in the context of competing packs. We might be genetically wired to be vulnerable to the lure of the mob.

One of the most wonderful things about the rise of the Web and other Internet-based communication schemes is how anti-mob they have been. I was in heaven 10 years ago watching millions of people build web sites for the first time as a form of expression. I'm just as excited

1

2

3

4

5

Introduction: Here Lanier sets the stage, so to speak, as he introduces his argument.

Narration: Lanier states his point about people and groups.

Lanier tries to get readers thinking: Do people really act differently in groups than they do individually? What does he mean by "the lure of the mob"? Can you think of any examples from your own experience? Are you willing to give up some of your own personal attributes and qualities to be a member of some group? Does the Internet change people's behavior in the manner Lanier describes?

Confirmation: Lanier provides some evidence here to support his claim.

Confirmation: More evidence on how the Internet works and affects people and their work.

But now Lanier hints of a change in the way the Internet affects people— a negative change.

Example.

Another example.

Personal example.

today when I run across a creative web page, MySpace site, YouTube video or whatever. There are zillions of people out there who are developing themselves, reaching out to others, becoming more creative, better educated, and richer than they otherwise would have been. My personal favorite of the current batch of fast growing sites might be Second Life, where people create avatars of themselves to share in a virtual world. Bravo!

In the last few years, though, a new twist has appeared. Along with all the sites that encourage individual expression, we are seeing a flood of schemes that celebrate collective action by huge numbers of bland, anonymous people. A lot of folks love this stuff. My worry is that we're playing with fire.

6

There are a lot of recent examples of collectivity online. There's the Wikipedia, which has absorbed a lot of the energy that used to go into individual, expressive web sites, into one bland, master description of reality. Another example is the automatic mass-content collecting schemes like DIGG. Yet another, which deserves special attention, is the unfortunate design feature in most blog software that practically encourages spontaneous pseudonym creation. That has led to the global flood of anonymous mob-like commentary.

7

I remember the first time I noticed myself becoming mean when I left an anonymous comment on a blog. What is it about that situation that seems to bring out the worst in people so often? It's a shame, because the benefits of blogs (such as that citizen journalists can pool resources to do research that otherwise might not get done) get cancelled out. Blogs often lead to such divisiveness that people end up caring more about clan membership than truth after a while.

8

There's a pattern in recent online businesses that is sometimes called Web 2.0 that I think is distinct from the collectivity problem, but for some reason seems to be leading a lot of entrepreneurs into promoting collectives.

9

The Web 2.0 notion is that an entrepreneur comes up with some scheme that attracts huge numbers of people to participate in an activity online—like the video sharing on YouTube, for instance. Then you can "monetize" at an astronomical level by offering a way to bring ads or online purchasing to people in your gigantic crowd of participants. What is amazing about this idea is that the people are the value—and they also pay for the value they provide instead of being paid for it. For instance, when you buy something that is advertised, part of the price goes to the ads—but in the new online world, you yourself were the bait for the ad you saw. The whole cycle is remarkably efficient and concentrates giant fortunes faster than any other business scheme in history.

10

So what's wrong with this pretty picture? All too many entrepreneurs seem to think that if you reduce the human element, the scheme will become more efficient. Instead of asking people to create videos or avatars, which require creativity and commitment, just watch their clicks, have them take surveys, have them tweak collective works, add anonymous, unconsidered remarks, etc. This trend is lousy, in my opinion, because it encourages people to lose themselves into groupthink.

But (Lanier provides an objection to his own argument here) the Web does some wonderful things, provides wonderful new and exciting ways for people to interact.

Refutation: Lanier answers the objection: reducing the human aspect leads to impersonal behavior. Back to his mob analogy.

What's to stop an online mass of anonymous but connected people from suddenly turning into a mean mob, just like masses of people have time and time again in the history of every human culture? It's amazing that details in the design of online software can bring out such varied potentials in human behavior. It's time to think about that power on a moral basis.

Conclusion: Asks readers to think, to consider what we're becoming. Note the power of Lanier's last line.

WRITING ACTIVITY

With several of your classmates, find an essay in a newsmagazine (such as *Time* or *Newsweek*) that is written in the form of a classical argument. Identify each part of the argument:

- Introduction
- Narration
- Confirmation
- Refutation
- Conclusion

Toulmin Strategies for Arguing

Another important model of argument was developed by philosopher Stephen Toulmin in his 1958 book *The Uses of Argument.* As with Aristotle's classical scheme, you already use the main aspects of Toulmin's approach: Every day you make assertions ("All students need to be involved in the upcoming election") and then use *"because* statements" to provide support for those assertions ("because if they are not, they won't have their needs and positions represented to those

Stephen Toulmin

in power"). Toulmin calls your assertion or thesis a **claim** and your *because* statement your **data**—the information supporting your claim, your assertion.

What Toulmin adds to this fairly intuitive way of constructing any text is the notion of a **warrant:** *why* the data support the claim. Sometimes you need to say why explicitly; other times you can assume that your reader understands this connection.

In Toulmin's model of argumentation, then, three components are considered essential to any argument:

- **Claim:** the conclusion or point that you will argue and hope to convince readers to agree with. For example, your claim might be "A major objective of this country's space program should be to land a crew of astronauts on Mars."

- **Data:** the reasons you give to support your claim. Your data may take the form of *because* statements. You might support your claim about Mars by saying "because knowing about Mars will help us understand our own planet and the life it supports because Mars may have had water—and life—at one time."

- **Warrant:** the connection between the claim and the data, explaining why the data support the claim. Often this connection is obvious and can go unstated. For example, the data and claim above are connected by the idea that it is important that we understand our planet, an assumption your readers undoubtedly would share.

Three other components of an argument are considered optional: the *backing*, the *rebuttal*, and the *qualifier*.

- **Backing:** If you are not sure that your readers will see the connection between data and claim, you need to state the warrant and support it as well. The support for the warrant is the **backing.** If you felt you could not assume the warrant about understanding our planet, you might need to state it explicitly: "Understanding our own planet and the life it supports is crucial to our survival as a species, and knowing about Mars will help us do that."

- **Rebuttal:** When you **rebut** the opposition's position, you prove that your position is better, for example, that it is acceptable to more people.

- **Qualifier:** In response to opposing positions and points, you may need to in some way limit or modify, or **qualify,** your claim. You can do this by indicating precisely the conditions under which your claim does and does not apply. Qualifiers often include words such as *sometimes, possibly, may,* and *perhaps.*

Example: the Toulmin Model in Action

STANLEY FISH

But I Didn't Do It!

Both a professor and an attorney, Stanley Fish has held teaching as well as administrative positions in several large American universities. A world-renowned scholar of the seventeenth-century poet John Milton, Dr. Fish is the author of more than a hundred articles and books and review articles, many of which have been translated into other languages.

Dr. Fish has also won many awards and honors, including the Hanford Book Award, the PEN/Spielvogel-Diamonstein Award, and the Milton Society Award. He also received a nomination for the National Book Award. The following opinion piece was first published in the *New York Times* in 2006.

Emboldened by the State of Virginia's apology for slavery—the measure passed both houses unanimously—some Georgia lawmakers are in the process of introducing a similar resolution in their legislature. The reasoning behind the apology movement is straightforward: a great wrong was done for centuries to men and women who contributed in many ways to the prosperity of their country and were willing to die for it in battle; it's long past time to say we're sorry.

Resistance to the apology movement is also straightforward. There is the fear that because an apology is an admission of responsibility for a prior bad act, apologizing might establish a legal or quasi-legal basis for reparations. And there is also the objection that after so many years an apology would be merely ceremonial and would therefore be nothing more than a "feel good" gesture.

But the objection most often voiced is that the wrong people would be apologizing to the wrong people. That was the point made by Tommie Williams, the Georgia Senate majority leader, when he said: "I personally believe apologies need to come from feelings that I've done wrong," and "I just don't feel like I did something wrong."

Williams's counterpart in the house, Speaker Glenn Richardson, made the same claim of innocence on behalf of his colleagues. "I'm not sure what we ought to be apologizing for," given that "nobody here was in office."

Mr. Richardson's statement at least has the merit of recognizing that an apology would not be made by an individual—the idea isn't to go to some slave cemetery and speak to a gravestone—but by an

1

2

3

4

5

Unstated warrant: Slavery was and is a horrible part of American history. Fish probably assumes that he does not need a *because* statement since readers will agree that slavery was terrible.

This is the issue Fish is dealing with. He is rebutting the assertion that an apology for slavery is a bad idea because no one who is currently alive, including the individual members of the Georgia legislature, kept slaves.

Fish's claim: The Georgia lawmaker's resistance to an apology is based on faulty reasoning.

Data: The members of the Supreme Court, by relying on precedent, carry on the work of the members who preceded them and are responsible for earlier members' actions because they are all part of that institution.

Unstated warrant: The Supreme Court's authority derives from its reliance on, and respect for, precedent.

Warrant: Justices should overrule previous decisions in which the court ruled incorrectly.

Warrant: Legislatures are analogous to courts.

Data: Case where the U.S. Congress passed legislation providing reparations to Japanese-Americans unjustly treated during World War II.

Data: President George H. W. Bush formally apologized to Japanese-Americans.

Qualifier: Fish admits he doesn't intend to answer the greater question of whether or not an apology should be issued, but rather he limits his argument to addressing one reason offered by members of the Georgia legislature for not apologizing.

Conclusion: The fact that the Georgia legislators did not personally keep slaves is not a valid reason to resist apologizing.

institution. He just thinks that because no present member of the institution was around at the time of the injury, an apology would make no sense.

But this is very bad reasoning, and you can see why if you read just 6 a few recent Supreme Court cases on any subject. Invariably, the justice delivering the court's opinion will cite a precedent from a case decided 50 or 100 years ago, and say something like, "In Smith v. Jones, we ruled that . . ." But of course he or she didn't actually—that is, personally—rule on anything in 1940 or 1840, so what's with the "we"?

The answer is that by using "we" to refer to an action taken before 7 any present member of the court had reached the age of reason or was even alive, the justices acknowledge that they are part of an ongoing enterprise, and as such are responsible for its history; not as individuals, but as persons charged with the duty of carrying on a project that precedes them and will survive them.

At times "carrying on" includes revising and even repudiating ear- 8 lier stages in that project. By overruling a precedent—a rare occurrence, to be sure—the justices say, collectively and on behalf of everyone who has ever donned the robe, "Oops, we got that one wrong; sorry, here's another try."

Legislatures do not overrule; they repeal, but the principle is the 9 same. Legislators meeting on the first day of a new term don't say, "O.K., let's start all over again and figure out what laws we would like to have on the books." Instead, they regard themselves as picking up a baton passed to them by their predecessors whose actions they now "own," even in those instances when no legislator now sitting performed them. The vast majority of those actions will continue in force, but a few will be revisited, and of those, a smaller number will be modified or even reversed.

Sometimes a mistake now acknowledged can be remedied by chang- 10 ing the law. Sometimes that remedy would come too late, and another form of response is called for, as when the United States passed the Civil Liberties Act of 1988, deploring the internment of Japanese-Americans during World War II and authorizing payments of $20,000 to each surviving internee.

Ronald Reagan signed that act into law, and two years later Presi- 11 dent George H. W. Bush formally apologized for "the wrongs of the past."

Does that mean that Georgia should apologize, too? Not necessarily. 12 The question is a political as well as a moral one, and it is not my intention here to answer it. All I am saying is that while there may be good reasons to resist apologizing, the "we didn't personally do it and those it was done to are dead" reason isn't one of them.

Consider some issue you think is important to you and to your classmates. Construct a brief Toulmin argument in which you identify your claim and the warrants that an audience of your classmates need to believe for them to accept your argument.

Rogerian Strategies for Arguing

Carl Rogers

Rogerian argument, which is based on the work of psychologist and mediator Carl Rogers, allows for the fact that at times we will inevitably take perspectives on issues that are different from those of the people with whom we have important relationships. Suppose you and a close friend disagree about how to solve the problem of alcohol-related traffic fatalities, for example. Although you could use classical argumentative strategies to win this argument, in the long term your relationship might not be as well served as it would be by a conversation in which you try to see the other point of view.

Differences of opinion occur in all four areas of life—the academic, the professional, the civic, and the personal. And in all four areas, we have relationships that we value enough to want to maintain. We might therefore do better to resolve our differences without trying to "win."

The ultimate goal of Rogerian argument is to negotiate differences and cooperate to reach a resolution that benefits or is in some way acceptable to both parties. Thus, in Rogerian argument, it is useful to begin by thinking about commonalities, that is, by thinking about and understanding opposing views and asking yourself, "Even though we may have some differences, what do we have in common?" or "Even though we may not think alike, how can we work together effectively to solve this problem?"

Rogerian arguments have several component parts:

- **Introduction:** The introduction includes a description of the issue you hope to come to a consensus on. As you state a positive goal—solving a problem, reaching a consensus on some issue—keep your tone positive and invite others to participate in developing the solution to the problem, or reaching agreement if the issue does not call for a solution to a problem.

- **Summary of Opposing Views:** Be as accurate and as neutral as you can be in stating the views of those who may disagree with you. Show that you have the skills, character, and fairness to see and to appreciate the merits of opposing views.

- **Statement of Understanding:** After you have stated the opposing views, demonstrate that you understand why others might hold such views, especially in certain situations. If possible, indicate the conditions under which you too could share those views.
- **Statement of Writer's Position:** The previous three parts have prepared your readers to listen to your views, and here is the place to state them. Invite your audience to consider your views in the same way that you have considered theirs.
- **Statement of Contexts:** Building on the statement of your position, be specific about the kinds of conditions under which you hope others will find merit in your position.
- **Statement of Benefit:** Explain how your position or, if applicable, your solution to the problem, will benefit those who might oppose you. End on a positive and hopeful note, saying that you hope that your readers will accept the validity of your position.

Example: Rogerian Strategies in Action

RICK REILLY
Nothing but Nets

Rick Reilly has been voted National Sportswriter of the Year eight times. He currently writes the weekly "Life of Reilly" column for *Sports Illustrated* and also frequently contributes to *Time* magazine. Reilly's nonfiction books include *Who's Your Caddy?* and *The Life of Reilly: The Best of* Sports Illustrated's *Rick Reilly*. Reilly also has published the novel *Missing Links* and is the winner of many awards, including the New York Newspaper Guild's Page One Award for Best Magazine Story. The following article was first published in *Sports Illustrated* in 2006.

Problem: Reilly is a sportswriter who is not writing about game nets, but the need for mosquito nets.
Introduction: Reilly outlines the severity of the problem.

I've never asked for anything before, right? Well, sorry, I'm asking now. 1

We need nets. Not hoop nets, soccer nets or lacrosse nets. Not New 2
Jersey Nets or dot-nets or clarinets. *Mosquito* nets.

See, nearly 3,000 kids die every day in Africa from malaria. And 3
according to the World Health Organization, transmission of the disease
would be reduced by 60% with the use of mosquito nets and prompt
treatment for the infected.

Three thousand kids! That's a 9/11 every day! 4

Put it this way: Let's say your little Justin's Kickin' Kangaroos have a 5
big youth soccer tournament on Saturday. There are 15 kids on the team,

10 teams in the tourney. And there are 20 of these tournaments going on all over town. Suddenly, every one of these kids gets chills and fever, then starts throwing up and then gets short of breath. And in seven to 10 days, they're all dead of malaria.

6   We *gotta* get these nets. They're coated with an insecticide and cost between $4 and $6. You need about $10, all told, to get them shipped and installed. Some nets can cover a family of four. And they last four years. If we can cut the spread of disease, 10 bucks means a kid might get to live. Make it $20 and more kids are saved.

7   So, here's the ask: If you have ever gotten a thrill by throwing, kicking, knocking, dunking, slamming, putting up, cutting down or jumping over a net, please go to a special site we've set up through the United Nations Foundation. The address is: *UNFoundation.org/malaria*. Then just look for the big *SI's Nothing But Net* logo (or call 202–887–9040) and donate $20. *Bang*. You might have just saved a kid's life.

8   Or would you rather have the new Beastie Boys CD?

9   You're a coach, parent, player, gym teacher or even just a fan who likes watching balls fly into nets, send $20. You saved a life. Take the rest of the day off.

10   You have *ever* had a net in the driveway, front lawn or on your head at McDonald's, send $20. You ever imagined Angelina Jolie in fishnets, $20. So you stay home and eat on the dinette. You'll live.

11   Hey, Dick's Sporting Goods. You have 255 stores. How about you kick in a dime every time you sell a net? Hey, NBA players, hockey stars and tennis pros, how about you donate $20 every time one of your shots hits the net? Maria Sharapova, you don't think this applies to you just because you're Russian? Nyet!

12   I tried to think how many times I have said or written the word "net" in 28 years of sports writing, and I came up with, conservatively, 20,000. So I've already started us off with a $20,000 donation. That's a whole lot of lives. Together, we could come up with $1 million, net. How many lives would that save? More than 50 times the population of Nett Lake, Minn.

13   I know what you're thinking: *Yeah, but bottom line, how much of our $1 million goes to nets?* All of it. Thanks to Ted Turner, who donated $1 billion to create the U.N. Foundation, which covers *all* the overhead. "Every cent will go to nets," says Andrea Gay, the U.N. Foundation's Director of Children's Health.

14   Nets work! Bill and Melinda Gates have just about finished single-handedly covering every bed in Zambia. Maybe we can't cover an entire Zambia, but I bet we could put a serious dent in Malawi.

15   It's not like we're betting on some scientist somewhere coming up with a cure. And it's not like warlords are going to hijack a truckload of

Reilly works hard to put the problem into a language that everyone can understand.

Reilly points out how inexpensive the nets are.

Benefit: For $10 you can save a child's life. Note how Reilly writes about a shared, common ground with any reader who ever played a sport (which would include almost everyone).

Writer's Position: Reilly works to defuse the money objection to his proposal, and he does so in a humorous way. Sure, he says, he wants to raise a million dollars . . . but then he shows how that large amount can come from many small donations.

Benefit: no overhead costs— all donations pay for nets.

Benefit: Look at how many lives could be saved.

nets. "Theoretically, if every person in Africa slept at night under a net," says Gay, "nobody need ever die of malaria again." You talk about a net profit.

My God, think of all the nets that are taken for granted in sports! 16 Ping-Pong nets. Batting cage nets. Terrell Owens's bassinet. If you sit behind the plate at a baseball game, you watch the action *through* a net. You download the highlights on Netscape and forward it on the net to your friend Ben-net while eating Raisinets. Sports is nothing *but* net. So next time you think of a net, go to that website and click yourself happy. Way more fun than your fantasy bowling league, dude.

One last vignette: A few years back, we took the family to Tanzania, 17 which is ravaged by malaria now. We visited a school and played soccer with the kids. Must've been 50 on each team, running and laughing. A taped-up wad of newspapers was the ball and two rocks were the goal. Most fun I ever had getting whupped. When we got home, we sent some balls and nets.

I kick myself now for that. How many of those kids are dead because 18 we sent the wrong nets?

WRITING ACTIVITY

With several of your classmates, construct a Rogerian argument, focusing on some campus or national issue or problem (see the list on p. 433). Your instructor may want you to share your argument with the rest of the class.

Some Common Flaws in Arguments

Any argument, no matter how effective, can be marred by **logical fallacies,** or flaws in reasoning. Although sometimes introduced deliberately into an argument with the aim of misleading readers, such flaws are often inadvertent, and avoiding them requires the kinds of critical thinking discussed in Chapter 2 of this book. The following list of flaws in arguments is by no means exhaustive, but it does include the most common and easily avoided ones.

- **Appealing to irrational fears:** All humans have fears, and it is often easy to exploit those fears. Someone making the argument that even though there have been only a few isolated cases of Mad Cow Disease in the United States, cattle ranchers should test each cow every month would be exploiting an irrational fear.

- **Appealing to pity:** Although appeals to pity and other emotions can be justified at times, this kind of appeal can mask an otherwise weak case. If a student who is earning a failing grade in a course because she has missed many class sessions, neglected to hand in assignments, and performed poorly on examinations appeals to her instructor by pleading tearfully, "If I fail this course, I won't graduate on time," she is obviously masking a weak case.

- **Appealing to prejudice:** Also known as *"ad populum,"* this fallacy occurs when the writer appeals to a preexisting positive or negative prejudice. A common example is the practice of putting an image of the American flag on a bumper sticker that advocates a particular product or stance, with an appeal to patriotism thus substituting for an argument for the product or stance.

- **Appealing to tradition:** The most common form of this appeal is the statement "We've always done it this way in the past."

- **Arguing from a lack of knowledge or evidence:** We can illustrate both forms of this flaw with the following example: You have looked for a needle in a haystack, and your search has been unsuccessful. From this lack of evidence, one person might argue that there must be a needle in that haystack if you would only search more carefully. From the same lack of evidence, a second person might argue that there is no needle in the haystack. In reality, of course, neither conclusion can be supported.

- **Attacking the opponent's character:** Often called an *ad hominem* attack, this fallacy is sometimes used in an attempt to direct attention away from the logic of a case—usually a strong case—by evoking a negative emotional response to the person making the case.

- **Attributing false causes:** Usually called *post hoc, ergo propter hoc* ("after this, therefore because of this"), this fallacy occurs when someone assumes that Event A caused Event B because Event A occurred before Event B. A common example is superstitious thinking: "I've been having so much bad luck recently because I broke a mirror/walked under a ladder/crossed the path of a black cat."

- **Bandwagon appeal:** Here the arguer is essentially saying "Many people are doing it, especially people whom you admire, so it must be a good thing to do. You should do it too."

- **Begging the question (circular reasoning):** This fallacy treats a questionable assertion as if it has already been answered or fully explained, as in the following example: "My friend would never cheat because he's an honest person."

- **Either-or reasoning:** Also known as "false dichotomy," this fallacy occurs when writers give readers two opposing choices (either A or B) when other possibilities also exist. For instance, a person might state, "You can major in business administration, or you can plan on getting a crummy job." Many attractive jobs do not require a degree in business administration, of course.

- **Faulty analogy:** In this fallacy, the writer makes a comparison that is in some way misleading or incomplete—or that does not even relate to the topic being discussed. A reporter who writes "The President hit a home run with his labor bill" is using a faulty baseball analogy. The President is not a baseball player and is supposed to be working with Congress, not "playing" against them.

- **Guilt by association:** This fallacy occurs when a writer seeks to discredit an opponent by associating the opponent with some unpopular person, group, or idea, as when politicians attempt to brand their opponents with labels such as "free-spending liberal" or "hard-right conservative." Such labels imply that *all* liberals are "free spending" or that all conservatives are "hard-right"—and both terms (*free-spending* and *hard-right*) have negative connotations.

- **Overgeneralization:** This fallacy occurs when someone reaches a conclusion based on insufficient evidence, especially atypical examples. For instance, your best friend engages in overgeneralization when, after an automobile accident in which she was not wearing a seatbelt but sustained only minor injuries, she says, "See. Seatbelts aren't necessary." Of course, anyone who has read studies on seatbelt use knows that they save many lives each year.

- **Red herring (or non sequiter):** This fallacy occurs when the writer introduces irrelevant material to divert attention from the issue being considered. The fallacy gets its name from the practice of dragging a red herring—a fish—along the ground to distract hunting dogs from the scent that they are following. A student who says to the teacher, "I know that I was late for class today, but I've been on time every other day" is using a red herring to throw the teacher off the scent of the real issue: the student is late.

- **Slippery slope:** This fallacy claims that once something starts, it must continue, just like a person sliding down a slippery slope. The person will not be able to stop sliding. An example is the student who says, "We've got to fight that proposed fee for using the computer center. If that fee is enacted, pretty soon they'll be charging fees for using the restrooms on campus."

- **Stacking the deck:** Here the writer presents evidence for only one side of the case. A student who says, "I should get an 'A' in this class because I handed in all my homework," while neglecting to mention that she got a "C" on the midterm and final exams, is stacking the deck in a rather blatant way.

- **Straw person:** This fallacy occurs when an arguer distorts the opponent's argument and then attacks that distorted argument. For instance, a few decades ago when equal rights for women was a hotly contested issue, some people made statements such as "Equal rights for women means that women will have the right to use men's restrooms. What is this country coming to?" Unisex restrooms were not part of what women's rights advocates were arguing for—so they served as a straw person.

WRITING ACTIVITY

To help you learn to identify logical fallacies, in your local or campus newspaper, find several instances of logical fallacies (hint: often, letters to the editor provide rich material!). Bring copies to class, share them, and explain the logical fallacies to your classmates.

Chapter

15

Using Strategies for Collaboration

Although writing can be a solitary activity, it is often a collaborative endeavor. For instance, researchers in the sciences, education, and engineering often co-author research proposals and reports. In business, teams often write project proposals and reports. In local, state, or national legislatures, many people collaborate to write bills to present to their colleagues. When groups of neighbors or parents are concerned about some local problem, they will often collaborate on a letter to the editor of their local newspaper or to the school board. In your writing classroom, you will probably have the opportunity to get feedback on your writing from your classmates, and in other courses throughout your college career, you are likely to encounter assignments that require you to work as part of a team.

Working with Peers on Your Single-Authored Projects

As you work on your own writing projects, working with peers can yield many benefits. Early in the process of crafting a project, peers can help you generate ideas by challenging you to consider perspectives that you may not consider on your own. Later in the process, peers can point out ways to revise your writing so that readers will find it more understandable, informative, or persuasive. Peers can also help edit your prose by seeing problems that your tired eyes might miss.

In the chapters in Parts 2 and 3 of this book, you will find various Writer's Workshop activities that will help you solicit feedback from peers. As you gather comments from peers, it is your responsibility to encourage reviewers to offer candid assessments of your work. Peers should not be nasty, of course, but they *should* give you a clear sense of how well your writing is fulfilling its purpose.

Strategies for Working with Peers on Your Projects

Peers can offer perspectives that can help you at any point in a project—invention, research, revising, editing. Although it is important to seek and use the perspectives that peers can offer, it is equally important to remember that you—not your peers—are ultimately responsible for the project. Given this principle of responsibility, the following guidelines can be useful:

1. Peers can indicate what is working well—and not so well—in a draft. When peers ask questions that are requests for more information, you should consider adding that information to your next draft.
2. Peers' questions are usually more helpful than their suggestions. Questions keep the responsibility for the project on your shoulders.

Using Digital Tools for Peer Review

Digital tools for peer review can help you when it is a challenge finding time to meet face-to-face outside of class. Even if it is easy to meet face-to-face, though, writers still work with digital texts, and therefore need to use digital tools. Here are some common tools that you can use:

1. The track-changes feature of your word-processing software makes it easy to see the changes that different reviewers are suggesting in a document. You can then accept or reject any or all suggested changes.

2. The "comment" feature of most word-processing software makes it easy to offer a suggestion or pose a question to the writer.

3. Many instructors use *WebCT, Blackboard*, or some other course-management system to offer courses either completely or partially online.

Working with Peers on Multiple-Authored Projects

Working with your classmates on multiple-authored projects can have many benefits. One long-term benefit is that it will prepare you for co-authoring documents with your colleagues in the workplace. Another benefit is that working with a group can infuse a project with a rich array of perspectives.

Group work also presents challenges, however. Some members of the writing team may be inclined to contribute too much to the project while others sometimes seem to contribute too little. Another challenge is that some co-authors may insist on doing things their way without listening to potentially effective ideas from others.

Strategies for Working with Peers Effectively

Working with peers can be challenging because they can question your thinking in new and sometimes uncomfortable ways. In college, this kind of interaction is especially likely because your classmates may have personalities and/or cultural backgrounds that differ substantially from yours. Although encountering a variety of backgrounds and perspectives can move you out of your comfort zone, it can also be a powerful catalyst for learning.

To make the most of your work with peers, try some of the following strategies:

1. **Listen empathically to your group members' comments and questions.** Empathic listeners strive to understand why someone is making a particular comment or raising a particular question.

2. **Assign roles to members of the group.** One member of the group can be the *recorder*, whose duty is to keep track of who says

> ### TechNote
>
> When working in groups with other students, remember that not everyone in the class will have the same level of access to the Internet or to computer technologies. Among any given group of college students, the level of experience with and knowledge about computers will vary.
>
> Never assume that everyone uses the same programs on his or her personal computer. Some students do not even own computers, although most college campuses and dormitories have computer labs available for student use. It is a good idea to ask your friends and classmates what kinds of programs they use regularly, rather than simply assuming everyone is familiar with the services you use most often.

what. Another member of the group can be the *question-asker*, posing questions to encourage everyone to think more critically or deeply. Yet another group member can be the *facilitator*, whose role is to keep the discussion focused and moving forward, to keep everyone on task. It is important that every group member have some *specific responsibility* to perform for the whole group to succeed.

3. **Provide positive and constructive feedback.** Every piece of feedback can be stated more-or-less negatively or more-or-less positively. Further, every negative or less positive statement can be recast into a more positive form:

Less Positive	**More Positive**
There's an error in his sentence.	You could edit the sentence this way:
This paragraph is underdeveloped.	You could develop this paragraph by adding this:
You don't have a conclusion.	What are you planning to say in the conclusion?

4. **Pay attention to interpersonal dynamics.** Before the group begins discussing the assigned topic, ask each member of the group to respond to the following kinds of questions:

   a. What can the group do to function most effectively?

   b. What seems to impede our group from functioning effectively?

   c. What encourages you to contribute effectively to the group?

5. **Do round-robin sharing.** Sometimes some group members contribute more than their fair share to the discussion while others contribute less than they could. To ensure that every member of the group contributes equally, go around the table clockwise, with each

person contributing one after the other. Keep going around the table as many times as necessary to solicit everyone's contributions.

6. **If possible, keep the group relatively small—three or four members.** Larger groups become hard to manage, and it becomes difficult to coordinate calendars or to come to consensus.

7. **Consider your class and your peer group to be intertwined communities.** Make a commitment to improve the work of each community and each member of the community. If every member of the class and the group makes such a commitment, everyone will benefit.

8. **Celebrate your accomplishment.** When the project is completed, treat yourselves in some way, perhaps by enjoying coffee or lunch together.

One way to ensure the success of any group endeavor is to plan. The tasks that follow will help you to plan various aspects of your work with your group.

DEFINE SUCCESS FOR THE GROUP

What will count as success, and how can the group achieve it? You might use the following chart, for example, to define success and to identify the means for achieving that success.

Defining Group Success

Sign of Success	Method(s) for Achieving
Everyone shows up for our out-of-class meetings at the agreed-upon time.	Add meetings to daily planners and/or PDAs.
Everyone participates equally.	Use a round-robin approach for sharing ideas during discussions.

DEVELOP A PLAN FOR DEALING WITH GROUP PROBLEMS

Potential problems include a group member who dominates a discussion, doesn't carry a fair share of the load, or misses a deadline. If a problem does surface, deal with it immediately. Dealing with small problems immediately can keep them from becoming bigger problems. If a problem arises, do *not* focus on who is to blame; instead, focus on finding a solution.

SET SHORT-TERM AND LONG-TERM GOALS

Before the group begins a particular work session, decide what you want to accomplish in the session, your short-term goal. As you work, stay focused on that goal until you achieve it. If the group will work together over multiple sessions, decide on a long-term goal to achieve by the last session. Then establish short-term goals for each session along the way.

Project Goals

Long-Term Goals	Short-Term Goals
Complete the project by November 16.	Complete library research by October 3.
	Complete interviews by October 10.

DEVELOP A PLAN FOR COMPLETING THE PROJECT

Identify the subtasks that need to be completed along the way, as well as a timeline for completing each subtask. Write down who is responsible for each task, and make certain that each member of the group has a list of everyone's responsibilities. As each deadline for a subtask approaches, ask the responsible member or members to report on progress.

MAKE A CALENDAR OF GROUP MEETINGS

Group meetings can be held face-to-face, by telephone, or in online chat rooms. For each meeting, establish an agenda and identify what each person needs to do before the meeting. Also, decide who will serve as the discussion leader for each meeting and assign a different discussion leader for each meeting so that no one group member dominates.

Calendar for Meetings

Meeting Date	Agenda Item(s)	Individuals' Preparation	Discussion Leader
October 11	Examine interviews	**Hanna:** Bring three copies of transcripts of interviews with rental-property owners.	Hanna
		Molly: Bring three copies of transcripts of interviews with renters.	Molly
		Meghan: Bring three copies of transcript of interview with city attorney.	Meghan

Using Digital Tools for Facilitating Multiple-Authored Projects

Here are some tried-and-true suggestions for using digital tools so that your co-authoring experience is a happy, productive one:

1. Agree on a sequence for working on each digital file to avoid duplication of effort.

2. For revising, use the track-changes and the comment features of your word-processing software. That way other members of the group can see the changes that you are making.

3. When you send a file to another member of the group for it is his or her turn to do the next round of revising or editing, copy the other members of the group so that they can be certain who is working on the document and can see the progress on the project.

4. When you name files, make certain to include the current date in the file name, such as "rental_paper_10–18–08." Don't delete older versions of files because you may need them to recover a deleted paragraph or to recover a file that has become corrupted.

Making Effective Oral Presentations

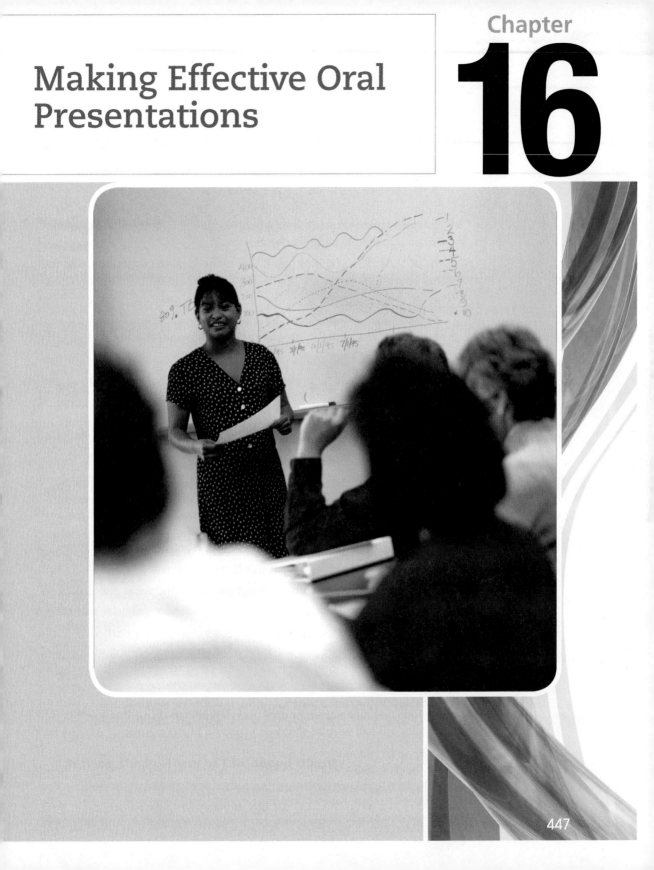

Along with invention, arrangement, memory, and style, *delivery*—the way you present a message—is one of the five "canons" of rhetoric. In most of this book, we have dealt with written or visual forms of delivery. In this chapter, however, we will consider oral presentations, a form of delivery that is becoming increasingly important in all areas of life.

- In your **academic life**, you will be asked to make presentations in some of your classes.
- In your **professional life**, you will often be asked to present your ideas to your colleagues and to clients.
- In your **civic life**, you may speak before the local school board, or to the city council, or in front of any number of civic or political organizations.
- In your **personal life**, you may be called upon to give a speech at an occasion such as a wedding, a funeral, or a school reunion, or you may speak at a less formal gathering of your family or friends.

As with written communication, oral presentations are *rhetorical acts*. To prepare an effective oral presentation, you need to ask yourself the same questions that you would ask for any writing situation:

- **What** do I want to accomplish? In other words, what is the purpose of this presentation? To inform? To persuade? To explain? To analyze?
- **Who** is my audience? What do they already know about my topic? What information do I need to supply in order to achieve my purpose? What is the best way to present this information—charts, graphs, photos, handouts, a *PowerPoint* presentation, overhead slides?
- What is the **context** surrounding this presentation? Will I make a classroom presentation, or will I present in a more formal setting? Why have I been asked to speak to this group at this particular time and place?
- How much do I already know about my **topic,** and what else do I need to learn about it?

Once you decide what you want to accomplish with a particular audience on a specific occasion, you will have a better understanding of how you need to prepare: what kind of research you need to conduct, the types of information you need to collect, and whether you should prepare handouts or *PowerPoint* or overhead slides.

Developing Your Presentation

To develop an oral presentation, you can use several approaches. For more formal presentations on complex topics, you might decide to write the full text of your presentation, using the composing strategies detailed in Parts 2 and 3 of this textbook. In some situations you might decide to read that full text, especially if you have to use specific words at specific moments during your presentation. In other situations you might write the full text and then prepare an outline of it. You might then speak from that outline on a sheet of paper and/or on a set of *PowerPoint* slides.

Establishing a Clear Structure

As with any piece of discourse that you construct, an oral presentation needs to have a clear organization that helps you to achieve your purpose. For most oral presentations, you will need to do the following:

- Construct an effective, thought-provoking, and attention-grabbing **introduction.** Remember that during your presentation, your listeners may be tempted to let their attention wander. Therefore, part of your job is to draw them in, to tell them something that will interest them, and to indicate quickly how your topic affects them.

- Let your audience know the **main point(s)** that you plan to make. Often called **forecasting,** this technique is especially important in oral presentations because your audience will not usually have something they can refer back to, as they can with a written text. If you have five main points that you want to cover, name them. Each time you move to the next point, make note of that, too ("The third point I want to make is . . ."). It often helps to provide the audience with a written outline of your points.

- Include sufficient evidence to **support** each one of your claims. You will be much more credible as a speaker if you support your claims with facts, examples, statistics, and testimony from experts.

  For more on supporting claims with evidence, see Chapters 8 and 14.

- Always be sure to **point back** to your main point so that it will be easy for your listeners to understand exactly how each point that you make or piece of information that you provide relates to your thesis.

  For more on using transitions, see Chapter 13.

- Use **visual aids** to outline the structure of your talk, if the situation calls for them. Your *PowerPoint* or overhead slides should outline the points you want to make, which you will then elaborate on (for more on using visuals, see the box that follows). The message of each visual needs to be readily apparent.

- Use your **conclusion** to summarize and emphasize your main point, and to outline briefly how everything in your presentation supports it.

VISUALIZING VARIATIONS

Effective Visual Aids

Consider the most **ineffective** ways to use overhead slides or a *PowerPoint* presentation:

- The speaker uses very small type, so any text would be hard for the audience to read.
- The speaker spends part of the designated speaking time setting up or becoming familiar with the projection equipment.
- The speaker simply reads the visuals to the audience, without adding any new information or ideas.
- The speaker uses every *PowerPoint* special effect on every slide.
- The speaker faces *away from* the audience as she reads the text on the screen.
- The speaker walks to the screen and uses a finger to point to words on the screen.

Ouch! Now contrast that to a presentation like the following:

- Each visual aid uses appropriate type sizes, colors, and graphics to illustrate the speaker's main points.
- Before the presentation the speaker learns how to use the equipment and sets it up. He or she has already made sure needed equipment is available and functional.
- The speaker talks directly to the audience, using the text on each visual only as starting points, which he or she then elaborates and explains.
- The speaker uses *PowerPoint* special effects sparingly—perhaps to help emphasize major points.
- The speaker talks directly to the audience, making eye contact, looking for signs of affirmation (smiles, nodding heads) that the audience is "getting" what the presentation is about.
- If necessary, the speaker uses an inexpensive laser pointer to point to specific words on the screen.

Now that's better, isn't it?

If you were assigned to write the academic paper in Chapter 6, focusing on whether or not college students are "slobs," for example (see p. 123), and you needed to prepare an oral presentation as part of that assignment, the slide in Figure 16.1 is one possible way for you to start a *PowerPoint* presentation on that topic.

The photograph can help you get your audience's attention and focus them on your topic. Each subsequent *PowerPoint* slide can contain the same heading, but provide the points you want to discuss in your presentation. Your second slide (Figure 16.2) might offer examples that suggest that students really are *not* slobs.

You will elaborate on these **talking points** as you make your presentation, discussing each one in detail and providing more information to support each point as you make it. For example, for the first point you make—that students help with the campus recycling program—you could add the following information:

For more on visuals for presentations, see Chapter 18.

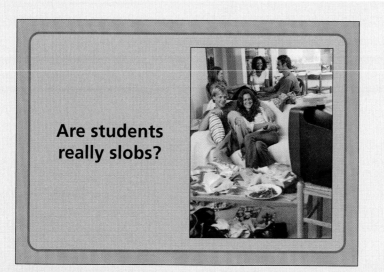

FIGURE 16.1   An Opening Slide for a Presentation

FIGURE 16.2   A Second Slide

- Student organizations collect all recycled products in classrooms and office buildings.

- Student groups make money through this recycling effort.

- Students work together in the dorms to collect recycled products.

- Several student leaders serve on the Campus Recycling Board (CRB), which is responsible for making all decisions regarding the recycling program.

As you speak, then, you will flesh out each point with specific examples that are not on the slide, but that provide information and details for your audience.

Considering Your Audience

Your *audience* is your primary concern as you plan, develop, and deliver your presentation. Every decision you make depends on your awareness of that audience, from considering what they already know about your subject to what they need to know to believe what you tell them to how you should present yourself to that audience. So consider: How do you want to come across to your audience? As informed and logical? As thoughtful? Probably. Or as someone shouting at them? Or droning at them? Probably not.

TechNote

Using graphic, audio, and video files to enhance your oral presentations is not just a good idea—in this day and age, it's often expected. Audiences are not usually critical of video that is less than perfect as long as it illustrates an important point. Before incorporating media into your oral presentation, however, use the following checklist to make sure your presentation goes smoothly:

- Examine the room, lecture hall, or space where you will be presenting— note the size and shape of the room, the seating arrangements, and the available equipment.

- If you are using video or sound media, make sure you have allowed enough time within your allotted presentation time for the video or audio clip to play.

- Keep it brief. Do not give the audience time to get uncomfortable or restless while the video or sound is playing.

- *Always* plan a fallback handout, visual chart, or anecdote in the event that the technologies available in the room suddenly fail.

- Choose music, video clips, and images that are relevant to your presentation, and that strengthen your claims and positions. (Importing the *Saturday Night Live* "More Cowbell" skit may make the audience laugh, but it will not improve your presentation unless it is directly relevant to it.)

- Practice your presentation, including the time it takes to start and stop each video or sound element.

- Ask a friend, coworker, or classmate to be your test audience and be open to this person's feedback. Video and sound elements should illustrate, add meaning to, and clarify main points, not distract or confuse your audience. If your test audience tells you that it's not clear why you have incorporated media, ask for comments and suggestions.

- Give the audience time to react. If they *do* enjoy the media you've incorporated, give them a moment or two to laugh, applaud, or just babble exuberantly before you continue with your presentation.

One way to move your audience in the direction you would like them to go is through what magician and author Steve Cohen calls "command [of] the room." He recommends that you do the following:

- Look listeners in the eye. This might seem hard to do, especially if you are speaking before a large crowd, but you can always find someone to look at and speak to directly. Find these folks in several parts of your audience, and soon it will look like you are speaking personally to *everyone* in that audience.

- Hold that eye contact longer than you might expect to.

- Speak in a conversational tone and manner.

- Remember the 45-degree rule: If you are concerned that you might "wobble" as you speak, make sure to put one foot in front of the other, at about a 45-degree angle. It's impossible to wobble when you stand that way.

Finally, always make certain that your listeners can hear you, projecting your voice to the farthest member of your audience. To make certain that the audience can hear you, begin your presentation by asking, "Can folks in the back of the room hear me if I speak at this volume?" It's also a good idea to ask people to raise their hands and cup their ears if your volume becomes so low that they can't hear you.

Eliminating the Fear of Speaking in Public

In every list of the common fears that people have, the fear of speaking in public is always at or close to the top of the list.

In fact, a bit of nervousness before a presentation can be a positive thing. If you are not nervous, you can be overconfident and not do a very effective job. Here are some techniques that can help you overcome stage fright:

- Always be overprepared. Know what you want to say. Know your subject. If you plan to use visual aids, be prepared for the unexpected— for example, a broken projector.

- Practice *out loud* several times before your presentation. The more you practice, the better your presentation will be, period. *Thinking* what you want to say and actually *saying it aloud* are really two different things. When you just think about a presentation, your mind tends to fill in the gaps and blanks and words you leave out. But when you force yourself to practice presenting out loud, you will end up with a much more thoughtful, articulate, and polished presentation.

- Time your presentation, so you will know that it fits whatever time parameters you have been given. There's nothing worse than having your host hold up a sign that says "TWO MINUTES LEFT" when you still have eight minutes of material left in your presentation.

- Another way to eliminate the fear of speaking, or at least to avoid showing that fear, is always to use a clipboard to hold your notes. A piece of paper held in your hand might shake, but a clipboard will not.

- *Visualize* making a successful presentation before you make it. *See yourself* in front of your audience. *Listen* to them applaud. *See* them nod in agreement. *See yourself speaking with them* afterwards, as they congratulate you for your effective speech. Picture what you want to happen, and it will.

- As you speak, do not let minor distractions bother you. If you hear noise from an adjoining room or from the street outside, ignore it. Do not assume that the person in the back row who appears to be laughing is laughing at you. If you hear a cell phone ring, do not stop speaking and glare at the offending party. Any number of things will distract you. You need to ignore them and concentrate on what you want to say.

Other Tips for Making Effective Oral Presentations

- Show enthusiasm.
- Use hand gestures purposefully.
- Finally, always say "thank you" at the end of your presentation. You will be surprised at how many speakers do *not* use this ending, and you will find it to be surprisingly effective (and thoughtful).

ACTIVITY

Making an Oral Presentation

Using one of the papers that you wrote for Part 2 or 3 of this textbook, prepare and deliver an oral presentation. Revise and adapt your paper to suit your new medium and purpose, by establishing a clear structure, using effective visual aids, and considering your audience, according to the strategies described in this chapter.

If you have a video camera and can record your presentation so you can play it back and critique yourself, so much the better. But in any case when you practice, think of your work as *rehearsal:* Go through your presentation from start to finish, without stopping. If you get tongue-tied or drop your notes or the projector does not work, just continue as if you were actually giving your speech.

This is the kind of work actors or professional entertainers do to get good—try it!

PART FIVE

Technologies for Effective Communication

Choosing a Medium, Genre, and Technology for Your Communication

As long as humans have recorded their experiences, they have used technologies that act as tools to record their ideas.

A portion of a prehistoric cave painting from caves in Lascaux, France, the image that opens this chapter is approximately 17,000 years old. While we know little about the person or people who made this image, we can surmise that painting was a useful technology for communicating with the intended audience. We do know that this medium (painting on a cave wall) allowed ancient humans to record images that might be decorative, might be symbolic, might tell a story, or might have performed a combination of these functions. Although the form of communication—or *genre*—this cave painting was created in has been lost, its medium is certainly durable, having survived for thousands of years.

Communication technologies are as varied as paint on a cave wall or a canvas, a piece of chalk, a ballpoint pen, or a word-processing program. Whatever a writer's purpose, the availability of a particular tool often helps to determine what **medium**—method of delivery—that writer uses to communicate. Depending on the tools at a writer's disposal, he or she might write a message on a chalkboard, print it on paper, or publish it in an electronic format such as a newsgroup posting or a Web page.

When writers use a specific communication technology, they need to understand the impact that the technology will have on that communication. You do not always have a choice of which technology or medium you can use, but when you do, you need to understand the potential and limitations of each and you need to make your choice in a rhetorically sound way. This chapter will provide guidelines for choosing the most effective genre and medium for your written work, a brief discussion of your options for publishing and designing documents (more detailed guidelines for designing documents are provided in Chapter 18), and an overview of the technologies for computer-mediated communication.

Communication Technologies

As we have seen, a **communication technology** is not necessarily an electronic device. Because writing is itself a technology, every tool that we use to write is a kind of communication technology. Some communication technologies, such as word-processing software, encourage revision while others, such as pen and paper, act to discourage it. On the other hand, a handwritten letter, while difficult to revise, may make a more personal connection with your reader than a word-processed document. And pens and note paper are easier to carry than laptop computers and do not require an electrical outlet, a battery, or an Internet connection to function.

Writing is inextricably linked to the technology that produces it. Understanding your own process and what communication technologies will work most effectively and efficiently for you in a given writing situation is important to your success as a writer.

For an overview of technologies for computer-mediated communication, see pages 462–69.

Publishing Your Work

When you write letters or even when you write for an academic purpose, you are usually writing to one person or to a small number of people. As a result, your communication is generally private—between you and that small audience. When you *publish* your written work, however, you make it public. You can publish your writing in a variety of ways, from printing a newsletter and distributing copies to a limited group of people to constructing a page on the World Wide Web that is accessible to anyone in the world who has a computer connected to the Internet. Although publishing your work can be exciting, it also involves both responsibilities and risks.

As recently as the 1970s, the only way to publish a piece of writing was in some kind of print medium. Publishing meant typesetting a manuscript and reproducing it on a printing press, a process that was both time-consuming and expensive. With the advent of the Internet, however and specifically the hypertext environment of the World Wide Web, today's students have technology and publishing options and opportunities that were unheard of in the past. Now anyone who constructs a Web page on a server connected to the Internet publishes a document that is available to the entire world.

If you publish to a broad audience, and especially if you publish on the Web, you need to remember that those who view your work will be forming an opinion of you and your ideas that is based solely on what they see and read. Comments made in haste, without thought and reflection, can sometimes come back to "haunt" their authors. Members of your audience will also respond in some way to the design of your document or Web page—to the colors, the typeface, the size of type, how items are arranged on the page or screen. If you make assertions, they will expect you to provide proof. As with any other form of written communication, they will also expect you to follow the conventions of spelling, grammar, punctuation, and mechanics. If you do not, you will weaken the credibility of your document or Web page.

Whether you publish in print or in an electronic medium, you will enhance your credibility with your audience if you choose an appropriate genre for your message.

Selecting a Genre and a Medium

At the beginning of any writing task that has an audience beyond their immediate circle, then, writers need to decide which established form of writing, or **genre,** to write in and the best medium in which to publish their work.

So how should you make these decisions? You need to consider carefully the audience, the context, and the purpose for your writing. For example, if you are writing a set of instructions for the operation of a propane camp stove, you can expect that the people who will read those instructions will usually be outdoors and often in isolated locations. The instructions will be more useful and effective, then, if they are published in print and in a size that is easy to pack and carry. On the other hand, if you are providing information about the academic support resources available on your college campus and most of the students on the campus have high-speed Internet access, the best way to reach this audience may be to publish the information on a Web site. You may even decide to use sound, video, or animation.

Deciding on a Genre for Your Work

Because the genre you choose is usually determined by your purpose, it is a rhetorical decision. If your purpose is to obtain funding for a project or permission to implement a change, you will usually write a proposal (a type of writing covered in Chapter 11), a relatively easy decision. However, if your purpose is to provide information about a project you are working on, you have many choices. You might write a formal, authoritative report, called a white paper, a brochure, or a set of frequently asked questions (FAQs) among other genres for informative writing (for more on informative writing, see Chapter 6). Determining what genre you use in this situation will depend on not only your purpose but also your audience. Ultimately, you will have to decide which genre will be most effective for the people you are trying to reach. (For more on some common genres, see Appendix C.)

Once you have decided on the genre (say you decide on a brochure), you will have to decide which medium will be most effective in presenting that brochure to your audience (you might provide it in print form and as a PDF file on the Web, for example).

Deciding Whether to Use Print, Electronic, or Oral Media

Although in-class essay examinations are usually written by hand, few academic papers are handwritten these days. Usually, you need to turn in an assignment printed in type on paper or in some kind of electronic medium. Often you have no choice; your instructor will specify a medium and format. However, in other situations, your instructor might not specify the medium and format and, instead, expects you to make the proper rhetorical choice.

Because the same information can usually be provided in both print and electronic forms, the medium you choose often depends on how that information is going to be used. Consider how each one also helps you accomplish different tasks better than the other.

Features of Paper and Electronic Documents

Criteria	Medium: Print on paper	Medium: Electronic
Portability	Easily portable	Needs devices for portability such as a laptop, PDA, or Smartphone.
Control of design	Relatively easy to control	Less easy to control—issues can be screen size and resolution
Ability to search	More difficult to search—needs a good index	Easy to search—can use hot-linked keywords
Transportability	Needs to be carried or mailed over distance	Can be sent almost instantly over the Internet
Revision	Once printed, paper is difficult to revise. You must go back to the electronic version	Most electronic documents are easy to revise

Paper documents work best when you are providing information in a narrative or sequential organization. Much academic writing, which is often argumentative, works well in print form because argument, which involves presenting and supporting a thesis, is best presented as a linear sequence of points. On the other hand, if you are providing information that does not need to be read sequentially or chronologically, then hypertextual electronic formats, in which readers can use links to move easily from one section to another, offer a distinct advantage over paper documents.

WRITING ACTIVITY

Selecting a Medium

With several of your classmates, consider the following writing tasks. For each one, decide what medium might be appropriate to get your message across to the audience indicated.

- A group consisting of you and your neighbors wants to collect comments and information on a problem with an illegal dump near a school and present them to the town council.

- To increase public awareness of the different organizations on campus, your group has been asked to send information to various civic clubs such as the Rotary, Kiwanis, and Elks. With the material will be a request for donations for your school organizations.

Considering Design

In addition to choosing a genre and medium for your work, you will need to decide on a design for it. We know that many people are visual learners: They seem to absorb information more readily when it is presented in a diagram or a chart. And we know that how a document (an advertisement, for instance) looks will affect our response to it. Chapter 18 covers the principles of good design and provides guidelines for incorporating visual material effectively in your writing.

No matter what design functions you use, your goal in using them should be to make your message more effective.

Technologies for Computer-Mediated Communication

Your choice of a medium for your work may depend not only on the writing situation and the genre you have chosen, but also on the availability of computers and the Internet to you and your audience and your—and their—comfort level with using them.

When you think about the way you use computers during your writing process, you probably think about using word-processing software to compose, revise, and edit your various drafts. While these uses are important, they are not the only way that computers can help you during your writing process. You might use a computer to find information on the Internet or to access a variety of library databases. In addition, you can use word-processing software at other stages of the process besides composing, such as when you are taking notes or using brainstorming, listing, and other invention strategies. You can even use other technologies, such as e-mail and instant messaging, for exploring topics and sharing ideas and drafts with peer reviewers.

The following technologies give you additional tools and options for writing and publishing your work in different media.

E-mail

Many of us use **e-mail** frequently. Familiar though it may be, e-mail is a powerful technology. To make the best use of it, you need to be aware of some basic rhetorical issues.

- **Tone:** E-mail messages range from very informal to formal, depending on your audience. If you are writing to a close friend, a family member, or even a classmate, you may feel comfortable using non-standard words such as "gonna" or "dunno" or acronyms such as BTW (by the way), or ASAP (as soon as possible). However, using non-standard language in your e-mail correspondence with supervisors, instructors, or people you don't know may harm your credibility with your audience.

- **Audience:** While you may send an e-mail to a specific person, *that* person might forward your e-mail or include it in another e-mail to someone you don't even know, so be aware of and cautious about what you say.

- **Ethos:** Your e-mail address will be seen by everyone you send e-mail to. If you send e-mail from work or school, your address is often assigned to you—and usually consists of a form of your name. However, when you set up a personal e-mail account, you can choose your own address, which will therefore say something about you. Like a vanity license plate on a car, addresses that are overly cute (FroggyBoy), might be fine for your closest friends but are likely to be highly inappropriate in a professional environment. Consider using different addresses for different purposes.

For more on e-mail as a genre, see Appendix C, page A-22.

Threaded Discussions

A **threaded discussion** is simply e-mail that, instead of being sent to individual addresses, is posted on the virtual equivalent of a bulletin board, usually as part of a Web site. Participants simply add their comments on a particular topic in the appropriate place—either as an extension of a previous message or as a new topic or "thread." The advantage is that everyone who is participating in the discussion can see what the other participants are saying.

Threaded discussions can help instructors and students perform a variety of writing tasks. If the class is being offered entirely online, threaded discussions are a substitute for in-class discussions. If the class meets face-to-face, then threaded discussions are one way to work collaboratively on a class assignment or participate in a discussion outside of class.

Synchronous Chat

At its most basic level, **synchronous chat** is simply a way to communicate with someone else in real time using text. Two types of synchronous chat that may be familiar to you are the virtual text-based worlds in MUDs (Multi User Domains) and MOOs (MUDs Object Oriented). These days most people who use synchronous chat are likely to be using some kind of instant messaging (IM).

Although instant messaging and other forms of synchronous chat are a great way to communicate with distant friends or relatives, you can also

For a definition of brainstorming, see Chapter 3, page 34.

use the same technology for a variety of group or team activities. Synchronous chat provides an incredibly powerful environment for brainstorming. Because most chat software has a logging function, you can keep a written record of your conversation or brainstorming session and use it later in your writing.

Blogs

TechNote Use the barter system to discover how you and your classmates can help one another become more proficient with various software applications:

1. Make a list of all of the computer programs (software applications) you have used.

2. Beside each one, rate your familiarity with the application on a scale of 1 to 5. Give a rating of "1" to programs you have opened and used only once or twice. Give a "5" to programs you use frequently, and whose features and flaws you know well.

3. Now list all of the programs you rate either 4 or 5, ranking them in order from the most difficult or complicated to the least difficult or complicated.

4. Make another list of the programs you rated 5, ranking them from most to least popular among your classmates (this will be a guess, but it can help you think through what kind of knowledge you have to share vs. what kind of knowledge will be in demand).

5. Compare your list with those of your classmates, and agree to help one another with programs that you would like to learn, or learn to use more effectively.

For more on effective document design and the use of visuals, see Chapter 18, pages 470–98.

Blogs or **Web logs** are a type of online journal. Like pen and paper journals, blogs often feature personal, reflective writing, but blogs are posted on the Web and are therefore public documents. Because blogs are consciously written as public documents, they are often about subjects that might interest large numbers of people such as politics or sports or entertainers. However, they tend to retain their personal flavor because there is seldom, if ever, any accountability for what gets written in a blog. While some blogs are the work of a single author, others are interactive. They allow, and even encourage, multiple writers to take part in the conversation. An Internet site like Globe of Blogs (www.globeofblogs.com) lists thousands of blogs on a wide variety of topics and interests.

Word-Processing Software

Word processors such as Microsoft *Word, OpenOffice,* and *WordPerfect* have always performed four basic functions: inserting text, deleting text, copying and moving text, and formatting text. One important advantage that word processors offer is that they are a very forgiving technology. Changes are incredibly easy to make—whether you spot a misspelled word or need to rephrase a sentence or rewrite a paragraph. This ability to revise texts easily opens up all kinds of possibilities for writers. Major revisions become easier because moving chunks of text from one place to another takes only a few simple manipulations of the mouse. Editing your text becomes easier because you can make minor changes with just a few keystrokes instead of retyping the entire paper. In addition, other functions allow a writer or writers to edit a text and peer reviewers to make comments on it.

Finally, the options for designing a word-processed document are increasing all the time. While all documents need to be well written, their content can no longer be divorced from their format, and readers now expect word-processed documents to look professional. Formatting options include, but are not limited to, type fonts in different sizes, tables, boxes, and visual effects such as numbered and bulleted lists. If a writer needs to include graphics, they can be inserted directly into the word-processed document.

WRITING ACTIVITY

Using Editing Features

Using whatever word-processing software you have available, investigate some of its editing features. Is there a "track-changes" feature? If so, try it. Use the help function to learn how to turn this feature on and off. Is there a "comment" feature?

Working in teams of two, each student should write a paragraph or two on what you think is the most interesting or challenging feature of your word-processing program. Save your writing as an electronic file and then share it with your teammate. Edit your teammate's file, using the track-changes and comment features.

Peer-Review Applications

As increasing numbers of writers use computer software to collaborate in both educational and workplace environments, the software that facilitates collaborative writing keeps improving. The programs that writers use for this purpose fall into two distinct categories: collaborative tools built into standard word-processing programs, as discussed on page 464 in the preceding section, and web-based editing programs.

One type of Web-based editing program is a Wiki: software that allows for open editing of Web documents. When a document is placed in a Wiki, it can be edited by anyone who views it through any Web browser, using any computer operating system. Some Wikis, however, require that users be logged in before they are allowed to edit a document. A Wiki is useful when writing teams work over distance and do not necessarily share the same computer operating systems or Web browsing software. This flexibility makes Wikis useful for student projects. However, since a Wiki is a Web page, unless it is password protected or sits on an intranet (a private computer network), any document in a Wiki becomes accessible to anyone in the world with Internet access.

One Web-based program that allows peers to comment on your work is available to you as part of the Online Learning Center for this text. This software permits you and the other members of your assigned peer group to make comments about one another's writing and to view and respond to those comments.

Graphics Software

Today, it is possible to enhance your documents using a variety of visual information: tables, charts, and graphs as well as photos, drawings, and other

TechNote Computers are like toothbrushes: people really don't like to share. Letting someone use your computer can result in downloads and icons you don't want or need and resource issues that can mean an expensive visit to a tech support service. It's better to limit the number of people who use your college computer and to resist the urge to use someone else's computer. Most colleges provide computer labs on campus, and the staff at the computer lab can usually help you with any problems that arise.

visual images. Although you can design some tables in your word-processing program and graphs and charts using a spreadsheet, other images need to be digitized (that is, put into a form that can be read by a computer) in order to include them as part of your computer document. The easiest way to render many visuals in a digital format is to use a graphics program such as *Paint-ShopPro*, *Illustrator*, or *FreeHand*. If you are taking photographs yourself, you can use a digital camera. If you have a printed image, however, you can easily digitize it by using a scanner.

Once the image is digitized, you can manipulate it in a variety of ways by using graphic editing software such as *PhotoShop*. Image-editing software allows you to change the size or resolution of the digital image, crop out unneeded elements, or change the contrast so that the image becomes clearer. However, image editing software also makes it possible to change images inappropriately. Just because it is easy to change a photo does not mean that you *should* change it. The ease with which we can now alter images raises serious ethical questions.

We have all seen examples of famous photographs that have been altered to include a person who was not in the original image, a relatively easy change to make with the right software. Although some doctored photos might be considered funny, others are fabricated with the intention of misleading readers. For example, a fake photo of a young John Kerry attending an anti-war rally with Jane Fonda surfaced during the 2004 presidential campaign season. Figure 17.1 shows the fake photo, along with the two photos that were combined to construct the fake.

The fake photo enraged many people because John Kerry, who was using his status as a Vietnam War veteran as part of his presidential campaign, is standing next to Jane Fonda, well known for her controversial visit to North Vietnam during that war. Perhaps not surprisingly, this fake photo was cited as evidence that Kerry was unpatriotic. Clearly, some people were fooled by the fake.

A WRITER'S RESPONSIBILITIES
Using Image-Editing Software Ethically

If you are thinking of altering a photo, the first question you need to ask yourself has both ethical and legal implications: Do I have the right to change someone else's image without that person's permission? Unless you already own the image or have the owner's permission to use it and alter it, making changes may very well violate the creator's copyright. Because you will need the owner's permission to use the image, make sure you also get permission to change the image if you would like to do so. You may think that cropping out what you consider to be unnecessary parts of a photo might not be an issue, but the copyright owner might see the issue differently. Second, you need to be sure that by making changes you are not misrepresenting your subject or misleading your readers.

Fonda Speaks To Vietnam Veterans At Anti-War Rally

Actress And Anti-War Activist Jane Fonda Speaks to a crowd of Vietnam Veterans as Activist and former Vietnam Vet John Kerry (LEFT) listens and prepares to speak next concerning the war in Vietnam (AP Photo)

FIGURE 17.1 This photograph of John Kerry and Jane Fonda, supposedly appearing together at an anti-war rally, is fake. It was fabricated by combining the two photographs shown below it.

Desktop Publishing Software

Desktop publishing software such as *Quark, Pagemaker,* or *InDesign* allows writers to produce documents on their personal computers that are ready to be professionally printed. While people who are comfortable with computers and have some training in layout and design can readily do some simple tasks in desktop publishing software, most people need either training or practice to get comfortable in its use. Most desktop publishing software programs are designed to construct short documents, and people often use them to prepare flyers, brochures, newsletters, and similar publications. Such software gives you control over your document, including more precision in placing and manipulating images and more control over *leading,* the spacing between the lines, and *kerning,* the spacing between letters.

Presentation Software

Chapter 16 covers strategies for effective oral presentations

At some point in their careers, almost all professionals make oral presentations, and you will most likely be asked to make presentations to some of your classmates while you are still a student. Sometimes professionals need to make a presentation to an audience of peers or higher-level employees. At other times they may need to do a sales presentation, or present a new idea or report on a project in a more informal setting. Most professional presenters include some kind of visual component in their presentations in order to help keep their audience's attention focused on the presentation. In the past, presenters often used large charts or posters, slides, or overhead transparencies. Now, most professionals use presentation software such as *PowerPoint* to complement their oral presentations. Presentation software allows you to format slides for a presentation easily and professionally. If you do not have access to *PowerPoint,* you can use *Impress,* a compatible, open source (free) program that is part of the *OpenOffice* desktop software suite. *Google Docs,* another free Web-based presentation program, allows you to import *PowerPoint* files and easily share and collaborate on presentations online.

For more on oral presentations and presentation software, see Chapter 16.

When using presentation software, you need to remember that your slides should complement your presentation, not be its focus. When you give a presentation, you want your listeners to pay the most attention to what you say, not to the slides being shown behind you. If you use a graphic, the graphic should add to, not detract from, the content of the slide. Think of your bullet points as "talking points" or even as hyperlinks. What you actually say is the equivalent of clicking on a link in a Web page for more information.

Technologies for Constructing Web Pages

Web pages are computer files that can be viewed using software called a **browser.** Examples of browsers are *Internet Explorer, Netscape,* and *Firefox.* Web pages are coded using hypertext markup language (html). The html coding places information in the document that allows the browser to display the page properly. There are many ways to construct a Web page:

- Use the "save as a Web page" option in your word-processing software. This option has the advantage of being easy and is appropriate for very simple, straightforward Web pages. For more complex pages, you may need to choose one of the other options.

- "Hand code" the html (this means writing the actual mark-up tags in a text editor like *Notepad* or *TextEdit*). This option gives you more control over the design of your site, but it is time-consuming.
- Use an html editor like *Dreamweaver*. Because html has become increasingly complex, most professionals now use html editors.
- Use a Web-based page construction tool like *Google Page Creator*. Web-based tools usually have both visual (word processor-like) and html editor modes. They also have the added advantage of instantly providing you with an opportunity to view your page exactly as it will appear online before you publish it.

Constructing effective Web pages involves making appropriate rhetorical choices, just as with any other kind of document. While you need to be sensitive to the look and feel of your Web pages, ultimately what will matter most is their content. The most important question will be, "How effectively am I getting my message across to the audience that I am targeting?"

For more on writing Web pages, see Appendix C.

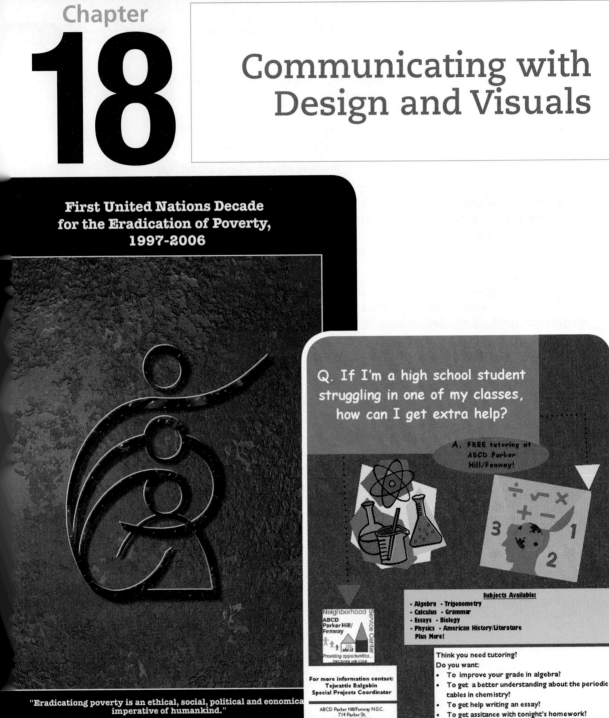

First United Nations Decade for the Eradication of Poverty, 1997-2006

"Eradicationg poverty is an ethical, social, political and eonomical imperative of humankind."

Millennium development goal:

"...To halve, by the year 2015, the proportion of the world's people whose income is less than one dollar a day

Q. If I'm a high school student struggling in one of my classes, how can I get extra help?

A. FREE tutoring at ABCD Parker Hill/Fenway!

Neighborhood Service Center
ABCD Parker Hill/Fenway
Providing opportunities... because we care

For more information contact:
Tejwattie Balgobin
Special Projects Coordinator

ABCD Parker Hill/Fenway N.S.C.
714 Parker St.
Roxbury, MA 02120

Phone: 617-445-6000 ext. 232
Fax: 617-445-6005
Email: balgobin@bostonabcd.org

Subjects Available:
- Algebra · Trigonometry
- Calculus · Grammar
- Essays · Biology
- Physics · American History/Literature
Plus More!

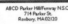

Think you need tutoring?
Do you want:
- To improve your grade in algebra?
- To get a better understanding about the periodic tables in chemistry?
- To get help writing an essay?
- To get assitance with tonight's homework?

If you answered yes to any of the above questions you may qualify for our FREE tutoring program! Call us today for more information!

The two documents that open this chapter combine both written and visual elements. To craft a poster like the one for the International Day for the Eradication of Poverty, a writer needs specialized graphics software, which is commonly available in university or college computing labs. To design a flyer similar to the one for the tutoring program for high school students offered by the Fenway Neighborhood Service Center, however, a writer can use any of several widely available word-processing software programs, which provide graphics such as the image of the beakers and the shading in the text box. Whether you are designing an elaborate document like the poster or a simpler document like the flyer, you can use the same standard design principles that are the focus of this chapter.

Any time you apply the principles of design, and any time you decide to use images in your own texts, you need to consider your writing situation and make rhetorical choices. Here are some questions to consider:

- What are you trying to accomplish with your text, and how might your design and images (photographs, charts, diagrams, tables) help you achieve your goals?

- Who is your audience? What kind(s) of design elements and images (or data presented in graphic form) might interest and appeal to your audience? What might make it easier for your readers to understand the information you are providing?

- What is the context in which you are writing? How does that context limit the kinds of design choices you might make and the images you might use? Many academic writing situations, for example, require the use of specific styles such as the one recommended by the Modern Language Association (MLA).

- How might the available technology affect the design and image choices you make? If you do not have access to a color printer, for example, that obviously restricts your use of color in your document.

In addition to discussing the principles of document design that you can apply to any document that you prepare, this chapter offers guidelines for choosing suitable visuals for your paper.

For a discussion of reading visuals critically, see Chapter 2.

Principles of Document Design

Whatever their rhetorical choices might be, writers can use the design principles of proximity, contrast, alignment, and repetition to craft more effective texts.

Proximity

Whenever you vary the amount of space between and around text elements so that related items are close to one another and unrelated items are separated from one another, you are employing the principle of **proximity.** For instance, consider the following three versions of a shopping list:

Version A	Version B	Version C
wireless network router	wireless network router	wireless network router
water colors	wireless mouse	wireless mouse
English dictionary	blank CDs	blank CDs
blank CDs	English dictionary	
pastels	thesaurus	English dictionary
thesaurus	book of quotations	thesaurus
wireless mouse	oil paints	book of quotations
oil paints	water colors	
book of quotations	pastels	oil paints
		water colors
		pastels

Which list would make it easier for you to find these nine items in the shortest amount of time?

For some documents, such as brochures and newsletters, writers can also use borders and color to group common items and separate them from dissimilar items. (Color type may not be appropriate for many academic papers.) Most word processors allow you to add these elements to your document.

As illustrated by the flyer advertising tutoring services at the beginning of this chapter, borders can also make sections of your written text stand out.

Contrast

You can use **contrast** by employing design features such as bold or italic type, underlining, indentation, and color to indicate the hierarchy of importance among text elements and to create certain effects. For instance, you can use contrast to make headings at different levels of importance visually distinct.

Color can also add visual interest and contrast to your texts. If you use more than one color in a document, however, consult the color wheel shown in Figure 18.1 to determine which colors work best together.

As the color wheel indicates, the **primary colors** are red, yellow, and blue. The **secondary colors,** located at points halfway between the three primary colors on the wheel, are formed by combining primary colors: Red and yellow combine to make orange; blue and yellow combine to make green; and red and blue combine to make violet. Other colors are formed by combining primary colors with secondary colors.

Complementary colors are directly across from each other on the wheel—for instance, yellow and violet, red and green, and blue and orange. Placing complementary colors next to each other has the effect of **jarring** the reader. Placing adjacent colors together, on the other hand, has a **pleasing** effect. Pairing colors separated by two or three positions on the color wheel can have a **vivid** or **bold** effect.

Colors are sometimes considered to be "warm" and "cool." Warm colors—red, orange, and yellow—are energetic and bold. Cool colors—

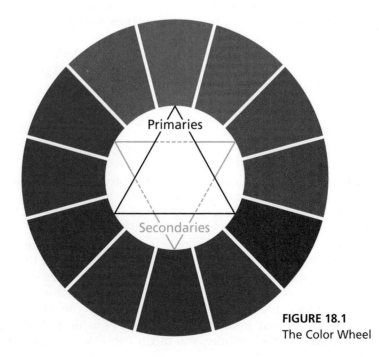

FIGURE 18.1
The Color Wheel

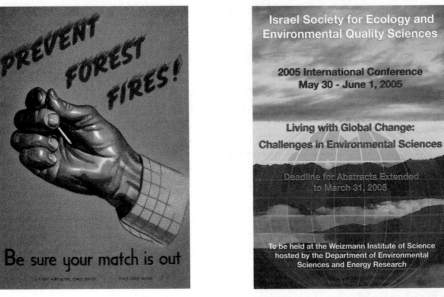

FIGURE 18.2   A Poster Using Warm Colors   **FIGURE 18.3**   A Poster Using Cool Colors

green, blue, and violet—sometimes have a soothing, calming effect. Consider the poster shown in Figure 18.2 above. Two warm colors, yellow and red, appear together in this poster. Because red and yellow are also both primary colors, the red text on the yellow background is especially eye-catching.

Now consider another poster, shown in Figure 18.3, this one announcing a conference on ecology and environment. The background for this poster includes green and blue, both cool colors that have a calming effect.

Alignment

Writers also use **alignment** to indicate relationships among text elements and make their documents easier for readers to process. As readers of English, we are accustomed to text that is aligned on the left side of the page. Other alignments are possible, however, and you can vary alignments to achieve different effects.

Unless your text is very brief, your best choice for most academic writing is usually to align your text at the left margin to make it easier for your readers to process. For other contexts—for example, for a professional report— you might align your text at both margins, or *justify* it, for a professional look; most books and periodicals make extensive use of this type of alignment. If your text is short and you want to achieve an eye-catching effect on a poster or a brochure, you might consider using right or center alignment.

Repetition (or Consistency)

When you use **repetition** or **consistency,** you apply the same design features to text elements with similar rhetorical functions. The general principle is that a writer should use design features consistently throughout the text. For example, note how the consistent use of bullets in front of the items in our grocery list sets them off even more for readers.

SHOPPING LIST

Computer Store

- Wireless network router
- Wireless mouse
- Blank CDs

Bookstore

- English dictionary
- Thesaurus
- Book of quotations

Art Supply Store

- Oil paints
- Water colors
- Pastels

There are many ways to follow the principle of repetition or consistency in a document: following a documentation style accurately; using typefaces and fonts consistently; using a carefully developed heading structure; and using bullets, numbers, and graphics consistently.

USING A SINGLE DOCUMENTATION FORMAT

Chapter 20 provides guidelines for the systems for citing sources and formatting academic papers recommended by the Modern Language Association (MLA) and the American Psychological Association (APA). Following a single, consistent format throughout your paper makes it easier for readers to determine the type of source you are citing (a book or a periodical article, for instance), find it in your works-cited or references list, and consult it themselves if they choose to do so.

USING TYPEFACES AND TYPE SIZES CONSISTENTLY

A typeface is a design for the letters of the alphabet, numbers, and other symbols. A type font consists of all of the different styles and sizes that one typeface is available in. For most academic documents, you probably need to use only one or possibly two typefaces. Typefaces belong to one of two general categories: **serif** and **sans serif.** A serif typeface has small strokes or extenders at the top and the bottom of the letter, and letters may vary in thickness. Sans serif ("without serif") type has no small strokes or extenders, and the letters have a uniform thickness. Usually, serif type is considered easier to read, especially in longer texts. For that reason, most newspapers, magazines, and books, including this one, use serif type for body text and sans serif type in headings and other kinds of displayed type, for contrast. Here are some examples of serif and sans serif type:

Serif Typefaces	Sample Sentence
Times New Roman	Carefully select the typeface that you use in your texts because the type can affect how easily readers can process your text.
Courier New	Carefully select the typeface that you use in your texts because the type can affect how easily readers can process your text.

Sans Serif Type	Sample Sentence
Arial	Carefully select the typeface that you use in your texts because the type can affect how easily readers can process your text.
Century Gothic	Carefully select the typeface that you use in your texts because the type can affect how easily readers can process your text.

All of the samples above are in 12-point type, which is a standard size for academic papers (a point is equivalent to 1/72 of an inch). Notice that different typefaces take up different amounts of space. In some writing situations, space costs money; if so, you should consider a smaller face such as Times New Roman or Arial over a larger one such as Courier or Century Gothic. In other situations, such as a slide presentation, you may need a larger face because it will be easier to read from a distance.

Most computers offer a wide range of typefaces to choose from, including unusual and ornate varieties. You should use these typefaces sparingly, however, because they can be difficult to read, especially for longer texts.

USING HEADINGS CONSISTENTLY

Headings signal the content of your paper and help readers understand its organization. When headings are worded and styled consistently, readers know which sections are at a higher or lower level of generality than others. You can use different sizes of type; different typefaces; and underlining, bold, and italics to signal different levels of generality. When you use headings to signal different levels of generality, it is important that you treat headings at the same level the same way—the same font size and style (for example, 12 point Times New Roman), the same location on the page (for example, at the left margin, centered, or indented), and the same capitalization.

You should also use parallel structure for all headings at a given level, as in the following example:

Parts of the City
    Shopping in the Business District
    Discovering the Residential Areas
    Enjoying the Waterfront
    Relaxing in the Parks

TechNote

Projects written for digital media should integrate visual and graphical elements in ways that make logical and intuitive sense to your audience. Here are some suggestions:

- Break up long blocks of text into paragraphs or boxes.
- Choose color schemes that are easy on the readers' eyes.
- Create labels and captions that clarify visual information.
- Use elements that explain and contextualize images, video, and sound—don't assume that the image, video, or audio by itself will indicate to online visitors the point you are trying to get across.
- Be prepared to prove ownership and/or rights to the media and images you have incorporated.

USING BULLETS, NUMBERS, ROMAN NUMERALS, OR LETTERS CONSISTENTLY

You can use bullets, numbers, Roman numerals, or letters—or some combination of these elements—for several purposes. Most frequently, they are used to indicate items in a list or an outline. Any of these markers can be effective for a short list of items, as shown on page 478.

If you are presenting steps in a process or items in a certain order, numbers are usually a better choice, and a combination of Roman numerals, letters, and numbers is standard in outlines. Bullets can be used to set off the

Bullets	Numbers (with Bullets)	Roman Numerals (with Letters)	Letters (with Numbers)
Car Models	Car Models	Car Models	Car Models
• Ford	1. Ford	I. Ford	A. Ford
• Taurus	• Taurus	A. Taurus	1. Taurus
• Focus	• Focus	B. Focus	2. Focus
• Mustang	• Mustang	C. Mustang	3. Mustang
• Chevrolet	2. Chevrolet	II. Chevrolet	B. Chevrolet
• Impala	• Impala	A. Impala	1. Impala
• Malibu	• Malibu	B. Malibu	2. Malibu
• Corvette	• Corvette	C. Corvette	3. Corvette

For more on how to construct an outline, see Chapter 13, pages 414–16.

items in a list effectively, although they can be problematic in longer lists because readers may have to count down the list of items if they need to discuss a particular point in the list ("Joe, look at the fourteenth bullet item in the list" or "Joe, look at the item that begins with . . ."). Of course, you should use bullets, numbers, Roman numerals, and/or letters consistently throughout a text to make it easier for readers to process your writing.

USING WHITE SPACE CONSISTENTLY

White space is any part of a document that is not covered by type or graphics. The margins at the edges of a document are white space, as are the spaces between lines and above and below titles, headings, and other elements. Use white space consistently throughout a document. You should always leave the same amount of space above headings at the same level. (If you are using MLA or APA style, you will need to follow the guidelines provided by the style you are following for margins and spacing—see Chapter 20.)

USING GRAPHICS EFFECTIVELY

Graphics—photographs, charts, drawings, diagrams, cartoons, graphs, and tables—can appear in academic papers as well as a number of other types of documents that you might prepare. The different kinds of graphics that a writer might choose are discussed on pages 480–94. Generally, you should use the same kind of graphic to illustrate similar points or concepts. To achieve consistency, you need to consider the following:

- What you want to accomplish with the graphic
- The overall look of the image
- How the graphics are marked in the text with labels and captions
- How you should introduce the graphics within your text

Select the kind of graphic that best accomplishes your purpose—what you are trying to show to your readers. To most effectively indicate the composition of a pizza, for example, you might choose a pie chart like that shown in Figure 18.4, which shows the ingredients used to make a sausage and mushroom pizza weighing 1.6 kg. The sum of the numbers shown equals 1.6 kg, the weight of the pizza. The size of each slice shows us the fraction of the pizza made up from that ingredient.

Figure 18.5 shows the same data but given as a bar graph—as you can tell, the bar graph does not explain or present the information as effectively as the pie chart does.

To present graphics effectively, follow these guidelines:

- Give the graphics in your document a consistent look. For example, use one-color or multi-color drawings rather than mixing one-color and multi-color drawings. If you use multiple colors, use the same ones in each graphic (for more on the use of color, see pp. 473–74).

FIGURE 18.4 An Example of a Pie Chart Showing the Composition of Pizza

Source: Math League[1]

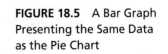

FIGURE 18.5 A Bar Graph Presenting the Same Data as the Pie Chart

---

[1] Complete source information for the figures in this section can be found in the Credits on pages C-2–C-3.

- Be sure you introduce and explain each graphic, just as you need to do with each quotation you insert into your text. If you do not do so, then it is possible that your readers will not "see" the image in the same way that you do. They may not understand why it is there or what it is intended to convey. For the bar graph in Figure 18.5, for example, you would want both to introduce it before putting it into your text ("This next graph shows how mushrooms make up the least amount, in weight, of the ingredients in a typical pizza") and to follow the image with an explanation of how the bar graph connects to your topic.

- Place graphics in a document strategically. To help your readers connect your words with your graphics, place each visual as close to the text discussion that refers to it as possible. If you are following APA style, however, you have the option of placing visuals at the end of your paper.

Common Kinds of Visual Texts

When you consider adding a visual image or images to a document, you should do so to help accomplish your overall purpose: to persuade or inform your readers, to help demonstrate something to your readers, or to entertain your readers. Do not add a visual just to have a picture or chart or table in your text; rather, use it as a way to support your thesis and achieve your goal for that piece of writing. Visuals such as tables, bar and line graphs, drawings, diagrams, maps, and cartoons can help you in various ways.

Tables

Tables organize information in columns and rows for readers, helping them make comparisons between or among pieces of information or sets of numerical data. Consider, for instance, the following table, which compares cereal use across many countries. This table shows what percentage of the total domestic cereal supply was used for direct human consumption, was used for feeding animals, or was wasted.

The same data given in a paragraph would be difficult to compare. By reviewing the table, however, readers can easily make comparisons up and down rows, across columns, and across rows and columns. Notice how the table focuses on cereal as food for humans rather than feed for cattle or waste by listing countries in descending order in terms of the percentage of cereal that is used for human food.

USING TABLES EFFECTIVELY IN YOUR TEXTS

Word-processing programs will usually allow you to format information into tables automatically—consult the Help screen for the program you are using. Spreadsheet programs also allow you to construct tables.

Domestic Cereal Supply: Food, Feed, Waste

	Food	Feed	Waste
Sri Lanka	92.2	0.5	4.7
Pakistan	88.9	3.5	2.8
India	88.0	0.9	4.4
Viet Nam	84.6	2.6	7.8
Nepal	83.9	2.2	11.0
China	72.3	18.5	5.2
Egypt	70.3	18.0	9.0
Philippines	68.2	23.9	1.1
Korea DPR	68.0	6.1	6.8
World	**57.1**	**32.5**	**4.7**
Malaysia	54.7	40.4	2.8
Korea Rep.	50.3	31.5	2.7
Japan	44.3	44.2	0.8
Germany	23.9	59.1	2.8
U.S.A.	12.6	68.5	0.2
Denmark	8.8	80.3	3.7

Source: FAOSTAT, 1997

To decide if a table will be appropriate for your purpose and audience, answer the following questions:

- Do I have data or information that could appear in tabular form?
- How would a table help me organize this data or information for readers?
- How do I want or need to organize the data or information in the table so that readers can find the information they need, or that I want them to see?

Bar and Line Graphs

Bar and line graphs provide another way to present numerical information to your readers. Both types of graphs plot data along a horizontal line (the *x* axis) and a vertical line (the *y* axis). Like a table, a **bar graph** allows readers to make comparisons. For example, the graph in Figure 18.6 allows readers

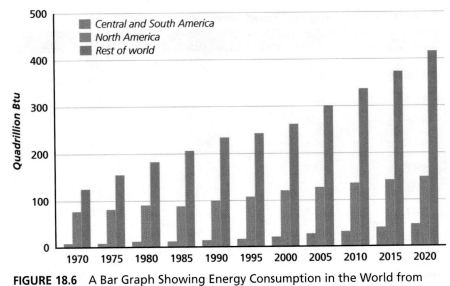

FIGURE 18.6 A Bar Graph Showing Energy Consumption in the World from 1970 to 2020 *Source:* U.S. Government Energy Information Administration

to compare actual or projected energy use in three different parts of the world over a period of fifty years.

A **line graph** shows readers a change or changes over a period of time. Figure 18.7 is a line graph illustrating the relationship between a car's mileage and its value.

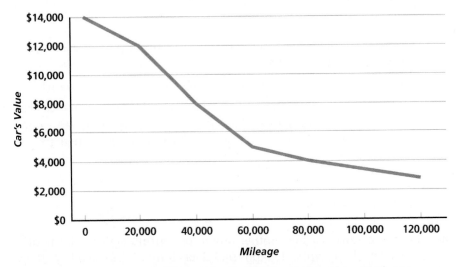

FIGURE 18.7 A Line Graph Illustrating the Relationship between Mileage and Value *Source:* Math League

WRITING ACTIVITY

Analyzing Bar and Line Graphs

Analyze the preceding bar and line graphs by responding to the following questions:

- What are the components of the graphs?
- How has the writer used color in the bar graph?
- How has the writer organized the data in the graphs?
- What would happen if the writer reversed the *x* axis and the *y* axis in either of the graphs?
- What stories do these graphs tell?

USING GRAPHS EFFECTIVELY IN YOUR TEXTS

You can use bar or line graphs that have been constructed by others in your paper as long as you give proper credit to the source of the graph. You can also use a spreadsheet program or *PowerPoint* to construct your own graphs from data you have discovered or generated on your own, or you can use an online graphing site, such as "Create a Graph" (http://nces.ed.gov/nceskids/ Graphing/), hosted by the National Center for Educational Statistics. If you do not have access to a computer, however, you can always construct the graph yourself, using graph paper. If you use data from a source to construct your graph, you need to give credit to that source.

See Chapter 20 for help with citing sources for your data.

To use bar and line graphs effectively in your texts, consider the following questions:

- Do I have sets of numerical data that I would like readers to compare?
- Do I have data that indicate a change over a period of time?
- What could a bar or line graph add to my text?
- If I am using a bar graph, how should I organize it?
- How should I explain the graph in my text?
- Do I have access to the technology (a color printer, for example) that will enable me to construct the graph and/or present it effectively?

Charts

A **chart** is a visual text that allows you to show the relationships among different items or among the parts of a whole. Consider Figure 18.8 on page 484, which shows what various stain colors look like on oak. Notice how the chart holds one variable constant—the kind of wood—so that readers can make consistent comparisons among stain colors.

FIGURE 18.8   A Chart Showing Wood Stains
Source: ComeToBuy.com

Two kinds of charts that are very common in academic writing, as well as in writing for other areas, are pie charts and flowcharts.

A **pie chart** shows readers the components that make up the whole of something. Pie charts are ideal for showing the percentages of each part of an item. The pie chart in Figure 18.4 on page 479 shows the ingredients used to make a sausage and mushroom pizza.

FLOWCHARTS

A flowchart shows how a process works. Although you can usually describe processes with words alone, a flowchart can do so in a visual way. Many readers find it easier to understand processes when they see flowcharts. Figure 18.9 on page 485 illustrates the complex process of launching a water rocket. Notice that the chart is also a kind of *decision tree,* with yes or no responses that direct readers' progress through the chart.

Bigfoot Rocket Launcher Flowchart

FIGURE 18.9
A Flowchart That Is
Also a Decision Tree
Source: Gary Ensmenger

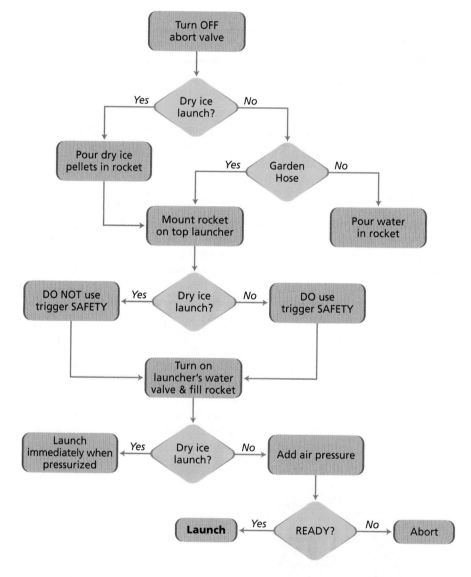

USING CHARTS EFFECTIVELY IN YOUR TEXTS

As with graphs, you can use charts that have been produced by others in your paper as long as you give proper credit to the source of the chart. You can also construct your own chart the old-fashioned way—drawing it by hand—or by using a drawing program. Spreadsheet programs and *PowerPoint* also enable you to produce charts and import them into your paper.

To use charts effectively in your texts, consider the following questions:

- Is there a process, a key relationship, or the components of something within my text that I could illustrate with a chart?
- How will the chart help my audience better understand a particular point in my paper?
- How will a chart support my purpose?
- How can I organize the chart so that readers can see patterns in the information?
- Do I have access to the technology (a color printer, for example) that will enable me to construct the chart and/or present it effectively?

Photographs

Photographs are common in our lives. We collect photographs of friends and family, and we see them daily in magazines and newspapers, as well as on Web sites, billboards, and posters. Because photographs are filled with details, a single photograph can replace hundreds or even thousands of words. Imagine how difficult it would be to describe your best friend's physical appearance to a stranger using words alone, without a photograph. On the other hand, a photograph could not give your reader a detailed view of your friend's personality; for those characteristics, words are needed.

Consider two well-known photographs of Abraham Lincoln. The first photo (Figure 18.10) portrays Lincoln with his son Tad. The second photograph (Figure 18.11) portrays Lincoln with Allan Pinkerton, who developed the federal Secret Service and who headed the Union spying operations, and Major General John A. McClernand. A writer could use either photograph to illustrate what Lincoln's life was like during the Civil War years, which corresponded with his years in the White House. The photograph that shows Lincoln reading

FIGURE 18.10 Abraham Lincoln with His Son Tad *Source:* Library of Congress

FIGURE 18.11 Lincoln with Allan Pinkerton (left) and Major General John A. McClernand   *Source:* Library of Congress

to his son gives readers a sense of his personal life, specifically his closeness to his sons. It does not tell the whole story, however, including his love for Tad and his other two children—Willie and Robert—and his heartbreak when his favorite child, Willie, died from typhoid fever in 1862, at the age of eleven. These are details that a writer would include in the text. Similarly, the photograph of Lincoln with Pinkerton and McClernand does not give a complete picture of his working relationship with them; for that, words are needed.

WRITING ACTIVITY

Considering Photos

With your classmates, prepare a list of six well-known places, people, or objects—for example, the Alamo, Martin Luther King, Jr., a castle. Bring one photograph of each place, person, or object to class. Compare and contrast your photos with those that other students have brought by responding to the following questions:

- What does each photograph reveal about its subject? What does each photograph leave out?
- What does each photograph reveal about the person who took it?
- How could you use each photograph in a piece of writing?
- What purposes could each photograph have in a given type of writing?

USING PHOTOGRAPHS EFFECTIVELY IN YOUR WRITING

With the advent of inexpensive digital photography, it is easy to store, retrieve, manipulate, and send photographs. Although it is easy to integrate digital photographs into your documents, note that low-resolution photos are grainy when printed on paper. *Resolution* refers to the number of pixels (or dots) in the image. High-resolution photos have more pixels per inch than low-resolution photos. The following table gives the recommended resolutions (300 dots per inch) for several photograph sizes:

Size of Photo	Recommended Resolution for Printed Photograph
2" × 2"	600 × 600 pixels
2" × 3"	600 × 900 pixels
4" × 6"	1200 × 1800 pixels
5" × 7"	1500 × 2100 pixels

In your written texts, you may use photographs that have been produced by others if you give proper credit to the source of the photograph. If you are publishing the photograph on a Web site or in some other print or electronic medium, you will need to obtain permission to use it from the copyright holder unless it is in the public domain. (If a photograph is in the **public domain,** no one owns the copyright for the image, and you may use it without obtaining permission.)

To decide when and how to use photographs in your writing, consider the following questions:

- What kind of photograph will best support my purpose?
- What impact will a photograph have on my text?
- How will my audience respond to each of the photographs that I am considering?
- Where might I place the photograph in my text? Why?

- Do I need permission to use a particular photograph?
- How might I ethically manipulate the photograph to use in my text? For example, can I cut out, or "crop," part of the photograph that includes extraneous material?
- If the photograph is an electronic document, is the resolution high enough for use in a print document?
- Will the technology that is available to me accurately reproduce the photograph?

Drawings

Like photographs, **drawings** enable readers to visualize a subject. Drawings are common in technical and scientific writing because writers in those fields frequently need to give readers detailed descriptions of objects, many of which are so small (atoms or strands of DNA) or so far away (stars in other galaxies) that it is difficult to see and photograph them. Consider the drawing of a cell nucleus in Figure 18.12 below. Notice how this drawing of a cell nucleus includes **labels,** words that name its parts. What is missing from this drawing, however, is an explanation of the functions of the nucleus and its many parts. Only words can provide that information, and only writers can provide those words. In other words, the visual and verbal elements in a text need to complement and supplement each other.

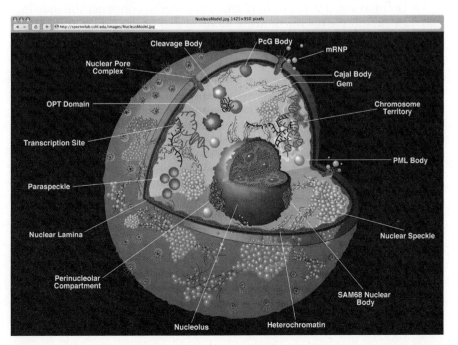

FIGURE 18.12
A Drawing of a Cell Nucleus
Source: Spector Lab

WRITING ACTIVITY

Considering Drawings

Find an example of a drawing in one of your textbooks, in a newspaper, in a magazine, or on a Web site. Discuss how successfully the text and drawing you have found work together to achieve the writer's purpose.

USING DRAWINGS EFFECTIVELY IN YOUR TEXTS

You can produce a drawing by hand. If you have access to a scanner, you can then scan your finished drawing, generating a computer file. Alternately, a drawing program allows you to generate a digital file directly on your computer. If you pick up a drawing from a source for use in your paper, you will need to give proper credit to that source. If you are publishing the drawing, you will need to obtain permission to use it.

To use drawings effectively in your texts, consider the following questions:

- What in my text could I illustrate with a drawing?
- How could a drawing meet the needs of my audience?
- How would a drawing support the purpose of my text?
- Can I use an existing drawing, or do I need to construct one?
- Do I need permission to use an existing drawing?
- Do I have access to software that I can use to construct the drawing? Or should I make the drawing by hand and scan it?

Diagrams

Diagrams are drawings that illustrate and explain the arrangement of and relationships among parts of a system. Venn diagrams, for example, consist of circles representing relationships among sets. Consider the Venn diagram shown in Figure 18.13, which illustrates how sustainable development depends on relationships among the environment, the economy, and equity. Of course, this diagram by itself does not explain the exact nature of these relationships. To do that, a writer needs to define each of the terms in the diagram—*environment, economy, equity*—and then explain how they interact to form sustainable development.

USING DIAGRAMS EFFECTIVELY IN YOUR WRITING

As with drawings, you can either construct a diagram by hand and scan it or use a drawing program. If you use a diagram from a source in your paper, you will need to give proper credit to that source. If you are publishing the diagram, you will need to obtain permission to use it.

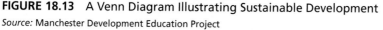

FIGURE 18.13 A Venn Diagram Illustrating Sustainable Development
Source: Manchester Development Education Project

To use diagrams effectively in your writing, consider the following questions:

- What in my text could I illustrate with a diagram?
- What effect will the diagram have on my readers?
- How would a diagram support my purpose?
- Can I use an existing diagram, or do I need to construct one?
- Do I need permission to use an existing diagram?
- Do I have access to software that I can use to construct the diagram? Or should I construct the diagram by hand and scan it?

Maps

Cartographers use **maps** to record and show where countries, cities, streets, buildings, colleges, lakes, rivers, and mountains are located in the world or in a particular part of it. Of course, consumers of maps use them to find these places. We use printed or downloaded maps to drive from one location to another. On the evening news we see maps showing where events take place and what kind of weather is occurring in neighboring states and countries. We even use maps to help us visualize fictional places such as the territories described in the *Lord of the Rings* trilogy (Figure 18.14).

FIGURE 18.14 A Map from the *Lord of the Rings* Trilogy

Source: NewLine/Saul Zaentz/Wing Nut/The Kobal Collection

Many different academic disciplines use maps. Anthropologists use maps to illustrate where species have lived, as in the map in Figure 18.15, which shows the range of the Neanderthals—an extinct species of human—in Europe.

FIGURE 18.15 Neanderthal Range Map *Source:* National Geographic Society

WRITING ACTIVITY

Analyzing Maps

Choose one of the two maps in Figures 18.4 and 18.5 and respond to the following questions:

- What is the purpose of this map?
- What additional information would make the map more useful?
- What would a writer need to explain to readers within the text so that they could use the map effectively?
- How does the map adhere to the principles of proximity and contrast (see pp. 472–74)?
- How might the captions for the maps be revised to be more informative?

USING MAPS EFFECTIVELY IN YOUR TEXTS

In most cases, you will need to use maps from other sources, giving credit and obtaining permission to use them if necessary. To use maps effectively in your texts, consider the following questions:

- What information could a map offer to my audience?
- If there is an existing map that will serve my purpose, do I need permission to use it?
- If I need to draw my own map, what tools do I need?
- What data do I need to create the map?
- What information do I need to include in the caption for the map?
- Do I have the technology available to present the map effectively?

Cartoons

To find evidence of how much people enjoy cartoons, you need only walk the halls of any office building on your campus. You will notice that people display cartoons on their office doors, cubicle walls, and bulletin boards. Cartoons make humorous—and sometimes poignant—observations about people and events. Consider the cartoon in Figure 18.16 on page 494, for example. One feature of most cartoons is that their visual and verbal elements complement each other. The visual part of the cartoon gives the topic a human or human-like face, and the verbal part offers a specific comment.

FIGURE 18.16
Cartoon
Reprinted by
permission of
Randy Glasbergen

GLASBERGEN

"My presentation lacks power and it has no point.
I assumed the software would take care of that!"

USING CARTOONS EFFECTIVELY IN YOUR TEXTS

In most cases, when you use cartoons in your text, they probably will have been produced by other people. Make sure that you are able to give the source information for any cartoon that you include. If you are publishing your paper on the Web or in another medium, you will need to obtain permission to use the cartoon from the copyright holder. If you draw your own cartoon, you will need to draw it by hand and scan it to produce a computer file that you can incorporate into your text.

To use cartoons effectively in your texts, consider the following questions:

- How will a cartoon support my purpose?
- Given that readers usually associate cartoons with humor and/or satire, how might humor or satire affect my readers?
- Do I need permission to use a published cartoon, or is it in the public domain?

Using Visuals Rhetorically

As you consider using the visuals covered in this chapter, you need to think about using them rhetorically to achieve some specific purpose with a specific audience.

Considering Your Audience

Readers are more likely to expect visuals in some genres than in others. Lab reports, for example, commonly include tables and graphs. This principle applies to any visuals that you plan to use in your writing as much as to the words that you write. As you consider using a particular visual, ask yourself the following questions:

- Does my audience need this visual, or is it showing something that my readers already know very well? What information might a visual add?
- How will this audience respond to this visual? How do I know what their response will be?
- What other visual might they respond to more favorably?
- Will this audience understand the subtleties of this visual?
- How do I need to explain this visual for this particular audience?

Considering Your Purpose

As we have seen throughout Parts 2 and 3 of this book, you will have a general purpose for any writing project—to record and share experiences, to explore, to inform, to analyze, to convince or persuade, to evaluate, to explain causes and effects, to solve problems, or to analyze creative works. To the extent possible, every section, paragraph, and sentence of your paper should contribute to that purpose. Any phrase, clause, sentence, paragraph, or section of your paper that does not support your purpose needs to be revised or deleted. The same principle applies to any visual that you are considering. Diagrams, for example, most often have an informative purpose. A cartoon, by contrast, is almost always humorous but often makes a statement. Photographs are often used to make the rhetorical appeal of *pathos*, as they can create an emotional response in the reader. Figure 18.17 below, for example,

FIGURE 18.17 A Photograph from the Web Page for Feed the Children, a Charitable Organization   *Source:* Feed the Children

is a photograph from the Web page for Feed the Children, a well-known charitable organization.

Before using any visual, you should ask yourself these questions:

- How will this visual support my purpose?
- How might this visual detract from my purpose?
- Why is this visual necessary?
- What other visual or visuals might support my purpose more effectively?

Using Visuals Responsibly

Just as you need to consider the purpose of using any visual, you also need to consider how using visuals responsibly will enhance your credibility as a writer.

Permissions

Whenever you plan to use a visual, you need to make certain that you have permission to use that visual. If you have constructed a table, graph, or chart from data that you have gathered, then permission is not needed. If you use a visual prepared by someone else, or use data from a source to produce a visual, you should always give credit to your source, even if the visual or data are from a government source and/or are in the public domain (that is, outside of copyright and available to anyone who wants to use it). For most academic papers, it is usually not necessary to request permission to use a visual. If your writing will be made available to an audience beyond your classroom, however, you will need to ask for permission to use any visual from a source that you include. Some visuals that you find on the Web are in public domain, but if you are in doubt about a particular visual, contact the Web manager of the site where you found it to ask what permissions are required.

The subjects of photographs have certain rights as well. If you take a photograph of a friend, you need to ask your friend for permission to use it if your project will have an audience beyond the two of you. If your friend does not want the photo used in a course paper or on a Web site, you are ethically and legally obligated to honor those wishes. To be certain that there is no misunderstanding, ask your friend to sign an agreement granting you permission to use the photo for clearly specified purposes. If you later want to use the photo for other purposes, ask your friend to sign another agreement. You should never put undue pressure on someone to sign such an agreement.

Distortions

Just as you should not distort quoted or paraphrased material (see Chapter 20), you should also be careful not to distort the content and the physical

properties of any visuals you include in your paper. In Chapter 17, for
instance, we show a fabricated photo of Jane Fonda and John Kerry on stage
together (p.467). Sometimes the data in charts and graphs is misrepre-
sented—consider, for example, Figure 18.18, which shows the pass rates for
students in English 101. Clearly, the pass rate improved by year 3 and has
remained fairly stable since then. *If* this chart maker wanted to show a dramatic improvement in the pass rate, then it makes sense to use a "scale" that
runs from 75% to 100%. On the other hand, a full scale (from 0 to 100%)
makes the improvement in pass rates much less obvious and dramatic, as
shown in Figure 18.19.

There may be times, however, when some forms of distortion can be
helpful and ethical. For instance, consider the two maps shown in Figure
18.20 on page 498. The first one shows the forty-eight contiguous states as
they typically appear on a map. Such maps show the relative sizes—measured in square miles—of the states. The second map, on the other hand, is
designed to show the distribution of wire-service news stories about certain
cities and states. Notice that New York and Washington, DC, get lots of attention in wire-service news stories. This deliberately distorted image helps to
make a serious point about the news.

FIGURE 18.18
A Chart That Distorts
Information

FIGURE 18.19
A Chart That Presents
the Same Information
Honestly

FIGURE 18.20

A Regular Map of the United States and a Distorted Map That Illustrates a Point about News

Source: Maps by M. E. J. Newman and M. T. Gastner

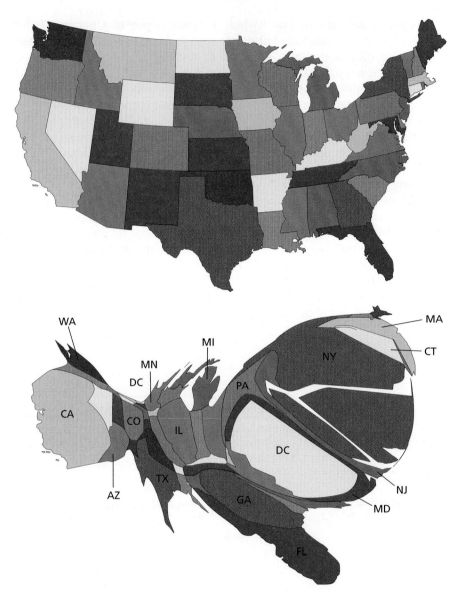

6

Using Research for Informed Communication

Finding and Evaluating Information from Sources and the Field

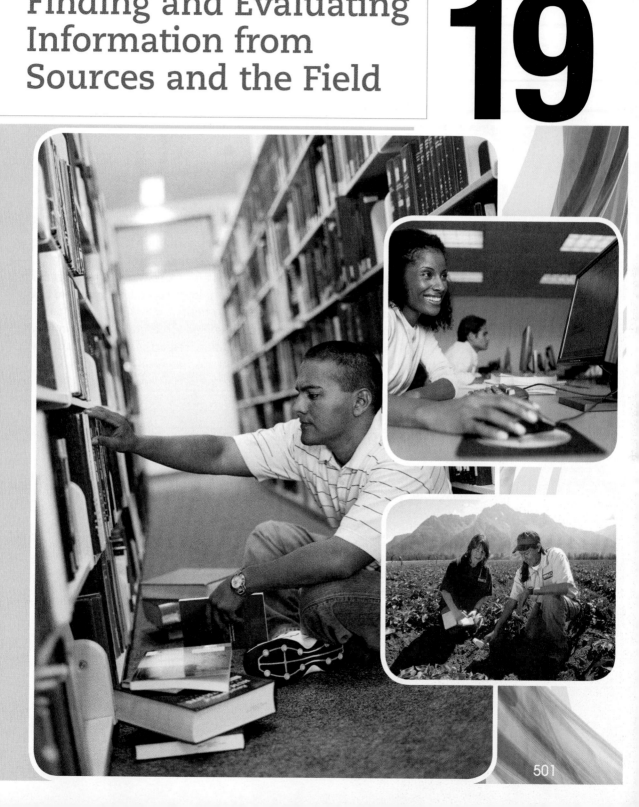

To older generations, **research** meant searching through actual library stacks. Because of the almost instant access to a wealth of sources that technology makes possible, however, finding information today may appear to be much easier than it was in the past, but the reality is that it is simply different. Although you can still find books and print journals on library shelves, and they are still useful resources, today researchers often start a project with a search of the library's online catalog or database or a search of the World Wide Web.

Before the advent of electronic sources, researchers usually assumed that they could generally rely on the accuracy of the printed texts found in college or university libraries. Although those sources still exist, of course, anyone can now publish anything on the World Wide Web or more easily self-publish content as a book. So much information is available on the Internet that it is vital to focus your search as carefully as possible so that you turn up only the most relevant sources. It is also more critical than ever for researchers to learn effective ways not just to locate useful information, but also to evaluate the quality of what they do find.

Finally, researchers still go "out into the field" to conduct other kinds of research. In this kind of hands-on investigation, researchers gather information through observation and experimentation as well as, when working with humans, interviews and surveys.

Conducting Effective Research: An Example

You already have plenty of experience in conducting research. Have you ever determined a classmate's opinion of an author or a band and tried to use it to influence a friend to read that author's book or to see that band? If so, you were using the results of a type of *field research* called *interviewing* as evidence.

For more on field research, see pages 525–30.

The research that you do for any writing task—whether for a college class, in a letter to a friend, or for a report to your supervisor—is a rhetorical act. That is, you conduct research for a specific purpose, with a particular audience in mind, in a specific writing situation. Consider how you might approach the following assignment for a psychology class:

> Respond to this question: Why do adolescent males (and sometimes females) change their behavior when they join a gang? Based on your own research, write a 3- to 4-page paper that provides compelling reasons for this behavior, providing specific evidence to support your position.

This assignment is fairly straightforward: Your purpose is to fulfill this assignment, and your audience is your psychology professor. The assignment even provides you with a **research question:** Why do adolescent males (and sometimes females) change their behavior when they join gangs? Your answer to this question will form the thesis of your research paper. But where will you find the evidence that will help you decide on your answer to this question—your thesis—and support that thesis? How will you locate it? How will you be able to tell if the evidence is credible and reliable?

Sometimes your instructor will provide you with a **research question**, as in the example cited above. However, often it will be your responsibility to formulate your own research question. When you find yourself in that situation, keep these principles in mind:

- Keep the question focused. For example, "What caused the Civil War?" is a huge question. However, "Why did Confederate forces fire on Fort Sumter on April 12, 1861?" is much more manageable.

- Make sure you will be able to get good information on your question. You may be interested in the role Venezuelan oil plays in the U.S. economy, especially from the Venezuelan perspective. However, if you discover that most of the information for this topic is in Spanish and you can't read that language, you will probably not be able to go forward with this question.

- Consider whether you can find an adequate number of resources to answer your question. For example, are the people you hope to interview available and willing to speak with you? Can you really arrange to do field research at some far-off location?

Library Research

Often the first place to look when conducting research to answer a question is the reference section of your college library. There you will find sources such as general and specialized encyclopedias and dictionaries that can give you background on a given topic. For example, you might start your research for the psychology paper about gangs and adolescents by defining the word "adolescent," perhaps by looking it up in a medical dictionary:

> A young person who has undergone puberty but who has not reached full maturity; a teenager.
>
> —The American Heritage® *Stedman's Medical Dictionary*

Based on this definition, you determine that your research will focus on males and females between the ages of thirteen and nineteen. You decide to conduct a search in your online college library catalog. While you may decide to begin your search before you actually go to the library, asking the Research Librarian at your college library's Reference Desk for help is also a good idea. (Librarians are also available online in many libraries, in some cases twenty-four hours a day, seven days a week.) He or she will probably be able to point you to some reference sources that might be useful in your research project.

All college libraries have a book **catalog** of some kind—usually that catalog is online. In addition to the book catalog, your library probably subscribes to various electronic **databases** such as *Academic Search Premier*. Databases are indexes of articles that are available in periodicals; many also provide complete texts of the articles themselves. To look for articles in popular or trade magazines, for instance, you would search one database, while you would use another database to find articles in academic journals, and still another library database for articles in newspapers.

TechNote

Here are some popular academic databases that can help you with research in different disciplines. Keep in mind that the names of academic databases do change; your reference librarian can help you find a database that will be useful for your particular project.

Academic Search Premier: A valuable resource that provides the full-text articles for more than 8,000 scholarly publications.

ERIC: A popular education database with articles going back to 1966. It also provides access to over 100,000 full-text documents.

General Science Index: A helpful index for science students, especially for introductory courses.

Humanities Index: An index that lists articles from publications in the humanities

disciplines, including modern languages and literature, history, and philosophy.

JSTOR: An electronic archive of scholarly journals in different disciplines.

LexisNexis Academic: An online service that offers full-text articles from over 6,000 newspapers and other publications.

ProQuest: A resource that offers access to journals and other publications, including the full texts of many articles, going back to 1996. It also offers information on sources going back to 1986 and historical sources that date to the nineteenth century, including a Historical Newspapers database.

Social Science Index: An index that lists articles from publications in the social sciences, including economics, psychology, political science, and sociology.

SEARCHING A LIBRARY CATALOG

For any electronic search, you need to come up with an appropriate word or phrase, or **keyword,** that will be found in the kind of source you are seeking. To find useful keywords for a search of your library's catalog, it is often a good idea to start by consulting the *Library of Congress Subject Headings* (LCSH), a book that lists subject headings in use in most library systems. It will tell you how subject areas are categorized in the library and will therefore help you come up with search terms that will turn up books on your subject.

Note that the search term "gang behavior" is just one of a range of possibilities. It is often useful to use a number of search terms because that will provide you with a range of sources to choose from. You can also pull up more information on each entry and examine other relevant references there that might be useful to your research (Figure 19.1).

Here is a research hint: Whenever you find a book on your research subject in your college library, spend a few minutes examining the *other* texts that surround the one you just located. Books about the same topic are shelved together, so once you find one book on the topic you are researching,

FIGURE 19.1 Information on the First Book Listed on the Results Page, Using the Search Term "Gang Behavior"   Reprinted by permission of Arizona State University Libraries many others will be nearby. Because you are standing right there, it is easy for you to conduct further library research.

SEARCHING AN ONLINE DATABASE

Now that you have several books that you might want to examine for information on gang behavior, you should also search one or more of the databases your college's library subscribes to. A search of a typical database—in this case, *Academic Search Premier*—using the keywords "male" and "gang" might turn up abstracts (summaries) of articles like this one:

> <u>*GANG* WORLD</u>. By: Papachristos, Andrew V.. Foreign Policy, Mar/Apr2005 Issue 147, p48–55, 8p, 3c, 1bw; Abstract: The article discusses the rise of street *gangs* around the world. The image of a young, minority, "inner-city," *male gang* member is transmitted, exploited, and glamorized across the world. The increasing mobility of information via cyberspace, films, and music makes it easy for *gangs, gang* members, and others to get information, adapt personalities, and distort *gang* behaviors. Two images of street *gangs* dominate the popular consciousness—*gangs* as posses of drug-dealing thugs and, more recently, *gangs* as terrorist organizations. Although the media like to link *gangs* and drugs, only a small portion of all *gangs* actually deal in them. Similarly, the name Jose Padilla is inevitably followed by two epithets—al Qaeda terror suspect and street *gang* member. The link between the two is extremely misleading. One of the most urgent challenges for policymakers is distinguishing between the average street *gang* and groups that operate as criminal networks. Globalization and street *gangs* exist in a paradox: *Gangs* are a global phenomenon not because the groups themselves have become transnational organizations, but because of the recent hypermobility of *gang* members and their culture. Individual *gangs* flaunt their Internet savvy by posting complex Web sites, including some with password protection. As the global economy creates a growing number of disenfranchised groups, some will inevitably meet their needs in a *gang*. INSETS: Want to Know More?; When *Gangs* Go Bad.; (*AN 16195307*)
> 📄 **HTML Full Text** 📄 **PDF Full Text** (1.7MB)

Note that the abstract indicates that this article deals with "gang culture," so this one seems especially promising (and because the full text of the article is available online, you can print the essay with a click of your mouse). Note also that *Academic Search Premier*, the search database we used for this search, may not be available in all libraries. We use it here to illustrate a possible search database; your college or university will provide a similar search database.

Another online database that many colleges offer their students is *Lexis-Nexis*, which indexes a range of newspapers, other periodicals, and a wide range of other kinds of documents. Figure 19.2 shows the first part of a search using the keyword "adolescent gangs," a search term that focuses on both the subject of gangs and the youth involved in those activities.

FIGURE 19.2 A Search of the LexisNexis Database Using the Search Term "Adolescent Gangs"

LexisNexis and *Knowledge Burst* logo are registered trademarks of Reed Elsevier Properties Inc. Used with permission of *LexisNexis*

Several of the articles listed by *LexisNexis* appear to be potentially useful. Since they are available as full-text articles, you can click on the title and immediately check them for relevance.

Research on the World Wide Web

You continue your search on the **World Wide Web,** which is the largest part of the global network of computers known as the **Internet.** The Web is hyperlinked, which means that one useful site will often provide you with links to many more.

If you have conducted Web searches, you probably quickly learned that different **search engines,** software programs that find sites on the Web, locate different information—that the search engine Google (www.google.com), for example, will give you different results from what does Yahoo! (www.yahoo.com), and both return somewhat different lists of sites for a given keyword than would be provided by a search conducted using AltaVista (www.AltaVista.com). You may also have used a "meta-search" engine such as Dogpile (www.dogpile.com), which searches *other* search engines, so the results you retrieve are from a range of searches. Usually, it is a good idea to use several different search engines.

A search of the Web using Google, one of the most commonly used search engines, and the keywords "gang behavior," for example, turns up over 1,470,000 hits. Clearly, this result provides an unmanageable number of choices. The best way to limit the number of hits that a search engine returns is to narrow what the search engine is looking for. You can do this easily on Google by enclosing multiple keywords within quotation marks so that the search engine looks for them when they appear together as a phrase. (To see how to narrow search terms on another search engine, consult the Help screens for that engine.) Simply by enclosing the search term "Gang Behavior" in quotation marks, you can limit the result to 46,700 hits, for example. This helps, but 46,700 options are still far too many. As a next step, you might qualify the search even more. If you are looking for information about female gangs, for example, you might try searching with the keywords "gang behavior" + "female." Doing so gives you a list of 13,000 hits. While that's still better, it's not really good enough. You can then modify the search even further by trying this combination of keywords: "gang behavior" + "adolescent female." This time the response, shown in Figure 19.3, is only twenty-four hits, a manageable number. By closely defining your search terms and using them in combination, you can narrow your search and come up with the best possible online sources. Most search engines such as Google also have an advanced search screen that can help you narrow your search.

One other option you might consider using if you are working on an academic paper is Google Scholar, which searches only scholarly Web sites. Searching Google Scholar using the keywords "gang behavior" + "adolescent female" gives you the result shown in Figure 19.4 on page 510. You can also search for images on the World Wide Web. Using an image search on Google, for example, you may find a photo of gang activity which you can use to illustrate your paper.

WRITING ACTIVITY

Develop a List of Questions and a Research Plan

For one of your current writing projects, develop a list of intriguing research questions. These are questions that require complex answers, not just facts. After each question, indicate where you would go to find answers (for example, the library) and what you would do there (for example, search a database for newspaper articles on your topic).

Your instructor may ask you to share your lists and research plans with several of your classmates.

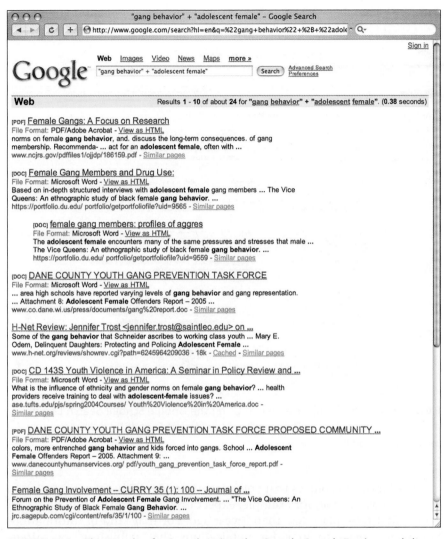

FIGURE 19.3   The Result of a Search Using the Google Search Engine and the Keywords "Gang Behavior" + "Adolescent Female"   Reprinted by permission of Google Brand Features

Selecting Sources

Whenever you do research you will encounter a wide range of sources. You have to determine what sources will be useful to you for your particular writing situation. We will outline a number of sources here, and then discuss how you might *evaluate* the various kinds of information you locate.

FIGURE 19.4   The Result of a Search Using the Google Scholar Search Engine and the Keywords "Gang Behavior" + "Adolescent Female"   Reprinted by permission of Google Brand Features

The kind(s) of sources that you select depend on what you are trying to learn. You would not, for example, expect to find information in books on events that took place less than a year ago. For that kind of information, you would need to look for publications that publish more current information.

Each type of source has advantages and disadvantages, so it is usually best to use a variety of sources.

Books

A Book from
Cambridge University
Press

Books such as the one shown here have historically been a researcher's first choice for much academic research because what you learn from them has almost always been well-researched and the statistical information validated. However, even books have to be subjected to more intensive questioning these days, as it is now relatively easy for just about anyone to publish a book. Books in an academic library, however, have been carefully evaluated by librarians and are usually reputable. One disadvantage of the research you will find in a printed book is that it often takes several years to write, review, and publish a book—so the information often is not as current as that in newspapers, academic journals, the Internet, and other media.

Academic Journals

Academic essays appear in **journals** such as the *American Journal of Psychiatry*, shown on the right. Journals are most often sponsored by universities. Because journals are nonprofit, many do not carry advertisements. Essays in most academic journals are written by scholars in the field and are "peer reviewed," which means that other scholars have read, commented on, and made a judgment about the article's validity and usefulness. Journal articles are usually well-researched. Also, academic essays most often come with a "works cited" or "references" page, which lists all of the sources the writer used in his or her essay. Often, these lists are gold mines of information for you, as they point to useful sources about the topic you are working on.

American Journal of Psychiatry

For example, your library search focusing on adolescent males and females and gangs might turn up this essay, published in the *American Journal of Psychiatry*: "What Happens to 'Bad' Girls? A Review of the Adult Outcomes of Antisocial Adolescent Girls" by Kathleen A. Pajer, M.D., M.P.H. In addition to the essay, which might contain useful information, you find a "works cited" section with eighty-three entries, references to other journal articles and books that Dr. Pajer used in her text. These will lead you to more information about teenage gangs.

Newspapers

Newspapers, especially those with a national focus such as the *New York Times*, the *Washington Post*, the *Los Angeles Times*, and the *Wall Street Journal*, are considered reliable sources. Often, local papers will get their information from national sources. They always acknowledge when they do—so you can tell where their information comes from. Local newspapers are a useful source for just what you might expect: local news and information.

A *LexisNexis* search for newspaper articles on a topic will provide you with recent information. You do need to remember, however, that while newspapers are very current sources, because they are following stories in progress, sometimes the information they provide may change as more complete information on a story becomes available.

Newsweek Magazine

Popular Magazines

Magazines, especially newsmagazines such as *Time* and *Newsweek*, have a broad perspective on national issues and often provide useful background and historical information. Most magazines now have online versions. Many make the contents of the print magazine available online, either to anyone who visits the site or to registered users. Often the magazine will offer additional content online, as well as forums for readers to respond to articles and to one another.

A search at Time.com, for example, turns up possible sources for your paper on gangs, as shown in Figure 19.5.

TIME Magazine – Search Results

http://www.time.com/time/searchresults?N=0&Ntk=NoBody&Nty=1&Nr=OR%28p_record

TIME

Tuesday, September 4, 2007

▸ Home | Gangs | (Search)

Refine Your Search

Refine By Dates
▸ Past 7 Days (2)
▸ Past 30 Days (17)
▸ Past Year (146)

From
Ma   17   1923
To
Se   10   2007
(Refine)

Years limited by available results

Refine by Section
▸ Politics (5)

Refine by Author
▸ Corliss, Richard (162)
▸ Lacayo, Richard (24)
▸ McGirk, Tim (36)
▸ Morrow, Lance (33)
▸ Schickel, Richard (50)
▸ More...

Refine by Publication
▸ Time Domestic (5267)
▸ Time Asia (166)
▸ Time Europe (106)

Refine by Type
▸ Articles (5608)
▸ Blog (13)

Refine by Article Length
▸ Long (1948)
▸ Medium (2140)
▸ Short (1533)
▸ Cover Story (250)

Search Results:

Your search for **"Gangs"** found **5,621** results

Page: 1 | 2 | 3 | 4 | 5 | 6 | 7 | 8 | 9 | 10 | Next >>

Sponsored Links

Gangs
www.ask.com Better pictures & more relevant results on Ask.com. Use Ask.com.

See Sponsored Links For: Gangs

Sorted by **newest** | oldest | relevance

Making a Difference at Home
Sep. 10, 2007 | By Caroline Kennedy
Inspired by their work abroad, Peace Corps volunteers return to the U.S. as teachers, bringing the lessons they learned to the kids who need them most
844 words | view cover

Postcard: Philadelphia
Sep. 3, 2007 | By Brendan Lowe
...was seen as closely linked to more violent crimes, whether explicitly as **gang** markings or simply as a sign of neighborhoods in disrepair. But in...
605 words | view cover

Making a Difference at Home
Aug. 29, 2007 | By Caroline Kennedy
Inspired by their work abroad, Peace Corps volunteers return to the U.S. as teachers, bringing the lessons they learned to the kids who need them most
846 words

Healing Katrina's Racial Wounds
Aug. 27, 2007 | By Russell McCulley/New Orleans
Amid all the problems that New Orleans has faced, relieving black-white distrust has proven to be one of the toughest
965 words

Covers
Apr. 24, 1972

▸ Table of Contents
▸ Large Cover

Featured Cover Stories

THE YOUTH CRIME PLAGUE
Jul. 11, 1977 | view cover

A Boy and His Gun
Aug. 2, 1993 | view cover

Life In Hell: A Baghdad Diary
Aug. 14, 2006 | view cover

More Cover Stories (250)

Photo Essays
Jul. 10, 2007

FIGURE 19.5 A Search of the Time.com Web Site Using the Keyword "Gangs"

Trade or Commercial Magazines

Trade or commercial/professional magazines have a specific audience, which consists of the members of a group with a common interest or profession. If the magazine is published for a professional organization, a portion of the members' dues usually pays for the magazine. Other magazines are for-profit publications that serve the industry as a whole. These publications often have a point of view and are written specifically for their target audience. They also can provide lots of information from an insider's perspective, so you may need to be very familiar with the field to really understand the context.

Business Traveler
Magazine

Public Affairs Magazines

Magazines that focus on public affairs, such as *Harpers*, *Public Affairs*, or *Foreign Affairs,* generally publish articles on large national issues, so they are useful sources for papers about these issues. Their essays are usually thoughtfully researched and documented.

Specialty Magazines

Magazines about travel, different regions of the country, cooking, and other specialized topics are often useful if you are searching for the kinds of information they provide. Examples include *Alaska*, *Southern Living*, and *Arizona Highways*. Others, like *BusinessWeek,* cater to a specific field and often have useful statistics and other types of information related to that field.

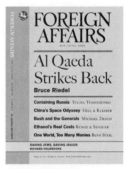

Foreign Affairs
Magazine

The Internet

The Internet, especially the hyperlinked part of it known as the World Wide Web, offers a huge and expanding range of information, all available very quickly and often in great detail. As you will see on pages 515–24, in the discussion of evaluating sources, it sometimes takes a bit of work to figure out exactly who controls a Web site and the information it presents, so information you obtain from the Web must be used with caution, depending on its source.

It is extremely difficult to generalize about the Internet because it remains a dynamic, ever-evolving source of information and, often, misinformation. Any attempt to categorize Internet sources is, at best, a rough estimate, but we can point to at least five different kinds of online resources.

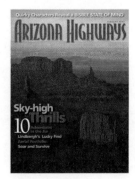

Arizona Highways
Magazine

1. **Web sites that serve as what used to be called the "home page" of an organization.** Most of these are now much more complex and sophisticated than they were in the early years of the Web, but

they may very well be the first place you choose to look for information about any organization or group, no matter whether it is an educational institution, a business, or a nonprofit agency. While the quality of the information you find on these Web sites may be good, you need to remember that because they are maintained by the organization itself, they tend to give a very positive view of the organization.

2. **Web sites that provide information to the general public.** Many of these Web sites are maintained by governmental agencies. Their subject matter and complexity vary depending on whether they are constructed and maintained by local municipalities, state agencies, or the federal government. In most instances the information found on these sites is very reliable. Figure 19.6, for example, is the home page for the site maintained by the Internal Revenue Service, a highly reliable source for information on the federal income tax.

3. **Online periodicals and newspapers.** As noted in the discussion of popular magazines on page 512, almost every print publication now has its own online version. Some local newspapers, such as the *Daily Hampshire Gazette* (www.gazettenet.com) of Northampton, Massachusetts, have a free news section and a section only for paid subscribers. Much of the content from each day's edition of the *New York Times* (www.nytimes.com), considered by many to be a national newspaper, is

FIGURE 19.6
The Home Page for the Internal Revenue Service

available for free online, but only to those who have registered for free. Many magazines allow online viewers to read most of their articles, while others publish snippets online and allow full access only to subscribers.

Some academic journals such as *Kairos* (http://english.ttu.edu/ Kairos/) are published only online. Like most academic journals, they are peer-reviewed and the information in them is as reliable as that found in print academic journals.

4. **Blogs.** A Weblog, or **blog,** is a kind of Web journal, usually maintained by one person who shares his or her thoughts on a given topic or set of topics and may post links to other sites on the Web as well as comments from other writers. It is sometimes difficult to determine the soundness of the information that you find in a blog. While some blogs are maintained by experts in a particular field, others are written by people who want to spread their own point of view on anything from politics to what kind of software is better and most everything in between. Use them with caution. Figure 19.7 on page 516 is an example of a blog on dieting.

See the information on evaluating sources on pages 515–24.

5. ***Wikipedia.*** *Wikipedia* is a collaborative online encyclopedia. All the articles on *Wikipedia* are written by volunteers, and it is possible for anyone to edit already existing articles. Though there are some safeguards to protect certain pages, it is possible that some information found on *Wikipedia* may be suspect. You may think of it as a good starting place, in much the same way that a traditional encyclopedia, whether in print or online, is a place to start for background on your research topic—but you should not rely on it for all of your information on a topic. It is always wise to look for additional sources of information beyond *Wikipedia.* You should also be cautious about citing it as a source in your academic papers. Figure 19.8 on page 516 shows the *Wikipedia* entry for "textbook."

For more about Wikipedia, *see "Growing* Wikipedia *Revises Its 'Anyone Can Edit' Policy" by Katie Hafner, in Chapter 6.*

Evaluating Your Sources: Asking the Reporter's Questions

Finding sources is only the beginning of your task in conducting research; you also need to evaluate the information you locate. How do you determine that a source is credible and accurate? Usually, asking the questions a reporter asks when he or she is working on a story will help you.

Who Is the Author?

Who is the author of the research? What can you learn about that author? If the work is an essay or an entire book, you may be able to

FIGURE 19.7
A Page from
Diet Blog
Reprinted by permission of
Jim Foster, Editor, www
.diet-blog.com

FIGURE 19.8
The *Wikipedia* Entry
for "Textbook"

find biographical information about the author or authors. For example, let's say you were conducting research on gangs and found this book in your college library: *Teen Gangs: A Global View*, edited by Maureen P. Duffy and Scott Edward Gillig. This book was published by Greenwood Press. Here is what the publisher says about the two editors in its online catalog:

A Scholarly Book on the Subject of Gangs

> **MAUREEN P. DUFFY** is Associate Professor and Chair of the Counseling Department at Barry University, Miami Shores, Florida.

> **SCOTT EDWARD GILLIG** is Professor and Coordinator of the mental health counseling specialization at Barry University.

Both editors are university professors, which means the book most likely contains thoroughly researched and well-documented articles by respected authors. In fact, each of the editors has written one chapter of the book, and Duffy has also written the introduction. If you examine Greenwood's catalog or Web site, you will see that it specializes in nonfiction books primarily for schools—middle school through college level—and that it also publishes library reference titles. So you know the editors are both professors and the book is not self-published, and although you cannot tell much about the reputation of Greenwood Press from its Web site alone, all of the information you have found indicates that the articles in this text were probably written by people who are credible authorities in their field.

What Is the Text About? What Is the Quality of the Information?

To determine the answer to this question, you will need to ask the following additional questions:

- What is the focus of the printed or online text you are considering?
- How thoughtful and research-based is it?
- Does the text seem designed to sensationalize its topic, or does it take a more balanced, thoughtful approach?

You'll also want to make sure the text is relevant to your topic. It is possible to find interesting and well-researched information that may not have much to do with your topic.

For instance, in your research on why adolescent males or females change their behavior when they join gangs, suppose you visit the Web site at www.streetgangs.com. The mission statement shown in Figure 19.9 on page 518 indicates that the site appears to be controlled by an individual and has been since 1995. This does not mean the information on the site is not credible, only that you will need to consider this information about the source if you decide to use anything from this Web site.

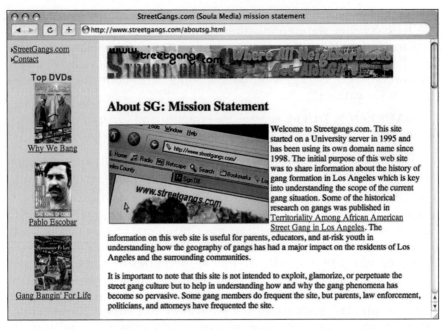

FIGURE 19.9 The Mission Statement for the Web Site Streetgangs.com

Reprinted by permission of Alex Alonso, Editor, www. streetgangs.com

The final paragraph of the section about the history of the Web site adds this information:

> We receive dozens of email every day so forgive us if we cannot personally respond to your message, but we will do our best to answer ALL serious questions. We receive over 6 million page visits monthly so please do not email us to help you with your high school paper or to ask silly questions. Please see the *bibliography* for tips on good books to read and for articles to download, or visit the *topics* to read recent news articles. If you have a serious question about gangs visit the *billboard* where your question may have already been asked. If you would like to write an article for *Street Gangs Magazine* please follow the *submission guidelines* and forward your essay. Media requests should be made from the *contact page*.

With so much interest in street gangs, it is certainly possible that this Web site gets "over 6 million page visits monthly." How does the tone of these comments (to not ask silly questions, for example) affect how you think about this site?

At the same time, even at sites or blogs maintained by individuals (and blogs are a good example of this), you can sometimes learn valuable information and find useful links. For example, Streetgangs.com offers a "100 page bibliography" for sale, but the site includes a few sample pages to give you a sense of the information the site makes available.

When Was the Text Published or the Web Site Last Updated?

Generally, the more current the information a source provides, the more useful it is to you. In academic research, new data is generally a response to *older* data. In fact, one of the benefits of reading books and articles by university scholars is that they almost always refer to earlier research as they outline how their new research relates to it, giving you the best of both worlds—the older information as well as the latest data.

At www.streetgangs.com, there is no notice that tells you when the Web page was last updated, but in the copyright section you will find the following notice:

> **Copyright © Notice, Terms & Conditions**
> **Copyright © 1995–2006, Street Gangs, Gangs in Los Angeles**
> **P.O. Box 18238, Los Angeles CA, 90018, USA**
> **800.249.1324**
> **All Rights Reserved**

This notice tells you that someone has worked on this Web site sometime in 2006. The page also includes a link to the biography and contact information for A. Alonso, who is evidently responsible for the site, another bit of evidence that the site is controlled by a person rather than by a group or company.

Why Was This Information Published?

What can you determine about why the information was published? What is the text's purpose? Who appears to be the target audience for this text? If you can determine to whom the text appeals, you might gain a sense of its purpose.

Of course, you cannot know for sure why an essay was published, or a book printed, or a Web site constructed, but you can make some good educated guesses:

- **Essays in academic journals** are often published to share new knowledge. This is especially true of articles in scientific journals, which publish the results of scientific research, but even in journals that focus on the humanities or on professional fields, professors publish what they have learned and concluded from their reading and thinking.

  Because articles in academic journals are peer-reviewed, other scholars in the field will get the chance to comment on and make suggestions (and criticisms) about any essay before it is published. So generally you can expect the information in journal articles to be reliable. Journals are also one of the major ways that scholars and practitioners communicate and share information within professional and scientific fields: Attorneys read law journals, physicians read medical journals, and writing teachers read journals about composition and rhetoric.

- **Academic books** provide professors with a way to distribute large amounts of information and insight to their peers, and while some make money for their author and publisher, many do not, so the profit motive is not a strong factor in publishing an academic text. Academic texts are also peer-reviewed, just as academic essays are, so other scholars in the field will have examined the information, data, and conclusions in a text prior to publication. During the publishing process, those peer reviewers will have the opportunity to contribute their ideas, criticisms, and suggestions—always with the goal of making the text the best possible. Academic texts are generally published by university presses (Harvard University Press, for instance).

- **Articles in newsmagazines and newspapers** present items in the local, national, or worldwide news. Most often, editors work diligently to present the news in an unbiased manner, but most newspapers and even some magazines have editorial pages or sections.

  As with anyone else, newspaper and magazine editors and writers have their own particular viewpoints and ways of looking at what they report on—in other words, there always is *some* bias in anything that is said or written. At any particular time and place, you might be able to label newspapers and magazines according to their general tendencies. But these ways of seeing and writing about the news vary over time, as editors and writers come and go.

  How can you, as a reader, get some sense of the biases of the newsmagazines and newspapers you read for your research? One way is to compare how the same information is presented in the different magazines or newspapers you are looking at. Reading two or more editorials on the same topic will give you some sense of how the editors of each newspaper see the world. Look for facts related to a story that appear in one publication but that do not appear in the other: What might that tell you about each publication? Consider how the same story is presented in two different publications. What photographs are included? How big is the headline? How much space is devoted to the article? Is it on the front page or on an interior page?

- **Web sites** give all kinds of information. However, not all Web sites give completely accurate and reliable information. You have to evaluate the value of a Web site just as you would any other source. You'll need to ask yourself questions like the following:

  - Who constructed the Web site?
  - What makes that person or organization credible?

- What clues can you find within the Web site that indicate it is more or less credible? For example, what kind of sites do the links lead to?

WRITING ACTIVITY

Newspaper Analysis

Most newspapers do have a particular political slant, which is often clear in their editorials but is also evident in the way various news stories are presented. If you examine the newspapers from several large cities, such differences will be readily apparent. Your college library will have copies of major newspapers such as the *New York Times* and the *Washington Post*, and all major newspapers now have online versions. Select a major story that is currently in the news and compare how three newspapers cover it. What kind of photographs have they printed about the story? What do their editorials say about it? How much "newsprint" space is devoted to the story? Where do the stories appear?

Compare what you have learned with the information that several of your classmates have gathered about coverage of the same story or another similar story.

WRITING ACTIVITY

Examine a Web Site to Determine Its Audience

Select one of the following Web sites and, in no more than two pages, outline who you think is the intended audience for the site, what you think its purpose is, and why you make that assertion. Indicate who maintains the site (if you can tell) and when it was last updated. Use examples from the site to help prove your claim about the intended audience and purpose.

http://www.gangwar.com/dynamics.htm
http://www.csun.edu/~hcchs006/gang.html
http://ojjdp.ncjrs.org/pubs/reform/ch2_e.html
http://www.gangstyle.com/

Your instructor may ask you to share your findings with several of your classmates.

Where Was the Item Published?

It is becoming more and more difficult to differentiate between library research and online research because so many traditional library resources are now located online. In addition, many libraries provide portals to online databases and other online sites. As a result, whether information resides in a physical building or is stored on a server, you will need your critical thinking skills more than ever to determine its value.

As with any research activity, your decision about where to search for information depends on what you are trying to learn. If the answer to your research question requires demographic data, you might find that all the best and most current census information you need is on different Web sites maintained by a variety of agencies of the U.S. government. Web-based research is rarely sufficient for a project of any depth, however. For example, you probably can learn more about local census trends and data from your local newspaper.

Articles and other source materials published on the World Wide Web can appear professional and unbiased, but it is often difficult to find information that allows you to evaluate fully the credibility of a Web page. To do so, you need to determine what person, company, or organization constructed the site and stands behind it. If you learn that you are examining a personal Web site instead of one sponsored by a government agency or a university, you need to take that fact into account when judging its reliability. Although organizations will often have their own agenda, of course, usually an organization can devote more resources to the construction and maintenance of a Web site than an individual can. Web suffixes generally indicate the source of a Web site:

- **.edu** indicates an educational institution (www.asu.edu, for instance, is the Web address for Arizona State University). Information you find at such a location has generally been approved by the college or university. However, many colleges and universities also provide Web space for students and faculty members, and those individuals may post information that has *not* necessarily been approved by the school.

- **.com** indicates a for-profit company (www.cnn.com is the Web address for the Cable News Network). The suffix *.com* is a shortened form of the word *commercial* and usually designates a business-oriented site.

- **.org** indicates an organization (www.pbs.org is the Web address for the Corporation for Public Broadcasting). The *.org* Web suffix is generally used for nonprofit organizations.

- **.gov** indicates some level of government (state, national, or local). The URL http://www.loc.gov/ is the Web address for the site maintained by the Library of Congress.

- **.net** These Web sites are generally used by Internet service providers (ISPs) and companies that provide Web hosting like www.concentric .net. Some commercial businesses also use the *.net* extension, but usually not as their main Web site. Some Internet service providers allow their customers to use their "net" extension for sharing things like photographs, such as www.photo.net.

- **.biz** is most often used for small business Web sites such as www .minimus.biz, a Web site that sells travel-size products.

- **.info** is, like *.com*, an unrestricted domain. Anyone can use it. According to Network Associates, the company that assigns and allocates Web addresses, *info* is the most popular extension beyond *.com, .net,* and *.org.* An example is www.microbes.info, a portal for information on microbiology.

For more information on Web suffixes and addresses, see http://www .networksolutions.com/. Network Solutions offers a "WhoIs" search function for nearly all sites on the Web except personal ones. Conducting a "WhoIs" search will give you information about the creator of any particular Web page. This search not only tells you who "owns" the domain name, but also provides e-mail contact information. If the Web page you're looking for is not listed, then it is probably a personal page.[1]

How Accurate Is the Information in This Source?

Do you believe everything you read? Anyone who checks out in a supermarket and sees newspaper headlines about aliens and Elvis sightings understands that not all news stories that appear in print are necessarily accurate. How do you know what information to believe and what information to view with skepticism?

- One of the best ways of determining accuracy in any publication is finding out who published it. As we have noted, books published by university presses and articles published in academic journals are peer-reviewed. You can usually expect that large newspapers such as the *New York Times* will print the most accurate information available at the time. Over time, some information published in reliable periodicals or newspapers may change or be corrected. The publication is then likely to publish the updated information. Publications of this caliber also tend to be credible because they have a history of firing writers who knowingly publish false information.

- Another way of determining accuracy is to investigate the author's track record. You might check the author's academic credentials, for example, as we have done for authors Duffy and Gillig on page 517. Of course, it's important to make sure that the author's area of expertise is in the

---

[1] Thanks to William Sherman, University of Northern Colorado, for this information.

subject you are researching. A famous actor who writes a diet book may or may not be a credible source of information on proper nutrition.

To determine the accuracy of information on a Web site, you might consider the Web sites the site provides links to. Often, following some of the links will give you a good deal of information about the site's credibility. For example, the Web site Streetgangs.com showed these links in December of 2006:

> ➤ Gang Member receives 50 years, Dec 8, 2006
> ➤ Stopping gang activity is a noble goal, but the end doesn't always justify the means, Nov 30, 2006
> ➤ Delgadillo names U.S. prosecutor as 'gang czar', Nov 28, 2006
> ➤ Police, FBI target San Fernando Valley gang crimes, Nov 22, 2006

Links that connect to reputable newspapers or television stations would indicate that whoever is maintaining the Web site is providing readers with connections to legitimate news articles, thus adding to the credibility of the Web site. However, the links listed above lead to stories that have bylines but give little indication of what organization the writer works for. Some simply say "Times Staff." What impact do links such as these have on the way you view the information available on this site?

A WRITER'S RESPONSIBILITIES

Evaluating Web Sites

Ask yourself the following questions when evaluating the credibility of a Web site.

- Who is the author or sponsor of the site? What can you find out about the author or sponsor?
- What does the site's address tell you about it? What does the suffix that appears at the end of the address tell you about it: *edu* for educational, for example, or *com* for commercial? Is there a tilde (~) in the address, which indicates a personal site?
- What is the purpose of the site? Is the purpose to provide information? Is the site trying to sell a product or service? To persuade readers to accept a particular point of view?
- How professional is the tone, and how well designed is the site? How carefully has it been edited and proofread? How many grammatical and spelling errors are there?
- Consider the quality of the author's arguments. Does the content contain logical fallacies? How fairly does the author deal with opposing views?
- Can you find a date when the site was published or most recently updated?
- What kinds of links does the site provide? How legitimate or credible are the sites the links lead to? Are there links to questionable sites or to sites that no longer exist?

Field Research

As we have seen, much of the time you will gather information for your research projects from books, periodicals, the World Wide Web, and other preexisting sources. At other times, you may need to gather first-hand information. Sometimes you can get the information you need by simply observing people, wildlife, or natural phenomena. At other times, the best method of gathering information from human subjects may be to ask questions of individual people or groups of people, either directly or in writing. However you do it, the act of gathering information on your own, instead of relying solely on information obtained in the library, on the Internet, or in a laboratory setting is called **field research** because, to obtain this information, you need to go out "into the field." The most common kinds of field research you might find yourself doing are observation, personal interviews, and surveys.

Working with Human Subjects

Much of what you may study as you conduct field research has to do with human behavior. Any time you are doing research that involves human subjects, you are expected to behave ethically and to do or say nothing that might in any way hurt your subjects. To ensure that researchers follow ethical practices, all academic institutions (and many private organizations) have Institutional Review Boards (IRBs). All research projects that use human subjects must be approved by your organization's IRB or its designated representative. All IRBs have their own rules. Check with your instructor about your school's human subject policy.

Informed Consent

Whether you are required to submit a formal proposal to your school's IRB or simply need to work closely with your instructor, if you are going to be working with human subjects, you need to get their permission by having all of the participants in your field research—whether it is an interview, an observation, or a survey—sign an Informed Consent Form. Most institutions have templates for these forms readily available.

Observations

Sometimes, seeing really is believing: Watching and recording what you see might be the best way to get good information that will help you answer your research question. If viewing people, animals, or other phenomena over a short period of time will provide you with good information, you may choose observation as your research method. On the other hand, though a phenomenon like soil erosion may be observable, it usually takes place over too long a period of time for personal observation to be useful.

OBSERVING HUMANS

If you are writing an informative or analytical paper, you may need to observe human behavior as part of your research. To make your observations, you might station yourself at a particular place in a shopping mall, at an athletic event, or at a busy intersection and record, in detail, certain behaviors. For example, you might record how many vehicles passing through an intersection near your college actually come to a complete stop at the stop sign. You would need to keep track of the total number of vehicles passing by as well as the specific number of vehicles that demonstrate the particular behavior you are watching for. It is, of course, possible to make even more detailed observations, such as what car models drivers who run stop signs are driving? To make detailed observations such as these, it helps to make preparations before you start your observation by setting up categories. Once you are in the field observing and recording, you probably won't have time to develop new ones.

OBSERVING OTHER PHENOMENA

For writing projects that lend themselves to observation, see Chapters 5, 6, and 7.

You can also observe other natural and human-influenced phenomena, of course. Some researchers observe animal behavior; others watch volcanoes, tornadoes and other weather patterns, or cosmic activity. The specific nature of what you are observing will determine the tools you will need as well as the appropriate methods you will use.

WRITING ACTIVITY

Conduct an Observation

People often comment on how tied to technology students are. Do you think this is true? One way to test this assumption might be to sit for an hour in your student union or some other place where students from your campus gather. Watch the behavior of the students. Are students talking with one another in person, or are they using technology to, for example, communicate with one another, listen to music, or watch videos? Take notes of what you see. You might want to establish some categories. Are students talking on cell phones? Are they using laptops? Are they listening to iPods? After you've watched and taken notes, write a short report on your findings.

Interviews

Because most of us are comfortable talking with other people, we often think
that interviewing someone will be easy. Interviews are rarely an easy way to
do meaningful research, however. Effective interviews that yield useful information happen only when the interviewer prepares ahead of time. As you
prepare, it's important to remember that some of the interviews you may see
on television or listen to on the radio are not necessarily good examples of
interviewing. The aggressive, "in your face" nature of many media interview-
ers is rarely suitable for the purpose of gathering information.

You can employ several strategies to prepare and conduct a successful
interview:

- Be sure to call ahead to make an appointment instead of just showing up in your subject's office. A little bit of courtesy will often
  make your subject more comfortable and, as a result, you might
  obtain more information than you might otherwise have been able
  to get.

- Do your homework ahead of time so that you have good questions
  ready to ask, have anticipated the nature of the responses, and have
  good follow-up questions at hand. While it is impossible to predict
  exactly what your subject will say, being able to anticipate the nature
  of the interview will enable you to steer the interview in the direction
  in which you need it to go.

- Be prepared to take notes using either a laptop computer or paper and
  pencil. Before you interview someone for an assignment, practice
  (using your interview questions) with a classmate or a friend.

- Consider bringing along some kind of recording device. If you plan to
  record the interview, make sure you have your subject's permission
  before the interview begins. Some people are willing to talk but do not
  wish to be recorded. They have the right to say "no" to you.

- Be polite and friendly during the interview. It is usually a good idea to
  follow up an interview with a thank-you note.

While your specific interview questions will depend on your topic
and the person you are interviewing, you will usually want to prepare two
kinds of questions: open-ended and directed. **Open-ended questions**
let the person being interviewed develop his or her answers at length. You
ask **directed questions** to get more specific kinds of information. As
part of her research for a paper on violence in the movies, for example,
Magda is interested in learning about how people actually react when
they are watching violent movies. To find out, she has decided to interview the local manager of a theater chain that sometimes shows violent,
R-rated movies. To prepare for the interview, Magda has come up with the
following list of questions:

1. What would you consider a violent movie?

2. What specific content in a movie makes it violent?

3. Are all movies that contain scenes with (the content from the previous questions) necessarily violent? If not, why not? What's the determining factor?

4. Do you show many movies like that? If so, how many per month?

5. Why do you think people like violent movies?

6. What age groups seem to like violent movies?

7. Do audiences at violent movies behave differently from audiences at other types of movies, such as comedies?

8. Are audiences at violent movies likely to buy more at the concession stand?

9. Do audiences at violent movies leave behind more trash in the theater?

10. Are audiences at violent movies more likely to leave through an unauthorized exit?

11. Are audiences at violent movies generally noisier, rowdier?

Some of the questions in Magda's list, such as the first three, are open-ended. Others, such as questions 7–11, are more directed and may indicate the direction of her thinking as she develops her thesis.

You should always avoid what can be called "forced-choice questions," questions that presuppose only a few specific choices and force your subject to answer one of them. Asking "Do you think the football team is bad or just plain awful this year?" assumes the team really is bad and that your subject will agree. A better question would be, "What's your opinion of the football team this year?"

You should also stay away from leading questions that have built-in *assumptions* the person you are interviewing might not agree with. A question like "Don't you think that conducting surveys provides a richness that

WRITING ACTIVITY

Conduct an Interview

Assume that you are a reporter for your school's newspaper. Your editor has assigned you to interview the president of your campus on a topic of your choice. Develop a list of ten questions, some open-ended, some directed, that you want to ask the president.

other research methods can't match?" assumes (1) that the interviewee will interpret "richness" in the same way you do, and (2) that both of your definitions of "can't match" will also agree. It would be more effective to ask the question in a more neutral way: "Are there any advantages, in your view, to surveys over other kinds of field research? If so, what might they be?"

Surveys and Questionnaires

Although interviews are helpful sources of information and have the advantage of enabling a direct exchange between the subject and the interviewer, the number of people that one person can interview is of course limited. Some research projects require you to collect information from a larger number of people than you could possibly interview. To get information from a large number of people quickly and efficiently, you can use a **survey** or **questionnaire.** Though on the surface a survey may look like just a set of questions, a good survey is carefully designed, and its questions are very specifically framed. A good survey will either target a particular group of people or solicit information about the participants to provide you with a context for their answers.

Several strategies will enable you to put together an effective survey:

- Keep the survey a reasonable length. Ask only those questions that are really necessary. Many people think that all surveys need to start with questions that ask for certain basic demographic information, but you need gather only information that is important for your research. If you are not going to sort your data by age groupings, for example, there is no need to ask your respondents their age.

- Make sure the questions you ask call for an appropriate response. If a reasonable answer to the question is "yes," or "no," make sure there are only two possible responses. If a wider range of responses is appropriate, a scale such as "strongly agree, agree, no opinion, disagree, strongly disagree" may be more useful.

- Consider whether you want to ask only *closed-ended* or *directed* questions that call for specific answers, such as "List your age," or if you also want to ask *open-ended* questions, such as "Describe your experience at the Math Testing Center." Closed-ended questions are easier to tabulate, but open-ended questions will provide you with more examples and narrative detail.

- If you ask open-ended questions that call for written responses, make sure that you give your respondents enough room on the form to answer fully.

- Make sure that the question itself doesn't influence the response. Asking a question like "Do you think there are not enough parking spaces on campus?" leads the respondent to say "yes." A more effective way to get the same information would be to ask, "What is your opinion of the campus parking situation?"

- Make sure you have a way of tabulating the open-ended responses. Are you going to try to categorize them? Are you planning to use them as anecdotal examples?

ADMINISTERING YOUR SURVEY

Test your survey before you administer it. That way, if a question or two prove to be faulty, you have a chance to make changes. Have several people respond to your survey, asking them to indicate any confusing questions. Also consider whom you would like to respond to your survey, targeting your audience as specifically as possible. A general rule of thumb is that the more people you can ask to take your survey—the larger the data set—the more useful the results will be. It is also important to make sure that you are surveying the right population. If you are looking for information on what kind of coffee drinks are most popular on your campus (mochas, lattes, cappuccinos, and the like), for example, you will need to make sure you survey only coffee drinkers.

WRITING ACTIVITY

Develop a Survey

Often people who are thinking of opening a small business conduct a survey of their potential clientele to test their business plan's chances for success. Think of a possible product or service that seems to be lacking in your community. Then identify the customers your business will serve. Develop a set of survey questions that will give you a good sense of whether others share your perceived need for this business.

Synthesizing and Documenting Sources

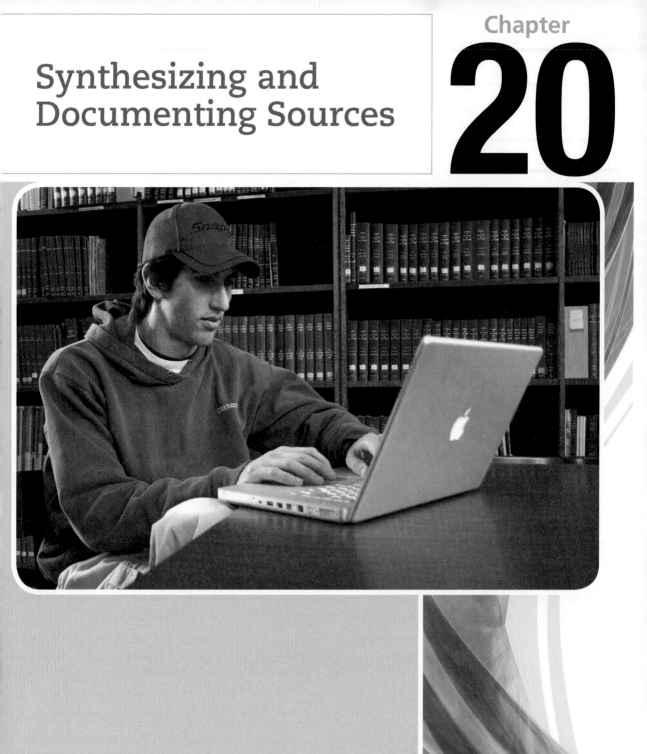

Effective academic writing does not just emerge out of a writer's mind. Academic writers are expected to know what others have said on their topic, using the work of other writers to help establish a foundation for an argument, substantiate an argument, or set up a point that they will then challenge or support. This process of building your own arguments using support and arguments from other writers is called **synthesis.** As they synthesize ideas, all academic writers need to use sources, acknowledging the thinking that already exists on an issue and giving credit to those who developed it. When developing an argument in an academic essay, for instance, you will be expected to review the relevant work of previous researchers and summarize their results. You will then be able to build your own arguments, working from theirs. And you will need to give these researchers credit.

For more on synthesis, see Chapter 2, pages 28–30.

When you document sources appropriately, you accomplish several important purposes.

- Documentation indicates what you as the writer did not produce—in effect, it indicates where you have used summary and paraphrase: "This isn't my idea and here is where it came from." Or it indicates a quotation: "These aren't my words, and here is the name of the person who wrote them."

- Documentation that follows a system such as the one recommended by the Modern Language Association (MLA) or the American Psychological Association (APA) provides readers with a list of sources—called the list of Works Cited in MLA style or References in APA style—so if a reader wants to learn more about the topic, he or she can consult the works listed.

- Proper documentation, within the text and in the list of sources, makes it easy for the reader to locate and read a particular source the writer has cited or even a specific quotation in that source. In this way sources function like hyperlinks do in Web-based documents.

- Proper documentation of appropriate sources lends ethos and credibility to you as a writer and enhances your argument.

Different academic disciplines have different style guides that offer a range of conventions for writers to follow, including conventions for documentation; to some extent, the differences among these style guides reflect the different needs of the disciplines that use them. Here we will present the conventions for documentation given in the style guides of the MLA and the APA. MLA style is used for papers in humanities disciplines, including English; APA style is used for papers in social science disciplines. The current editions of both manuals are as follows:

Gibaldi, Joseph. *MLA Handbook for Writers of Research Papers*. 6th ed. New York: MLA, 2003.

American Psychological Association. (2001). *Publication manual of the American Psychological Association* (5th ed.). Washington, DC: Author.[1]

Although we are concentrating here on the documentation styles recommended by the MLA and APA, other disciplines recommend a variety of styles. Here are some of those other options:

- *Scientific Style and Format: The CSE Manual for Authors, Editors and Publishers* (7th ed.). If your academic work is in the sciences, you may be required to use the style suggested by the Council of Scientific Editors (CSE), formerly the Council of Biology Editors (CBE).

- *Information for Authors,* published by the Institute of Electrical and Electronics Engineers (IEEE), is used by engineers, both academics and practicing professionals.

- *The Chicago Manual of Style* (15th ed.) (CMS) is another widely used style. In fact, if you are expected to do on-the-job writing that requires documentation, more likely than not you will use CMS.

When you use information from sources to support your thesis, you must be careful to give appropriate credit to the author of each source. Failing to do so is plagiarism. You can choose from among several options for presenting information that you have taken from other writers' work: quotations, paraphrases, or summaries.

For help with avoiding plagiarism, see pages 535–37.

Quotations

When the most effective way to make a point is to use another author's exact words, you are using a **quotation.** Use a direct quotation in the following situations:

- When the exact wording is particularly striking, such as in a literary quotation
- When the author is considered to be especially authoritative
- When you take issue with the author's statement

If you are using MLA style and your quotation is shorter than five lines, you should enclose it in quotation marks and incorporate it into your text. Because the quotation is incorporated into the sentence, a comma is used after the introductory phrase. At first it might feel a bit awkward or clumsy when you integrate quoted material into your writing; however, you will get better with

---

[1] APA has also published the *APA Style Guide to Electronic References* (2007), which covers electronic sources.

For information on how to cite quotations, paraphrases, and summaries within text, see pages 538–41 for MLA style and pages 566–68 for APA style.

practice. Using verbs such as *notes, comments, observes, explains,* or similar words will help you introduce quotations smoothly and meaningfully.

> Writing about the power of computers, Sherry Turkle says, "When I want to write and don't have a computer, I tend to wait until I do" (29).

When the quotation is longer than four lines and you are using MLA style, start the quotation on a new line and indent all lines of the quotation ten spaces. The quotation should be double spaced and does not need to be enclosed in quotation marks. Because the quotation is introduced with an independent clause, that clause is followed by a colon.

> An early researcher in virtual environments writes of their compelling nature:
>> Why is it so hard for me to turn away from the screen? The windows on my computer desktop offer me layers of material to which I have simultaneous access: field notes; previous drafts of this book; a list of ideas not yet elaborated but which I want to include; transcripts of interviews with computer users; and verbatim logs of sessions on computer networks, on bulletin boards, and in virtual communities. (Turkle 29)

If you are using APA style, quotations of fewer than forty words should be enclosed in quotation marks and incorporated into the text, as follows:

> Writing about the power of computers, Sherry Turkle (1995) says, "When I want to write and don't have a computer, I tend to wait until I do" (p. 29).

Block quotations are used in APA style when the quotation is at least forty words long. They are indented only five spaces and double spaced, and are not enclosed in quotation marks.

> An early researcher in virtual environments writes eloquently of their compelling nature:
>> Why is it so hard for me to turn away from the screen? The windows on my computer desktop offer me layers of material to which I have simultaneous access: field notes; previous drafts of this book; a list of ideas not yet elaborated but which I want to include; transcripts of interviews with computer users; and verbatim logs of sessions on computer networks, on bulletin boards, and in virtual communities. (Turkle, 1995, p. 29)

Paraphrases

Use **paraphrases** when you put someone else's ideas into your own words. It is important to understand that because you are using someone else's ideas in a paraphrase, you need to make appropriate citations. However, in a paraphrase you will use your own words and sentence structure. If you choose to borrow unique phrases from the original, those phrases should be placed in quotation marks. Here, for example, is a block quotation in APA style:

> In his book, *The World Is Flat, New York Times* columnist Thomas
> L. Friedman (2005) notes that when Netscape went public in 1995, it
> had significant ramifications for the emerging global economy:
>> Looking back, what enabled Netscape to take off was the existence,
>> from the earlier phase, of millions of PC's, many already equipped with
>> modems. Those are the shoulders Netscape stood on. What Netscape
>> did was bring a new killer app—the browser—to this installed base of
>> PC's making the computer and its connectivity inherently more useful
>> for millions of people. (p. 57)

If you don't want to use a direct quotation, you can paraphrase Friedman's information by changing it into your own words. However, you need to be careful in paraphrasing that you do not commit **plagiarism** by using language and/or sentence structures that are too close to the original. The following paraphrase is guilty of using language that too closely mimics the original. (The language that is too close to the original is highlighted.)

Faulty Paraphrase

> In *The World Is Flat* (2005), Thomas L. Friedman looks back to
> 1995 and notes that what enabled Netscape to take off when it
> went public was that it could stand on the shoulders of the millions
> of already existing PC's, many already equipped with modems.
> Its new killer app—the browser—helped millions of people make
> connecting more useful. (57)

By contrast, the following paraphrase is entirely in the writer's own words and sentence structures, yet it contains essentially the same ideas as the original quotation from Friedman.

Acceptable Paraphrase

> In *The World Is Flat* (2005), Thomas L. Friedman looks back to 1995 and notes that Netscape could make a significant impact on the emerging global economy when it went public because of its browser. When Netscape brought this new software application—the browser—to the users of modem-enhanced PC's, it made those connected computers much more useful. (57)

Suppose you were writing about the film *Harry Potter and the Sorcerer's Stone* and wanted to cite ideas from Roger Ebert's review of it. Here is a paragraph from Ebert's review (the entire review appears in Chapter 9):

> *Harry Potter and the Sorcerer's Stone* is a red-blooded adventure movie, dripping with atmosphere, filled with the gruesome and the sublime, and surprisingly faithful to the novel. A lot of things could have gone wrong, and none of them have: Chris Columbus' movie is an enchanting classic that does full justice to a story that was a daunting challenge. The novel by J. K. Rowling was muscular and vivid, and the danger was that the movie would make things too cute and cuddly. It doesn't. Like an Indiana Jones for younger viewers, it tells a rip-roaring tale of supernatural adventure, where colorful and eccentric characters alternate with scary stuff like a three-headed dog, a pit of tendrils known as the Devil's Snare and a two-faced immortal who drinks unicorn blood. Scary, yes, but not too scary—just scary enough.

A faulty paraphrase would mimic Ebert's sentence structure in the original text. Here is an excerpt from Ebert's paragraph:

> The novel by J. K. Rowling was muscular and vivid, and the danger was that the movie would make things too cute and cuddly. It doesn't.

A poor paraphrase would look similar:

Faulty Paraphrase

> According to Ebert, the novel by J. K. Rowling was brawny and brilliant, and the danger was that the movie would make things too delightful and cuddly. It does not.

The following acceptable version conveys Ebert's idea but with a different sentence structure:

Acceptable Paraphrase

According to Ebert, the film avoids the trap of making Harry's story too cutesy while remaining true to the novel's power.

Summaries

When you include a **summary** of your source's ideas, you condense the material presented by another author into a briefer form. While similar to paraphrasing, summaries condense information into a substantially smaller number of words. Paraphrases might be similar in length to the original. Summaries vary in length depending on what is being summarized. You might summarize a paragraph or even a page of material in only a sentence or two. To summarize a chapter, you might need several paragraphs. A summary of a larger work might be several pages in length. Once again, however, a summary must be entirely in your own words and sentence structure to avoid plagiarizing the original. Here are acceptable and unacceptable summaries of the Ebert passage on page 536 (in the unacceptable passage, wording from the original and sentence structure that is too close to the original are highlighted):

Unacceptable Summary

Roger Ebert notes that the film is an adventure movie with lots of atmosphere and that it does full justice to Rowling's challenging novel. Colorful and eccentric characters alternate with scenes that are scary but not too scary.

Acceptable Summary

In Roger Ebert's opinion, the film is a faithful rendition of the first Harry Potter novel, a rousing adventure story in the tradition of the *Indiana Jones* films. It offers a not overly frightening experience along with Rowling's "colorful and eccentric characters."

Note that if you use phrases from the original in your summary, you should enclose them in quotation marks.

For more on writing a summary, see Chapter 2, page 28.

Ellipses

If you decide that a quotation is too long and you want to condense it, you can do so by placing an ellipsis (three periods with a space between each) in place of the omitted words. If the ellipsis occurs at the end of the sentence, you will need to place the sentence's period preceding the first ellipsis with a space between the first ellipsis period and the period of the sentence. Make sure when you use an ellipsis that you are careful not to change the meaning of the original quotation. For example, compare the original quotation from Marshall McLuhan and the condensed version.

> As the alphabet neutralized the divergencies of primitive cultures by translation of their complexities into simple visual terms, so representative money reduced the moral values in the nineteenth century.

> In <u>Understanding Media</u>, Marshall McLuhan compares the visual technology inherent in the alphabet with money, saying, "As the alphabet neutralized the divergencies of primitive cultures . . . so representative money reduced moral values in the nineteenth century" (141).

Brackets

If you find that something within a quotation is not clear and you need to add information so that your readers will understand it better, you can do so by using square brackets [ ]:

> In their book <u>Freakonomics</u>, Steven D. Leavitt and Stephen J. Dubner confirm that often commonly held stereotypes seem to apply to reality:
> > For instance, men [on online dating sites] who say they want a long-term relationship do much better than men looking for an occasional lover. But women [on the same sites] looking for an occasional lover do great. (82)

■ MLA Documentation Style

There are two components to MLA style: parenthetical in-text citations and a works-cited list that appears at the end of the paper. Every source cited within the body of the paper appears in the works-cited list.

MLA Style: In-Text Citation

In MLA style, parenthetical in-text citations are used in conjunction with the list of works cited to give readers the information they would need to locate the sources that you have quoted, paraphrased, or summarized. The intent in MLA style is to give only as much information in the text as the reader needs to find the detailed bibliographical information in the list of works cited—generally, the author and the page number of the material cited. The following are examples of how to cite different types of sources within your text using MLA style, starting with the most basic citation: a work with one author.

A WORK WITH ONE AUTHOR

Suppose that you quote from page 282 of Deborah Tannen's *You Just Don't Understand: Women and Men in Conversation*, published in 1990. In MLA style, your in-text citation would be *(Tannen 282)*. MLA in-text citations do not include punctuation, and the page number is given simply as a number.

The parenthetical citation is placed directly after the cited material. Here is an example using a block quotation in MLA style:

> In talking about gender differences, this phenomenon is noted:
>
> > Complementary schismogenisis commonly sets in when women and men have divergent sensitivities and hypersensitivities. For example, a man who fears losing freedom pulls away at the first sign he interprets as an attempt to "control" him, but pulling away is just the signal that sets off alarms for the woman who fears losing intimacy. (Tannen 282)

In this example, the author's name is not mentioned in the text that precedes the quotation. When the author's name is mentioned in the preceding sentence, however, the parenthetical citation includes only the page number, as in the following example:

> Deborah Tannen, a researcher who has written extensively about the language differences of men and women, notes, "Understanding each other's styles, and the motives behind them, is a first move in breaking this destructive cycle" (282).

Note that when a quotation is given within a sentence of your text, the period ends *your sentence*.

A WORK WITH MORE THAN ONE AUTHOR

Use all the authors' last names. If there are more than three authors, you can use the first author's last name with *et al.* following it.

> Glassick, Huber, and Maeroff state that "teaching, too, must in the end be judged not merely by process but by results, however eloquent a teacher's performance" (29).

> Ultimately, it is the results of teaching, not the method or the quality of the teacher's performance, that we must evaluate (Glassick, Huber, and Maeroff 29).

TWO OR MORE WORKS BY THE SAME AUTHOR

If you are citing ideas from two or more works by the same author, use the title of the work (in a shortened version if appropriate) to distinguish which source you are citing.

> It is important to establish good relations with the people you work with by engaging in non-work related conversation. Both men and women do so, but the subjects of their conversations differ (Tannen, Talking from 9 to 5 64).

AN UNKNOWN AUTHOR

Use a shortened version of the title.

> Employees of Google believe their corporate culture to be antithetical to that of Microsoft ("Google" 15).

A GOVERNMENT AGENCY OR A CORPORATE AUTHOR

Use the name of the organization. You can shorten lengthy names in the parenthetical citation.

> Policy makers and citizens are warned that "Arizona is not positioned well to attract and keep the knowledge workers it needs" (Morrison Institute 6).

AN ANTHOLOGIZED WORK

Cite the author of the anthologized piece, not the editor of the collection. However, give the page numbers used in the collection.

John Perry Barlow asks the important question: "The enigma is this: If our property can be infinitely reproduced and instantaneously distributed all over the planet without cost, without our knowledge, without its even leaving our possession, how can we protect it?" (319).

A SECONDARY SOURCE

Whenever possible, cite the original source. However, if you do need to use a quotation from a secondary source, use *qtd. in* to let your readers know that you are doing so.

Jonathan Shaw muses, "I don't think mankind is ready, spiritually or mentally, for the transformations it's undergoing in the technological era: tattooing is a mute plea for a return to human values" (qtd. in Dery 284).

AN ONLINE SOURCE

Unless your source has some kind of numbering system or is a pdf file, you will not usually be able to provide page numbers for your quotation or paraphrase. Give the author or, if the author's name is not available, the title of the online work you are citing.

According to Christopher Beam, there are a number of methods that Internet service providers can use to block Web sites if a government orders them to do so.

MLA Style: Constructing a List of Works Cited

Because the list of works cited at the end of your paper is intended to work together with your in-text citations, it includes only the sources you cite within your text, not the works that you read but did not cite. The list should be double-spaced, and its entries are listed alphabetically by the last name of the first author. The first line of each entry is even with the left margin; any subsequent lines are indented by one-half inch or five spaces so that it is easy for a reader to skim down the left side of the page and find the author he or she is looking for.

All entries in the list are formatted following the same rules—this standardized format makes it easy for readers to understand the information in each entry. In the following pages you will find, for each common type of entry, a sample entry for a work in MLA style and, on pages 566–81, for many of the same works in APA style. First, though, to see some important differences between the two styles, consider these pairs of entries:

MLA   Paivio, Allan. <u>Mental Representations</u>. New York: Oxford UP, 1986.

APA   Paivio, A. (1986). *Mental representations*. New York: Oxford University Press.

MLA   Miller, George A. "The Magical Number Seven, Plus or Minus Two: Some Limits on Our Capacity for Processing Information." <u>Psychological Review</u> 63 (1956): 81–97.

APA   Miller, G. A. (1956). The magical number seven, plus or minus two: Some limits on our capacity for processing information. *Psychological Review, 63,* 81–97.

Notice in particular the following:

- In both styles, entries consist of three essential pieces of information, separated by periods: author, source (a book in the first pair, an article from an academic journal in the second), and publication information for the source (place of publication and publisher for the book; journal title and volume number for the article). Note the difference in the placement of information: Because of the importance of the year of publication to social scientists, in APA style it immediately follows the author's name rather than coming later in the entry as it does in MLA style.
- In MLA style, authors' first and middle names are given in full if that is how they are given in the source; in APA style, only initials are given.
- In MLA style, all major words in titles are capitalized; in APA style, only the first word, words following a colon, and names are capitalized in the titles of books and articles. All major words are capitalized in the titles of periodicals, however.
- In MLA style, titles of books and periodicals are underscored, and titles of articles are enclosed in quotation marks; in APA style, titles of books and periodicals are given in italics, and titles of articles are not enclosed in quotation marks.

The section that follows includes model entries for different types of print and nonprint sources in MLA style. Figure 20.1 provides you with a flowchart that will help you find the model entry that is closest to the source that you need to cite.

Is My Source a Complete Print Book or Part of a Print Book?

No	Yes, go to the next question below.	Go to this entry.
	Is it a book with only one author?	1 (p.546)
	Are you citing more than one book by this author?	2 (p.547)
	Is it a book with multiple authors?	3 (p.547)
	Is the book by an organization of some kind?	4 (p.547)
	Is the author unknown or unnamed?	5 (p.547)
	Does the book also have a translator?	11 (p.548)
	Is it a later publication or edition of the book?	6, 7 (p.547)
	Is it a multivolume work or part of a multivolume work?	13 (p.548)
	Is it part of a series?	14 (p.548)
	Does the book have an editor or a translator?	8, 11 (p.547, 548)
	Is the book an edited collection or anthology?	8 (p.547)
	Is it a work in a collection or anthology?	9 (p.548)
	Is it an introduction, a preface, a foreword, or an afterword?	12 (p.548)
	Is it an entry in a dictionary or reference work?	22 (p.551)
	Is it a published interview?	10 (p.548)

Is My Source from a Print Periodical Such as a Journal, a Magazine, or a Newspaper?

No	Yes, go to the next question below.	Go to this entry.
	Is it from a scholarly journal?	
	Do the journal's page numbers continue from one issue to the next?	15 (p.549)
	Does each issue start with page 1?	16 (p.549)
	Is it from a magazine?	17 (p.550)
	Is it a review?	20 (p.551)
	Is it from a newspaper?	18 (p.551)
	Is it an editorial?	19 (p.551)
	Is it a letter to the editor?	21 (p.551)

Is My Source a Print Source but Not from a Journal, a Magazine, or a Newspaper?

No	Yes, go to the next question below.	Go to this entry.
	Is it an entry in a dictionary or reference work?	22 (p.551)
	Is it a government document?	23 (p.552)
	Is it a pamphlet?	24 (p.552)
	Is it the proceedings from a conference?	25 (p.552)
	Is it an unpublished doctoral dissertation?	26 (p.552)
	Is it a published or an unpublished letter?	27 (p.552)
	Is it a map or chart?	28 (p.553)
	Is it a cartoon?	29 (p.553)
	Is it an advertisement?	30 (p.553)

FIGURE 20.1

MLA Style: A Flowchart for Determining the Model Works-Cited Entry You Need

(cont'd)

FIGURE 20.1
Continued

Is My Source a Nonprint Source from an Online Subscription Database or the World Wide Web?

No Yes, go to the next question below.	Go to this entry.
Is it a professional or personal Web site?	31 (p.553)
Is it an article?	
Is it a scholarly article retrieved from a database?	32 (p.553)
Is it an article from an online journal?	34 (p.555)
Is it an article from an online magazine?	35 (p.555)
Is it an article from an online newspaper?	36 (p.555)
Is it an online book?	33 (p.555)
Is it a blog entry?	37 (p.555)
Is it an entry on a wiki?	38 (p.556)
Is it a posting to an electronic forum?	39 (p.556)
Is it an e-mail message?	40 (p.556)

Is My Source a Nonprint Source That Is Not Published Online?

No Yes, go to the next question below.	Go to this entry.
Is it a television or radio program?	41 (p.556)
Is it an audio recording?	42 (p.556)
Is it a film, video recording, or DVD?	43 (p.556)
Is it a nonperiodical publication on CD-ROM?	44 (p.557)
Is it a personal, e-mail, or telephone interview?	45 (p.557)
Is it an oral presentation?	46 (p.557)
Is it a performance?	47 (p.557)
Is it a work of art?	48 (p.557)

Consult with Your Instructor about How to Cite Your Source.

PRINT DOCUMENTS

Books

The basic items in an entry for a book are the author's name or authors' names, the title, and the publication information, consisting of the place of publication, publisher, and date of publication. See Figure 20.2 on pages 545–46 for guidelines on where to find the elements of a works-cited entry for a book in MLA style.

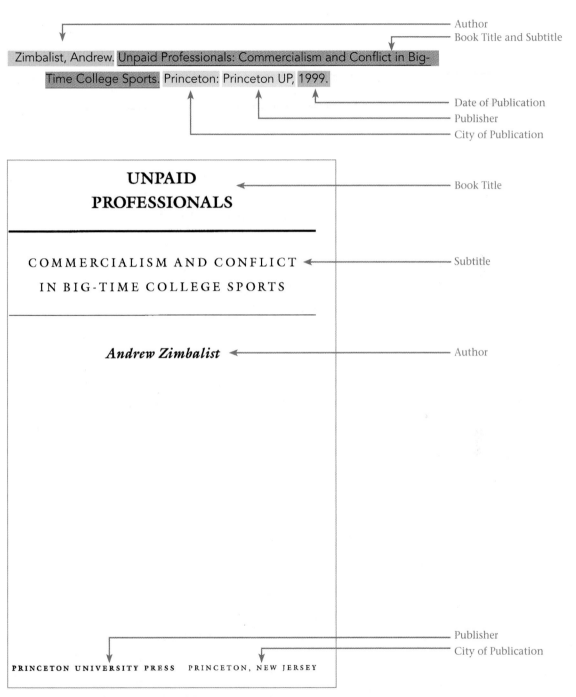

Author
Book Title and Subtitle

Zimbalist, Andrew. Unpaid Professionals: Commercialism and Conflict in Big-Time College Sports. Princeton: Princeton UP, 1999.

Date of Publication
Publisher
City of Publication

UNPAID PROFESSIONALS ← Book Title

COMMERCIALISM AND CONFLICT ← Subtitle
IN BIG-TIME COLLEGE SPORTS

Andrew Zimbalist ← Author

Publisher
City of Publication

PRINCETON UNIVERSITY PRESS   PRINCETON, NEW JERSEY

FIGURE 20.2 The Parts of a Works-Cited Entry for a Book in MLA Style

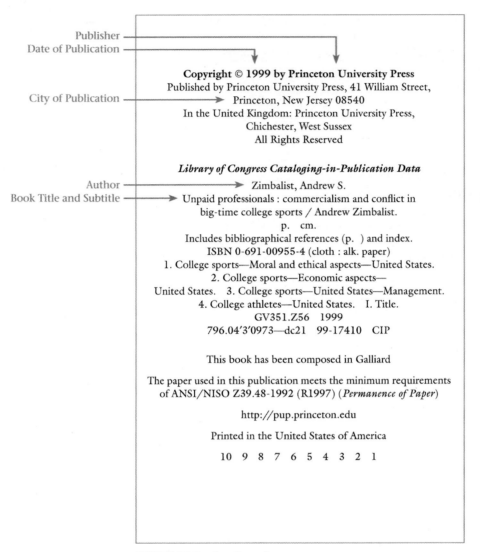

Publisher ——
Date of Publication ——

City of Publication ——

Copyright © 1999 by Princeton University Press
Published by Princeton University Press, 41 William Street,
Princeton, New Jersey 08540
In the United Kingdom: Princeton University Press,
Chichester, West Sussex
All Rights Reserved

Library of Congress Cataloging-in-Publication Data

Author ——
Book Title and Subtitle ——

Zimbalist, Andrew S.
Unpaid professionals : commercialism and conflict in
big-time college sports / Andrew Zimbalist.
p.   cm.
Includes bibliographical references (p.   ) and index.
ISBN 0-691-00955-4 (cloth : alk. paper)
1. College sports—Moral and ethical aspects—United States.
2. College sports—Economic aspects—
United States.   3. College sports—United States—Management.
4. College athletes—United States.   I. Title.
GV351.Z56   1999
796.04′3′0973—dc21   99-17410   CIP

This book has been composed in Galliard

The paper used in this publication meets the minimum requirements
of ANSI/NISO Z39.48-1992 (R1997) (*Permanence of Paper*)

http://pup.princeton.edu

Printed in the United States of America

10   9   8   7   6   5   4   3   2   1

FIGURE 20.2   Continued

1. Book with one author: The most basic form includes the author's name, the title of the book, underlined, and the publication information.

　　　　　　　　　　　　　　　　　　　　　　publication information
　　author　　　　　　　　　　title　　　　　city　　publisher
Gould, Stephen Jay. <u>The Mismeasure of Man</u>. New York: Norton,

date
1981.

2. Two books by the same author: MLA style gives the author's name only in the first entry. For all subsequent entries, three hyphens are used instead of the name. The entries are listed in alphabetical order according to title.

Tannen, Deborah. Talking from 9 to 5. New York: Morrow, 1994.

- - -. You Just Don't Understand: Women and Men in Conversation. New
York: Ballantine, 1990.

3. Book with multiple authors: In MLA style, only the first author's name is inverted; the other authors' names are given first name first. MLA style uses *and* before the last author's name. In MLA style, if a book has more than three authors, you may give all the names or give the name of the first author followed by *et al.* (For an example of the use of *et al.*, see #8.)

Covey, Stephen R., A. Roger Merrill, and Rebecca R. Merrill. First Things
First. New York: Simon, 1994.

4. Book by a corporate entity or organization:

Adobe Systems Inc. Adobe Acrobat 5.0: Getting Started. San Jose, CA:
Adobe, 2001.

5. Book by an unknown author:

The Chicago Manual of Style: The Essential Guide for Writers, Editors, and
Publishers. 15th ed. Chicago: Chicago UP, 2003.

6. Republished book: Including the original date of publication is optional in MLA style. If you do include this date, place it immediately following the title.

Dickens, Charles. Hard Times. 1854. Ed. David Craig. Baltimore: Penguin,
1969.

7. Book in a later edition:

Corbett, Edward P. J. Classical Rhetoric for the Modern Student. 3rd ed.
New York: Oxford UP, 1990.

8. Edited collection:

Inman, James A., and Donna N. Sewell, eds. Taking Flight with Owls:
Examining Electronic Writing Center Work. Mahwah: Erlbaum, 2000.

Harrington, Susanmarie, et al., eds. The Outcomes Book: Debate and Consensus after the WPA Outcomes Statement. Logan: Utah State UP, 2005.

9. Work in a collection or an anthology: In MLA style the page ranges come at the end of the citation.

Anson, Chris M., and Richard Jewell. "Shadows of the Mountain." Moving a Mountain: Transforming the Role of Contingent Faculty in Composition Studies and Higher Education. Ed. Eileen E. Schell and Patricia Lambert Stock. Urbana: NCTE, 2001. 47–75.

10. Published interview:

Hawisher, Gail. "Making the Map: An Interview with Gail Hawisher." Feminist Cyberscapes: Mapping Gendered Academic Spaces. Interview with Kristine Blair and Pamela Takayoshi. Ed. Kristine Blair and Pamela Takayoshi. Stamford: Ablex, 1999. 177–91.

11. Translation:

Eliade, Mircea. The Sacred and the Profane: The Nature of Religion. Trans. Willard R. Trask. New York: Harcourt, 1959.

12. Introduction, preface, foreword, or afterword:

Burns, Hugh. Foreword. Technology and Literacy in the Twenty-First Century: The Importance of Paying Attention. By Cynthia L. Selfe. Carbondale: Southern Illinois UP, 1999. ix-xvii.

13. A multivolume work: If you have used more than one volume of a multivolume work, place that information after the title.

Campbell, Joseph. The Masks of God. 4 vols. New York: Viking, 1972.

If you have used only one volume of a multivolume work, however, cite only the volume you have used.

Elias, Norbert. The History of Manners. Vol. 1. New York: Pantheon, 1982.

14. A book in a series: If you are using a book that is part of a series, include the title of the series with no underlining or quotation marks before the publication information. Include the number of the series as well if it is present.

Marshall, Margaret J. <u>Response to Reform: Composition and the</u>

  <u>Professionalization of Teaching</u>. Studies in Writing & Rhetoric.

  Carbondale: Southern Illinois UP, 2004.

PERIODICAL ARTICLES

The basic items in an entry for a periodical article are the author's name or authors' names, the title of the article, and information about the publication in which the article appeared, including its title, volume number (if applicable), date, and the page range for the article. See Figure 20.3 for guidelines on where to find the elements of a works-cited entry for a periodical article in MLA style.

15. Article in a scholarly journal with continuous pagination: The volume number follows the title.

  authors   title of article
Thayer, Alexander, and Beth E. Kolko. "Localization of Digital Games:

  The Process of Blending for the Global Games Market."

  title of periodical   volume no. and date   page range
  <u>Technical Communication</u> 51 (2004): 477–88.

16. Article in a scholarly journal that is paginated by issue: When an article is from a journal that restarts its page numbers with each issue, the issue number follows the volume number and a period.

Howard, Rebecca Moore. "Power Revisited: Or, How We Became a

  Department." <u>Journal of the Council of Writing Program</u>

  <u>Administrators</u> 16.3 (1993): 37–49.

17. Magazine article: Magazines may or may not include volume and issue numbers. In any case, in MLA style volume numbers are not given. Instead, dates are provided. If magazines are published weekly or biweekly, the day is included along with the month, which is abbreviated. If the entire article does not appear on consecutive pages, give only the first page number and a plus sign (+).

Foust, Dean, Michael Eidem, and Brian Bremner. "AFLAC: Its Ducks Are

  Not in a Row." <u>BusinessWeek</u> 2 Feb. 2004: 52–53.

Wilson, Chauncey E. "Usability and User Experience Design: The Next

  Decade." <u>Intercom</u> Jan 2005: 6–9.

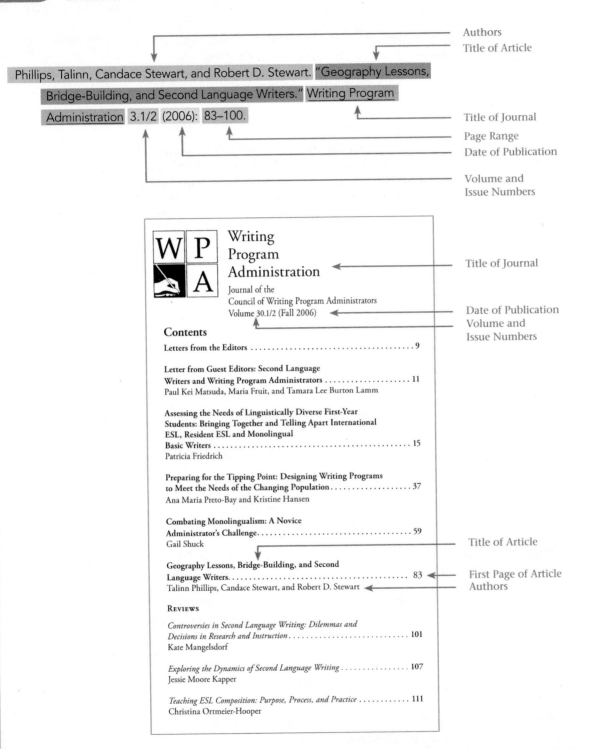

FIGURE 20.3 The Parts of a Works-Cited Entry for a Journal Article in MLA Style

18. Newspaper article: Entries for newspaper articles include the edition, when it is given (since different editions print different items), along with the date of publication and the section and page numbers. You should include the city of origin of a local newspaper within square brackets if it is not part of the title of the newspaper (for example, *Capital Times [Madison, WI]*). You should also eliminate *The* at the beginning of the names of newspapers. When articles appear on discontinuous pages, as they often do, MLA style calls for using a + sign.

> Fatsis, Stefan. "A More Modern Masters." Wall Street Journal 9 Apr. 2002:
>
> B1+.

19. Editorial:

> "Moral Scoreboard." Editorial. Arizona Republic [Phoenix, AZ] 18 Feb.
>
> 2004: B10.

20. Review: If there is no author for the review, alphabetize it by the title of the review. If the review also has no title, alphabetize by the title of what is being reviewed. When citing a review, use the format appropriate for its place of publication. If it appears in a magazine, use the format for magazines. If it appears in a newspaper, use the format for newspapers.

> Jablonski, Jeffrey. Rev. of The New Careers: Individual Action and Economic
>
> Change, by Michael B. Arthur, Kerr Inkson, and Judith K. Pringle.
>
> Technical Communication Quarterly 12 (2003): 230–34.

21. Letter to the editor:

> Rosati, Colette. Letter. Arizona Republic [Phoenix, AZ] 18 Feb. 2004: B10.

Other Print Sources

22. Entry in a dictionary or reference work: In MLA style, entries in reference works are treated like entries in collections. If the author is known, begin with the author. Otherwise, start with the title of the entry. If the reference work is commonly known and regularly updated, you can simply give the edition and the date of publication. Otherwise, full publication information is necessary.

> "Express Mail." Merriam-Webster's Collegiate Dictionary. 10th ed. 1993.

> Pfeiffer, Robert H. "Sumerian Poetry." Princeton Encyclopedia of Poetry
>
> and Poetics. Ed. Alex Preminger. Enlarged Ed. Princeton: Princeton
>
> UP, 1974.

23. Government document: When the author of the document is not known, the agency is given as the author. Most publications from the U.S. federal government are published by the Government Printing Office (GPO). Give GPO as the publisher unless the title page indicates otherwise, as in the citation below.

> United States. Dept. of Health and Human Services. National Institutes of Health. <u>Toxicology and Carcinogenesis Studies of Resorcinal (CAS No. 108-46-3) in F344/N Rats and B6C3F$_1$ Mice (Gavage Studies)</u>. Research Triangle Park: National Institutes of Health, 1992.

24. Pamphlet: Pamphlets are short documents and are usually held together by staples rather than a more formal binding. They are treated as books.

> <u>A Guide to Visiting the Lands of Many Nations & to the Lewis & Clark Bicentennial</u>. St. Louis: National Council of the Lewis & Clark Bicentennial, 2004.

25. Published conference proceedings: The entire collection is treated as a book. Individual articles are treated as though they were in a collection by different authors.

> Buchanan, Elizabeth, and Nancy Morris. "Designing a Web-Based Program in Clinical Bioethics: Strategies and Procedures." <u>Proceedings of the 15th Annual Conference on Distance Teaching & Learning</u>. Madison: U of Wisconsin, 1999. 65–70.

26. Unpublished doctoral dissertation:

> Edminster, Judith R. "The Diffusion of New Media Scholarship: Power, Innovation, and Resistance in Academe." Diss. U. of South Florida, 2002.

27. Letter: If the letter you are citing has been published, treat it as you would a work in an anthology, but also include the date.

> Hemingway, Ernest. "To Maxwell Perkins." 7 February 1936. <u>Ernest Hemingway: Selected Letters, 1917–1961</u>. Ed. Carlos Baker. New York: Scribner's, 1981. 437–38.

If the letter you are citing is a personal letter, start with the writer's name followed by *Letter to the author* and the date.

> Morris, Patricia M. Letter to the author. 28 Dec. 2005.

28. Map or chart:

> San Francisco Bay. Map. San Francisco: California State Automobile
>   Association, 2004.

29. Cartoon:

> Benson, Steve. Cartoon. Arizona Republic [Phoenix, AZ] 28 Dec.
>   2006: 17.

30. Advertisement: Identify the product or company being advertised. If the ad appears in print or in the media, give the appropriate publication information.

> Bristol-Myers Squibb. Advertisement. Time. 25 Dec. 2006: 81.

ONLINE SOURCES

Because online sources change constantly, citing them is more complicated than citing print sources, although the principles, and many of the specifics, are the same. In addition to the author's name (if known) and the title and date of the document, MLA asks for the date the document was accessed and for its electronic address or Uniform Resource Locator (URL). Since some URLs are very long and complicated, MLA suggests giving URLs for pages containing links that will lead to the document, such as search pages for large sites. When the document you are citing has a print as well as an electronic version, MLA requires you to provide publication information for both versions. See Figure 20.4 for guidelines on where to find the elements of a works-cited entry for an article accessed from an online database.

TechNote MLA style calls for placing URLs inside angle brackets. However, when you type a period after the closing angle bracket, your word processor's "auto-correct" function will probably eliminate both angle brackets, so you will have to go back and retype them. To avoid having to do this step each time, modify your word processor's auto-correct settings so that they do not include angle brackets. Try to avoid breaking URLs across lines; if you must break them, break them only after a slash (/).

31. Basic professional or personal Web site:

> American Medical Association. Home page. 17 Feb. 2004
>   <http://www.ama-assn.org/>.

Publication Information about the Print Version of the Article →

Online Subscription Service →

Home Page of Service

Library System

Date of Access

Hayes, Matt. "College Football Inside Dish." Sporting News 29 Sept. 2003: 31.

Academic Search Premier, Arizona State U. Libraries. 5 Apr. 2007

http://www.ebscohost.com>.

Link to Home Page (to Get Home Page URL)

Publication Information for Article

Author

Title of Article

FIGURE 20.4   The Parts of a Works-Cited Entry for a Periodical Article Accessed from an Online Subscription Database

32. Scholarly article retrieved from a database:

author   title of article
Selber, Stuart A. "Beyond Skill Building: Challenges Facing Technical

Communication Teachers in the Computer Age." Technical

title of journal   volume no., date, page range   database
Communication Quarterly 3 (1994): 365–91. EBSCOHost.

subscribing system   date of access
Arizona State University. 18 Feb. 2004

URL of database
<http://www.ebsco.com/home/>.

Bennet-Kastor, Tina. "Spelling Abilities of University Students in
Developmental Writing Classes." Journal of College Reading and
Learning, 35.1 (2004): 67–82. ERIC. Arizona State University.
30 March 2007 <http://www.eric.ed.gov/ERICDocs/data/
ericdocs2/content_storage_01/0000000b/80/2c/a4/f2.pdf>.

33. Online book:

Howells, William Dean. Familiar Spanish Travels. Project Gutenberg.
18 Feb. 2004 <http://www.gutenberg.net/etext05/sptrv10.txt>.

34. Article from an online journal: When the online article is a digitized version of a print document, include the page numbers that you would find in print. However, if the document appears only in electronic form, as in the example below, page numbers will not exist.

Salvo, Michael J. "Deafened to Their Demands: An Ethnographic
Study of Accommodation." Kairos 7.1 (2002). 17 Feb. 2004
<http://english.ttu.edu/kairos/7.1/binder2.html?coverweb/salvo/
ctx.html>.

35. Article from an online magazine: If the online source is a digitized version of an original print source, give the page numbers.

Cooper, Matthew, and Karen Tumulty. "Bring on the Cash!" Time. 16
Feb. 2004. 17 Feb. 2004: 18–21 <http://www.time.com/time/
election2004/article/0,18471,591298,00.html>.

36. Article from an online newspaper:

Novovitch, Barbara. "It's Home Stupid Home, but the 'Clods' Can
Read." New York Times. 17 Feb. 2004. 23 Feb. 2005 <http://
www.nytimes.com/2004/02/17/education/17PROF.html>.

37. Blog entry: Use the MLA format for general Web sites. Include the name of the author (bloggers often use pseudonyms), the name of the entry, enclosed in quotation marks, the name of the blog, the date of the entry (if available), the date of access, and the URL.

> Rice, J. "Network Academics." Yellow Dog. 30 Mar. 2007 <http://
> ydog.net/?page_id=345>.

38. Wiki entry: Include the title of the entry, in quotation marks, the title of the wiki, underscored, the date you accessed the entry, and the URL for the entry.

> "Rhetoric." Wikipedia, 30 Mar. 2007 <http://en.wikipedia.org/wiki/
> Rhetoric>.

39. Posting to an electronic forum such as a mailing list (listserv): This basic format is used for all online forums including Web-based postings.

> Peckham, Irvin. "Re: Update on AP and Dual Enrollment." Online posting.
> 21 Sept. 2003. WPA-L. 17 Feb. 2004 <http://lists.asu.edu/cgi-bin/
> wa?A2=ind0309&L=wpal&D=1&O=D&F=&S=&P=52156>.

40. E-mail message:

> Bernhardt, Stephen B. "RE: Congrats!" E-mail to the author. 17 Feb. 2004.

OTHER NONPRINT SOURCES

41. Television and radio programs: The basic elements for entries that cite radio and television programs include the following: the title of the episode, the title of the program, the title of the series, the name of the network, the call letters and the city of the local station, and the broadcast date.

> "Dogs and More Dogs." Nova. Narr. John Lithgow. PBS. KAET, Phoenix.
> 3 Feb. 2004.

> "Scientists Succeed in Cloning Human Embryo." All Things Considered.
> Narr. Joe Palca. NPR. WGBH, Boston. 12 Feb. 2004.

42. Audio recording:

> Jackson, Alan. "Drive." Perf. Jackson. Drive. Arista, 2002.

43. Film, video recording, or DVD: In MLA style the citation starts with the title and the director. The distributor and year of release are necessary. Other items, such as performers, are optional.

The Lord of the Rings: The Two Towers. Dir. Peter Jackson. Perf. Elijah
      Wood and Ian McKellan. 2002. DVD. New Line Home
      Entertainment, 2003.

44. A nonperiodical publication on a CD-ROM:

The OWL Construction and Maintenance Guide. Ed. James A. Inman and
      Clinton Gardner. CD-ROM. Emmitsburg: IWCA, 2002.

45. Personal, e-mail, or telephone interview: Indicate whether the interview was conducted in person (*Personal interview*), by e-mail (*E-mail interview*), or by telephone (*Telephone interview*) following the name of the person you interviewed.

Schwalm, D. Personal interview. 21 Feb. 2004.

46. Oral presentation:

Russell, David R. "Teacher's Perception of Genre across the Curriculum: Making
      Classroom/Culture Connections Visible." Conf. on College Composition
      and Communication Convention. Atlanta Hilton, Atlanta, 26 Mar. 1999.

47. Performance: If you are citing a play, an opera, a concert, or a ballet performance, start with the title, followed by the authors (*By*), and any other pertinent information (such as the director, identified as *Dir*), the site where performed, the city, and performance date.

The Norse Family. By Jerry Jones. Dir. Walter Onger. Mesa Performing Arts
      Center, Mesa. 28 Dec. 2007.

48. Work of art:

di Chirico, Giorgio. The Philosopher's Conquest, 1914. Joseph
      Winterbotham Collection. Art Institute of Chicago, Chicago.

MLA Style: Sample Student Paper

Follow these guidelines if you are required to use MLA style:

- A separate title page is not required in MLA style. Instead, on the first page, put your name, your professor's name, the course number, and the date in the upper-left-hand corner, one inch from the top of the page, and follow with the title of your paper. The title should be centered, with every word capitalized except articles and prepositions, and should not be underlined or in a special typeface.

- Double-space the entire paper, including the information mentioned above as well as block quotations and the entries in your list of works cited.
- Leave one-inch margins on all sides.
- Put page numbers in the upper-right-hand corner, one-half inch from the top. Just before each page number, put your last name.
- Indent paragraphs one-half inch, or five spaces, from the left-hand margin.
- Begin your list of works cited on a new, consecutively numbered page. Include the title *Works Cited* one inch from the top. Center the title; do not use a special typeface for it.
- In quoting and citing sources, use the guidelines for MLA style given in this chapter.

The student paper that follows, "Money for Nothing" by Jessie Katz, is an example of a paper that uses MLA style.

↕ ½"
Katz 1

↕ 1"

Jessie Katz

Professor Wilson

English 105

15 February 2006

Money for Nothing

    For followers of college sports, February is a particularly exciting time of year. With the recent culmination of the football season in the bowl games and the anticipation of upcoming March Madness, all eyes seem glued to ESPN and the sports section of the newspaper as the drama of the season's games, rivalries, and players unfolds. In this charged atmosphere, the public turns its attention toward student-athletes and has ample occasion to contemplate the extraordinary lives that these young people lead. Indeed, some student-athletes apparently have it all: Aside from their national recognition and virtual stardom on and off of their campuses, these athletes also often receive special on-campus housing, state-of-the-art training facilities, and, perhaps most notably, substantial scholarships from their schools.

    According to the National Collegiate Athletic Association (NCAA), colleges and universities award $1 billion in athletic scholarships annually to over 126,000 student-athletes (Online). NCAA defines athletic aid as "a grant, scholarship, tuition waiver, or other assistance from a college or university that is awarded on the basis of a student's athletic ability"; and a student-athlete is a member of the student body who receives athletic aid from his or her school sometime during his or her freshman year. Regardless of financial need or academic promise, athletic scholarships may cover tuition, fees, room and board, and books. Although nearly all Division I and Division II schools grant athletic scholarships, awarding this type of aid does little to benefit the academic prestige, community, or economic condition of colleges or universities. Giving scholarships based solely on athletic merit may in fact undermine the purpose of institutions of higher education, so colleges and universities need to reexamine the extraordinary amounts of money they currently spend on athletic aid to their students.

↕ 1"

Margin notes (right column):

Student's name

Professor's name

Course title

Date

Title centered; important words capitalized

Shortened version of the title of an online source is enclosed in parentheses.

Thesis statement

Katz 2

Like any social institution, colleges and universities exist to promote a certain set of goals. Even though mission statements differ from school to school, these organizations usually share three major objectives: academic scholarship through instruction and research, service to the university's community, and economic development of the university and its surroundings. For instance, Arizona State University, one of the nation's premier research institutions and member of the PAC-10, has a mission statement typical of a state university. Its 2005–2006 General Catalog reads as follows:

> Arizona State University's goal is to become a world-class university in a multicampus setting. Its mission is to provide outstanding programs in instruction, research, and creative activity, to promote and support economic development, and to provide service appropriate for the nation, the state of Arizona, and the state's major metropolitan area. To fulfill its mission, ASU places special emphasis on the core disciplines and offers a full range of degree programs—baccalaureate through doctorate, recognizing that it must offer quality programs at all degree levels in a broad range of fundamental fields of inquiry. ASU will continue to dedicate itself to superior instruction; to excellent student performance; to original research, creative endeavor, and scholarly achievement; and to outstanding public service and economic development activities. (23)

Universities, including ASU, promote their goals through their facilities, through their academic and community programs, and especially through their people, the large majority of whom are students. Students represent both a college's main source of income and its main product; and when a school awards a scholarship, it makes an investment in an individual who it feels will make a special contribution to its goals. However, granting athletes aid does not directly contribute to the three primary goals that most colleges and universities share.

Although they are part of institutions that society entrusts with the passage and creation of knowledge through scholarship and research, people often suspect that athletics departments disregard the academic success of student-athletes.

Quotation longer than four lines is indented 1 inch or 10 spaces and double-spaced. The sentence that introduces it ends with a colon. Page number is given at the end.

Katz 3

Certainly not all student-athletes fit the "dumb jock" stereotype, but an alarming amount of data shows that these individuals fall behind their peers in the classroom. Academic underachievement in student-athletes starts at the recruitment level. To become a member of the NCAA and gain the privilege of practicing and playing sports and obtaining a sports scholarship at a Division I or Division II college, incoming freshmen must graduate from high school, complete at least fourteen core courses (including English, math, and physical and social sciences), have a minimum grade point average of 2.0, and achieve a minimum score of 820 on the SAT (Online). While these requirements appear reasonable, NCAA receives too many applicants and has a staff that is too small to carefully examine each potential student's high school record. Thus, academic advisors "cheat the system," as is evidenced in a 1997 scandal in which exceptional high school athletes attended and paid certain high schools that adjusted their deficient standardized test scores (Zimbalist 35). In the most extreme cases of academic under-preparedness, student-athletes enter institutes of "higher" education without basic literacy and math skills. Since NCAA evaluates high school courses rather than college courses, after student-athletes are accepted into college, the regulation of student-athlete academic education becomes less centralized, falling to the universities' athletic departments, which may be motivated to keep student-athletes in the game and not on the academic chopping block. Instances abound in which advisors recommend lenient professors and classes with titles like "Leisure and the Quality of Life," "Sports Officiating," and "Popular Music" (Arizona State University). Surely, if and when academic education becomes subordinate to athletics, colleges and universities are counterproductive in funding their student-athletes' "scholarship."

One of the most disturbing facts concerning athletics in colleges and universities is that a substantial number of athletes are leaving these schools without a degree. In an effort to remedy the academic deficiencies prevalent in college sports, NCAA instituted the Academic Progress Rate (APR) program in 2004 (Bartter 1). Using a complex formula to assign each team an APR, NCAA supports teams with an APR of 925, the minimum value that predicts that the team will graduate at least half of its athletes, and higher. According to

> Source is cited in parentheses, with page number.

> Organization as author.

Katz 4

a recent study by the University of Central Florida, of the fifty-six Division I
football teams selected to play in the 2006 Bowl games, twenty-three teams
(including the previous national champion, University of Southern California)
received an APR below 925, and twenty-seven teams had a graduation rate
under 50%. For all Division I student-athletes, the U.S. Department of Education reports a 62% graduation rate, although the graduation rates for "the elite
sports" (men's basketball and football) are considerably lower, with a basketball
graduation rate of 44% and a football graduation rate of 54% (Wolverton). Ad-
mittedly, the total student-athlete graduation rate exceeds the graduation rate
(60%) of non-athletes, but the success of many of these student-athletes may
be bolstered by the financial support they receive. Consequently, a vast sum
of the money that colleges give to their athletic students does not support the
achievement of a degree, the most important tangible reward that a college or
university can give a student. Indeed, unlike academic or music scholarships,
which directly contribute to a college degree, athletic scholarships fund a
pursuit unrelated, and at times even counterproductive, to what ASU's mission
statement calls "fundamental fields of inquiry." Considering the tough odds of
playing professional sports (1 in 1,233), student-athletes who do not graduate
miss out on the invaluable and marketable skills and knowledge that a degree
signifies (Zimbalist 31). Thus, granting athletic scholarships does not necessarily
lead to academic returns for the university or the student-athlete.

> Katz cites
> studies to
> support her
> thesis about
> athletic aid.

Despite the academic arguments against granting athletic scholarships,
some institutions defend their awarding of financial aid based solely upon
athletic performance with the argument that athletics contribute to
the community service facet of a college's or university's stated mission.
Certainly, a strong athletic program may benefit the community in a variety
of healthy ways; a winning team engenders school spirit in its students and
faculty, entices the citizens who live near the college to take an active interest
in at least one aspect of the school, and earns state and national recognition
and exposure, which may attract students and lead to increased enrollment.
However, college athletics can be seen as having as many detrimental as positive effects on its community. In some instances, the same school spirit that

Katz 5

fills the students with a sense of pride and place leads to very disreputable, unsportsmanlike conduct in the student body. In 2001, about 2,000 University of Arizona basketball fans flooded streets, destroyed cars, and set fires after the NCAA tournament in Minneapolis (Rotstein); and in 2003, University of West Virginia students set over 100 fires and rioted in the streets after their football team defeated Virginia Tech (French 89). The athletes themselves also sometimes engage in activities that harm the communities; underage drinking and drug use occur in the athlete population as they do the general college population, and more serious events (such as allegations of rape against members of the University of Colorado football team in 2001 and the 2005 Baylor University incident in which one basketball player murdered his team-mate) become highly publicized scandals. These events weaken considerably the positive impacts college athletics may have on schools' communities and undermine other community services, such as volunteer work, that students without any sort of scholarship perform. While athletics may benefit the community in many ways, they also have too many harmful effects on the community for colleges to justify the current levels of spending that many of them devote to athletic scholarships.

Katz responds to a counterargument about the possible benefits of student athletics.

Perhaps the most common justification for granting student-athletes athletic scholarships is that college athletics is a major source of revenue for institutes of higher learning: through scholarships, athletes are allowed a portion of the money that they bring to their schools. This justification operates on the assumption that athletics do indeed attract capital to colleges and universities; yet an increasing amount of evidence shows that athletics departments actually cause a substantial deficit to the institutions that house them. The financial information from college athletics departments can be very misleading: in 1994, NCAA reported that Division I-A athletics programs earned an average of about $13,632,000 and spent about $12,972,000, yielding an apparent profit of $660,000 (French 80). These numbers, though, did not account for the fact that some universities subsidized their athletic departments. If the direct transfers to athletics programs from their universities that year were subtracted from the average earnings, the result would reveal that these programs actually had

Katz 6

a $174,000 deficit. In fact, some athletics departments had so little money that they could not even afford to fund their athletes' scholarships; instead, there is evidence of some universities dipping into the scholarship funds reserved for students with demonstrated financial need or academic merit (French 82).

Another misconception about athletic funding is that winning teams attract more monetary gifts from donors and alumni. A study by Cornell University management and economics professor Robert Frank, discussed in a 2004 Sports Illustrated article, demonstrates that "the presumed indirect benefits of sports, such as the spike in alumni giving and an enlarged applicant pool, are by all indications minimal." In fact, Frank discovered that "the revenues needed to compete have escalated to the point where the average big-time athletic program runs in the red. And when success brings a spike in donations, the money is routinely earmarked for the athletic program—not the general university fund" (Fish). Therefore, even if a profit from student athletics is earned, universities usually cannot and do not use the money to advance their missions. Southern Methodist University President Gerald Turner confirms these conclusions: "I've been a university president now for about 20 years and I have never found any relationship between alumni giving to academic programs and the success of the athletic program" (qtd. in Fish). When colleges and universities award athletic scholarships, it may be less of a sound financial investment than boosters hope.

Without a doubt, athletics have an important entertainment role in a university setting. Yet, behind the Rose Bowl and March Madness, athletics programs are not as beneficial to their scholarly institutions as they may seem. It's time for colleges and universities to concentrate on their central missions—to promote academic scholarship, service to the university's community, and economic development of the university and its surroundings—instead of justifying the exorbitant expenditures of funds on programs that are more popular than they are useful to the school, the student, and the community at large.

Information from an authoritative source introduced by a signal phrase within the text.

Katz responds to two additional counter-arguments. She responds to the second counter-argument by citing a study and quoting an expert.

Secondary source introduced in text, with *qtd. in* used in parenthetical citation.

Katz 7

Works Cited

Arizona State University. Office of the Executive Vice President and Provost of the University. Arizona State University: 2005–2006 General Catalog. Tempe: Academic and Administrative Documents, 2005.

Bartter, Jessica. "Institute Study by Lapchick Looks at APR Rates and Gradua- tion Rates for 2005–06 Bowl-Bound Teams." 5 Dec. 2005. Devos Sport Business Management Program, College of Business Administration, University of Central Florida. 8 Feb. 2006 <http://www.bus.ucf.edu/sport/ public/downloads/2005_Football_APR_Grad_Rate.pdf>.

Fish, Mike. "Separate Worlds: Studies Show Big-Time Athletics Don't Impact Academic Donations." Sports Illustrated. 14 Sept. 2004. 9 Feb. 2006. http://sportsillustrated.cnn.com/2004/writers/mike_fish/09/14/ straight.shooting/index.html.

French, Peter A. Ethics and College Sports: Ethics, Sports, and the University. Lanham: Rowman, 2004.

The Online Resource for the National Collegiate Athletic Association. 2005. NCAA. 7 Feb. 2006 <http://www.ncaa.org/wps/portal>.

Rotstein, Arthur H. "Arizona Fans Turn Rowdy." Associated Press. 3 Apr. 2001. 12 Feb. 2006 <http://www.usatoday.com/sports/other/ 2002-04-09-fan-violence.htm>.

Wolverton, Brad. "Under New Formula, Graduation Rates Rise." Chronicle of Higher Education. 52.21 (2006): A41. 10 Feb. 2006 <http:// chronicle.com/weekly/v52/i21/21a04101.htm>.

Zimbalist, Andrew. Unpaid Professionals: Commercialism and Conflict in Big- Time College Sports. Princeton: Princeton UP, 1999.

New page, title centered; double space between title and first line of works- cited list.

Entries double spaced, in alphabetical order

First line of each entry at left margin; all other lines indented 5 spaces or 1/2 inch.

APA Documentation Style

APA Style: In-Text Citation

In APA style, parenthetical in-text citations are used in conjunction with the list of references at the end of a paper to give readers the information they would need to locate the sources that you have quoted, paraphrased, or summarized. In research in the fields in which APA style is used (the social sciences, business, and so on), often currency is crucial and dates of publication are extremely relevant, so in-text citations include year of publication along with the author and page number. Suppose, for example, that you are quoting from page 282 of Deborah Tannen's *You Just Don't Understand: Woman and Men in Conversation*, published in 1990. In APA style, a parenthetical in-text citation would be *(Tannen, 1990, p. 282)*. If you give the author's name within your sentence, however, the date appears in parentheses following the name. APA parenthetical citations have commas between the elements and "p." before the page number. Page numbers are needed only when you are citing a quotation or specific information.

The following are examples of how to cite different types of sources within your text using APA style.

A WORK WITH ONE AUTHOR

> Deborah Tannen (1990), in talking about gender differences, observes, "Complementary schismogenisis commonly sets in when women and men have divergent sensitivities and hypersensitivities" (p. 282).

A WORK WITH MORE THAN ONE AUTHOR

For a source with up to five authors, use all the authors' last names in the first citation. If you give their names in parentheses, put an ampersand (&) between the last two names. After the first citation, use the first author's name followed by *et al.* for a work by three or more authors.

> Glassick, Huber, and Maeroff (1999) state that "Teaching, too, must in the end be judged not merely by process but by results, however eloquent a teacher's performance" (p. 29).

> Ultimately, it is the results of teaching, not the method or the quality of the teacher's performance, that we must evaluate (Glassick, Huber, & Maeroff, 1999, p. 29).

For a source with six or more authors, use *et al.* with every citation, including the first.

AN UNKNOWN AUTHOR

Use a shortened version of the title.

> Employees of Google believe their corporate culture to be antithetical to that of Microsoft ("Google," 2006).

A GOVERNMENT AGENCY OR A CORPORATE AUTHOR

Give the complete name of most organizations every time you use them. After the first use, however, you can use an abbreviation for organizations with unwieldy names and well-known or easily understood abbreviations.

> The Federal Emergency Management Agency (FEMA) (2007) offers officials many suggestions in a new brochure. You can obtain a copy of FEMA's brochure at our main office.

A SECONDARY SOURCE

If you need to use a quotation from a secondary source, use *as cited in* to let your readers know that you are doing so.

> Jonathan Shaw muses, "I don't think mankind is ready, spiritually or mentally, for the transformations it's undergoing in the technological era: tattooing is a mute plea for a return to human values" (as cited in Dery, 1996, p. 284).

AN ONLINE SOURCE

Cite in the same way that you would cite a print source. For a source with paragraph numbers, use *para.* or ¶ for *p.* If you cannot find a date for the source, use the abbreviation *n.d.* (for "no date").

> According to Christopher Beam (2006), there are a number of methods that Internet service providers can use to block Web sites if a government orders them to.

A BLOCK QUOTATION

In APA style, block quotations are used for quotations of more than forty words and are indented one-half inch or five spaces, as in the following example:

> Tannen (1990), in talking about gender differences, notes this phenomenon:
>> Complementary schismogenesis commonly sets in when women and men have divergent sensitivities and hypersensitivities. For example, a

man who fears losing freedom pulls away at the first sign he interprets as an attempt to "control" him, but pulling away is just the signal that sets off alarms for the woman who fears losing intimacy. (p. 282)

Note that the year of publication is given in parentheses immediately following the author's name and not with the page number.

APA Style: Constructing a References List

For a comparison of the MLA and APA styles for citing books and periodical articles, see page 542.

The section that follows includes model entries for different types of print and nonprint sources in APA style. Figure 20.5 provides you with a flowchart that will help you find the model entry that is closest to the source that you need to cite.

Is My Source a Complete Print Book or Part of a Print Book?

No	Yes, go to the next question below.	Go to this entry.
	Is it a book with only one author?	1 (p.571)
	Are you citing more than one book by this author?	2 (p.572)
	Is it a book with multiple authors?	3 (p.572)
	Is the author unknown or unnamed?	5 (p.572)
	Is the book by an organization of some kind?	4 (p.572)
	Does the book also have a translator?	10 (p.573)
	Is it a later publication or edition of the book?	6, 7 (p.572)
	Is it a multivolume work?	12 (p.573)
	Does the book have an editor or a translator?	8,10 (p.573)
	Is the book an edited collection or anthology?	8, 9 (p.573)
	Is it a work in a collection or an anthology?	9 (p.573)
	Is it an introduction, a preface, a foreword, or an afterword?	11 (p.573)
	Is it a published interview?	13 (p.573)
	Is it an entry in a dictionary or reference work?	22 (p.576)

Is My Source from a Print Periodical Such as a Journal, a Magazine, or a Newspaper?

No	Yes, go to the next question below.	Go to this entry.
	Is it from a scholarly journal?	
	Do the journal's page numbers continue from one issue to the next?	14 (p.574)
	Does each issue start with page 1?	15 (p.574)
	Is it from a magazine?	16 (p.574)
	Is it a review?	19 (p.576)
	Is it from a newspaper?	17 (p.576)
	Is it an editorial?	18 (p.576)
	Is it a letter to the editor?	20 (p.576)
	Is it an article in a newsletter?	21 (p.576)

FIGURE 20.5 APA Style: A Flowchart for Determining the Model References Entry You Need

Is My Source a Print Source but Not from a Journal, a Magazine, or a Newspaper?

No	Yes, go to the next question below.	Go to this entry.
	Is it an entry in a dictionary or reference work?	22 (p.576)
	Is it a government document?	23 (p.577)
	Is it an unpublished doctoral dissertation?	24 (p.577)
	Is it an academic report	25 (p.577)

Is My Source a Nonprint Source from an Online Subscription Database or the World Wide Web?

No	Yes, go to the next question below.	Go to this entry.
	Is it a professional or personal Web site?	26 (p.578)
	Is it an article?	
	Is it a scholarly article retrieved from a database?	27 (p.578)
	Is it from an online journal?	29 (p.579)
	Is it from an online magazine?	30 (p.579)
	Is it from an online newspaper?	31 (p.579)
	Is it an online book?	28 (p.579)
	Is it a posting to an electronic forum?	32 (p.579)
	Is it an e-mail message?	33 (p.580)
	Is it a blog entry?	34 (p.580)
	Is it an entry in a wiki?	35 (p.580)
	Is it computer software?	36 (p.580)

Is My Source a Nonprint Source That Is Not Published Online?

No	Yes, go to the next question below.	Go to this entry.
	Is it a television or radio program?	37 (p.580)
	Is it an audio recording?	38 (p.580)
	Is it a film, video recording, or DVD?	39 (p.581)
	Is it an oral presentation?	40 (p.581)

Consult with Your Instructor about How to Cite Your Source.

FIGURE 20.5
Continued

PRINT DOCUMENTS

Books

The basic elements in an entry for a book are the author's name or authors' names, the date of publication, the title, and the publication information, consisting of the place of publication and the publisher. See Figure 20.6 for guidelines on where to find the elements of an entry in a list of references for an edited collection in APA style.

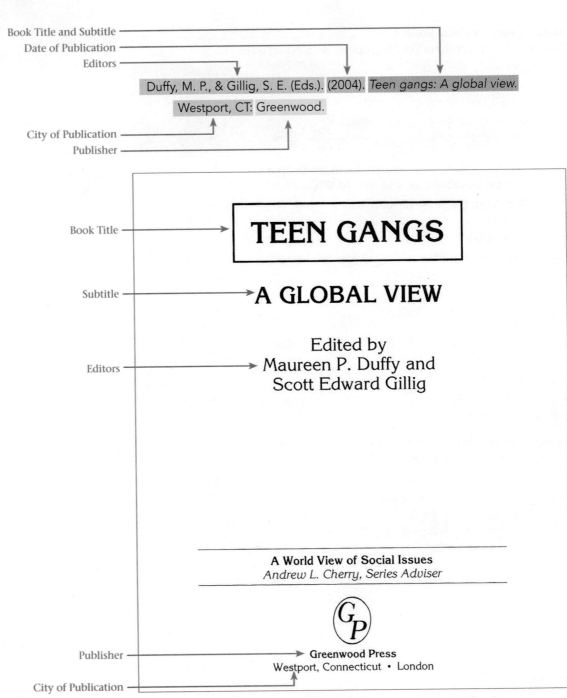

Book Title and Subtitle ————————————————————

Date of Publication ————————

Editors ————————

Duffy, M. P., & Gillig, S. E. (Eds.). (2004). *Teen gangs: A global view.*
Westport, CT: Greenwood.

City of Publication ————————

Publisher ————————

Book Title ————————→

TEEN GANGS

A GLOBAL VIEW

Subtitle ————————→

Edited by
Maureen P. Duffy and
Scott Edward Gillig

Editors ————————→

A World View of Social Issues
Andrew L. Cherry, Series Adviser

Publisher ————————→ **Greenwood Press**
Westport, Connecticut • London

City of Publication ————————

FIGURE 20.6   The Parts of a Reference Entry for an Edited Collection

Library of Congress Cataloging-in-Publication Data ——— Book Title

Teen gangs : a global view / edited by Maureen P. Duffy and Scott Edward Gillig. ◄——— Editors
      p. cm.—(A world view of social issues, ISSN 1526–9442)
   Includes bibliographical references and index.
   ISBN 0–313–32150–7 (alk. paper)
   1. Gangs—Cross-cultural studies.   2. Juvenile delinquency—Cross-cultural studies.
I. Duffy, Maureen P.   II. Gillig, Scott Edward.   III. Series.
   HV6437.T44   2004
   364.1'06'60835—dc22   2003060015

British Library Cataloguing in Publication Data is available.

Copyright © 2004 by Maureen P. Duffy and Scott Edward Gillig ◄——— Date of Publication

All rights reserved. No portion of this book may be
reproduced, by any process or technique, without the
express written consent of the publisher.

Library of Congress Catalog Card Number: 2003060015
ISBN: 0–313–32150–7
ISSN: 1526–9442

First published in 2004 ——— Publisher

Greenwood Press, 88 Post Road West, Westport, CT 06881
An imprint of Greenwood Publishing Group, Inc.
www.greenwood.com ——— City of Publication

Printed in the United States of America

∞

The paper used in this book complies with the
Permanent Paper Standard issued by the National
Information Standards Organization (Z39.48–1984).

10 9 8 7 6 5 4 3 2 1

FIGURE 20.6   Continued

1. Book with one author: In APA style, the date of publication follows the author's name. The author's first and middle name are given as initials, and the title of the book is italicized, not underlined. Only the first word of the title is capitalized, as well as any proper nouns and the first word following a colon.

author   date of publication   title   city   publisher
Gould, S. J. (1981). *The mismeasure of man.* New York: Norton.

2. Two entries by the same author: The entries are listed in chronological order, with the earliest publication first. If more than one work was published in the same year, the works are ordered alphabetically based on the first letter of the title. Each work is given a lowercase letter after the date: for example, (2004a) for the first entry published in 2004 and (2004b) for the second entry. These letters would appear with the dates in the in-text citations.

> Tannen, D. (1990). *You just don't understand: Women and men in conversation.* New York: Ballantine Books.

> Tannen. D. (1994). *Talking from 9 to 5.* New York: Morrow.

3. Book with multiple authors: All authors' names are inverted. Use an ampersand to separate the last two entries. Give the names of all authors for up to six authors; if there are more authors, follow the sixth name with *et al.*

> Covey, S. R., Merrill, A. R., & Merrill, R. R. (1994). *First things first.* New York: Simon & Schuster.

4. Book by a corporate entity or organization: When the publisher is the same as the author, use the word *Author* where the publisher's name is usually given.

> Adobe Systems Inc. (2001). *Adobe acrobat 5.0: Getting started.* San Jose, CA: Author.

5. Book by an unknown author:

> *The Chicago manual of style: The essential guide for writers, editors, and publishers* (15th ed.). (2003). Chicago: Chicago University Press.

6. Republished book: Including the original date of publication is obligatory in APA style.

> Dickens, C. (1969). *Hard times.* (D. Craig, Ed.). Baltimore: Penguin Books. (Original work published 1854)

7. Book in a later edition:

> Corbett, E. P. J. (1990). *Classical rhetoric for the modern student* (3rd ed.). New York: Oxford University Press.

8. Edited collection:

> Inman, J. A., & Sewell, D. N. (Eds.). (2000). *Taking flight with owls: Examining electronic writing center work*. Mahwah, NJ: Erlbaum.

See also Figure 20.6 on pages 570–71.

9. Work in a collection or an anthology: In APA style the page numbers come after the title and before the publication information.

> Anson, C. M., & Jewell, R. (2001). Shadows of the mountain. In E. E. Schell & P. L. Stock (Eds.), *Moving a mountain: Transforming the role of contingent faculty in composition studies and higher education* (pp. 47–75). Urbana, IL: NCTE.

10. Translation:

> Eliade, M. (1959). *The sacred and the profane: The nature of religion* (W. R. Trask, Trans.). New York: Harcourt. (Original work published 1957)

11. Introduction, preface, foreword, or afterword:

> Burns, H. (1999). Foreword. In C. L. Selfe, *Technology and literacy in the twenty-first century: The importance of paying attention* (pp. ix–xvii). Carbondale: Southern Illinois University Press.

12. A multivolume work published over more than one year:

> Campbell, J. (1959–1968) *The masks of god* (Vols. 1–4). New York: Viking.

13. Published interview:

> Blair, K., & Takayoshi, P. (1999). Making the map: An interview with Gail Hawisher. [Interview with G. Hawisher] In K. Blair & P. Takayoshi (Eds.), *Feminist cyberspaces: Mapping gendered academic spaces* (pp. 177–191). Stamford, CT: Ablex.

You should cite an interview published in a periodical as you would a periodical article (see #s 14, 15, and 16). APA categorizes personal interviews as personal communications: Because such an interview cannot be recovered, there is no need to include an entry for it in a reference list, but the interview should be cited in the body of the text (see #s 33 and 40).

Periodical Articles

The basic items in an entry for a periodical article are the author's name or authors' names, the date of publication in parentheses, the title of the article, and information about the publication in which the article appeared, including its title, volume and issue number (if applicable), and the page range for the article. See Figure 20.7 below and on page 575 for guidelines on where to find the elements of a reference entry for a periodical article in APA style.

14. Article in a scholarly journal with continuous pagination: In APA style the volume number is italicized. APA style also uses full page numbers.

> authors   date of publication   title
> Thayer, A., & Kolko, B. E. (2004). Localization of digital games: The
>
>   title of periodical
>   process of blending for the global games market. *Technical*
>
>   volume no. and page range
>   *Communication, 51,* 477–488.

15. Article in a scholarly journal that is paginated by issue: When an article is from a journal that restarts the page numbers with each issue, the issue number follows the volume number in parentheses in APA style.

> Howard, R. M. (1993). Power revisited: Or, how we became a department.
>   *Writing Program Administration: Journal of the Council of Writing*
>   *Program Administrators, 16*(3), 37–49.

16. Magazine article: Magazines may or may not include volume and issue numbers. In an entry in APA style, the volume number should be included, placed within commas between the name of the magazine and the page numbers of the article (*Scientific American, 290,* 54–61). In the first example below, *Business Week* is a magazine that does not use volume numbers.

> Foust, D., Eidem, M., & Bremner, B. (2004, February 2). AFLAC: Its ducks
>   are not in a row. *Business Week,* 52–53.

> Wilson, C. E. (2005, January). Usability and user experience design: The
>   next decade. *Intercom, 52,* 6–9.

Authors
Date of Publication
Title of Article

Kiesner, J., & Pastore, M. (2005). Differences in the relations between antisocial behavior and peer acceptance across contexts and across adolescence. *Child Development, 26*, 1278–1293.

Page Numbers
Volume Number
Title of Journal

Volume Number
Date of Publication
Title of Journal

Child Development, November/December 2005, Volume 76, Number 6, Pages 1129–1317

Contents

Title of Article
First Page of Article
Authors

FIGURE 20.7   The Parts of a Reference Entry for a Journal Article

17. Newspaper article: When articles appear on discontinuous pages, as they often do, APA style requires you to list all the page numbers.

> Fatsis, S. (2002, April 9). A more modern masters. *The Wall Street Journal*,
>
> pp. B1, B4.

18. Editorial: If there is a title, it should precede [*Editorial*].

> Moral scoreboard. (2004, February 18). [Editorial]. *The Arizona Republic*,
>
> p. B10.

19. Review: If the review is titled, give the title in the usual position, preceding the bracketed information.

> Jablonski, J. (2003). [Review of the book *The new careers: Individual*
>
> *action and economic change*]. *Technical Communication Quarterly*,
>
> *12*, 230–234.

20. Letter to the editor:

> Rosati, C. (2004, February 18). Let's throw the book at Valley street racers
>
> [Letter to the editor]. *The Arizona Republic*, p. B10.

21. Newsletter article, no author: Unsigned articles should be alphabetized in the list of references by the first word of the title. If there is a volume number, place it between the name of the publication and the page numbers, separated by commas. The following example from the newsletter of the Heard Museum of Native Cultures and Art has no volume number.

> Shared images: The jewelry of Yazzie Johnson and Gail Bird. (2007),
>
> (January/February), *Earthsong*, 8.

Other Print Sources

22. Entry in dictionary or reference work: APA style uses page numbers even when the entries are alphabetical.

> Express Mail. (1993). In *Merriam-Webster's new collegiate dictionary*
>
> (p. 411). Springfield, MA: Merriam-Webster.

Pfeiffer, R. H. (1974). Sumerian Poetry. In *Princeton Encyclopedia of Poetry and Poetics* (pp. 820–821). Princeton: Princeton University Press.

23. Government document: Like MLA style, APA style lists the agency as the author of the report when the author is not known. If you list a sub-department or agency, make certain that you also list the higher department if the sub-department is not well-known. If the publisher is not the Government Printing Office (GPO), list the highest known agency or department as the author. If the document has a specific publication number, list it after the title.

National Institutes of Health. (1992). *Toxicology and carcinogenesis studies of Resorcinol (CAS No. 108-46-3) in F344/N rats and B6C3F$_1$ mice (Gavage Studies)* (NIH Publication No. 92-2858). Research Triangle Park, NC: Author.

24. Unpublished doctoral dissertation:

Edminster, J. R. (2002). *The diffusion of new media scholarship: Power, innovation, and resistance in academe.* Unpublished doctoral dissertation, University of South Florida.

25. Academic report:

Melnick, R., Welch, N., & Hart, B. (2005). *How Arizona compares: Real numbers and hot topics.* Tempe: Arizona State University, Morrison Institute for Public Policy.

ONLINE SOURCES

Unlike MLA, APA prefers that the exact URL be given in the reference entry. When the document being cited has a print as well as an electronic version, APA requires you to provide publication information for both versions. If the content is likely to change, give a retrieval date. For content that is fixed, such as a journal article, no date is necessary. See Figure 20.8 for guidelines on where to find the elements of a reference entry for an article accessed from an online database in APA style.

Publication Information
about the Print Version
of the Article

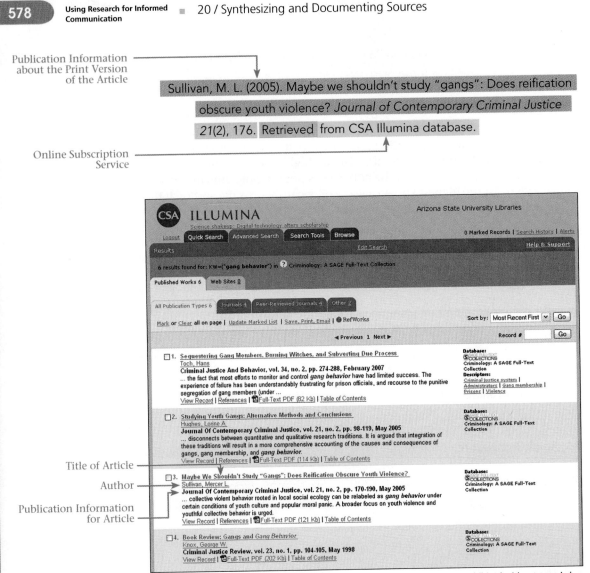

Online Subscription
Service

Image published with permission of ProQuest CSA. Further reproduction is prohibited without permission

FIGURE 20.8   The Parts of a Reference Entry for a Journal Article Accessed from an Online Subscription Database

26. Basic professional or personal Web site:

American Medical Association. (2004). Home page. Retrieved February 17, 2004, from http://www.ama-assn.org/

27. Scholarly article retrieved from a database: Include the issue number as well as the volume number.

author   date of publication   title of article

Selber, S. A. (1994). Beyond skill building: Challenges facing technical

communication teachers in the computer age.

    title of journal   volume no. and page range

Technical Communication Quarterly, 3(4), 365–391. Retrieved

name of database

from EBSCOHost database.

28. Online book:

Howells, W. D. (1913). *Familiar Spanish travels.* Retrieved from

http://www.gutenberg.net/etext05/sptrv10.txt

29. Article from an online journal: In APA style the volume number is italicized.

Salvo, M. J. (2002). Deafened to their demands: An ethnographic study

of accommodation. *Kairos 7*(1). Retrieved from http://english.ttu.

edu/kairos/7.1/binder2.html?coverweb/salvo/ctx.html

Note: For journal articles that are published online and are unchanged from their print version, you can use the format for a journal article (#14 or 15) but add [*Electronic version*] following the title of the article. A retrieval statement is not necessary.

30. Article from an online magazine:

Cooper, M., & Tumulty, K. (2004, February 16). Bring on the cash! *Time.*

Retrieved from http://www.time.com/time/election2004/

article/0,18471,591298,00.html

31. Article from an online newspaper:

Novovitch, B. (2004, February 17). It's home stupid home, but the "clods"

can read. *New York Times.* Retrieved from http://www.nytimes.com/

2004/02/17/education/17PROF.html

32. Posting to an electronic forum such as a mailing list (listserv): In APA style, list only electronic references that have been archived and are retrievable.

Peckham, I. (2004, February 17). Update on AP and dual enrollment.

Message posted to WPA-L. electronic mailing list, archived at http://lists.asu.edu/cgi-bin/wa?A2=ind0309&L=wpal&D=1&O=

D&F=&S=&P=52156

33. E-mail message: In APA style, e-mail is cited only in the text as "personal communication," followed by the date of the e-mail. Because personal communications are not recoverable data, they are not listed in the references.

34. Blog entry: Provide the name of the author (bloggers often use pseudonyms), date, title of entry, the words *Message posted to,* name of blog, and the URL.

Rice, J. (2007, March 30). Re: Network academics. Message posted to

http://ydog.net/?page_id=345

35. Wiki entry:

Rhetoric. (n.d.). Retrieved March 30, 2007, from *Wikipedia*: http://

en.wikipedia.org/wiki/Rhetoric

36. Computer software: If you download software, include *Available from* and the URL.

AllWrite! 2.0 with Online Handbook. (2003). [Computer software]. New

York: McGraw-Hill.

OTHER NONPRINT SOURCES

37. Television and radio programs: In APA style the names of the writers, directors, and producers are given as appropriate. After the name of the series, indicate whether the source is a television or radio broadcast in square brackets.

Buckner, N., & Whittlesey, R. (Writers, Directors, Producers). (2004,

February 3). Dogs and more dogs. *Nova* [Television broadcast].

Boston and Washington, DC: Public Broadcasting Service.

Turpin, C. (Executive Producer). (2004, February 12). Scientists succeed

in cloning human embryo. *All things considered* [Radio broadcast].

Washington, DC: National Public Radio.

38. Audio recording:

Jackson, A. (2002). Drive. On *Drive* [CD]. New York: Arista.

39. Film, video recording, or DVD:

> Jackson, P. (Director). (2002). *The lord of the rings: The two towers* [DVD].
> United States: New Line Home Entertainment.

40. Oral presentation: Because live lectures are not recoverable data, in APA style they are cited parenthetically in the text but are not included in the list of references. However, when professional presentations are made from texts that can be recovered, they are cited.

> Russell, D. R. (1999, March). Teacher's perception of genre across the
> curriculum: Making classroom/culture connections visible. Paper
> presented at the Conference on College Composition and
> Communication Convention, Atlanta, GA.

APA Style: Sample Student Paper

The student paper that follows, "How Do Gangs Affect Adolescent Behavior" by Aaron Zook, is an example of a paper that uses APA style.

If you write a paper using APA style, follow these guidelines:

- Include a separate title page. Center the title one-third of the way down the page, using capital and lowercase letters, and do not use a special typeface for it. Give your name, the course number, and the date, all also centered and double spaced, on separate lines below the title. In the upper-right-hand corner give the page number, preceded by a short version of the title, which you will include on each page of your paper.

- On the second page of your paper, provide an abstract of the paper if your instructor requires one. The abstract should be a short (approximately 100–120 words) summary of your paper's contents. If you include an abstract, the paper itself begins on the third page. Repeat the title on the first page of your paper, centering it one inch from the top. Double-space to the first line of your text.

- Double-space the entire paper, including any block quotations and the items in your list of references.

- Leave one-inch margins on all sides.

- Place page numbers in the upper-right-hand corner after the running head, five spaces after the shortened version of the title.

- Indent paragraphs one-half inch from the left margin.

- Some papers use headings to label sections of the text. If you use headings, center them and double-space above and below them.

- Put your list of references on a new page, with the title "References" centered at the top.

How Do Gangs Affect Adolescent Behavior?

Aaron Zook

Psychology 101

Professor Jones

March 23, 2007

Title is centered, one-third of the way down the page.

Name, title of course, name of professor, and date all centered and double-spaced on separate lines below the title.

↑1″
↕½″
How Do Gangs 2

How Do Gangs Affect Adolescent Behavior?

1″

Since the early 1920s, researchers have closely studied the relationship between street gangs and violent crime from a variety of perspectives: criminological, sociological, and psychological (Thabit, 2005). Whatever the underlying causes for gang membership, the results seem clear; members of street gangs admit to a far greater rate of serious crime, and to far more severe acts of violence (Penly Hall, Thornberry, & Lizotte, 2006) than non-gang members of the same age, race, and socioeconomic background (Battin-Pearson, Thornberry, Hawkins, & Krohn, 1998). According to the Web site Safeyouth.org (n.d.), gang violence is certainly cause for concern:

> Gang members are responsible for much of the serious violence in the United States. . . . Teens that are gang members are much more likely than other teens to commit serious and violent crimes. For example, a survey in Denver found that while only 14% of teens were gang members, they were responsible for committing 89% of the serious violent crimes.

Many researchers have therefore come to the conclusion that gangs necessarily cause violence and deviant behavior. As a matter of policy, then, it seems clear that the solution to a number of social ills is to break up, disrupt, or prevent the formation of gangs. Other programs seek to prevent young people from joining gangs through interventions of various types and levels of effectiveness. Most of these efforts take it as a given that gangs seriously distort behavior, even among individuals who already belong to "high-risk" demographic groups. Adolescents living in poverty or other disadvantaged circumstances; those attending violent and/or failing schools; members of criminalized peer groups; and children from violent and/or extremely dysfunctional households or demonstrating a predisposition toward antisocial behavior all seem to be at greater risk for future gang membership (Battin-Pearson et al., 1998), but a number of studies have shown that their own behaviors are considerably more violent while they belong to a gang than they were before or after membership (Gordon et al., 2004). After years of study, researchers still do not clearly understand how and why gangs exert such a powerful influence on behavior.

↕1″

Title repeated on first page of paper, centered.

Double-space from title to first line of paper.

Information from sources cited with parenthetical references.

Quotation longer than forty words is indented 1/2 inch or 5 spaces and double-spaced. The sentence that introduces it ends with a colon. Because no date is given in the source, the abbreviation *n.d.* is included.

Et al. used after the first citation for multiple authors. *Et al.* used for first citation of a work with six authors

How Do Gangs   3

A crucial answer might be found in the typical composition of a gang. Overwhelmingly, gangs are made up of adolescents and young adults. The median age of violent gang members has been estimated to be eighteen; members tend to join in their late teens, and contrary to popular fallacies and urban legends, youths generally leave a gang with few or no consequences within a year of joining (Thomas, 2005). Clearly, then, the gang problem can and should be understood in large part as a youth problem; researchers might come to a deeper understanding of the nature and impact of gangs by shifting some emphasis in their research from violence to adolescent adjustment behaviors.

The research community has by no means reached a consensus as to the precise definition of street gangs, however. The telltale sign that a group is a gang—one that most researchers, police organizations, the popular media, and gang members themselves agree on—is a tendency to commit violent acts (Katz & Jackson-Jacobs, 2004), but violence is not an adequate condition in itself. Why, for example, are Crips and Bloods considered gangs, but not Skinheads? Likewise, organized crime is now rarely considered "gang behavior," though early studies included these types of organizations. Yet all of these form distinct social groups and are involved in criminal behaviors (Thomas, 2005). One common distinction researchers draw is based on the motivation behind the group's violent activities. Does the group sell drugs or stolen merchandise? Do they operate according to an ideology or shared set of racial or cultural prejudices? Or are they primarily concerned with "turf," status, or violence for its own sake (U.S. Department of Education, n.d.)? Contemporary studies tend to maintain that only the latter group of motives typify "gangs" and have been particularly concerned with the seemingly random nature of the various criminal behaviors that many such gangs exhibit. The criminal acts seem to have largely symbolic value, consistent with the way many street gangs are associated with the use of emblems, dress, and a shared name easily identified by all of their members (Katz & Jackson-Jacobs, 2004).

Experts in gang behavior have advanced numerous explanations for the most troubling examples of violent gang behavior: random drive-by shootings, seemingly unmotivated killings and aggravated assaults, car-jackings, and

Opening paragraph sets up the issue.

Government agency given as author.

First point: Difficulty of defining gangs.

so on. Ritual initiations, turf wars, cycles of retribution between competing gangs, and intra-gang status have all been identified as motivators (Fagan & Wilkinson, 1998). Other hypotheses focus on the greater availability of guns and drugs, and still others on the model of shared or diffuse moral culpability (Thornberry, Krohn, Lizotte, & Chard-Wierschem, 1993), a phenomenon that has also been observed in riots and cases where soldiers have committed wartime atrocities. Yet another explanation has involved the culpability of the media and the police in promoting gang imagery: The very definition of gangs as violent entities increases members' levels of violence. In other words, certain youths seek the rewards they think gang membership will afford them—status; protection; group identity; and entertainment, drugs, and sex (U.S. Department of Education, n.d.)—and are willing to engage in violent acts because "that's what a gang is." The image is reinforced by the news and popular media and by the folklore of the gang itself. It has also been argued that both gang members' own accounts of their activities and police statistics may be misleading. Because of the status violence confers on a perpetrator, a subject could conceivably exaggerate his or her criminal behavior in surveys and interviews as a means of bragging. Further, crime statistics reflect arrest and incarceration rates which, considering the general conspicuousness of gang members and police efforts to target these groups, could conceivably skew higher for gang offenders than for criminals who do not belong to gangs. A number of studies, less sensational in their findings and therefore less visible in the mainstream media, have found that most gang members spend the majority of their time simply "hanging out," albeit often within the context of drug or alcohol use (Katz & Jackson-Jacobs, 2004). In a sense, then, lacking any overarching objective such as profit or ideology, some gangs may see continued violence as a means of justifying their own existence and retaining members who would otherwise grow restless and leave.

Second point: Various explanations of gang behavior, leading to the most satisfactory one.

If retention is indeed the motivation for violent gang behavior, then it seems unlikely that some special feature of gangs in their day-to-day operation enables violent extremes of behavior; rather, it is the symbolic value of the gang "family" that makes them sufficiently attractive to justify violence, the risk of death or imprisonment, and the common perception (however false) that one can never leave the gang. It seems likely that certain characteristics typical of adolescents—the desire to create a self-identity, establish a sense of belonging, and both derive status from and earn status within groups (Ausubel, 2002)—make them vulnerable to the allure of such symbolism. It also seems likely that, in addition to environmental and psychological factors such as peer pressure and/or facilitation (Gifford-Smith, Dodge, Dishion, & McCord, 2005) or poor self-esteem ("At last," 1995), cultural factors also aggravate the problem of gang violence. That is to say, while many studies have rightly focused on how crumbling inner cities, poverty, and lack or loss of opportunity and hope affect a teen's predisposition toward gang affiliation, it might be worthwhile to examine how society itself provides gangs with false or mythical status that might add to their attraction.

Citation of a source with no author indicated.

Concludes with assertion that his arguments have led to: cultural factors contribute to gang violence.

How Do Gangs   6

References

At last—a rejection detector! (1995, November). *Psychology Today*. Retrieved from http://www.psychologytoday.com/articles/pto-19951101-000034.html

Ausubel, D. P. (2002). *Theory and problems of adolescent development* (2nd ed.). Lincoln, NE: iUniverse.

Battin-Pearson, S. R., Thornberry, T. P., Hawkins, J. D., & Krohn, M. D. (1998, October). Gang membership, delinquent peers, and delinquent behavior. *Juvenile Justice Bulletin*. Retrieved from http://www.ncjrs.gov/pdffiles/171119.pdf

Fagan, J., & Wilkinson, D. L. (1998). Social contexts and functions of adolescent violence. In D. S. Elliott, B. Hamburg, & K. R. Williams (Eds.), *Violence in American schools: A new perspective* (pp. 55–93). New York: Cambridge University Press. Retrieved from http://www.colorado.edu/cspv/publications/factsheets/schoolviolence/FS-SV03.html

Gifford-Smith, M., Dodge, K. A., Dishion, T. J., & McCord, J. (2005). Peer influence in children and adolescents: Crossing the bridge from developmental to intervention science. *Journal of Abnormal Child Psychology, 33*(3), 255–265. Retrieved from SpringerLink.

Gordon, R. A., Lahey, B. B., Kawai, E., Loeber, R., Stouthamer-Loeber, M., & Farrington, D. P. (2004). Antisocial behavior and youth gang membership: Selection and socialization. *Criminology, 42*(1), 55–88. Abstract retrieved from Blackwell Synergy.

Katz, J., & Jackson-Jacobs, C. (2004). The criminologists' gang. [Electronic version]. In C. Sumner (Ed.), *The Blackwell companion to criminology*. Malden, MA: Blackwell Publishers.

National Youth Violence Prevention Center. (n.d.). *Youth gangs*. Retrieved February 13, 2007, from http://www.safeyouth.org/scripts/teens/gangs.asp

Penly Hall, G., Thornberry, T. P., & Lizotte, A. J. (2006). The gang facilitation effect and neighborhood risk: Do gangs have a stronger influence on delinquency in disadvantaged areas? In J. F. Short, Jr., & L. Hughes (Eds.), *Studying youth gangs*. Lanham, MD: Altamira Press.

New page, title centered; double-space between title and first line of reference list.

Entries double-spaced, in alphabetical order.

First line of each entry at left margin; all other lines indented 1/2 inch or 5 spaces.

Thabit, W. (2005). How did East New York become a ghetto? Retrieved
February 13, 2007, from http://faculty.ncwc.edu/toconnor/301/
301lect08.htm

Thomas, C. (2005). Serious delinquency and gang membership. *Psychiatric
Times 22*(4). Retrieved from http://www.psychiatrictimes
.com/showArticle.jhtml?articleID=162100156

Thornberry, T. P., Krohn, M. D., Lizotte, A. J., & Chard-Wierschem, D. (1993).
The role of juvenile gangs in facilitating delinquent behavior. *Journal of
Research in Crime and Delinquency, 30*(1), *55–87.* Abstract retrieved from
Sage Journals Online.

U.S. Department of Education. (n.d.). *Youth gangs: Going beyond the myths
to address a critical problem.* Retrieved from http://www.ed.gov/admins/
lead/safety/training/gangs/problem_pg3.html

Walker-Barnes, C. J., & Mason, C. A. (2001). Ethnic differences in the effect of
parenting on gang involvement and gang delinquency: A longitudinal,
hierarchical linear modeling perspective. *Child Development, 72*(6),
1814–1831. Abstract retrieved from IngentaConnect.

Appendix A
Constructing a Writing Portfolio

Constructing a writing portfolio gives you the opportunity to select, display, and reflect on the work you have done in this course. An important purpose for constructing the portfolio is to provide you with support for the claims that you will make about your writing in the course. In short, a portfolio helps you support this statement: "Here is what I have learned this semester, and here is the evidence that I have learned these writing strategies and conventions."

What Is a Portfolio and Why Should I Construct One?

In the past, graphic artists or photographers tended to keep portfolios of their work to give potential clients a sense of what to expect in the future. More recently, other professionals, such as technical or professional writers, have found that keeping a portfolio is helpful when they look for work.

While no one will deny that the quality of the final product is important, how you arrived at that final product may be just as important as, or even more important than, the result. By looking at your process in a portfolio, your instructor can better assess your strengths and weaknesses as a writer.

Because the portfolio represents what you have learned throughout the course, the ideal time to begin constructing your portfolio is during the first week of the course. That will give you many opportunities to select and reflect on your work while that work is still fresh in your mind.

Selecting Materials for Your Portfolio

As you decide what to include as part of your portfolio, consider the following questions:

1. What have I learned about writing in each of the four areas of life—academic, professional, civic, personal?
2. What have I learned about writing for various purposes?
3. What rhetorical skills and knowledge have I developed?
4. What critical thinking and reading skills have I developed?
5. What have I learned about the writing process?

6. What have I learned about working effectively with peers?
7. What knowledge of conventions have I developed?
8. What have I learned about writing responsibly?
9. What have I learned about using technology?

As you respond to each of the questions above, consider a follow-up question: *What evidence will demonstrate that I have developed this set of skills or knowledge?* Among the print or electronic evidence available to you are the following:

- Invention work (listing; brainstorming; clustering; freewriting)
- Research notes (from your library and online research; field research; interviews)
- Reading notes (comments you made on the reading you did for the class)
- Drafts of papers
- Peers' comments on your work
- Polished versions of your papers
- Reflections on your papers (that you write when you submit your papers)

Among the evidence that may not appear on paper or disk are the following:

- Discussions with peers about your writing
- Discussions with your instructor about your writing

Reflecting on What You Have Written

As noted earlier, it is helpful to reflect on your work regularly throughout the semester while that work is fresh in your mind. Remember that *reflective writing* asks you to think back on, to consider, to reflect on the work you did for the course. Consider answering the questions at the end of each chapter in Parts 2 and 3 as a way to start that reflective process.

As you reflect on the work that you use as evidence in your portfolio, you might consider another question: *Why does this piece of evidence effectively demonstrate that I have developed a certain set of skills or knowledge?* Your response to that question should also appear in your portfolio because it illustrates that you are confident about what you have learned during the course.

Organizing Your Portfolio

There are many ways to organize your portfolio, and your instructor will let you know how he or she would like your portfolio arranged and organized. Sometimes, your teacher will ask you to organize your portfolio in a *chronological* manner: Start with the first piece of writing you did for the class and end with the final piece of writing. Other organizational schemes you may find especially useful include the following:

- **By Learning Goals:** The Writing Program Administrators Outcomes Statement, which is prominent in this book, includes four categories of learning goals which you could use as headings in your portfolio: (1) Rhetorical Knowledge; (2) Critical Thinking, Reading, and Writing; (3) Processes; and (4) Knowledge of Conventions.

- **By Purpose:** If you use this organizational scheme, you could list the chapter titles from Parts 2 and 3 of this book as your headings—for example, "Writing to Explore," "Writing to Convince," "Writing to Propose Solutions."

For an example from a writing portfolio organized by learning goals, see pages A-3–A-7.

Portfolio Formats

You may decide to submit—or your instructor may request that you submit—your portfolio in one of the following formats:

- **As a print document** in a three-ring binder.
- **As an electronic file,** on a floppy disk, flash drive, or CD. If you use this format, consider constructing a hypertext document so that readers can click on links to see other parts of your portfolio.
- **As a Web site.** This format enables you to provide links to other parts of your own portfolio as well as links to other Web sites or pages that you have found useful during the semester.

In the example shown in Figure A.1, note how student Eileen Holland has organized her electronic portfolio. As background for her work in her first-year writing course, she provides examples of her writing from elementary and secondary school. She also provides information about several of her favorite writers, and she includes materials to demonstrate that she has learned skills and knowledge from the four areas of the Writing Program Administrators Outcomes Statement. Finally, she discusses what she hopes to learn in upcoming semesters.

A Portion of a Sample Portfolio

The following portfolio excerpt comes from Chelsea Rundle, who constructed it in a second-semester writing course. Note how she uses evidence from her work to demonstrate what she has learned.

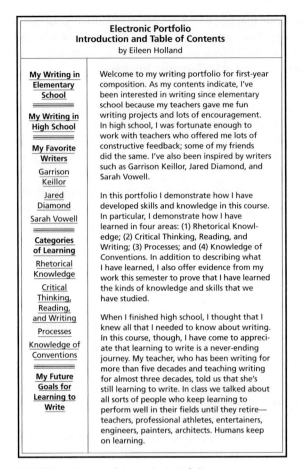

Electronic Portfolio
Introduction and Table of Contents
by Eileen Holland

My Writing in Elementary School
═══════
My Writing in High School
═══════
My Favorite Writers
Garrison Keillor
Jared Diamond
Sarah Vowell
═══════
Categories of Learning
Rhetorical Knowledge
Critical Thinking, Reading, and Writing
Processes
Knowledge of Conventions
═══════
My Future Goals for Learning to Write

Welcome to my writing portfolio for first-year composition. As my contents indicate, I've been interested in writing since elementary school because my teachers gave me fun writing projects and lots of encouragement. In high school, I was fortunate enough to work with teachers who offered me lots of constructive feedback; some of my friends did the same. I've also been inspired by writers such as Garrison Keillor, Jared Diamond, and Sarah Vowell.

In this portfolio I demonstrate how I have developed skills and knowledge in this course. In particular, I demonstrate how I have learned in four areas: (1) Rhetorical Knowledge; (2) Critical Thinking, Reading, and Writing; (3) Processes; and (4) Knowledge of Conventions. In addition to describing what I have learned, I also offer evidence from my work this semester to prove that I have learned the kinds of knowledge and skills that we have studied.

When I finished high school, I thought that I knew all that I needed to know about writing. In this course, though, I have come to appreciate that learning to write is a never-ending journey. My teacher, who has been writing for more than five decades and teaching writing for almost three decades, told us that she's still learning to write. In class we talked about all sorts of people who keep learning to perform well in their fields until they retire—teachers, professional athletes, entertainers, engineers, painters, architects. Humans keep on learning.

FIGURE A.1   An Electronic Portfolio

In English 102, I learned that a good paper topic is one that I am passionate about and is feasible. Picking topics related to my major—applied biology—helped me explore different issues/trends in the field of biology and medical science through writing my English papers.

In my first paper, I explored the concept of personalized medicine by researching what others thought about it and then forming my opinion on the topic. For the second paper, writing to convince, I addressed a topic I am very passionate about—CT scans causing radiation cancer. I was able to look at how these two topics affect one another because CT scans are an integral process in personalized medicine.

While writing these papers and revising them, I have expanded my writing knowledge and have learned how to strengthen my writing skills. I will demonstrate what I have learned in this portfolio.

RHETORICAL KNOWLEDGE

- Focus on a Purpose

In writing the first argument, I stayed focused on a purpose: persuading the audience to see the dangers of CT scans. To do this, I used a claim, support for my claim, and the refutation of counterarguments. In refuting counterarguments I addressed multiple viewpoints on the issue while showing the reader why my claim is correct, such as in this example:

> Some argue that radiation cancer is not caused by CT scans, but can be caused by other factors. This is absolutely true, for radiation, or the release of energy, can be given off by a number of sources including household electrical appliances, heaters, the sun, and x-ray machines. For example, I recall my parents telling me that they were always warned as children not to stand too close to the microwave, or they would get cancer. This is hardly the case, for the type of radiation given off by electrical appliances and heaters isn't harmful enough to cause cancer. However, radiation cancer is caused by high exposure to the sun and x-ray machines. Therefore, as exposure to CT scans—a form of x-ray technology—increases, so does the risk of radiation cancer.

- Respond to the Needs of Different Audiences

When writing a paper particular to my major, I had to think about the needs of my audience. It is important to give background information at the beginning of the paper since It is hard for the reader to form an opinion if they don't understand the topic you are writing about. It is also important to not offend your audience, so I had to determine how to use the three appeals—logos (logic), ethos (ethics), and pathos (emotions)—appropriately. Peer reviews helped me determine where more background information was needed.

To provide background information to the reader in a draft of my argument on the topic of CT scans, I wrote:

> The word <u>tomography</u> originates from the Greek word <u>tomos</u>, meaning "slice," and <u>graphia</u>, or "describing." CT scans, a form of tomography, have been used for years as the predominate method for medical imaging. The scans produce a three-dimensional image of an object's internal structure based on several x-ray images. Original uses of CT scans are to diagnose different cancers, guide biopsies and similar procedures, and to plan surgery or radiation treatment ("Computed").

I also learned that it is crucial to maintain a negotiable stance while writing an argument. Arguments are rarely two-sided, so it is important to be open to all sides. If you form an opinion without getting all the facts and hearing other viewpoints, you can't honestly say your claim is correct. It is difficult to persuade your audience to see things from your perspective if you don't know all the perspectives yourself.

- Adopt Appropriate Voice, Tone, and Level of Formality

Different tones and levels of formality should be used for different genres of writing and in different writing situations. For example, in my argument paper it was important to present the technical background information in a way that could be easily understood by the reader. A semiformal tone was appropriate because it informed the reader without seeming too wordy or technical. However, some genres of writing allowing the writer to incorporate more of his or her own voice. For example, a short narrative from my learning log is much more informal:

> Earlier this evening, I was reading Leonard Pitts Jr.'s argument entitled "Spare the Rod, Spoil the Parenting." At the same time, my sister and dad were having an argument about I don't know what, but my sister wouldn't stop talking back. She was saying, "It's a free country, I can say whatever I want." To which my dad replied, "Yah, but the family is more of a dictatorship." Still reading Pitts' argument, I came to the sentence "As a culture, we seem to have forgotten that the family is not a democracy, but a benign dictatorship." What a coincidence . . . it made me laugh!

- Write in Several Genres

In English 102, I learned the structural aspects of various genres of writing. In the analysis essay, for example, I began with an introduction that included a question I wanted to answer: *How can treatment for disease be adapted to an individual's genetic makeup?* I then gave brief summaries of two texts that answered the question. Next, I analyzed the texts. Finally, I synthesized the texts with my thoughts and opinions to answer the beginning question.

In the argument paper, however, I began with my claim: *CT scans cause radiation cancer due to the high amount of radiation a person is exposed to.* Next, I provided any background information on the topic my audience might need. Then, I provided evidence to support my claim. Finally, I addressed and refuted counterarguments to my claim and concluded.

Writing Effective Essay Examinations

In many of your college classes, you will be asked to take essay examinations: to sit and write (sometimes on a computer, most often by hand), for a specified period of time, about the material you have learned. Writing essay exams differs in several ways from writing academic papers that you might work on for several weeks. When you write an essay exam, you will find that the following is true:

- You usually have to rely on your memory.
- You don't have much time to figure out what you would like to say.
- You can't get feedback from your instructor and classmates.
- You usually do not have much time for revision.

It is no wonder, then, that some students worry about in-class essay examinations. Our purpose here is to help you overcome fears about essay examinations by giving you some specific strategies to use before and during such tests.

Keep in mind that essay-examination situations may come along throughout your life. In your career or in a civic organization, for example, you may be asked to write quickly and without the luxury of invention work or peer feedback:

- As a small business owner, you might have to draft and complete a cost estimate and quotation in a customer's home.
- As a member of a city council or town board, you may need to comment on a political issue at a town meeting or in response to a question from the media.
- If you write advertising copy or are a journalist, you will frequently have tight deadlines to contend with.

Think of college essay examinations as a way of preparing for life after college, when you often will have to write from memory in a short period of time.

To write an effective response to a question on an essay examination, you will need to do the following:

- Know and understand the information that the examination will cover.
- Be able to relate that information to other topics and ideas you have read about and discussed in class.

- Analyze and understand the question(s) that you are asked to address.

- Construct a thoughtful answer to the question(s) and get your ideas down onto paper, in the available time.

- Deal with any pre-exam stress issues that you might have (much of what causes stress for any kind of examination occurs when students are not prepared for the exam, so just being ready can make a big difference in your anxiety level).

- Deal with the examination *scene*—whether you are writing by hand or with computer, what distractions there might be (other students, noise), and so on.

Getting Ready: Information Gathering, Storage, and Retrieval

When you read and take notes for your college classes, remember that one day you probably will be tested on this information.

Chapter 2 provides useful strategies for reading effectively, and Chapter 3 offers strategies for writing about course material, so we suggest you revisit those chapters with an eye to using them to help prepare you for essay examinations. Teachers don't expect students to remember everything covered in classes, but you will be expected to recall and understand the main concepts and to relate them to other ideas. As you read and listen in class, make note of the major concepts, and be sure you can explain them.

Considering Questions

As you read and listen to class lectures and participate in class discussions, consider the kinds of questions an instructor might ask you to write about. What are the big issues or ideas that have been covered in class or that you have encountered in your reading? As you think of possible questions, record them in your journal. Then set aside some time to write responses to those questions.

For example, in your history class, you may be asked to explain how the historical events that took place over a period of time led to the start of a war. The important thing for you is to realize that you probably can make an informed guess at what questions a teacher will ask on an essay examination, so it is worthwhile for you to consider what those questions might be—before the exam—and how you might answer them.

▌ Analyzing Questions

In addition to thinking about what questions you might be asked, it is equally important to understand what the questions are asking you to do.

Because instructors know that students have only a limited time to respond to an essay examination, they generally will ask questions that have a narrow focus. When you see the test question(s) for your essay examination, ask yourself what the questions ask you to *do*. In most cases, your instructor will be asking you to employ a strategy we discuss in more detail elsewhere in this text:

Sample Essay Examination Question	Key Strategy	Where to Find More
Analyze the use of the magic of flying in relation to the other illusions in the *Harry Potter* films.	Analyze	Chapter 7, Writing to Analyze (pp. 154-86)
Of the short stories we read in our English class this semester, explain which makes the most effective use of *imagery*.	Evaluate	Chapter 9, Writing to Evaluate (pp. 226-64)
How did the Gulf of Tonkin incident influence the start of the Vietnam War?	Relate Causes and Effects	Chapter 10, Writing about Causes and Effects (pp. 266-305)
Briefly compare Canada's and Australia's reactions to the second Iraq war.	Compare and Contrast	Chapter 13, Using Strategies That Guide Readers (Writing about Comparisons and Contrasts, pp. 412-14)
Define *oligopoly* in relation to the California energy crisis.	Define	Chapter 13, Using Strategies That Guide Readers (Writing Definitions, pp. 409-11)
Illustrate, using examples from your reading, how educators' growing awareness of different learning styles is influencing elementary school teaching practices.	Inform, Analyze, Relate Causes and Effects	Chapter 6, Writing to Inform (pp. 118-53), Chapter 7, Writing to Analyze (pp. 154-86), and Chapter 10, Writing about Causes and Effects (pp. 266-305)
Critique William Faulkner's use of *time* in "A Rose for Emily."	Evaluate	Chapter 9, Writing to Evaluate (pp. 226-64)
Explain how Thailand, though surrounded by nations who have been colonized by former imperial powers such as France and Great Britain, has avoided being colonized by another nation.	Describe, Inform, Convince	Chapter 13, Using Strategies That Guide Readers (Writing Descriptions, pp. 405-08), Chapter 6, Writing to Inform (pp. 118-53), and Chapter 8, Writing to Convince (pp. 188-225)
Outline the three major theories of social change.	Summarize, Inform	Chapter 2, Reading Critically for College and for Life (Writing Effective Summaries, p. 28) and Chapter 6, Writing to Inform (pp. 118-53).

If you are faced with a multiple-part question that perhaps seems impossible to answer, draw some lines between each section—in effect, segment the question into its component parts. For example, here is a multi-part question:

Noting the recent changes in campus safety problems, argue that your campus needs more or less police protection, but without fostering a siege or locked-in mentality for the student body.

Go through and mark each part of a multi-part question (here set off with |||):

		Noting the recent changes in campus safety problems		
		argue that your campus needs more or less police protection		
		but without fostering a siege mentality		
		or locked-in mentality for the student body		

The first part of the question (*Noting the recent changes in campus safety problems*) asks that you outline what campus safety issues have recently taken place.

The second part of the question (*argue that your campus needs more or less police protection*) asks that you take a position on the amount of police protection your campus needs (if you argue for more protection, what does that mean: more police on campus? More police on foot patrol? Bicycle police? Should they be more heavily armed? Should there be police dogs?).

The third part of the question (*but without fostering a siege [mentality]*) asks that you define what a "siege mentality" would be for the teachers as well as the students. The last part of the question asks much the same: for a definition and explanation of what a "locked-in mentality" means.

Breaking down a complex question in this manner allows you to see and thus consider each part of the question, an analysis that helps ensure that you will answer all of its parts.

Constructing Thoughtful Answers

Once you understand exactly what the question is asking you, it is a good idea to jot down your main ideas quickly. Then think about what organizational method you might use.

Also think about whether your professor considers the exam to be a *short-* or *long-answer* essay examination. If you have an hour for the essay exam, for example, and there are ten questions, that gives you an average of six minutes to answer each question, a fairly good tip-off that you are working with a *short-answer* examination. For your answers to be effective, you will need to get right to the point and then state any supporting evidence as concisely as possible.

On the other hand, if you have 90 minutes to respond to one question on an exam, then you have time, perhaps, for some brainstorming about the ideas you think you might like to present, to construct a brief cluster diagram of how the parts of your answer relate to each other, and other invention work. And as you are writing the examination, you will have time to explain each aspect of your answer in greater detail than you could with only a few minutes to answer the question.

One type of organization that works well for essay examinations is what is commonly called the "Classical Scheme." If you follow the Classical Scheme, you will do the following:

For more on the Classical Scheme, see Chapter 14, pages 423–26.

- Construct a solid thesis statement, clearly indicating the main point that you want to make in your answer.

- State your main point right at the start, forcing you to use supporting details that always relate back to that main idea.

- Provide an effective and logical organizational pattern to follow.

- Acknowledge the other side of an issue or situation or idea, which tells your instructor that you are aware that there are other perspectives or approaches.

- Tie everything together at the end.

Dealing with the Examination Scene

You probably have your favorite place to write, where it is quiet (or there is music) and where everything you need is at hand (pen, computer, paper, coffee). But, you *rarely* will have such an ideal setting for an in-class examination— unless you construct it.

Since you usually know when an exam will take place, it is helpful to prepare your test-taking environment as thoroughly as you can, so the writing situation the examination presents is as normal and comfortable as possible. If you usually use a pencil to write, then make sure you have several sharpened pencils with you—or better yet, a good quality mechanical pencil. If you are allowed to use notes as you write the exam, make sure your notes are clearly written and legible. Here are some other ways to prepare:

See Chapter 3, Writing to Learn for College and for Life, for more on study strategies.

- Know the material that you will be tested on, by using effective studying techniques (tape recording and then listening to your notes, rewriting your in-class notes on your computer, working with others in study groups, and so on).

- Construct your own test questions. This activity forces you to look at the material from an instructor's viewpoint by asking, What would I like my students to know and understand about this material?

- Think about how you will spend the time you are allotted for the examination, *before* taking the examination. Surprisingly, few students really think about how they will spend the hour or 90 minutes or whatever time they will be given for the exam. If you have a plan of attack, so to speak, going into the exam, then you will use your time more wisely. Consider how much time you might plan to spend understanding the question, getting some ideas onto paper, organizing those ideas, actually writing the exam, revising your response, and so on.

Note whether some questions are worth more points than others; if so, then it makes sense to spend *more time* on the questions that are worth more. If you encounter a question that you cannot immediately answer, skip it and go on to other questions. That gives you some time to think about it as you work on other answers.

Terry Dolan Writes an Essay Examination

College student Terry Dolan received this prompt for a 50-minute essay examination:

PROMPT

In his 2005 book *The World Is Flat*, Thomas Friedman talks of "ten forces that flattened the world." Name three of Friedman's ten forces and explain how they helped to flatten the world.

TERRY DOLAN'S RESPONSE

In his book *The World Is Flat*, Thomas Friedman talks of ten forces that flattened the world. I will discuss how three of these forces—the fall of the Berlin Wall, Netscape going public, and open-sourcing—helped to flatten the twenty-first-century world.

On November 9, 1989, the Berlin Wall fell. While this was a major victory for the forces of democracy in East Berlin and East Germany, it also stood as a symbol for the eventual fall of communism in all of Europe. By opening up Eastern Europe, and eventually the old Soviet Union, to free market capitalism, the end of the Berlin Wall was Friedman's first "flattener." Friedman also talks about the IBM PC computer and how its introduction helped to facilitate the flattening process begun by the fall of the Berlin Wall. The computer with a modem helped to connect people in the old communist bloc with new computer and economic networks.

Friedman's second flattening force happened when the browser Netscape went public. Netscape was a major force because it really opened up the World Wide Web and the Internet for the general population. Before Netscape, the only way people had access to the Internet was in text-only environments. While that type of access may have been interesting, it mainly attracted scientists and educators. Netscape let people use graphics, and eventually sound and video, online as well. One of the important advantages Netscape offered is that it could be used on any type of computer—PCs, Macs, or Unix boxes.

Another flattener, according to Friedman, is the open-source movement. Unlike most software, you can download open-source software for free. People participate in developing the software for the good of the group. The main open-source software that Friedman discusses is the Apache Web server. Friedman talks about how many of the main Internet Web sites run on Apache servers. Because there is no cost involved in buying the software, just about anyone who knows how can run a Web server.

An even more important example of open-source software is probably the Linux operating system. Linux is a kind of Unix, a powerful computer operating system. The advantage to Linux is that it's cheap (you can download it for free) and flexible (lots of computer people are constantly working to make it even better). The disadvantage to Linux is that most software is written to run on PCs. But more and more open-source software is being written to run on Linux boxes. You can now get *OpenOffice* and similar open-source programs that will let you do just about anything you could do with Microsoft software. In other parts of the world, lots of computers run on Linux and use open-source software.

Finally, what I think is the most interesting point about all of Friedman's flatteners is that they're all about technology, mainly computer technology, and how that helps all of us connect to one another faster and better.

Standard Document Forms

Selecting and using a particular "form" for any text you construct involves making rhetorical choices. Before selecting any kind of format for any text you construct then, you first need to ask (and answer) the following questions:

- What do you want your writing to accomplish?
- What form will best serve your purpose?
- Who is your audience?

This appendix presents guidelines for designing ten types of print or online documents, along with examples of each type.

For more on designing documents, see Chapter 18, Communicating with Design and Visuals.

Business Letters

Features of an Effective Business Letter

As with any text, business letters have real audiences and purposes, and the form that you use needs to fit your readers' expectations of business correspondence:

- Use margins of at least one inch on all four sides of the letter.
- Use a standard 12-point font such as Times New Roman.
- Single-space addresses and paragraphs.
- Double-space between sections of the letter—return address of sender, date, name and address of person to whom the letter is being sent, salutation, paragraphs, and closing. If you use an indented format, you do not need to double-space between paragraphs.
- Use a colon after the salutation.
- Use formal, but not stilted, language.
- After the closing (usually "Sincerely"), use a comma.
- After the closing, include four blank lines for your signature; then type your name, and give your professional title, if applicable.
- After your name and professional title, include a "cc:" (copy) line and/ or an "Enc:" (enclosure) line if necessary.
- Because error-free letters give readers a positive impression, proofread your letter carefully and ask a friend or colleague to proofread it if possible.

Figure C.1 is an example of a business letter.

Hanna Olsen	Return address of sender
1111 Lutefisk Lane	
Olso, WI 55555	
	Double-space between sections
October 1, 2005	Date
Kirsti Andersen, Director	Name and address of person to
Office of the Registrar	whom letter is being sent
413 Lefse Hall	
Oslo College	
Oslo, WI 55555	
Dear Ms. Andersen:	Salutation

I am writing to request that you adjust my tuition payment for this semester. Because of health problems, I have been forced to withdraw from two of my courses. I am requesting a partial tuition refund for those six credit hours.   Double-space between paragraphs

Three weeks after the semester began, I was diagnosed with mono-nucleosis, which has limited the number of hours that I can attend class and study. Fortunately, I am doing well in my other two courses, and I am confident that I will be able to carry a full course load next semester.

To document my illness, I have attached a note from the Campus Medical Center. If you need further evidence, I will be happy to provide it.

I look forward to hearing from you soon.

Sincerely,	Closing
	4 blank lines
Hanna Olsen	Signature
Hanna Olsen	Name
Enc: Note from Campus Medical Center	Enclosure line

FIGURE C.1   Business Letter (Block Format)

Letters of Application

Your purpose in writing a letter of application is to *get* something—most often a job interview (and sometimes even the job itself).

Features of an Effective Letter of Application

- Use the features of the business-letter format described on page A-15.
- Use the exact job title from the job announcement to indicate the position for which you are applying.

- Briefly summarize your qualifications for the job. Don't simply repeat what is on your résumé, which will be attached to your letter.
- If the job announcement includes "required qualifications" and "desired qualifications," you must discuss all of the required ones, and you should discuss as many of the desired ones as possible.
- Indicate how you can meet the needs of the hiring organization.
- Subtly show that you have done your homework in learning as much as possible about the organization and the job itself.
- Never misrepresent your skills, knowledge, or background. Honesty is the best approach.

Figure C.2 is an example of a letter of application.

Kirsti Brones   Return address of sender
1234 Raaen Way
Modum, MN 55555
                                       Double-space between sections

July 5, 2007   Date

Anna Drolsum   Name and address of person to
Personnel Director   whom letter is being sent
Super Computer Company, Inc.
2222 E. Cyberspace Dr.
Minneapolis, MN 55444

Dear Ms. Drolsum: Salutation

I am writing to apply for the sales representative position recently advertised in the *Minneapolis Star-Tribune.* The skills that I have developed in my degree program support my strong interest in the position.
                          Double-space between paragraphs
In my recent internship with Excellent Computer Company, I had sales responsibilities similar to those described in your advertisement and on your Web site. Thus, I gained experience in maintaining sales accounts and in making cold-calls to prospective corporate customers. Prior to my internship, I learned how to handle customer concerns by working for several years at the Customer Service desk of a Bull's-Eye Department Store.

I am especially interested in working for Super Computer Company because you have such a strong reputation for offering quality products and being responsive to customers' needs.

I am eager to speak with you about the sales representative position. If you have any questions about my enclosed résumé, please call me at 400-555-4371. Thank you for considering my application.

Sincerely,   Closing

Kirsti Brones   Signature

Kirsti Brones   Name

Enclosure   Enclosure line

FIGURE C.2   Letter of Application

Memos

As with business letters, business memos have a rhetorical purpose and their own specific requirements as to format.

Features of an Effective Memo

- If your office or organization has a memo template, use that format. If it does not, follow the generic format: Include a separate line for a "To" entry, a "From" entry, the date, and a "Regarding" or "RE" designation.
- For printed memos, use margins of at least one inch on all four sides.
- In the "RE" line, use a clear, concise subject heading.
- For printed memos that have legal significance, include your initials or legal signature, in ink.
- For memos that need to be shared with other people besides the primary recipient(s), add a "cc" (copy) line after the body of the memo.
- Use bold type sparingly for emphasis and to highlight any information that requires immediate attention.

Figure C.3 is an example of a memo.

Date: March 29, 2006
To: Information Technology Staff
From: Norman Jones, Assistant Director, Division of Information Technology
RE: Installing New Computers

At the end of this fiscal year, we will be purchasing 124 new desktop computers for employees in the Division of Research and Development. The machines are scheduled to arrive on June 30.

Because we need to have all the new computers installed and fully operational by July 10, **all Information Technology staff need to be on the job between June 28 and July 10.** For that reason, I cannot approve any requests for vacation time during that period.

I hope that this early notice affords you ample time to plan your summer vacations accordingly. I regret any inconvenience.

Thank you for your good work.

cc: Linda Searcy, Director, Division of Information Technology

FIGURE C.3   Memo

Résumés

At first glance, writing a résumé might seem easy: just list your work history and when you did it. But constructing an effective résumé involves a great deal of time and effort. To begin with, you need to consider carefully the audience to which you are addressing your résumé: Who will see your résumé? What information will they need, and what format should it be in? If you are adapting your résumé for a specific position, what does the *job advertisement* call for? You want to ensure that everything the advertisement asks for is included.

Features of an Effective Résumé

- You may—or may not—choose to include a concise career objective at the beginning of your résumé. Although such job objectives were common until recently, some experts now advise résumé writers not to include an objective because the objective is to acquire the job for which you are applying.

- Include current contact information—name, mailing address, e-mail address, phone numbers.

- Use descriptive headings to label the sections of your résumé, such as "Education," "Work Experience," "Skills," "Activities," "Awards," and "References."

- Do not include personal information such as age, race, ethnicity, marital status, sexual orientation, or health status.

- If requested to do so, list your references. Before you list someone as a reference, make certain that he or she knows your work and feels comfortable recommending you for a job. As an alternative, you can add the line "References available upon request." If you post your résumé on a Web site, do not list your references.

- If you limit your résumé to a single page, hiring personnel can read it quickly. However, it is more important to include the information that will help you get a job, so consider your audience and their expectations. In business, for example, one-page résumés are common; in colleges and universities, résumés are usually much longer and more detailed.

- If you post your résumé on a Web site, keep in mind that readers will see it one screen at a time rather than one page at a time.

- Although it is easy to embellish an online résumé with ornate graphics, a simple online résumé is actually more effective.

- Because employers sometimes conduct Web searches for résumés, adding some key terms such as the word *résumé* itself to your online résumé will make it more likely that a search engine will detect your résumé.

- A résumé must not have any errors, so be sure to proofread carefully. Ask friends to help with this task if possible.

Different Kinds of Résumés

The two most common kinds of résumés are the chronological résumé and the functional résumé. In a **chronological résumé,** you list all of the jobs you have held in the past in reverse chronological order with the most recent listed first. Your work history should appear just below your personal information. Figure C.4 is an example of a chronological résumé. In a **functional résumé,** you make sure to highlight skills you possess or tasks you have accomplished in previous jobs. Another option is to combine the two formats by listing jobs chronologically and highlighting the tasks that you performed while employed in each job.

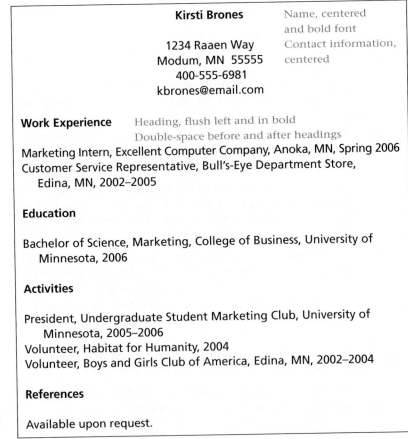

Kirsti Brones — Name, centered and bold font

1234 Raaen Way
Modum, MN 55555 — Contact information, centered
400-555-6981
kbrones@email.com

Work Experience — Heading, flush left and in bold
Double-space before and after headings

Marketing Intern, Excellent Computer Company, Anoka, MN, Spring 2006
Customer Service Representative, Bull's-Eye Department Store,
    Edina, MN, 2002–2005

Education

Bachelor of Science, Marketing, College of Business, University of
    Minnesota, 2006

Activities

President, Undergraduate Student Marketing Club, University of
    Minnesota, 2005–2006
Volunteer, Habitat for Humanity, 2004
Volunteer, Boys and Girls Club of America, Edina, MN, 2002–2004

References

Available upon request.

FIGURE C.4
A Chronological
Résumé

Electronic Résumés

As you enter today's employment market, you are likely to encounter employers who ask you to submit electronic résumés. Sometimes the electronic résumé can be nothing more than a digital copy (a *Word* document or a pdf) of your paper résumé. However, you might be asked to fill out a web-form that will serve as a résumé. When you are submitting an electronic résumé of any kind, in all likelihood the first reader of your résumé will not be a human but a machine, machines are programmed to search for predetermined keywords or phrases. That means that every résumé that contains the right keyword or phrase will go on to the next phase of screening— maybe by a human. Reading job ads closely will give you a good idea of what keywords or phrases might be important for the specific job you're applying for. While you already know the importance of proofreading a paper résumé, proofreading becomes even more important with electronic résumés. Figure C.5 is an example of a mixed chronological and functional résumé. Potential keywords or phrases that would be helpful in an electronic résumé are highlighted.

FIGURE C.5 A Mixed Chronological and Functional Résumé, with Keywords Highlighted

E-mail Messages

Especially in business environments, e-mail is everywhere, and often everyone seems to be checking e-mail all the time, every day. Constructing an e-mail, like any other kind of text, requires that you consider the rhetorical situation, who your audience is, and what you want the e-mail to accomplish.

In addition, because it is so easy to forward an e-mail, it is important to understand that what you say to one person in an e-mail *might* be shared widely with others.

Features of an Effective E-mail Message

- Use relatively short block paragraphs to make it easier for your readers to read the message. Single space, and include a blank line between paragraphs.
- Be very careful when using "reply to all."
- Use a font that is easy to read on a screen, such as 10-point or 12-point Times New Roman or Arial.
- In business e-mail, it is best to not use emoticons such as smiley faces.
- If you use an electronic signature for your e-mail, make certain that it includes relevant contact information. For business messages, use a signature that is suitable for business.

Figure C.6 is an example of an e-mail.

Date: Thu, 24 May 2007 16:58:31 -0400

From: O_DOOL@XYandZ.com

To: needshybrid@cox.net

Subject: Your new vehicle

I am happy to tell you that your new Toyota Prius has arrived. We will have it prepared for you to pick up after 5:00 pm tomorrow evening.

I think you'll find the colors you chose to your liking.

Please respond to this e-mail to tell us when you'll pick up your new Prius. Could you also please make sure to bring a copy of your proof of insurance card? Our finance officer forgot to make a copy when she was doing your paperwork. We do need a copy for the files.

Thanks for your business,

Oscar Doolittle
Sales Manager
X,Y, & Z Toyota/Scion
Yuma, AZ 85365
(928) 555-4567

FIGURE C.6
E-mail Message

Threaded Discussion Groups and Listserv Postings

A number of publicly available Web sites such as Yahoo!, MSN, and Google offer online discussion groups (sometimes called **threaded discussions**). Organized by topic or interest area, these groups allow members to view and participate in written discussions over the Web. After a member posts a message about a particular topic, others may then post their responses. As the discussion proceeds, a Web page is automatically built around the discussion. Threaded discussions allow members to see all the postings in context on one Web page. This makes participating in and viewing the discussion easy.

A **listserv** is another kind of online forum facilitated by e-mail that allows participants to transmit information to large numbers of people who share an interest or are involved in an organization. A listserv distributes e-mail to the addresses of all people who have subscribed to that listserv. That is, when a subscriber sends a message to a listserv, the listserv automatically distributes it to all other subscribers.

Features of an Effective Threaded Discussion or Listserv Posting

- If you are posting a message as part of an ongoing discussion, become familiar with previous postings on the topic so that you do not repeat what has already been written.
- Stay on the topic at hand unless it is appropriate to move to a new topic.
- If you disagree with someone's opinion on a topic, express your views politely. Do not engage in personal attacks, called **flaming.**
- Do not post personal messages ("thanks for the information, Joe") to the group or listserv, when your message is intended for just one person.

For an example of a threaded discussion, see p.463. Figure C.7 below is an example of a listserv posting.

```
Date:        Tue, 19 Oct 2005 23:00:10  –0500
Reply-To:    Writing Program Administration <[log in to unmask]>
Sender:      Writing Program Administration <[log in to unmask]>
From:        CJ <[log in to unmask]>
Subject:     Re: names for FYC 2

Our FYC sequence is titled

Semester 1: College Writing and Rhetoric
Semester 2: College Writing and Research

Could be better . . . . could be a lot worse . . . .

Best,

CeeJ
```

FIGURE C.7
Listserv Posting

Brochures

As with your résumé, you want a brochure to accomplish something: to sell a product or service (or to get a reader more interested in a product or service), perhaps, or to provide information (a voter's guide, for example).

Features of an Effective Brochure

- Include a headline that is informative and attention-getting.
- Include a visual element such as a photo or drawing if it adds to the content of the brochure and if it grabs readers' attention.
- If the brochure advertises an event, make certain that you include all relevant information—date, time, place, cost (if any), phone number, Web site address.
- Your layout will depend on the number of folds that your brochure has. If you are using standard 8-1/2″ × 11″ paper, you may decide to have no fold, a bi-fold, or a tri-fold.
- Consider the principles of proximity, contrast, alignment, and repetition described in Chapter 18.
- If you use photos or graphics that are not your own, make certain that you have permission to display them publicly.

Figure C.8 is an example of a brochure.

FIGURE C.8
A Brochure for an
Art Show Reprinted by
permission of Friends of
Patuxent Wildlife Research
Center and Patuxent
Research Refuge, Inc.

Posters

When constructing a poster, consider its rhetorical purpose: What do you want a poster to *do*? Provide information? Show people how to get somewhere? Explain something?

Features of an Effective Poster

- Include a headline that is informative and will grab viewers' attention.
- Include a visual element such as a photograph or drawing if it adds to the content of the poster and if it grabs viewers' attention.
- Determine what size poster and what size font will be necessary for readers. Both will depend on the location of the poster and how close to the poster readers will be.
- Consider the principles of proximity, contrast, alignment, and repetition described in Chapter 18.
- If you use photos or stock graphics, make certain that you have permission to display them publicly.
- If the poster advertises an event, make certain that you include all relevant information—date, time, place, cost (if any), phone number or Web site address.

Figure C.9 is an example of an effective poster.

FIGURE C.9 A Poster Advertising an Event

Newsletters

Newsletters most often have a specific audience (usually employees or members of a club or organization of some kind). Those who produce newsletters for a group also have specific purposes. At our university, for example, we get newsletters from a number of places, including the following:

- The university itself, including a "wellness newsletter," which tells of various workshops employees can attend to lose weight, stop smoking, become better managers, learn new computer software, and so on.
- The faculty senate, which lets us know about political issues on campus.
- Our department, letting us know about upcoming speakers, recent publications by our colleagues, and other news of interest.

Features of an Effective Newsletter

- Determine who your readers will be and include information that will be interesting and useful to those readers.
- Determine a purpose for the newsletter, and keep that purpose in mind as you decide what to include and what to exclude.
- Use headlines to indicate the content of the stories that follow them.
- Consider the principles of proximity, contrast, alignment, and repetition described in Chapter 18.
- If you use photos or graphics that are not your own, make certain that you have permission to include them in your publication.

Figure C.10 is an example of a newsletter.

FIGURE C.10
A Newsletter for
a Community
Organization

Web Sites

Do you have your own Web site? Would you like to? As a student, you might develop a portfolio as a Web site, in which you display your work (see Appendix A). As a member of an organization, you might develop a Web site that describes the activities of the organization. Or, like many people, you might develop a Web site in which you tell your family's history. A related option is to establish a **blog** (or Web log), which is a specific kind of Web site that operates like an online journal and often has an interactive function which enables viewers to post comments about each blog entry.

Features of an Effective Web Site

When designing a Web site or a blog, you should keep both your purpose and audience in mind. That means that you will design a personal Web site, intended to be viewed by your friends and family very differently from a Web site that is intended to portray you as a professional. Similarly, you will construct a personal-interest blog differently than a blog aimed at a larger audience. For example, the design of a blog intended to inform and interact with others about your hobbies or daily life will be different from a blog to inform and discuss politics with a wider readership.

Other factors to keep in mind include the following:

- Break text into smaller chunks, and write as concisely as possible. Give readers "breathers." Bulleted lists work especially well on the Web.

- Provide readers with a clear way to navigate your site. You might have a navigation bar along the top or on the side, with buttons that link to different pages on the site, including the homepage.

- Organization and navigation work hand-in-hand on the Web. Organize material on the site so that organizational principle is apparent to readers. Web designers frequently organize sites hierarchically, which means you begin with the most important or most general topic and then have your viewers "drill down" further into the site for specific details. Blogs typically display entries in reverse chronological order but can be reorganized, if a different order better suits your purpose and audience.

- Each page on your Web site should have a design that is consistent with the other pages on your site. A lack of consistency may make your viewers suspect that they have left your site for another.

- Graphics can enhance the informational value and aesthetic appeal of Web pages, including blogs, but they can also make pages download more slowly.

- If you include links to external sites, periodically check to see if any links are "dead"—links to sites that are no longer active.

- To make pages usable to a wide audience, make them accessible to people with visual impairments. To determine if your site is accessible, you can use *Bobby*, a free, Web-based tool that will analyze your site and tell you if you need to make changes so that people with disabilities will be able to view it (http://bobby.watchfire.com/bobby/html/en/index.jsp). There are also pages on the site that will give you information on how to design your site so that it is more accessible.

- Keep in mind online readers' attention spans. Try to design each page of your Web site so that readers can view each page with only a minimal amount of scrolling. Limit your blog posts to reasonable lengths and consider focusing on a single topic in each post. Shorter, more frequent posts may help generate readership and interactivity.

- Regularly examine your Web pages and blog entries to make sure that the information is current. Including a "last date updated" line on your homepage helps to assure your viewers that you are keeping the site current.

Figure C.11 is a Web page from a student oral history project. Notice the navigation bar on the left side and the title identifying the project at the top.

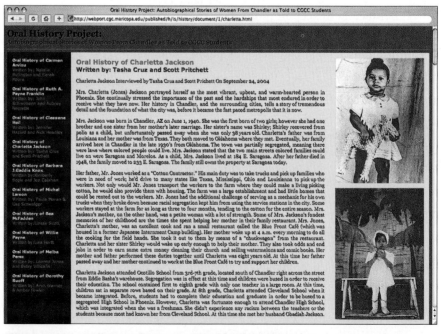

FIGURE C.11   Web Page from a Student Oral History Project

Credits

TEXT CREDITS

Front matter
WPA Outcomes Statement for First-Year Composition is reprinted by permission of the Council of Writing Program Administrators.

Chapter 2
pp. 20–21: "A Purpose Greater Than Oneself," Miss Hall's School. Reprinted by permission of Miss Hall's School, www.misshalls.org; **p. 27:** "Choosing the Sex of Your Baby," *The New York Times,* September 30, 2001. Copyright © 2001 by The New York Times Co. Reprinted with permission.

Chapter 4
p. 49: Excerpt from "Katrina & The Waves," Richard Connelly, Ray Hafner & Todd Spivak, *Houston Press,* September 8, 2005. Reprinted by permission of the Houston Press; **pp. 60–64:** Excerpt from *Growing Up* by Russell Baker. Copyright © 1982 by Russell Baker. New York: Congdon & Weed, Inc.; **pp. 60–64:** "Se Habla Espanol," Tanya Barrientos from *Border-Line Personalities* by Michelle Herrera-Mulligan and Robyn Moreno. Compilation copyright © 2004 by Michelle Herrera-Mulligan and Robyn Moreno. Reprinted by permission of HarperCollins Publishers.

Chapter 5
pp. 92–96: "Scientist at Work—Terence Tao: Journeys to the Distant Fields of Prime," Kenneth Chang, *The New York Times,* March 13, 2007. Copyright © 2007 by The New York Times Co. Reprinted with permission; **pp. 97–101:** "Bipolar Iraq," Michael Wolff, *New York Magazine,* November 17, 2003. Reprinted by permission of *New York Magazine.*

Chapter 6
p. 120: *The New York Times* online front page from February 23, 2007 is reprinted by permission of The New York Times Co; **pp. 128–130:** "Clocking Cultures," Carol Ezzell, *Scientific American,* September 2002. Reprinted with permission. Copyright 2002 by Scientific American, Inc. All rights reserved; **pp. 131–135:** "Growing Wikipedia Revises Its 'Anyone Can Edit' Policy," Katie Hafner, *The New York Times,* June 17, 2006. Copyright © 2006 by The New York Times Co. Reprinted with permission; **p. 137, Fig. 6.2:** Bar graph showing the U.S. National debt is reprinted by permission of Ed Hall; **p. 142:** "Easy Voter Guide: California Edition" is reprinted by permission of the League of Women Voters of California, www.easyvoter.org; **p. 148:** Table 1 Rates of Biodegradability is reprinted by permission of Worldwise, Inc.; **p. 149:** "Did You Know" note from the University of Nebraska at Lincoln is reprinted by permission of the University of Nebraska-Lincoln Landscape Services.

Chapter 7
pp. 164–167: "Putting in the Hours," James M. Lang, *The Chronicle of Higher Education,* May 16, 2003. Copyright © 2003, The Chronicle of Higher Education. Reprinted with permission; **pp. 168–170:** "All Work and No Play" from *Strapped: Why America's 20-And 30-Somethings Can't Get Ahead* by Tamara Draut. Copyright © 2005 by Tamara Draut. Used by permission of Doubleday, a division of Random House Inc., and the author; **p. 171, Fig. 7.1:** Flowchart, "Value Added, Cost Added Only" is reprinted by permission of RFF Electronics.

Chapter 8
pp. 199–201: "When Women Go To War," Anne Applebaum, *The Washington Post,* March 26, 2003. Reprinted by permission of the author; **pp. 202–203:** "Our Own Warrior Princess," Maureen Dowd, *The New York Times,* June 1, 2003. Copyright © 2003 by The New York Times Co. Reprinted with permission; **p. 204:** "Letter Responding to Dowd," Brian J.G. Pereira, *The New York Times,* September, 2004. Reprinted by permission of Dr. Brian J.G. Pereira; **p. 212:** Chart and data on temperature differences is reprinted by permission of Dr. Charles Ophardt, Professor of Chemistry, Elmhurst College, Elmhurst, IL.

Chapter 9

p. 229: American Film Institute's List of 100 Greatest American Movies is reprinted by permission of the American Film Institute; **pp. 239–241:** Review of *Harry Potter and the Sorcerer's Stone* by Roger Ebert is reprinted from the *Roger Ebert* column by Roger Ebert © 2001. Reprinted with permission of Universal Press Syndicate. All rights reserved; **pp. 241–245:** "The Sorcerer's Apprentice," Elvis Mitchell, *The New York Times*, November 16, 2001. Copyright © 2001 by The New York Times Co. Reprinted with permission; **pp. 246–247:** "How Safe Are Worn Tires?" Copyright © 2004 by Consumers Union of U.S., Inc. Yonkers, NY 10703-1057, a nonprofit organization. Reprinted with permission from the February 2004 issue of *Consumer Reports*® for educational purposes only. No commercial use or reproduction permitted. www.ConsumerReports.org®.

Chapter 10

p. 269: "Sunspots Cause Trouble" from Space and Weather News Web site, October 27, 2003. Reprinted by permission of Dr. Tony Phillips; **pp. 277–281:** "The Ruling That Changed America," Juan Williams is reprinted with permission from *American School Board Journal*, April 2004. Copyright © 2004 National School Boards Association. All rights reserved; **pp. 282–284:** "Where Are the Jobs?" Bruce Nussbaum, *BusinessWeek*, March 22, 2004; **p. 287, Fig. 10.1:** 1895 Earthquake shaking intensity map is reprinted by permission of David J. Rogers; **p. 301:** From "Study Hints at Extreme Climate Change," Environmental News Network, October 28, 1999. Reprinted by permission of ENN.com; **p. 308:** Map showing temperatures in the Sargasso Sea during the last ice age from "Study hints at extreme climate change," Environmental News Network, October 28, 1999. Reprinted by permission of ENN.com.

Chapter 11

p. 308: "Why Microlending," Accion, is reprinted by permission; **pp. 316–320:** "The Nursing Crisis: The Solution Lies Within," Michele Mise was originally published in the *Journal of Undergraduate Nursing Scholarship*, Fall 2002. Reprinted by permission of the author, Michele Mise; **pp. 321–323:** "How to End Grade Inflation," Michael Bérubé, *The New York Times*, May 4, 2002. Copyright © 2004, The New York Times Co. Reprinted by permission.

Chapter 12

p. 347: "Geometry" from *The Yellow House on the Corner* by Rita Dove. Copyright © 1980 by Rita Dove. Reprinted by permission of the author; **pp. 354–358:** "Videotape" is reprinted with permission of Scribner, an imprint of Simon & Schuster Adult Publishing Group from *Underworld* by Don DeLillo. Copyright © 1997 by Don DeLillo. Originally appeared in *Antaeus:* Fall 1994 under the title "Videotape." All rights reserved; **pp. 359–368:** "Alien Relative" Amy Tan. Copyright © Amy Tan. Reprinted by permission of the author and the Sandra Dijkstra Literary Agency.

Chapter 13

pp. 396–397: "Child Survival" is reprinted by permission of RESULTS Educational Fund; **p. 397:** Excerpt from "Poverty Up as Welfare Enrollment Declines: Nation's Social Safety Net in Tatters as More People Lose Their Jobs," Griff Witte, *The Washington Post*, September 26, 2004. Copyright © 2004, The Washington Post. Reprinted with permission; **p. 407:** "What Is Good Bread?" is reprinted by permission of Ken Forkish, Ken's Artisan Bakery and Café; **p. 410:** Definition of "Mugwump" is reprinted by permission of Michael Quinion, World Wide Words; **pp. 410–411:** Definition of "Luddite" from TechTargetNetwork is reprinted by permission of WhatIs.com.

Chapter 14

pp. 427–429: "Beware the Online Collective," Jaron Lanier, *Time* magazine, August 27, 2007. Copyright © 2007 Time, Inc. Reprinted by permission of Time, Inc., via RightsLink, Copyright Clearance Center; **pp. 431-432:** "But I Didn't Do It!" Stanley Fish, *The New York Times*, March 21, 2007. Copyright © 2007 The New York Times Co. Reprinted by permission; **pp. 434–436:** "Nothing But Nets," Rick Reilly, *Sports Illustrated*, May 1, 2006.

Chapter 18

p. 470: ESOL Flyer from Fenway Neighborhood Service Center is reprinted by permission of Action for Boston Community Development, Inc.; **p. 473, Fig. 18.1:** Colorwheel is reprinted by permission of Stanford Brands, Newell Rubbermaid, Inc; **p. 474, Fig. 18.3:** Poster for Israel Society for Ecology and Environmental Quality Sciences is reprinted by permission of Weizmann Institute of Science; **p. 479, Fig. 18.4:** Pie chart showing composition of a slice of pizza is reprinted by permission of Mathematics Leagues, Inc; **p. 481:** "Domestic Cereal Supply: Food; Feed,

Waste" is compiled by the Land Use Change Program of the International Institute for Applied Systems Analysis (IIASA) using data from the Food and Agriculture Organization of the United Nations. Reprinted with permission; **p. 482, Fig. 18.7:** Relationship between a Car's Mileage and Its Value is reprinted by permission of Mathematics Leagues, Inc.; **p. 484, Fig. 18.8:** Universal Stain Color Selection Guide is reprinted by permission of Come To Buy, Inc., www.ComeToBuy.com; **p. 485, Fig. 18.9:** Bigfoot Water Rocket Launcher Flowchart is reprinted by permission of Gary Ensmenger, President, Bigfoot Stilt Company; **p. 489, Fig. 18.12:** Drawing of a cell nucleus is reprinted by permission of David L. Spector, Cold Spring Harbor Laboratory, New York; **p. 491, Fig. 18.13:** Venn diagram on sustainable development is reprinted by permission of Manchester Development Education Project; **p. 493, Fig. 18.15:** Neanderthal Range Map is reprinted by permission of Richard G. Klein; **p. 498, Fig. 18.20:** Two maps of the U.S., one plain and one distorted, from "Diffusion-based methods for producing density-equalizing maps," Michael Gastner and Mark Newman, *PNAS*, May 18, 2004. Copyright © 2004 National Academy of Sciences, USA. Reprinted with permission.

Chapter 19

p. 503: Definition of "adolescent" copyright © 2007 by Houghton Mifflin Company. Adapted and reproduced by permission from *The American Heritage Medical Dictionary;* **p. 506:** Search result for keywords "male" and "gang" are reprinted by permission of EBSCO Publishing; **p. 517:** Blurb about authors Duffy and Gillig from the Greenwood Press online catalog is reproduced with permission of Greenwood Publishing Group, Inc., Westport, CT.

Chapter 20

pp. 545–546, Fig. 20.2: Title and copyright pages from *Unpaid Professionals* by Andrew Zimbalist are reprinted by permission of Princeton University Press; **p. 550, Fig. 20.3:** Journal table of contents is reprinted by permission of Council of Writing Program Administrators; **pp. 570 – 571, Fig. 20.6:** Title and copyright pages from *Teen Gangs* are copyright © 2004 by Maureen P. Duffy and Scott Edward Gillig. Reproduced with permission of Greenwood Publishing Group, Inc., Westport, CT; **p. 575, Fig. 20.7:** Journal table of contents is reprinted by permission of Blackwell Publishing.

PHOTO CREDITS

Chapter 1
p. 3: Getty Images/Digital Vision, (inset) DigitalVues/Alamy.

Chapter 2
p. 15: Getty Images/Digital Vision.

Chapter 3
p. 31: Stockbyte/PunchStock; **p. 35:** © SuperStock, Inc./SuperStock.

Chapter 4
p. 48: © AP/Wide World Photos, (inset) Courtesy of Todd Spivak/Houston Press; **p. 57:** Jeffrey MacMillan for WGBH/ Masterpiece Theatre; **p. 60:** David Cruz/Newscom; **p. 66, p. 68, p. 69:** Courtesy of the authors.

Chapter 5
p. 84: Courtesy of NASA, (top inset) NASA Jet Propulsion Laboratory, (bottom inset) Courtesy of NASA and STScI; **p. 92:** Courtesy of The New York Times; **p. 97:** © Najlah Feanny/Corbis SABA; **p. 109:** Quarter-dollar coin image from the United States Mint.

Chapter 6
p. 124: © BananaStock/PunchStock; **p. 128:** Photo courtesy of Carol Ezzell Webb; **p. 131:** © The New York Times/ Redux Pictures.

Chapter 7
p. 156: © AP/Wide World Photos; **p. 164:** Photo courtesy of James Lang; **p. 168:** Courtesy Demos: A Network for Ideas & Action www.demos.org.

Chapter 8
p. 190: Courtesy of Mexico Tourism Board; **p. 199:** Photo courtesy of Anne Applebaum; **p. 202:** Fred R. Conrad/The New York Times/Redux; **p. 204:** Courtesy of Dr. Brian Pereira; **p. 212:** © Brand X Pictures/PunchStock.

Chapter 9
p. 228: © RF/Corbis, (inset) RKO Radio Pictures Inc./Photofest; **p. 232:** © RF/Corbis; **p. 233:** © The McGraw-Hill Companies, Inc./Lars A. Niki, photographer; **p. 239:** © Frank Trapper/Corbis; **p. 241:** Michael Germana/SSI Photo/Landov; **p. 247:** © 2004 by Consumers Union of U.S., Inc. Yonkers, NY 10703-1057, a nonprofit organization. Reprinted with permission from the February 2004 issue of *Consumer Reports* (r) for educational purposes only. No commercial use or reproduction permitted. www.ConsumerReports.org; **p. 254:** Jules Frazier/Getty Images.

Chapter 10
p. 268: © Lauri Kangas; **p. 277:** PRNewsFoto/SeniorNet/Newscom; **p. 282:** Courtesy Business Week; **p. 286:** © moodboard/Corbis.

Chapter 11
p. 316: Courtesy of Michelle Mise Pollard; **p. 321:** © Steve Tressler; **p. 324:** Courtesy SkySong, The ASU Scottsdale Innovation Center, rendering by Pei Cobb Freed Architects; **p. 330:** (top) Courtesy SkySong, The ASU Scottsdale Innovation Center, rendering by Todd & Associates. Architects, (bottom) Courtesy SkySong, The ASU Scottsdale Innovation Center, rendering by Pei Cobb Freed Architects.

Chapter 12
p. 346: JP Beato III Photography; **p. 354:** © Jurgen Frank/Corbis; **p. 359:** © Marc Brasz/Corbis; **p. 369, p. 370:** Warner Bros./Photofest; **p. 371:** Twentieth Century Fox/Photofest; **p. 372:** © Marvel Entertainment, Inc.

Chapter 13
p. 391: BananaStock/JupiterImages; **p. 408:** Jim Wehtje/Getty Images.

Chapter 14
p. 418: © Mike Segar/Reuters/Corbis, (inset) Courtesy of MacNeil/Lehrer Productions; **p. 423:** © SuperStock, Inc./SuperStock; **p. 427:** PRNewsFoto/Newscom; **p. 429:** © sijmen hendriks; **p. 431:** Courtesy of Stanley Fish; **p. 433:** © Roger Ressmeyer/Corbis; **p. 434:** Courtesy of Sports Illustrated.

Chapter 15
p. 440: BananaStock/JupiterImages.

Chapter 16
p. 447: Keith Brofsky/Getty Images; **p. 451:** BananaStock/JupiterImages.

Chapter 17
p. 457: © images-of-france/Alamy; **p. 467:** (top) Ken Light, (bottom left) © Ken Light/Corbis, (bottom right) © Owen Franken/Corbis.

Chapter 18
p. 470: United Nations Graphic Design Unit/Outreach Division/DPI, (inset) Courtesy of ABCD Parker Hill/Fenway Neighborhood Service Center; **p. 474:** (left) USDA Forest Service; **p. 484:** Courtesy of FUHR Industrial, www.furhindustrial.com; **p. 486:** Library of Congress, Prints and Photographs Division, LC-USZ62-11897; **p. 487:** Library of Congress, Prints and Photographs Division, LC-DIG-cwpb-04326; **p. 492:** NEW LINE/SAUL ZAENTZ/WING NUT/THE KOBAL COLLECTION; **p. 495:** Courtesy of Feed the Children, Inc.

Chapter 19
p. 501: BananaStock/JupiterImages, (top inset) © Stockbyte/PunchStock, (bottom inset) USDA; **p. 510:** Reprinted with permission of Cambridge University Press; **p. 511:** Courtesy of American Psychiatric Publishing, Inc.; **p. 512:** PRNewsFoto/NEWSWEEK/AP/Wide World Photos; **p. 513:** (top) Courtesy of Foreign Affairs, (bottom) Courtesy *Arizona*

Highways; **p. 517:** Maureen Duffy, *Teen Gangs: A Global View*, Copyright © 2004 by Greenwood Press. Reproduced with permission of Greenwood Publishing Group, Inc. Westport, CT.

Chapter 20
p. 531: The McGraw-Hill Companies, Inc./Christopher Kerrigan, photographer.

Appendix C
p. A-24: Courtesy Friends of Patuxent; **p. A-25:** Courtesy Mayor's Office of Special Events, Chicago, IL.

Index

Useful Boxes in *The Concise McGraw-Hill Guide*

Guide to MLA Documentation Models in Chapter 20